Applied Linguistics and Language Study

GENERAL EDITOR: C. N. CANDLIN

Language Tests
at School

A Pragmatic Approach

JOHN W. OLLER, Jr.

University of New Mexico
Albuquerque

LONGMAN

LONGMAN GROUP LIMITED
London

*Associated companies, branches and
representatives throughout the world*

© Longman Group Ltd. 1979

First published 1979

Oller, John W
    Language tests at school. – (Applied
linguistics and language study.)
    1. Language and languages – Ability
testing
    I. Title II. Series
407'.6 P53 78-41005

ISBN 0-582-55365-2
ISBN 0-582-55294-X Pbk

Printed in Great Britain by
Butler & Tanner Ltd, Frome and London.

ACKNOWLEDGEMENTS

We are grateful to the following for permission to reproduce copyright material:

Longman Group Ltd., for an extract from *Bridge Series: Oliver Twist* edited by Latif
Doss; the author, John Pickford for his review of 'The Scandaroon' by Henry
Williamson from *Bookcase Broadcast* on the BBC World Service January 6th 1973,
read by John Pickford; Science Research Associates Inc., for extracts from 'A Pig Can
Jig' by Donald Rasmussen and Lynn Goldberg in *The SRA Reading Program – Level A*
Basic Reading Series © 1964, 1970 Donald E. Rasmussen and Lenina Goldberg.
Reprinted by permission of the publisher Science Research Associates Inc. Board of
Education of the City of New York, from 'New York City Language Assessment
Battery'; reproduced from the Bilingual Syntax Measure by permission. Copyright ©
1975 by Harcourt Brace Jovanovich, Inc. All rights reserved; Center for Bilingual
Education, Northwest Regional Educational Laboratory from 'Oral Language Tests
for Bilingual Students'; McGraw-Hill Book Company, from 'Testing English as a
Second Language' by Harris; McGraw-Hill Book Company from 'Language Testing'
by Lado; Language Learning (North University Building) from 'Problems in Foreign
Language Testing'; Newbury House Publishers from 'Oral Interview' by Ilyin; 'James
Language Dominance Test', copyright 1974 by Peter James, published by Teaching
Resources Corporation, Boston, Massachusetts, U.S.A.; 'Black American Cultural
Attitude Scale', copyright 1973 by Perry Alan Zirkel, Ph.D, published by Teaching
Resources Corporation, Boston, Massachusetts, U.S.A.

Contents

v

LIST OF FIGURES

LIST OF TABLES

TABLES IN THE APPENDIX

Acknowledgements

George Miller once said that it is an 'ill-kept secret' that many people other than the immediate author are involved in the writing of a book. He said that the one he was prefacing was no exception, and neither is this one. I want to thank all of those many people who have contributed to the inspiration and energy required to compile, edit, write, and re-write many times the material contained in this book. I cannot begin to mention all of the colleagues, students, and friends who shared with me their time, talent, and patience along with all of the other little joys and minor agonies that go into the writing of a book. Neither can I mention the teachers of the extended classroom whose ideas have influenced the ones I have tried to express here. For all of them this is probably a good thing, because it is not likely that any of them would want to own some of the distillations of their ideas which find expression here.

Allowing the same discretion to my closer mentors and collaborators, I do want to mention some of them. My debt to my father and to his Spanish program published by Encyclopaedia Britannica Educational Corporation, will be obvious to anyone who has used and understood the pragmatic principles so well exemplified there. I also want to thank the staff at Educational Testing Service, and the other members of the Committee of Examiners for the *Test of English as a Foreign Language* who were kind enough both to tolerate my vigorous criticisms of that test and to help fill in the many lacunae in my still limited understanding of the business of tests and measurement. I am especially indebted to the incisive thinking and challenging communications with John A. Upshur of the University of Michigan who chaired that committee for three of the four years that I served on it. Alan Hudson of the University of New Mexico and Robert Gardner of the University of Western Ontario stimulated my interest in much of the material on attitudes and sociolinguistics which has found its way into this book. Similarly, doctoral research by Douglas Stevenson, Annabelle Scoon, Rose Ann Wallace, Frances Hinofotis, and Herta Teitelbaum has had a significant impact on recommendations contained here. Work in Alaska with Eskimo children by Virginia Streiff, in the African primary schools by John Hofman, in Papua New Guinea by Jonathon Anderson, in Australia by Norman Hart and Richard Walker, and in Canada and Europe by John McLeod has fundamentally influenced what is said concerning the testing of children.

In addition to the acknowledgements due to people for contributing to the thinking embodied here, I also feel a debt of gratitude towards those colleagues who indirectly contributed to the development of this book by making it possible to devote concentrated periods of time thinking and studying on the topics discussed here. In the spring of 1974, Russell Campbell, now Chairman of the TESL group at UCLA, contributed to the initial work on this text by inviting me to give a series of lectures on pragmatics and language testing at the American University, English Language Institute in Cairo, Egypt. Then, in the fall semester of 1975, a six week visit to the University of New Mexico by Richard Walker, Deputy Director of Mount Gravatt College of Advanced Education in Brisbane, Australia, resulted in a stimulating exchange with several centers of activity in the world where child language development is being seriously studied in relation to reading curricula. The possibility of developing tests to assess the suitability of reading materials to a given group of children and the discussion of the relation of language to curriculum in general is very much a product of the dialogue that ensued.

More recently, the work on this book has been pushed on to completion thanks to a grant from the Center for English as a Second Language and the Department of Linguistics at Southern Illinois University in Carbondale. Without that financial support and the encouragement of Patricia Carrell, Charles Parish, Richard Daesch, Kyle Perkins, and others among the faculty and students there, it is doubtful that the work could have been completed.

Finally, I want to thank the students in the testing courses at Southern Illinois University and at Concordia University in Montreal who read all or parts of the manuscript during various stages of development. Their comments, criticisms, and encouragement have sped the completion of the work and have improved the product immensely.

Preface

It is, in retrospect, with remarkable speed that the main principles and assumptions have become accepted of what can be called the teaching and learning of language as communication. Acceptance, of course, does not imply practical implementation, but distinctions between language as form and language as function, the meaning potential of language as discourse and the role of the learner as a negotiator of interpretations, the match to be made between the integrated skills of communicative actuality and the procedures of the classroom, among many others, have all been widely announced, although not yet adequately described. Nonetheless, we are certain enough of the plausibility of this orientation to teaching and learning to suggest types of exercise and pedagogic procedures which are attuned to these principles and assumptions. Courses are being designed, and textbooks written, with a communicative goal, even if, as experiments, they are necessarily partial in the selection of principles they choose to emphasise.

Two matters are, however, conspicuously lacking. They are connected, in that the second is an ingredient of the first. Discussion of a communicative approach has been very largely concentrated on syllabus specifications and, to a lesser extent, on the design of exercise types, rather than on any coherent and consistent view of what we can call the *communicative curriculum*. Rather than examine the necessary interdependence of the traditional curriculum components: purposes, methods and evaluations, from the standpoint of a communicative view of language and language learning, we have been happy to look at the components singly, and at some much more than others. Indeed, and this is the second matter, *evaluation* has hardly been looked at at all, either in terms of assessment of the communicative abilities of the learner or the efficacy of the programme he is following. There are many current examples, involving materials and methods aimed at developing communicative interaction among learners, which are preceded, interwoven with or followed by evaluation instruments totally at odds with the view of language taken by the materials and the practice with which they are connected. Partly because we have not taken the curricular view, and partly because we have directed our innovations towards animation rather than evaluation, teaching and testing are out of joint. Teachers are unwilling to adopt novel materials because they can see that they no longer emphasise exclusively the formal items of language structure which make up the 'psychometric-structuralist' (in Spolsky's phrase) tests another generation of applied linguists have urged them to use. Evaluators of programmes expect satisfaction in terms of this testing paradigm even at points within the programme when quite other aspects of communicative ability are being encouraged. Clearly, this is an undesirable and unproductive state of affairs.

It is to these twin matters of communication and curriculum that John Oller's major contribution to the *Applied Linguistics and Language Study Series* is addressed. He poses two questions: *how can language testing relate to a pragmatic view of language as communication* and *how can language testing relate to educational measurement in general?*

Chapter 1 takes up both issues; in a new departure for this Series John Oller shows how language testing has general relevance for all educationalists, not just those concerned with language. Indeed, he hints here at a topic he takes up later, namely the *linguistic* basis of tests of intelligence, achievement and aptitude. Language testing, as a branch of applied linguistics, has cross-curricular relevance for the learner at school. The major emphasis, however, remains the connection to be made between evaluation, variable learner characteristics, and a psycho-socio-linguistic perspective on 'doing' language-based tasks.

This latter perspective is the substance of the four Chapters in Part One of the book. Beginning from a definition of communicative proficiency in terms of 'accuracy' in a learner's *'expectancy grammar'* (by which Oller refers to the learner's predictive competence in formal, functional and strategic terms) he proceeds to characterise communication as a functional, context-bound and culturally-specific use of language involving an integrated view of receptive and productive skills. It is against such a yardstick that he is able, both in Chapters 3 and 4 of Part One, and throughout Part Two, to offer a close, detailed and well-founded critical assessment of the theories and methods of discrete point testing. Such an approach to testing,

Oller concludes, is a natural corollary of a view of language as form and usage, rather than of process and use. If the view of language changes to one concerned with the communicative properties of language in use, then our ways of evaluating learners' competences to communicate must also change.

In following Spolsky's shift towards the 'integrative-sociolinguistic' view of language testing, however, John Oller does not avoid the frequently-raised objection that although such tests gain in apparent validity, they do so at a cost of reliability in scoring and handling. The immensely valuable practical recommendations for pragmatically-orientated language tests in Part Three of the book constantly return to this objection, and show that it can be effectively countered. What is more, and this is a strong practical theme throughout the argument of the book, it is necessary to invoke a third criterion in language testing, that of *classroom utility*. Much discrete point testing, he argues, is not only premissed on an untenable view of language for the teacher of communication, but in requiring time-consuming and often arcane pre-testing, statistical evaluation and rewriting techniques, poses quite impractical burdens on the classroom teacher. What is needed are effective testing procedures, linked to the needs of particular instructional programmes, reflecting a communicative view of language learning and teaching, but which are within the design and administrative powers of the teacher. Pragmatic tests must be reliable and valid: they need also to be practicable and to be accessible without presupposing technical expertise. If, as the examples in Part Three of the book show, they can be made to relate and be relevant to other subjects in the curriculum than merely *language* alone, then the evaluation of pragmatic and communicative competence has indeed cross-curricular significance.

Finally, a word on the book's organisation: although it is lengthy, the book has clear-cut divisions: the Introduction in Chapter 1 provides an overview; Part One defines the requirements on pragmatic testing; Part Two defines and critically assesses current and overwhelmingly popular discrete point tests, and the concluding Part Three exemplifies and justifies, in practical and technical terms, the shape of alternative pragmatic tests. Each Chapter is completed by a list of *Key Points* and *Discussion Questions*, and *Suggested Readings*, thus providing the valuable and necessary working apparatus to sustain the extended and well-illustrated argument.

Christopher N Candlin, General Editor

Lancaster, July 1978.

Author's Preface

A simple way to find out something about how well a person knows a language (or more than one language) is to ask him. Another is to hire a professional psychometrist to construct a more sophisticated test. Neither of these alternatives, however, is apt to satisfy the needs of the language teacher in the classroom nor any other educator, whether in a multilingual context or not. The first method is too subject to error, and the second is too complicated and expensive. Somewhere between the extreme simplicity of just asking and the development of standardized tests there ought to be reasonable procedures that the classroom teacher could use confidently. This book suggests that many such usable, practical classroom testing procedures exist and it attempts to provide language teachers and educators in bilingual programs or other multilingual contexts access to those procedures.

There are several textbooks about language testing already on the market. All of them are intended primarily for teachers of foreign languages or English as a second language, and yet they are generally based on techniques of testing that were not developed for classroom purposes but for institutional standardized testing. The pioneering volume by Robert Lado, *Language Testing* (1961), the excellent book by Rebecca Valette, *Modern Language Testing: A Handbook* (1967), the equally useful book by David Harris, *Testing English as a Second Language* (1969), *Foreign Language Testing: Theory and Practice* (1972) by John Clark, *Testing and Experimental Methods* (1977) by J. P. B. Allen and Alan Davies, and Valette's 1977 revision of *Modern Language Testing* all rely heavily (though not exclusively) on techniques and methods of constructing multiple choice tests developed to serve the needs of mass production.

Further, the books and manuals oriented toward multilingual education such as *Oral Language Tests for Bilingual Students* (1976) by R. Silverman, *et al*, are typically aimed at standardized published tests. It would seem that all of the previously published books attempt to address classroom needs for assessing proficiency in one or more languages by extending to the classroom the techniques of standardized testing. The typical test format discussed is generally the multiple-choice discrete-item type. However, such techniques are difficult and often impracticable for classroom use. While Valette, Harris, and Clark briefly discuss some of the so-called 'integrative' tests like dictation (especially Valette), composition, and oral interview, for the most part they concentrate on the complex tasks of writing, pre-testing, statistically evaluating, and re-writing discrete point multiple-choice items.

The emphasis is reversed in this book. We concentrate here on pragmatic testing procedures which generally do not require pre-testing, statistical evaluation, or re-writing before they can be applied in the classroom or some other educational context. Such tests can be shown to be as appropriate to monolingual contexts as they are to multilingual and multicultural educational settings.[1]

Most teachers whether in a foreign language classroom or in a multilingual school do not have the time nor the technical background necessary for multiple choice test development, much less for the work that goes into the standardization of such tests. Therefore, this book focusses on how to make, give, and evaluate valid and reliable language tests of a pragmatic sort. Theoretical and empirical reasons are given, however, to establish the practical foundation and to show why teachers and educators can confidently use the recommended testing procedures without a great deal of prerequisite technical training. Although such training is desirable in its own right, and is essential to the researcher in psychometry, psycholinguistics, sociolinguistics, or education *per se*, this book is meant as a handbook for those many teachers and educators who do not have the time to master fully (even if that were possible) the highly technical fields of statistics, research design, and applied linguistics. The book is addressed to educators at the consumer end of educational research. It tries to provide practical information without presupposing technical expertise. Practical examples of testing procedures are given wherever they are appropriate.

---

[1] Since it is believed that a multilingual context is normally also multicultural, and since it is also the case that language and culture are mutually dependent and inseparable, the term 'multilingual' is often used as an abbreviation for the longer term 'multilingual-multicultural' in spite of the fact that the latter term is often preferred by many authors these days.

The main criterion of success for the book is whether or not it is useful to educators. If it also serves some psychometrists, linguists and researchers, so much the better. It is hoped that it will fill an important gap in the resources available to language teachers and educators in multilingual and in monolingual contexts. Thoughtful suggestions and criticism are invited and will be seriously weighed in the preparation of future editions or revisions.

John Oller
Albuquerque, New Mexico, 1979

1

Introduction

A. What is a language test?
B. What is language testing research about?
C. Organization of this book

This introduction discusses language testing in relation to education in general. It is demonstrated that many tests which are not traditionally thought of as language tests may actually be tests of language more than of anything else. Further, it is claimed that this is true both for students who are learning the language of the school as a second language, and for students who are native speakers of the language used at school. The correctness of this view is not a matter that can be decided by preferences. It is an empirical issue, and substantiating evidence is presented throughout this book. The main point of this chapter is to survey the overall topography of the crucial issues and to consider some of the angles from which the salient points of interest can be seen in bold relief. The overall organization of the rest of the book is also presented here.

A. What is a language test?

When the term 'language test' is mentioned, most people probably have visions of students in a foreign language classroom poring over a written examination. This interpretation of the term is likely because most educated persons and most educators have had such an experience at one time or another. Though only a few may have really learned a second language (and practically none of them in a classroom context), many have at least made some attempt. For them, a language test is a device that tries to assess how much has

1

been learned in a foreign language course, or some part of a course.

But written examinations in foreign language classrooms are only one of the many forms that language tests take in the schools. *For any student whose native language or language variety is not used in the schools, many tests not traditionally thought of as language tests may be primarily tests of language ability.* For learners who speak a minority language whether it is Spanish, Italian, German, Navajo, Digueño, Black English, or whatever language, coping with any test in the school context may be largely a matter of coping with a language test. *There are, moreover, language aspects to tests in general even for the student who is a native speaker of the language of the test.*

In one way or another, *practically every kind of significant testing of human beings depends on a surreptitious test of ability to use a particular language.* Consider the fact that the psychological construct of 'intelligence' or IQ, at least insofar as it can be measured, may be no more than language proficiency. In any case, substantial research (see Oller and Perkins, 1978) indicates that language ability probably accounts for the lion's share of variability in IQ tests. It remains to be proved that there is some unique and meaningful variability that can be associated with other aspects of intelligence once the language factor has been removed. And, conversely, it is apparently the case that the bulk of variability in language proficiency test scores is indistinguishable from the variability produced by IQ tests. In Chapter 3 we will return to consider what meaningful factors language skill might consist of (also see the Appendix on this question). It has not yet been shown conclusively that there are unique portions of variability in language test scores that are not attributable to a general intelligence factor.

Psycholinguistic and sociolinguistic research rely on language test results in obvious ways. As Upshur (1976) has pointed out, so does research on the nature of psychologically real grammars. Whether the criterion measure is a reaction time to a heard stimulus, the accuracy of attempts to produce, interpret, or recall a certain type of verbal material, or the amount of time required to do so, or a mark on a scale indicating agreement or disagreement with a given statement, language proficiency (even if it is not the object of interest *per se*) is probably *a* major factor in the design, and may often be *the* major factor.

The renowned Russian psychologist, A. R. Luria (1959) has argued that even motor tasks as simple as pushing or not pushing a button in response to a red or green light may be rather directly related to language skill in very young children. On a much broader scale, achievement testing may be much more a problem of language testing than is commonly thought.

For all of these reasons the problems of language testing are a large subset of the problems of educational measurement in general. The methods and findings of language testing research are of crucial importance to research concerning psychologically real grammatical systems, and to all other areas that must of necessity make assumptions about the nature of such systems. Hence, all areas of educational measurement are either directly or indirectly implicated. Neither intelligence measurement, achievement testing, aptitude assessment, nor personality gauging, attitude measurement, or just plain classroom evaluation can be done without language testing. It therefore seems reasonable to suggest that educational testing in general can be done better if it takes the findings of language testing research into account.

B. What is language testing research about?

In general, the subject matter of language testing research is the use and learning of language. Within educational contexts, the domain of foreign language teaching is a special case of interest. Multilingual delivery of curricula is another very important case of interest. However, the phenomena of interest to research in language testing are yet more pervasive.

Pertinent questions of the broader domain include: (1) How can levels of language proficiency, stages of language acquisition (first or second), degrees of bilingualism, or language competence be defined? (2) How are earlier stages of language learning different from later stages, and how can known or hypothesized differences be demonstrated by testing procedures? (3) How can the effects of instructional programs or techniques (or environmental changes in general) be demonstrated empirically? (4) How are levels of language proficiency and the concomitant social interactions that they allow or deny related to the acquisition of knowledge in an educational setting? This is not to say that these questions have been or even will be answered by language testing research, but that they are indicative of some of the kinds of issues that such research is in a unique position to grapple with.

Three angles of approach can be discerned in the literature on language testing research. First, language tests may be examined as tests *per se*. Second, it is possible to investigate learner characteristics using language tests as elicitation procedures. Third, specific hypotheses about psycholinguistic and sociolinguistic factors in the performance of language based tasks may be investigated using language tests as research tools.

It is important to note that regarding a subject matter from one angle rather than another does not change the nature of the subject matter, and neither does it ensure that what can be seen from one angle will be interpretable fully without recourse to other available vantage points. The fact is that in language testing research, it is never actually possible to decide to investigate test characteristics, or learner traits, or psycholinguistic and sociolinguistic constraints on test materials without making important assumptions about all three, regardless which happens to be in focus at the moment.

In this book, we will be concerned with the findings of research from all three angles of approach. When the focus is on the tests themselves, questions of *validity*, *reliability*, *practicality*, and *instructional value* will be considered. The validity of a test is related to how well the test does what it is supposed to do, namely, to inform us about the examinee's progress toward some goal in a curriculum or course of study, or to differentiate levels of ability among various examinees on some task. Validity questions are about what a test actually measures in relation to what it is supposed to measure.

The reliability of a test is a matter of how consistently it produces similar results on different occasions under similar circumstances. Questions of reliability have to do with how consistently a test does what it is supposed to do, and thus cannot be strictly separated from validity questions. Moreover, a test cannot be any more valid than it is reliable.

A test's practicality must be determined in relation to the cost in terms of materials, time, and effort that it requires. This must include the preparation, administration, scoring, and interpretation of the test.

Finally, the instructional value of a test pertains to how easily it can be fitted into an educational program, whether the latter involves teaching a foreign language, teaching language arts to native speakers, or verbally imparting subject matter in a monolingual or multilingual school setting.

When the focus of language testing research is on learner characteristics, the tests themselves may be viewed as elicitation procedures for data to be subsequently analyzed. In this case, scores on a test may be treated as summary statistics indicating various positions on a developmental scale, or individual performances may be analyzed in a more detailed way in an attempt to diagnose specific aspects of learner development. The results of the latter sort of analysis, often referred to as 'error analysis' (Richards, 1970a, 1971) may subsequently enter into the process of prescribing therapeutic intervention – possibly a classroom procedure.

When the focus of language testing research is the verbal material in the test itself, questions usually relate to the psychologically real grammatical constraints on particular phonological (or graphological) sequences, syllable structures, vocabulary items, phrases, clauses, and higher level patterns of discourse. Sociological constraints may also be investigated with respect to the negotiability of those elements and sequences of them in interactional exchanges between human beings or groups of them.

For any of the stated purposes of research, and of course there are others which are not mentioned, the tests may be relatively formal devices or informal elicitation procedures. They may require the production or comprehension of verbal sequences, or both. The language material may be heard, spoken, read, written (or possibly merely thought), or some combination of these. The task may require recognition only, or imitation, or delayed recall, memorization, meaningful conversational response, learning and long term storage, or some combination of these.

Ultimately, any attempt to apply the results of language testing research must consider the total spectrum of tests *qua* tests, learner characteristics, and the psychological and sociological constraints on test materials. Inferences concerning psychologically real grammars cannot be meaningful apart from the results of language tests viewed from all three angles of research outlined above. Whether or not a particular language test is valid (or better, the degree to which it is valid or not valid), whether or not an achievement test or aptitude test, or personality inventory, or IQ test, or whatever other sort of test one chooses to consider is a language test, is dependent on what language competence really is and what sorts of verbal sequences present a challenge to that competence. This is essentially the question that Spolsky (1968) raised in the paper entitled: 'What does it mean to know a language? Or, How do you get someone to perform his competence?'

C. Organization of this book

A good way, perhaps the only acceptable way to develop a test of a given ability is to start with a clear definition of the capacity in question. Chapter 2 begins Part One on *Theory and Research Bases for Pragmatic Language Testing* by proposing a definition for language proficiency. It introduces the notion of an expectancy grammar as a way of characterizing the psychologically real system that governs the use of a language in an individual who knows that language. Although it is acknowledged that the details of such a system are just beginning to be understood, certain pervasive characteristics of expectancy systems can be helpful in explaining why certain kinds of language tests apparently work as well as they do, and how to devise other effective testing procedures that take account of those salient characteristics of functional language proficiency.

In Chapter 3, it is hypothesized that a valid language test must press the learner's internalized expectancy system into action and must further challenge its limits of efficient functioning in order to discriminate among degrees of efficiency. Although it is suggested that a statistical average of native performance on a language test is usually a reasonable upper bound on attainable proficiency, it is almost always possible and is sometimes essential to discriminate degrees of proficiency among native speakers, e.g. at various stages of child language learning, or among children or adults learning to read, or among language learners at any stage engaged in normal inferential discourse processing tasks. Criterion referenced testing, where passing the test or some portion of it means being able to perform the task or tasks at some desired level of adequacy (which may be native-like performance in some cases) is also discussed. Pragmatic language tests are defined and exemplified as tasks that require the meaningful processing of sequences of elements in the target language (or tested language) under normal time constraints. It is claimed that time is always involved in the processing of verbal sequences.

Chapter 4 extends the discussion to questions often raised in reference to bilingual-bicultural programs and other multilingual contexts in general. The implications of the now famous Lau versus Nichols case are discussed. Special attention is given to the role of socio-cultural attitudes in language acquisition and in education in general. It is hypothesized that other things being equal, attitudes expressed and perceived in the schools probably account for more variance in rate and amount of learning than do educational methodologies related to the transmission of the traditionally conceived curriculum. Some of the special problems that arise in multilingual contexts are considered, such as, cultural bias in tests, difficulties in translating test items, and methods of assessing language dominance.

Chapter 5 concludes Part One with a discussion of the measurement of attitudes and motivations. It discusses in some detail questions related to the hypothesized relationship between attitudes and language learning (first or second), and considers such variables as the context in which the language learning takes place, and the types of measurement techniques that have been used in previous research. Several hypotheses are offered concerning the relationship between attitudes, motivations, and achievement in education. Certain puzzling facts about apparent interacting influences in multilingual contexts are noted.

Part Two, *Theories and Methods of Discrete Point Testing*, takes up some of the more traditional and probably less theoretically sound ways of approaching language testing. Chapter 6 discusses some of the difficulties associated with testing procedures that grew out of contrastive linguistics, syntax based structure drills, and certain assumptions about language structure and the learning of language from early versions of transformational linguistics.

Pitfalls in relying too heavily on statistics for guiding test development are discussed in Chapter 7. It is shown that different theoretical assumptions may result in contradictory interpretations of the same statistics. Thus it is argued that such statistical techniques as are normally applied in test development, though helpful if used with care, should not be the chief criterion for deciding test format. An understanding of language use and language learning must take priority in guiding format decisions.

Chapter 8 shows how discrete point language tests may produce distorted estimates of language proficiency. In fact, it is claimed that some discrete point tests are probably most appropriate as measures of the sorts of artificial grammars that learners are sometimes encouraged to internalize on the basis of artificial contexts of certain syntax dominated classroom methods. In order to measure communicative effectiveness for real-life settings in and out of the classroom, it is reasoned that the language tests used in the classroom (or in any educational context) must reflect certain crucial properties of the normal use of language in ways that some discrete point tests apparently cannot. Examples of discrete point items which attempt to examine the pieces of language structure apart from some of their systematic interrelationships are considered. The chapter concludes by proposing that the diagnostic aims of discrete point tests can in fact be achieved by so-called integrative or pragmatic tests. Hence, a reconciliation between the apparently irreconcilable theoretical positions is possible.

In conclusion to Part Two on discrete point testing, Chapter 9 provides a natural bridge to Part Three, *Practical Recommendations for Language Testing*, by discussing multiple choice testing procedures which may be of the discrete point type, or the integrative type, or anywhere on the continuum in between the two extremes. However, regardless of the theoretical bent of the test writer, multiple choice tests require considerable technical skill and a good deal of energy to prepare. They are in some respects less practical than some of the pragmatic procedures recommended in Part Three precisely because of the technical skills and the effort necessary to their preparation. Multiple choice tests need to be critiqued by some native speaker, other than the test writer. This is necessary to avoid the pitfalls of ambiguities and subtle differences of interpretation that may not be obvious to the test writer. The items need to be pretested, preferably on some group other than the population which will ultimately be tested with the finished product (this is often not feasible in classroom situations). Then, the items need to be statistically analyzed so that non-functional or weak items can be revised before they are used and interpreted in ways that affect learners. In some cases, recycling through the whole procedure is necessary even though all the steps of test development may have been quite carefully executed. Because of these complexities and costs of test development, multiple choice tests are not always suitable for meeting the needs of classroom testing – or for broader institutional purposes in some cases.

The reader who is interested mainly in classroom applications of pragmatic testing procedures may want to begin reading at Chapter 10 in Part Three. However, unless the material in the early chapters (especially 2 through 9) is fairly well grasped, the basis for many of the recommendations in Part Three will probably not be appreciated fully. For instance, many educators seem to have acquired the impression that certain pragmatic language tests, such as those based on the cloze procedure for example (see Chapter 11), are 'quick and dirty' methods of acquiring information about language proficiency. This idea, however, is apparently based only on intuitions and is disconfirmed by the research discussed in Part One. Pragmatic tests are typically *better* on the whole than any other procedures that have been carefully studied. Whereas the prevailing techniques of language testing that educators are apt to be most familiar with are based on the discrete point theories, these methods are rejected in Part Two. Hence, were the reader to skip over to Part Three immediately, he might be left in a quandary as to why the pragmatic testing techniques discussed there are recommended instead of the more familiar discrete point (and typically multiple choice) tests.

Although pragmatic testing procedures are in some cases deceptively simple to apply, they probably provide more accurate information concerning language proficiency (and even specific achievement objectives) than the more familiar tests produced on the basis of discrete point theory. Moreover, not only are pragmatic tests apparently more valid, but they are more practicable. It simply takes less premeditation, and less time and effort to prepare and use pragmatic tests. This is not to say that great care and attention is not necessary to the use of pragmatic testing procedures, quite the contrary. It is rather to say that hour for hour and dollar for dollar the return on work and money expended in pragmatic testing will probably offer higher dividends to the learner, the educator, and the taxpayer. Clearly, much more research is needed on both pragmatic and discrete point testing procedures, and many suggestions for possible studies are offered throughout the text.

Chapter 10 discusses some of the practical classroom applications of the procedure of dictating material in the target language. Variations of the technique which are also discussed include the procedure of 'elicited imitation' employed with monolingual, bilingual, and bidialectal children.

In Chapter 11 attention is focussed on a variety of procedures requiring the use of productive oral language skills. Among the ones discussed are reading aloud, story retelling, dialogue dramatization, conversational interview techniques, and specifically the Foreign Service Institute Oral Interview, the *Ilyin Oral Interview*, the Upshur *Oral Communication Test*, and the *Bilingual Syntax Measure* are also discussed.

Increasingly widely used cloze procedure and variations of it are considered in Chapter 12. Basically the procedure consists of deleting words from prose (or auditorily presented material) and asking the examinee to try to replace the missing words. Because of the simplicity of application and the demonstrated validity of the technique, it has become quite popular in recent years. However, it is probably not any more applicable to classroom purposes than some of the procedures discussed in other chapters. The cloze procedure is sometimes construed to be a measure of reading ability, though it may be just as much a measure of writing, listening and speaking ability (see Chapter 3, and the Appendix).

Chapter 13 looks at writing tasks *per se*. It gives considerable space to ways of approaching the difficulties of scoring relatively free essays. Alternative testing methods considered include various methods of increasing the constraints on the range of material that the examinee may produce in response to the test procedure. Controls range from suggesting topics for an essay to asking examinees to rephrase heard or read material after a time lapse. Obviously, many other control techniques are possible, and variations on the cloze procedure can be used to construct many of them.

Chapter 14 considers ways in which testing procedures can be related to curricula. In particular it asks, 'How can effective testing procedures be invented or adapted to the needs of an instructional program?' Some general guidelines are tentatively suggested for both developing or adapting testing procedures and for studying their effectiveness in relation to particular educational objectives. To illustrate one of the ways that curriculum (learning, teaching, and testing) can be related to a comprehensive sort of validation research, the Mount Gravatt reading research project is discussed. This project provides a rich source of data concerning preschool children, and children in the early grades. By carefully studying the kinds of language games that children at various age levels can play and win (Upshur, 1973), that is, the kinds of things that they can explore verbally and with success, Norman Hart, Richard Walker, and their colleagues have provided a model for relating theories of language learning via careful research to the practical educational task of teaching reading. There are, of course, spin off benefits to all other areas of the curriculum because of the fundamental part played by language use in every area of the educational process. It is strongly urged that language testing procedures, especially for assessing the language skills of children, be carefully examined in the light of such research.

Throughout the text, wherever technical projects are referred to, details of a technical sort are either omitted or are explained in nontechnical language. More complete research reports are often referred to in the text (also see the Appendix) and should be consulted by anyone interested in applying the recommendations contained here to the testing of specific research hypotheses. However, for classroom purposes (where at least *some* of the technicalities of research design are luxuries) the suggestions offered here are intended to be sufficient. Additional readings, usually of a non-technical sort, are suggested at the end of each chapter. A complete list of technical reports and other works referred to in the text is included at the end of the book in a separate Bibliography. The latter includes all of the Suggested Readings at the end of each chapter, plus many items *not* given in the Suggested Readings lists. An Appendix reporting on recent empirical study of many of the pressing questions raised in the body of the text is included at the end. The fundamental question addressed there is whether or not language proficiency can be parsed up into components, skills, and the like. Further, it is asked whether language proficiency is distinct from IQ, achievement, and other educational constructs. The Appendix is not included in the body of the text precisely because it is somewhat technical.

It is to be expected that a book dealing with a subject matter that is changing as rapidly as the field of language testing research should soon be outdated. However, it seems that most current research is pointing toward the refinement of existing pragmatic testing procedures and the discovery of new ones and new applications. It seems unlikely that there will be a substantial return to the strong versions of discrete point theories and methods of the 1960s and early 1970s. In any event the emphasis here is on pragmatic language testing because it is believed that such procedures offer a richer yield of information.

KEY POINTS

1. Any test that challenges the language ability of an examinee can, at least in part, be construed as a language test. This is especially true for examinees who do not know or normally use the language variety of the test, but is true in a broader sense for native speakers of the language of the test.
2. It is not known to what extent language ability may be co-extensive with IQ, but there is evidence that the relationship is a very strong one. Hence, IQ tests (and many other varieties of tests as well) may be tests of language ability more than they are tests of anything else.
3. Language testing is crucial to the investigation of psychologically real grammars, to research in all aspects of distinctively human symbolic

behavior, and to educational measurement in general.

4. Language testing research may focus on tests, learners, or constraints on verbal materials.

5. Among the questions of interest to language testing research are: (a) how to operationally define levels of language proficiency, stages of language learning, degrees of bilingualism, or linguistic competence; (b) how to differentiate stages of learning; (c) how to measure possible effects of instruction (or other environmental factors) on language learning; (d) how language ability is related to the acquisition of knowledge in an educational setting.

6. When the research is focussed on tests, validity, reliability, practicality, and instructional value are among the factors of interest.

7. When the focus is on learners and their developing language systems, tests may be viewed as elicitation procedures. Data elicited may then be analyzed with a view toward providing detailed descriptions of learner systems, and/or diagnosis of teaching procedures (or other therapeutic interventions) to facilitate learning.

8. When research is directed toward the verbal material in a given test or testing procedure, the effects of psychological or sociological constraints built into the verbal sequences themselves (or constraints which are at least implicit to language users) are at issue.

9. From all of the foregoing it follows that the results of language tests, and the findings of language testing research are highly relevant to psychological, sociological, and educational measurement in general.

DISCUSSION QUESTIONS

1. What tests are used in your school that require the comprehension or production of complex sequences of material in a language? Reading achievement tests? Aptitude tests? Personality inventories? Verbal IQ tests? Others? What evidence exists to show that the tests are really measures of different things?

2. Are tests in your school sometimes used for examinees whose native language (or language variety) is not the language (or language variety) used in the test? How do you think such tests ought to be interpreted?

3. Is it possible that a non-verbal test of IQ could have a language factor unintentionally built into it? How are the instructions given? What strategies do you think children or examinees must follow in order to do the items on the test? Are any of those strategies related to their ability to code information verbally? To give subvocal commands?

4. In what ways do teachers normally do language testing (unintentionally) in their routine activities? Consider the kinds of instructions children or adults must execute in the classroom.

5. Take any standardized test used in any school setting. Analyze it for its level of verbal complexity. What instructions does it use? Are they more or less complex than the tasks which they define or explain? For what age level of children or for what proficiency level of second language learners would such instructions be appropriate? Is guessing necessary in order to understand the instructions of the test?

6. Consider any educational research project that you know of or have access to. What sorts of measurements did the research use? Was there a testing technique? An observational or rating procedure? A way of recording behaviors? Did language figure in the measurements taken?

7. Why do you think language might or might not be related to capacity to perform motor tasks, particularly in young children? Consider finding your way around town, or around a new building, or around the house. Do you ever use verbal cues to guide your own stops, starts, turns? Subvocal ones? How about in a strange place or when you are very tired? Do you ever ask yourself things like, *Now what did I come in here for?*

8. Can you conceive of any way to operationalize notions like language competence, degree of bilingualism, stages of learning, effectiveness of language teaching, rate of learning, level of proficiency without language tests?

9. If you were to rank the criteria of *validity, reliability, practicality* and *instructional value* in their order of importance, what order would you put them in? Consider the fact that validity without practicality is certainly possible. The same is true for validity without instructional value. How about instructional value without validity?

10. Do you consider the concept of intelligence or IQ to be a useful theoretical construct? Do you believe that researchers and theorists know what they mean by the term apart from some test score? How about grammatical knowledge? Is it the same sort of construct?

11. Can you think of any way(s) that time is normally involved in a task like reading a novel – when no one is holding a stop-watch?

SUGGESTED READINGS

1. George A. Miller, 'The Psycholinguists,' *Encounter* 23, 1964, 29–37. Reprinted in Charles E. Osgood and Thomas A. Sebeok (eds.) *Psycholinguistics: A Survey of Theory and Research Problems.* Bloomington, Indiana: Indiana University, 1965.

2. John W. Oller, Jr. and Kyle Perkins, *Language in Education: Testing the Tests.* Rowley, Massachusetts: Newbury House, 1978.

3. Bernard Spolsky, 'Introduction: Linguists and Language Testers' in *Advances in Language Testing: Series 2, Approaches to Language Testing.* Arlington, Virginia: Center for Applied Linguistics, 1978, v–x.

PART ONE
Theory and Research Bases
for Pragmatic Language Testing

2

Language Skill
as a Pragmatic Expectancy
Grammar

A. What is pragmatics about?
B. The factive aspect of language use
C. The emotive aspect
D. Language learning as grammar
   construction and modification
E. Tests that invoke the learner's
   grammar

Understanding what is to be tested is prerequisite to good testing of any sort. In this chapter, the object of interest is language as it is used for communicative purposes – for getting and giving information about (or for bringing about changes in) facts or states of affairs, and for expressing attitudes toward those facts or states of affairs. The notion of *expectancy* is introduced as a key to understanding the nature of psychologically real processes that underlie language use. It is suggested that expectancy generating systems are constructed and modified in the course of language acquisition. Language proficiency is thus characterized as consisting of such an expectancy generating system. Therefore, it is claimed that for a proposed measure to qualify as a language test, it must invoke the expectancy system or grammar of the examinee.

A. What is pragmatics about?

The newscaster in Albuquerque who smiled cheerfully while speaking of traffic fatalities, floods, and other calamities was expressing an entirely different attitude toward the facts he was referring to than was probably held by the friends and relatives of the victims, not to

16

mention the more compassionate strangers who were undoubtedly watching him on the television. There might not have been any disagreement about what the facts were, but the potent contrast in the attitudes of the newscaster and others probably accounts for the brevity of the man's career as the station's anchorman.

Thus, two aspects of language use need to be distinguished. Language is usually used to convey information about people, things, events, ideas, states of affairs, *and* attitudes toward all of the foregoing. It is possible for two or more people to agree entirely about the facts referred to or the assumptions implied by a certain statement but to disagree markedly in their attitudes toward those facts. The newscaster and his viewers probably disagreed very little or not at all concerning the facts he was speaking of. It was his manner of speaking (including his choice of words) and the attitude conveyed by it that probably shortened his career.

Linguistic analysis has traditionally been concerned mainly with what might be called the *factive* (or cognitive) aspect of language use. The physical stuff of language which codes factive information usually consists of sequences of distinctive sounds which combine to form syllables, which form words, which get hooked together in highly constrained ways to form phrases, which make up clauses, which also combine in highly restricted ways to yield the incredible diversity of human discourse. By contrast, the physical stuff of language which codes *emotive* (or affective, attitudinal) information usually consists of facial expression, tone of voice, and gesture. Psychologists and sociologists have often been interested more in the emotive aspect of language than in the cognitive complexities of the factive aspect. Certainly cognitive psychology and linguistics, along with philosophy and logic, on the other hand, have concentrated on the latter.

Although the two aspects are intricately interrelated, it is often useful and sometimes essential to distinguish them. Consider, for instance, the statement that *Some of Richard's lies have been discovered*. This remark could be taken to mean that there is a certain person named Richard (whom we may infer to be a male human), who is guilty of lying on more than one or two occasions, and some of whose lies have been found out. In addition, the remark implies that there are other lies told by Richard which may be uncovered later. Such a statement relates in systematic ways to a speaker's asserted beliefs concerning certain states of affairs. Of course, the speaker may be lying, or sincere but mistaken, or sincere and correct, and these are only some of the many possibilities. In any case, however, as persons who know English, we understand the remark about Richard partly by inferring the sorts of facts it would take to make such a statement true. Such inferences are not perfectly understood, but there is no doubt that language users make them. A speaker (or writer) must make them in order to know what his listener (or reader) will probably understand, and the listener (or reader) must make them in order to know what a speaker (or writer) means.

In addition to the factive information coded in the words and phrases of the statement, a person who utters that statement may convey attitudes toward the asserted or implied states of affairs, and may further code information concerning the way the speaker thinks the listener should feel about those states of affairs. For instance, the speaker may appear to hate Richard, and to despise his lies (both those that have already been discovered and the others not yet found out), or he may appear detached and impersonal. In speaking, such emotive effects are achieved largely by facial expression, tone of voice, and gesture, but they may also be achieved in writing by describing the manner in which a statement is made or by skillful choice of words. The latter, of course, is effective either in spoken or written discourse as a device for coding emotive information. Notice the change in the emotive aspect if the word *lies* is replaced by *half-truths*: *Some of Richard's half-truths have been discovered*. The disapproval is weakened still further if we say: *Some of Richard's mistakes have been discovered*, and further still if we change *mistakes* to *errors of judgement*.

In the normal use of language it is possible to distinguish two major kinds of context. First, there is the physical stuff of language which is organized into a more or less linear arrangement of verbal elements skillfully and intricately interrelated with a sequence of rather precisely timed changes in tone of voice, facial expression, body posture, and so on. To call attention to the fact that in human beings even the latter so-called 'paralinguistic' devices of communication are an integral part of language use, we may refer to the verbal and gestural aspects of language in use as constituting *linguistic context*. With reference to speech it is possible to decompose *linguistic context* into *verbal* and *gestural contexts*. With reference to writing, the terms *linguistic context* and *verbal context* may be used interchangeably.

A second major type of context has to do with the world, outside of language, as it is perceived by language users in relation to themselves and valued other persons or groups. We will use the term *extralinguistic context* to refer to states of affairs constituted by things, events, people, ideas, relationships, feelings, perceptions, memories, and so forth. It may be useful to distinguish *objective* aspects of extralinguistic context from *subjective* aspects. On the one hand, there is the world of existing things, events, persons, and so forth, and on the other, there is the world of self-concept, other-concept, interpersonal relationships, group relationships, and so on. In a sense, the two worlds are part of a single totality for any individual, but they are not necessarily so closely related. Otherwise, there would be no need for such terms as schizophrenia, or paranoia.

Neither linguistic nor extralinguistic contexts are simple in themselves, but what complicates matters still further and makes meaningful communication possible is that there are systematic correspondences between linguistic contexts and extralinguistic ones. That is, sequences of linguistic elements in normal uses of language are not haphazard in their relation to people, things, events, ideas, relationships, attitudes, etc., but are systematically related to states of affairs outside of language. Thus we may say that linguistic contexts are pragmatically mapped onto extralinguistic contexts, and vice versa.

We can now offer a definition of pragmatics. Briefly, it addresses the question: how do utterances relate to human experience outside of language? It is concerned with the relationships between linguistic contexts and extralinguistic contexts. It embraces the traditional subject matter of psycholinguistics and also that of sociolinguistics. Pragmatics is about how people communicate information about facts and feelings to other people, or how they merely express themselves and their feelings through the use of language for no particular audience, except possibly an omniscient God. It is about how meaning is both coded and in a sense invented in the normal intercourse of words and experience (to borrow a metaphor from Dewey, 1929).

B. The factive aspect of language use

Language, when it is used to convey information about facts, is always an abbreviation for a richer conceptualization. We know more about objects, events, people, relationships, and states of affairs than we are ever fully able to express in words. Consider the difficulty of saying all you know about the familiar face of a friend. The fact is that your best effort would probably fail to convey enough information to enable someone else to single out your friend in a large crowd. This simply illustrates the fact that you know more than you are able to say.

Here is another example. Not long ago, a person whom I know very well, was involved in an accident. He was riding a ten-speed bicycle around a corner when he was hit head-on by a pick-up. The driver of the truck cut the corner at about thirty miles an hour leaving no room for the cyclist to pass. The collision was inevitable. Blood gushed from a three inch gash in the top of his head and a blunt handlebar was rammed nearly to the bone in his left thigh. From this description you have some vivid impressions about the events referred to. However, no one needs to point out the fact that you do not know as much about the events referred to as the person who experienced them. Some of what you do know is a result of the linguistic context of this paragraph, and some of what you know is the result of inferences that you have correctly made concerning what it probably feels like to have a blunt object rammed into your thigh, or to have a three inch gash in your head, but no matter how much you are told or are able to infer it will undoubtedly fall short of the information that is available to the person who experienced the events in his own flesh. Our words are successful in conveying only part of the information that we possess.

Whenever we say anything at all we leave a great deal more unsaid. We depend largely for the effect of our communications not only on what we say but also on the creative ability of our listeners to fill in what we have left unsaid. The fact is that a normal listener supplies a great deal of information by creative inference and in a very important sense is always anticipating what the speaker will say next. Similarly, the speaker is always anticipating what the listener will infer and is correcting his output on the basis of feedback received from the listener. Of course, some language users are more skillful in such things than others.

We are practically always a jump or two ahead of the person that we are listening to, and sometimes we even outrun our own tongues when we are speaking. It is not unusual in a speech error for a speaker to say a word several syllables ahead of what he intended to say, nor is it uncommon for a listener to take a wrong turn in his thinking and fail to understand correctly, simply because he was expecting something else to be said.

It has been shown repeatedly that tampering with the speaker's own feedback of what he is saying has striking debilitating effects

(Chase, Sutton, and First, 1959). The typical experiment illustrating this involves delayed auditory feedback or sidetone. The speaker's voice is recorded on a tape and played back a fraction of a second later into a set of headphones which the speaker is wearing. The result is that the speaker hears not what he is saying, but what he has just said a fraction of a second earlier. He invariably stutters and distorts syllables almost beyond recognition. The problem is that he is trying to compensate for what he hears himself saying in relation to what he expects to hear. After some practice, it is possible for the speaker to ignore the delayed auditory feedback and to speak normally by attending instead to the so-called kinesthetic feedback of the movements of the vocal apparatus and presumably the bone conducted vibrations of the voice.

The pervasive importance of expectations in the processing of all sorts of information is well illustrated in the following remark by the world renowned neurophysiologist, Karl Lashley:

> ... The organization of language seems to me to be characteristic of almost all other cerebral activity. There is a series of hierarchies of organization; the order of vocal movements in pronouncing the word, the order of words in the sentence, the order of sentences in the paragraph, the rational order of paragraphs in a discourse. Not only speech, but all skilled acts seem to involve the same problems of serial ordering, even down to the temporal coordinations of muscular contractions in such a movement as reaching and grasping (1951, p. 187).

A major aspect of language use that a good theory must explain is that there is, in Lashley's words, 'a series of hierarchies of organization.' That is, there are units that combine with each other to form higher level units. For instance, the letters in a written word combine to form the written word itself. The word is not a letter and the letter is not a word, but the one unit acts as a building block for the other, something like the way atoms combine to form molecules. Of course, atoms consist of their own more elementary building blocks and molecules combine in complex ways to become the building blocks of a great diversity of higher order substances.

Words make phrases and the phrases carry new and different meanings which are not part of the separate words of which they are made. For instance, consider the meanings of the words *head*, *red*, *the*, and *beautiful*. Now consider their meanings again in the phrase *the beautiful redhead* as in the sentence, *She's the beautiful redhead I've been telling you about*. At each higher level in the hierarchy, as John

Dewey (1929) put it, new meanings are bred from the copulating forms. This in a nutshell is the basis of the marvelous complexity and novelty of language as an instrument for coding information and for conceptualizing.

Noam Chomsky, eminent professor of linguistics at the Massachusetts Institute of Technology, is mainly responsible for the emphasis in modern linguistics on the characteristic novelty of sentences. He has argued convincingly (cf. especially Chomsky, 1972) that novelty is the rule rather than the exception in the everyday use of language. If a sentence is more than part of a ritual verbal pattern (such as, 'Hello. How are you?'), it is probably a novel concoction of the speaker which probably has never been heard or said by him before. As George Miller (1964) has pointed out, a conservative estimate of the number of possible twenty-word sentences in English is on the order of the number of seconds in one hundred million centuries. Although sentences may share certain structural features, any particular one that happens to be uttered is probably invented, new on the spot. The probability that it has been heard before and memorized is very slight.

The novelty of language, however, is a kind of freedom within limits. When the limits on the creativity allowed by language are violated, many versions of nonsense result. They may range from unpronounceable sequences like *gbntmbwk* (unpronounceable in English at least) to pronounceable nonsense such as *nox ems glerf onmo kebs* (from Osgood, 1955). They may be syntactically acceptable but semantically strange concoctions like the much overused example of Jabberwocky or Chomsky's (now trite) illustrative sentence, *Colorless green ideas sleep furiously*.[1]

A less well known passage of nonsense was invented by Samuel Foote, one of the best known humorists of the nineteenth century, in order to prove a point about the organization of memory. Foote had been attending a series of lectures by Charles Macklin on oratory. On one particular evening, Mr Macklin boasted that he had mastered the principles of memorization so thoroughly that he could repeat any paragraph by rote after having read it only once. At the end of the lecture, the unpredictable Foote handed Mr Macklin a piece of paper on which he had composed a brief paragraph during the

---

[1] At one Summer Linguistics Institute, someone had bumper stickers printed up with Chomsky's famous sentence. One of them found its way into the hands of my brother, D. K. Oller, and eventually onto my bumper to the consternation of many Los Angeles motorists.

lecture. He asked Mr Macklin to kindly read it aloud once to the audience and then to repeat it from memory. So Mr Macklin read:

> So she went into the garden to cut a cabbage leaf to make an apple pie; and at the same time a great she-bear coming up the street pops its head in the shop. 'What! No soap!' So he died, and she very imprudently married the barber: and there were present the Picninnies, the Joblillies, and the Garcelies, and the Great Panjandrum himself, with the little round button at the top, and they all fell to playing the game of catch-as-catch-can, till the gunpowder ran out the heels of their boots (Samuel Foote, ca. 1854; see Cooke, 1902, p. 221f).[2]

The incident probably improved Mr Macklin's modesty and it surely instructed him on the importance of the reconstructive aspects of verbal memory. We don't just happen to remember things in all their detail; rather, we remember a kind of skeleton, or possibly a whole hierarchy of skeletons, to which we attach the flesh of detail by a creative and reconstructive process. That process, like all verbal and cognitive activities, is governed largely by what we have learned to expect. The fact is that she-bears rarely pop their heads into barber shops, nor do people cut cabbage leaves to make apple pies. For such reasons, Foote's prose is difficult to remember. It is because the contexts, outside of language, which are mapped by his choice of words are odd contexts in themselves. Otherwise, the word sequences are grammatical enough.

Perhaps the importance of our normal expectancies concerning words and what they mean is best illustrated by nonsense which violates those expectancies. The sequence *gbntmbwk* forces on our attention things that we know only subconsciously about our language – for example, the fact that *g* cannot immediately precede *b* at the beginning of a word, and that syllables in English must have a vowel sound in them somewhere (unless *shhhh!* is a syllable). These are facts we know because we have acquired an expectancy grammar for English.

Our internalized grammar tells us that *glerf* is a possible word in English. It is pronounceable and is parallel to words that exist in the

---

[2] I am indebted to my father, John Oller, Sr., for this illustration. He used it often in his talks on language teaching to show the importance of meaningful sequence to recall and learning. He often attributed the prose to Mark Twain, and it is possible that Twain used this same piece of wit to debunk a supposed memory expert in a circus contest as my father often claimed. I have not been able to document the story about Twain, though it seems characteristic of him. No doubt he knew of Foote and may have consciously imitated him.

language such as *glide, serf,* and *slurp*; still, *glerf* is not an English word. Our grammatical expectancies are not completely violated by Lewis Carroll's phrase, *the frumious bandersnatch,* but we recognize this as a novel creation. Our internalized grammar causes us to suppose that *frumious* must be an adjective that modifies the noun *bandersnatch.* We may even imagine a kind of beast that, in the context, might be referred to as a *frumious bandersnatch.* Our inferential construction may or may not resemble anything that Carroll had in mind, if in fact he had any 'thing' in mind at all. The inference here is similar to supposing that Foote was referring to Macklin himself when he chose the phrase *the Great Panjandrum himself, with the little round button at the top.* In either case, similar grammatical expectancies are employed.

But it may be objected that what we are referring to here as *grammatical* involves more than what is traditionally subsumed under the heading *grammar.* However, we are not concerned here with grammar in the traditional sense as being something entirely abstract and unrelated to persons who know languages. Rather, we are concerned with the psychological realities of linguistic knowledge as it is internalized in whatever ways by real human beings. By this definition of grammar, the language user's knowledge of how to map utterances pragmatically onto contexts outside of language and vice versa (that is, how to map contexts onto utterances) must be incorporated into the grammatical system. To illustrate, the word *horse* is effective in communicative exchanges if it is related to the right sort of animal. Pointing to a giraffe and calling it a horse is not an error in syntax, nor even an error in semantics (the speaker and listener may both know the intended meaning). It is the pragmatic mapping of a particular exemplar of the category GIRAFFE (as an object or real world thing, *not* as a word) that is incorrect. In an important sense, such an error is a grammatical error.

The term *expectancy grammar* calls attention to the peculiarly sequential organization of language in actual use. Natural language is perhaps the best known example of the complex organization of elements into sequences and classes, and sequences of classes which are composed of other sequences of classes and so forth. The term *pragmatic expectancy grammar* further calls attention to the fact that the sequences of classes of elements, and hierarchies of them which constitute a language are available to the language user in real life situations because they are somehow indexed with reference to their appropriateness to extralinguistic contexts.

In the normal use of language, no matter what level of language or mode of processing we think of, it is always possible to predict partially what will come next in any given sequence of elements. The elements may be sounds, syllables, words, phrases, sentences, paragraphs, or larger units of discourse. The mode of processing may be listening, speaking, reading, writing, or thinking, or some combination of these. In the meaningful use of language, some sort of pragmatic expectancy grammar must function in all cases.

A wide variety of research has shown that the more grammatically predictable a sequence of linguistic elements is, the more readily it can be processed. For instance, a sequence of nonsensical syllables as in the example from Osgood, *Nox ems glerf onmo kebs*, is more difficult than the same sequence with a more obvious structure imposed on it, as in *The nox ems glerfed the onmo kebs*. But the latter is still more difficult to process than, *The bad boys chased the pretty girls*. It is easy to see that the gradation from nonsense to completely acceptable sequences of meaningful prose can vary by much finer degrees, but these examples serve to illustrate that as sequences of linguistic elements become increasingly more predictable in terms of grammatical organization, they become easier to handle.

Not only are less constrained sequences more difficult than more constrained ones, but this generalization holds true regardless of which of the four traditionally recognized skills we are speaking of. It is also true for learning. In fact, there is considerable evidence to suggest that as organizational constraints on linguistic sequences are increased, ease of processing (whether perceiving, producing, learning, recalling, etc.) increases at an accelerating rate, almost exponentially. It is as though our learned expectations enable us to lie in wait for elements in a highly constrained linguistic context and make much shorter work of them than would be possible if they took us by surprise.

As we have been arguing throughout this chapter, the constraints on what may follow in a given sequence of linguistic elements go far beyond the traditionally recognized grammatical ones, and they operate in every aspect of our cognition. In his treatise on thinking, John Dewey (1910) argued that the 'central factor in thinking' is an element of expectancy. He gives an example of a man strolling along on a warm day. Suddenly, the man notices that it has become cool. It occurs to him that it is probably going to rain; looking up, he sees a dark cloud between himself and the sun. He then quickens his steps (p. 6f). Dewey goes on to define thinking as '*that operation in which present facts suggest other facts (or truths) in such a way as to induce belief in the latter upon the ground or the warrant of the former'* (p. 8f).

C. The emotive aspect

To this point, we have been concerned primarily with the factive aspect of language and cognition. However, much of what has been said applies as well to the emotive aspect of language use. Nonetheless there are contrasts in the coding of the two types of information. While factive information is coded primarily in distinctly verbal sequences, emotive information is coded primarily in gestures, tone of voice, facial expression, and the like. Whereas verbal sequences consist of a finite set of distinctive sounds (or features of sounds), syllables, words, idioms, and collocations, and generally of discrete and countable sequences of elements, the emotive coding devices are typically non-discrete and are more or less continuously variable.

For example, a strongly articulated *p* in the word *pat* hardly changes the meaning of the word, nor does it serve much better to distinguish *a pat on the head* from *a cat in the garage*. Shouting the word *garage* does not imply a larger garage, nor would whispering it necessarily change the meaning of the word in terms of its factive value. Either you have a garage to talk about or you don't, and there isn't much point in distinguishing cases in between the two extremes. With emotive information things are different. A wildly brandished fist is a stronger statement than a mere clenched fist. A loud shout means a stronger degree of emotion than a softer tone. In the kinds of devices typically used to code emotion information, variability in the strength of the symbol is analogically related to similar variability in the attitude that is symbolized.

In both speaking and writing, choice of words also figures largely in the coding of attitudinal information. Consider the differences in the attitudes elicited by the following sentences: (1) *Some people say it is better to explain our point of view as well as give the news*; (2) *Some people say it is better to include some propaganda as well as give the news*. Clearly, the presuppositions and implications of the two sentences are somewhat different, but they could conceivably be used in reference to exactly the same immediate states of affairs or extralinguistic contexts. Of the people polled in a certain study, 42.8 % agreed with the first, while only 24.7 % agreed with the second (Copi, 1972, p. 70). The 18.1 % difference is apparently attributable to the difference between explaining and propagandizing.

Although the facts referred to by such terms as exaggerating and lying may be the same facts in certain practical cases, the attitudes expressed toward those facts by selecting one or the other term are quite different. Indeed, the accompanying facial expression and tone of voice may convey attitudinal information so forcefully as to even contradict the factive claims of a statement. For instance, the teacher who says to a young child in an irritated tone of voice to 'Never mind about the spilled glue! It won't be any trouble to clean it up!' conveys one message factively and a very different one emotively. In this case, as in most such cases, the tone of voice is apt to speak louder than the words. Somehow we are more willing to believe a person's manner of speaking than whatever his words purport to say.

It is as if emotively coded messages were higher ranking and therefore more authoritative messages. As Watzlawick, Beavin, and Jackson (1967) point out in their book on the *Pragmatics of Human Communication*, it is part of the function of emotive messages to provide instructions concerning the interpretation of factively coded information. Whereas the latter can usually be translated into propositional forms such as 'This is what I believe is true', or 'This is what I believe is not true', the former can usually be translated into propositional forms about interpersonal relationships, or about how certain factive statements are to be read. For instance, a facetious remark may be said in such a manner that the speaker implies 'Take this remark as a joke' or 'I don't really believe this, and you shouldn't either.' At the same time, people are normally coding information emotively about the way they see each other as persons. Such messages can usually be translated into such propositional forms as 'This is the way I see you' or 'This is the way I see myself' or 'This is the way I see you seeing me' and so on.

Although attitudes toward the self, toward others, and toward the things that the self and others say may be more difficult to pin down than are tangible states of affairs, they are nonetheless real. In fact, Watzlawick *et al*, contend that emotive messages concerning such abstract aspects of interpersonal realities are probably much more important to the success of communicative exchanges than the factively coded messages themselves. If the self in relationship to others is satisfactorily defined, and if the significant others in interactional relationships confirm one's definition of self and others, communication concerning factive information can take place. Otherwise, relationship struggles ensue. Marital strife over whether or not one party loves the other, children's disputes about who said what and whether or not he or she meant it, labor and management disagreements about fair wages, and the arms race between the major world powers, are all examples of breakdowns in factive communication once relationship struggles begin.

What is very interesting for a theory of pragmatic expectancy grammar is that in normal communication, ways of expressing attitudes are nearly perfectly coordinated with ways of expressing factive information. As a person speaks, boundaries between linguistic segments are nearly perfectly synchronized with changes in bodily postures, gestures, tone of voice, and the like. Research by Condon and Ogston (1971) has shown that the coordination of gestures and verbal output is so finely grained that even the smallest movements of the hands and fingers are nearly perfectly coincident with boundaries in linguistic segments clear down to the level of the phoneme. Moreover, through sound recordings and high resolution motion photography they have been able to demonstrate that when the body movements and facial gestures of a speaker and hearer 'are segmented and displayed consecutively, the speakers and hearer look like puppets moved by the same set of strings' (p. 158).

The demonstrated coordination of mechanisms that usually code factive information and devices that usually code emotive information shows that the anticipatory planning of the speaker and the expectations of the listener must be in close harmony in normal communication. Moreover, from the fact that they are so synchronized we may infer something of the complexity of the advance planning and hypothesizing that normal internalized grammatical systems must enable language users to accomplish. Static grammatical devices which do not incorporate an element of real time would seem hard put to explain some of the empirical facts which demand explanation. Some sort of expectancy grammar, or a system incorporating temporal constraints on linguistic contexts seems to be required.

D. Language learning as grammar construction and modification

In a sense language is something that we learn, and in another it is a medium through which learning occurs. Colin Cherry (1957) has said that we never feel we have fully grasped an idea until we have 'jumped on it with both verbal feet.' This seems to imply that language is not just a means of expressing ideas that we already have, but rather that it is a means of discovering ideas that we have not yet fully discovered.

John Dewey argued that language was not just a means of 'expressing antecedent thought', rather that it was a basis for the very act of creative thinking itself. He wryly observed that the things that a person says often surprise himself more than anyone else. Alice in *Through the Looking Glass* seems to have the same thought instilled in her own creative imagination through the genius of Lewis Carroll. She asks, 'How can I know what I am going to say until I have already said it?'

Because of the nature of human limitations and because of the complexities of our universe of experience, in order for our minds to cope with the vastness of the diversity, it categorizes and systematizes elements into hierarchies and sequences of them. Not only is the universe of experience more complex than we can perceive it to be at a given moment of time, but the depths of our memories have registered untold millions of details about previous experience that are beyond the grasp of our present consciousness.

Our immediate awareness can be thought of as an interface between external reality and the mind. It is like a corridor of activity where incoming elements of experience are processed and where the highly complex activities of thinking and language communication are effected. The whole of our cognitive experience may be compared to a more or less constant stream of complex and interrelated objects passing back and forth through this center of activity.

Because of the connections and interrelationships between incoming elements, and since they tend to cluster together in predictable ways, we learn to expect certain kinds of things to follow from certain others. When you turn the corner on the street where you live you expect to see certain familiar buildings, yards, trees, and possibly your neighbor's dog with teeth bared. When someone speaks to you and you turn in his direction, you expect to see him by looking in the direction of the sound you have just heard. These sorts of expectations, whether they are learned or innate, are so commonplace that they seem trivial. They are not, however. Imagine the shock of having to face a world in which such expectations stopped being correct. Think what it would be like to walk into your living room and find yourself in a strange place. Imagine walking toward someone and getting farther from him with every step. The violations of our commonest expectations are horror-movie material that make earthquakes and hurricanes seem like Disneyland.

Man's great advantage over other organisms which are also prisoners of time and space, is his ability to learn and use language to systematize and organize experience more effectively. Through the use of language we may broaden or narrow the focus of our attention much the way we adjust the focus of our vision. We may think in terms of this sentence, or today, or this school year, or our lifetime, or known history, and so on. Regardless of how broad or narrow our perspective, there is a sequence of elements attended to by our consciousness within that perspective. The sequence itself may consist of relatively simple elements, or sets of interrelated and highly structured elements, but there must be a sequence because the totality of even a relatively simple aspect of our universe is too complex to be taken in at one gulp. We must deal with certain things ahead of others. In a sense, we must take in elements single file at a given rate, so that within the span of immediate consciousness, the number of elements being processed does not exceed certain limits.

In a characteristic masterpiece publication, George Miller (1956) presented a considerable amount of evidence from a wide variety of sources suggesting that the number of separate things that our consciousness can handle at any one time is somewhere in the neighborhood of seven, plus or minus one or two. He also pointed out that human beings overcome this limitation in part by what he calls 'chunking'. By treating sequences or clusters of elements as unitary chunks (or members of paradigms or classes) the mind constructs a richer cognitive system. In other words, by setting up useful categories of sequences, and categories of sequences of categories, our capacity to have correct expectations is enhanced – that is, we are enabled to have correct expectations about more objects, or more complex sorts of objects (in the most abstract sense of 'object') without any greater cost to the cognitive system.

All of this is merely a way of talking about learning. As sequences of elements at one level are organized into classes at a higher order of abstraction, the organism can be said to be constructing an appropriate expectancy grammar, or learning. A universal consequence of the construction and modification of an appropriate expectancy grammar is that the processing of sequences of elements that conform to the constraints of the grammar is thus enhanced. Moreover, it may be hypothesized that highly organized sequences of elements that are presented in contexts where the basis for the organization can be discovered will be more conducive to the construction of an appropriate expectancy grammar than the presentation of similar sequences without appropriate sorts of context.

We are drawn to the generalization that there is an extremely important parallel between the normal use of language and the learning of a language. The learner is never quite in the position of having no expectations to begin with. Even the newborn infant apparently has certain innate expectancies, e.g., that sucking its mother's breast will produce a desired effect. In fact, experiments by Bower (1971, 1974) seem to point to the conclusion that an infant is born with certain expectations of a much more specific sort – for example, the expectation that a seen object should have some tangible solidity to it. He proved that infants at surprisingly early ages were astonished when they passed their hands through the space occupied by what appeared to be a tangible object. However, his experiments show that infants apparently have to learn to expect entities (such as mother) to appear in only one place at one time. They also seem to have to *learn* that a percept of a moving object is caused by the same object as the percept of that same moving object when it comes to rest.

The problem, it would seem, from an educational point of view is how to take advantage of the expectancies that a learner has already acquired in trying to teach new material. The question is, what does the learner already know, and how can that knowledge be optimally utilized in the presentation of new material? It has been demonstrated many times over that learning of verbal material is enhanced if the meaningfulness of the material is maximized from the learner's point of view. An unpronounceable sequence of letters like *gbntmbwk* is more difficult to learn and to recall than say, *nox ems glerf*, in spite of the fact that the latter is a longer sequence of letters. The latter is easier because it conforms to some of the expectations that English speakers have acquired concerning phonological and graphological elements. A phrase like *colorless green ideas* conforms less well to our acquired expectancies than *beautiful fall colors*. Given appropriate contexts for the latter and the lack of them for the most part for the former, the latter should also be easier to learn to use appropriately than the former. A nonsensical passage like the one Mr Foote invented to stump Mr Macklin would be more difficult to learn than normal prose. The reason is simple enough. Learners know more about normal prose before the learning task begins.

Language programs that employ fully contextualized and maximally meaningful language necessarily optimize the learner's ability to use previously acquired expectancies to help discover the pragmatic mappings of utterances in the new language onto extralinguistic contexts. Hence, they would seem to be superior to programs that expect learners to acquire the ability to use a language on the basis of disconnected lists of sentences in the form of pattern drills, many of which are not only unrelated to meaningful extralinguistic contexts, but which are intrinsically unrelatable.

If one carefully examines language teaching methods and language learning settings which seem to be conducive to success in acquiring facility in the language, they all seem to have certain things in common. Whether a learner succeeds in acquiring a first language because he was born in the culture where that language was used, or was transported there and forced to learn it as a second language; whether a learner acquires a second language by hiring a tutor and speaking the language incessantly, or by marrying a tutor, or by merely maintaining a prolonged relationship with someone who speaks the language; whether the learner acquires the language through the command approach used successfully by J. J. Asher (1969, 1974), or the old silent method (Gattegno, 1963), or through a set of films of communicative exchanges (Oller, 1963–65), or by joining in a bilingual education experiment (Lambert and Tucker, 1972), certain sorts of data and motivations to attend to them are always present. The learner must be exposed to linguistic contexts in their peculiar pragmatic relationships to extralinguistic contexts, and the learner must be motivated to communicate with people in the target language by discovering those pragmatic relationships.

Although we have said little about education in a broader sense, everything said to this point has a broader application. In effect, the hypothesis concerning pragmatic expectancy grammar as a basis for explaining success and failure in language learning and language teaching can be extended to all other areas of the school curriculum in which language plays a large part. We will return to this issue in Chapter 14 where we discuss reading curricula and other language based parts of curricula in general. In particular we will examine research into the developing language skills of children in Brisbane, Australia (Hart, Walker, and Gray, 1977).

E. Tests that invoke the learner's grammar

When viewed from the vantage point assumed in this chapter, language testing is primarily a task of assessing the efficiency of the pragmatic expectancy grammar the learner is in the process of constructing. In order for a language test to achieve validity in terms of the theoretical construct of a pragmatic expectancy grammar, it will have to invoke and challenge the efficiency of the learner's developing grammar. We can be more explicit. Two closely interrelated criteria of construct validity may be imposed on language tests: first, they must cause the learner to process (either produce or comprehend, or possibly to comprehend, store, and recall, or some other combination) temporal sequences of elements in the language that conform to normal contextual constraints (linguistic and extralinguistic); second, they must require the learner to understand the pragmatic interrelationship of linguistic contexts and extra-linguistic contexts.

The two validity requirements just stated are like two sides of the same coin. The first emphasizes the sequential constraints specified by the grammar, and the second emphasizes the function of the grammar in relating sequences of elements in the language to states of affairs outside of language. In subsequent chapters we will often refer to these validity requirements as the *pragmatic naturalness criteria*. We will explore ways of accomplishing such assessment in Chapter 3, and in greater detail in Part Three which includes Chapters 10 through 14. Techniques that fail to meet the naturalness criteria are discussed in Part Two – especially in Chapter 8. Multiple choice testing procedures are discussed in Chapter 9.

KEY POINTS

1. To understand the problem of constructing valid language tests, it is essential to understand the nature of the skill to be tested.
2. Two aspects of language in use need to be distinguished: the *factive* (or cognitive) aspect of language use has to do with the coding of information about states of affairs by using words, phrases, clauses, and discourse; the *emotive* (or affective) aspect of language use has to do with the coding of information about attitudes and interpersonal relationships by using facial expression, gesture, tone of voice, and choice of words. These two aspects of language use are intricately interrelated.
3. Two major kinds of context are distinguished: *linguistic context* consists of verbal and gestural aspects; and *extralinguistic context* similarly consists of objective and subjective aspects.
4. The systematic correspondences between linguistic and extralinguistic contexts are referred to as pragmatic mappings.
5. *Pragmatics* asks how utterances (and of course other forms of language in use) are related to human experience.
6. In relation to the factive aspect of coding information about states of affairs outside of language, it is asserted that language is always an abbreviation for a much more complete and detailed sort of knowledge.
7. An important aspect of the coding of information in language is the anticipatory planning of the speaker and the advance hypothesizing of the listener concerning what is likely to be said next.

8. A *pragmatic expectancy grammar* is defined as a psychologically real system that sequentially orders linguistic elements in time and in relation to extralinguistic contexts in meaningful ways.

9. As linguistic sequences become more highly constrained by grammatical organization of the sorts illustrated, they become easier to process.

10. Whereas coding devices for factive information are typically digital (either on or off, present or absent), coding devices for emotive information are usually analogical (continuously variable). A tone of voice which indicates excitement may vary with the degree of excitement, but a digital device for, say, referring to a pair of glasses cannot be whispered to indicate very thin corrective lenses and shouted to indicate thick ones. The word *eyeglasses* does not have such a continuous variability of meaning, but a wild-eyed shout probably does mean a greater degree of intensity than a slightly raised voice.

11. Where there is a conflict between emotively coded information and factive level information, the former usually overrides the latter.

12. When relationship struggles begin, factive level communication usually ends. Examples are the wage-price spiral and the arms race.

13. The coding of factive and emotive information are very precisely synchronized, and the gestural movements of speaker and listener in a typical communicative exchange are also timed in surprisingly accurate cadence.

14. Some sort of grammatical system incorporating the element of real time and capable of substantial anticipatory-expectancy activity seems required to explain well known facts of normal language use.

15. Language is both an object and a tool of learning. Cherry suggests that we not only express ideas in words, but that we in fact discover them by putting them into words.

16. Language learning is construed as a process of constructing an appropriate expectancy generating system. Learning is enhancing one's capacity to have correct expectations about the nature of experience.

17. It is hypothesized that language teaching programs (and by implication educational programs in general) will be more effective if they optimize the learner's opportunities to take advantage of previously acquired expectancies in acquiring new knowledge.

18. It is further hypothesized that the data necessary to language acquisition are what are referred to in this book as pragmatic mappings – i.e., the systematic correspondences between linguistic and extralinguistic contexts. In addition to opportunity, the only other apparent necessity is sufficient motivation to operate on the requisite data in appropriate ways.

19. Valid language tests are defined as those tests which meet the pragmatic naturalness criteria – namely, those which invoke and challenge the efficiency of the learner's expectancy grammar, first by causing the learner to process temporal sequences in the language that conform to normal contextual constraints, and second by requiring the learner to understand the systematic correspondences of linguistic contexts and extralinguistic contexts.

DISCUSSION QUESTIONS

1. Why is it so important to understand the nature of the skill you are trying to test? Can you think of examples of tests that have been used for educational or other decisions but which were not related to a careful consideration of the skill or knowledge they purported to assess? Study closely a test that is used in your school or that you have taken at some time in the course of your educational experience. How can you tell if the test is a measure of what it purports to measure? Does the label on the test really tell you what it measures?

2. Look for examples in your own experience illustrating the importance of grammatically based expectancies. Riddles, puns, jokes, and parlor games are good sources. Speech errors are equally good illustrations. Consider the example of the little girl who was asked by an adult where she got her ice cream. She replied, 'All over me,' as she looked sheepishly at the vanilla and chocolate stains all over her dress. How did her expectations differ from those of the adult who asked the question?

3. Keep track of listening or reading errors where you took a wrong turn in your thinking and had to do some retreading farther down the line. Discuss the source of such wrong turns.

4. Consider the sentences: (a) The boy was bucked off by the pony, and (b) The boy was bucked off by the barn (example from Woods, 1970). Why does the second sentence require a mental double-take? Note similar examples in your reading for the next few days. Write down examples and be prepared to discuss them with your class.

SUGGESTED READINGS

1. George A. Miller, 'The Magical Number Seven Plus or Minus Two: Some Limits on Our Capacity for Processing Information,' *Psychological Review* 63, 1956, 81–97.

2. Donald A. Norman, 'In Retrospect,' *Memory and Attention*. New York: Wiley, 1969, pp. 177–181.

3. Part VI of *Focus on the Learner*. Rowley, Mass.: Newbury House, 1973, pp. 265–300.

4. Bernard Spolsky, 'What Does It Mean to Know a Language or How Do You Get Someone to Perform His Competence?' In J. W. Oller, Jr. and J. C. Richards (eds.) *Focus on the Learner*. Rowley, Mass.: Newbury House, 1973, 164–76.

3

Discrete Point,
Integrative,
or Pragmatic Tests

Not all that glitters is gold, and not everything that goes by the name is twenty-four karat. Neither are all tests which are called *language* tests necessarily worthy of the name, and some are better than others. This chapter deals with three classes of tests that are called measures of *language* – but it will be argued that they are not equal in effectiveness. It is claimed that only tests which meet the pragmatic naturalness criteria defined in Chapter 2 are *language* tests in the most fundamental sense of what language is and how it functions.

A. Discrete point versus integrative testing

In recent years, a body of literature on language testing has developed which distinguishes two major categories of tests. John Carroll (1961, see the Suggested Readings at the end of this chapter) was the person credited with first proposing the distinction between *discrete point* and *integrative* language tests. Although the types are not always different for practical purposes, the theoretical bases of the two approaches contrast markedly and the predictions concerning the effects and relative validity of different testing procedures also differ in fundamental ways depending on which of the two approaches one selects. The contrast between these two philosophies, of course, is not limited to language testing *per se*, but can be seen throughout the whole spectrum of educational endeavor.

Traditionally, a *discrete point* test is one that attempts to focus attention on one point of grammar at a time. Each test item is aimed at one and only one element of a particular component of a grammar (or perhaps we should say hypothesized grammar), such as phonology, syntax, or vocabulary. Moreover, a discrete point test purports to assess only one skill at a time (e.g., listening, or speaking, or reading, or writing) and only one aspect of a skill (e.g., productive versus receptive or oral versus visual). Within each skill, aspect, and component, discrete items supposedly focus on precisely one and only one phoneme, morpheme, lexical item, grammatical rule, or whatever the appropriate element may be. (See Lado, 1961, in Suggested Readings at the end of this chapter.) For instance, a phonological discrete item might require an examinee to distinguish between minimal pairs, e.g., *pill* versus *peel*, auditorily presented. An example of a morphological item might be one which requires the selection of an appropriate suffix such as *-ness* or *-ity* to form a noun from an adjective like *secure*, or *sure*. An example of a syntactic item might be a fill-in-the-blank type where the examinee must supply the suffix *-s* as in *He walk — to town each morning now that he lives in the city.*[1]

The concept of an *integrative* test was born in contrast with the definition of a discrete point test. If discrete items take language skill apart, integrative tests put it back together. Whereas discrete items attempt to test knowledge of language one bit at a time, integrative tests attempt to assess a learner's capacity to use many bits all at the same time, and possibly while exercising several presumed components of a grammatical system, and perhaps more than one of the traditionally recognized skills or aspects of skills.

However, to base a definition of integrative language testing on

---

[1] Other discrete item examples are offered in Chapter 8 where we return to the topic of discrete point tests and examine them in greater detail.

what would appear to be its logical antithesis and in fact its competing predecessor is to assume a fairly limiting point of view. It is possible to look to other sources for a theoretical basis and rationale for so-called integrative tests.

B. A definition of pragmatic tests

The term *pragmatic test* has sometimes been used interchangeably with the term *integrative test* in order to call attention to the possibility of relating integrative language testing procedures to a theory of pragmatics, or pragmatic expectancy grammar. Whereas integrative testing has been somewhat loosely defined in terms of what discrete point testing is not, it is possible to be somewhat more precise in saying what a pragmatic test is: it is any procedure or task that causes the learner to process sequences of elements in a language that conform to the normal contextual constraints of that language, and which requires the learner to relate sequences of linguistic elements via pragmatic mappings to extralinguistic context.

Integrative tests are often pragmatic in this sense, and pragmatic tests are always integrative. There is no ordinary discourse situation in which a learner might be asked to listen to and distinguish between isolated minimal pairs of phonological contrasts. There is no normal language use context in which one's attention would be focussed on the syntactic rules involved in placing appropriate suffixes on verb stems or in moving the agent of an active declarative sentence from the front of the sentence to the end in order to form a passive (e.g., *The dog bit John* in the active form becoming *John was bitten by the dog* in the passive). Thus, *discrete point tests cannot be pragmatic, and conversely, pragmatic tests cannot be discrete point tests.* Therefore, pragmatic tests must be integrative.

But integrative language tasks can be conceived which do not meet one or both of the naturalness criteria which we have imposed in our definition of pragmatic tests. If a test merely requires an examinee to use more than one of the four traditionally recognized skills and/or one or more of the traditionally recognized components of grammar, it must be considered integrative. But to qualify as a pragmatic test, more is required.

In order for a test user to say something meaningful (valid) about the efficiency of a learner's developing grammatical system, the pragmatic naturalness criteria require that the test invoke and challenge that developing grammatical system. This requires processing sequences of elements in the target language (even if it is the learner's first and only language) subject to temporal contextual constraints. In addition, the tasks must be such that for examinees to do them, linguistic sequences must be related to extralinguistic contexts in meaningful ways.

Examples of tasks that do not qualify as pragmatic tests include all discrete point tests, the rote recital of sequences of material without attention to meaning; the manipulation of sequences of verbal elements, possibly in complex ways, but in ways that do not require awareness of meaning. In brief, if the task does not require attention to meaning in temporally contrained sequences of linguistic elements, it cannot be construed as a pragmatic language test. Moreover, the constraints must be of the type that are found in normal uses of the language, not merely in some classroom setting that may have been contrived according to some theory of how languages should be taught. Ultimately, the question of whether or not a task is pragmatic is an empirical one. It cannot be decided by theory based preferences, or opinion polls.

C. Dictation and cloze procedure as examples of pragmatic tests

The traditional dictation, rooted in the distant past of language teaching, is an interesting example of a pragmatic language testing procedure. If the sequences of words or phrases to be dictated are selected from normal prose, or dialogue, or some other natural form of discourse (or perhaps if the sequences are carefully contrived to mirror normal discourse, as in well-written fiction) and if the material is presented orally in sequences that are long enough to challenge the short term memory of the learners, a simple traditional dictation meets the naturalness requirements for pragmatic language tests. First, such a task requires the processing of temporally constrained sequences of material in the language and second, the task of dividing up the stream of speech and writing down what is heard requires understanding the meaning of the material – i.e., relating the linguistic context (which in a sense is given) to the extralinguistic context (which must be inferred).

Although an inspection of the results of dictation tests with appropriate statistical procedures (as we will see below) shows the technique to be very reliable and highly valid, it has not always been looked on with favor by the experts. For example, Robert Lado (1961) said:

> Dictation ... on critical inspection ... appears to measure very little of language. Since the word order is given ... it does not test word order. Since the words are given ... it does not test vocabulary. It hardly tests the aural perception of the examiner's pronunciation because the words can in many cases be identified by context. ... The student is less likely to hear the sounds incorrectly in the slow reading of the words which is necessary for dictation (p. 34).

Other authors have tended to follow Lado's lead:

> As a testing device ... dictation must be regarded as generally uneconomical and imprecise (Harris, 1969, p. 5). Some teachers argue that dictation is a test of auditory comprehension, but surely this is a very indirect and inadequate test of such an important skill (Anderson, 1953, p. 43). Dictation is primarily a test of spelling (Somaratne, 1957, p. 48).

More recently. J. B. Heaton (1975), though he cites some of the up-to-date research on dictation in his bibliography, devotes less than two pages to dictation as a testing procedure and concludes that

> dictation ... as a testing device measures too many different language features to be effective in providing a means of assessing any one skill (p. 186).

Davies (1977) offers much the same criticism of dictation. He suggests that it is too imprecise in diagnostic information, and further that it is apt to have an unfortunate 'washback' effect (namely, in taking on 'the aura of language goals'). Therefore, he argues

> it may be desirable to abandon such well-worn and suspect techniques for less familiar and less coherent ones (p. 66).

In the rest of the book edited by Allen and Davies (1977) there is only one other mention of dictation. Ingram (1977) in the same volume pegs dictation as a rather weak sort of spelling test (see p. 20).

If we were to rely on an opinion poll, the weight of the evidence would seem to be against dictation as a useful language testing procedure. However, the validity of a testing procedure is hardly the sort of question that can be answered by taking a vote.

Is it really necessary to read the material very slowly as is implied by Lado's remarks? The answer is no. It is possible to read slowly, but it is not necessary to do so. In fact, unless the material is presented in sequences long enough to challenge the learner's short term memory, and quickly enough to simulate the normal temporal nature of speech sequences, then perhaps dictation would become a test of spelling as Somaratne and Ingram suggest. However, it is not even necessary to count spelling as a criterion for correctness. Somaratne's remark seems to imply that one must, but research shows that one shouldn't. We will return to this question in particular, namely, the scoring of dictation, and other practical questions in Chapter 10.

The view that a language learner can take dictation (which is presented in reasonably long bursts, say, five or more words between pauses, and where each burst is given at a conversational rate) without doing some very active and creative processing is credible only from the vantage point of the naive examiner who thinks that the learner automatically knows what the examiner knows about the material being dictated. As the famous Swiss linguist pointed out three quarters of a century ago,

> ... the main characteristic of the sound chain is that it is linear. Considered by itself it is only a line, a continuous ribbon along which the ear perceives no self-sufficient and clear-cut division ... (quoted from lectures compiled by de Saussure's students, Bally, Sechehaye, and Riedlinger, 1959, pp. 103–104).

To prove that the words of a dictation are not necessarily 'given' from the learner's point of view, one only needs to try to write dictation in an unknown language. The reader may try this test: have a speaker of Yoruba, Thai, Mandarin, Serbian or some other language which you do not know say a few short sentences with pauses between them long enough for you to write them down or attempt to repeat them. Try something simple like, *Say Man what's happening*, or *How's life been treating you lately*, at a conversational rate. If the proof is not convincing, consider the kinds of errors that non-native speakers of English make in taking dictation.

In a research report circulated in 1973, Johansson gave examples of vocabulary errors: *eliquants, elephants,* and *elekvants* for the word *eloquence*. It is possible that the first rendition is a spelling error, but that possibility does not exist for the other renditions. At the phrase level, consider *of appearance* for *of the period, person in facts* for *pertinent facts, less than justice, lasting justice, last in justice* for *just injustice.*Or when a foreign student at UCLA writes, *to find particle man living better and mean help man and boy tellable damage* instead of *to find practical means of feeding people better and means of helping them avoid the terrible damage of windstorms*, does it make sense to say that the words and their order were 'given'?

Though much research remains to be done to understand better what learners are doing when they take dictation, it is clear from the above examples that whatever mental processes they are performing must be active and creative. There is much evidence to suggest that there are fundamental parallels between tasks like taking dictation and using language in a wide variety of other ways. Among closely related testing procedures are sentence repetition tasks (or 'elicited imitation') which have been used in the testing of children for proficiency in one or more languages or language varieties. We return to this topic in detail in Chapter 10.

All of the research seems to indicate that in order for examinees to take dictation, or to repeat utterances that challenge their short term memory, it is necessary not only to make the appropriate discriminations in dividing up the continuum of speech, but also to understand the meaning of what is said.

Another example of a pragmatic language testing procedure is the cloze technique. The best known variety of this technique is the sort of test that is constructed by deleting every fifth, sixth, or seventh word from a passage of prose. Typically each deleted word is replaced by a blank of standard length, and the task set the examinee is to fill in the blanks by restoring the missing words. Other varieties of the procedure involve deleting specific vocabulary items, parts of speech, affixes, or particular types of grammatical markers.

The word *cloze* was invented by Wilson Taylor (1953) to call attention to the fact that when an examinee fills in the gaps in a passage of prose, he is doing something similar to what Gestalt psychologists call 'closure', a process related to the perception of incomplete geometric figures, for example. Taylor considered words deleted from prose to present a special kind of closure problem. From what is known of the grammatical knowledge the examinee brings to bear in solving such a closure problem, we can appreciate the fact that the problem is a very special sort of closure.

Like dictation, cloze tests meet both of the naturalness criteria for pragmatic language tests. In order to give correct responses (whether the standard of correctness is the exact word that originally appeared at a particular point, or any other word that fully fits the context of the passage), the learner must operate _____ the basis of, both immediate and long-range _____ constraints. Whereas some of the blanks in a cloze test (say of the standard variety deleting every *n*th word) can be filled by attending only to a few words on either side of the blank, as in the first blank in the preceding sentence, other blanks in a typical cloze passage require attention to longer stretches of linguistic context. They often require inferences about extralinguistic context, as in the case of the second blank in the preceding sentence.

The word *on* seems to be required in the first blank by the words *operate* and *the basis of,* without any additional information. However, unless long range constraints are taken into account, the second blank offers many possibilities. If the examinee attended only to such constraints as are afforded by the words from *operate* onward, it could be filled by such words as *missile, legal,* or *leadership.* The intended word was *contextual.* Other alternatives which might have occurred to the reader, and which are in the general semantic target area might include *temporal, verbal, extralinguistic, grammatical, pragmatic, linguistic, psycholinguistic, sociolinguistic, psychological, semantic,* and so on.

In taking a cloze test, the examinee must utilize information that is inferred about the facts, events, ideas, relationships, states of affairs, social settings and the like that are pragmatically mapped by the linguistic sequences contained in the passage. Examples of cases where extralinguistic context and the linguistic context of the passage are interrelated are obvious in so-called deictic words such as *here* and *now, then* and *there, this* and *that,* pronouns that refer to persons or things, tense indicators, aspect markers on verbs, adverbs of time and place, determiners and demonstratives in general, and a host of others.

For a simple example, consider the sentence, *A horse was fast when he was tied to a hitching post, and the same animal was also fast when he won a horse-race.* If such a sentence were part of a larger context, say on the difficulties of the English language, and if we deleted the first *a,* the blank could scarcely be filled with the definite article *the* because no horse has been mentioned up to that point. On the other hand, if we deleted the *the* before the words *same animal,* the indefinite article could not be used because of the fact that the horse referred to by the phrase *A horse* at the beginning of the sentence is the same horse referred to by the phrase *the same animal.* This is an example of a pragmatic constraint. Consider the oddity of saying, *The horse was fast when he was tied to a hitching post, and a same animal was also fast when he won a horse-race.*

Even though the pragmatic mapping constraints involved in normal discourse are only partially understood by the theoreticians, and though they cannot be precisely characterized in terms of grammatical systems (at least not yet), the fact that they exist is well-known, and the fact that they can be tested by such pragmatic procedures and the cloze technique has been demonstrated (see Chapter 12).

All sorts of deletions of so-called content words (e.g., nouns, adjectives, verbs, and adverbs), and especially grammatical connectors such as subordinating conjunctions, negatives, and a great many others carry with them constraints that may range backward or forward across several sentences or more. Such linguistic elements may entail restrictions that influence items that are widely separated in the passage. This places a strain on short term memory which presses the learner's pragmatic expectancy grammar into operation. The accuracy with which the learner is able to supply correct responses can therefore be taken as an index of the efficiency of the learner's developing grammatical system. Ways of constructing, administering, scoring, and interpreting cloze tests and a variety of related procedures for acquiring such indices are discussed in Chapter 12.

D. Other examples of pragmatic tests

Pragmatic testing procedures are potentially innumerable. The techniques discussed so far, dictation, cloze, and variations of them, by no means exhaust the possibilities. Probably they do not even begin to indicate the range of reasonable possibilities to be explored. There is always a danger that minor empirical advances in educational research in particular, may lead to excessive dependence on procedures that are associated with the progress. However, in spite of the fact that some of the pragmatic procedures thus far investigated do appear to work substantially better than their discrete point predecessors, there is little doubt that pragmatic tests can also be refined and expanded. It is important that the procedures which now exist and which have been studied should not limit our vision concerning other possibilities. Rather, they should serve as guideposts for subsequent refinement and development of still more effective and more informative testing procedures.

Therefore, the point of this section (and in a broader sense, this entire book) is not to provide a comprehensive list of possible pragmatic testing procedures, but rather to illustrate some of the possible types of procedures that meet the naturalness criteria concerning the temporal constraints on language in use, and the pragmatic mapping of linguistic contexts onto extralinguistic ones. Below, in section E of this chapter, we will discuss evidence concerning the validity of pragmatic tests. (Also, see the Appendix.)

Combined cloze and dictation. The examinee reads material from which certain portions have been deleted and simultaneously (or subsequently) hears the same material without deletions either live or on tape. The examinee's task is to fill in the missing portions the same as in the usual cloze procedure, but he has the added support of the auditory signal to help him fill in the missing portions. Many variations on this procedure are possible. Single words, or even parts of words, or sequences of words, or even whole sentences or longer segments may be deleted. The less material one deletes, presumably, the more the task resembles the standard cloze procedure, and the more one deletes, the more the task looks like a standard dictation.

Oral cloze procedure. Instead of presenting a cloze passage in a written format, it is possible to use a carefully prepared tape recording of the material with numbers read in for the blanks, or with pauses where blanks occur. Or, it is possible merely to read the material up to the blank, give the examinee the opportunity to guess the missing word, record the response, and at that point either tell the examinee the right answer (i.e., the missing word), or simply go on without any feedback as to the correctness of the examinee's response. Another procedure is to arrange the deletions so that they always come at the end of a clause or sentence. Any of these oral cloze techniques have the advantage of being usable with non-literate populations.

Dictation with interfering noise. Several varieties of this procedure have been used, and for a wide range of purposes. The best known examples are the versions of the Spolsky-Gradman noise tests used with non-native speakers of English. The procedure simply involves superimposing white noise (a wide spectrum of random noise sounding roughly like radio static or a shhhhshing sound at a constant level) onto taped verbal material. If the linguistic context under the noise is fully meaningful and subject to the normal extralinguistic constraints, this procedure qualifies as a pragmatic testing technique. Variations include noise throughout the material versus noise over certain portions only. It is argued, in any event, that the noise constitutes a situation somewhat parallel to many of the everyday contexts where language is used in less than ideal acoustic conditions, e.g., trying to have a conversation in someone's livingroom when the television and air conditioner are producing a high level of competing noise, or trying to talk to or hear someone else in the crowded lobby of a hotel, or trying to hear a message over a public address system in a busy air terminal, etc.

Paraphrase recognition. In one version, examinees are asked to read a sentence and then to select from four or five alternatives the best paraphrase for the given sentence. The task may be made somewhat more difficult by having examinees read a paragraph or longer passage and then select from several alternatives the one which best represents the central meaning or idea of the given passage. This task is somewhat similar to telling what a conversation was about, or what the main ideas of a speech were, and the like. Typically, such tests are interpreted as being tests of reading comprehension. However, they are pragmatic language tests inasmuch as they meet the naturalness criteria related to meaning and temporal constraints.

A paraphrase recognition task may be either in a written format or an oral format or some combination of them. An example of an oral format comes from the *Test of English as a Foreign Language* produced by Educational Testing Service, Princeton, New Jersey. Examinees hear a sentence like, *John dropped the letter in the mailbox.* Then they must choose between (a) *John sent the letter*; (b) *John opened the letter*; (c) *John lost the letter*; (d) *John destroyed the letter.*[2] Of course, considerably more complicated items are possible. The discrete point theorist might object that since the first stimulus is presented auditorily and since the choices are then presented in a written format, it becomes problematic to say what the test is a test of – whether listening comprehension, or reading comprehension, or both. This is an issue that we will return to in Chapters 8 and 9, and which will be addressed briefly in the section on the validity of pragmatic tests below. Also, see the Appendix.

Question answering. In one section of the *TOEFL*, examinees are required to select the best answer from a set of written alternatives to an auditorily presented question (either on record or tape). For instance, the examinee might hear, *When did Tom come here?* In the test booklet he reads, (a) *By taxi*; (b) *Yes, he did*; (c) *To study history*; and (d) *Last night.* He must mark on his answer sheet the letter corresponding to the best answer to the given question.

[2] This example and subsequent ones from the TOEFL are based on mimeographed hand-outs prepared by the staff at Educational Testing Service to describe the new format of the TOEFL in relation to the format used from 1961–1975.

A slightly different question answering task appears in a different section of the test. The examinee hears a dialogue such as:

MAN'S VOICE: Hello Mary. This is Mr Smith at the office. Is Bill feeling any better today?

WOMAN'S VOICE: Oh, yes, Mr Smith. He's feeling much better now. But the doctor says he'll have to stay in bed until Monday.

THIRD VOICE: Where is Bill now?

Possible answers from which the examinee must choose include: (a) *At the office*; (b) *On his way to work*; (c) *Home in bed*; and (d) *Away on vacation*.

Perhaps the preceding example, and other multiple choice examples may seem somewhat contrived. For this and other reasons to be discussed in Chapter 9, good items of the preceding type are quite difficult to prepare. Other formats which allow the examinee to supply answers to questions concerning less contrived contexts may be more suitable for classroom applications. For instance, sections of a television or radio broadcast in the target language may be taped. Questions formed in relation to those passages could be used as part of an interview technique aimed at testing oral skills.

A colorful, interesting, and potentially pragmatic testing technique is the *Bilingual Syntax Measure* (Burt, Dulay, and Hernandez, 1975). It is based on questions concerning colorful cartoon style pictures like the one shown in Figure 1, on page 48.

The test is intended for children between the ages of four and nine, from kindergarten through second grade. Although the authors of the test have devised a scoring procedure that is essentially aimed at assessing control of less than twenty so-called functors (morphological and syntactic markers like the plural endings on nouns, or tense markers on verbs), the procedure itself is highly pragmatic. First, questions are asked in relation to specific extralinguistic contexts in ways that require the processing of sequences of elements in English, or Spanish, or possibly some other language. Second, those meaningful sequences of linguistic elements in the form of questions must be related to the given extralinguistic contexts in meaningful ways.

For instance, in relation to a picture such as the one shown in Figure 1, the child might be asked something like, *How come he's so skinny*? The questioner indicates the guy pushing the wheelbarrow. The situation is natural enough and seems likely to motivate a child to

Figure 1. A cartoon drawing illustrating the style of the *Bilingual Syntax Measure.*

want to respond. We return to the *Bilingual Syntax Measure* and a number of related procedures in Chapter 11.

Oral interview. In addition to asking specific questions about pictured or real situations, oral tests may take a variety of other forms. In effect, every opportunity a learner is given to talk in an educational setting can be considered a kind of oral language test. The score on such a test may be only the subjective impression that it makes on the teacher (or another evaluator), or it may be based on some more detailed plan of counting errors. Surprisingly perhaps, the so-called objective procedures are not necessarily more reliable. In fact, they may be less reliable in some cases. Certain aspects of language performances may simply lend themselves more to subjective judgement than they do to quantification by formula. For instance, Richards (1970b) has shown that naive native speakers are fairly reliable judges of word frequencies. Also, it has been known for a long time that subjective rankings of passages of prose are sometimes more reliable than rankings (for relative difficulty) based on readability formulas (Klare, 1974).

An institutional technique that has been fairly well standardized by the Foreign Service Institute uses a training procedure for judges who are taught to conduct interviews and to judge performance on the basis of carefully thought-out rating scales. This procedure is discussed along with the *Ilyin Oral Interview* (Ilyin, 1972) and Upshur's *Oral Communication Test* (no date), in Chapter 11.

Composition or essay writing. Most free writing tasks necessarily qualify as pragmatic tests. Because it is frequently difficult to judge examinees relative to one another when they may have attempted to say entirely different sorts of things, and because it is also difficult to say what constitutes an error in writing, various modified writing tasks have been used. For example, there is the so-called dehydrated sentence, or dehydrated essay. The examinee is given a telegraphic message and is asked to expand it. An instance of the dehydrated sentence is *child/ride/bicycle/off embankment/last month.* A dehydrated narrative might continue, *was taken to hospital/lingered near death/family reunited/back to school/two weeks in hospital.*

Writing tasks may range from the extreme case of allowing examinees to select their own topic and to develop it, to maximally controlled tasks like filling in blanks in a pre-selected (or even contrived) passage prepared by the teacher or examiner. The blanks might require open-ended responses on the order of whole paragraphs, or sentences, or phrases, or words. In the last case, we have arrived back at a rather obvious form of cloze procedure.

Another version of a fairly controlled writing task involves either listening to or reading a passage and then trying to reproduce it from recall. If the original material is auditorily presented, the task becomes a special variety of dictation. This procedure and a variety of others are discussed in greater detail in Chapter 13.

Narration. One of the techniques sometimes used successfully to elicit relatively spontaneous speech samples is to ask subjects to talk about a frightening experience or an accident where they were almost 'shaded out of the picture' (Paul Anisman, personal communication). With very young children, story re-telling, which is a special version of narration, has been used. It is important that such tasks seem natural to the child, however, in order to get a realistic attempt from the examinee. For instance, it is important that the person to whom the child is expected to re-tell the story is not the same person who has just told the story in the first place (he obviously knows it). It should rather be someone who has not (as far as the child is aware) heard the story before – or at least not the child's version.

Translation. Although translation, like other pragmatic procedures, has not been favored by the testing experts in recent years, it still remains in at least some of its varieties as a viable pragmatic procedure. It deserves more research. It would appear from the study by Swain, Dumas, and Naiman (1974) that if it is used in ways that approximate its normal application in real life contexts, it can provide valuable information about language proficiency. If the sequences of verbal material are long enough to challenge the short-term memory of the examinees, it would appear that the technique is a special kind of pragmatic paraphrase task.

E. Research on the validity of pragmatic tests

We have defined language use and language learning in relation to the theoretical construct of a pragmatic expectancy grammar. Language use is viewed as a process of interacting plans and hypotheses concerning the pragmatic mapping of linguistic contexts onto extralinguistic ones. Language learning is viewed as a process of developing such an expectancy system. Further, it is claimed that a language test must invoke and challenge the expectancy system of the learner in order to assess its efficiency. In all of this discussion, we are concerned with what may be called the *construct validity* of pragmatic language tests. If they were to stand completely alone, such considerations would fall far short of satisfactorily demonstrating the validity of pragmatic language tests. Empirical tests must be applied to the tests themselves to determine whether or not they are good tests according to some purpose or range of purposes (see Oller and Perkins, 1978).

In addition to *construct validity* which is related to the question of whether the test meets certain theoretical requirements, there is the matter of so-called *content validity* and of *concurrent validity*. *Content validity* is related to the question of whether the test requires the examinee to perform tasks that are really the same as or fundamentally similar to the sorts of tasks one normally performs in exhibiting the skill or ability that the test purports to measure. For instance, we might ask of a test that purports to measure listening comprehension for adult foreign students in American universities: does the test require the learner to do the sort of thing that it supposedly measures his ability to do? Or, for a test that purports to measure the degree of dominance of bilingual children in classroom contexts that require listening and speaking, we might ask: does the test require the children to say and do things that are similar in some fundamental way to what they are normally required to do in the classroom? These are questions about *content validity*.

With respect to *concurrent validity*, the question of interest is to what extent do tests that purport to measure the same skill(s), or component(s) of a skill (or skills) correlate statistically with each other? Below, we will digress briefly to consider the meaning of statistical correlation. An example of a question concerning concurrent validity would be: do several tests that purport to measure the same thing actually correlate more highly with each other than with a set of tests that purport to measure something different? For instance, do language tests correlate more highly with each other than with tests that are labeled IQ tests? And vice versa. Do tests which are labeled tests of listening comprehension correlate better with each other than they do with tests that purport to measure reading comprehension? And vice versa.

A special set of questions about concurrent validity relate to the matter of test *reliability*. In the general sense, concurrent validity is about whether or not tests that purport to do the same thing actually do accomplish the same thing (or better, the degree to which they accomplish the same thing). Reliability of tests can be taken as a special case of concurrent validity. If all of the items on a test labeled as a test of writing ability are supposed to measure writing ability, then there should be a high degree of consistency of performance on the various items on that test. There may be differences of difficulty level, but presumably the type of skill to be assessed should be the same. This is like saying there should be a high degree of concurrent validity among items (or tests) that purport to measure the same thing. In order for a test to have a high degree of validity of any sort, it can be shown that it must first have a high degree of reliability.

In addition to these empirical (and statistically determined) requirements, a good test must also be *practical* and, for educational purposes, we might want to add that it should also have *instructional value*. By being *practical* we mean that it should be usable within the limits of time and budget available. It should have a high degree of cost effectiveness.

By having *instructional value* we mean that it ought to be possible to use the test to enhance the delivery of instruction in student populations. This may be accomplished in a foreign language classroom by diagnosing student progress (and teacher effectiveness) in more specific ways. In some cases the test itself becomes a teaching procedure in the most obvious sense. In multilingual contexts better knowledge of student abilities to process information coded verbally in one or more languages can help motivate curricular decisions. Indeed, in monolingual contexts curricular decisions need to be related as much as is possible to the communication skills of students (see Chapter 14).

It has been facetiously observed that what we are concerned with when we add the requirements of practicality and instructional value is something we might call true validity, or valid validity. With so many kinds of validity being discussed in the literature today, it does not seem entirely inappropriate to ask somewhat idealistically (and sad to say, not superfluously) for a valid variety of validity that teachers and educators may at least aim for. Toward this end we might examine the results of theoretical investigations of *construct* validity, practical analyses of the *content* of tests, and careful study of the intercorrelations among a wide variety of testing procedures to address questions of *concurrent* validity.[3]

We will return to the matter of validity of pragmatic tests and their patterns of interrelationship as determined by concurrent validity studies after a brief digression to consider the meaning of *correlation* in the statistical sense of the term. The reader who has some background in statistics or in the mathematics underlying statistical correlation may want to skip over the next eleven paragraphs and go directly to the discussion of results of statistical correlations between various tests that have been devised to assess language skills.

1. *The meaning of correlation.* The purpose here is not to teach the reader to apply correlation necessarily, but to help the non-

---

[3] Another variety of validity sometimes referred to in the literature is *face validity*. Harris (1969) defines it as 'simply the way the test *looks* – to the examinees, test administrators, educators, and the like' (p. 21). Since these kinds of opinions are often based on mere experiences with things that have been called tests of such and such a skill in the past, Harris notes that they are not a very important part of determining the validity of tests. Such opinions are ultimately important only to the extent that they affect performance on the test. Where judgements of face validity can be shown to be ill-informed, they should not serve as a basis for the evaluation of testing procedures at all.

statistically trained reader to understand the meaning of correlation enough to appreciate some of the interesting findings of recent research on the reliability and validity of various language testing techniques. There are many excellent texts that deal with correlation more thoroughly and with its application to research designs. The interested reader may want to consult one of the many available references.[4] No attempt is made here to achieve any sort of mathematical rigor – and perhaps it is worth noting that most practical applications of statistical procedures do not conform to all of the niceties necessary for mathematical precision attainable in theory (see Nunnally, 1967, pp. 7–10, for a discussion of this point). Few researchers, however, would therefore deny the usefulness of the applications.

Here we are concerned with simple correlation, also known as Pearson product-moment correlation.To understand the meaning of this statistic, it is first necessary to understand the simpler statistics of the arithmetic mean, the variance, and the standard deviation on which it is based. The arithmetic mean of a set of scores is computed by adding up all of the scores in the set of interest and dividing by the number of scores in the set. This procedure provides a measure of central tendency of the scores. It is like an answer to the question, if we were to take all the amounts of whatever the test measures and distribute an equal amount to each examinee, how much would each one get with none left over? Whereas the mean is an index of where the true algebraic center of the scores is, the variance is an index of how much scores tend to differ from that central point.

Since the true degree of variability of possible scores on a test tends to be somewhat larger than the variability of scores made by a given group of examinees, the computation of test variance must correct for this bias. Without going into any detail, it has been proved mathematically that the best estimate of true test variance can be made as follows: first, subtract the mean score from each of the scores on the test and record each of the resulting deviations from the mean (the deviations will be positive quantities for scores larger than the mean, and negative quantities for scores less than the mean); second, square each of the deviations (i.e., multiply each deviation by itself) and record the result each time; third, add up all of the squares (note that all of the quantities must be either zero or a positive value since

[4] An excellent text written principally for educators is Merle Tate, *Statistics in Education and Psychology: A First Course.* New York: Macmillan, 1965, especially Chapter VII. Or, see Nunnally (1967), or Kerlinger and Pedhazur (1973).

the square of a negative value is always a positive value); fourth, divide the sum of squares by the number of scores minus one (the subtraction of one at this point is the correction of estimate bias noted at the beginning of this paragraph). The result is the best estimate of the true variance in the population sampled.

The standard deviation of the same set of scores is simply the square root of the variance (i.e., the positive number which times itself equals the variance). Hence, the standard deviation and the variance are interconvertible values (the one can be easily derived from the other). Each of them provides an index of the overall tendency of the scores to vary from the mathematically defined central quantity (the mean). Conceptually, computing the standard deviation is something like answering the question: if we added to the mean and subtracted from the mean amounts of whatever the test measures, how much would we have to add and subtract on the average to obtain the original set of scores? It can be shown mathematically that for *normal* distributions of scores, the mean and the standard deviation tell everything there is to know about the distribution of scores. The mean defines the central point about which the scores tend to cluster and their tendency to vary from that central point is the standard deviation.

We can now say what Pearson product-moment correlation means. Simply stated, it is an index of the tendency for the scores of a group of examinees on one test to covary (that is, to differ from their respective mean in similar direction and magnitude) with the scores of the same group of examinees on another test. If, for example, the examinees who tend to make high scores on a certain cloze test also tend to make high scores on a reading comprehension test, and if those who tend to make low scores on the reading test also tend to make low scores on the cloze, the two tests are positively correlated.

The square of the correlation between any two tests is an index of the variance overlap between them. Perfect correlation will result if the scores of examinees on two tests differ exactly in proportion to each other from their respective means.

One of the conceptually simplest ways to compute the product-moment correlation between two sets of test scores is as follows: first, compute the standard deviation for each test; second, for each examinee, compute the deviation from the mean on the first test and the deviation from the mean on the second test; third, multiply the deviation from the mean on test one times the deviation from the mean on test two for each examinee (whether the value of the deviation is positive or negative is important in this case because it is possible to get negative values on this operation); fourth, add up the products of deviations from step three (note that the resulting quantity is conceptually similar to the sum of squares of deviations in the computation of the variance of a single set of scores); finally, divide the quantity from step four by the standard deviation of test one times the standard deviation of test two times one less than the number of examinees. The resulting value is the correlation between the two tests.

Correlations may be positive or negative. We have already considered an example of positive correlation. An instance of negative correlation would result if we counted correct responses on say, a cloze test, and errors, say, on a dictation. Thus, a high score on the cloze test would (if the tests were correlated positively, as in the previous example) correspond to a low score on the other. High scorers on the cloze test would typically be low scorers on the dictation (that is, they would make fewer errors), and low scorers on the cloze would be high scorers on the dictation (that is, they would make many errors). However, if the score on the cloze test were converted to an error count also, the correlation would become positive instead of negative. Therefore, in empirical testing research, it is most often the magnitude of correlation between two tests that is of interest rather than the direction of the relationship. However, the value of the correlation (plus or minus) becomes interesting whenever it is surprising. We will consider several such cases in Chapter 5 when we discuss empirical research with attitudes and motivations.

What about the magnitude of correlations? When should a correlation be considered high or low? Answers to such questions can be given only in relation to certain purposes, and then only in general and somewhat imprecise terms. In the first place, the size of correlations cannot be linearly interpreted. A correlation of .90 is not three times larger than a correlation of .30 – rather it is nine times larger. It is necessary to square the correlation in each case in order to make a more meaningful comparison. Since .90 squared is .81 and .30 squared is .09, and since .81 is nine times larger than .09, a correlation of .90 is actually nine times larger than a correlation of .30. Computationally (or perhaps we should say mathematically), a correlation is like a standard deviation, while the square of the correlation (or the *coefficient of determination* as it is called) is on the same order as the variance. Indeed, the square of the correlation of two tests is an index of the amount of variance overlap between the two tests – or put differently, it is an index of the amount of variance that they have in common. (For more thorough discussion, see Tate, 1965, especially Chapter VII.)

With respect to reliability studies, correlations above .95 between, say, two alternate forms of the same test are considered quite adequate. Statistically, such a correlation means that the test forms overlap in variance at about the .90 level. That is, ninety percent of the total variance in both tests is present in either one by itself. One could feel quite confident that the tests would tend to produce very similar results if administered to the same population of subjects. What can be known from the one is almost identical to what can be known from the other, with a small margin of error.

On the other hand, a reliability index of .60 for alternate forms of the same test would not be considered adequate for most purposes. The two tests in this latter instance are scarcely interchangeable. It would hardly be justifiable to say that they are very reliable measures of whatever they are aimed at assessing. (However, one cannot say that they are necessarily measuring different things on the basis of such a correlation. See Chapter 7 on statistical traps.)

In general, whether the question concerns reliability or validity, low correlations are less informative than high correlations. An observed low correlation between two tests that are expected to correlate highly is something like the failure of a prospector in search of gold. It may be that there is no gold or it may be that the prospector simply hasn't turned the right stones or panned the right spots in the stream. A low correlation may result from the fact that one of the tests is too easy or too hard for the population tested. It may mean that one of the tests is unreliable. Or that both of them are unreliable. Or a low correlation may result from the fact that one or both tests do not measure what they are supposed to measure (i.e., are not valid), or merely that one of them (or both) has (or have) a low degree of validity.

A very high correlation is less difficult to interpret. It is more like a gold strike. The richer the strike, that is, the higher the correlation, the more easily it can be interpreted. A correlation of .85 or .90 between two tests that are superficially very different would seem to be evidence that they are tapping the same underlying skill or ability. In any event, it means at face value that the two tests share .72 or .81 of the total variance in both tests. That is, between 72 and 81 percent of what can be known from the one can be known equally well from the other.

A further point regarding the interpretation of reliability estimates should be made. Insofar as a reliability estimate is accurate, its square may be interpreted as the amount of non-random variance in the test in question. It follows that the validity of a test can never exceed its reliability, and further that validity indices can equal reliability indices only in very special circumstances – namely, when all the reliable (non-random) variance in one test is also generated by the other. We shall return to this very important fact about correlations as reliability indices and correlations as validity indices below. In the meantime, we should keep in mind that a correlation between two tests should normally be read as a reliability index if the two tests are considered to be different forms of the *same* test or testing procedure. However, if the two tests are considered to be *different* tests or testing procedures, the correlation between them should normally be read as a validity index.

2. *Correlations between different language tests.* One of the first studies that showed surprisingly high correlations between substantially different language tests was done by Rebecca Valette (1964) in connection with the teaching of French as a foreign language at the college level. She used a dictation as part of a final examination for a course in French. The rest of the test included: (1) a listening comprehension task in a multiple choice format that contained items requiring (a) identification of a phrase heard on tape, (b) completion of sentences heard on tape, and (c) answering of questions concerning paragraphs heard on tape; (2) a written sentence completion task of the fill-in-the-blank variety; and (3) a sentence writing task where students were asked to answer questions in the affirmative or negative or to follow instructions entailed in an imperative sentence like, *Tell John to come here*, where a correct written response might be, *John, come here.*

For two groups of subjects, all first semester French students, one of which had practiced taking dictation and the other of which had not, the correlations between dictation scores and the other test scores combined were .78 and .89, respectively. Valette considered these correlations to be notably high and concluded that the 'dictee' was measuring the same basic overall skills as the longer and more difficult to prepare French examination.

Valette concluded that the difference in the two correlations could be explained as a result of a practice effect that reduced the validity of dictation as a test for students who had practiced taking dictation.

However, the two groups also had different teachers which suggests another possible explanation for the differences. Moreover, Kirn (1972) in a study of dictation as a testing technique at UCLA found that extensive practice in taking dictation in English did *not* result in substantially higher scores. Another possible explanation for the differences in correlations between Valette's two groups might be that dictation is a useful teaching procedure in which case the difference might be evidence for real learning.

Nevertheless, one of the results of Valette's study has been replicated on numerous occasions with other tests and with entirely different populations of subjects – namely, that dictation does correlate at surprisingly high levels with a vast array of other language tests. For instance, in a study at UCLA a dictation task included as part of the UCLA *English as a Second Language Placement Examination Form 1* correlated better with every other part of that test than any other two parts correlated with each other (Oller, 1970, Oller and Streiff, 1975). This would seem to suggest that dictation was accounting for more of the total variance in the test than any other single part of that test. The correlation between dictation and the total score on all other test parts not including the dictation (Vocabulary, Grammar, Composition, and Phonology – for description see Oller and Streiff, 1975, pp. 73–5) was .85. Thus the dictation was accounting for no less than 72 % of the variance in the entire test.

In a later study, using a different form of the UCLA placement test (Form 2C), dictation correlated as well with a cloze test as either of them did with any of the other subtests on the *ESLPE 2C* (Oller and Conrad, 1971). This was somewhat surprising in view of the striking differences in format of the two tests. The dictation is heard and written, while the cloze test is read with blanks to be filled in. The one test utilizes an auditory mode primarily whereas the other uses mainly a visual mode.

Why would they not correlate better with more similar tasks than with each other? For instance, why would the cloze test not correlate better with a reading comprehension task or a vocabulary task (both were included among the subtests on the *ESLPE 2C*)? The correlation between cloze and dictation was .82 while the correlations between cloze and reading, and cloze and vocabulary were .80 and .59, respectively. This surprising result confirmed a similar finding of Darnell (1968) who found that a cloze task (scored by a somewhat complicated procedure to be discussed in Chapter 12) correlated better with the Listening Comprehension subscore on the *TOEFL* than it did with any other part of that examination (which also includes a subtest aimed at reading comprehension and one aimed at vocabulary knowledge). The correlation between the cloze test and the Listening Comprehension subtest was .73 and the correlation with the total score on all subtests of the *TOEFL* combines was .82.

In another study of the UCLA *ESLPE 2A Revised*, correlations of .74, .84, and .85 were observed between dictations and cloze tests (Oller, 1972). Also, three different cloze tests used with different populations of subjects (above 130 in number in each case) correlated above .70 in six cases with grammar tasks and paraphrase recognition tasks. The cloze test was scored by the contextually-appropriate ('acceptable word') method; see Chapter 12.

While Valette was looking at the performance of students in a formal language classroom context where the language being studied was not spoken in the surrounding community, the studies at UCLA and the one by Darnell (at the University of Colorado) examined populations of students in the United States who were in social contexts where English was in fact the language of the surrounding community. Yet the results were similar in spite of the contrasts in tested populations and regardless of the contrasts in the tests used (the various versions of UCLA *ESLPE*, the *TOEFL*, and the foreign language French exams).

Similar results are available, however, from still more diverse settings. Johansson (1972) reported on the use of a combined cloze and dictation procedure which produced essentially the same results as the initial studies with dictation at UCLA. He found that his combined cloze and dictation procedure correlated better with scores on several language tests than any of the other tests correlated with each other. It is noteworthy that Johansson's subjects were Swedish college students who had learned English as a foreign language. The correlation between his cloze-dictation and a traditional test of listening comprehension was .83.

In yet another context, Stubbs and Tucker (1974) found that a cloze test was generally the best predictor of various sections on the American University at Beirut *English Entrance Examination*. Their subject population included mostly native speakers of Arabic learning English as a foreign or second language. The cloze test appeared to be superior to the more traditional parts of the *EEE* in spite of greater ease of preparation of the cloze test. In particular, the cloze blanks seemed to discriminate better between high scorers and low scorers than did the traditional discrete point types of items (see Chapter 9 on item analysis and especially item discrimination).

A study by Pike (1973) with such diverse techniques as oral interview (FSI type), essay ratings, cloze scores, the subscores on the *TOEFL* and a variety of other tasks yielded notably strong correlations between tasks that could be construed as pragmatic tests. He tested native speakers of Japanese in Japan, and Spanish speakers in Chile and Peru. There were some interesting surprises in the simple correlations which he observed. For instance, the essay scores correlated better with the subtest labeled Listening Comprehension for all three populations tested than with any of the other tests, and the cloze scores (by Darnell's scoring method) correlated about as highly with interview ratings as did any other pairs of subtests in the data.

The puzzle remains. Why should tests that look so different in terms of what they require people to do correlate so highly? Or more mysterious still, why should tests that purport to measure the same skill or skills fail to correlate as highly with each other as they correlate with other tests that purport to measure very different skills? A number of explanations can be offered, and the data are by no means all in at this point. It would appear that the position once favored by discrete point theorists has been excluded by experimental studies – that position was that different forms of discrete point tests aimed at assessing the same skill, or aspect of a skill, or component of a skill, ought to correlate better with each other than with, say, integrative (especially, pragmatic) tests of a substantially different sort. This position now appears to have been incorrect.

There is considerable evidence to show that in a wide range of studies with a substantial variety of tests and a diverse selection of subject populations, discrete point tests do not correlate as well with each other as they do with integrative tests. Moreover, integrative tests of very different types (e.g., cloze versus dictation) correlate even more highly with each other than they do with language tests which discrete point theory would identify as being more similar. The correlations between diverse pragmatic tests, in other words, generally exceed the correlations observed between quite similar discrete point tests. This would seem to be a strong disproof of the early claims of discrete point theories of testing, and one will search in vain for an explanation in the strong versions of discrete point approaches (see especially Chapter 8, and in fact all of Part Two).

Having discarded the strong version of what might be termed the discrete point hypothesis – namely, that tests aimed at similar elements, components, aspects of skills, or skills ought to correlate more highly than tests that are apparently requiring a greater diversity of performances – we must look elsewhere for an explanation of the pervasive results of correlation studies. Two explanations have been offered. One is based on the pragmatic theory advocated in Chapter 2 of this book, and the other is a modified version of the discrete point argument (Upshur, 1976, discusses this view though it is doubtful whether or not he thinks it is correct). From an experimental point of view, it is obviously preferable to avoid advocacy and let the available data or obtainable data speak for themselves (Platt, 1964).

One hypothesis is that pragmatic language tests must correlate highly if they are valid language tests. Therefore, the results of correlation studies can be easily understood or at least straightforwardly interpreted as evidence of the fundamental validity of the variety of language tests that have been shown to correlate at such remarkably high levels. The reason that a dictation and a cloze test (which are apparently such different tasks) intercorrelate so strongly is that both are effective devices for assessing the efficiency of the learner's developing grammatical system, or language ability, or pragmatic expectancy grammar, or cognitive network of the language or whatever one chooses to call it. There is substantial empirical evidence to suggest that there may be a single unitary factor that accounts for practically all of the variance in language tests (Oller, 1976a). Perhaps that factor can be equated with the learner's developing grammatical system.

One rather simple but convincing source of data on this question is the fact that the validity estimates on pragmatic tests of different sorts (i.e. the correlations between different ones) are nearly equal to the reliability estimates for the same tests. From this it follows that the tests must be measuring the same thing to a substantial extent. Indeed, if the validity estimates were consistently equal to, or nearly equal to the reliability estimates we would be forced to conclude that the tests are essentially measures of the same factor. This is an empirical question, however, and another plausible alternative remains to be ruled out.

Upshur (1976) suggests that perhaps the grammatical system of the learner will account for a large and substantial portion of the variance in a wide variety of language tests. This central portion of variance might explain the correlations mentioned above, but there could still be meaningful portions of variance left which would be attributable to components of grammar or aspects of language skill, or the traditional skills themselves.

Lofgren (1972) concluded that 'there appear to be four main factors which are significant for language proficiency. These have been named knowledge of words and structures, intelligence, pronunciation, and fluency' (p. 11). He used a factor analytic approach (a sophisticated variation on correlation techniques) to test 'Lado's idea ... that language' can be broken down into 'smaller components in order to find common elements' (p. 8). In particular, Lofgren wanted to test the view that language skills could be differentiated into listening, speaking, reading, writing, and possibly translating factors. His evidence would seem to support either the unitary pragmatic factor hypothesis, or the central grammatical factor with meaningful peripheral components as suggested by Upshur. His data seem to exclude the possibility that meaningful variances will emerge which are unique to the traditionally recognized skills. Clearly, more research is needed in relation to this important topic (see the Appendix).

Closely related to the questions about the composition of language skill (and these questions have only recently been posed with reference to native speakers of any given language), are questions about the important relation of language skill(s) to IQ and other psychological constructs. If pragmatic tests are actually more valid tests than other widely used measures of language skills, perhaps these new measurement techniques can be used to determine the relationship between ability to perform meaningful language proficiency tasks and ability to answer questions on so-called IQ tests, and educational tests in general. Preliminary results reported in Oller and Perkins (1978) seem to support a single factor solution where language proficiency accounts for nearly all of the reliable variance in IQ and achievement tests.

Most of the studies of language test validity have dealt with second or foreign language learners who are either adults or post-adolescents. Extensions to native speakers and to children who are either native or non-native speakers of the language tested are more recent. Many careful empirical investigations are now under way or have fairly recently been reported with younger subjects. In a pioneering doctoral study at the University of New Mexico, Craker (1971) used an oral form of the cloze procedure to assess language skills of children at the first grade level from four ethnic backgrounds. She reported significant discrimination between the four groups suggesting that the procedure may indeed be sensitive to variations in levels of proficiency for children who are either preliterate or are just beginning to learn to read.

Although data are lacking on many of the possible pragmatic testing procedures that might be applied with children, the cloze procedure has recently been used with literate children in the elementary grades in contexts ranging from the Alaskan bush country to the African primary school. Streiff (1977) investigated the effects of the availability of reading resources on reading proficiency among Eskimo children from the third to sixth grade using cloze tests as the criterion measure for reading proficiency. Hofman (1974) used cloze tests as measures of reading proficiency in Uganda schools from grades 2 through 9. Data were collected on children in 14 schools (12 African and 2 European). Since the tests were in a second language for many of the African children, and in the native language for many of the European children, some interesting comparisons are possible. Concerning test reliabilities and internal consistencies of the various cloze tests used, Hofman reports somewhat lower values for the 2nd graders, but even including them, the average reliability estimate for all nine test batteries is .91 – and none is below .85. These data were based on a mean sample size of 264 subjects. The smallest number for any test battery was 232.

In what may be the most interesting study of language proficiency in young children to date, Swain, Lapkin, and Barik (1976) have reported data closely paralleling results obtained with adult second language learners. In their research, 4th grade bilinguals (or English speaking children who are becoming bilingual in French) were tested. Tests of proficiency in French were used and correlated with a cloze test in French scored by the exact and acceptable word methods (see Chapter 12 for elaboration on scoring methods). Proficiency tests for English ability were also correlated with a cloze test in English (also scored by both methods). In every case, the correlations between cloze scores and the other measures of proficiency used (in both languages) were higher than the correlations between any of the other pairs of proficiency tests. This result would seem to support the conclusion that the cloze tests were simply accounting for more of the available meaningful variance in both the native language (English) and in the second language (French).

The authors conclude, 'this study has indicated that the cloze tests can be used effectively with young children . . . the cloze technique has been shown to be a valid and reliable means of measuring second language proficiency. These characteristics along with the fact that it is easy to construct, administer, and score combine to make the cloze technique an efficient tool to use in summative evaluations. In addition, a detailed analysis of the types of errors made on a cloze test shows promise as an excellent source of information in formative evaluations' (p. 40). Still more recently, Lapkin and Swain, (1977) cite further confirming evidence.

Regardless of the eventual answers yet to be obtained concerning some of the subtler questions still remaining about the developing field of pragmatic testing, it would seem that the substantial validity of such testing techniques is supported from a wide range of research angles. If language tests were like windows through which language proficiency might be viewed, and if language proficiency were thought of as a courtyard that could be seen from a number of different windows, it would seem that a clearer view of the courtyard is possible through some windows than through others. Pragmatic tests seem to be among the clearest windows available for determining what is in the courtyard. Moreover, very different pragmatic tests seem to be producing a very high degree of agreement about what is there – about what language proficiency really is.

3. *Error analysis as an independent source of validity data.* If language tests are viewed as elicitation procedures for acquiring data on examinees' performance in a certain language, one way of assessing the validity of the procedures themselves is to see what kinds of data they are capable of eliciting. Typically, the analysis of learner performance in this way has the objective of making 'an exhaustive description of an individual's grammar' (Swain, Dumas, and Naiman, 1974, p. 68), or at least this would seem to be the ideal. Usually such studies are referred to as *error analyses*. Richards (1970a, 1971) popularized the term *error analysis* in two widely read and often anthologized papers. Another term that has been used is *interlanguage analysis* following Selinker (1972). The fundamental objective of all such studies would appear to be to characterize in a useful way the developing language ability (whether in a first or other language) of a learner or group of learners.

It is, however, possible to use the analysis of learner performances on language tests as a basis for determining what it is that a certain test or type of test measures. We have seen above some rather strong evidence to suggest that at least certain types of so-called pragmatic language tests are apparently tapping the same underlying language ability. It is possible to raise the question whether error analyses based on pragmatic tasks used as elicitation procedures will support the same conclusion – whether pragmatic tests of many different kinds do indeed seem to be tests of the same basic ability.

For instance, if a learner, or if learners in general, tend to make the same sorts of errors in spontaneous speech that they make in a more controlled interview situation, our confidence in the interview technique would be strengthened. Or, suppose learners could be shown to make the same sorts of errors in a translation task, say from the native language to the target language, that they make in spontaneous speech in the target language. Since it takes a long time to collect sufficient samples of spontaneous speech data, and since it is relatively easier to set up a translation task, such a finding would be very useful and would make testing and data collection for interlanguage analysis much easier. Or, consider the possibility that a second language learner might tend to make similar sorts of errors in writing a dictation of heard material and in speaking. Such a finding could make the testing of speaking ability much more convenient.

The fact is that few carefully controlled studies that might shed light on these important possibilities have been done. One notable exception is a study of *elicited imitation* and *translation* by Swain, Dumas, and Naiman (1974). Elicited imitation is a kind of oral dictation procedure. That is, the material to be imitated is presented to the examinee auditorily and the examinee's task is to repeat it. Fraser, Bellugi, and Brown (1963) argued against this procedure as a test of language competence much the way Lado (1961) and others argued against dictation. They complained that the technique could only assess a relatively superficial aspect of 'perceptual-motor skills'. Other researchers (Menyuk, 1969, Ervin-Tripp, 1970, Slobin and Welsh, 1973, and Natalicio and Williams, 1971) disagreed. They argued that if the material to be repeated pushed the limits of the short-term memory of the examinees, it was in fact a valid test of both comprehension and production skills. With different aims in mind, Labov and Cohen (1967) and Baratz (1969) had used elicited imitation in studies of non-majority varieties of English. More recently, the technique has been extended to test proficiency in two major varieties of English by Politzer, Hoover, and Brown (1974).

However, with many of the arguments unresolved concerning the actual demands of the task, Swain, Dumas, and Naiman (1974) set out to study the validity of elicited imitation in relation to elicited translation (that is, both tasks were under the control of an examiner or experimenter; neither was spontaneous). They reasoned that if the sentences children were to repeat exceeded immediate memory span, then elicited imitation ought to be a test both of comprehension and production skills. Translation on the other hand could be done in two directions, either from the native language of the children (in this case English) to the target language (French), or from the target language to the native language. The first sort of translation, they reasoned, could be taken as a test of productive ability in the target language, whereas the second could be taken as a measure of comprehension ability in the target language (presumably, if the child could understand something in French he would have no difficulty in expressing it in his native language, English).

In order to rule out the possibility that examinees might be using different strategies for merely repeating a sentence in French as opposed to translating it into English, Swain, Dumas, and Naiman devised a careful comparison of the two procedures. One group of children was told before each sentence whether they were to repeat it or to translate it into English. If subjects used different strategies for the two tasks, this procedure would allow them to plan their strategy before hearing the sentence. A second group was given each sentence first and told afterward whether they were to translate it or repeat it. Since the children in this group did not know what they were to do with the sentence beforehand, it would be impossible for them consistently to use different strategies for the imitation task and the translation task. Differences in error types or in the relative difficulty of different syntactic structures might have implied different strategies of processing, but there were no differences. The imitation task was somewhat more difficult, but the types of errors and the rank ordering of syntactic structures were similar for both tasks and for both groups. (There were no significant differences at all between the two groups.)

There were some striking similarities in performance on the two rather different pragmatic tasks. 'For example, 75 % of the children who imitated the past tense by "a + the third person of the present tense of the main verb" made the same error in the production task. ... Also, 69 % of the subjects who inverted pronoun objects in imitation made similar inversions in production. ... In sum, these findings lead us to reject the view held by Fraser, Bellugi, and Brown (1963) and others that imitation is only a perceptual-motor skill' (Swain, Dumas, and Naiman, 1974, p. 72). Moreover, in a study by Naiman (1974), children were observed to make many of the same errors in spontaneous speech as they made in elicited translation from the native language to the target language.

In yet another study, Dumas and Swain (1973) 'demonstrated that when young second language learners similar to the ones in Naiman's study (Naiman, 1974) were given English translations of their *own* French spontaneous productions and asked to translate these utterances into French, 75% of their translations matched their original spontaneous productions' (Swain, Dumas, and Naiman, 1974, p. 73).

Although much more study needs to be done, and with a greater variety of subject populations and techniques of testing, it seems reasonable to say that there is already substantial evidence from studies of learner outputs that quite different pragmatic tasks may be tapping the same basic underlying competence. There would seem to be two explanations for differences in performance on tasks that require saying meaningful things in the target language versus merely indicating comprehension by, say, translating the meaning of what someone else has just said in the target language into one's own native language. Typically, it is observed that tasks of the latter sort are easier than the former. Learners can often understand things that they cannot say; they can often repeat things that they could not have put together without the support of a model; they may be able to read a sentence which is written down that they could not have understood at all if it were spoken; they may be able to comprehend written material that they obviously could not have written. There seems to be a hierarchy of difficulties associated with different tasks. The two explanations that have been put forth parallel the two competing explanations for the overlap in variance on pragmatic language tests.

Discrete point testers have long insisted on the separation of tests of the traditionally recognized skills. The extreme version of this argument is to propose that learners possess different grammars for different skills, aspects of skills, components of aspects of skills, and so on right down to the individual phonemes, morphemes, etc. The disproof of this view seems to have already been provided now many times over. Such a theoretical argument cannot embrace the data from correlation studies or the data from error analyses. However, it seems that a weaker version cannot yet be ruled out.

It is possible that there is a basic grammatical system underlying all uses of language, but that there remain certain components which are not part of the central core that account for what are frequently referred to as differences in productive and receptive repertoires (e.g.

phonology for speaking versus for listening), or differences in productive and receptive abilities (e.g. speaking and writing versus listening and reading), or differences in oral and visual skills (e.g. speaking and listening versus reading and writing), or components that are associated with special abilities such as the capacity to do simultaneous translation, or to imitate a wide variety of accents, and so on, and on. This sort of reasoning would harmonize with the hypothesis discussed by Upshur (1976) concerning unique variances associated with tests of particular skills or components of grammar.

Another plausible alternative exists, however, and was hinted at in the article by Swain, Dumas, and Naiman (1974). Consider the rather simple possibility that the differences in difficulties associated with different language tasks may be due to differences in the load they impose on the brain. It is possible that the grammatical system (call it an expectancy grammar, or call it something else) functions with different levels of efficiency in different language tasks – not because it is a different grammar – but because of differences in the load it must bear (or help consciousness to bear) in relation to different tasks. No one would propose that because a man can carry a one hundred pound weight up a hill faster than he can carry a one hundred and fifty pound weight that he therefore must have different pairs of legs for carrying different amounts of weight. It wouldn't even seem reasonable to suggest that he has more weight-moving ability when carrying one hundred pounds rather than when carrying one hundred and fifty pounds. Would it make sense to suggest that there is an additional component of skill that makes the one hundred pound weight easier to carry?

The case of, say, speaking versus listening skill is obviously much more complex than the analogy, which is intentionally a reduction to absurdity. But the argument can apply. In speaking, the narrow corridor of activity known as attention or consciousness must integrate the motor coordination of signals to the articulators telling them what moves to make and in what order, when to turn the voice on and off, when to push air and when not to; syllables must be timed, monitoring to make certain the right ones get articulated in the right sequence; facial expressions, tones, gestures, etc. must be synchronized with the stream of speech; and all of the foregoing must be coordinated with certain ill-defined intentions to communicate (or with pragmatic mappings of utterances onto extralinguistic contexts, if you like). In listening, somewhat less is required. While the speaker must both plan and monitor his articulatory output to make sure it catches up with what he intended to say in form and meaning all the while continuing to plan and actively construct further forms and meanings, the listener needs only to monitor his inferences concerning the speaker's intended meanings, and to help him do this, the listener has the already constructed sensory signals (that he can hear and see) which the speaker is outputting. A similar explanation can be offered for the fact that reading is somewhat less taxing than writing, and that reading is somewhat easier than listening, and so forth for each possible contrast. Swain, Dumas, and Naiman (1974) anticipate this sort of explanation when they talk about 'the influence of memory capacity on some of the specific aspects of processing involved in tasks of imitation and translation' (p. 75).

Crucial experiments to force the choice between the two competing explanations for hierarchies of difficulties in different language tasks remain to be done. Perhaps a double-edged approach from both correlation studies and error analysis will disprove one or the other of the two competing alternatives, or possibly other alternatives remain to be put forward. In the meantime, it would seem that the evidence from error analysis supports the validity of pragmatic tasks. Certainly, it would appear that studies of errors on different elicitation procedures are capable of putting both of the interesting alternatives in the position of being vulnerable to test. This is all that science requires (Platt, 1964).

Teachers and educators, of course, require more. We cannot wait for all of the data to come in, or for the crucial experiments to be devised and executed. Decisions must be made and they will be made either wisely or unwisely, for better or for worse. Students in classrooms cannot be left to sit there without a curriculum, and the decisions concerning the curriculum must be made with or without the aid of valid language tests. The best available option seems to be to go ahead with the sorts of pragmatic language tests that have proved to yield high concurrent validity statistics and to provide a rich supply of information concerning learner grammatical systems. In the next chapter we will consider aspects of language assessment in multilingual contexts. In Part Two, we will discuss reasons for rejecting certain versions of discrete point tests in favor of pragmatic testing, and in Part Three, specific pragmatic testing procedures are discussed in greater detail. The relevance of the procedures recommended there to educational testing in general is discussed at numerous points throughout Part Three.

KEY POINTS

1. Discrete point tests are aimed at specific elements of phonology, syntax, or vocabulary within a presumed aspect (productive or receptive, oral or visual) of one of the traditionally recognized language skills (listening, speaking, reading, or writing).
2. The strong version of the discrete point approach argues that different test items are needed to assess different elements of knowledge within each component of grammar, and different subtests are needed for each different component of each different aspect of each different skill. Theoretically, many different tests are required.
3. Integrative tests are defined as antithetical to discrete point tests. Integrative tests lump many elements and possibly several components, aspects and skills together and test them all at the same time.
4. While it can be argued that discrete point tests and integrative tests are merely two extremes on a continuum, pragmatic tests constitute a special class of integrative tests. It is possible to conceive of a discrete point test as being more or less integrative, and an integrative test as being more or less discrete, but pragmatic tests are more precisely defined.
5. Pragmatic language tests must meet two naturalness criteria: first, they must require the learner to utilize normal contextual constraints on sequences in the language; and, second, they must require comprehension (and possibly production also) of meaningful sequences of elements in the language in relation to extralinguistic contexts.
6. Discrete point tests cannot be pragmatic tests.
7. The question whether or not a task is pragmatic is an empirical one. It can be decided by logic (that is by definition) and by experiment, but not by opinion polls.
8. Dictation and cloze procedure are examples of pragmatic tests. First, they meet the requirements of the definition, and second, they function in experimental applications in the predicted ways.
9. Other examples include combinations of cloze and dictation, oral cloze tasks, dictation with interfering noise, paraphrase recognition, question-answering, oral interview, essay writing, narration, and translation.
10. A test is valid to the extent that it measures what it is supposed to measure. *Construct validity* has to do with theoretical justification of a testing procedure; *content validity* has to do with the faithfulness with which a test reflects the normal uses of language to which it is related as a measure of an examinee's skill; *concurrent validity* has to do with the strength of correlations between tests that purport to measure the same thing.
11. Correlation is a statistical index of the tendency of scores on two tests to vary proportionately from their respective means. It is an index of the square root of variance overlap, or variance common to two tests.
12. The square of the simple correlation between two tests is an unbiased estimate of their variance overlap. The technical term for the square of the correlation is the *coefficient of determination*. Correlations cannot be compared linearly, but their squares can be.

13. A high correlation is more informative and easier to interpret than a low one. While a high correlation does mean that some sort of strong relationship exists, a low correlation does not unambiguously mean that a strong relationship does not exist between the tested variables. There are many more explanations for low correlations than for high ones.

14. Generally, pragmatic tests of apparently very different types correlate at higher levels with each other than they do with other tests. However, they also seem to correlate better with the more traditional discrete point tests than the latter do with each other. Hence, pragmatic tests seem to be generating more meaningful variance than discrete item tests.

15. Two possibilities seem to exist: there may be a large factor of grammatical knowledge of some sort in every language test, with certain residual variances attributable to specific components, aspects, skills, and the like; or, language skill may be a relatively unitary factor and there may be no unique meaningful variances that can be attributed to specific components, etc.

16. The relation of language proficiency to intelligence (or more specifically to scores on so-called IQ tests) remains to be studied more carefully. Scores on achievement tests and educational measures of all sorts should also be examined critically with careful experimental procedures.

17. Error analysis, or interlanguage analysis, can provide additional validity data on language tests. If language tests are viewed as elicitation procedures, and if errors are analyzed carefully, it is possible to make very specific observations about whether certain tests measure different things or the same thing.

18. Available data suggest that very different pragmatic tasks, such as spontaneous speech, or elicited imitation, or elicited translation tend to produce the same kinds of learner errors.

19. Differences in difficulty across tasks may be explained by considering the relative load on mental mechanisms.

20. Teachers and educators can't wait for all of the research data to come in. At present, pragmatic testing seems to provide the most promise as a reliable, valid, and usable approach to the measurement of language ability.

DISCUSSION QUESTIONS

1. What sort of testing procedure is more common in your school or in educational systems with which you are familiar; discrete point testing, or integrative testing? Are pragmatic tests used in classrooms that you know of? Have you used dictation or cloze procedure in teaching a foreign language? Some other application? For instance, assessing reading comprehension, or the suitability of materials aimed at a certain grade level?

2. Discuss ways that you evaluate the language proficiency of children in your classroom, or students at your university, or perhaps how you might estimate your own language proficiency in a second language you have studied.

3. What are some of the drawbacks or advantages to a phonological

discrimination task where the examinee hears a sentence like, *He thinks he will sail his boat at the lake*, and must decide whether he heard *sell* or *sail*. Try writing several items of this type and discuss the factors that enter into determining the correct answer. What expectancy biases may arise?

4. In what way is understanding the sentence, *Shove off, Smith, I'm tired of talking to you*, dependent on knowing the meaning of *off*? Could you test such knowledge with an appropriate discrete item?
5. Try doing a cloze test and a dictation. Reflect on the strategies you use in performing one or the other. Or give one to a class and ask them to tell you what they attended to and what they were doing mentally while they filled in the blanks or wrote down what they had heard.
6. Propose other forms of tasks that you think would qualify as pragmatic tasks. Consider whether they meet the two naturalness criteria. If so try them out and see how they work.
7. Can you think of possible objections to a dictation with noise? What are some arguments for and against such a procedure?
8. Given a low correlation between two language tests, say, .30, what are some of the possible conclusions? Suppose the correlation is .90. What could you conclude for the latter?
9. Keep a diary on listening errors and speech errors that you or people around you make. Do the processes appear to be distinct? Interrelated?
10. Discuss Alice's query about not knowing what she would say next till she had already said it. How does this fit the strategies you follow when you speak? In what cases might the statement apply to your own speech?
11. Can a high correlation between two tests be taken as an indication of test validity? When is it merely an indication of test reliability? What is the difference? Can a test be valid without being reliable? How about the reverse?
12. Try collecting samples of learner outputs in a variety of ways. Compare error types. Do dissimilar pragmatic tests elicit similar or dissimilar errors?
13. Consider the pros and cons of the long despised technique of translation as a teaching and as a testing device. Are the potential uses similar? Can you define clearly abuses to be avoided?
14. What sorts of tests do you think will yield superior diagnostic information to help you to know what to do to help a learner by teaching strategies? Consider what you do now with the test data that are available. Are there reading tests? Vocabulary tests? Grammar tests? What do you do differently because of the information that you get from the tests you use?
15. Compute the means, variances, and standard deviations for the following sets of scores:

	Test A	Test B
George	1	5
Sarah	2	10
Mary	3	15

(Note that these data are highly artificial. They are contrived purely to

illustrate the meaning of correlation while keeping the computations extremely simple and manageable.)
16. What is the correlation between tests A and B?
17. What would your interpretation of the correlation be if Tests A and B were alternate forms of a placement test? What if they were respectively a reading comprehension test and an oral interview?
18. Repeat questions 15, 16, and 17 with the following data:

	Test C	Test D
George	5	7
Sarah	10	6
Mary	15	5

(Bear in mind that correlations would almost never be done on such small numbers of subjects. Answers: correlation between A and B is $+1.00$, between C and D it is -1.00.)

SUGGESTED READINGS

1. Anne Anastasi, *Psychological Testing*. New York: Macmillan, revised edition, 1976. See especially Chapters 5 and 6 on test validity.
2. John B. Carroll, 'Fundamental Considerations in Testing for English Language Proficiency of Foreign Students,' *Testing*, Washington, D.C.: Center for Applied Linguistics, 1961, 31–40. Reprinted in H. B. Allen and R. N. Campbell (eds.) *Teaching English as a Second Language: A Book of Readings*. New York: McGraw Hill, 1972, 313–320.
3. L. J. Cronbach, *Essentials of Psychological Testing*. New York: Harper and Row, 1970. See especially the discussion of different types of validity in Chapter 5.
4. Robert Lado, *Language Testing*. New York: McGraw Hill, 1961. See especially his discussion of discrete point test rationale pp. 25–29 and 39–203.
5. John W. Oller, Jr., 'Language Testing,' in Ronald Wardhaugh and H. Douglas Brown (eds.) *Survey of Applied Linguistics*. Ann Arbor, Michigan: University of Michigan, 1976, 275–300.
6. Robert L. Thorndike, 'Reliability,' *Proceedings of the 1963 Invitational Conference on Testing Problems*. Princeton, N.J.: Educational Testing Service, 1964. Reprinted in Glenn H. Bracht, Kenneth D. Hopkins, and Julian C. Stanley (eds.) *Perspectives in Educational and Psychological Measurement*. Englewood Cliffs, N.J.: Prentice-Hall, 1972, 66–73.

4

Multilingual Assessment

A. Need
B. Multilingualism versus multidialectalism
C. Factive and emotive aspects of multilingualism
D. On test biases
E. Translating tests or items
F. Dominance and proficiency
G. Tentative suggestions

Multilingualism is a pervasive modern reality. Ever since that cursed Tower was erected, the peoples of the world have had this problem. In the United States alone, there are millions of people in every major urban center whose home and neighborhood language is not one of the majority varieties of English. Spanish, Italian, German, Chinese and a host of other 'foreign' languages have actually become American languages. Furthermore, Navajo, Eskimo, Zuni, Apache, and many other native languages of this continent can hardly be called 'foreign' languages. The implications for education are manifold. How shall we deliver curricula to children whose language is not English? How shall we determine what their language skills are?

A. Need

Zirkel (1976) concludes an article entitled 'The why's and ways of testing bilinguality before teaching bilingually,' with the following paragraph:

The movement toward an effective and efficient means of testing bilinguality before teaching bilingually is in progress. In its wake is the hope that in the near future 'equality of educational opportunity' will become more meaningful for linguistically different pupils in our nation's elementary schools (p. 328).

Earlier he observes, however, that 'a substantial number of bilingual programs do not take systematic steps to determine the language dominance of their pupils' (p. 324).

Since the 1974 Supreme Court ruling in the case of Lau versus Nichols, the interest in multilingual testing in the schools of the United States has taken a sudden upswing. The now famous court case involved a contest between a Chinese family in San Francisco and the San Francisco school system. The following quotation from the Court's Syllabus explains the nature of the case:

> The failure of the San Francisco school system to provide English language instruction to approximately 1,800 students of Chinese ancestry who do not speak English denies them a meaningful opportunity to participate in the public educational program and thus violates §601 of the Civil Rights Act of 1964, which bans discrimination based 'on the ground of race, color, or national origin,' (Lau vs. Nichols, 1974, No. 72–6520).

In page 2 of an opinion by Mr. Justice Stewart concurred in by The Chief Justice and Mr. Justice Blackmun, it is suggested that 'no specific remedy is urged upon us. Teaching English to the students of Chinese ancestry who do not speak the language is one choice. Giving instruction to this group in Chinese is another' (1974, No. 72–6520). Further, the Court argued:

> Basic English skills are at the very core of what these public schools teach. Imposition of a requirement that, before a child can effectively participate in the educational program, he must already have acquired those basic skills is to make a mockery of public education. We know that those who do not understand English are certain to find their classroom experiences wholly incomprehensible and in no way meaningful (1974, No. 72–6520, p. 3).

As a result of the interpretation rendered by the Court, the U.S. Office of Civil Rights convened a Task Force which recommended certain so-called 'Lau Remedies'. Among other things, the main document put together by the Task Force requires language assessment procedures to determine certain facts about language use and it requires the rating of bilingual proficiency on a rough five point scale (1. monolingual in a language other than English; 2. more proficient in another language than in English; 3. balanced bilingual in English and another language; 4. more proficient in English than in another language; 5. monolingual in English). Multilingual testing seems to have come to stay for a while in U.S. schools, but as Zirkel and others have noted, it has come very late. It is late in the sense of antiquated and inhumane educational programs that placed children of language backgrounds other than English in classes for the 'mentally retarded' (Diana versus California State Education Department, 1970, No. C-7037), and it is late in terms of bilingual education programs that were started in the 1960s and even in the early 1970s on a hope and a promise but without adequate assessment of pupil needs and capabilities (cf. John and Horner, 1971, and Shore, 1974, cited by Zirkel, 1976). In fact, as recently as 1976, Zirkel observes, 'a fatal flaw in many bilingual programs lies in the linguistic identification of pupils at the critical point of the planning and placement process' (p. 324).

Moreover, as Teitelbaum (1976), Zirkel (1976), and others have often noted, typical methods of assessment such as surname surveys (to identify Spanish speakers, for instance) or merely asking about language preferences (e.g., teacher or student questionnaires) are largely inadequate. The one who is most likely to be victimized by such inadequate methods is the child in the school. One second grader indicated that he spoke 'English-only' on a rating sheet, but when 'casually asked later whether his parents spoke Spanish, the child responded without hesitation: Sí, ellos hablan español – pero yo, no.' Perhaps someone had convinced him that he was not supposed to speak Spanish?

Surely, for the sake of the child, it is necessary to obtain reliable and valid information about what language(s) he speaks and understands (and how well) *before* decisions are reached about curriculum delivery and the language policy of the classroom. 'But,' some sincere administrator may say, 'we simply can't afford to do systematic testing on a wide scale. We don't have the people, the budget, or the time.' The answer to such an objection must be indignant if it is equally sincere and genuine. Can the schools afford to do this year what they did last year? Can they afford to continue to deliver instruction in a language that a substantial number of the children cannot understand? Can they afford to do other wide scale standardized testing programs whose results may be less valid?

It may be true that the educators cannot wait until all the research results are in, but it is equally true that we cannot afford to play political games of holding out for more budget to make changes in ways the present budget is being spent, especially when those changes were needed years ago. This year's budget and next year's (if there is a next year) will be spent. People in the schools will be busy at many tasks, and all of the available time will get used up. Doing all of it the way it was done last year is proof only of the disappointing fact that a system that purports to teach doesn't necessarily learn. Indeed, it is merely another comment on the equally discouraging fact that many students in the schools (and universities no doubt) must learn in spite of the system which becomes an adversary instead of a servant to the needs of learners.

The problems are not unique to the United States. They are world-wide problems. Hofman (1974) in reference to the schools of Rhodesia says, 'It is important to get some idea, one that should have been reached ten years ago, of the state of English in the primary school' (p. 10). In the case of Rhodesia, and the argument can easily be extended to many of the world's nations, Hofman questions the blind and uninformed language policy imposed on teachers and children in the schools. In the case of Rhodesia, at least until the time his report was written, English was the required school language from 1st grade onward. Such policies have recently been challenged in many parts of the world (not just in the case of a super-imposed English) and reports of serious studies examining important variables are beginning to appear (see for instance, Bezanson and Hawkes, 1976, and Streiff, 1977). This is not to say that there may not be much to be gained by thorough knowledge of one of the languages of the world currently enjoying much power and prestige (such as English is at the present moment), but there are many questions concerning the price that must be paid for such knowledge. Such questions can scarcely be posed without serious multilingual testing on a much wider scale than has been common up till now.

B. Multilingualism versus multidialectalism

The problems of language testing in bilingual or multilingual contexts seem to be compounded to a new order of magnitude each time a new language is added to the system. In fact, it would seem that the problems are more than just doubled by the presence of more than one language because there must be social and psychological interactions between different language communities producing complexities not present in monolingual communities. However, there are some parallels between so-called monolingual communities and multilingual societies. The former display a rich diversity of language varieties in much the way that the latter exhibit a variety of languages. To the extent that differences in language varieties parallel differences in languages, there may be less contrast between the two sorts of settings than is commonly thought. In both cases there is the need to assess performance in relation to a plurality of group norms. In both cases there is the difficulty of determining what group norms are appropriate at different times and places within a given social order.

It has sometimes been argued that children in the schools should be compared only against themselves and never against group norms, but this argument implicitly denies the nature of normal human communication. Evaluating the language ability of an individual by comparing him only against himself is a little like clapping with one hand. Something is missing. It only makes sense to say that a person knows a language in relation to the way that other persons who also know that language perform when they use it. Becoming a speaker of a particular language is a distinctively socializing process. It is a process of identifying with and to some degree functioning as a member of a social group.

In multilingual societies, where many mutually unintelligible languages are common fare in the market places and urban centers, the need for language proficiency testing as a basis for informing educational policy is perhaps more obvious than in so-called monolingual societies. However, the case of monolingual societies, which are typically multidialectal, is deceptive. Although different varieties of a language may be mutually intelligible in many situations, in others they are not. At least since 1969, it has been known that school children who speak different varieties of English perform about equally badly in tests that require the repetition of sentences in the other group's variety (Baratz, 1969). Unfortunately for children who speak a non-majority variety of English, all of the other testing in the schools is done in the majority variety (sometimes referred to as 'standard English'). An important question currently being researched is the extent to which educational tests in general may contain a built-in language variety bias and related to it is the more general question concerning how much of the variance in educational tests in general can be explained by variance in language proficiency tests (see Stump, 1978 Gunnarsson, 1978 and

Pharis and Perkins, in press; also see the Appendix).

The parallel between multilingualism and multidialectalism is still more fundamental. In fact, there is a serious question of principle concerning whether it is possible to distinguish languages and dialects. Part of the trouble lies in the fact that for any given language (however we define it), there is no sense at all in trying to distinguish it from its dialects or varieties. The language *is* its varieties. The only sense in which a particular variety of a language may be elevated to a status above other varieties is in the manner of Orwell's pigs – by being a little more equal or in this case, a little more English or French or Chinese or Navajo or Spanish or whatever. One of the important rungs on the status ladder for a language variety (and for a language in the general sense) is whether or not it is written and whether or not it can lay claim to a long literary tradition. Other factors are who happens to be holding the reins of political power (obviously the language variety they speak is in a privileged position), and who has the money and the goods that others must buy with their money. The status of a particular variety of English is subject to many of the same influences that the status of English (in the broader sense) is controlled by.

The question, where does language X (or variety X) leave off and language Y (or variety Y) begin is a little like the question, where does the river stop and the lake begin. The precision of the answer, or lack of it, is not so much a product of clarity or unclarity of thought as it is a product of the nature of the objects spoken of. New terms will not make the boundaries between languages, or dialects, or between languages and language varieties any clearer. Indeed, it can be argued that the distinction between languages as disparate as Mandarin and English (or Navajo and Spanish) is merely a matter of degree. For languages that are more closely related, such as German and Swedish, or Portuguese and Spanish, or Navajo and Apache, it is fairly obvious that their differences are a matter of degree. However, in relation to abstract grammatical systems that may be shared by all human beings as part of their genetic programming, it may be the case that all languages share much of the same universal grammatical system (Chomsky, 1965, 1972).

Typically, varieties of a language that are spoken by minorities are termed 'dialects' in what sometimes becomes an unintentional (or possibly intentional) pejorative sense. For example, Ferguson and Gumperz (1971) suggest that a dialect is a 'potential language' (p. 34). This remark represents the tendency to institutionalize what may be appropriately termed the 'more equal syndrome'. No one would ever suggest that the language that a middle class white speaks is a potential language – of course not, it's a real language. But the language spoken by inner city blacks – that's another matter. A similar tendency is apparent in the remark by The Chief Justice in the Lau case where he refers to the population of Chinese speaking children in San Francisco (the 1,800 who were not being taught English) as 'linguistically deprived' children: (Lau versus Nichols, 1974, No. 72–6520, p. 3). Such remarks may reflect a modicum of truth, but deep within they seem to arise from ethno-centric prejudices that define the way I do it (or the way we do it) as intrinsically better than the way anyone else does it. It is not difficult to extend such intimations to 'deficit theories' of social difference like those advocated by Bernstein (1960), Bereiter and Engleman (1967), Herrnstein (1971), and others.

Among the important questions that remain unanswered and that are crucial to the differentiation of multilingual and monolingual societies are the following: to what extent does normal educational testing contain a language variety bias? And further, to what extent is that bias lesser or greater than the language bias in educational testing for children who come from a non-English speaking background? Are the two kinds of bias really different in type or merely in degree?

C. Factive and emotive aspects of multilingualism

Difficulties in communication between social groups of different language backgrounds (dialects or language varieties included) are apt to arise in two ways: first, there may be a failure to communicate on the factive level; or second, there may be a failure to communicate on the emotive level as well as the factive level. If a child comes to a school from a cultural and linguistic background that is substantially different from the background of the majority of teachers and students in the school, he brings to the communication contexts of the school many sorts of expectations that will be inappropriate to many aspects of the exchanges that he might be expected to initiate or participate in. Similarly, the representatives of the majority culture and possibly other minority backgrounds will bring other sets of expectations to the communicative exchanges that must take place.

In such linguistically plural contexts, the likelihood of misinterpretations and breakdowns in communication is increased. On the factive level, the actual forms of the language(s) may present some difficulties. The surface forms of messages may sometimes be uninterpretable, or they may sometimes be misinterpreted. Such problems may make it difficult for the child, teacher, and others in the system to communicate the factive-level information that is usually the focus of classroom activities – namely, transmitting the subject matter content of the curriculum. Therefore, such factive level communication problems may account for some portion of the variance in the school performance of children from ethnically and culturally different backgrounds, i.e., their generally lower scores on educational tests. As Baratz (1969) has shown, however, it is important to keep in mind the fact that if the tables were turned, if the majority were suddenly the minority, their scores on educational tests might be expected to plummet to the same levels as are typical of minorities in today's U.S. schools. Nevertheless, there is another important cluster of factors that probably affect variance in learning far more drastically than problems of factive level communication.

There is considerable evidence to suggest that the more elusive emotive or attitudinal level of communication may be a more important variable than the surface form of messages concerning subject matter. This emotive aspect of communication in the schools directly relates to the self-concept that a given child is developing, and also it relates to group loyalties and ethnic identity. Though such factors are difficult to measure (as we shall see in Chapter 5), it seems reasonable to hypothesize that they may account for more of the variance in learning in the schools that can be accounted for by the selection of a particular teaching methodology for instilling certain subject matter (factive level communication).

As the research in the Canadian experiments has shown, if the socio-cultural (emotive level) factors are not in a turmoil and if the child is receiving adequate encouragement and support at home, etc., the child can apparently learn a whole new way of coding information factively (a new linguistic system) rather incidentally and can acquire the subject matter and skills taught in the schools without great difficulty (Lambert and Tucker, 1972, Tucker and Lambert, 1973, Swain, 1976a, 1976b).

However, the very different experience of children in schools, say, in the Southwestern United States where many ethnic minorities do not experience such success requires a different interpretation. Perhaps the emotive messages that the child is bombarded with in the Southwest help explain the failure of the schools. Pertinent questions are: how does the child see his culture portrayed in the curriculum? How does the child see himself in relation to the other children who may be defined as successful by the system? How does the child's home experience match up with the experience in the school?

It is hypothesized that variance in rate of learning is probably more sensitive to the emotive level messages communicated in facial expressions, tones of voice, deferential treatment of some children in a classroom, biased representation of experiences in the school curriculum, and so on, than to differences in factive level methods of presenting subject matter. This may be more true for minority children than it is for children who are part of the majority. A similar view has been suggested by Labov (1972) and by Goodman and Buck (1973).

The hypothesis and its consequences can be visualized as shown in Figure 2 where the area enclosed by the larger circle represents the total amount of variance in learning to be accounted for (obviously the Figure is a metaphor, not an explanation or model). The area enclosed by the smaller concentric circle represents the hypothetical amount of variance that might be explained by emotive message factors. Among these are messages that the child perceives concerning his own worth, the value of his people and culture, the viability of his language as a means of communication, and the validity of his life experience. The area in the outer ring represents the hypothetical portion of variance in learning that may be accounted for by appeal to factive level aspects of communication in the schools, such as methods of teaching, subject matter taught, language of presentation of the material, IQ, initial achievement levels, etc.

Of all the ways struggles for ethnic identity manifest themselves, and of all the messages that can be communicated between different social groups in their mutual struggles to identify and define themselves, William James (as cited by Watzlawick, *et al*, 1967, p. 86) suggested that the most cruel possible message one human being can communicate to another (or one group to another) is simply to pretend that the other individual (or group) does not exist. Examples are too common for comfort in the history of education. Consider the statement that *Columbus discovered America in 1492* (Banks, 1972). Then ask, *who doesn't count?* (Clue: Who was already here before Columbus ever got the wind in his sails?) James said, 'No more fiendish punishment could be devised, ... than that one should be turned loose in a society and remain absolutely unnoticed by all the members thereof' (as cited by Watzlawick, *et al*, 1967, p. 86).

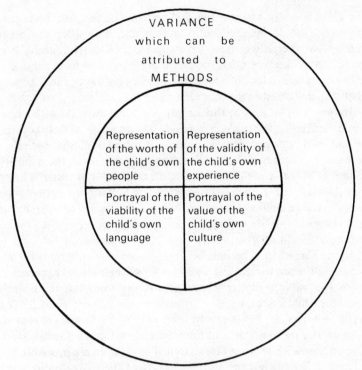

Figure 2. A hypothetical view of the amount of variance in learning to be accounted for by emotive versus factive sorts of information (methods of conveying subject matter are represented as explaining variance in the outer ring, while the bulk is explained by emotive factors).

The interpretation of low scores on tests, therefore, needs to take account of possible emotive conflicts. While a high score on a language test or any other educational test probably can be confidently interpreted as indicating a high degree of skill in communicating factive information as well as a good deal of harmony between the child and the school situation on the emotive level, a low score cannot be interpreted so easily. In this respect, low scores on tests are somewhat like low correlations between tests (see the discussion in Chapter 3, section E, and again in Chapter 7, section B); they leave a greater number of options open. A low score may occur because the test was not reliable or valid, or because it was not suited to the child in difficulty level, or because it created emotive reactions that interfered with the cognitive task, or possibly because the child is really weak in the skill tested. The last interpretation, however, should be used with caution and only after the other reasonable alternatives have been ruled out by careful study. It is important to keep in mind the fact that an emotive-level conflict is more likely to call for changes in the educational system and the way that it affects children than for changes in the children.

In some cases it may be that simply providing the child with ample opportunity to learn the language or language variety of the educational system is the best solution; in others, it may be necessary to offer instruction in the child's native language, or in the majority language and the minority language; and no doubt other untried possibilities exist. If the emotive factors are in harmony between the school and the child's experience, there is some reason to believe that mere exposure to the unfamiliar language may generate the desired progress (Swain, 1976a, 1976b).

In the Canadian experiments, English speaking children who are taught in French for the first several years of their school experience, learn the subject matter about as well as monolingual French speaking children, and they also incidentally acquire French. The term 'submersion' has recently been offered by Swain (1976b) to characterize the experience of minority children in the Southwestern United States who do not fare so well. The children are probably not all that different, but the social contexts of the two situations are replete with blatant contrasts (Fishman, 1976).

D. On test biases

A great deal has been written recently concerning cultural bias in tests (Brière, 1972, Condon, 1973). No doubt much of what is being said is true. However, some well-meaning groups have gone so far as to suggest a 'moratorium on all testing of minority children.' Their argument goes something like this. Suppose a child has learned a language that is very different from the language used by the representatives of the majority language and culture in the schools. When the child goes to school, he is systematically discriminated against (whether intentionally or not is irrelevant to the argument). All of the achievement tests, all of the classes, all of the informal teacher and peer evaluations that influence the degree of success or failure of the child is in a language (or language variety) that he has not yet learned. The entire situation is culturally biased against the child. He is regularly treated in a prejudicial way by the school system as a whole. So, some urge that we should aim to get the cultural bias out of the school situation as much as possible and especially out of the tests. A smaller group urges that all testing should be stopped indefinitely pending investigation of other educational alternatives.

The arguments supporting such proposals are persuasive, but the suggested solutions do not solve the problems they so graphically point out. Consider the possibility of getting the cultural bias out of language proficiency tests. Granted that language tests though they may vary in the pungency of their cultural flavor all have cultural bias built into them. They have cultural bias because they present sequences of linguistic elements of a certain language (or language variety) in specific contexts. In fact, it is the purpose of such tests to discriminate between various levels of skill, often, to discriminate between native and non-native performance. A language test is therefore intentionally biased against those who do not speak the language or who do so at different levels of skill.

Hence, getting the bias out of language tests, if pushed to the logical limits, is to get language tests to stop functioning as language tests. On the surface, preventing the cultural bias and the discrimination between groups that such tests provide might seem like a good idea, but in the long run it will create more problems than it can solve. For one, it will do harm to the children in the schools who most need help in coping with the majority language system by pretending that crucial communication problems do not exist. At the same time it would also preclude the majority culture representatives in schools from being exposed to the challenging opportunities of trying to cope in settings that use a minority language system. If this latter event is to occur, it will be necessary to evaluate developing learner proficiencies (of the majority types) in terms of the norms that exist for the minority language(s) and culture(s).

The more extreme alternative of halting testing in the schools is no real solution either. What is needed is more testing that is based on carefully constructed tests and with particular questions in mind followed by deliberate and careful analysis. Part of the difficulty is the lack of adequate data – not an overabundance of it. For instance, until recently (Oller and Perkins, 1978) there was no data on the relative importance of language variety bias, or just plain language bias in educational testing in general. There was always plenty of evidence that such a factor must be important to a vast array of educational tests, but how important? Opinions to the effect that it is not very important, or that it is of great importance merely accent the need for empirical research on the question. It is not a question that can be decided by vote – not even at the time honored 'grass roots level' – but that is where the studies need to be done.

There is another important way that some of the facts concerning test biases and their probable effects on the school performance of certain groups of children may have been over-zealously interpreted. These latter interpretations relate to an extension of a version of the strong contrastive analysis hypothesis familiar to applied linguists. The reasoning is not unappealing. Since children who do poorly on tests in school, and on tasks such as learning to read, write, and do arithmetic, are typically (or at least often) children who do not use the majority variety of English at home, their failure may be attributed to differences in the language (or variety of English) that they speak at home and the language that is used in the schools. Goodman (1965) offered such an explanation for the lower performance of inner city black children on reading tests. Reed (1973) seemed to advocate the same view. They suggested that structural contrasts in sequences of linguistic elements common to the speech of such children accounted for their lower reading scores. Similar arguments have been popular for years as an explanation of the 'difficulties' of teaching or learning a language other than the native language of the learner group. There is much controverting evidence, however, for either application of the contrastive analysis hypothesis (also see Chapter 6 below).

For instance, contrary to the prediction that would follow from the contrastive analysis hypothesis, in two recent studies, black children understood majority English about as well as white children, but the white children had greater difficulty with minority black English (Norton and Hodgson, 1973, and Stevens, Ruder, and Tew, 1973). While Baratz (1969) showed that white children tend to transform sentences presented in black English into their white English counterparts, and similarly, black children render sentences in white English into their own language variety, it would appear from her remarks that at least the black children had little difficulty understanding white English. This evidence does not conclusively eliminate the position once advocated by Goodman and Reed, but it does suggest the possibility of looking elsewhere for an explanation of reading problems and other difficulties of minority children in the schools. For example, is it not possible that sociocultural factors that are of an essentially non-linguistic sort might play an equal if not greater part in explaining school performance? One might ask whether black children in the communities where differences have been observed are subject to the kinds of reinforcement and punishment contingencies that are present in the experience of comparable groups of children in the majority culture. Do they see their parents reading books at home? Are they encouraged to read by parents and older siblings? These are tentative attempts at phrasing the right questions, but they hint at certain lines of research.

As to the contrastive explanation of the difficulties of language learners in acquiring a new linguistic system, a question should suffice. Why should Canadian French be so much easier for some middle class children in Montreal to acquire, than English is for many minority children in the Southwest? The answer probably does not lie in the contrasts between the language systems. Indeed, as the data continues to accummulate, it would appear that many of the children in bilingual programs in the United States (perhaps most of the children in most of the programs) are dominant in English when they come to school. The contrastive explanation is clearly inapplicable to those cases. For a review of the literature on second language studies and the contrastive analysis approaches, see Oller (1979). For a systematic study based on a Spanish–English bilingual program in Albuquerque, New Mexico, see Teitelbaum (1976).

If we reject the contrastive explanation, what then? Again it seems we are led to emotive aspects of the school situation in relation to the child's experience outside of the school. If the child's cultural background is neglected by the curriculum, if his people are not represented or are portrayed in an unfavorable light or are just simply misrepresented (e.g., the Plains Indian pictured in a canoe in a widely used elementary text, Joe Sando, personal communication), if his language is treated as unsuitable for educational pursuits (possibly referred to as the 'home language' but not the 'school language'), probably just about any teaching method will run into major difficulties.

It is in the area of cultural values and ways of expressing emotive level information in general (e.g., ethnic identity, approval, disapproval, etc.) where social groups may contrast more markedly and in ways that are apt to create significant barriers to communication between groups. The barriers are not so much in the structural systems of the languages (nor yet in the educational tests) as they are in the belief systems and ways of living of different cultures. Such differences may create difficulties for the acceptance of culturally distinct groups and the people who represent them. The failure of the minority child in school (or the failure of the school) is more likely to be caused by a conflict between cultures and the personalities they sustain rather than a lack of cognitive skills or abilities (see Bloom, 1976).

In any event, none of the facts about test bias lessens the need for sound language proficiency testing. Those facts merely accent the demands on educators and others who are attempting to devise tests and interpret test results. And, alas, as Upshur (1969b) noted *test* is still a four letter word.

E. Translating tests or items

Although it is possible to translate tests with little apparent loss of information, and without drastically altering the task set the examinees under some conditions, the translation of items for standardized multiple choice tests is beset by fundamental problems of principle. First we will consider the problems of translating tests item by item from one multiple choice format into another, and then we will return to consider the more general problem of translating pragmatic tasks from one language to another. It may seem surprising at the outset to note that the former translation procedure is probably not feasible while the latter can be accomplished without great difficulty.

A doctoral dissertation completed in 1974 at the University of New Mexico investigated the feasibility of translating the *Boehm Test of Basic Concepts* from English into Navajo (Scoon, 1974). The test attempts to measure the ability of school children in the early grades to handle such notions as sequence in time (before versus after) and location in space (beside, in front of, behind, under, and so on). It was reasoned by the original test writer that children need to be able to understand such concepts in order to follow everyday classroom instructions, and to carry out simple educational tasks. Scoon hoped to be able to get data from the translated test which would help to define instructional strategies to aid the Navajo child in the acquisition and use of such concepts.

Even though skilled bilinguals in English and Navajo helped with the translation task, and though allowances were made for unsuccessful translations, dialect variations, and the like, the tendency for the translated items to produce results similar to the original items was surprisingly weak. It is questionable whether the two tests can be said to be similar in what they require of examinees. Some of the items that were among the easiest ones on the English test turned out to be very difficult on the Navajo version, and vice versa.

The researcher began the project hoping to be able to diagnose learning difficulties of Navajo children in their own language. The study evolved to an investigation of the feasibility of translating a standardized test in a multiple choice format from English into Navajo. Scoon concluded that translating standardized tests is probably not a feasible approach to the diagnosis of educational aptitudes and skills.

All of this would lead us to wonder about the wisdom of translating standardized tests of 'intelligence' or achievement. Nevertheless, such translations exist. There are several reasons why translating a test, item by item, is apt to produce a very different test than the one the translators began with.

Translation of factive-level information is of course possible. However, much more is required. Translation of a multiple choice test item requires not only the maintenance of the factive information in the stem (or lead-in part) of the item, but the maintenance of it in roughly the same relation to the paradigm of linguistic and extralinguistic contexts that it calls to mind. Moreover, the relationships between the distractors and the correct answer must remain approximately the same in terms of the linguistic and extralinguistic contexts that they call to mind and in terms of the relationships (similarities and differences) between all of those contexts. While it may sometimes be difficult to maintain the factive content of one linguistic form when translating it into another language, this may be possible. However, to maintain the paradigm of interrelationships between linguistic and extralinguistic contexts in a set of distractors is probably not just difficult – it may well be impossible.

Translating delicately composed test items (on some of the delicacies, see Chapter 9) is something like trying to translate a joke, a pun, a riddle, or a poem. As 'Robert Frost once remarked, when a poem is translated, the poetry is often lost' (Kolers, 1968, p. 4). With test items (a lesser art form) it is the meaning and the relationship between alternative choices which is apt to be lost. A translation of a joke or poem often has to undergo such changes that if it were literally translated back into the source language it would not be recognizable. With test items it is the meaning of the items in terms of their effects on examinees that is apt to be changed, possibly beyond recognition.

A very common statement about a very ordinary fact in English may be an extremely uncommon statement about a very extraordinary fact in Navajo. A way of speaking in English may be incomprehensible in Navajo; for instance, the fact that you *cut down a tree* before you *cut it up* which is very different from *cutting up in a class* or *cutting down your teacher*. Conversely, a commonplace saying in Navajo may be enigmatic if literally translated into English.

Successful translation of items requires maintaining roughly the same style level, the same frequency of usage of vocabulary and idiom, comparable phrasing and reference complexities, and the same relationships among alternative choices. In some cases this simply cannot be done. Just as a pun cannot be directly translated from one language into another precisely because of the peculiarities of the particular expectancy grammar that makes the pun possible, a test item cannot always be translated so as to achieve equal effect in the target language. This is due quite simply to the fact that the real grammars of natural languages are devices that relate to paradigms of extralinguistic contexts in necessarily unique ways.

The bare tip of the iceberg can be illustrated by data from word association experiments conducted by Paul Kolers and reported in *Scientific American* in March 1968. He was not concerned with the word associations suggested by test items, but his data illustrate the nature of the problem we are considering. The method consists of presenting a word to a subject such as *mesa* (or *table*) and asking him to say whatever other word comes to mind, such as *silla* (or *chair*). Kolers was interested in determining whether pairs of associated words were similar in both of the languages of a bilingual subject. In fact, he found that they were the same in only about one-fifth of the cases. Actually he complicated the task by asking the subject to respond in the same language as the stimulus word on two tests (one in each of the subject's two languages), and in the opposite language in two other tests (e.g., once in English to Spanish stimulus words, and once in Spanish to English stimulus words). The first two tests can be referred to as *intralingual* and the second pair as *interlingual*.

The chart given below illustrates typical responses in Spanish and English under all four conditions. It shows that while the response in English was apt to be *girl* to the stimulus *boy*, in Spanish the word *muchacho* generated the response *hombre*. As is shown in the chart, the interlingual associations tended to be the same in about one out of five cases.

In view of such facts, it is apparent that it would be very difficult indeed to obtain similar associations between sets of alternative

INTRALINGUAL INTERLINGUAL

ENGLISH	ENGLISH
table	dish
boy	girl
king	queen
house	window

SPANISH	SPANISH
mesa	silla
muchacho	hombre
rey	reina
casa	madre

ENGLISH	SPANISH
table	silla
boy	niña
king	reina
house	blanco

SPANISH	ENGLISH
mesa	chair
muchacho	trousers
rey	queen
casa	mother

TYPICAL RESPONSES in a word-association test were given by a subject whose native language was Spanish. He was asked to respond in Spanish to Spanish stimulus words, in English to the same words in English and in each language to stimulus words in the other.

choices on multiple choice items. Scoon's results showed that the attempt at translating the Boehm test into Navajo did not produce a comparable test. This, of course, does not prove that a comparable test could not be devised, but it does suggest strongly that other methods for test development should be employed. For instance, it would be possible to devise a concept test in Navajo by writing items in Navajo right from the start instead of trying to translate items from an existing English test.

Because of the diversity of grammatical systems that different languages employ, it would be pure luck if a translated test item should produce highly similar effects on a population of speakers who have internalized a very different grammatical system for relating language sequences to extralinguistic contexts. We should predict in advance that a large number of such translation attempts would produce markedly different effects in the target language.

Is translation therefore never feasible? Quite the contrary. Although it is difficult to translate puns, jokes, or isolated test items in a multiple choice format, it is not terribly difficult to translate a novel, or even a relatively short portion of prose or discourse. Despite the idiosyncrasies of language systems with respect to the subtle and delicate interrelationships of their elements that make poetry and multiple choice test items possible, there are certain robust features that all languages seem to share. All of them have ways of coding factive (or cognitive) information and all of them have ways of expressing emotive (or affective) messages, and in doing these things, all languages are highly organized. They are both redundant and creative (Spolsky, 1968). According to recent research by John McLeod (1975), many languages are probably about equally redundant.

These latter facts about similarities of linguistic systems suggest the possibility of applying roughly comparable pragmatic testing procedures across languages with equivalent effects. For instance, there is empirical evidence in five languages that translations and the original texts from which they were translated can be converted into cloze tests of roughly comparable difficulty by following the usual procedures (McLeod, 1975; on procedures see also Chapter 12 of this book). The languages that McLeod investigated included Czech, Polish, French, German, and English. However, using different methods, Oller, Bowen, Dien, and Mason (1972) showed that it is probably possible to create cloze tests of roughly comparable difficulty (assuming the educational status, age, and socioeconomic factors are controlled) even when the languages are as different as English, Thai, and Vietnamese.

In a different application of cloze procedure, Klare, Sinaiko, and Stolurow (1972) recommend 'back translation' by a translator who has not seen the original passage. McLeod (1975) used this procedure to check the faithfulness of the translations used in his study and referred to it as 'blind back translation'. Whereas in the item-by-item translation that is necessary for multiple choice tests of the typical standardized type there will be a systematic one-for-one correspondence between the original test items and the translation version, this is not possible in the construction of cloze tests over translation of equivalent passages. In fact it would violate the normal use of the procedure to try to obtain equivalences between individual blanks in the passages.

Other pragmatic testing procedures besides the cloze technique could perhaps also be translated between two or more languages in order to obtain roughly equivalent tests in different languages. Multiple choice tests that qualify as pragmatic tasks should be translatable in this way (for examples, see Chapter 9). Passages in English and Fante were equated by a translation procedure to test reading comprehension in a standard multiple choice format by Bezanson and Hawkes (1976).

Kolers (1968) used a brief paragraph carefully translated into French as a basis for investigating the nature of bilingualism. He also constructed two test versions in which either English or French phrases were interpolated into the text in the opposite language. The task required of subjects was to read each passage aloud. Kolers was interested in whether passages requiring switching between English and French would require more time than the monolingual passages. He determined that each switch on the average required an extra third of a second. The task, however, and the procedure for setting up the task could be adapted to the interests of bilingual or multilingual testing in other settings.

Ultimately, the arguments briefly presented here concerning the feasibility of setting up equivalent tests by translation between two or more languages are related to the controversy about discrete point and integrative or pragmatic tests. Generally speaking it should be difficult to translate discrete point items in a multiple choice (or other) format while maintaining equivalence, though it is probably quite feasible to translate pragmatic tests and thereby to obtain equivalent tests in more than one language. For any given discrete item, translation into another language will produce (in principle and of necessity) a substantially different item. For any given pragmatic testing procedure on the other hand, translation into another language (if it is done carefully) can be expected to produce a substantially similar test. In this respect, discrete items are delicate whereas pragmatic procedures are robust. Of course, the possibility of translating tests of either type merits a great deal more empirical study.

F. Dominance and proficiency

We noted above that the 'Lau Remedies' require data concerning language use and dominance. The questions of importance would seem to be, what language does the child prefer to use (or feel most comfortable using) with whom and in what contexts of experience? And, in which of two or more languages is the child most competent? The most common way of getting information concerning language use is by either interviewing the children and eliciting information from them, or by addressing a questionnaire to the teacher(s) or some other person who has the opportunity to observe the child. Spolsky, Murphy, Holm, and Ferrel (1972) offer a questionnaire in Spanish and one in Navajo (either of which can also be used in English) to 'classify' students roughly according to the same basic categories that are recommended in the 'Lau Remedies' (see Spolsky, et al, p. 79).

Since the 'Remedies' came more than two years later than the Spolsky, *et al* article, it may be safe to assume that the scale recommended in the 'Remedies' derives from that source. The teacher questionnaire involves a similar five point scale (see Spolsky, *et al*, p. 81).

Two crucial questions arise. Can children's responses to questions concerning their language-use patterns be relied upon for the important educational decisions that must be made? And, second, can teachers judge the language ability of children in their classrooms (bear in mind that in many cases the teachers are not bilingual themselves; in fact, Spolsky, 1974, estimates that only about 5% of the teachers on the Navajo reservation and in BIA schools speak Navajo)? Related to these crucial questions is the empirical problem of devising careful testing procedures to assess the validity of self-reported data (by the child), and teacher-reported judgements.

Spolsky, *et al* made several assumptions concerning the interview technique which they used for assessing dominance in Spanish and English:

1. ... bilingual dominance varies from domain to domain. Subscores were therefore given for the domains of home, neighborhood, and school.

2. A child's report of his own language use is likely to be quite accurate.

3. Vocabulary fluency (word-naming) is a good measure of knowledge of a language and it is a good method of comparing knowledge of two languages.

4. The natural bias of the schools in Albuquerque as a testing situation favors the use of English; this needs to be counteracted by using a Spanish speaking interviewer (p. 78).

If such assumptions can be made safely, it ought to be possible to make similar assumptions in other contexts and with little modification extend the 'three functional tests of oral proficiency' recommended by Spolsky, *et al*. Yet they themselves say, somewhat ambiguously:

> Each of the tests described was developed for a specific purpose and it would be unwise to use it more widely without careful consideration, but the general principles involved may prove useful to others who need tests that can serve similar purposes (p. 77).

One is inclined to ask what kind of consideration? Obviously a local meeting of the School Board or some other organization will not suffice to justify the assumptions listed above, or to guarantee the success of the testing procedures, with or without adaptations to fit a particular local situation (Spolsky, 1974). What is required first is some careful logical investigation of possible outcomes from the procedures recommended by Spolsky, *et al*, and other procedures which can be devised for the purpose of crossvalidation. Second, empirical study is required as illustrated, for example, in the Appendix below.

Zirkel (1974) points out that it is not enough merely to place a child on a dominance scale. Simple logic will explain why. It is possible for two children to be balanced bilinguals in terms of such a scale but to differ radically in terms of their developmental levels. An extreme case would be children at different ages. A more pertinent case would be two children of the same age and grade level who are balanced bilinguals (thus both scoring at the mid point of the dominance scale, see p. 76 above), but who are radically different in language skill in both languages. One child might be performing at an advanced level in both languages while the other child is performing at a much lower level in both languages. Measuring for dominance-only would not reveal such a difference.

No experimentation is required to show the inadequacy of any procedure that merely assesses dominance – even if it does the job accurately, and it is doubtful whether some of the procedures being recommended can do even the job of dominance assessment accurately. Besides, there are important considerations in addition to mere language dominance which can enter the picture only when valid proficiency data are available for both languages (or each of the several languages in a multilingual setting). Moreover, with care to insure test equivalence across the languages assessed, dominance scores can be derived directly from proficiency data – the reverse is not necessarily possible.

Hence, the question concerning how to acquire reliable information concerning language proficiency in multilingual contexts, including the important matter of determining language dominance, is essentially the same question we have been dealing with throughout this book. In order to determine language dominance accurately, it is necessary to impose the additional requirement of equating tests across languages. Preliminary results of McLeod (1975), Klare, Sinaiko, and Stolurow (1972), Oller, Bowen, Dien, and Mason (1972), and Bezanson and Hawkes (1976) suggest that careful translation may offer a solution to the equivalence problem, and no doubt there are other approaches that will prove equally effective.

There are pitfalls to be avoided, however. There is no doubt that it is possible to devise tests that do not accomplish what they were designed to accomplish – that are not valid. Assumptions of validity are justifiable only to the extent that assumptions of lack of validity have been disposed of by careful research. On that theme let us reconsider the four assumptions quoted earlier in this section. What is the evidence that bilingual dominance 'varies from domain to domain'?

In 1969, Cooper reported that a word-naming task (the same sort of task used in the Spanish-English test of Spolsky, *et al*, 1972) which varied by domains such as 'home' versus 'school' or 'kitchen' versus 'classroom' produced different scores depending on the domain referred to in a particular portion of the test. The task set the examinee was to name all the things he could think of in the 'kitchen', for example. Examinees completed the task for each domain (five in all in Cooper's study) in both languages without appropriate counterbalancing to avoid an order effect. Since there were significant contrasts between relative abilities of subjects to do the task in Spanish and English across domains, it was concluded that their degree of dominance varied from one domain to another. This is a fairly broad leap of inference, however.

Consider the following question: does the fact that I can name more objects in Spanish that I see in my office than objects that I can see under the hood of my car mean that I am relatively more proficient in Spanish when sitting in my office than when looking under the hood of my car? What Cooper's results seem to show (and Teitelbaum, 1976, found similar results with a similar task) is that the number of things a person can name in reference to one physical setting may be smaller or greater than the number that the same person can name in reference to another physical setting. This is not evidence of a very direct sort about possible changes in language dominance when sitting in your living room, or when sitting in a classroom. Not even the contrast in 'word-naming' across languages is necessarily an indication of any difference whatsoever in language dominance in a broader sense. Suppose a person learned the names of chess pieces in a language other than his native language, and suppose further that he does not know the names of the pieces in his native language. Would this make him dominant in the foreign language when playing chess?

A more important question is not whether there are contrasts across domains, but whether the 'word-naming' task is a valid indication of language proficiency. Insufficient data are available. At face value such a task appears to have little relation to the sorts of things that people normally do with language, children especially. Such a task does not qualify as a pragmatic testing procedure because it does not require time-constrained sequential processing, and it is doubtful whether it requires mapping of utterances onto extralinguistic contexts in the normal ways that children might perform such mappings – naming objects is relatively simpler than even the speech of median-ranged three-and-a-half year old children (Hart, 1974, and Hart, Walker, and Gray, 1977).

Teitelbaum (1976) correlated scores on word-naming tasks (in Spanish) with teacher-ratings; and self-ratings differentiated by four domains ('kitchen, yard, block, school'). For a group of kindergarten through 4th grade children in a bilingual program in Albuquerque (nearly 100 in all), the correlations ranged from .15 to .45. Correlations by domain with scores on an interview task, however, ranged from .69 to .79. These figures hardly justify the differentiation of language dominance by domain. The near equivalence of the correlations across domains with a single interview task seems to show that the domain differentiation is pointless. Cohen (1973) has adapted the word-naming task slightly to convert it into a story-telling procedure by domains. His scoring is based on the number of different words used in each story-telling domain. Perhaps other scoring techniques should also be considered.

The second assumption quoted above was that a child's own report of his language use is apt to be 'quite accurate'. This may be more true for some children than for others. For the children in Teitelbaum's study neither the teacher's ratings nor the children's own ratings were very accurate. In no case did they account for more than 20% of the variance in more objective measures of language proficiency.

What about the child Zirkel (1976) referred to? What if some children are systematically indoctrinated concerning what language they are supposed to use at school and at home as some advocates of the 'home language/school language' dichotomy advocate? Some research with bilingual children seems to suggest that at an early age they may be able to discriminate appropriately between occasions when one language is called for and occasions when the other language is required (e.g., answering in French when spoken to in French, but in English when spoken to in English, Kinzel, 1964), without being able to discuss this ability at a more abstract level (e.g., reporting when you are supposed to speak French rather than English). Teitelbaum's data reveal little correlation between questions about language use and scores on more objective language proficiency measures. Is it possible that a bilingual child is smart enough to be sensitive to what he thinks the interviewer expects him to say? Upshur (1971a) observes, 'it isn't fair to ask a man to cut his own throat, and even if we should ask, it isn't reasonable to expect him to do it. We don't ask a man to rate his proficiency when an honest answer might result in his failure to achieve some desired goal' (p. 58). Is it fair to expect a child to respond independently of what he may think the interviewer wants to hear?

We have dealt earlier with the third assumption quoted above, so we come to the fourth. Suppose that we assume the interviewer should be a speaker of the minority language (rather than English) in order to counteract an English bias in the schools. There are several possibilities. Such a provision may have no effect, the desired effect (if indeed it is desired as it may distort the picture of the child's true capabilities along the lines of the preceding paragraph), or an effect that is opposite to the desired one. The only way to determine which result is the actual one is to devise some empirical measure of the relative magnitude of a possible interviewer effect.

G. Tentative suggestions

What methods then can be recommended for multilingual testing? There are many methods that can be expected to work well and deserve to be tried – among them are suitable adaptations of the methods discussed in this book in Part Three. Some of the ones that have been used with encouraging results include oral interview procedures of a wide range of types (but designed to elicit speech from the child and data on comprehension, not necessarily the child's own estimate of how well he speaks a certain language) – see Chapter 11. Elicited imitation (a kind of oral dictation procedure) has been widely used – see Chapter 10. Versions of the cloze procedure (particularly ones that may be administered orally) are promising and have been used with good results – see Chapter 12. Variations on composition tasks and story telling or retelling have also been used – see Chapter 13. No doubt many other procedures can be devised – Chapter 14 offers some suggestions and guidelines.

In brief, what seems to be required is a class of testing procedures providing a basis for equivalent tests in different languages that will yield proficiency data in both languages and that will simultaneously provide dominance scores of an accurate and sensitive sort. Figure 3 offers a rough conceptualization of the kinds of equivalent measures needed. If Scale A in the diagram represents a range of possible scores on a test in language A, and if Scale B represents a range of possible scores on an equivalent test in language B, the relative difference in scores on A and B can provide the basis for placement on the dominance scale C (modelled after the 'Lau Remedies' or the Spolsky, *et al*, 1972, scales).

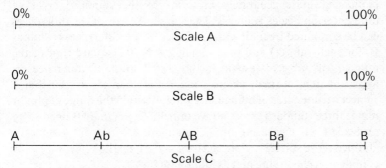

Figure 3. A dominance scale in relation to proficiency scales. (Scales A and B represent equivalent proficiency tests in languages A and B, while scale C represents a dominance scale, as required by the Lau Remedies. It is claimed that the meaning of C can only be adequately defined in relation to scores on A and B.)

It would be desirable to calibrate both of the proficiency scales with reference to comparable groups of monolingual speakers of each language involved (Cowan and Zarmed, 1976, followed such a procedure) in order to be able to interpret scores in relation to clear criteria of performance. The dominance scale can be calibrated by defining distances on that scale in terms of units of difference in proficiency on Scales A and B.

This can be done as follows: first, subtract each subject's score on A from the score on B. (If the tests are calibrated properly, it is not likely that anyone will get a perfect score on either test though there may be some zeroes.) Then rank order the results. They should range from a series of positive values to a series of negative values. If the group tested consists only of children who are dominant in one language, there will be only positive or only negative values, but not both. The ends of the rank will define the ends of the dominance scale (with reference to the population tested) – that is the A and B points on Scale C in Figure 3. The center point, AB on Scale C, is simply the zero position in the rank. That is the point at which a subject's scores in both languages are equal. The points between the ends and the center, namely, Ab and Ba, can be defined by finding the mid point in the rank between that end (A or B) and the center (AB).

The degree of accuracy with which a particular subject can be classed as A = monolingual in A, Ab = dominant in A, AB = equally bilingual in A and B, Ba = dominant in B, B = monolingual in B, can be judged quite accurately in terms of the standard error of differences on Scales A and B. The standard error of the differences can be computed by finding the variance of the differences (A minus B, for each subject) and then dividing it by the square root of the number of subjects tested. If the distribution of differences is approximately normal, chances are better than 99 in 100 that a subject's true degree of bilinguality will fall within the range of plus or minus three standard errors above or below his actual attained score on Scale C. If measuring off ± 3 standard errors from a subject's attained score still leaves him close to, say, Ab on the Scale, we can be confident in classifying him as 'dominant in A'.

Thus, if the average standard error of differences in scores on tests A and B is large, the accuracy of Scale C will be less than if the average standard error is small. A general guideline might be to require at least six standard errors between each of the five points on the dominance scale. It remains to be seen, however, what degree of accuracy will be possible. For suggestions on equating scales across languages, see Chapter 10, pp. 289–295.[1]

KEY POINTS

1. There is a serious need for multilingual testing in the schools not just of the United States, but in many nations.
2. In the Lau versus Nichols case in 1974, the Supreme Court ruled that the San Francisco Schools were violating a section of the Civil Rights Code which 'bans discrimination based on the ground of race, color, or national origin' (1974, No. 72–6520). It was ruled that the schools should either provide instruction in the native language of the 1,800 Chinese speaking children in question, or provide special instruction in the English language.
3. Even at the present, in academic year 1978–9, many bilingual programs

[1] Also see discussion question number 10 at the end of Chapter 10. Much basic research is needed on these issues.

and many schools which have children of multilingual backgrounds are not doing adequate language assessment.

4. There are important parallels between multilingual and multidialectal societies. In both cases there is a need for language assessment procedures referenced against group norms (a plurality of them).

5. In a strong logical sense, a language *is* its varieties or dialects, and the dialects or varieties are languages. A particular variety may be elevated to a higher status by virtue of the 'more equal syndrome', but this does not necessitate that other varieties must therefore be regarded as less than languages – mere 'potential languages'.

6. Prejudices can be institutionalized in theories of 'deficits' or 'deprivations'. The pertinent question is, from whose point of view? The institutionalization of such theories into discriminatory educational practices may well create real deficits.

7. It is hypothesized that, at least for the minority child, and perhaps for the majority child as well, variance in learning in the schools may be much more a function of the emotive aspects of interactions within and outside of schools than it is a function of methods of teaching and presentation of subject matter *per se*.

8. When emotive level struggles arise, factive level communication usually stops altogether.

9. Ignoring the existence of a child or social group is a cruel punishment. Who discovered America?

10. Getting the cultural bias out of language tests would mean making them into something besides language tests. However, adapting them to particular cultural needs is another matter.

11. Contrastive analysis based explanations for the generally lower scores of minority children on educational tests run into major empirical difficulties. Other factors appear to be much more important than the surface forms of different languages or language varieties.

12. Translating discrete point test items is roughly comparable to translating jokes, or puns, or poems. It is difficult if not impossible.

13. Translating pragmatic tests or testing procedures on the other hand is more like translating prose or translating a novel. It can be done, not easily perhaps, but at least it is feasible.

14. 'Blind back translation' is one procedure for checking the accuracy of translation attempts.

15. Measures of multilingual proficiencies require valid proficiency tests. The validity of proposed procedures is an empirical question. Assumptions must be tested, or they remain a threat to every educational decision based on them.

16. Measuring dominance is not enough. To interpret the meaning of a score on a dominance scale, it is useful to know the proficiency scores which it derives from.

17. It is suggested that a dominance scale of the sort recommended in the Lau Remedies can be calibrated in terms of the average standard error of the differences in test scores against which the scale is referenced.

18. Similarly, it is recommended that scores on the separate proficiency tests be referenced against (and calibrated in terms of) the scores of

monolingual children who speak the language of the test. (It is realized
that this may not be possible to attain in reference to some very small
populations where the minority language is on the wane.)

DISCUSSION QUESTIONS

1. How are curricular decisions regarding the delivery of instructional
   materials made in your school(s)? Schools that you know of?
2. If you work in or know of a bilingual program, what steps are taken in
   that program to assess language proficiency? How are the scores
   interpreted in relation to the curriculum? If you knew that a substantial
   number of the children in your school were approximately equally
   proficient in two languages, what curricular decisions would you
   recommend? What else would you need to know in order to recommend
   policies?
3. If you were asked to rank priorities for budgetary expenditures, where
   would language testing come on the list for tests and measurements? Or,
   would there be any such list?
4. What is wrong with 'surname surveys' as a basis for determining
   language dominance? What can be said about a child whose name is
   Ortiz? Smith? Reitzel? What about asking the child concerning his
   language preferences? What are some of the factors that might influence
   the child's response? Why not just have the teachers in the schools judge
   the proficiency of the children?
5. What price would you say would be a fair one for being able to
   communicate in one of the world's power languages (especially English)?
   Consider the case for the child in the African primary schools as
   suggested by Hofman. Is it worth the cost?
6. Try to conceive of a language test that need not make reference to group
   norms. How would such a test relate to educational policy?
7. Consider doing a study of possible language variety bias in the tests used
   in your school. Or perhaps a language bias study, or combination of the
   two would be more appropriate. What kinds of scores would be available
   for the study? IQ? Aptitude? Achievement? Classroom observations?
   What sorts of language proficiency measures might you use? (Anyone
   seriously considering such a study is urged to consult Part Three, and to
   ask the advice of someone who knows something about research design
   before actually undertaking the project. It could be done, however, by
   any teacher or administrator capable of persuading others that it is
   worth doing.) Are language variety biases in educational testing different
   in type?
8. Begin to construct a list of the sociocultural factors that might be
   partially accountable for the widely discussed view that has been put
   forth by Jensen and Herrnstein to the effect that certain races are
   superior in intelligence. What is intelligence? How is it measured with
   reference to your school or school populations that you know of?
9. Spend a few days as an observer of children in a classroom setting. Note
   ways in which the teacher and significant others in the school
   communicate emotive information to the children. Look especially for

contrasts in what is said and what is meant from the child's perspective. Consider the school curriculum with a view to its representation of different cultures and language varieties. Observe the behaviour of the children. What kinds of messages do they pick up and pass on? What kinds of beliefs and attitudes are they being encouraged to accept or reject?

10. Discuss the differences between 'submersion' and 'immersion' as educational approaches to the problem of teaching a child a new language and cultural system. (See Barik and Swain, 1975, in Suggested Readings at the end of this chapter.)

11. Consider an example or several of them of children who are especially low achievers in your school or in a school that you know of. Look for sociocultural factors that may be related to the low achievement. Then, consider some of the high achievers in the same context. Consider the probable effects of sociocultural contexts. Do you see a pattern emerging?

12. To what extent is 'cultural bias' in tests identical to 'experiential bias' – i.e., simply not having been exposed to some possible set of experiences? Can you find genuine cultural factors that are distinct from experiential biases? Examine a widely used standardized test. If possible discuss it with someone whose cultural experience is very different from your own. Are there items in it that are clearly biased? Culturally? Or merely experientially?

13. Discuss factors influencing children who learn to read before they come to school. Consider those factors in relation to what you know of children who fail to learn to read after they come to school. Where does language development fit into the picture? Books in the home? Models who are readers that the child might emulate? Do children of widely different dialect origins in the United States (or elsewhere) learn to read much the same material? Consider Great Britain, Ireland, Australia, Canada, and other nations.

14. Consider the fact that *test* is a four letter word (Upshur, 1969b). Why? How have tests been misused or simply used to make them seem so ominous, portentous, even wicked? Reconsider the definition of language tests offered in Chapter 1. Can you think of any innocuous and benign procedures that qualify as tests? How could such procedures be used to reduce the threat of tests?

15. Try translating a few discrete items on several types of tests. Have someone else who has not seen the original items do a 'blind back translation'. Check the comparability of the results. Try the same with a passage of prose. Can corrections be made to clear up the difficulties that arise? Are there substantial contrasts between the two tasks?

16. Try a language interview procedure that asks children how well they understand one or more languages and when they use it. A procedure such as the one suggested for Spanish-English bilinguals by Spolsky, *et al* (1972, see Suggested Readings for Chapter 4) should suffice. Then test the children on a battery of other measures – teacher evaluations of the type suggested by Spolsky, *et al* (1972) for Navajo-English bilinguals might also be used. Intercorrelate the scores and determine empirically

104 LANGUAGE TESTS AT SCHOOL

their degree of variance overlap. To what extent can the various procedures be said to yield the same information?

17. What kinds of tests can you conceive of to assess the popular opinion that language dominance varies from domain to domain? Be careful to define 'domain' in a sociolinguistically meaningful and pragmatically useful way.

18. Devise proficiency tests in two or more languages and attempt to calibrate them in the recommended ways – both against the scores of monolingual reference groups (if these are accessible) and in terms of the average standard error of the differences on the two tests. Relate them to a five point dominance scale such as the one shown in Figure 3 above. Correlate scores on the proficiency tests that you have devised with other standardized tests used in the school from which your sample population was drawn. To what extent are variances on other tests accounted for by variances in language proficiencies (especially in English, assuming that it is the language of practically all standardized testing in the schools)?

SUGGESTED READINGS

1. H. C. Barik and Merrill Swain, 'Three-year Evaluation of a Large Scale Early Grade French Immersion Program: the Ottawa study,' *Language Learning* 25, 1975, 1–30.

2. Andrew Cohen, 'The Sociolinguistic Assessment of Speaking Skills in a Bilingual Education Program,' in L. Palmer and B. Spolsky (eds.) *Papers on Language Testing*. Washington, D.C.: *TESOL*, 1975, 173–186.

3. Paul A. Kolers, 'Bilingualism and Information Processing,' *Scientific American* 218, 1968, 78–84.

4. 'OCR Sets Guidelines for Fulfilling *Lau* Decision,' *The Linguistic Reporter* 18, 1975, 1, 5–7. (Gives addresses of Lau Centers and quotes the text of the 'Lau Remedies' recommended by the Task Force appointed by the Office of Civil Rights.)

5. Patricia J. Nakano, 'Educational Implications of the *Lau v. Nichols* Decision,' in M. Burt, H. Dulay, and M. Finocchinaro (eds.) *Viewpoints on English as a Second Language*. New York: Regents, 1977, 219–34.

6. Bernard Spolsky, 'Speech Communities and Schools,' *TESOL Quarterly* 8, 1974, 17–26.

7. Bernard Spolsky, Penny Murphy, Wayne Holm, and Allen Ferrel, 'Three Functional Tests of Oral Proficiency,' *TESOL Quarterly* 6, 1972, 221–235. (Also in Palmer and Spolsky, 75–90, see reference 2 above. Page references in this text are to the latter source.)

8. Perry A. Zirkel, 'A Method for Determining and Depicting Language Dominance,' *TESOL Quarterly* 8, 1974, 7–16.

9. Perry A. Zirkel, 'The Why's and Ways of Testing Bilinguality Before Teaching Bilingually,' *The Elementary School Journal*, March 1976, 323–330.

5

Measuring Attitudes and Motivations

    A. The need for validating affective measures
    B. Hypothesized relationships between affective variables and the use and learning of language
    C. Direct and indirect measures of affect
    D. Observed relationships to achievement and remaining puzzles

A great deal of research has been done on the topic of measuring the affective side of human experience. Personality, attitudes, emotions, feelings, and motivations, however, are subjective things and even our own experience tells us that they are as changeable as the wind. The question here is whether or not they can be measured. Further, what is the relationship between existing measures aimed at affective variables and measures aimed at language skill or other educational constructs?

A. The need for validating affective measures

No one seems to doubt that attitudinal factors are related to human performances.[1] In the preceding chapter we considered the hypothesis that emotive or affective factors play a greater part in determining success or failure in schools than do factive or cognitive factors (particularly teaching methodologies). The problem is how to determine what the affective factors might be. It is widely believed

---

[1] Throughout this chapter and elsewhere in the book, we often use the term 'attitudes' as a cover term for all sorts of affective variables. While there are many theories that distinguish between many sorts of attitudinal, motivational and personality variables, all of them are in the same boat when it comes to validation.

that a child's self-concept (confidence or lack of it, willingness to take social risks, and all around sense of well-being) must contribute to virtually every sort of school performance – or performance outside of the school for that matter. Similarly, it is believed that the child's view of others (whether of the child's own ethnic and social background, or of a different cultural background, whether peers or non-peers) will influence virtually every aspect of his interpersonal interactions in positive and negative ways that contribute to success or failure (or perhaps just to happiness in life, which though a vaguer concept, may be a better one).

It is not difficult to believe that attitude variables are important to a wide range of cognitive phenomena – perhaps the whole range – but it is difficult to say just exactly what attitude variables are. Therefore, it is difficult to prove by the usual empirical methods of science that attitudes actually have the importance usually attributed to them. In his widely read and often cited book, *Beyond Freedom and Dignity*, B. F. Skinner (1971) offers the undisguised thesis that such concepts as 'freedom' and 'dignity' not to mention 'anxiety', 'ego', and the kinds of terms popular in the attitude literature are merely loose and misleading ways of speaking about the kinds of events that control behavior. He advocates sharpening up our thinking and our ways of controlling behavior in order to save the world – 'not ... to destroy [the] environment or escape from it ... [but] to redesign it' (p. 39). To Skinner, attitudes are dispensable intervening variables between behavior and the consequences of behavior. They can thus be done away with. If he were quite correct, it ought to be possible to observe behaviors and their consequences astutely enough to explain all there is to explain about human beings – however, there is a problem for Skinner's approach. Even simpler systems than human beings are not fully describable in that way – e.g., try observing the input and output of a simple desk calculator and see if it is possible to determine how it works inside – then recall that human beings are much more complex than desk calculators.

Only very radical and very narrow (and therefore largely uninteresting and very weak theories) are able to dispense completely with attitudes, feelings, personalities, and other difficult-to-measure internal states and motives of human beings. It seems necessary, therefore, to take attitudes into account. The problem begins, however, as soon as we try to be very explicit about what an attitude is. Shaw and Wright (1967) say that 'an attitude is a hypothetical, or latent, variable' (p. 15). That is to say, an attitude is not the sort of variable that can be observed directly. If someone reports that he is angry, we must either take his word for it, or test his statement on the basis of what we see him doing to determine whether or not he is really angry. In attitude research, the chain of inference is often much longer than just the inference from a report to an attitude or from a behavioral pattern to an attitude. The quality or quantity of the attitude can only be inferred from some other variable that can be measured.

For instance, a respondent is frequently asked to evaluate a statement about some situation (or possibly a mere proposition about a very general state of affairs). Sometimes he is asked to say how he would act or feel in a given described situation. In so-called 'projective' techniques, it is further necessary for some judge or evaluator to rate the response of the subject for the degree to which it displays some attitude. In some of these techniques there are so many steps of inference where error might arise that it is amazing that such techniques ever produce usable data, but apparently they sometimes do. Occasionally, we may be wrong in judging whether someone is happy or sad, angry or glad, anxious or calm, but often we are correct in our judgements, and a trained observer *may* (not necessarily *will*) become very skilled in making such judgements.

Shaw and Wright (1967) suggest that 'attitude measurement consists of the assessment of an individual's responses to a set of situations. The set of situations is usually a set of statements (items) about the attitude object, to which the individual responds with a set of specific categories, e.g., agree and disagree. ... The ... number derived from his scores represents his position on the latent attitude variable' (p. 15). Or, at least, that is what the researcher *hopes* and often it is what the researcher merely *asserts*. For example, Gardner and Lambert (1972) assert that the degree of a person's agreement with the statement that 'Nowadays more and more people are prying into matters that should remain personal and private' is a reflection of their degree of 'anti-democratic ideology' (p. 150). The statement appears in a scale supposed by its authors (Adorno, Frenkel-Brunswick, Levinson, and Sanford, 1950) to measure 'prejudice and authoritarianism'. The scale was used by Gardner and Lambert in the 1960s in the states of Maine, Louisiana, and Connecticut. Who can deny that the statement was substantially true and was becoming more true as the Nixon regime grew and flourished?

The trouble with most attitude measures is that they have never been subjected to the kind of critical scrutiny that should be applied to *any* test that is used to make judgements (or to refute judgements) about human beings. In spite of the vast amounts of research completed in the last three or four decades on the topic of attitudes, personality, and measures of related variables, precious little has been learned that is not subject to severe logical and empirical doubts. Shaw and Wright (1967) who report hundreds of attitude measures along with reliability statistics and validity results, where available, lament their 'impression that much effort has been wasted. ...' and that 'nowhere is this more evident than in relation to the instruments used in the measurement of attitudes' (p. ix).

They are not alone in their disparaging assessment of attitude measures. In his preface to a tome of over a thousand pages on *Personality: Tests and Reviews*, Oscar K. Buros (1970) says:

> Paradoxically, the area of testing which has outstripped all others in the quantity of research over the past thirty years is also the area in which our testing procedures have the generally least accepted validity. ... In my own case, the preparation of this volume has caused me to become increasingly discouraged at the snail's pace at which we are advancing compared to the tremendous progress being made in the areas of medicine, science, and technology. As a profession, we are prolific researchers; but somehow or other there is very little agreement about what is the resulting verifiable knowledge (p. ixx).

In an article on a different topic and addressed to an entirely different audience, John R. Platt offered some comments that may help to explain the relative lack of progress in social psychology and in certain aspects of the measurement of sociolinguistic variables. He argued that a thirty year failure to agree is proof of a thirty year failure to do the kind of research that produces the astounding and remarkable advances of fields like 'molecular biology and high-energy physics' (1964, p. 350). The fact is that the social sciences generally are among the 'areas of science that are sick by comparison because they have forgotten the necessity for alternative hypotheses and disproof' (p. 350). He was speaking of his own field, chemistry, when he coined the terms 'The Frozen Method, The Eternal Surveyor, The Never Finished, The Great Man with a Single Hypothesis, The Little Club of Dependents, The Vendetta, The All Encompassing Theory which Can Never Be Falsified' (p. 350), but do these terms not have a certain ring of familiarity with reference to the social sciences? What is the solution? He proposes a return to the old-fashioned method of inductive inference – with a couple of embellishments.

It is necessary to form multiple working hypotheses instead of merely popularizing the ones that we happen to favor, and instead of trying merely to support or worse yet to prove (which strictly speaking is a logical impossibility for interesting empirical) hypotheses, we should be busy eliminating the plausible alternatives – alternatives which are rarely addressed in the social sciences. As Francis Bacon stressed so many years ago, and Platt re-emphasizes, science advances only by disproofs.

Is it the failure to disprove that explains the lack of agreement in the social sciences? Is there a test that purports to be a measure of a certain construct? What else might it be a measure of? What other alternatives are there that need to be ruled out? Such questions have usually been neglected. Has a researcher found a significant difference between two groups of subjects? What plausible explanations for the difference have not been ruled out? In addition to forming multiple working hypotheses (which will help to keep our thinking impartial as well as clear), it is necessary always to recycle the familiar steps of the Baconian method: (1) form clear hypotheses; (2) design crucial experiments to eliminate as many as possible; (3) carry out the experiments; and (4) 'refine the possibilities that remain' (Platt, 1964, p. 347) and do it all over again, and again, and again, always eliminating some of the plausible alternatives and refining the remaining ones. By such a method, the researcher enhances the chances of formulating a more powerful explanatory theory on each cycle from data-to-theory to data-to-theory with maximum efficiency. Platt asks if there is any virtue in plodding almost aimlessly through thirty years of work that might be accomplished in two or three months with a little forethought and planning.

In the sequel to the first volume on personality tests, Buros offers the following stronger statement in 1974 (*Personality Tests and Reviews* II):

> It is my considered belief that most standardized tests are poorly constructed, of questionable or unknown validity, pretentious in their claims, and likely to be misused more often than not (p. xvii).

In another compendium, one that reviews some 3,000 sources of psychological tests, E. Lowell Kelly writes in the Foreword (see Chun, Cobb, and French, 1975):

> At first blush, the development of such a large number of assessment devices in the past 50 years would appear to reflect remarkable progress in the development of the social sciences.

Unfortunately, this conclusion is not justified, ... nearly three out of four of the instruments are used but once and often only by the developer of the instrument. Worse still, ... the more popular instruments tend to be selected more frequently not because they are better measuring instruments, but primarily because of their convenience (p. v).

It is one thing to *say* that a particular attitude questionnaire, or rating procedure of whatever sort, measures a specific attitude or personality characteristic (e.g., authoritarianism, prejudice, anxiety, ego strength/weakness, or the like) but it is an entirely different matter to *prove* that this is so. Indeed, it is often difficult to conceive of any test whatsoever that would constitute an adequate criterion for 'degree of authoritarianism' or 'degree of empathy', etc. Often the only validity information offered by the designer or user of a particular procedure for assessing some hypothetical (at best latent) attitudinal variable is the label that he associates with the procedure. Kelly (1975) classes this kind of validity with several other types as what he calls 'pseudo-validity'. He refers to this kind of validity as 'nominal validity' – it consists in 'the assumption that the instrument measures what its name implies'. It is related closely to 'validity by fiat' – 'assertion by the author (no matter how distinguished!) that the instrument measures variable X, Y, or Z' (p. vii, from the Foreword to Chun, *et al*, 1975). One has visions of a king laying the sword blade on either shoulder of the knight-to-be and declaring to all ears, 'I dub thee Knight.' Hence the test author gives 'double' (or 'dubious', if you prefer) validity to his testing instrument – first by authorship and then by name.

Is there no way out of this difficulty? Is it not possible to require more of attitude measures than the pseudo-validities which characterize so many of them? In a classic paper on 'construct validity' Cronbach and Meehl (1955) addressed this important question. If we treat attitudes as theoretical constructs and measures of attitudes (or measures that purport to be measures of attitudes) as tests, then the tests are subject to the same sorts of empirical and theoretical justification that are applied to any construct in scientific study. Cronbach and Meehl say, 'a construct is some postulated attribute of people assumed to be reflected in performance' (p. 283). They continue, 'persons who possess this attribute will, in situation X, act in manner Y (with a stated probability)' (p. 284).

Among the techniques for assessing the validity of a test of a postulated construct are the following: select a group whose behavior is well known (or can be determined) and test the hypothesis that the behavior is related to an attitude (e.g., the classic example used by Thurstone and others was church-goers versus non-church-goers). Or, if the attitude or belief of a particular group is known, some behavioral criterion can be predicted and the hypothesized outcome can be tested by the usual method.

These techniques are rather rough and ready, and can be improved upon generally (in fact they must be improved upon if attitude measures are to be more finely calibrated) by devising alternative measures of the attitude or construct and assessing the degree (and pattern) of variance overlap on the various measures by correlation and related procedures (e.g., factor analysis and multiple regression techniques). For instance, as Cronbach and Meehl (1955) observe, 'if two tests are presumed to measure the same construct, a correlation between them is predicted ... If the obtained correlation departs from the expectation, however, there is no way to know whether the fault lies in test A, test B, or the formulation of the construct. A matrix of intercorrelations often points out profitable ways of dividing the construct into more meaningful parts, factor analysis being a useful computational method in such studies' (p. 287).

Following this latter procedure, scales which are supposed to assess the same construct can be correlated to determine whether in fact they share some variance. The extent of the correlation, or of their tendency to correlate with a mathematically defined factor (or to 'load' on such a factor), may be taken as a kind of index of the validity of the measure. Actually, the latter techniques are related to the general internal consistency of measures that purport to measure the same thing. To prove a high degree of internal consistency between a variety of measures of, say, 'prejudice' is not to prove that the measures are indeed assessing degree of prejudice, but if any one of them on independent grounds can be shown to be a measure of prejudice then confidence in all of the measures is thereby strengthened. (For several applications of rudimentary factor analysis, see the Appendix.)

Ultimately, there may be no behavioral criterion which can be proposed as a basis for validating a given attitude measure. At best there may be only a range of criteria, which taken as a whole, cause us to have confidence in the measurement technique (for most presently used measures, however, there is no reason at all to have confidence in them). As Cronbach and Meehl (1955) put it, 'personality tests, and some tests of ability, are interpreted in terms of attributes for which there is no criterion' (p. 299). In such cases, it is principally through statistical and empirical methods of assessing the internal consistency of such devices that their construct validity is to be judged. They give the example of the measurement of temperature. One criterion we might impose on any measuring device is that it would show higher temperature for water when it is boiling than when it is frozen solid, or when it feels hot to the touch rather than cold to the touch – but the criterion can be proved to be more crude than the degrees of temperature a variety of thermometers are capable of displaying. Moreover, the subjective judgement of temperature is more subject to error than are measurements derived directly from the measuring techniques.

The trouble with attitudes is that they are so out of reach, and at the same time they are apparently subject to a kind of fluidity that allows them to change (or perhaps be created on the spot) in response to different social situations. Typically, it is the effects of attitudes that we are interested in rather than the attitudes *per se*, or alternatively, it is the social situations that give rise to both the attitudes and their effects which are the objects of interest. Recently, there has been a surge of interest in the topic of how attitudes affect language use and language behavior. We turn now to that topic and return below to the kinds of measures of attitudes that have been widely used in the testing of certain research hypotheses related to it.

B. Hypothesized relationships between affective variables and the use and learning of language

At first look, the relationship of attitudes to the use and learning of language may appear to be a small part of the problem of attitudes in general – what about attitude toward self, significant others, situations, groups, etc.? But a little reflection will show that a *very* wide range of variables are compassed by the topic of this subsection. Moreover, they are variables that have received much special attention in recent years. In addition to concern for attitudes and the way they influence a child's learning and use of his own native language (or possibly his native languages in the event that he grows up with more than one at his command), there has been much concern for the possible effects that attitudes may have on the learning of a second or third language and the way such attitudes affect the choice of a particular linguistic code (language or style) in a particular context. Some of the concern is generated by actual research results – for instance, results showing a significant relationship between certain attitude measures or motivation indices and attainment in a second language. Probably most of it, however, is generated by certain appealing arguments that often accompany meager or even contradictory research findings – or no findings at all.

A widely cited and popular position is that of Guiora and his collaborators (see Guiora, Paluszny, Beit-Hallahmi, Catford, Cooley, and Dull, 1975). The argument is an elaborate one and has many interesting ramifications and implications, but it can be capsulized by a few selected quotations from the cited article. Crucial to the argument are the notions of *empathy* (being able to put yourself in someone else's shoes – apropos to Shakespeare's claim that 'a friend is another self'), and *language ego* (that aspect of self awareness related to the fact that 'I' sound a certain way when 'I' speak and that this is part of 'my' identity):

> We hypothesized that this ability to shed our native pro-
> nunciation habits and temporarily adopt a different pro-
> nunciation is closely related to empathic capacity (p. 49).

One wonders whether having an empathic spirit is a necessary criterion for acquiring a native-like pronunciation in another language? A sufficient one? But the hypothesis has a certain appeal as we read more.

> With pronunciation viewed as the core of language ego, and as
> the most critical contribution of language ego to self-
> representation, we see that the early flexibility of ego
> boundaries is reflected in the ease of assimilating native-like
> pronunciation by young children; the later reduced flexibility is
> reflected in the reduction of this ability in adults (p. 46).

Apart from some superfluity and circularity (or perhaps because of it) so far so good. They continue,

> At this point we can link empathy and pronunciation of a
> second language. As conceived here, both require a temporary
> relaxation of ego boundaries and thus a temporary modifi-
> cation of self-representation. Although psychology tradi-
> tionally regards language performance as a cognitive-
> intellectual skill, we are concerned here with that particular
> aspect of language behavior that is most critically tied to self-
> representation (p. 46).

But the most persuasive part of the argument comes two pages later:

> ... superimposed upon the speech sounds of the words one
> chooses to utter are sounds which give the listener information

about the speaker's identity. The listener can decide whether
one is sincere or insincere. Ridicule the way I sound, my dialect,
or my attempts at pronouncing French and you will have
ridiculed me.

(One might, however, be regarded as oversensitive if one spoke very
bad French, mightn't one?)

Ask me to change the way I sound and you ask me to change
myself. To speak a second language authentically is to take on a
new identity. As with empathy, it is to step into a new and
perhaps unfamiliar pair of shoes (p. 48).

What about the empirical studies designed to test the relationship
between degree of empathy and acquisition of unfamiliar phonological systems? What does the evidence show? The empirical data is
reviewed by Schumann (1975), who, though he is clearly sympathetic
with the general thesis, finds the empirical evidences for it excessively
weak. The first problem is in the method for measuring 'empathy' by
the Micro Momentary Expression test – a procedure that consists
of watching silent psychiatric interviews and pushing a button
everytime a change is noticed in the expression on the face of the
person being interviewed by the psychiatrist (presumably the film
does not focus on the psychiatrist, but Guiora, et al, are not clear on
this in their description of the so-called measure of empathy).
Reasonable questions might include, is this purported measure of
empathy correlated with other purported measures of the same
construct? Is the technique reliable? Are the results similar on
different occasions under similar circumstances? Can trained
'empathizers' do the task better than untrained persons? Is there any
meaningful discrimination on the MME between persons who are
judged on other grounds to be highly empathetic and persons who are
judged to be less so? Apparently, the test, as a measure of empathy
must appeal to 'nominal validity'.

A second problem with the empirical research on the Guiora, et al,
hypothesis is the measure of pronunciation accuracy, the Standard
Thai Procedure:

The STP consists of a master tape recording of 34 test items
(ranging in length from 1 to 4 syllables) separated by a 4 second
pause. The voicer is a female Thai native speaker. ... Total
testing time is $4\frac{1}{2}$ minutes. ... (p. 49).
    The scoring procedure is currently under revision. The basic
evaluation method involves rating tone, vowel and consonant
quality for selected phonetic units on a scale of 1 (poor), 2 (fair),

or 3 (native-like). Data tapes are rated independently by three native Thai speakers, trained in pronunciation evaluation. A distinct advantage of the STP is that it can be used with naive subjects. It bypasses the necessity of first teaching subjects a second language (p. 50).

A distinct advantage to test people who have not learned the language? Presumably the test ought to discriminate between more and less native-like pronouncers of a language that the subjects have already learned. Does it? No data are offered. Obviously, the STP would not be a very direct test of, say, the ability to pronounce Spanish utterances with a native-like accent – or would it? No data are given. Does the test discriminate between persons who are judged to speak 'seven languages in Russian' (said with a thick Russian accent) and persons who are judged by respective native speaker groups to speak two or more languages so as to pass themselves for a native speaker of each of the several languages? Reliability and validity studies of the test are conspicuously absent.

The third problem with the Guiora, et al, hypothesis is that the empirical results that have been reported are either only weakly interpretable as supporting their hypothesis, or they are not interpretable at all. (Indeed, it makes little sense to try to interpret the meaning of a correlation between two measures about which it cannot be said with any confidence what they are measures of.) Their prediction is that empathetic persons will do better on the STP than less empathetic persons.

Two empirical studies attempted to establish the connection between empathy and attained skill in pronunciation – both are discussed more fully by Schumann (1975) than by Guiora, et al, (1975). The first study with Japanese learners failed to show any relationship between attained pronunciation skill and the scores on the MME (the STP was not used). The second study, a more extensive one, found significant correlations between rated pronunciation in Spanish (for 109 subjects at the Defense Language Institute in a three month intensive language course), Russian (for 201 subjects at DLI), Japanese (13 subjects at DLI), Thai (40 subjects), and Mandarin (38).

There was a difficulty however. The correlations were positive for the first three languages and negative for the last two. This would seem to indicate that if the MME measures empathy, for some groups it is positively associated with the acquisition of pronunciation skills in another language, and for other groups, it is negatively associated with the same process. What can be concluded from such data? Very little of any substance – except that the validity of the measures, and the hypothesis is in serious doubt.

In spite of all of the foregoing weaknesses in the empirical methods of Guiora, *et al*, their reasoning seems to have merit independently. Perhaps this is because the arguments they propose for relating language use and learning to affective variables find some kind of historical appeal inasmuch as they may relate to the feelings that people experience and report about the process of learning a language and the sense of personal identity that goes with the process. Schumann (1975) relates the argument to a variety of other viewpoints on how affective variables play a part in the acquisition of a second language. Earlier, Brown (1973) was apparently sympathetic to the position advocated by Guiora *et al*. He suggested that, 'the very definition of communication implies a process of revealing one's self to another' (pp. 233–4), hence the 'ego' is very much involved in any process of language use and language learning by any definition.

Brown suggests serious investigation of such ego related factors as the role of imitative behaviors (related to model figures, admired persons), self-knowledge, self-esteem, and self-confidence. He reports that an unpublished study in 1973 (Lederer, see Brown's references p. 244) 'revealed that the self-concept of Detroit high school students was an overwhelming indicator of success in a foreign language' (p. 234). He also recommends investigation of variables such as empathy, introversion/extroversion, and aggression. (See Suggested Readings at the end of this chapter.)

Another very substantial tradition of research revolves around the work of Lambert and Gardner and their co-workers. That research paradigm hinges on the distinction between two major motives for learning the language of another group, integrative versus instrumental, and several satellite concepts. It is generally argued that if a learner wants to be like valued members of the target language community, he is more apt to be a successful learner of that target language. A learner who can be shown to have such an orientation can be assumed to have an *integrative* motive, whereas a learner who wants to acquire the language for utilitarian reasons is said to have an *instrumental* motive. In the early research on the topic one gets the impression that integratively oriented learners were expected to outperform instrumentally motivated learners (other things being equal), but in later studies the sharpness of this distinction faded somewhat.

For instance, in their first study Gardner and Lambert (1959) concluded that 'the integratively oriented students are generally more successful in acquiring French than those who are instrumentally oriented' (p. 196). Later, Anisfeld and Lambert (1961) weakened their original hypothesis substantially: 'our results may suggest that the reasons for studying a language, whether instrumental or integrative, are not important in themselves' (p. 224) whereas what is important is 'attitudes toward the language community' (p. 225). However, in yet another study, Lambert, Gardner, Barik, and Tunstall (1962) weaken the position still further:

> Our previous studies indicated that favorable attitudes and orientations toward the other language contributed to a strong motivation to learn the other group's language and consequently correlated with achievement measures. In the present case, even the instrumentally oriented advanced students have strong motivations to learn the language, thereby reducing the relation of Orientation Index [which gives a 1 for an instrumental motive and a 2 for an integrative motive] scores to achievement (p. 241).

In a more recent study by Lukmani (1972), an instrumental motive seemed to be more strongly related to attainment in English as a second language in India than an integrative motive. Hence, all three possibilities concerning the original hypothesis have been obtained: in some cases, the integrative motive has been stronger (as was originally predicted, and as Gardner and Lambert, 1972, p. 16 still maintained), in others there has been no advantage of one over the other, and in still others, the instrumental motive appears to be the stronger.

What is to become of such a position? Should it not be rejected or substantially modified? It would seem that the empirical data only serve to confuse the issue – at least the data do not clearly support the 'working hypothesis' and the hypothesis keeps on working without ever drawing unemployment benefit (see Johnson and Krug, in press).

The same sort of difficulties arise with respect to the satellite concepts of *anomie* (the sense of being cut loose from one's roots that may arise in the course of becoming a member of a different language and culture group), and *ethnocentrism* (like egocentrism, except that one's group rather than one's self is the center of attention). Early in Lambert's writing, the hypothesis that anomie was correlated with the learning of a second language – that is, the more anomic one felt about one's own culture and language, the more rapidly one might want to acquire another (see Lambert, 1955, and Gardner and Lambert, 1959). A similar claim was offered for ethnocentrism although it was expected to be negatively correlated with attainment in the target language. Neither of these hypotheses (if they can be termed hypotheses) has proved to be any more susceptible to empirical test than the one about types of motivation. The arguments in each case have a lot of appeal, but the hypotheses themselves do not seem to be borne out by the data – the results are either unclear or contradictory. We will return to consider some of the specific measuring instruments used by Gardner and Lambert in section C.

Yet another research tradition in attitude measurement is that of Joshua Fishman and his co-workers. Perhaps his most important argument is that there must be a thoroughgoing investigation of the factors that determine who speaks what language (or variety) to whom and under what conditions.

In a recent article, Cooper and Fishman (1975), twelve issues of interest to researchers in the area of 'language attitude' are discussed. The authors define language attitudes either narrowly as related to how people think people ought to talk (following Ferguson, 1972) or broadly as 'those attitudes which influence language behavior and behavior toward language' (pp. 188–9). The first definition they consider to be too narrow and the second 'too broad' (p. 189).

Among the twelve questions are: (1) Does attitude have a characteristic structure? ... ; (2) To what extent can language attitudes be componentialized? ... ; (3) Do people have characteristic beliefs about their language? (e.g., that it is well suited for logic, or poetry, or some special use); (4) Are language attitudes really attitudes toward people who speak the language in question, or toward the language itself? Or some of each? (5) What is the effect of context on expressed stereotypes? Is one language considered inappropriate in some social settings but appropriate in others? (6) Where do language attitudes come from? Stereotypes that are irrational? Actual experiences? (7) What effects do they have? ('Typically, only modest relationships are found between attitude measures and the overt behaviors which such scores are designed to predict' p. 191); (8) Is one language apt to be more effective than another for persuading bilinguals under different circumstances? (9) 'What relationships exist among attitude scores obtained from different classes of attitudinal measurements (physiological or psychological reaction, situational behavior, verbal report)?' (p. 191); (10) How about breaking down the measures into ones that assess reactions 'toward an object, toward a situation, and toward the object in that situation' (p. 191)? What would the component structure be like then? (11) 'Do indirect measures of attitude (i.e., measures whose purpose is not apparent to the respondent) have higher validities than direct measures'? ... (p. 192); (12) 'How reliable are indirect measures ... ?' (p. 192).

It would seem that attitude studies generally share certain strengths and weaknesses. Among the strengths is the intuitive appeal of the argument that people's feelings about themselves (including the way they talk) and about others (and the way they talk) ought to be related to their use and learning of any language(s). Among the weaknesses is the general lack of empirical vulnerability of most of the theoretical claims that are made. They stand or fall on the merits of their intuitive appeal and quite independently of any experimental data that may be accumulated. They are subject to wide differences of interpretation, and there is a general (nearly complete) lack of evidence on the validity of purported measures of attitudinal constructs. What data are available are often contradictory or uninterpretable – yet the favored hypothesis still survives. In brief, most attitude studies are not empirical studies at all. They are mere attempts to support favored 'working' hypotheses – the hypotheses will go right on working even if they turn out to predict the wrong (or worse yet, all possible) experimental outcomes.

Part of the problem with measures of attitudes is that they require subjects to be honest in the 'throat-cutting' way – to give information about themselves which is potentially damaging (consider Upshur's biting criticism of such a procedure, cited above on p. 98). Furthermore, they require subjects to answer questions or react to statements that sometimes place them in the double-bind of being damned any way they turn – the condemnation which intelligent people can easily anticipate may be light or heavy, but why should subjects be expected to give meaningful (indeed, non-pathological) responses to such items? We consider some of the measurement techniques that are of the double-bind type in the next section. As Watzlawick, Beavin, and Jackson (1967) reason, such double-bind situations are apt to generate pathological responses ('crazy' and irrational behaviors) in people who by all possible non-clinical standards are 'normal'.

And there is a further problem which even if the others could be resolved remains to be dealt with – it promises to be knottier than all of the rest. Whose value system shall be selected as the proper criterion for the valuation of scales or the interpretation of responses? By whose standards will the questions be interpreted? This is the essential validity problem of attitude inventories, personality measures, and affective valuations of all sorts. It knocks at the very doors of the unsolved riddles of human existence. Is there meaning in life? By whose vision shall it be declared? Is there an absolute truth? Is there a God? Will I be called to give an accounting for what I do? Is life on this side of the grave all there is? What shall I do with this man Jesus? What shall I do with the moral precepts of my own culture? Yours? Someone else's? Are all solutions to the riddles of equivalent value? Is none of any value? Who shall we have as our arbiter? Skinner? Hitler? Kissinger?

Shaw and Wright (1967) suggest that 'the only inferential step' in the usual techniques for the measurement of attitudes 'is the assumption that the evaluations of the persons involved in scale construction correspond to those of the individuals whose attitudes are being measured' (p. 13). One does not have to be a logician to know that the inferential step Shaw and Wright are describing is clearly not the only one involved in the 'measurement of attitudes'. In fact, if that were the only step involved it would be entirely pointless to waste time trying to devise measurement instruments – just ask the test constructors to divulge their own attitudes at the outset. Why bother with the step of inference?

There are other steps that involve inferential leaps of substantial magnitude, but the one they describe as the 'only' one is no doubt the crucial one. There is a pretense here that the value judgements concerning what is a prejudice or what is not a prejudice, or what is anxiety or what is not anxiety, what is aggressiveness or acquiescence, what is strength and what is weakness, etc. *ad infinitum*, can be acceptably and impartially determined by some group consensus. What group will the almighty academic community pick? Or will the choice of a value system for affective measurement in the schools be made by political leaders? By Marxists? Christians? Jews? Blacks? Whites? Chicanos? Navajos? Theists? Atheists? Upper class? Middle class? Humanists? Bigots? Existentialists? Anthropologists? Sexists? Racists? Militarists? Intellectuals?

The trouble is the same one that Plato discussed in his *Republic* – it is not a question of how to interpret a single statement on a questionnaire (though this is a question of importance for each such statement), it is a question of how to decide cases of disagreement. Voting is one proposal, but if the minority (or a great plurality of minorities, down to the level of individuals) get voted down, shall their values be repressed in the institutionalization of attitude measures?

C. Direct and indirect measures of affect

So many different kinds of techniques have been developed for the purpose of trying to get people to reveal their beliefs and feelings that it would be impossible to be sure that all of the types had been covered in a single review. Therefore, the intent of this section is to discuss the most widely used types of attitude scales and other measurement techniques and to try to draw some conclusions concerning their empirical validities – particularly the measures that have been used in conjunction with language proficiency and the sorts of hypotheses considered in section B above.

Traditionally, a distinction is made between 'direct' and 'indirect' attitude measures. Actually we have already seen that there is no direct way of measuring attitudes, nor can there ever be. This is not so much a problem with measuring techniques *per se* as it is a problem of the nature of attitudes themselves. There can be no direct measure of a construct that is evidenced only indirectly, and subjectively even then.

As qualities of human experience, emotions, attitudes, and values are notoriously ambiguous in their very expression. Joy or sadness may be evident by tears. A betrayal or an unfeigned love may be demonstrated with a kiss. Disgust or rejoicing may be revealed by laughter. Approval or disapproval by a smile. Physiological measures might offer a way out, but they would have to be checked against subjective judgements. An increase in heart rate might be caused by fear, anger, surprise, etc. But even if a particular constellation of glandular secretions, palmar sweating, galvanic skin response, and other physiological responses were thought to indicate some emotional state, presumably the test would have to be validated against subjective judgement by asking the patient displaying the pertinent constellation of factors, 'Do you feel angry now?' As D. M. MacKay (1951) noted in his insightful article 'Mindlike Behavior in Artefacts,' we could know all about the inner workings of a neon sign without knowing the meaning of the words that it displays. The problem of attitudes is like that; it is distinctly a matter of interpretation.

What measures of attitudinal variables have been used or

recommended in studies of language use and language learning? We have mentioned a few above; we will look more closely at a number of them below. They include the notoriously unreliable 'projective' techniques such as the *Thematic Apperception Test* (see Anastasi, 1976, pp. 565–7, and 579–85) which is a Rorschach-like test consisting of 19 deliberately vague pictures concerning which subjects are asked to tell stories. They also use the ranking of statements concerning how well they describe the respondent. More often attitude scales are of the more traditional agree-disagree type originated by Likert (1932). Recently, a variant on the Likert scale technique has been developed by Zirkel and Jackson (1974) for use with children from four different ethnic backgrounds. It employs line drawings of faces supposedly ranging from very happy to very sad.

First, we will consider three of the attitude scales of the Likert-type used by Gardner and Lambert (1972) – the F Scale, the E Scale, and the Anomie Scale. The instructions used for each scale were similar:

> The following statements are opinions which have often been expressed by students about your age. They cover a wide range of topics and it has been found that many people agree with each statement and many disagree. There are no right or wrong answers. You are asked to mark each statement in the left-hand margin according to your agreement or disagreement as follows:

> +1: slight support, agreement   −1: slight opposition, disagreement
>
> +2: moderate support, agreement   −2: moderate opposition, disagreement
>
> +3: strong support, agreement   −3: strong opposition, disagreement

MODIFIED F SCALE

1. Obedience and respect for authority are the most important virtues children should learn.
2. What youth needs most is strict discipline, rugged determination, and the will to work and fight for family and country.
3. Nowadays when so many different kinds of people move around and mix together so much, a person has to protect himself especially carefully against catching an infection or disease from them.
4. What this country needs most, more than laws and political programs, is a few courageous, tireless, devoted leaders in whom the people can put their faith.

5. No weakness or difficulty can hold us back if we have enough will power.
6. Human nature being what it is, there will always be war and conflict.
7. A person who has bad manners, habits, and breeding can hardly expect to get along with decent people.
8. People can be divided into two distinct classes: the weak and the strong.
9. There is hardly anything lower than a person who does not feel a great love, gratitude, and respect for his parents.
10. The true American way of life is disappearing so fast that force may be necessary to preserve it.
11. Nowadays more and more people are prying into matters that should remain personal and private.
12. If people would talk less and work more, everybody would be better off.
13. Most people don't realize how much our lives are controlled by plots hatched in secret places.

According to Gardner and Lambert (1972, p. 150), all of the foregoing statements 'reflect antidemocratic ideology'. In fact, the original authors of the scale developed items from research on 'the potentially fascistic individual' (Adorno, et al, 1950, p. 1) which 'began with anti-Semitism in the focus of attention' (p. 2). Sources for the items were subject protocols from 'factual short essay questions pertaining to such topics as religion, war, ideal society, and so forth; early results from projective questions; finally, and by far the most important, material from the interviews and the *Thematic Apperception Tests*' (p. 225). The thirteen scales given above were selected from Forms 45 and 40 of the Adorno, et al (1950) F Scale consisting of some 46 items according to Gardner and Lambert (1972). Actually, item 10 given above was from Form 60 (an earlier version of the F Scale).

There are two major sources of validity on the Fascism Scale (that is, the F Scale) that are easily accessible. First, there are the intercorrelations between the early versions of the F Scale with measures that were supposed (by the original authors of the F Scale) to be similar in content, and second, there are the same data in the several correlation tables offered by Gardner and Lambert which can be examined. According to Adorno, et al (1950, pp. 222–24) the original purpose in developing the F Scale was to try to obtain a less obvious measure of 'antidemocratic *potential*' (p. 223, their italics) than was available in the E Scale (or Ethnocentrism Scale) which they had already developed.

Immediately following is the Gardner and Lambert adaptation of a selected set of the questions on the E Scale which was used in much of their attitude research related to language use and language learning. Below, we return to the question of the validity of the F Scale in relation to the E Scale:

MODIFIED E SCALE

1. The worst danger to real Americanism during the last fifty years has come from foreign ideas and agitators.
2. Now that a new world organization is set up, America must be sure that she loses none of her independence and complete power as a sovereign nation.
3. Certain people who refuse to salute the flag should be forced to conform to such a patriotic action, or else be imprisoned.
4. Foreigners are all right in their place, but they carry it too far when they get too familiar with us.
5. America may not be perfect, but the American way has brought us about as close as human beings can get to a perfect society.
6. It is only natural and right for each person to think that his family is better than any other.
7. The best guarantee for our national security is for America to keep the secret of the nuclear bomb.

These items were selected by Gardner and Lambert from 20 original items recommended for the final form of the Adorno, et al E Scale. The original authors reason, 'the social world as most ethnocentrists see it is arranged like a series of concentric circles around a bull's-eye. Each circle represents an ingroup-outgroup distinction; each line serves as a barrier to exclude all outside groups from the center, and each group is in turn excluded by a slightly narrower one. A sample "map" illustrating the ever-narrowing ingroup would be the following: Whites, Americans, native-born Americans, Christians, Protestants, Californians, my family, and finally – I' (p. 148). Thus, the items on the E Scale are expected to reveal the degree to which the respondent is unable 'to identify with humanity' (p. 148).

How well does the E Scale, and its more indirect counterpart the F Scale, accomplish its purpose? One way of testing the adequacy of both scales is to check their intercorrelation. This was done by Adorno, *et al*, and they found correlations ranging from a low of .59 to a high of .87 (1950, p. 262). They concluded that if the tests were lengthened, or corrected for the expected error of measurement in any such test, they should intercorrelate at the .90 level (see their footnote, p. 264). From these data the conclusion can be drawn that if either scale is tapping an 'authoritarian' outlook, both must be. However, the picture changes radically when we examine the data from Gardner and Lambert (1972).

In studies with their modified (in fact, shortened) versions of the F and E Scales, the correlations were .33 (for 96 English speaking high school students in Louisiana), .39 (for 145 English speaking high school students in Maine), .33 (for 142 English speaking high school students in Connecticut), .33 (for 80 French-American high school students in Louisiana), and .46 (for 98 French-American high school students in Maine). In none of these studies does the overlap in variance on the two tests exceed 22 % and the pattern is quite different from the true relationship posited by Adorno, *et al* between F and E (the variance overlap should be nearly perfect).

What is the explanation? One idea that has been offered previously (Liebert and Spiegler, 1974, and their references) and which seems to fit the data from Gardner and Lambert relates to a subject's tendency merely to supply what are presumed to be the most socially acceptable responses. If the subject were able to guess that the experimenter does in fact consider some responses more appropriate than others, this would create some pressure on sensitive subjects to give the socially acceptable responses. Such pressure would tend to result in positive correlations across the scales.

Another possibility is that subjects merely seek to appear consistent from one answer to the next. The fact that one has agreed or disagreed with a certain item on either the E or F Scale may set up a strong tendency to respond as one has responded on previous items – a so-called 'response set'. If the response set factor were accounting for a large portion of the variance in measures like E and F, then this would also account for the high correlations observed between them.

In either event, shortening the tests as Gardner and Lambert did would tend to reduce the amount of variance overlap between them because it would necessarily reduce the tendency of the scales to establish a response set, or it would reduce the saliency of socially desirable responses. All of this could happen even if neither test had anything to do with the personality traits they are trying to measure.

Along this line, Crowne and Marlowe (1964) report:

> Acquiescence has been established as a major response determinant in the measurement of such personality variables as authoritarianism (Bass, 1955, Chapman and Campbell, 1957, Jackson and Messick, 1958). The basic method has been

to show, first of all, that a given questionnaire – say the California F Scale (Adorno, et al, 1950) – has a large proportion of items keyed *agree* (or *true* or *yes*). Second, half the items are reversed, now being scored for disagreement. Correlations are then computed between the original and the reversed items. Failure to find high negative correlations is, then, an indication of the operation of response acquiescence. In one study of the F Scale, in fact, significant *positive* correlations – strongly indicative of an acquiescent tendency – were found (Jackson, Messick, and Solley, 1957), (p. 7).

Actually, the failure to find high negative correlations is not necessarily indicative only of a response acquiescence tendency; there are a number of other possibilities, but all of them are fatal to the claims of validity for the scale in question.

Another problem with scales like E and F involves the tendency for respondents to differentiate factive and emotive aspects of statements with which they are asked to agree or disagree. One may agree with the factive content of a statement and disagree with the emotive tone (both of which in the case of written questionnaires are coded principally in choice of words). Consider, for instance, the factive content and emotive tone of the following statements (the first version is from the Anomie Scale which is discussed below):

A.   The big trouble with our country is that it relies, for the most part, on the law of the jungle: 'Get him before he gets you.'
B.   The most serious problem of our people is that too few of them practice the Golden Rule: 'Do unto others as you would have them do unto you.'
C.   The greatest evil of our country is that we exist, for the most part, by the law of survival: 'Speak softly and carry a big stick.'

Whereas the factive content of the preceding statements is similar in all cases, and though each might be considered a rough paraphrase of the others, they differ greatly in emotive tone. Concerning such differences (which they term 'content' and 'style' respectively), Crowne and Marlowe (1964) report:

Applying this differentiation to the assessment of personality characteristics or attitudes, Jackson and Messick (1958) contended that both stylistic properties of *test items* and habitual expressive or response styles of *individuals* may outweigh the importance of item content. The way an item is worded – its style of expression – may tend to increase its frequency of endorsement (p. 8).

Their observation is merely a special case of the hypothesis which we discussed in Chapter 4 (p. 82f) on the relative importance of factive and emotive aspects of communication.

Taking all of the foregoing into account, the validity of the E and F Scales is in grave doubt. The hypothesis that they are measures of the same basic configuration of personality traits (or at least of similar configurations associated with 'authoritarianism') is not the only hypothesis that will explain the available data – nor does it seem to be the most plausible of the available alternatives. Furthermore, if the validity of the E and F Scales is in doubt, their pattern of interrelationship with other variables – such as attained proficiency in a second language – is essentially uninterpretable.

A third scale used by Gardner and Lambert is the Anomie Scale adapted partly from Srole (1951, 1956):

ANOMIE SCALE

1. In the U.S. today, public officials aren't really very interested in the problems of the average man.
2. Our country is by far the best country in which to live. (The scale is reversed on this item and on number 8.)
3. The state of the world being what it is, it is very difficult for the student to plan for his career.
4. In spite of what some people say, the lot of the average man is getting worse, not better.
5. These days a person doesn't really know whom he can count on.
6. It is hardly fair to bring children into the world with the way things look for the future.
7. No matter how hard I try, I seem to get a 'raw deal' in school.
8. The opportunities offered young people in the United States are far greater than in any other country.
9. Having lived this long in this culture, I'd be happier moving to some other country now.
10. In this country, it's whom you know, not what you know, that makes for success.
11. The big trouble with our country is that it relies, for the most part, on the law of the jungle: 'Get him before he gets you.'
12. Sometimes I can't see much sense in putting so much time into education and learning.

This test is intended to measure 'personal dissatisfaction or discouragement with one's place in society' (Gardner and Lambert, 1972, p. 21).

Oddly perhaps, Gardner and Lambert (1972, and their other works reprinted there) have consistently predicted that higher scores on the preceding scale should correspond to higher performance in learning a second language – i.e., that degree of anomie and attainment of proficiency in a second language should be positively correlated – however, they have predicted that the correlations for the E and F Scales with attainment in a second language should be negative. The difficulty is that other authors have argued that scores on the Anomie Scale and the E and F Scales should be positively intercorrelated with each other – that, in fact, 'anomia is a factor related to the formation of negative rejective attitudes toward minority groups' (Srole, 1956, p. 712).

Srole cites a correlation of .43 between a scale designed to measure prejudice toward minorities and his 'Anomia Scale' (both 'anomie' and 'anomia' are used in designating the scale in the literature) as evidence that 'lostness is *one* of the basic conditions out of which some types of political authoritarianism emerge' (p. 714, footnote 20). Yet other authors have predicted no relationship at all between Anomie scores and F scores (Christie and Geis, 1970, p. 360).

Again, we seem to be wrestling with hypotheses that are flavored more by the preferences of a particular research technique than they are by substantial research data. Even 'nominal' validity cannot be invoked when the researchers fail to agree on the meaning of the name associated with a particular questionnaire. Gardner and Lambert (1972) report generally positive correlations between Anomie scores and E and F scores. This, rather than contributing to a sense of confidence in the Anomie Scale, merely makes it, too, suspect of a possible response set factor – or a tendency to give socially acceptable responses, or possibly to give consistent responses to similarly scaled items (negatively toned or positively toned). In brief, there is little or no evidence to show that the scale in fact measures what it purports to measure.

Christie and Geis (1970) suggest that the F Scale was possibly the most studied measure of attitudes for the preceding twenty year period (p. 38). One wonders how such a measure survives in the face of data which indicate that it has no substantial claims to validity. Further, one wonders why, if such a studied test has produced such a conglomeration of contradictory findings, any one should expect to be able to whip together an attitude measure (with much less study) that will do any better. The problems are not merely technical ones associated with test reliability and validity, they are also moral ones having to do with the uses to which such tests are intended to be put.

The difficulties are considered severe enough for Shaw and Wright (1967) to put the following statement in a conspicuous location at the end of the Preface to their book on *Scales for the Measurement of Attitudes*:

> The attitude scales in this book are recommended for research purposes and for group testing. We believe that the available information and supporting research does not warrant the application of many of these scales as measures of individual attitude for the purpose of diagnosis or personnel selection or for any other individual assessment process (p. xi).

In spite of such disclaimers, application of such measurement techniques to the diagnosis of individual performances – e.g., prognosticating the likelihood of individual success or failure in a course of study with a view to selecting students who are more likely to succeed in 'an overcrowded program' (Brodkey and Shore, 1976) – is sometimes suggested:

> A problem which has arisen at the University of New Mexico is one of predicting the language-learning behavior of students in an overcrowded program which may in the near future become highly selective. This paper is a progress report on the design of an instrument to predict good and poor language learning behavior on the basis of personality. Subjects are students in the English Tutorial Program, which provides small sized classes for foreign, Anglo-American, and minority students with poor college English skills. Students demonstrate a great range of linguistic styles, including English as a second language, English as a second dialect, and idiosyncratic problems, but all can be characterized as lacking skill in the literate English of college usage – a difficult 'target' language (p. 153).

In brief, Brodkey and Shore set out to predict teacher ratings of students (on 15 positively scaled statements with which the teacher must agree or disagree) on the basis of the student's own preferential ordering of 40 statements about himself – some of the latter are listed below. The problem was to predict which students were likely to succeed. Presumably, students judged likely to succeed would be given preference at time of admission.

Actually, the student was asked to sort the 40 statements twice – first, in response to how he would like to be and second, how he was at the time of performing the task. A third score was derived by computing the difference between the first two scores. (There is no way to determine on the basis of information given by Brodkey and

Shore how the items were scaled – that is, it cannot be determined whether agreeing with a particular statement contributed positively or negatively to the student's score.)

THE Q-SORT STATEMENTS
(from Appendix B of Brodkey and Shore, 1976, pp. 161–2)

1. My teacher can probably see that I am an interesting person from reading my essays.
2. My teachers usually enjoy reading my essays.
3. My essays often make me feel good.
4. My next essay will be written mainly to please myself.
5. My essays often leave me feeling confused about my own ideas.
6. My writing will always be poor.
7. No matter how hard I try, my grades don't really improve much.
8. I usually receive fair grades on my assignments.
. . . .
10. My next essay will be written mainly to please my teacher.
11. I dislike doing the same thing over and over again.
. . . .
18. I often get my facts confused.
19. When I feel like doing something I go and do it now.
. . . .
22. I have trouble remembering names and faces.
. . . .
28. I am more interested in the details of a job than just getting it done.
29. I sometimes have trouble communicating with others.
30. I sometimes make decisions too quickly.
31. I like to get one project finished before starting another.
32. I do my best work when I plan ahead and follow the plan.
. . . .
34. I try to get unpleasant tasks out of the way before I begin working on more pleasant tasks.
. . . .
36. I always try to do my best, even if it hurts other people's feelings.
37. I sometimes hurt other people's feelings without knowing it.
38. I often let other people's feelings influence my decisions.
39. I am not very good at adapting to changes.
40. I am usually very aware of other people's feelings.

On the basis of what possible theory of personality can the foregoing statements be associated with a definition of the successful student? Suppose that some theory is proposed which offers an unambiguous basis for scaling the items as positive or negative. What is the relationship of an item like 37 to such a theory? On the basis of careful thought one might conclude that statement 37 is not a valid description of any possible person since if such a person hurt other people's feelings without knowing it, how would he know it? In such a case the score might be either positively or negatively related to logical reasoning ability – depending on whether the item is positively or negatively scaled. Note also the tendency throughout to place the student in the position of potential double-binds. Consider item 28 about the details of a job versus getting it done. Agreeing or disagreeing may be true and false at the same time.

Further, consider the fact that if the items related to the teacher's attitudes are scaled appropriately (that is in accord with the teacher's attitudes about what a successful learner is), the test may be a measure of the subject's ability to perceive the teacher's attitudes – i.e., to predict the teacher's evaluation of the subject himself. This would introduce a high degree of correlation between the personality measure (the Q-Sort) and the teacher's judgements (the criterion of whether or not the Q-Sort is a valid measure of the successful student) – but the correlation would be an artefact (an artificially contrived result) of the experimental procedure. Or consider yet another possibility. Suppose the teacher's judgements are actually related to how well the student understands English – is it not possible that the Q-Sort task might in fact discriminate among more and less proficient users of the language? These possibilities might combine to produce an apparent correlation between the 'personality' measure and the definition of 'success'.

No statistical correlation (in the sense of Chapter 3 above) is reported by Brodkey and Shore (1976). They do, however, report a table of correspondences between grades assigned in the course of study (which themselves are related to the subjective evaluations of teachers stressing 'reward for effort, rather than achievement alone', p. 154). Then they proceed to an individual analysis of exceptional cases: the Q-Sort task is judged as not being reliable for '5 Orientals, 1 reservation Indian, and 3 students previously noted as having serious emotional problems' (p. 157). The authors suggest, 'a general conclusion might be that the Q-sort is not reliable for Oriental students, who may have low scores but high grades, and is slightly less reliable for women than men.... [for] students 30 or older, ... Q-sort scores seemed independent of grades ...' (p. 157). No explanations are offered for these apparently deviant cases, but the authors conclude nonetheless that 'the Q-sort is on the way to providing us with a useful predictive tool for screening Tutorial Program applicants' (p. 158).

In another study, reported in an earlier issue of the same journal, Chastain (1975) correlated scores on several personality measures with grades in French, German, and Spanish for students numbering 80, 72, and 77 respectively. In addition to the personality measures (which included scales purporting to assess anxiety, outgoingness, and creativity), predictor variables included the verbal and quantitative sub-scores on the Scholastic Aptitude Test, high school rank, and prior language experience. Chastain observes, 'surprising as it may seem, the direction of correlation was not consistent [for test anxiety]' (p. 160). In one case it was negative (for 15 subjects enrolled in an audio-lingual French course, $-.48$), and in two others it was positive (for the 77 Spanish students, .37; and for the 72 German students, .21). Chastain suggests that 'perhaps some concern about a test is a plus while too much anxiety can produce negative results' (p. 160). Is his measure valid? Chastain's measure of Test Anxiety came from Sarason (1958, 1961). An example item given by Sarason (1958) is 'While taking an important examination, I perspire a great deal' (p. 340). In his 1961 study, Sarason reports correlations with 13 measures of 'intellectual ability' and the Test Anxiety scale along with five other measures of personality (all of them subscales on the *Autobiographical Survey*). For two separate studies with 326 males and 412 females (all freshman or sophomore students at the University of Washington, Seattle), no correlations above .30 were reported. In fact, Test Anxiety produced the strongest correlations with high school grade averages (divided into six categories) and with scores on Cooperative English subtests. The highest correlation was $-.30$ between Test Anxiety and the ACE Q (1948, presumably a widely used test since the author gives only the abbreviation in the text of the article). These are hardly encouraging validity statistics.

A serious problem is that correlations of above .4 between the various subscores on the *Autobiographical Survey* may possibly be explained in terms of response set. There is no reason for concluding that Test Anxiety (as measured by the scale by the same name) is a substantial factor in variance obtained in the various 'intellectual' variables. Since in no case did Chastain's other personality variables account for as much as 10 % of the variance in grades, they are not discussed here. We only note in passing that he is probably correct in saying that 'course grade may not be synonymous with achievement' (p. 159) – in fact it may be sensitive to affective variables precisely because it may involve some affectively based judgement (see especially the basis for course grades recommended by Brodkey and Shore, 1976, p. 154).

We come now to the empathy measure used by Guiora, Paluszny, Beit-Hallahmi, Catford, Cooley, and Dull (1975) and by Guiora and others. In studying the article by Haggard and Isaacs (1966), where the original MME (Micro-Momentary Expression) test had its beginnings, it is interesting to note that for highly skilled judges the technique adapted by Guiora, *et al*, had average reliabilities of only .50 and .55. The original authors (Haggard and Isaacs) suggest that 'it would be useful to determine the extent to which observers differ in their ability to perceive accurately rapid changes of facial expressions and the major correlates of this ability' (p. 164). Apparently, Guiora and associates simply adapted the test to their own purpose with little change in its form and without attempting (or at least without reporting attempts) to determine whether or not it constituted a measure of empathy.

From their own description of the MME, several problems become immediately apparent. The subject is instructed to push a button, which is attached to a recording device, whenever he sees a change in facial expression on the part of a person depicted on film. The first obvious trouble is that there is no apparent way to differentiate between hits and misses – that is, there is no way to tell for sure whether the subject pushed the button when an actual change was taking place or merely when the subject thought a change was taking place. In fact, it is apparently the case that the higher the number of button presses, the higher the judged empathy of the subject. Isn't it just as reasonable to assume that an inordinately high rate of button presses might correspond to a high rate of false alarms? In the data reported by Haggard and Isaacs, even highly skilled judges were not able to agree in many cases on when changes were occurring, much less on the meaning of the changes (the latter would seem to be the more important indicator of empathy). They observe, 'it is more difficult to obtain satisfactory agreement when the task is to identify and designate the impulse or affect which presumably underlies any particular expression or expression change' (p. 158). They expected to be able to tell more about the nature and meaning of changes when they slowed down the rate of the film. However, in that condition (a condition also used by Guiora and associates, see p. 51) the reliability was even lower on the average than it was in the normal speed condition (.50 versus .55, respectively).

Since it is axiomatic (though perhaps not exactly true for all empirical cases) that the validity of a test cannot exceed the square of its reliability, the validity estimates for the MME would have to be in the range of .25 to .30 – this would be only for the case when the test is a measure of someone's ability to notice changes in facial expressions, or better, as a measure of interjudge agreement on the task of noticing changes in facial expressions. The extrapolation from such judgements to 'empathy' as the construct to be measured by the MME is a wild leap indeed. No validity estimates are possible on the basis of available data for an inferential jump of the latter sort.

Another widely used measure of attitudes – one that is somewhat less direct than questions or statements concerning the attitudes of the subject toward the object or situation of interest – is the semantic differential technique which was introduced by Osgood, Suci, and Tannenbaum (1957) for a wider range of purposes. In fact, they were interested in the measurement of meaning in a broader sense. Their method, however, was adapted to attitude studies by Lambert and Gardner, and by Spolsky (1969a). Several follow up studies on the Spolsky research are discussed in Oller, Baca, and Vigil (1977).

Gardner and Lambert (1972) reported the use of seven point scales of the following type (subjects were asked to rate themselves, Americans, how they themselves would like to be, French-Americans, and their French teacher):

SEMANTIC DIFFERENTIAL SCALES, BIPOLAR VARIETY

1.	Interesting	__:__:__:__:__:__:__ Boring
2.	Prejudiced	__:__:__:__:__:__:__ Unprejudiced
3.	Brave	__:__:__:__:__:__:__ Cowardly
4.	Handsome	__:__:__:__:__:__:__ Ugly
5.	Colorful	__:__:__:__:__:__:__ Colorless
6.	Friendly	__:__:__:__:__:__:__ Unfriendly
7.	Honest	__:__:__:__:__:__:__ Dishonest
8.	Stupid	__:__:__:__:__:__:__ Smart
9.	Kind	__:__:__:__:__:__:__ Cruel
10.	Pleasant	__:__:__:__:__:__:__ Unpleasant
11.	Polite	__:__:__:__:__:__:__ Impolite
12.	Sincere	__:__:__:__:__:__:__ Insincere
13.	Successful	__:__:__:__:__:__:__ Unsuccessful
14.	Secure	__:__:__:__:__:__:__ Insecure
15.	Dependable	__:__:__:__:__:__:__ Undependable
16.	Permissive	__:__:__:__:__:__:__ Strict
17.	Leader	__:__:__:__:__:__:__ Follower
18.	Mature	__:__:__:__:__:__:__ Immature
19.	Stable	__:__:__:__:__:__:__ Unstable

20. Happy   __:__:__:__:__:__:__ Sad
21. Popular   __:__:__:__:__:__:__ Unpopular
22. Hardworking __:__:__:__:__:__:__ Lazy
23. Ambitious   __:__:__:__:__:__:__ Not Ambitious

Semantic differential scales of a unipolar variety were used by Gardner and Lambert (1972) and by Spolsky (1969a) and others (see Oller, Baca, and Vigil, 1977). In form they are very similar to the bipolar scales except that the points of the scales have to be marked with some value such as 'very characteristic' or 'not at all characteristic' or possibly 'very much like me' or 'not at all like me'. Seven point and five point scales have been used.

In an evaluation of attitudes toward the use of a particular language Lambert, Hodgson, Gardner, and Fillenbaum (1960) used a 'matched guise' technique. Fluent French–English bilinguals recorded material in both languages. The recordings from several speakers were then presented in random order and subjects were asked to rate the speakers. (Subjects were, of course, unaware that each speaker was heard twice, once in English and once in French.)

SEMANTIC DIFFERENTIAL SCALES, UNIPOLAR VARIETY
1. Height very little __:__:__:__:__:__:__ very much
. . . .

and so on for the attributes: good looks, leadership, thoughtfulness, sense of humor, intelligence, honesty, self-confidence, friendliness, dependability, generosity, entertainingness, nervousness, kindness, reliability, ambition, sociability, character, and general likability.

Spolsky (1969a) and others have used similar lists of terms presumably defining personal attributes: helpful, humble, stubborn, businesslike, shy, nervous, kind, friendly, dependable, and so forth. The latter scales in Spolsky's studies, and several modeled after his, were referenced against how subjects saw themselves to be, how they would like to be, and how they saw speakers of their native language, and speakers of a language they were in the process of acquiring.

How reliable and valid are the foregoing types of scales? Little information is available. Spolsky (1969a) reasoned that scales such as the foregoing should provide more reliable data than those which were based on responses to direct questions concerning a subject's agreement or disagreement with a statement rather bald-facedly presenting a particular attitude bias, or than straightforward questions about why subjects were studying the foreign language and the like. The semantic differential type scales were believed to be more indirect measures of subject attitudes and therefore more valid than more direct questions about attitudes. The former, it was reasoned, should be less susceptible to distortion by sensitive respondents.

Data concerning the tendency of scales to correlate in meaningful ways are about the only evidence concerning the validity of such scales. For instance, negatively valued scales such as 'stubborn' 'nervous' and 'shy' tend to cluster together (by correlation and factor analysis techniques) indicating at least that subjects are differentiating the semantic values of scales in meaningful ways. Similarly, scales concerning highly valued positive traits such as 'kind' 'friendly' 'dependable' and the like also tend to be more highly correlated with each other than with very dissimilar traits.

There is also evidence that views of persons of different national, ethnic, or linguistic backgrounds differ substantially in ways that are characteristic of known attitudes of certain groups. For instance, Oller, Baca, and Vigil (1977) report data showing that a group of Mexican American women in a Job Corps program in Albuquerque generally rate Mexicans substantially higher than they rate Americanos (Anglo-Americans) on the same traits. It is conceivable that such scales could be used to judge the strength of self-concept, attitude toward other groups, and similar constructs. However, much more research is needed before such measures are put forth as measures of particular constructs. Furthermore, they are subject to all of the usual objections concerning self-reported data.

Little research has been done with the measurement of attitudes in children (at least this is true in relation to the questions and research interests discussed in section B above). Recently, however, Zirkel and Jackson (1974) have offered scales intended for use with children of Anglo, Black, Native American, and Chicano heritages. These scales are of the Likert-type (agree versus disagree on a five point scale with one position for 'don't know'). The innovation in their technique involves the use of line drawings of happy versus sad faces as shown in Figure 4. Strickland (1970) may have been the first to use such a method with children. It is apparently a device for obtaining scaled responses to attitude objects (such as, food, dress, games, well known personalities who are models of a particular cultural group, and symbols believed important in the definition of a culture). The scales are used for non-readers and preliterate children. The Cultural Attitude Scales exist in four forms (one for each of the above designated ethnic groups).

The Technical Report indicates test-retest reliabilities ranging from

MEASURING ATTITUDES AND MOTIVATIONS   137

Figure 4. Example of a Likert-type attitude scale intended for children. (From Zirkel (1973), *Black American Cultural Attitude Scale.* The scale has five points with a possible 'don't know' answer as represented at the extreme left – scales are referenced against objects presumed important to defining cultural attitudes and of a sort that can be pictured easily.)

.52 to .61, and validity coefficients ranging from .15 to .46. These are not impressive if one considers that only about 4% to 25% of the variance in the scales is apt to be related to the attitudes they purport to measure.

No figures on reliability or validity are given in the *Test Manual.* The authors caution, 'the use of the *Cultural Attitude Scales* to diagnose the acculturation of individual children in the classroom is at this time very precarious' (p. 27). It seems to be implied that 'acculturation' is a widely accepted goal of educational programs, and this is questionable. Further, it seems to be suggested that the scales might someday be used to determine the level of acculturation of individual children – this implication seems unwarranted. There is not any reason to expect reliable measures of such matters ever to be forthcoming. Nonetheless, the caution is commendable.

The original studies with the *Social Distance Scale* (Bogardus, 1925, 1933), from which the *Cultural Attitude Scales* very indirectly derive, suggest that stereotypes of outgroups are among the most stable attitudes and that the original scale was sufficiently reliable and valid to use with some confidence (see Shaw and Wright, 1967). With increasing awareness of crosscultural sensitivities, it may be that measures of social distance would have to be recalibrated for today's societal norms (if indeed such norms exist and can be defined) but the original studies and several follow ups have indicated reliabilities in the range of .90 and 'satisfactory' validity according to Newcomb (1950, as cited by Shaw and Wright, 1967, p. 408). The original scales required the respondent to indicate whether he would marry into, have as close friends, as fellow workers, as speaking acquaintances, as visitors to his country, or would debar from visiting his country members of a specific minority or designated outgroup. The Bogardus definition of 'social distance', however, is considerably narrower than that proposed more recently by Schumann (1976). The latter is, at this point, a theoretical construct in the making and is therefore not reviewed here.

D. Observed relationships to achievement and remaining puzzles

The question addressed in this section is, how are affective variables related to educational attainment in general, and in particular to the acquisition of a second language? Put differently, what is the nature and the strength of observed relationships? Gardner (1975) and Gardner, Smythe, Clement, and Gliksman (1976) have argued that attitudes are somewhat indirectly related to attainment of proficiency in a second language. Attitudes, they reason, are merely one of the types of factors that give rise to motivations which are merely one of the types of factors which eventually result in attainment of proficiency in a second language. By this line of reasoning, attitudes are considered to be causally related to achievement of proficiency in a second language even though the relationship is not apt to be a very strong one.

In a review of some 33 surveys of 'six different grade levels (grades 7 to 12) from seven different regions across Canada' (p. 32) involving no less than about 2,000 subjects, the highest average correlation between no less than 12 different attitude scales with two measures of French achievement in no case exceeded .29 (Gardner, 1975). Thus, the largest amount of variance in language proficiency scores that was predicted on the average by the attitude measures was never greater than $8\frac{1}{2}\%$. This result is not inconsistent with the claim that the relationship between attitude measures and attainment in a second language is quite indirect.

However, such a result also leaves open a number of alternative explanations. It is possible that the weakness of the observed relationships is due to the unreliability or lack of validity of the attitude measures. If this explanation were correct, there might be a much stronger relationship between attitudes and attained proficiency than has or ever would become apparent using those attitude measures. Another possibility is that the measures of language proficiency used are themselves low in reliability or validity. Yet another possibility is that attitudes do not cause attainment of proficiency but rather are caused by the degree of proficiency attained – though weakly perhaps. And, many other possibilities exist.

Backman (1976) in a refreshingly different approach to the assessment of attitudes offers what she calls the 'chicken or egg' puzzle. Do attitudes in fact cause behaviors in some way, or are attitudes rather the result of behaviors? Savignon (1972) showed that in the foreign language classroom positive attitudes may well be a *result* of success rather than a *cause*.

It seems quite plausible that success in learning a second language might itself give rise to positive feelings toward the learning situation and everything (or everyone) associated with it. Similarly, failure might engender less positive feelings. Yet another plausible alternative is that attitudes and behaviors may be complexly interrelated such that both of them influence each other. Bloom (1976) prefers this latter alternative. Another possibility is that attitudes are associated with the planning of actions and the perception of events in some way that influences the availability of sensory data and thus the options that are perceivable or conceivable to the doer or learner.

The research of Manis and Dawes (1961) showing that cloze scores were higher for subjects who agreed with the content of a passage than for those who disagreed would seem to lend credence to this last suggestion. Manis and Dawes concluded that it wasn't just that subjects didn't want to give right answers to items on passages with which they disagreed, but that they were in fact less able to give right answers. Such an interpretation would also fit the data from a wide variety of studies revealing expectancy biases of many sorts. However, Doerr (in press) raises some experimental questions about the Manis and Dawes design.

Regardless of the solution to the (possibly unsolvable) puzzle about what causes what, it is still possible to investigate the strength of the relationship of attitudes as expressed in response to questionnaires and scores on proficiency measures of second language ability for learners in different contexts. It has been observed that the relationship is apparently stronger in contexts where learners can avail themselves of opportunities to talk with representatives of the target language group(s), than it is in contexts where the learners do not have an abundance of such opportunities.

For instance, a group of Chinese adults in the Southwestern United States (mostly graduate students on temporary visas) performed somewhat better on a cloze test in English if they rated Americans as high on a factor defined by such positive traits as helpfulness, sincerity, kindness, reasonableness, and friendliness (Oller, Hudson, and Liu, 1977). Similarly, a group of Mexican-American women enrolled in a Job Corps program in Albuquerque, New Mexico scored somewhat higher on a cloze test if they rated themselves higher on a factor defined by traits such as calmness, conservativeness, religiosity, shyness, humility, and sincerity (Oller, Baca, and Vigil, 1977). The respective correlations between the proficiency measures and the attitude factors were .52 and .49.

In the cases of two populations of Japanese subjects learning English as a foreign language in Japan, weak or insignificant relationships between similar attitude measures and similar proficiency measures were observed (Asakawa and Oller, 1978, and Chihara and Oller, 1978). In the first mentioned studies, where learners were in a societal context rich in occasions where English might be used, attitudinal variables seemed somewhat more closely related to attained proficiency than in the latter studies, where learners were presumably exposed to fewer opportunities to communicate in English with representatives of the target language culture(s).

These observed contrasts between second language contexts (such as the ones the Chinese and Mexican-American subjects were exposed to) and foreign language contexts (such as the ones the Japanese subjects were exposed to) are by no means empirically secure. They seem to support the hunch that attitudes may have a greater importance to learning in some contexts than in others, and the direction of the contrasts is consistently in favor of the second language contexts. However, the pattern of sociocultural variables in the situations referred to is sufficiently diverse to give rise to doubts about their comparability. Further, the learners in the second language contexts generally achieved higher scores in English.

Probably the stickiest and most persistent difficulty in obtaining reliable data on attitudes is the necessity to rely on self-reports, or worse yet, someone else's evaluative and second-hand judgement. The problem is not *just* one of honesty. There *is* a serious question whether it is reasonable to expect someone to give an unbiased report of how they feel or think or behave when they are smart enough to know that such information may in some way be used against them, but this is not the *only* problem. There is the question of how reliable and valid are a person's judgements even when there is no aversive stimulus or threat to his security. How well do people know how they would behave in such and such a hypothetical situation? Or, how does someone know how they feel about a statement that may not have any relevance to their present experience? Are average scores on such tasks truly indicative of group tendencies in terms of attitudes and their supposed correlative behaviors, or are they merely indicative of group tendencies in responding to what may be relatively meaningless tasks?

The foregoing questions may be unanswerable for precisely the same reasons that they are interesting questions. However, there are other questions that can be posed concerning subjective self-ratings that are more tractable. For instance, how reliable are the self-ratings of subjects of their own language skills in a second language, say? Can subjects reliably judge their own ability in reading, writing, or speaking and listening tasks? Frequently in studies of attitude, the measures of attitude are correlated only with subject's own reports of how well they speak a certain language in a certain context with no objective measures of language skill whatsoever. Or, alternatively, subjects are asked to indicate when they speak language X and to whom and in what contexts. How reliable are such judgements?

In the cases where they can be compared to actual tests of language proficiency, the results are not too encouraging. In a study with four different proficiency measures (grammar, vocabulary, listening comprehension, and cloze) and four self-rating scales (listening, speaking, reading, and writing), in no case did a correlation between a self-rating scale and a proficiency test reach .60 (there were 123 subjects) – this indicates less than 36 % overlap in variance on any of the self-ratings with any of the proficiency tests (Chihara and Oller, 1978). In another study (Oller, Baca, Vigil, 1977) correlations between a single self-rating scale and a cloze test in English scored by exact and acceptable methods (see Chapter 12) were .33 and .37 respectively (subjects numbered 60).

Techniques which require others to make judgements about the attitudes of a person or group seem to be even less reliable than self-ratings. For instance, Jensen (1965) says of the widest used 'projective' technique for making judgements about personality variables, 'put frankly, the consensus of qualified judgement is that the Rorschach is a very poor test and has no practical worth for any of the purposes for which it is recommended by its devotees' (p. 293).

Careful research has shown that the Rorschach (administered to about a million persons a year in the 1960s in the U.S. alone, according to Jensen, at a total cost of 'approximately 25 million dollars', p. 292) and other projective techniques like it (such as the Thematic Apperception Test, mentioned at the outset of this chapter) generate about as much variability across trained judges as they do across subjects. In other words, when trained psychologists or psychiatrists use projective interview techniques such as the TAT or Rorschach to make judgements about the personality of patients or clients, the judges differ in their judgements about as much as the patients differ in their judged traits. On the basis of such tests it would be impossible to tell the difference (even if there was one) between the level of, say anxiety, in Mr Jones and Mr Smith. In the different ratings of Mr Jones, he would appear about as different from himself as he would from Mr Smith.[2]

In conclusion, the measurement of attitudes does not seem to be a promising field – though it offers many challenges. Chastain urges in the conclusion to his 1975 article that 'each teacher should do what he or she can to encourage the timid, support the anxious, and loose the creative' (p. 160). One might add that the teacher will probably be far more capable of determining who is anxious, timid, creative, and we may add empathetic, aggressive, outgoing, introverted, eager, enthusiastic, shy, stubborn, inventive, egocentric, fascistic, ethnocentric, kind, tender, loving, and so on, without the help of the existing measures that purport to discriminate between such types of personalities. Teachers will be better off relying on their own intuitions based on a compassionate and kind-hearted interest in their students.

---

[2] In spite of the now well-known weaknesses of the Rorschach (Jensen, 1965) and the TAT (Anastasi, 1976), Ervin (1955) used the TAT to draw conclusions about contrasts between bilingual subject's performances on the test in each of their two languages. The variables on which she claimed they differed were such things as 'physical aggression', 'escaping blame', 'withdrawal', and 'assertions of independence' (p. 391). She says, 'it was concluded that there are systematic differences in the content of speech of bilinguals according to the language being spoken, and that the differences are probably related to differences in social roles and standards of conduct associated with the respective language communities' (p. 391). In view of recent studies on the validity of the TAT (for instance, see the remarks by Anastasi, 1976, pp. 565–587), it is doubtful that Ervin's results could be replicated. Perhaps someone should attempt a similar study to see if the same pattern of results will emerge. However, as long as the validity of the TAT and other projective techniques like it is in serious doubt, the results obtained are necessarily insecure. Moreover, it is not only the validity of such techniques as measures of something in particular that is in question – but their reliability as measures of anything at all is in question.

KEY POINTS

1. It is widely believed that attitudes are factors involved in the causation of behavior and that they are therefore important to success or failure in schools.

2. Attitudes toward self and others are probably among the most important.

3. Attitudes cannot be directly observed, but must be inferred from behavior.

4. Usually, attitude tests (or attempts to measure attitudes) consist of asking a subject to say how he feels about or would respond to some hypothetical situation (or possibly merely a statement that is believed to characterize the attitude in question in some way).

5. Although attitude and personality research (according to Buros, 1970) received more attention from 1940-1970 than any other area of testing, attitude and personality measures are generally the least valid sort of tests.

6. One of the essential ingredients of successful research that seems to have been lacking in many of the attitude studies is the readiness to entertain multiple hypotheses instead of a particular favored viewpoint.

7. Appeal to the label on a particular 'attitude measure' is not satisfactory evidence of validity.

8. There are many ways of assessing the validity of a proposed measure of a particular hypothetical construct such as an attitude or motivational orientation. Among them are the development of multiple methods of assessing the same construct and checking the pattern of correlation between them; checking the attitudes of groups known to behave differently toward the attitude object (e.g., the institutionalized church, or possibly the schools, or charitable organizations); and repeated combinations of the foregoing.

9. For some attitudes or personality traits there may be no adequate behavioral criterion. For instance, if a person says he is angry, what behavioral criterion will unfailingly prove that he is not in fact scared instead of angry?

10. Affective variables that relate to the ways people interact through language compass a very wide range of conceivable affective variables.

11. It has been widely claimed that affective variables play an important part in the learning of second languages. The research evidence, however, is often contradictory.

12. Guiora, et al tried to predict the ease with which a new system of pronunciation would be acquired on the basis of a purported measure of empathy. Their arguments, however, probably have more intuitive appeal than the research justifies.

13. In two cases, groups scoring lower on Guiora's test of empathy did better in acquiring a new system of pronunciation than did groups scoring higher on the empathy test. This directly contradicts Guiora's hypothesis.

14. Brown (1973) and others have reported that self-concept may be an important factor in predicting success in learning a foreign or second language.

15. Gardner and Lambert have argued that integratively motivated learners should perform better in learning a second language than instrumentally motivated learners. The argument has much appeal, but the data confirm every possible outcome – sometimes integratively motivated learners do excel, sometimes they do not, and sometimes they lag behind instrumentally motivated learners. Could the measures of motivation be invalid? There are other possibilities.

16. The fact that attitude scales require subjects to be honest about potentially damaging information makes those scales suspect of a built-in distortion factor (even if the subjects try to be honest).

17. A serious moral problem arises in the valuation of the scales. Who is to judge what constitutes a prejudicial view? An ethnocentric view? A bias? Voting will not necessarily help. There is still the problem of determining who will be included in the vote, or who is a member of which ethnic, racial, national, religious, or non-religious group. It is known that the meaning of responses to a particular scale is essentially uninterpretable unless the value of the scale can be determined in advance.

18. Attitude measures are all necessarily indirect measures (if indeed they can be construed as measures at all). They may, however, be straightforward questions such as 'Are you prejudiced?' or they may be cleverly designed scales that conceal their true purpose – for example, the F, or Fascism Scale by Adorno, et al.

19. A possible interpretation of the pattern of correlations for items on the F Scale and the E Scale (Adorno, et al and Gardner and Lambert) is response set. Since all of the statements are keyed in the same direction, a tendency to respond consistently though independently of item content would produce some correlation among the items and overlap between the two scales. However, the correlations might have nothing to do with fascism or ethnocentrism which is what the two scales purport to measure.

20. It has been suggested that the emotive tone of statements included in attitude questionnaires may be as important to the responses of subjects as is the factive content of those same statements.

21. As long as the validity of purported attitude measures is in question, their pattern of interrelationship with any other criteria (say, proficiency attained in a second language) remains essentially uninterpretable.

22. Concerning the sense of lostness presumably measured by the Anomie Scale, all possible predictions have been made in relation to attitudes toward minorities and outgroups. The scale is moderately correlated with the E and F Scales in the Gardner and Lambert data which may merely indicate that the Anomie Scale too is subject to a response set factor.

23. Experts rarely recommend the use of personality inventories as a basis for decisions that will affect individuals.

24. A study of anxiety by Chastain (1975) revealed conflicting results: for one group higher anxiety was correlated with better instead of worse grades.

25. Patterns of correlation between scales of the semantic differential type as applied to attitude measurement indicate some possible validity.

Clusters of variables that are distilled by factor analytic techniques show semantically similar scales to be more closely related to each other than to semantically dissimilar scales.

26. Attitude scales for children of different ethnic backgrounds have recently been developed by Zirkel and Jackson (1974). No validity or reliability information is given in the *Test Manual*. Researchers and others are cautioned to use the scales only for group assessment – not for decisions affecting individual children.

27. There may be no way to determine the extent to which attitudes cause behavior or are caused by it, or both. The nature of the relationship may differ according to context.

28. There is some evidence that attitudes may be more closely associated with second language attainments in contexts that are richer in opportunities for communication in the target language than in contexts that afford fewer opportunities for such interaction.

29. In view of all of the research, teachers are probably better off relying on their own compassionate judgements than on even the most highly researched attitude measures.

DISCUSSION QUESTIONS

1. Reflect back over your educational experience. What factors would you identify as being most important in your own successes and failures in school settings? Consider the teachers you have studied under. How many of them really influenced you for better or for worse? What specific events can you point to that were particularly important to the inspirations, discouragements, and day-to-day experiences that have characterized your own education. In short, how important have attitudes been in your educational experience and what were the causes of those attitudes in your judgement?

2. Read a chapter or two from B. F. Skinner's *Verbal Behavior* (1957) or *Beyond Freedom and Dignity* (1971) or better yet, read all of his writings on one or the other topics. Discuss his argument about the dispensability of intervening variables such as ideas, meaning, attitudes, feelings, and the like. How does his argument apply to what is said in Chapter 5 of this book?

3. What evidences would you accept as indicating a belligerent attitude? A cheerful outgoing personality? Can such evidences be translated into more objective or operational testing procedures?

4. Discuss John Platt's claims about the need for disproof in science. Can you make a list of potentially falsifiable hypotheses concerning the nature of the relationship between attitudes and learning? What would you take as evidence that a particular view had indeed been disproved? Why do you suppose that disproofs are so often disregarded in the literature on attitudes? Can you offer an explanation for this? Are intuitions concerning the nature and effects of attitudes apt to be less reliable than tests which purport to measure attitudes?

5. Pick a test that you know of that is used in your school and look it up in the compendia by Buros (see the bibliography at the end of this book).

What do the reviewers say concerning the test? Is it reliable? Does it have a substantial degree of validity? How is it used in your school? How does the use of the test affect decisions concerning children in the school?

6. Check the school files to see what sorts of data are recorded there on the results of personality inventories (The Rorschach? The Thematic Apperception Test?). Do a correlation study to determine what is the degree of relationship between scores on available personality scales and other educational measures.

7. Discuss the questions posed by Cooper and Fishman (p. 118f, this chapter). What would you say they reveal about the state of knowledge concerning the nature and effects of language attitudes and their measurement?

8. Consider the moral problem associated with the valuation of attitude scales: Brodkey and Shore (1976) say that 'A student seems to exhibit an enjoyment of writing for its own sake, enjoyment of solitary work, a rejection of Puritanical constraints, a good deal of self-confidence, and sensitivity in personal relationships' (p. 158). How would you value the statements on the Q-sort p. 130 above with respect to each of the attitudinal or personality constructs offered by Brodkey and Shore? What would you recommend the English Tutorial Program do with respect to subjects who perform 'poorly' by someone's definition on the Q-sort? The Native American? The subjects over 30? Orientals?

9. Discuss with a group the valuation of the scale on the statement: 'Human nature being what it is, there will always be war and conflict.' Do you believe it is moral and just to say that a person who agrees strongly with this statement is to that extent fascistic or authoritarian or prejudiced? (See the F Scale, p. 122f.)

10. Consider the meaning of disagreement with the statement: 'In this country, it's whom you know, not what you know, that makes for success.' What are some of the bases of disagreement? Suppose subjects think success is not possible? Will they be apt to agree or disagree with the statement? Is their agreement or disagreement characteristic of Anomie in your view? Suppose a person feels that other factors besides knowing the right people are more important to success. What response would you expect him to give to the above statement on the Anomie scale? Suppose a person felt that success was inevitable for certain types of people (such a person might be regarded as a fatalist or an unrealistic optimist). What response would you predict? What would it mean?

11. Pick any statement from the list given from the Q-sort on p. 130. Consider whether in your view it is indicative of a person who is likely to be a good student or not a good student. Better yet, take all of the statements given and rank them from most characteristic of good students to least characteristic. Ask a group of teachers to do the same. Compare the rank orderings for degree of agreement.

12. Repeat the procedure of question 11 with the extremes of the scale defined in terms of Puritanism (or, say, positive self concept) versus non-Puritanism (or, say, negative self concept) and again compare the rank orders achieved.

13. Consider the response you might give to a statement like: 'While taking

an important examination, I perspire a great deal.' What factors might influence your degree of agreement or disagreement independently of the degree of anxiety you may or may not feel when taking an important examination? How about room temperature? Body chemistry (some people normally perspire a great deal)? Your feelings about such a subject? Your feelings about someone who is brazen enough to ask such a socially obtuse question? The humor of mopping your brow as you mark the spot labeled 'never' on the questionnaire?

14. What factors do you feel enter into the definition of empathy? Which of those are potentially measurable by the MME? (See the discussion in the text on pp. 133–4.)

15. How well do you think semantic differential scales, or Likert-type (agree–disagree) scales in general can be understood by subjects who might be tested with such techniques? Consider the happy-sad faces and the neutral response of 'I don't know' indicated in Figure 4. Will children who are non-literate (pre-readers) be able to perform the task meaningfully in your judgement? Try it out on some relatively non-threatening subject such as recess (play-time, or whatever it is called at your school) compared against some attitude object that you know the children are generally less keen about (e.g., arithmetic? reading? sitting quietly?). The question is can the children do the task in a way that reflects their known preferences (if indeed you do know their preferences)?

16. How reliable and consistent are self-reports about skills, feelings, attitudes, and the like in general? Consider yourself or persons whom you know well, e.g., a spouse, sibling, room-mate, or close friend. Do you usually agree with a person's own assessment of how he feels about such and such? Are there points of disagreement? Do you ever feel you have been right in assessing the feelings of others, who claimed to feel differently than you believed they were actually feeling? Has someone else ever enlightened you on how you were 'really' feeling? Was he correct? Ever? Do you ever say everything is fine when in fact it is lousy? What kinds of social factors might influence such statements? Is it a matter of honesty or kindness or both or neither in your view?

17. Suppose you have the opportunity to influence a school board or other decision-making body concerning the use or non-use of personality tests in schools. What kinds of decisions would you recommend?

SUGGESTED READINGS

1. Anne Anastasi, 'Personality Tests,' Part 5 of the book by the same author entitled *Psychological Testing* (4th ed). New York: Macmillan, 1976, 493–621. (Much of the information contained in this very thorough book is accessible to the person not trained in statistics and research design. Some of it is technical, however.)

2. H. Douglas Brown, 'Affective Variables in Second Language Acquisition,' *Language Learning* 23, 1973, 231–44. (A thoughtful discussion of affective variables that need to be more thoroughly studied.)

3. Robert L. Cooper and Joshua A. Fishman, 'Some Issues in the Theory and Measurement of Language Attitudes,' in L. Palmer and B. Spolsky (eds.) *Papers on Language Testing: 1967–1974*. Washington, D.C.: Teachers of English to Speakers of Other Languages, 187–98.

4. John Lett, 'Assessing Attitudinal Outcomes,' in June K. Phillips (ed.) *The Language Connection: From the Classroom to the World*: ACTFL Foreign Language Education Series. New York: National Textbook, in press.

5. Paul Pimsleur, 'Student Factors in Foreign Language Learning: A Review of the Literature,' *Modern Language Journal* 46, 1962, 160–9.

6. Sandra J. Savignon, *Communicative Competence*. Montreal: Marcel Didier, 1972.

7. John Schumann, 'Affective Factors and the Problem of Age in Second Language Acquisition,' *Language Learning* 25, 1975, 209–35. (Follows up on Brown's discussion and reviews much of the recent second language literature on the topic of affective variables – especially the work of Guiora, et al.)

PART TWO
Theories and Methods of Discrete Point Testing

6

Syntactic Linguistics as a Source for Discrete Point Methods

A. From theory to practice, exclusively?
B. Meaning-less structural analysis
C. Pattern drills without meaning
D. From discrete point teaching to discrete point testing
E. Contrastive linguistics
F. Discrete elements of discrete aspects of discrete components of discrete skills – a problem of numbers

This chapter explores the effects of the linguistic theory that contended language was primarily syntax-based – that meaning could be dispensed with. That theoretical view led to methods of language teaching and testing that broke language down into ever so many little pieces. The pieces and their patterns were supposed to be taught in language classrooms and tested in the discrete items of discrete sections of language tests. The question is whether language can be treated in this way without destroying its essence. Humpty Dumpty illustrated that some things, once they are broken apart, are exceedingly difficult to put together again. Here we examine the theoretical basis of taking language apart to teach and test it piece by piece. In Chapter 8, we will return to the question of just how feasible this procedure is.

A. From theory to practice, exclusively?

Prevailing theories about the nature of language influence theories about language learning which in their turn influence ways of teaching and testing language. As Upshur observed (1969a) the direction of the influence is usually from linguistic theory to learning theory to teaching methods and eventually to testing. As a result of the direction of influence, there have been important time lags – changes in theory at one end take a long time to be realized in changes at the other end. Moreover, just as changes in blueprints are easier than changes in buildings, changes in theories have been made often without any appreciable change in tests.

Although the chain of influence is sometimes a long and indirect one, with many intervening variables, it is possible to see the unmistakable marks of certain techniques of linguistic analysis not only on the pattern drill techniques of teaching that derive from those methods of analysis, but also on a wide range of discrete point testing techniques.

The unidirectional influence from theory to practice is not healthy. As John Dewey put it many years ago:

> That individuals in every branch of human endeavor be experimentalists engaged in testing the findings of theorists is the sole guarantee for the sanity of the theorist (1916, p. 442).

Language theorists are not immune to the bite of the foregoing maxim. In fact, because it is so easy to speculate about the nature of language, and because it has been such an immensely popular pastime with philosophers, psychologists, logicians, linguists, educators, and others, theories of language – perhaps more than other theories – need to be constantly challenged and put to the test in every conceivable laboratory.

Surely the findings of classroom teachers (especially language teachers or teachers who have learned the importance of language to all aspects of an educational curriculum) are as important to the theories of language as the theories themselves are to what happens in the classroom. Unfortunately, the direction of influence has been much too one-sided. Too often the teacher is merely handed untried and untested materials that some theory says ought to work – too often the materials don't work at all and teachers are left to invent their own curricula while at the same time they are expected to perform the absorbing task of delivering it. It's something like trying to write the script, perform it, direct the production, and operate the theater all at the same time. The incredible thing is that some teachers manage surprisingly well.

If the direction of influence between theory and practice were mutual, the interaction would be fatal to many of the existing theories. This would wound the pride of many a theorist, but it would generally be a healthy and happy state of affairs. As we have seen, empirical advances are made by disproofs (Platt, 1964, citing Bacon). They are not made by supporting a favored position – perhaps by refining a favored position some progress is made, but what progress is there in empirical research that merely supports a favored view while pretending that there are no plausible competing alternatives? The latter is not empirical research at all. It is a form of idol worship where the theory is enshrined and the pretence of research is merely a form – a ritual. Platt argues that a theory which cannot be 'mortally endangered' is not alive. We may add that empirical research that does not mortally endanger the hypotheses (or theories) to which it is addressed is not empirical research at all.

How have linguistic theories influenced theories about language learning and subsequently (or simultaneously in some cases) methods of language teaching and testing? Put differently, what are some of the salient characteristics of theoretical views that have influenced practices in language teaching and testing? How have discrete point testing methods, in particular, found justification in language teaching methods and linguistic theories? What are the most important differences between pragmatic testing methods and discrete point testing methods?

The crux of the issue has to do with meaning. People use language to inform others, to get information from others, to express their feelings and emotions, to analyze and characterize their own thoughts in words, to explain, cajole, reply, explore, incite, disturb, encourage, plan, describe, promise, play, and much much more. The crucial question, therefore, for any theory that claims to be a theory of natural language (and as we have argued in Part One, for any test that purports to assess a person's ability to use language) is how it addresses this characteristic feature of language – the fact that language is used in meaningful ways. Put somewhat differently, language is used in ways that put utterances in pragmatic correspondences with extra-linguistic contexts. Learning a language involves discovering how to create utterances in accord with such pragmatic correspondences.

B. Meaning-less structural analysis

We will briefly consider how the structural linguistics of the Bloomfieldian era dealt with the question of meaning and then we will consider how language teaching and eventually language testing methodologies were subsequently affected. Bloomfield (1933, p. 139) defined the meaning of a linguistic form as the situation in which the speaker utters it, and the response it calls forth in the hearer. The behavioristic motivation for such strict attention to observables will be obvious to anyone familiar with the basic tenets of behaviorism (see Skinner, 1953, and 1957). There are two major problems, however, with such a definition of meaning. For one it ignores the inferential processes that are always involved in the association of meanings with linguistic utterances, and for another it fails to take account of the importance of situations and contexts that are part of the history of experience that influence the inferential connection of utterances to meanings.

The greatest difficulties of the Bloomfieldian structuralism, however, arise not directly from the definition of meaning that Bloomfield proposed, but from the fact that he proposed to disregard meaning in his linguistic theory altogether. He argued that 'in order to give a scientifically accurate definition of meaning we should have to have a scientifically accurate knowledge of everything in the speaker's world' (p. 139). Therefore, he contended that meaning should not constitute any part of a scientific linguistic analysis. The implication of his definition was that since the situations which prompt speech are so numerous, the number of meanings of the linguistic units which occur in them must consequently be so large as to render their description infeasible. Hence, Bloomfieldian linguistics tried to set up inventories of phonemes, morphemes, and certain syntactic patterns without reference to the ways in which those units were used in normal communication.

What Bloomfield appeared to overlook was the fact that the communicative use of language is systematic. If it were not people could not communicate as they do. While it may be impossible to describe *each* of an infinitude of situations, just as it is impossible to count up to even the lowest order of infinities, it is not impossible in principle to characterize a generative system that will succeed where simple enumeration fails. The problem of language description (or better the characterization of language) is not a problem of merely enumerating the elements of a particular analytical paradigm (e.g., the phonemes or distinctive sounds of a given language). The problem of characterizing language is precisely the one that Bloomfield ruled out of bounds – namely, how people learn and use language meaningfully.

What effect would such thinking have on language teaching and eventually on language testing? A natural prediction would be that it ought to lead to a devastating disregard for meaning in the pragmatic sense of the word. Indeed it did. But, before we examine critically some of the debilitating effects on language teaching it is necessary to recognize that Bloomfield's deliberate excision of meaning from linguistic analyses was not a short-lived nor narrowly parochial suggestion – it was widely accepted and persisted well into the 1970s as a definitive characteristic of American linguistics. Though Bloomfield's limiting assumption was certainly not accepted by all American linguists and was severely crititized or ignored in certain European traditions of considerable significance,[1] his particular variety of structural linguistics was the one that unfortunately was to pervade the theories and methods of language teaching in the United States for the next forty or so years (with few exceptions, in fact, until the present).

The commitment to a meaning-less linguistic analysis was strengthened by Zellig Harris (1951) whose own thinking was apparently very influential in certain similar assumptions of Noam Chomsky, a student of Harris. Harris believed that it would be possible to do linguistic analyses on the basis of purely formal criteria having to do with nothing except the observable relationships between linguistic elements and other linguistic elements. He said:

> The whole schedule of procedures ... which is designed to begin with the raw data and end with a statement of grammatical structure, is essentially a twice made application of two major steps: the setting up of elements and the statement of the distribution of these elements relative to each other ... The elements are determined relatively to each other, and on the basis of the distributional relations among them (Harris, 1951, p. 6f).

There is a problem, however, with Harris's method. How will the first element be identified? It is not possible to identify an unidentified element on the basis of its yet to be discovered relationships to other yet to be discovered elements. Neither is it conceivable as Harris recommends (1951, p. 7) that 'this operation can be carried out ... only if it is carried out for all elements simultaneously'. If it cannot

---

[1] For instance, Edward Sapir (1921) was one of the Americans who was not willing to accept Bloomfield's limiting assumption about meaning. The Prague School of linguistics in Czechoslovakia was a notable European stronghold which was little enamored with Bloomfield's formalism (see Vachek, 1966 on the Prague group).

work for one unidentified element, how can it possibly work for all of them? The fact is that *it cannot work at all. Nor has anyone ever successfully applied the methods Harris recommended.* It is not a mere procedural difficulty that Harris's proposals run aground on, it *is* the procedure itself that creates the difficulty. It is intrinsically unworkable and viciously circular (Oller, Sales, and Harrington, 1969).

Further, how can unidentified elements be defined in terms of themselves or in terms of their relationships to other similarly undefined elements? We will see below that Harris's recommendations for a procedure to be used in the discovery of the grammatical elements of a language, however indirectly and through whatever chain of inferential steps, has been nearly perfectly translated into procedures for teaching languages in classroom situations – procedures that work about as well as Harris's methods worked in linguistics.

Unfortunately, Bloomfield's limiting assumption about meaning did not end its influence in the writings of Zellig Harris, but persisted right on through the Chomskyan revolution and into the early 1970s. In fact, it persists even today in teaching methods and standardized instruments for assessing language skills of a wide variety of sorts as we will see below.

Chomsky (1957) found what he believed were compelling reasons for treating grammar as an entity apart from meaning. He said:

> I think that we are forced to conclude that grammar is autonomous and independent of meaning (p. 17).

and again at the conclusion to his book *Syntactic Structures*:

> Grammar is best formulated as a self-contained study independent of semantics (p. 106).

He was interested in

> attempting to describe the structure of language with no explicit reference to the way in which this instrument is put to use (p. 103).

Although Chomsky stated his hope that the syntactic theory he was elaborating might eventually have 'significant interconnections with a parallel semantic theory' (p. 103), his early theorizing made no provision for the fact that words and sentences are used for meaningful purposes – indeed that fact was considered, only to be summarily disregarded. Furthermore, he later contended that the communicative function of language was subsidiary and derivative – that language as a syntactically governed system had its real essence in some kind of 'inner totality' (1964, p. 58) – that native speakers of a language are capable of producing 'new sentences ... that are immediately understood by other speakers although they bear no physical resemblance to sentences which are "familiar"' (Chomsky, 1966, p. 4).

The hoped for 'semantic theory' which Chomsky alluded to in several places seemed to have emerged in 1963 when Katz and Fodor published 'The Structure of a Semantic Theory'. However, they too contended that a speaker was capable of producing and understanding indefinitely many sentences that were '*wholly novel to him*' (their italics, p. 481). This idea, inspired by Chomsky's thinking, is an exaggeration of the creativity of language – or an understatement depending on how the coin is turned.

If everything about a particular utterance is completely new, it is not an utterance in any natural language, for one of the most characteristic facts about utterances in natural languages is that they conform to certain systematic principles. By this interpretation, Katz and Fodor have overstated the case for creativity. On the other hand, for everything about a particular utterance to be completely novel, that utterance would conform to none of the pragmatic constraints or lower order phonological rules, syntactic patterns, semantic values and the like. By this rendering, Katz and Fodor have underestimated the ability of the language user to be creative within the limits set by his language.

The fact is that precisely because utterances are used in communicative contexts in particular correspondences to those contexts, practically everything about them is familiar – their newness consists in the fact that they constitute new combinations of known lexical elements and known sequences of grammatical categories. It is in this sense that Katz and Fodor's remark can be read as an understatement. The meaningful use of utterances in discourse is always new and is constantly a source of information and meaning that would otherwise remain undisclosed.

The continuation of Bloomfield's limiting assumption about meaning was only made quite clear in a footnote to *An Integrated Theory of Linguistic Descriptions* by Katz and Postal (1964). In spite of the fact that they claimed to be integrating Chomsky's syntactic theory with a semantic one, they mentioned in a footnote that 'we exclude aspects of sentence use and comprehension that are not explicable through the postulation of a generative mechanism as the reconstruction of the speaker's ability to produce and understand sentences. In other words, we exclude conceptual features such as the physical and sociological setting of utterances, attitudes, and beliefs of the speaker and hearer, perceptual and memory limitations, noise level of the settings, etc.' (p. 4). It would seem that in fact they excluded just about everything of interest to an adequate theory of language use and learning, and to methods of language teaching and testing.

It is interesting to note that by 1965, Chomsky had waivered from his originally strong stand on the separation of grammar and meaning to the position that 'the syntactic and semantic structure of natural languages evidently offers many mysteries, both of fact and of principle, and any attempt to delimit these domains must certainly be quite tentative' (p. 163). In 1972, he weakened his position still further (or made it stronger from a pragmatic perspective) by saying, 'it is not clear at all that it is possible to distinguish sharply between the contribution of grammar to the determination of meaning, and the contribution of so-called "pragmatic considerations", question of fact and belief and context of utterance' (p. 111).

From the argument that grammar and meaning were clearly autonomous and independent, Chomsky had come a long way indeed. He did not correct the earlier errors concerning Bloomfield's assumption about meaning, but at least he came to the position of questioning the correctness of such an assumption. It remains to be seen how long it will take for his relatively recently acquired skepticism concerning some of his own widely accepted views to filter back to the methods of teaching and testing for which his earlier views served as after-the-fact supports if not indeed foundational pillars. It may not have been Chomsky's desire to have his theoretical thinking applied as it has been (see his remarks at the Northeast Conference, 1966, reprinted in 1973), but can anyone deny that it has been applied in such ways? Moreover, though some of his arguments may have been very badly misunderstood by some applied linguists, his argument about the autonomy of grammar is simple enough not to be misunderstood by anyone.

C. Pattern drills without meaning

What effects, then, have the linguistic theories briefly discussed above had on methods of language teaching and subsequently on methods of language testing? The effects are direct, obvious, and unmistakable. From meaning-less linguistic analysis comes meaning-less pattern drill to instill the structural patterns or the distributional 'meanings' of linguistic forms as they are strung together in utterances. In the Preface (by Charles C. Fries) to the first edition of *English Sentence Patterns* (see Lado and Fries, 1957), we read:

> The 'grammar' lessons here set forth ... consist basically of *exercises to develop habits* ...

What kinds of habits? Exactly the sort of habits that Harris believed were the essence of language structure and that his 'distributional analysis' aimed to characterize. The only substantial difference was that in the famed Michigan approach to teaching English as a second or foreign language, it was the learner in the classroom who was to apply the distributional discovery procedure (that is the procedure for putting the elements of language in proper perspective in relation to each other). Fries continues:

> The habits to be learned consist of patterns or molds in which the 'words' must be grasped. 'Grammar' from the point of view of these materials is the particular system of devices which a language uses to signal one of its various layers of meaning – structural meaning (...). 'Knowing' this grammar for practical use means being able to produce and to respond to these signals of structural meaning. To develop such habits efficiently demands practice and more practice, especially oral practice. These lessons provide the exercises for a sound sequence of such practice to cover a basic minimum of production patterns in English (p. v).

In his Foreword to the later edition, Lado suggests,

> The lessons are most effective when used simultaneously with *English Pattern Practices*, which provides additional drill for the patterns introduced here (Lado and Fries, 1957, p. iii).

In his introduction to the latter mentioned volume, Lado continues, concerning the *Pattern Practice Materials*, that

> they represent a new theory of language learning, the idea that *to learn a new language one must establish orally the patterns of the language as subconscious habits.* These oral practices are directed specifically to that end. (His emphasis, Lado and Fries, 1958, p. xv)
> ....
> ... in these lessons, the student is lead to practise a pattern, changing some element of that pattern each time, so that normally he never repeats the same sentence twice.

Furthermore, his attention is drawn to the changes, which are stimulated by pictures, oral substitutions, etc., and thus the *pattern itself, the significant framework of the sentence*, rather than the particular sentence, is driven intensively into his habit reflexes.

It would be false to assume that Pattern Practice, because it aims at habit formation, is unworthy of the educated mind, which, it might be argued, seeks to control language through conscious understanding. There is no disagreement on the value of having the human mind understand in order to be at its learning best. But nothing could be more enslaving and therefore less worthy of the human mind than to have it chained to the mechanics of the patterns of the language rather than free to dwell on the message conveyed through language. It is precisely because of this view that we discover the highest purpose of *pattern practice: to reduce to habit what rightfully belongs to habit in the new language*, so that the mind and the personality may be freed to dwell in their proper realm, that is, on the meaning of the communication rather than the mechanics of the grammar (pp. xv–xvi).

And just how do these pattern practices work? An example or two will display the principle adequately. For instance, here is one from Lado and Fries (1957):

Exercise 1c.1. (To produce affirmative short answers.) Answer the questions with YES, HE IS; YES, SHE IS; YES, IT IS; ... For example:

Is John busy?	YES, HE IS.
Is the secretary busy?	YES, SHE IS.
Is the telephone busy?	YES, IT IS.
Am I right?	YES, YOU ARE.
Are you and John busy? ·	YES, WE ARE.
Are the students homesick?	YES, THEY ARE.
Are you busy?	YES, I AM.

(Continue:)

1. Is John busy?
2. Is the secretary busy?
3. Is the telephone busy?
4. Are you and John busy?
5. Are the students homesick?
6. Are you busy?
7. Is the alphabet important?
8. Is Mary tired?
9. Is she hungry?
10. Are you tired?
11. Is the teacher right?
12. Are the students busy?
13. Is the answer correct?
14. Am I right?
15. Is Mr. Brown a doctor?

Suppose that the well-meaning student wants to discover the meaning of the sentences that are presented as Lado and Fries suggest. How could it be done? How, for instance, will it be possible for the learner to discover the differences between a phone being busy and a person being busy? Or between being a doctor and being correct? Or between being right and being tired? Or between the appropriateness of asking a question like, 'Are you hungry?' on certain occasions, but not 'Are you the secretary busy?'

While considering these questions, consider a series of pattern drills selected more or less at random from a 1975 text entitled *From Substitution to Substance*. The authors purport to take the learner from 'manipulation to communication' (Paulston and Bruder, 1975, p. 5). This particular series of drills (supposedly progressing from more manipulative and mechanical types of drills to more meaningful and communicative types) is designed to teach adverbs that involve the manner in which something is done as specified by *with* plus a noun phrase:

Model: c [Cue]	He opened the door with a key.
	can/church key
R [Response]	He opened the can with a church key.

T [Teacher says]	s [Student responds]
bottle/opener	He opened the bottle with an opener.
box/his teeth	He opened the box with his teeth.
letter/knife	He opened the letter with a knife.

M_1 [Mechanical type of practice]
Teaching Point: *Contrast* WITH $+ N$/BY $+ N$

Model: c [Cue]	He used a plane to go there.
R [Response]	He went there by plane.
c	He used his teeth to open it.
R	He opened it with his teeth.

T [Teacher]	He used a telegram to answer it.
s [Student]	He answered it by telegram.
T	He used a key to unlock it.
s	He unlocked it with a key.
T	He used a phone to contact her.
s	He contacted her by phone.
T	He used a smile to calm them.
s	He calmed them with a smile.
T	He used a radio to talk to them.
s	He talked to them by radio.

M_2 [Meaningful drill according to the authors]
Teaching Point: *Use of* HOW *and Manner Adverbials*

| Model: c [Cue | open a bottle |
| R_1 [one possible response] | How do you open a bottle? |

R₂ [another]	(With an opener.)
c [Cue]	finance a car
R₁	How do you finance a car?
R₂	(With a loan from the bank.)
	(By getting a loan.)

T [Teacher]

light a fire
sharpen a pencil
make a sandwich
answer a question

c [Communicative drill according to the authors]
Teaching Point: *Communicative Use*

Model: c [Cue]	How do you usually send letters to your country?
R	(By airmail.) (By surface mail.)
c	How does your friend listen to your problems?
R	(Patiently.) (With a smile.)

T [Teacher]   How do you pay your bills here?
How do you find your apartment here?
How will you go on your next vacation?
How can I find a good restaurant?

In the immediately foregoing pattern drills the point of the exercise is specified in each case. The pattern that is being drilled is the only motivation for the collection of sentences that appears in a particular drill. That is why at the outset of this section we used the term 'syntactically-based pattern drills'. The drills that are selected are not exceptional in any case. They are in fact characteristic of the major texts in English as a second language and practically all of the texts produced in recent years for the teaching of foreign languages (in ESL/EFL see National Council of Teachers of English, 1973, Bird and Woolf, 1968, Nadler, Marelli, and Haynes, 1971, Rutherford, 1968, Wright and McGillivray, 1971, Rand, 1969a, 1969b, and many others). They all present learners with lists of sentences that are similar in structure (though not always identical, as we will see shortly) but which are markedly different in meaning.

How will the learner be able to discover the differences in meaning between such similar forms? Of course, we must assume that the learner is not already a native speaker – otherwise there would be no point in studying ESL/EFL or a foreign language. The native speaker knows the fact that saying, 'He used a plane to go there,' is a little less natural than saying, 'He went there in an airplane,' or 'He flew,' but how will the non-native speaker discover such things on the basis of the information that can be made available in the drill? Perhaps the authors of the drill are expecting the teacher to act out each sentence in some way, or creatively to invent a meaningful context for each sentence as it comes up. Anyone who has tried it knows that the hour gets by before you can make it through just a few sentences. Inventing contexts for sentences like, 'Is the alphabet important?' and 'Is the telephone busy?' is like trying to write a story where the characters, the plot, and all of the backdrops change from one second to the next. It is not just difficult to conceive of a context in which students can be homesick, alphabets important, the telephone, the secretary, and John busy, Mary tired, me right, Brown a doctor and so on, but before you get to page two the task is *impossible*.

If it is difficult for a native speaker to perform the task of inventing contexts for such bizarre collections of utterances, why should anyone expect a non-native speaker who doesn't know the language to be able to do it? The simple truth is that *they cannot do it*. It is no more possible to learn a language by such a method than it is to analyze a language by the form of distributional analysis proposed by Harris. It is necessary to get some data in the form of pragmatic mappings of utterances onto meaningful contexts – failing that it is not possible either to analyze a language adequately or to learn one at all.

Worse yet, the typical (not the exceptional, but the ordinary everyday garden variety) pattern drill is bristling with false leads about similarities that are only superficial and will lead almost immediately to unacceptable forms – the learner of course won't know that they are unacceptable because he is not a native speaker of the language and has little or no chance of ever discovering where he went wrong. The bewildered learner will have no way of knowing that for a person to be busy is not like a telephone being busy. What information is there to prevent the learner from drawing the reasonable conclusion that if telephones can be busy in the way that people can, that televisions, vacuum cleaners, telegraphs, and typewriters can be busy in the same sense? What will keep the learner from having difficulty distinguishing the meanings of alphabet, telephone, secretary, and doctor if he doesn't already know the meanings of those words? If the learner doesn't already know that *a doctor*, *a secretary*, and *a teacher* are phrases that refer to people with different occupational statuses, how will the drill help him to discover this information? What, from the learner's point of view is different about *homesick* and *a doctor*? What will prevent the learner from saying *Are the students doctor* and *Is the alphabet busy*?

Meaning would prevent such absurdities, but the nature of the pattern drill encourages them. It is an invitation to confusion. Without meaning to help keep similar forms apart, the result is simple. They cannot be kept apart – they become mixed together indiscriminately. This is not because learners are lacking in intelligence, rather it is because they are in fact quite intelligent and they use their intelligence to classify similar things together and to keep different things apart. But how can they keep different things apart when it is only the superficial similarities that have been constantly called to their attention in a pattern drill?

The drills proposed by Paulston and Bruder are more remarkable than the ones by Lado and Fries, because the Paulston-Bruder drills are supposed to become progressively more meaningful – but they do not. They merely become less obviously structured. The responses and the stimuli to elicit them don't become any more meaningful. The responses merely become less predictable as one progresses through the series of drills concerning each separate point of grammatical structure.

Who but a native speaker of English will know that *opening a door with a key* is not very much like *opening a can with a church key*? The two sentences are alike in fact primarily in terms of the way they sound. If the non-native knew the meanings before doing the drill there would be no need for doing the drill – but if he does need the drill it will do him absolutely no good and probably some harm. What will keep him from saying, *He opened the can with a hand*? Or, *He opened the bottle with a church key*? Or, *He opened the car with a door*? Or, *He opened the faucet with a wrench*? If he can say, *He opened the letter with a letter opener*, why not, *He opened the box with a box opener*? Or, *He opened the plane with a plane opener*? If the learner is encouraged to say, *He used a key to unlock it*, why not, *He used a letter to write her*, or *He used a call to phone her*?

In the drill above labelled M_1, which the authors describe as a mechanical drill, the object is to contrast phrases like *with a knife* and *by telegram*. Read over the drill and then try to say what will prevent the learner from coming up with forms like, *He went there with a plane, He contacted her with a phone, He unlocked it by key, He calmed them by smile, He used radio to talk to them, He used phone to contact her, He contacted her with telegram*, etc.

In the drill labelled M$_2$, which is supposed to be somewhat more
meaningful, additional traps are neatly laid for the non-native
speaker who is helplessly at the mercy of the patterns laid out in the
drill. When asked how to light a fire, sharpen a pencil, make a
sandwich, or answer a question, he has still fresh in his memory the
keyed answers to the question about how to open a bottle or finance a
car. He has heard that you can finance a car *by getting a loan* or that
you can open a bottle *with an opener*. What is to prevent the
unsuspecting and naive learner from saying that you can open a
bottle *by getting an opener* – structurally the answer is flawless and in
line with what he has just been taught. The answer is even creative.
But pragmatically it is not quite right. Because of a quirk of the
language that native speakers have learned, *getting an opener* does
not imply using it, though *with an opener* in response to the question
How do you open a bottle? does imply the required use of the opener.
What will keep the learner from creatively inventing forms like, *by
a match* in response to the question about starting a fire? Or *by a
pencil sharpener* in answer to how you sharpen a pencil? Would it not
be perfectly reasonable if when asked *How do you answer a question?*
the learner replied *with an answer?* or *by answering?*

The so-called 'Communicative Use' drill offers even more
interesting traps. How do you send your letters? By an airplane of
course. Or sometimes I send them with a ship. When I'm in a hurry
though I always send them with a plane. How does your friend listen
to your problems? By patience mostly, but sometimes he does so by
smiling. Bills? Well, I almost always bill them by mail or with a car –
sometimes in an airmail. My apartment? Easy. I found it by a friend.
We went there with a car. My next vacation? With an airplane. My
girl friend is wanting to go too, but she goes by getting a loan with a
bank. A good restaurant? You can go with a taxi.

Is there any need to say more? Is there an English teacher alive
anywhere who cannot write reams on the topic? What then, Oh
Watchman of the pattern drill? The pattern drill *without meaning*, my
Son, is as a door opening into darkness and leading nowhere but to
confusion.

If the preceding examples were exceptional, there might be reason
to hope that pattern drills of the sort illustrated above might be
transformed into more meaningful exercises. There is no reason for
such a hope, however. Pattern drills which are unrelated and
intrinsically unrelatable to meaningful extralinguistic contexts are
confusing precisely because they are well written – that is, in the sense

that they conform to the principles of the meaning-less theory of linguistic analysis on which they were based. They are unworkable as teaching methods for the same reason that the analytical principles on which they are based are unworkable as techniques of linguistic analysis. The analytical principles that disregard meaning are not just difficult to apply, but they are fundamentally inapplicable to the objects of interest – namely, natural languages.

D. From discrete point teaching (meaning-less pattern drills) to discrete point testing

One might have expected that the hyperbole of meaning-less language was fully expressed in the typical pattern drills that characterized the language teaching of the 1950s and to a lesser extent is still characteristic of most published materials today. However, a further step toward complete meaninglessness was possible and was advocated by two leading authorities of the 1960s. Brooks (1964) and Morton (1960, 1966) urged that the minds of the learners who were manipulating the pattern drills should be kept free and unencumbered by the meanings of the forms they were practicing. Even Lado and Fries (1957, 1958) at least argued that the main purpose of pattern drills was not only to instill 'habits' but was to enable learners to say meaningful things in the language. But, Brooks and Morton developed the argument that skill in the purely manipulative use of the language, as taught in pattern drills, would have to be fully mastered before proceeding to the capacity to use the language for communicative purposes. The analogy offered was the practicing of scales and arpeggios by a novice pianist, before the novice could hope to join in a concerto or to use the newly acquired habits expressively.

Clark (1972) apparently accepted this two stage model in relation to the acquisition of listening comprehension in a foreign language. Furthermore, he extended the model as a justification for discrete point and integrative tests:

> Second-level ability cannot be effectively acquired unless first-level perception of grammatical cues and other formal interrelationships among spoken utterances has become so thoroughly learned and so automatic that the student is able to turn most of his listening attention to 'those elements which seem to him to contain the gist of the message' (Rivers, 1967, p. 193, as quoted by Clark, 1972, p. 43).

Clark continues:

Testing information of a highly diagnostic type would be useful during the 'first stage' of instruction, in which sound discriminations, basic patterns of spoken grammar, items of functional vocabulary, and so forth were being formally taught and practised. ... As the instructional emphasis changes from formal work in discrete aspects to more extensive and less controlled listening practice, the utility (and also the possibility) of diagnostic testing is reduced in favor of evaluative procedures which test primarily the students' comprehension of the 'general message' rather than the apprehension of certain specific sounds or sound patterns (p. 43).

How successful has this two stage dichotomy proved to be in language teaching? Stockwell and Bowen hinted at the core of the difficulty in their introduction to Rutherford (1968):

The most difficult transition in learning a language is going from mechanical skill in reproducing patterns acquired by repetition to the construction of novel but appropriate sentences in natural social contexts. Language teachers ... not infrequently ... fumble and despair, when confronted with the challenge of leading students comfortably over this hurdle (p. vii).

What if the hurdle were an unnecessary one? What if it were a mere artefact of the attempt to separate the learning of the grammatical patterns of the language from the communicative use of the language? If we asked how often children are exposed to meaningless non-contextualized language of the sort that second language learners are so frequently expected to master in foreign language classrooms, the answer would be, never. Are pattern drills, therefore, necessary to language learning? The answer must be that they are not. Further, pattern drills of the non-contextualized and non-contextualizable variety are probably about as confusing as they are informative.

If as we have already seen above, pattern drills are associated with the 'first stage' of a two stage process of teaching a foreign language and if the so-called 'diagnostic tests' (or discrete point tests) are also associated with that first stage, it only remains to show the connection between the pattern drills and the discrete point items themselves. Once this is accomplished, we will have illustrated each link in the chain from certain linguistic theories to discrete point methods of language testing.

Perhaps the area of linguistic analysis which developed the most rapidly was the level of phonemics. Accordingly, a whole tradition of pattern drills was created. It was oriented toward the teaching of 'pronunciation', especially the minimal phonemic contrasts of various target languages. For instance, Lado and Fries (1954) suggested:

> A very simple drill for practicing the recognition of ... distinctive differences can be made by arranging minimal pairs of words on the blackboard in columns thus:

(The words they used were offered in phonetic script but are presented here in their normal English spellings.)

man	men
lass	less
lad	led
pan	pen
bat	bet
sat	set

The authors continue:

> The teacher pronounces pairs of words in order to make the student aware of the contrast. When the teacher is certain that the students are beginning to hear these distinctions he can then have them actively participate in the exercise (p. iv).

In a footnote the reader is reminded:

> Care must be taken to pronounce such contrasts with the same intonation on both words so that the sole difference between the words will be the sound under study (op cit).

It is but a short step to test items addressed to minimal phonological contrasts. Lado and Fries point out in fact that a possible test item is a picture of a woman watching a baby versus a woman washing a baby. In such a case, the examinee might hear the statement, *The woman is washing the baby*, and point to or otherwise indicate the picture to which the utterance is appropriate.

Harris (1969) observes that the minimal pair type of exercise, of the sort illustrated above, 'is, in reality, a two-choice "objective test", and most sound discrimination tests are simply variations and expansions of this common classroom technique' (pp. 32–3). Other variations for which Harris offers examples include heard pairs of words where the learner (or in this case, the examinee) must indicate whether the two words are the same or different; or a heard triplet where the learner must indicate which of three words (e.g., *jump*, *chump*, *jump*) was different from the other two; or a heard sentence in which either member of a minimal pair might occur (e.g., *It was a large ship*, versus, *It was a large sheep*) where the examinee must indicate either a picture of a large ship or a large sheep depending on what was heard. Harris refers to the last case as an example of testing minimal pairs 'in context' (p. 33–4). It is not difficult to see, however, that the types of contexts in which one might expect to find both ships and sheep are relatively few in number – certainly a very small minority of possible contexts in which one might expect to find ships without sheep or sheep without ships.

Vocabulary teaching by discrete point methods also leads rather directly to discrete point vocabulary tests. For instance, Bird and Woolf (1968) include a substitution drill set in a sentence frame of *That's a* _____, or *This is a* _____ with such items as *chair, pencil, table, book,* and *door*. It is a short step from such a drill to a series of corresponding test items. For example, Clark (1972) suggests a test item where a door, chair, table, and bed are pictured. Associated with each picture is a letter which the student may mark on an answer sheet for easy scoring. The learner hears in French, *Voici une chaise,* and should correspondingly mark the letter of the picture of the chair on the answer sheet.

Other item types suggested by Harris (1969) include: a word followed by several brief definitions from which the examinee must select the one that corresponds to the meaning of the given word; a definition followed by several words from which the examinee must select the one closest in meaning to the given definition; a sentence frame with an underlined word and several possible synonyms from which the examinee must choose the best alternative; and a sentence frame with a blank to be filled by one of several choices and where all but one of the choices fail to agree with the meaning requirements of the sentence frame.

Test items of the discrete point type aimed at assessing particular grammatical rules have often been derived directly from pattern drill formats. For example, in their text for teaching English as a foreign language in Mali, Bird and Woolf (1968) recommend typical transformation drills from singular statements to plural ones (e.g., *Is this a book?* to *Are these books?* and reverse, see p. 14a); from negative to negative interrogative (e.g., *John isn't here,* to *Isn't John here?* see p. 83); from interrogative to negative interrogative (e.g., *Are we going?* to *Aren't we going?* see p. 83); statement to question (e.g., *He hears about Takamba,* to *What does he hear about?* see p. 131); and so forth.

There are many other types of possible drills in relation to syntax, but the fact that drills of this type can and have been translated more or less directly into test items is sufficient perhaps to illustrate the trend. Spolsky, Murphy, Holm, and Ferrel (1972, 1975) give examples of test items requiring transformations from affirmative form to negative, or to question form, from present to past, or from present to future as part of a 'functional test of oral proficiency' for adult learners of English as a second language.

Many other examples could be given illustrating the connection between discrete point teaching and discrete point testing, but the foregoing examples should be enough to indicate the relationship, which is simple and fairly direct. Discrete point testing derives from the pattern drill methods of discrete point teaching and is therefore subject to many of the same difficulties.

E. Contrastive linguistics

One of the strongholds of the structural linguistics of the 1950s and perhaps to a lesser extent the 1960s was contrastive analysis. It has had less influence on work in the teaching of English as a second language in the United States than it has had on the teaching of English as a foreign language and the teaching of other foreign languages. There is no way to apply contrastive analysis to the preparation of materials for teaching English as a second language when the language backgrounds of the students range from Mandarin Chinese, to Spanish, to Vietnamese, to Igbo, to German, etc. It would be impossible for any set of materials to take into account all of the contrasts between all of the languages that are represented in many typical college level classes for ESL in the U.S. However, the claims of contrastive analysis are still relatively strong in the teaching of foreign languages and in recent years have been reasserted in relation to the teaching of the majority variety of English as a second dialect to children who come to school speaking some other variety.

The basic idea of contrastive analysis was stated by Lado (1957). It is,

> the assumption that we can predict and describe the patterns
> that will cause difficulty in learning, and those that will not
> cause difficulty, by comparing systematically the language and
> culture to be learned with the native language and culture of the
> student. In our view, the preparation of up-to-date pedagogical

and experimental materials must be based on this kind of comparison (p. vii).

Similar claims were offered by Politzer and Staubach (1961), Lado (1964), Strevens (1965), Rivers (1964, 1968), Barrutia (1969), and Bung (1973). All of these authors were concerned with the teaching of foreign languages.

More recently, the claims of contrastive analysis have been extended to the teaching of reading in the schools. Reed (1973) says,

> the more 'radically divergent' the non-standard dialect (i.e., the greater the structural contrast and historical autonomy *vis-a-vis* standard English), the greater the need for a second language strategy in teaching Standard English (p. 294).

Farther on she reasons that unless the learner is

> enabled to bring to the level of consciousness, i.e., to *formalize* his intuitions about his dialect, it is not likely that he will come to understand and recognize the systematic points of contrast and interference between his dialect and the Standard English he must learn to control (p. 294).

Earlier, Goodman (1965) offered a similar argument based on contrastive analysis. He said,

> the more divergence there is between the dialect of the learner and the dialect of learning, the more difficult will be the task of learning to read (as cited by Richards, 1972, p. 250). (Goodman has since changed his mind; see Goodman and Buck, 1973.)

If these remarks were expected to have the same sort of effects on language testing that other notions concerning language teaching have had, we should expect other suggestions to be forthcoming about related (in fact derived) methods of language testing. Actually, the extension to language testing was suggested by Lado (1961) in what was perhaps the first major book on the topic. He reasoned that language tests should focus on those points of difference between the language of the learners and the target language. First, the 'linguistic problems' were to be determined by a 'contrastive analysis' of the structures of the native and target languages. Then,

> the test ... will have to choose a few sounds and a few structures at random hoping to give a fair indication of the general achievement of the student (p. 28).

More recently, testing techniques that focus on discrete points of difference between two languages or two dialects have generally fallen into disfavor. Exceptions however can be found. One example is the test used by Politzer, Hoover, and Brown (1974) to assess degree of control of two important dialects of English. Such items of difference between the majority variety of English and the minority variety at issue included the marking of possessives (e.g., *John's house* versus *John house*), and the presence or absence of the copula in the surface form (e.g., *He goin' to town* versus *He is going to town*). Interestingly, except for the manifest influence of contrastive analysis and discrete point theory on the scoring of the test used by Politzer, *et al*, it could be construed as a pragmatic test (i.e., it consisted of a sequential text where the task set the learner was to repeat sequences of material presented at a conversational rate).

Among the most serious difficulties for tests based on contrastive linguistics is that they should be suited (in theory at least) for only one language background – namely, the language on which the contrastive analysis was performed. Upshur (1962) argues that this very fact results in a peculiar dilemma for contrastively based tests: either the tests will not differentiate ability levels among students with the same native language background and experience, 'or the contrastive analysis hypothesis is invalid' (p. 127). Since the purpose of *all* tests is to differentiate success and failure or degrees of one or the other, *any* contrastively based test is therefore either not a test or not contrastively based. A more practical problem for contrastively based tests is that learners from different source languages (or dialects) would require different tests. If there are many source languages contrastively based tests become infeasible.

Further, from the point of view of pragmatic language testing as discussed in Part One above, the contrastive analysis approach is irrelevant to the determination of what constitutes an adequate language test. It is an empirical question as to whether tests can be devised which are more difficult for learners from one source language than for learners from other source languages (where proficiency level is a controlled variable). Wilson (in press) discusses this problem and presents some evidence suggesting that contrastive analysis is not helpful in determining which test items will be difficult for learners of a certain language background.

In view of the fact that contrastive analysis has proved to be a poor basis for predicting errors that language learners will make, or for hierarchically ranking points of structure according to their degree of difficulty, it seems highly unlikely that it will ever provide a substantial basis for the construction of language tests. At best, contrastive analysis provides heuristics only for certain discrete point test items. Any such items must then be subjected to the same sorts of validity criteria as are any other test items.

F. Discrete elements of discrete aspects of discrete components of discrete skills – a problem of numbers

One of the serious difficulties of a thoroughgoing analytical model of discrete point testing is that it generates an inordinately large number of tests. If as Lado (1961) claimed, we 'need to test the elements and the skills separately' (p. 28), and if as he further argued we need separate tests for supposedly separate components of language ability, and for both productive and receptive aspects of those components, we wind up needing a very large number of tests indeed. It might seem odd to insist on pronunciation tests for speaking and separate pronunciation tests for listening, but Lado did argue that the 'linguistic problems' to be tested 'will differ somewhat for production and for recognition' and that therefore 'different lists are necessary to test the student's pronunciation in speaking and in listening' (p. 45). Such distinctions, of course, are also common to tests in speech pathology.

Hence, what is required by discrete point testing theory is a set of items for testing the elements of phonology, lexicon (or vocabulary), syntax, and possibly an additional component of semantics (depending on the theory one selects) times the number of aspects one recognizes (e.g., productive versus receptive) times the number of separate skills one recognizes (e.g., listening, speaking, reading, writing, and possibly others).

In fact, several different models have been proposed. Figure 5 below illustrates the componential analysis suggested by Harris (1969); Figure 6 shows the analysis suggested by Cooper (1972); Figure 7 shows a breakdown offered by Silverman, Noa, Russell, and Molina (1967); and finally, Figure 8 shows a slightly different model of discrete point categories proposed by Oller (1976c) in a discussion of possible research recommended to test certain crucial hypotheses generated by discrete point and pragmatic theories of language testing.

Harris's model would require (in principle) sixteen separate tests or subtests; Cooper's would require twenty-four separate tests or subtests; the model of Silverman et al would require sixteen; and the model of Oller would require twelve.

What classroom teacher has time to develop so many different

Components	Language Skills			
	Listening	Speaking	Reading	Writing
Phonology/ Orthography				
Structure				
Vocabulary				
Rate and general fluency				

Figure 5. Componential breakdown of language proficiency proposed by Harris (1969, p. 11).

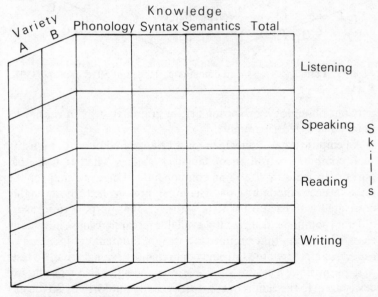

Figure 6. Componential analysis of language skills as a framework for test construction from Cooper (1968, 1972, p. 337).

tests? There are other grave difficulties in the selection of items for each test and in determining how many items should appear in each test, but these are discussed in Chapter 7 section A. The question is, are all the various tests or subtests necessary? We don't normally use

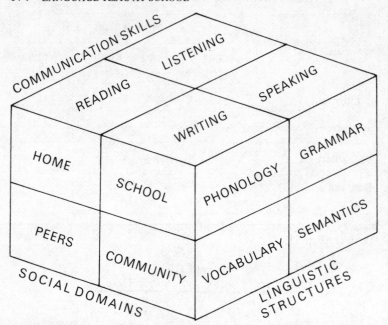

Figure 7. 'Language assessment domains' as defined by Silverman *et al* (1976, p. 21).

only our phonology, or vocabulary, or grammar; why must they be taught and tested separately?

An empirical question which must be answered in order to justify such componentialization of language skill is whether tests that purport to measure the same component of language skill (or the same aspect, modality, or whatever) are in fact more highly correlated with each other than with tests that purport to measure different components. Presently available research results show many cases where tests that purport to measure different components or aspects (etc.) correlate as strongly or even more strongly than do tests that purport to measure the same components. These results are devastating to the claims of construct validity put forth by advocates of discrete point testing.

For example, Pike (1973) found that scores on an essay task correlated more strongly with the Listening Comprehension subscore on the *TOEFL* than with the Reading Comprehension subscore for three different groups of subjects. This sort of result controverts the prediction that tasks in the reading-writing modality ought to be more highly intercorrelated with each other than with tasks in the listening-

Input–Output MODE / Sensory-Motor MODALITY	RECEPTIVE			PRODUCTIVE		
AUDITORY/ ARTICULATORY	Listening			Speaking		
	Phon-ology	Struc-ture	Vocab-ulary	Phon-ology	Struc-ture	Vocab-ulary
VISUAL/ MANUAL	Reading			Writing		
	Graph-ology	Struc-ture	Vocab-ulary	Graph-ology	Struc-ture	Vocab-ulary

Figure 8. Schematic representation of constructs posited by a componential analysis of language skills based on discrete point test theory, from Oller (1976c, p. 150).

speaking modality (of course, the *TOEFL* Listening Comprehension subtest does require reading). Perhaps more surprisingly, Darnell (1968) found that a cloze task was more highly correlated with the Listening Comprehension section on the *TOEFL* than with any of the other subscores. Oller and Conrad (1971) got a similar result with the UCLA *ESL Placement Examination Form 2C.* Oller and Streiff (1975) found that a dictation task was more strongly correlated with each other part of the UCLA *ESLPE Form 1* than any of the other parts with each other. This was particularly surprising to discrete point theorizing in view of the fact that the dictation was the only section of the test that required substantial listening comprehension. Except for the phonological discrimination task, which required distinguishing minimal pairs in sentence sized contexts, no other subsection required listening comprehension at all.

In conclusion, if tasks that bear a certain label (e.g., reading comprehension) correlate as well with tasks that bear different labels (e.g., listening comprehension, or vocabulary, or oral interview, etc.) as they do with each other, what independent justification can be offered for their distinct labels or for the positing of separate skills, aspects, and components of language? The only justification that comes to mind is the questionable theoretical bias of discrete point theory.

Such a justification is a variety, a not too subtle variety in fact, of validity by fiat, or nominal validity – for instance, the statement that a 'listening comprehension test' is a test of 'listening comprehension' because that is what it was named by its author(s); or that a 'reading' test is distinct from a 'grammar' test because they were assigned different labels by their creators. A 'vocabulary' test is different from a 'grammar' or 'phonology' test because they were dubbed differently by the theorists who rationalized the distinction in the first place.

There is a better basis for labeling tests. Tests may be referred to, not in terms of the hypothetical constructs that they are *supposed to* measure, but rather in terms of the sorts of operations they *actually require* of learners or examinees. A cloze test requires learners to fill in blanks. A dictation requires them to write down phrases, clauses or other meaningful segments of discourse. An imitation task requires them to repeat or possibly rephrase material that is heard. A reading aloud task requires reading aloud. And so forth. A synonym matching task is the most popular form of task usually called a 'Vocabulary Test'. If tests were consistently labeled according to what they require learners to do, a great deal of argumentation concerning relatively meaningless and misleading test labels could be avoided. Questions about test validity are difficult empirical questions which are only obscured by the careless assignment of test labels on the basis of untested theoretical (i.e., theory based) biases.

In the final analysis, the question of whether or not language skill can be split up into so many discrete elements, components, and so forth, is an empirical question. It cannot be decided *a priori* by fiat. It is true that discrete point tests can be made from bits and pieces of language, just as pumpkin pie can be made from pumpkins. The question is whether the bits and pieces can be put together again, and the extent to which they are characteristic of the whole. We explore this question more thoroughly in Chapter 8 below. Here, the intent has been merely to show that discrete point theories of testing are derived from certain methods of teaching which in their turn derive from certain methods of linguistic analysis.

KEY POINTS

1. Theories of language influence theories of language learning which in their turn influence theories of language teaching which in their turn influence theories and methods of language testing.
2. A unidirectinal influence from theory to practice (and not from practical findings to theories) is unhealthy.
3. A theory that cannot be mortally endangered is not alive.
4. Language is typically used for meaningful purposes – therefore, any theory of language that hopes to attain a degree of adequacy must encountenance this fact.
5. Structural analysis less meaning led to pattern drills without meaning.
6. Bloomfield's exclusion of meaning from the domain of interest to linguistics was reified in the distributional discovery procedure recommended by Zellig Harris.
7. The insistence on grammar without meaning was perpetuated by Chomsky in 1957 when he insisted on a grammatical analysis of natural languages with no reference to how those languages were used in normal communication.
8. Even when semantic notions were incorporated into the 'integrated theory' of the mid sixties, Katz and Fodor, and Katz and Postal insisted that the speaker's knowledge of how language is used in relation to extralinguistic contexts should remain outside the pale of interest.
9. Analysis of language without reference to meaning or context led to theories of language learning which similarly tried to get learners to internalize grammatical rules with little or no chance of ever discovering the meanings of the utterances they were encouraged to habitualize through manipulative pattern drill.
10. Pattern drills, like the linguistic analyses from which they derive, focussed on 'structural meaning' – the superficial meaning that was associated with the distributional patterns of linguistic elements relative to each other and largely independent of any pragmatic motivation for uttering them.
11. Typical pattern drills based on the syntactic theories referred to above are essentially noncontextualizable – that is, there is no possible context in which all of the diverse things that are included in a pattern drill could actually occur. (See the drills in most any ESL/EFL text – refer to the list of references given on p. 161 above.)
12. It is quite impossible, not just difficult, for a non-native speaker to infer pragmatic contexts for the sentences correctly in a typical syntax based pattern drill unless he happens to know already what the drill purports to be teaching.
13. Syntactically motivated pattern drills are intrinsically structured in ways that will necessarily confuse learners concerning similar forms with different meanings – there is no way for the learner to discover the pragmatic motivations for the differences in meaning.
14. The hurdle between manipulative drills and communicative use of the utterances in them (or the rules they are supposed to instill in the learner) is an artefact of meaning-less pattern drills in the first place.

15. Discrete point teaching, particularly the syntax based pattern drill approach, has been more or less directly translated into discrete point testing.

16. Contrastive linguistics contended that the difficult patterns of a particular target language could be determined in advance by a diligent and careful comparison of the native language of the learner with the target language.

17. The notion of contrastive linguistics was extended to the teaching of reading and to language tests in the claim that the points of difficulty (predicted by contrastive analysis) should be the main targets for teaching and for test items.

18. A major difficulty for contrastive linguistics is that it has never provided a very good basis for prediction. In many cases where the predictions are clear they are wrong, and in others, they are too vague to be of any empirical value.

19. Another serious difficulty is that every different native language background theoretically requires a *different language test* to assess knowledge of the *same target language* (e.g., English). Further, there seems to be no reason to expect a comparison of English and Spanish to provide a good test of either English or Spanish; rather, what appears to be required is something that can be arrived at independently of any comparison of the two languages – a test of one or the other language.

20. Many problems of test validity can be avoided if tests are labeled according to what they require examinees to do instead of according to what the test author thinks the test measures.

21. Finally, discrete point test theories require many subtests which are of questionable validity. Whether there exists a separable (and separately testable) component of vocabulary, another of grammar, and separable skills of listening, reading, writing, and so forth must be determined on an empirical basis.

DISCUSSION QUESTIONS

1. Take a pattern drill from any text. Ask what the motivation for the drill was. Consider the possibility (or impossibility) of contextualizing the drill by making obvious to the learner how the sentences of the drill might relate to realistic contexts of communication. Can it be done? If so, demonstrate how. If not, explain why not. Can contextualized or contextualizable drills be written? If so, how would the motivation for such drills differ from the motivation for noncontextualizable drills?

2. Examine pragmatically motivated drills such as those included in *El español por el mundo* (Oller, 1963–65). Study the way in which each sentence in the drill is relatable (in ways that can be and in fact are made obvious to the learner) to pragmatic contexts that are already established in the mind of the learner. How do such drills differ in focus from the drills recommended by other authors who take syntax as the starting point rather than meaning (or pragmatic mapping of utterance onto context)?

3. Work through a language test that you know to be widely used. Consider

which of the subparts of the test rely on discrete point theory for their justification. What sorts of empirical studies could you propose to see if the tests in question really measure what they purport to measure? What specific predictions would you make concerning the intercorrelations of tests with the same label as opposed to tests with different labels? What if the labels are not more than mere labels?

4. Consider the sentences of a particular pattern drill in a language that you know well. Ask whether the sentences of the drill would be apt to occur in real life. For instance, as a starter, consider the likelihood of ever having to distinguish between *She's watching the baby* versus *She's washing the baby*. Can you conceive of more likely contrasts? What contextual factors would cause you to prefer *She's giving the baby a bath*, or *She's bathing the infant*, etc.?

5. Following up on question 4, take a particular sentence from a pattern drill and try to say all that you know about its form and meaning. For instance, consider what other forms it calls to mind and what other meanings it excludes or calls to mind. Compare the associations thus developed for one sentence with the set of similar associations that come to mind in the next sentence in the drill, and the next and the next. Now, analyze some of the false associations that the drill encourages. Try to predict some of the errors that the drill will encourage learners to make. Do an observational study where the pattern drill is used in a classroom situation and see if the false association (errors) in fact arise. Or alternatively, record the errors that are committed in response to the sentences of a particular drill and see if you can explain them after the fact in terms of the sorts of associations that are encouraged by the drill.

6. As an exercise in distributional analysis, have someone give you a simple list of similarly structured sentences in a language that you do not know. Try to segment those sentences without reference to meaning. See if you can tell where the word boundaries are, and see if it is possible to determine what the relationships between words are – i.e., try to discover the structural meanings of the utterances in the foreign language without referring to the way those utterances are pragmatically mapped onto extralinguistic contexts. Then, test the success of your attempt by asking an informant to give you a literal word for word translation (or possibly a word for morpheme or phrase translation) along with any less literal translation into English. See how close your understanding of the units of the language was to the actual structuring that can be determined on the basis of a more pragmatic analysis.

7. Take any utterance in any meaningful linguistic context and assign to it the sort of tree structure suggested by a phrase structure grammar (or a more sophisticated grammatical system if you like). Now consider the question, what additional sorts of knowledge do I normally bring to bear on the interpretation of such sentences that is not captured by the syntactic analysis just completed? Extend the question. What techniques might be used to make a learner aware of the additional sorts of clues and information that native speakers make use of in coding and decoding such utterances? The extension can be carried one step further. What techniques could be used to test the ability of learners to utilize the kinds

180 LANGUAGE TESTS AT SCHOOL

of clues and information available to native speakers in the coding and decoding of such utterances?

8. Is there a need for pattern drills without meaning in language teaching? If one chose to dispense with them completely, how could pattern drills be constructed so as to maximize awareness of the pragmatic consequences of each formal change in the utterances in the pattern drill? Consider the naturalness constraints proposed for pragmatic language tests. Could not similar naturalness constraints be imposed on pattern drills? What kinds of artificiality might be tolerable in such a system and what kinds would be intolerable?

9. Take any discrete test item from any discrete test. Embed it in a context (if that is possible, for some items it is very difficult to conceive of a realistic context). Consider then the degree of variability in possible choices for the isolated discrete item and for the same item in context. Which do you think would produce results most commensurate with genuine ability to communicate in the language in question? Why? Alternatively, take an item from a cloze test and isolate it from its context (this is always possible). Ask the same questions.

SUGGESTED READINGS

1. J. Stanley Ahman, and Marvin D. Glock, *Measuring and Evaluating Educational Achievement* 2nd Ed. Boston: Allyn and Bacon, 1975. See especially Chapters 2, 3, and 4.

2. John L. D. Clark, *Foreign Language Testing: Theory and Practice*. Philadelphia: Center for Curriculum Development, 1972, 25–113.

3. David P. Harris, *Testing English as a Second Language*. New York: McGraw Hill, 1969, 1–11, 24–54.

4. J. B. Heaton, *Writing English Language Tests*. London: Longman, 1975.

5. Robert J. Silverman, Joslyn K. Noa, Randall H. Russell, and John Molina, *Oral Language Tests for Bilingual Students: An Evaluation of Language Dominance and Proficiency Instruments*. Portland, Oregon: Center for Bilingual Education (USOE, Department of HEW), 18–28.

7

Statistical Traps

There is an old adage that 'Figures don't lie', to which some sage added, 'But liars do figure'. While in the right contexts, both of these statements are true, both oversimplify the problems faced by anyone who must deal with the sorts of figures known as statistics produced by the figurers known as statisticians. Although most statistics can easily be misleading, most statisticians probably do not intend to be misleading even when they produce statistics that are likely to be misinterpreted.

The book by Huff (1954), *How to Lie with Statistics*, would probably be more widely read if it were on the topic, *How to Lie without Statistics*. Statistics *per se* is a dry and forbidding subject. The difficulty is probably not related to deliberate deception but to the difficulty of the objects of interest – namely, certain classes of numbers known as statistics. This chapter examines several common but misleading applications of statistics and statistical concepts. We are thinking here of *language* testing, but the problems are in fact very general in educational testing.

A. Sampling theory and test construction

One of the misapplications of statistical notions to language testing relates to the construction of tests. Discrete point theorists have suggested that the various 'parts' of the domain of 'language proficiency' must be defined and represented in appropriate proportions on the test ...

Item analysis statistics take on a different meaning ... The concern is ... with how well the items on the test represent the content domain (Petersen and Cartier, 1975, p. 108f) ...

At first glance, it might appear that, in principle, a test of general proficiency in a foreign language should be a sample of the entire language at large. In practice, obviously, this is neither necessary nor desirable. The average native speaker gets along quite well knowing only a limited sample of the language at large, so our course and test really only need to sample that sample. (Further discussion on *what* to sample will follow after touching on the problem of *how* to sample [p. 111]).

The reader will begin to appreciate the difficulty of determining just what domains to sample (within the sample of what the native speaker knows) a couple of paragraphs farther on in the Petersen-Cartier argument.

Most language tests, including DLI's tests [i.e., the tests of the Defense Language Institute], therefore make a kind of stratified random sample, assuring by plan that some items test grammatical features, some test phonological features, some test vocabulary, and so on. Thus, for example, the DLI's English Comprehension Level tests are constructed according to a fairly complex sampling matrix which requires that specific percentages of the total number of 120 items be devoted to vocabulary, sound discrimination, grammar, idioms, listening comprehension, reading comprehension, and so on.

The authors continue to point out that there was once an attempt to

determine the feasibility of establishing a universal item-selection matrix of this sort for all languages, or perhaps for all languages of a family, so that the problem of making a stratified sample for test construction purposes could be reduced to a somewhat standard procedure. However, such a procedure has not, as yet, been found, and until it is, we must use *some* method for establishing a rational sample of a language in our tests (p. 112).

The solution arrived at is to 'consider the present DLI courses as rational samples of the language and to sample them ... for the item objectives in our tests of general ability' (p. 113).[1]

---

[1] The authors indicate in personal communication that they reached this decision only 'with great reluctance'. They did not in their words 'arrive at these conclusions naively but, in fact, only with some considerable pain'. Therefore, the foregoing and following remarks should be interpreted accordingly.

Several crucial questions arise: What would a representative proportion of the phonology of the language be? How many items would be required to sample the component of phonology if such a component is in fact considered to be part of the larger domain of language proficiency? What percentage of the items on a language test should address the component of vocabulary (in order to be representative in the way that this component is sampled)? How many items should address the grammar component? What is a representative sampling of the grammatical structures of a language? How many noun phrases should it contain? Verb phrases? Left embedded clauses? Right branching relative clauses?

One is struck by the possibility that in spite of what anyone may say, there may be no answers to these questions. The suspicion that no answers exist is heightened by the admission that no procedure has yet been found which will provide a rational basis for 'making a stratified sample'. Indeed, if this is so, on what possible rational basis could specific percentages of a certain total number of items be determined?

Clearly, the motivation for separate items aimed at 'phonological features, vocabulary, grammar, idioms, listening comprehension, reading comprehension' and so forth is some sort of discrete point analysis that is presumed to have validity independent of any particular language test or portion thereof. However, the sort of questions that must be answered concerning the possible existence of such components of language proficiency cannot be answered by merely invoking the theoretical biases that led to the hypothesized components of language proficiency in the first place. The theoretical biases themselves must be tested – not merely assumed.

The problem for anyone proposing a test construction method that relies on an attempt to produce a representative (or even a 'rational') 'sampling of the language' is not merely a matter of how to parse up the universe of 'language proficiency' into components, aspects, skills, and so forth, but once having arrived at some division by whatever methods, the most difficult problem still remains – how to recognize a representative or rational sample in any particular portion of the defined universe.

It can be shown that *any* procedure that might be proposed to assess the representativeness of a particular sample of speech is doomed to failure because by any possible methods, all samples of real speech are either equally representative or equally unrepresentative of the universe of possible utterances. This is a natural and inevitable consequence of the fact that speech is intrinsically non-repetitive. Even an attempt to repeat a communicative exchange by using the same utterances with the same meanings is bound to fail because the context in which utterances are created is constantly changing. Utterances cannot be perfectly repeated. Natural discourse of the sort that is characteristic of the normal uses of human languages are even less repeatable – by the same logic. The universe to be sampled from is not just very large, it is infinitely large and non-repetitive.[2] To speak of a rational sampling of possible utterances is like speaking of a rational sampling of future events or even of historical happenings. The problem is not just where to dip into the possible sea of experience, but also how to know when to stop dipping – i.e., when a rational sample has been achieved.

To make the problem more meaningful, consider sampling the possible sentences of English. It is known that the number of sentences must be infinite unless some upper bound can be placed on the length of an allowable sentence. Suppose we exclude all sentences greater than twenty words in length. (To include them only strengthens the argument, but since we are using the method of reduction to absurdity tying our hands in this way is a reasonable way to start.) Miller (1964) conservatively estimated that the number of grammatical twenty-word sentences in English is roughly 10^{20}. This figure derives directly from the fact that if we interrupt someone who is speaking, on the average there are about 10 words that can be used to form an appropriate grammatical continuation. The number 10^{20} exceeds the number of seconds in 100,000,000 centuries.

Petersen and Cartier (1975) suggested that one way around the sampling problem was to 'sample the sample' of language that happened to appear in the particular course of study at the Defense Language Institute. Rather than trying to determine what would be a representative sample of the course, suppose we just took the whole course of an estimated '30 hours a week for 47 weeks' (p. 112). Suppose further that we make the contrary to fact assumption that in the course students are exposed to a minimum of one twenty-word sentence each second. If we then considered the entire course of study

---

[2] This is not the same as saying that every sentence is 'wholly novel' or 'totally unfamiliar' – a point of view that was argued against in Chapter 6 above. To say that normal communicative events cannot be repeated is like saying that you cannot relive yesterday or even the preceding moment of time. This does not mean that there is nothing familiar about today or that there will be nothing familiar about tomorrow. It is like saying, however, that tomorrow will not be identical to today, nor is today quite like yesterday, etc.

as a kind of language test, it would only be possible for such a test to cover about five million sentences – less than .000000000001 percent (one trillionth of one percent) of the possible twenty-word sentences in English. In what realistic sense could this 'sample' be considered representative of the whole? We are confronted here not just with a difficulty of how to select a 'sample', because it doesn't make any difference how we select the sample. It can never be argued that any possible sample of sentences is representative of the whole.

If we take a larger unit of discourse as our basic working unit, the difficulty of obtaining a representative sample becomes far greater since the number of possible discourses is many orders of magnitude larger than the number of possible twenty-word sentences. We are thus forced to the conclusion that the discrete point sampling notion is about as applicable to the problem of constructing a good language test as the method of *listing* sentences is to the characterization of the grammar of a particular natural language. No list will ever cover enough of the language to be interesting as a theory of grammar. It is fundamentally inadequate in principle – not just incomplete. Such a list could *never* be completed, and a test modeled after the same fashion could never be long enough even if we extended it for the duration of a person's life expectancy. In this vein, consider the fact that the number of twenty-word sentences by itself is about a thousand times larger than the estimated age of the earth (Miller, 1964).

The escape from the problem of sampling theory is suggested in the statement by Petersen and Cartier (1975) that 'the average native speaker gets along quite well knowing only a limited sample of the language at large, so our course and test really only need to sample that sample' (p. 111). Actually, the native speaker knows far more than he is ever observed to perform with his language. The conversations that a person has with others are but a small fraction of conversations that one could have if one chose to do so. Similarly, the utterances that one comprehends are but an infinitesimal fraction of the utterances that one could understand if they were ever presented. Indeed, the native speaker knows far more of his language than he will ever be observed to use – even if he talks a lot and if we observe him all the time. This was the original motivation for the distinction between competence and performance in the Chomskyan linguistics of the 1950s and 1960s.

The solution to the difficulty is not to shift our attention from many utterances (say, all of the ones uttered or understood by a given native speaker) to fewer utterances (say, all of those utterances presented to a language learner in a particular course of study at the DLI), but to remove our attention to an entirely different sort of object – namely, the grammatical system (call it a cognitive network, generative grammar, expectancy grammar, or interlanguage system) that the learner is in the process of internalizing and which when it is mature (i.e., like that of the native speaker) will generate not only the few meaningful utterances that happen to occur in a particular segment of time, but the many that the native speaker can say and understand.

Instead of trying to construct a language test that will 'representatively' or 'rationally sample' the universe of 'language', we should simply construct a test that requires the language learner to do what native speakers do with discourse (perhaps any discourse will do). Then the interpretation of the test is related not to the particular discourse that we happened to select, nor even to the universe of possible discourses in the sense of sampling theory. But thus it is related to the efficiency of the learner's internalized grammatical system in processing discourse. The validity of the test is related to how well it enables us to predict the learner's performance in other discourse processing tasks.

We can differentiate between segments of discourse that are easy to process and segments that are more difficult to process. Further, we can differentiate between segments of discourse that would be appropriate to the subject matter of mathematics, as opposed to say, geography, or gardening as opposed to architecture. The selection of segments of discourse appropriate to a particular learner or group of learners would depend largely on the kinds of things that would be expected later on of the same learner or group. Perhaps in this sense it would be possible to 'sample' types of discourse – but this is a very different sort of sampling than 'sampling' the phonological contrasts of a language, say, in appropriate proportion to the vocabulary items, grammatical rules, and the like. A language user can select portions of college level tests for cloze tests, but this is not the sort of 'sampling' that we have been arguing against. To make the selection analogous to the sort of sampling we have been arguing against is in principle impossible not just indefensible; one would have to search for prose with a specific proportion of certain phonological contrasts, vocabulary items, grammatical rules and the like in relation to a course syllabus for teaching the language of the test.

In short, sampling theory is either inapplicable or not needed. Where it might seem to apply, e.g., in the case of phonological contrasts, or vocabulary, it is not at all clear how to justify the weighting of subtests in relation to each other. Where sampling theory is clearly inapplicable, e.g., at the sentence or discourse levels, it is also obviously not needed. No elaborate sampling technique is needed to determine whether a learner can read college texts at a defined level of comprehension – nor is sampling theory necessary to the definition of the degree of comprehension that a given learner may exhibit.

B. Two common misinterpretations of correlations

Correlations between language tests have sometimes been misinterpreted in two ways: first, low correlations have sometimes been taken to mean that two tests with different labels are in fact measuring different skills, or aspects or components of skills; and, second, high correlations between dissimilar language processing tasks have sometimes been interpreted as indicating mere reliability or even a lack of validity. Depending upon the starting assumptions of a particular theoretical viewpoint, the same statistics may yield different interpretations – or may seem to support different, even mutually contradictory conclusions. When such contradictions arise, either one or both of the contradictory viewpoints must be wrong or poorly articulated.

For instance, it is not reasonable to interpret a low correlation between two tests as an indication that the two tests are measuring different skills and also that neither of them is reliable (or that one of them is not reliable). Since reliability is a prerequisite to validity, a given statistic cannot be taken as an indication of low reliability and high validity (yet this is sometimes suggested in the literature as we will see below). Similarly, a high correlation between two dissimilar language tests cannot be dismissed as a case of high reliability but low validity all in the same breath. This latter argument, however, is more complex, so we will take the simpler case first.

Suppose that the correlation between a particular test that bears the label 'Grammar' (or 'English Structure') and another language test that bears the label 'Vocabulary' (or 'Lexical Knowledge') is observed to be comparatively low, say, .40. Can it be concluded from such a low correlation that the two tests are therefore measuring different skills? Can we say on the basis of the low correlation between them that the so-called 'Grammar' test is a test of a 'grammar' component of language proficiency while the so-called

'Vocabulary' test is a test of a 'lexical' component? The answer to both questions is a simple, no.

The observed low correlation could result if both tests were in fact measures of the same basic factor but were both relatively unreliable measures of that factor. It could also result if one of the tests were unreliable; or if one of them were poorly calibrated with respect to the tested subjects (i.e., too easy or too difficult); or if one of the tests were in fact a poor measure of what it purported to measure even though it might be reliable; and so forth. In any case, a low correlation between two tests (even if it is expected on the basis of some theoretical reasoning) is relatively uninformative. It certainly cannot be taken as an indication of the validity of the correlated tests. Consider using recitation of poetry as a measure of empathy and quality of artistic taste as a measure of independence – would a low correlation between the two measures be a basis for claiming that one or both must be valid? Would a low correlation justify the assertion that the two tests are measures of different factors? The point is that low correlations would be expected if neither test were a measure of anything at all.

A low correlation between a 'Grammar' test and a 'Vocabulary' test might well be the product of poor tests rather than an independence of hypothesized components of proficiency. In fact, many failures to achieve very high correlations would not prove by any means that very high correlations do not in fact exist between something we might call 'knowledge of vocabulary' and something else that we might call 'knowledge of grammar'. Indeed the two kinds of knowledge might be one kind in reality and no number of low correlations between language tests labeled 'Grammar' tests on the one hand and 'Vocabulary' tests on the other would suffice to exclude such a possibility – and so on for all possible dichotomies. In fact the observation of low correlations between language tests where high correlations might be expected are a little like fishing trips which produce small catches where large catches were expected. Small catches do not prove that big catches do not exist. The larger catches may simply be beyond the depths of previously used nets.

To carry the example a little farther, consider the following remark by Bolinger (1975) in his introductory text on linguistics: 'There is a vast amount of grammatical detail still to be dug out of the lexicon – so much that by the time we are through there may be little point in talking about grammar and lexicon as if they were two different things' (p. 299). Take a relatively common word in English like *continue.* In a test such as the *TOEFL*, this word could appear as an item in the Vocabulary subsection. It might appear in a sentence frame something like, *The people want to* 'continue'. The examinees might be required to identify a synonymous expression such as *keep on* from a field of distractors. On the other hand, the word *continue* might just as easily appear in the English Structure section as part of a verb phrase, or on some other part of the test in a different grammatical form – e.g., *continuation, continual, continuity, discontinuity, continuous,* or the like. If the word appeared in the English Structure section it might be part of an item such as the following:

> SPEAKER A: 'But do you think they'll go on building?'
> SPEAKER B: 'Yes, I do because the contractor has to meet his deadline. I think _____.'
>
> (A) the people continue to will
> (B) will they want to continue
> (C) to continue the people will
> (D) they will want to continue

In an important sense, knowing a word is knowing how to use it in a meaningful context, a context that is subject to the normal syntactic (and other) constraints of a particular language. Does it make sense then to insist on testing word-knowledge independent of the constraints that govern the relationships between words in discourse? Is it possible? Even if it does turn out to be possible, the proof that it has been accomplished will have to come from sources of evidence other than mere low correlations between tests labeled 'Grammar' tests and tests called 'Vocabulary' tests. In particular, it will have to be shown that there exists some unique and meaningful variance associated with tests of the one type that is not also associated with tests of the other type – this has not yet been done. Indeed, many attempts to find such unique variances have failed (see the Appendix and references cited there).

In spite of the foregoing considerations, some researchers have contended that relatively low correlations between different language tests have more substantial meaning. For instance, the College Entrance Examination Board and Educational Testing Service recommended in their 1969 *Manual for Studies in Support of Score Interpretation* (for the *TOEFL*) that it may be desirable to 'study the intercorrelations among the parts [of the *TOEFL*] to determine the extent to which they are in fact measuring different abilities for the group tested' (p. 6).

The hint that low correlations might be taken as evidence that different subtests are in fact measuring different components of language proficiency or different skills is confirmed in two other reports. For instance, on the basis of the data in Table 1, the authors of the *TOEFL Interpretive Information* (Revised 1968) conclude: 'it appears that Listening Comprehension is measuring some aspect of English proficiency different from that measured by the other four parts, since the correlations of Listening Comprehension with each of the others are the four lowest in the table' (p. 14).

TABLE 1

Intercorrelation of the Part Scores on the *Test of English as a Foreign Language*. Averaged over Forms Administered through April 1967. (From *Manual for TOEFL Score Recipients*. Copyright © 1973 by Educational Testing Service. All rights reserved. Reprinted by permission.)

Subscores	(1)	(2)	(3)	(4)	(5)
(1) Listening Comprehension		.62	.53	.63	.55
(2) English Structure	.62		.73	.66	.79
(3) Vocabulary	.53	.73		.70	.77
(4) Reading Comprehension	.63	.66	.70		.72
(5) Writing Ability	.55	.79	.77	.72	

Later, in an update of the same interpretive publication, *Manual for TOEFL Score Recipients* (1973) on the basis of a similar table (see Table 2 below), it is suggested that 'the correlations between Listening Comprehension and the other parts of the test are the lowest. This is probably because skill in listening comprehension may be quite independent of skills in reading and writing; also it is not possible to standardize the administration of the Listening Comprehension section to the same degree as the other parts of the test' (p. 15). Here the authors offer what amount to mutually exclusive explanations. Both cannot be correct. If the low correlations between Listening Comprehension and the other subtests are the product of unreliability in the techniques for giving the Listening test (i.e., poor sound reproduction in some testing centers, or merely inconsistent procedures) then it is not reasonable to use the same low correlations as evidence that the Listening test is validly measuring something that the other subtests are not measuring. What might that something be? Clearly, if it is lack of

TABLE 2

Intercorrelations of the Part Scores on the *Test of English as a Foreign Language.* Averaged over Administrations from October 1966 through June 1971. (From *Manual for TOEFL Score Recipients.* Copyright © 1973 by Educational Testing Service. All rights reserved. Reprinted by permission.)

Subscores	(1)	(2)	(3)	(4)	(5)
(1) Listening Comprehension		.64	.56	.65	.60
(2) English Structure	.64		.72	.67	.78
(3) Vocabulary	.56	.72		.69	.74
(4) Reading Comprehension	.65	.67	.69		.72
(5) Writing Ability	.60	.78	.74	.72	

consistency in the procedure that produces the low correlations it is not listening ability as distinct from reading, or vocabulary knowledge, or grammar knowledge, etc. On the other hand if the low correlations are produced by real differences in the underlying skills presumed to be tested, the administrative procedures for the Listening test must have substantial reliability. It just can't go both ways.

In the 1973 manual, the authors continue the argument that the tests are in fact measuring different skills by noting that 'none of the correlations ... [in our Table 2] are as high as the reliabilities of the part scores' from which they conclude that 'each part is contributing something unique to the total score' (p. 15). The question that is still unanswered is what that 'something unique' is, and whether in the case of each subtest it is in any way related to the label on that subtest. Is the Reading Comprehension subtest more of a measure of reading ability than it is of writing ability or grammatical knowledge or vocabulary knowledge or mere test-taking ability or a general proficiency factor or intelligence? The fact that the reliability coefficients are higher than the correlations between different part scores is no proof that the tests are measuring different kinds of knowledge. In fact, they may be measuring the same kinds of knowledge and their low intercorrelations may indicate merely that they are not doing it as well as they could. In any event, it is axiomatic that validity cannot exceed reliability – indeed the general rule of thumb is that validity coefficients are not expected to exceed the square of the reliabilities of the intercorrelated tests (Tate, 1965). If a certain test has some error variance in it and a certain other test also has some error variance in it, the error is apt to be compounded in their intercorrelation. Therefore, the correlation between two tests can hardly be expected to exceed their separate reliabilities. It can equal them only in the very special case that the tests are measuring exactly the same thing.

From all of the foregoing, it is possible to see that low (or at least relatively low) correlations between different language tests *can* be interpreted as indications of low reliability or validity but hardly as proof that the tests are measuring different things.

If one makes the mistake of interpreting low correlations as evidence that the tests in question are measuring different things, how will one interpret higher correlations when they are in fact observed between equally diverse tests? For instance, if the somewhat lower correlations between *TOEFL* Listening Comprehension subtest and the Reading Comprehension subtest (as compared against the intercorrelations between the Reading Comprehension subtest and the other subtests) represented in Tables 1 and 2 above, are taken as evidence that the Listening test measures some skill that the Reading test does not measure, and vice versa, then how can we explain the fact that the Listening Comprehension subtest correlates more strongly with a cloze test (usually regarded as a reading comprehension measure) than the latter does with the Reading Comprehension subtest (see Darnell, 1968)?

Once high correlations between apparently diverse tests are discovered, the previous interpretations of low correlations as indicators of a lack of relationship between whatever skills the tests are presumed to measure are about as convincing as the arguments of the unsuccessful fisherman who said there were no fish to be caught. The fact is that the fish are in hand. *Surprisingly high correlations have been observed between a wide variety of testing techniques with a wide range of tested populations. The techniques range from a whole family of procedures under the general rubric of cloze testing, dictation, elicited imitation, essay writing, and oral interview.* Populations have ranged from children and adult second language learners, to children and adults tested in their native language (see the Appendix).

What then can be made of such high correlations? Two interpretations have been offered. One of them argues that the strong correlations previously observed between cloze and dictation, for instance, are merely indications of the reliability of both procedures and proof in fact that they are both measuring basically the same thing – further, that one of them is therefore not needed since they both give the same information. A second interpretation is that the high correlations between diverse tests must be taken as evidence not only of reliability but also of substantial test validity. In the first case, it is argued that part scores on a language proficiency test should produce low intercorrelations in order to attain validity, and in the second that just the reverse is true. It would seem that both positions cannot be correct.

It is easy to see that the expectation of low correlations between tests that purport to measure different skills, components, or aspects of language proficiency in accord with discrete point test philosophy necessitates some method of explaining away high correlations when they occur. The solution of treating the correlations merely as indications of test reliability, as Rand (1972) has done, runs into very serious logical trouble. Why should we expect a dictation which requires auditory processing of sequences of spoken material to measure the same thing as a cloze test which requires the learner to read prose and replace missing words? To say that these tests are tests of the same thing, or to interpret a high correlation between them as an indication of reliability (alone, and not something more) is to saw off the limb on which the whole of discrete point theory is perched. If cloze procedure is not different from dictation, then what is the difference between speaking and listening skills? What basis could be offered for distinguishing a reading test from a grammar test? Are such tasks more dissimilar than cloze and dictation? If we were to follow this line of reasoning just a short step further, we would be forced to conclude that low correlations between language tests of any sort are indicators of low reliabilities per force. This is a conclusion that no discrete point theorist, however, could entertain as it obliterates *all* of the distinctions that are crucial to discrete point testing.

What has been proposed by discrete point theorists, however, is that tests should be constructed so as to minimize, deliberately, the correlations between parts. If discrete point theorizing has substance to it, such a recommendation is not entirely without support. However, if the competing viewpoint of pragmatic or integrative test philosophy turns out to be more correct, test constructors should interpret low correlations as probable indicators of low validities and should seek to construct language tests that maximize the intercorrelation of part scores.

This does not mean that what is required is a test that consists of only one sort of task (e.g., reading without speaking, listening, or writing). On the contrary, unless one is interested only in ability to read with comprehension or something of the sort, to learn how well an individual understands, speaks, reads, and writes a language, it may well be necessary (or at least highly desirable) to require him to do all four sorts of performances. The question here is not which or how many tasks should be included on a comprehensive language test, but what sort of interrelationship between performances on language tasks in general should be expected.

If an individual happens to be much better at listening tasks than at speaking tasks, or at reading and writing tasks than at speaking and listening tasks, we would be much more apt to discover this fact with valid language tests than with non-valid ones. However, the case of a particular individual, who *may* show marked differences in ability to perform different language tasks, is not an argument against the possibility of a very high correlation between those same tasks for an entire population of subjects, or for subjects in general.

What if we go down the other road? What if we assume that part scores on language tests that intercorrelate highly are therefore redundant and that one of the highly correlated test scores should be eliminated from the test? The next step would be to look for some new subtest (or to construct one or more than one) which would assess some different component of language skill not included in the redundant tests. In addition to sawing the limb out from under the discrete point test philosophy, we would be making a fundamental error in the definition of *reliability* versus *validity*. Furthermore, we would be faced with the difficult (and probably intrinsically insoluble) problem of trying to decide how much weight to assign to which subskill, component, or aspect, etc. We have discussed this latter difficulty in section A above.

The matter of confusing reliability and validity is the second point to be attended to in this section. Among the methods for assessing test reliability are: the test-retest method; the technique of correlating one half of a test with the other half of the same test (e.g., correlating the average score on even numbered items with the average on odd numbered items for each presumed homogeneous portion of a test); and the alternate forms method (e.g., correlating different forms of the same test). In all of these cases, and in fact in all other measures of reliability (Kuder-Richardson formulas and other internal consistency measures included), *reliability* by definition has to do with tests or portions of tests that are in some sense the same or fundamentally similar.

To interpret high correlations between substantially different tests, or tests that require the performance of substantially different tasks, as mere indicators of reliability is to redefine reliability in an unrecognizable way. If one accepts such a definition, then how will one ever distinguish between measures of reliability and measures of validity? The distinction, which is a necessary one, evaporates.

In the case of language tests that require the performance of substantially different tasks, to interpret a high correlation between them as an indication of reliability alone is to treat the tasks as the same when they are not, and to ignore the possibility that even more diverse pragmatic language tasks may be equally closely related. In the case of language tests high correlations are probably the result of an underlying proficiency factor that relates to a psychologically real grammatical system. If such a factor exists, the ultimate test of validity of any language test is whether or not it taps that factor, and how well it does so. The higher the correlations obtained between diverse tasks, the stronger the confidence that they are in fact tapping such a factor. The reasoning may seem circular, but the circularity is only apparent. There are independent reasons for postulating the underlying grammatical system (or expectancy grammar) and there are still other bases for determining what a particular language test measures (e.g., error analysis). The crucial empirical test for the existence of a psychologically real grammar is in fact performance on language tests (or call them tasks) of different sorts. Similarly, the chief criterion of validity for any proposed language test is how well it assesses the efficiency of the learner's internalized grammatical system (or in the terms of Part One of this book, the learner's expectancy system).

On the basis of present research (see Oller and Perkins, 1978) it seems likely that Chomsky (1972) was correct in arguing that language abilities are central to human intelligence. Further, as is discussed in greater detail in the Appendix, it is apparently the case that language ability, school achievement, and IQ all constitute a relatively unitary factor. However, even if this latter conclusion were not sustained by further research, the discrete point interpretations of correlations as discussed above will still have to be radically revised. The problems there are logical and analytical whereas the unitary factor hypothesis is an empirical issue that requires experimental study.

C. Statistical procedures as the final criterion for item selection

Perhaps because of its distinctive jargon, perhaps because of its bristling mathematical formulas, or perhaps out of blind respect for things that one does not understand fully, statistical procedures (like budgets and curricula as we noted in Chapter 4) are sometimes elevated from the status of slaves to educational purposes to the status of masters which define the purposes instead of serving them. In Chapter 9 below we return to the topic of item analysis in greater detail. Here it is necessary to define briefly the two item statistics on which the fate of most test items is usually decided – i.e., whether to include a particular item, exclude it, or possibly rewrite it and pretest it again. The first item statistic is the simple percentage of students answering correctly (*item facility*) or the percentage answering incorrectly (*item difficulty*). For the sake of parsimony we will speak only of *item facility* (IF) – in fact, a little reflection will show that item difficulty is merely another way of expressing the same numerical value that is expressed as IF.

The second item statistic that is usually used by professional testers in evaluating the efficiency of an item is *item discrimination* (ID). This latter statistic has to do with how well the item tends to separate the examinees who are more proficient at the task in question from those examinees who are less proficient. There are numerous formulas for computing IDs, but all of them are in fact methods of measuring the degree of correlation between the tendency to get high and low scores on the total test (or subtest) and the tendency to answer correctly or incorrectly on a particular test item. The necessary assumption is that the whole test (or subtest) is apt to be a better measure of whatever the item attempts to measure (and the item can be considered a kind of miniature test) than any single item. If a given item is valid (by this criterion) it must correlate positively and significantly with the total test. If it does so, it is possible to conclude that high scorers on the test will tend to answer the item in question correctly more frequently than do low scorers. However, if the correlation is nil or worse yet, if it is negative, the item is in the former case giving no information about the proficiency assessed by the test as a whole, and in the latter is reversing the trends on the total test – i.e., if the correlation between the item and the test is negative it means that the examinees who get high scores on the test tend to miss the item more frequently than examinees who get low scores on the test.

For reasons that are discussed in more detail in Chapter 9, items with very low or very high IFs and/or items with very low or negative IDs are usually discarded from tests. Very simply, items that are too easy or too hard provide little or no information about the range of proficiencies in a particular group of examinees, and items that have nil or negative IDs either contribute nothing to the total amount of meaningful variance in the test (i.e., the tendency of the test to spread the examinees over a scale ranging from less proficient to more proficient) or they in fact tend to depress the meaningful variance by cancelling out some of it (in the case of negative IDs).

Probably any multiple choice test, or other test that is susceptible to item analysis, can be significantly improved by the application of the above criteria for eliminating weak items. In fact, as is argued in Chapter 9, multiple choice tests which have not been subjected to the requirements of such item analyses should probably not be used for the purposes of making educational decisions – unfortunately, they are used for such purposes in many educational contexts.

The appropriate use of item analysis then is to eliminate (or at least to flag for revision) items that are for whatever reason inconsistent with the test as a whole, or items that are not calibrated appropriately to the level of proficiency of the population to be tested. But what about the items that are left unscathed by such analyses? What about the items that seem to be appropriate in IF and ID? Are they necessarily, therefore, valid items? If such statistics can be used as methods for eliminating weak items, why not use them as the final criteria for judging the items which are not eliminated as valid – once and for all? There are several reasons why *acceptable item statistics cannot be used as the final basis for judging the validity of items to be included in tests*. It is necessary that test items conform to minimal requirements of IF and ID, but even if they do, this is not a sufficient basis for judging the items to be 'valid' in any fundamental sense.

One of the reasons that item statistics cannot be used as final criteria for item selection – and perhaps the most fundamental reason – relates to the assumption on which ID is based. Suppose that a certain Reading Comprehension test (or one that bears the label) is a fairly poor test of what it purports to measure. It follows that even items that correlate perfectly with the total score on such a test must also be poor items. For instance, if the test were really a measure of the learner's ability to recall dates or numbers mentioned in the reading selection and to do simple arithmetic operations to derive new dates, the items with the highest IDs might in actuality be the ones with the lowest validities (as tests of reading comprehension).

Another reason that item statistics cannot be relied on for the final selection of test items is that they may in fact push the test in a direction that it should not go. For example, suppose that one wants to test knowledge of words needed for college-level reading of texts in mathematics. (We ignore for the sake of the argument at this point the question of whether a 'vocabulary' test as distinct from other types of tests is really more of a measure of vocabulary knowledge than of other things. Indeed, for the sake of the argument at this point, let us assume that a valid test of 'vocabulary knowledge' can be constructed.) By selecting words from mathematics texts, we might construct a satisfactory test. But suppose that for whatever reason certain words like *ogle, rustle, shimmer, sheen, chiffonier, spouse, fettered, prune,* and *pester* creep into the examination, and suppose further that they all produce acceptable item statistics. Are they therefore acceptable items for a test that purports to measure the vocabulary necessary to the reading of mathematics texts?

Or change the example radically, do words like *ogle,* and *chiffonier,* belong in the *TOEFL* Vocabulary subtest? With the right field of distractors, either of these might produce quite acceptable item statistics – indeed the first member of the pair did appear in the *TOEFL.* Is it a word that foreign students applying to American universities need to know? As a certain Mr Jones pointed out, it did produce very acceptable item statistics. Should it therefore be included in the test? If such items are allowed to stand, then what is to prevent a test from gravitating further and further away from common forms and usages to more and more esoteric terms that produce acceptable item statistics?

To return to the example concerning the comprehension of words in mathematics texts, it is conceivable that a certain population of very capable students will know all the words included in the vocabulary test. Therefore, the items would turn out to be too easy by item statistics criteria. Does this necessarily mean that the items are not sufficiently difficult for the examinees? To claim this is like arguing that a ten foot ceiling cannot be measured with a ten foot tape. It is like arguing that a ten foot tape is the wrong instrument to use for measuring a ten foot ceiling because the ceiling is not high enough (or alternatively because the tape is too short).

Or, to look at a different case, suppose that all of the subjects in a certain population perform very badly on our vocabulary test. The item statistics may be unacceptable by the usual standards. Does it necessarily follow that the test must be made less difficult? Not necessarily, because it is possible that the subjects to be tested do not know any of the words in the mathematics texts – e.g., they may not know the language of the texts. To claim therefore that the test is not valid and/or that it is too difficult is like claiming that a tape measure is not a good measure of length, and/or that it is not short enough, because it cannot be used to measure the distance between adjacent points on a line.

For all of the foregoing reasons, test item statistics alone cannot be used to select or (in the limiting cases just discussed) to reject items. The interpretation of test item statistics must be subordinate to higher considerations. Once a test is available which has certain independent claims to validity, item analysis may be a useful tool for refining that test and for attaining slightly (perhaps significantly) higher levels of validity. Such statistics are by no means, however, final criteria for the selection of items.

D. Referencing tests against non-native performance

The evolution of a test or testing procedure is largely determined by the assumptions on which that test or procedure is based. This is particularly true of institutional or standardized tests because of their longer survival expectancy as compared against classroom tests that are usually used only once and in only one form. Until now, discrete point test philosophy has been the principal basis underlying standardized tests of all sorts.

Since discrete point theories of language testing were generally articulated in relation to the performance of non-native speakers of a given target language, most of the language tests based on such theorizing have been developed in reference to the performance of non-native speakers of the language in question. Generally, this has been justified on the basis of the assumption that native speakers should perform flawlessly, or nearly so, on language tasks that are normally included in such tests. However, native speakers of a language do vary in their ability to perform language related tasks. A child of six years may be just as much a native speaker of English as an adult of age twenty-five, but we do not expect the child to be able to do all of the things with English that we may expect of the adult – hence, there are differences in skill attributable to age or maturation. Neither do we expect an illiterate farmer who has not had the educational opportunities of an urbanite of comparable abilities to be able to read at the same grade level and with equal comprehension – hence, there are differences due to education and experience. Furthermore, recent empirical research, especially Stump (1978) has shown that normal native speakers do vary greatly in proficiency and that this variance may be identical with what has formerly been called IQ and/or achievement.

Thus, we must conclude that there is a real choice: language tests can either be referenced against the performance of native speakers or they may be referenced against the performance of non-native speakers. Put more concretely, the effectiveness of a test item (or a subtest, or an entire battery of tests) may be judged in terms of how it functions with natives or non-natives in producing a range of scores – or in producing meaningful variance between better performers and worse performers.

If a non-native reference population is used, test writers will tend to prepare items that maximize the variability within that population. If native speakers are selected as a reference population, test writers will tend to arrange items so as to maximize the variability within that population. Or more accurately, the test writers will attempt to make the test(s) in either case as sensitive as possible to the variance in language proficiency that is actually characteristic of the population against which the test is referenced.

In general, the attempt to maximize the sensitivity of a test to true variabilities in tested populations is desirable. This is what test validity is about. The rub comes from the fact that in the case of language tests, the ability of non-native speakers to answer certain discrete test items correctly may be unrelated to the kinds of ability that native speakers display when they use language in normal contexts of communication.

There are a number of salient differences between the performance of native speakers of a given language and the performance of non-natives who are at various stages of development in acquiring the same language as a second or foreign language. Among the differences is the fact that native speakers generally make fewer errors, less severe errors, and errors which have no relationship to another language system (i.e., native speakers do not have foreign accents, nor do they tend to make errors that originate in the syntactic, semantic, or pragmatic system of a competing language). Native speakers are typically able to process material in their native language that is richer in organizational complexities than the typical non-native can handle (other things such as age, educational experience, and the like being equal). Non-natives have difficulty in achieving the same level of skill that native speakers typically exhibit in handling jokes, puns, riddles, irony, sarcasm, facetious humor, hyperbole, double entendre, subtle inuendo, and so forth. Highly skilled native speakers are less susceptible to false analogies (e.g., *pronounciation* for *pronunciation, ask it to him* on analogy with forms like *tell it to him*) and are more capable of making the appropriate analogies afforded by the richness of their own linguistic system (e.g., the use of parallel phrasing across sentences, the use of metaphors, similes, contrasts, comparisons, and so on).

Because of the contrasts in native and non-native performance which we have noted above, and many others, the effect of referencing a test against one population rather than the other may be quite significant. Suppose the decision is made to use non-natives as a reference population – as, for instance, the *TOEFL* test writers decided to do in the early 1960s. What will be the effect on the eventual form of the test items? How will they be apt to differ from test items that are referenced against the performance of native speakers?

If the variance in the performance of natives is not completely similar to the variance in the performance of non-natives, it follows that items which work well in relation to the variance in one will not necessarily work well in relation to the variance in the other. In fact, we should predict that some of the items that are easy for native speakers should be difficult for non-natives and vice versa – some of the items that are easy for non-natives should be more difficult for native speakers. This last prediction seems anomalous. Why should non-native speakers be able to perform better on any language test item than native speakers? From the point of view of a sound theory of psycholinguistics, the fact is that native speakers should always outperform non-natives, other things being equal. However, if a given test of language proficiency is referenced against the performance of non-native speakers, and if the variance in their performance is different from the variance in the performance of natives, it follows that some of the items in the test will tend to gravitate toward portions of variance in the reference population that are not characteristic of normal language use by native speakers. Hence, some of the items on a test referenced against non-native performance will be more difficult for natives than for non-natives, and many of the items on such tests may have little or nothing to do with actual ability to communicate in the tested language.

Why is there reason to expect variance in the language skills of non-native speakers to be somewhat skewed as compared against the variance in native performance (due to age, education, and the like)? For one thing, many non-native speakers – perhaps most non-natives who were the reference populations for tests like the *TOEFL*, the *Modern Language Association Tests*, and many other foreign language tests – are exposed to the target language primarily in somewhat artificial classroom contexts. Further, they are exposed principally to materials (syntax based pattern drills, for instance) that are founded on discrete point theories of teaching and analyzing languages. They are encouraged to form generalizations about the nature of the target language that would be very uncharacteristic of native speaker intuitions about how to say and mean things in that same language. No native speaker, for example, would be apt to confuse *going to a dance in a car* with *going to a dance with a girl*, but non-natives may be led into such confusions. Forms like *going to a foreign country with an airplane* and *going to a foreign country in an airplane* are often confused due to classroom experience – see Chapter 6, section C.

The kinds of false analogies, or incorrect generalizations that non-natives are lured into by poorly conceived materials combined with good teaching might be construed as the basis for what could be called a kind of freak grammar – that is, a grammar that is suited only for the rather odd contexts of certain teaching materials and that is quite ill-suited for the natural contexts of communication. If a test then is aimed at the variance in performance that is generated by more or less effective internalization of such a freak grammar, it should not be surprising that some of the items which are sensitive to the knowledge that such a grammar expresses would be impervious to the knowledge that a more normal (i.e., native speaker) grammar specifies. Similarly, tests that are sensitive to the variance in natural grammars might well be insensitive to some of the kinds of discrete point knowledge characteristically taught in language materials.

If the foregoing predictions were correct, interesting contrasts in native and non-native performance on tests such as the *TOEFL* should be experimentally demonstrable. In a study by Angoff and Sharon (1971), a group of native speaking college students at the University of New Mexico performed less well than non-natives on 21 % of the items in the Writing Ability section of that examination. The Writing Ability subtest of the *TOEFL* consists primarily of items aimed at assessing knowledge of discrete aspects of grammar, style, and usage. The fact that some items are harder for natives than for non-natives draws into question the validity of those items as measures of knowledge that native speakers possess. Apparently some of the items are in fact sensitive to things that non-natives are taught but that native speakers do not normally learn. If the test were normed against the performance of native speakers in the first place, this sort of anomaly could not arise. By this logic, native performance is a more valid criterion against which to judge the effectiveness of test items than non-native performance is.

Another sense in which the performance of non-native speakers may be skewed (i.e., characteristic of unusual or freak grammars) is in the relationship between skills, aspects of skills, and components of skills. For instance, the fact that scores on a test of listening comprehension correlate less strongly with written tests of reading comprehension, grammatical knowledge (of the discrete point sort), and so-called writing ability (as assessed by the *TOEFL*, for instance), than the latter tests correlate with each other (see Tables 1 and 2 in section B above) may be a function of experiential bias rather than a consequence of the factorial structure of language proficiency.

Many non-native speakers who are tested on the *TOEFL*, for example, may not have been exposed to models who speak fluent American English. Furthermore, it may well be that experience with such fluent models is essential to the development of listening skill hand in hand with speaking, reading, and writing abilities. Hence, it is possible that the true correlation between skills, aspects, and components of skills is much higher under normal circumstances than has often been assumed. Further, the best approach if this is true would be to make the items and tests maximally sensitive to the meaningful variance present in native speaker performance (e.g., that sort of variance that is due to normal maturation and experience).

In short, referencing tests against the performance of non-native speakers, though statistically an impeccable decision, is hardly defensible from the vantage point of deeper principles of validity and practicality. In a fundamental and indisputable sense, native speaker performance is the criterion against which all language tests must be validated because it is the only observable criterion in terms of which language proficiency can be defined. To choose non-native performance as a criterion whenever native performance can be obtained is like using an imitation (even if it is a good one) when the genuine article is ready to hand. The choice of native speaker performance as the criterion against which to judge the validity of language proficiency tests, and as a basis for refining and developing them, guarantees greater facility in the interpretation of test scores, and more meaningful test sensitivities (i.e., variance).

Another incidental benefit of referencing tests against native performance is the exertion of a healthy pressure on materials writers, teachers, and administrators to teach non-native speakers to do what natives do – i.e., to communicate effectively – instead of teaching them to perform discrete point drills that have little or no relation to real communication. Of course, there is nothing surprising to the successful classroom teacher in any of these observations. Many language teachers have been devoting much effort to making all of their classroom activities as meaningful, natural, and relevant to the normal communicative uses of language as is possible, and that for many years.

KEY POINTS

1. Statistical reasoning is sometimes difficult and can easily be misleading.
2. There is no known rational way of deciding what percentage of items on a discrete point test should be devoted to the assessment of a particular skill, aspect, or component of a skill. Indeed, there cannot be any basis for componential analysis of language tests into phonology, syntax, and vocabulary subtests, because in normal uses of language all components work hand in hand and simultaneously.
3. The difficulty of representatively sampling the universe of possible sentences in a language or discourses in a language is insurmountable.
4. The sentences or discourses in a language which actually occur are but a small portion (an infinitesimally small portion) of the ones which could occur, and they are non-repetitive due to the very nature of human experience.
5. The discrete point method of sampling the universe of possible phrases, or sentences, or discourses, is about as applicable to the fundamental problem of language testing as the method of listing examples of phrases, sentences, or discourses is to the basic problem of characterizing language proficiency – or psychologically real grammatical systems.
6. The solution to the grammarian's problem is to focus attention at a

deeper level – not on the surface forms of utterances, but on the underlying capacity which generates not only a particular utterance, but utterances in general. The solution to the tester's problem is similar – namely to focus attention not on the sampling of phrases, sentences, or discourses *per se*, but rather on the assessment of the efficiency of the developing learner capacity which generates sequences of linguistic elements in the target language (i.e., the efficiency of the learner's psychologically real grammar that interprets and produces sequences of elements in the target language in particular correspondences to extralinguistic contexts).

7. Low correlations have sometimes been interpreted incorrectly as showing that tests with different labels are necessarily measures of what the labels name. There are, however, many other sources of low correlations. In fact, tests that are measures of exactly the same thing may correlate at low levels if one or both are unreliable, too hard or too easy, or simply not valid (e.g., if both are measures of nothing).

8. It cannot reasonably be argued that a low correlation between tests with different labels is due to a lack of validity for one of the tests and is also evidence that the tests are measuring different skills.

9. Observed high correlations between diverse language tests cannot be dismissed as mere indications of reliability – they must indicate that the proficiency factor underlying the diverse performances is validly tapped by both tests. Furthermore, such high correlations are not ambiguous in the way that low correlations are.

10. The expectation of low correlations between tests that require diverse language performances (e.g., listening as opposed to reading) is drawn from discrete point theorizing (especially the componentializing of language skills), but is strongly refuted when diverse language tests (e.g., cloze and dictation, sentence paraphrasing and essay writing, etc.) are observed to correlate at high levels.

11. To assume that high correlations between diverse tests are merely an indication that the tests are reliable, is to treat different tests as if they were the same. If they are not in fact the same, and if they are treated as the same, what justification remains for treating any two tests as different tests (e.g., a phonology test compared against a vocabulary test)? To follow such reasoning to its logical conclusion is to obliterate the possibility of recognizing different skills, aspects, or components of skills.

12. Statistical procedures merit the position of slaves to educational purposes much the way hammers and nails merit the position of tools in relation to building shelves. If the tools are elevated to the status of procedures for defining the shape of the shelves or what sort of books they can hold, they are being misused.

13. Acceptable item statistics do not guarantee valid test items, neither do unacceptable item statistics prove that a given item is not valid.

14. Tests must have independent and higher claims to validity before item statistics *per se* can be meaningfully interpreted.

15. Language tests may be referenced against the performance of native or non-native speakers.

16. Native and non-native performance on language tasks contrast in a number of ways including the frequency and severity of errors, type of errors (interference errors being characteristic only of non-native speech), and the subtlety and complexity of the organizational constraints that can be handled (humor, sarcasm, etc.).

17. Non-native performance is also apt to be skewed by the artificial contexts of much classroom experience.

18. If the foregoing generalizations were correct, we should expect natives to perform more poorly on some of the items aimed at assessing the knowledge that non-natives acquire in artificial settings.

19. Angoff and Sharon (1971) found that natives did more poorly than non-natives on 21 % of the items on the Writing Ability section of the *TOEFL* (a test referenced against the performance of non-natives to start with).

20. If, on the other hand, native performance is set as the main criterion, language tests can easily be made more interpretable and necessarily would achieve higher validity (other things being equal).

21. Another advantage of referencing language tests against the performance of native speakers is to place a healthy pressure on what happens in classrooms – a pressure toward more realistic uses of language for communicative purposes.

DISCUSSION QUESTIONS

1. Estimate the number of distinctive sounds there are in English (i.e., phonemes). Then, estimate the number of syllables that can be constructed from those sounds. Which number is greater? Suppose that there were no limit on the length or structure of a syllable (or say, a sequence of sounds). How many syllables would there be in English? Expressions like *John and Mary and Bill and* ... can be extended indefinitely. Therefore, how many possible sequences are there of the type? What other examples of recursive strings can you exemplify (i.e., strings whose length can always be increased by reapplying a principle already used in the construction of the string)? How many such strings are there in English? In any other language? Discuss the applicability of sampling theory to the problem of finding a representative set of such structures for a language test or subtest.

2. How could you demonstrate by logic that the number of possible sentences in a language must be smaller than the number of possible conversations? Or that the number of possible words must be smaller than the number of possible sentences? Or that in general (i.e., in all cases) the number of possible units of a lower order of structure must be smaller than the number of possible units of a higher order? Further, if it is impossible to sample representatively the phrases of a language, what does this imply with respect to the sentences? The discourses?

3. What unit of discourse is more highly constrained by rules of an expectancy system, a word or a phrase? A phrase or a sentence? A sentence or a dialogue? A chapter or an entire novel? Can you prove by logic that larger units of language are necessarily more highly

constrained by cognitive factors than lower order units? Can you show by logic that some of the constraints on phrases simply do not exist for words, and that some of the constraints on sentences do not exist for phrases and so forth? If so, what implications does your reasoning hold for language tests? What, for instance, is the difference between a vocabulary item without any additional context as opposed to say a vocabulary item in the context of a sentence, or in the context of a paragraph, or in the context of an entire essay or speech? Which sort of test is more apt to mirror faithfully what native speakers do when they use words – perhaps even when they use the word in question in the item?

4. Consider the problem of trying to decide what percentage of items on a language test should be devoted to phonology as opposed to vocabulary or syntax. What proportion of normal speech is represented by a strict attention to phonology as opposed to vocabulary?

5. Consider the meaning of a word in a particular context. For instance, suppose someone runs up to you and tells you that your closest friend has just been in an automobile accident. Is the meaning associated with the friend's name in that context the same as the meaning in a context where you are told that this friend will be leaving for Australia within a month? In what ways are the two uses of the friend's name (a proper noun, in these cases) similar? Different? What if the same person is standing nearby and you call him by name. Or suppose that he is not nearby and you mention his name to some other person. Or perhaps you refer to your friend by name in a letter addressed to himself, or to someone else. In what sense are all of these uses of the name the same, and in what sense are they different? If we extend the discussion then to other classes of words which are pragmatically more complex than proper nouns, or to grammatical forms that are more complex still, in what sense can any utterance be said to be a repetition of any other utterance? Discuss the implications for language teaching and language testing. If utterances and communicative events in general are non-repetitive, what does this imply for language tests? Be careful not to overlook the similarities between utterances on different occasions.

6. What crucial datum must be supplied to prove (or at least support) the notion that a test labeled a 'Vocabulary' test is in fact more a measure of vocabulary knowledge than of grammatical knowledge?

7. Why not interpret low correlations as proof that the intercorrelated tests are valid measures of what their labels imply?

8. Why not generally assume that high correlations are mere indications of test reliability? In what cases is such a claim justified? When is it not justified? What is the crucial factor that must be considered?

9. What evidence is there that syntactic and lexical knowledge may be more closely interrelated than was once thought? What does a learner have to know in order to select the best synonym for a given word when the choices offered and the given word are presented in isolation from any particular context?

10. Suppose that all of the items in a given test or subtest produce acceptable statistics. What additional criteria need to be met in order to prove that the test is a good test of whatever it purports to measure? Or, considered

from a different angle, what criteria might obtain which would make the test unacceptable in spite of the statistics?

11. Suppose the statistics indicate that some of the items on a test are not valid, or possibly that none are acceptable. What additional criteria should be considered before the test is radically revised?

12. Give a cloze test to a group of non-native speakers and to a group of native speakers. Compare the diversity of errors and the general degree of agreement on response choices. For instance, do natives tend to show greater or lesser diversity of responses on items that require words like *to, for, if, and, but, however, not,* and so forth than non-natives? What about blanks that require content words like nouns, verbs, and adjectives? What are the most obvious contrasts between native and non-native responses?

13. Analyze the errors of native speakers on an essay task (or any other pragmatic task) and compare them to those of a group of non-natives.

14. In what ways are tests influenced by classroom procedures and conversely how do tests influence what happens in classrooms? Has the *TOEFL*, for instance, had a substantial influence on the teaching of EFL abroad? Or consider the influence of tests like the *SAT*, or the *American College Tests*, or the *Comprehensive Tests of Basic Skills*, or IQ tests in general.

SUGGESTED READINGS

1. Anne Anastasi, 'Reliability,' Chapter 5 in *Psychological Testing*, 4th ed., New York: Macmillan, 1976, 103–133.

2. Anne Anastasi, 'Validity: Basic Concepts,' Chapter 6 in *Psychological Testing*, 4th ed., New York: Macmillan, 1976, 134–161.

3. Lee J. Cronbach and P. E. Meehl, 'Construct Validity in Psychological Tests.' *Psychological Bulletin* 1955, 52, 281–302.

4. Robert L. Ebel, 'Must All Tests Be Valid?' in G. H. Bracht, Kenneth D. Hopkins, and Julian C. Stanley (eds.) *Perspectives in Educational and Psychological Measurement*. Englewood Cliffs. New Jersey: Prentice-Hall, 1972, 74–87.

5. Calvin R. Petersen and Francis A. Cartier, 'Some Theoretical Problems and Practical Solutions in Proficiency Test Validity,' in R. L. Jones and B. Spolsky (eds.) *Testing Language Proficiency*. Arlington, Va.: Center for Applied Linguistics, 1975, 105–118.

8

Discrete Point Tests

A. What they attempt to do
B. Theoretical problems in isolating
   pieces of a system
C. Examples of discrete point items
D. A proposed reconciliation with
   pragmatic testing theory

Here several of the goals of discrete point theory are considered. The theoretical difficulty of isolating the pieces of a system is considered along with the diagnostic aim of specific discrete point test items. It is concluded that the virtues of specific diagnosis are preserved in pragmatic tests without the theoretical drawbacks and artificiality of discrete item tests. After all, the elements of language only express their separate identities normally in full-fledged natural discourse.

A. What they attempt to do

Discrete point tests attempt to achieve a number of desirable goals. Perhaps the foremost among them is the diagnosis of learner difficulties and weaknesses. The idea is often put forth that if the teacher or other test interpreter is able to learn from the test results exactly what the learner's strengths and weaknesses are, he will be better able to prescribe remedies for problems and will avoid wasting time teaching the learner what is already known.

Discrete point tests attempt to assess the learner's capabilities to handle particular phonological contrasts from the point of view of perception and production. They attempt to assess the learner's capabilities to produce and interpret stress patterns and intonations on longer segments of speech. Special subtests are aimed at knowledge of vocabulary and syntax. Separate tests for speaking, listening, reading, and writing may be devised. Always it is correctly assumed that individuals will differ, some being better in certain skills and components of knowledge while others are better in other skills and components. Moreover, it is assumed that a given individual (or group) may show marked differences in, say, pronunciation skills as opposed to listening comprehension, or in reading and writing skills as opposed to listening and speaking skills.

A second goal implicit in the first is the prescription of teaching remedies for the weaknesses in learner skills as revealed by discrete point tests. If it is possible to determine precisely what is the profile of a given learner with respect to the inventory of phonological contrasts that are possible in a given language, and with respect to each other skill, aspect or component of a skill as measured by some subtest which is part of a battery of discrete point tests, then it should be possible to improve course assignments, specific teaching objectives, and the like. For instance, if tests reveal substantial differences in speaking and listening skills as opposed to reading and writing skills, it might make sense to split students into two streams where in one stream learners are taught reading and writing skills while in the other they are taught listening and speaking skills.

Other breakdowns might involve splitting instructional groups according to productive versus receptive skills, that is, by putting speaking and writing skills into one course curriculum (or a series of course curricula advancing from the beginning level upward), or according to whatever presumed components all learners must acquire. For instance, phonology might be taught in one class where the curriculum would concentrate on the teaching of pronunciation or listening discrimination, or both. Another class (or period of time) might be devoted to enhancing vocabulary knowledge. Another could be devoted to the teaching of grammatical skills (pattern drills and syntax). Or, if one were to be quite consistent with the spirit of discrete point theorizing there should be separate classes for the teaching of vocabulary (and each of the other presumed components of language proficiency) for reading, writing, speaking, and listening. Correspondingly, there would be phonology for speaking, and phonology for listening, sound-symbol instruction for reading, and sound-symbol instruction for writing, and so on.

A third related goal for discrete point diagnostic testing would be to put discrete point teaching on an even firmer theoretical footing. Special materials might be devised to deal with precisely the points of difficulty encountered by learners in just the areas of skill that need attention. There could be pronunciation lessons focussing on specific phonological contrasts; vocabulary exercises focussing on the expansion of receptive or productive repertoires (or speaking or listening repertoires); syntax drills designed to teach certain patterns of structure for speaking, and others designed to teach certain patterns for listening, and others for reading and yet others for writing; and so on until all components and skills were exhausted.

These three goals, that is, diagnosing learner strengths and weaknesses, prescribing curricula aimed at particular skills, and developing specific teaching strategies to help learners overcome particular weaknesses, are among the laudable aims of discrete point testing. It should be noted, however, that the theoretical basis of discrete point teaching is no better than the empirical results of discrete point testing. The presumed components of grammar are no more real for practical purposes than they can be demonstrated to be by the meaningful and systematic results of discrete point tests aimed at differentiating those presumed components of grammar. Further, the ultimate effectiveness of the whole philosophy of discrete point linguistic analysis, teaching, and testing (not necessarily in any particular order) is to be judged in terms of how well the learners who are subjected to it are thereby enabled to communicate information effectively in the target language. In brief, the whole of discrete point methodology stands or falls on the basis of its practical results. The question is whether learners who are exposed to such a method (or family of methods) actually acquire the target language.

The general impotence of such methods can be attested to by almost any student who has studied a foreign language in a classroom situation. Discrete point methods are notoriously ineffective. Their nearly complete failure is demonstrated by the paucity of fluent speakers of any target language who have acquired their fluency exclusively in a classroom situation. Unfortunately, since classroom situations are predominantly characterized by materials and methods that derive more or less directly from discrete point linguistic analysis, the verdict seems inescapable: discrete point methods don't work.

The next obvious question is why. How is it that methods which have so much authority, and just downright rational analytic appeal, fail so widely? Surely it is not for lack of dedication in the profession. It cannot be due to a lack of talented teachers and bright students, nor that the methods have not been given a fair try. Then, why?

B. Theoretical problems in isolating pieces of a system

Discrete point theories are predicated on the notion that it is possible to separate analytically the bits and pieces of language and then to teach and/or test those elements one at a time without reference to the contexts of usage from which those elements were excised. It is an undeniable fact, however, that phonemes do not exist in isolation. A child has to go to school to learn that he knows how to handle phonemic contrasts – to learn that his language has phonemic contrasts. It may be true that he unconsciously makes use of the phonemic contrast between *see* and *say*, for instance, but he must go to school to find out that he has such skills or that his language requires them. Normally, the phonemic contrasts of a language are no more consciously available to the language user than harmonic intervals are to a music lover, or than the peculiar properties of chemical elements are to a gourmet cook. Just as the relations between harmonics are important to a music lover only in the context of a musical piece (and probably not at all in any other context), and just as the properties of chemical elements are of interest to the cook only in terms of the gustatory effects they produce in a roast or dish of stew, phonemic contrasts are principally of interest to the language user only in terms of their effects in communicative exchanges – in discourse.

Discrete point analysis necessarily breaks the elements of language apart and tries to teach them (or test them) separately with little or no attention to the way those elements interact in a larger context of communication. What makes it ineffective as a basis for teaching or testing languages is that crucial properties of language are lost when its elements are separated. The fact is that in any system where the parts interact to produce properties and qualities that do not exist in the parts separately, *the whole is greater than the sum of its parts*. If the parts cannot just be shuffled together in any old order – if they must rather be put together according to certain organizational constraints – those organizational constraints themselves become crucial properties of the system which simply cannot be found in the parts separately.

An example of a discrete point approach to the construction of a test of 'listening grammar' is offered by Clark (1972):

> Basic to the growth of student facility in listening comprehension is the development of the ability to isolate and appropriately interpret important syntactical and morphological aspects of the spoken utterance such as tense, number,

person, subject-object distinctions, declarative and imperative structures, attributions, and so forth. The student's knowledge of lexicon is not at issue here; and for that matter, a direct way of testing the aural identification of grammatical functions would be to use nonsense words incorporating the desired morphological elements or syntactic patterns. Given a sentence such as '*Le muglet a été candré par la friblonne*,' [roughly translated from French, *The muglet has been candered by the friblun*, where *muglet*, *cander*, and *friblun* are nonsense words] the student might be tested on his ability to determine: 1) the time aspect of the utterance (past time), 2) the 'actor' and 'acted upon' ('friblonne' and 'muglet', respectively), and the action involved ('candré') [p. 53f].

First, it is assumed that listening skill is different from speaking skill, or reading skill, or writing skill. Further, that lexical knowledge as related to the listening skill is one thing while lexical knowledge as related to the reading skill is another, and further still that lexical knowledge is different from syntactic (or morphological) knowledge as each pertains to listening skill (or 'listening grammar'). On the basis of such assumptions, Clark proposes a very logical extension: in order to separate the supposedly separate skills for testing it is necessary to eliminate lexical knowledge from consideration by the use of nonsense words like *muglet*, *cander*, and *friblun*. He continues,

If such elements were being tested in the area of reading comprehension, it would be technically feasible to present printed nonsense sentences of this sort upon which the student would operate. In a listening comprehension situation, however, the difficulty of retaining in memory the various strange words involved in the stimulus sentence would pose a listening comprehension problem independent of the student's ability to interpret the grammatical cues themselves. Instead of nonsense words (which would in any event be avoided by some teachers on pedagogical grounds), genuine foreign-language vocabulary is more suitably employed to convey the grammatical elements intended for aural testing [p. 54].

Thus, a logical extension of discrete point testing is offered for reading comprehension tests, but is considered inappropriate for listening tests. Let us suppose that such items as Clark is suggesting were used in reading comprehension tests to separate syntactic knowledge from lexical knowledge. In what ways would they differ from similar sentences that might occur in normal conversation, prose, or discourse? Compare *The muglet has been candered by the friblun* with *The money has been squandered by the freeloader*. Then consider the question whether the relationships that hold between the grammatical subject and its respective predicate in each case is the same. Add a third example. *The pony has been tethered by the barnyard.* It is entirely unclear in the nonsense example whether the relationship between the muglet and the friblun is similar to the relationship between the money and the freeloader or whether it is similar to the relationship between the pony and the barnyard. How could such syntactic relationships and the knowledge of them be tested by such items? One might insist that the difference between squandering something and tethering something is strictly a matter of lexical knowledge, but can one reasonably claim that the relationship between a subject and its predicate is strictly a lexical relationship? To do so would be to erase any vestige of the original distinction between syntax and vocabulary. The fact that the money is in some sense acted upon by the freeloader who does something with it, namely, squanders it, and that the pony is not similarly acted upon by the barnyard is all bound up in the syntax *and* in the lexical items of the respective sentences not to mention their potential pragmatic relations to extralinguistic contexts and their semantic relations to other similar sentences.

It is not even remotely possible to represent such intrinsically rich complexities with nonsense items of the sort Clark is proposing. What is the answer to questions like: *Can fribluns be candered by muglets? Is candering something that can be done to fribluns? Can it be done to muglets?* There are no answers to such questions, but there are clear and obvious answers to questions like: *Can barnyards be tethered by ponies? Is tethering something that can be done to barnyards? Can it be done to ponies? Can freeloaders be squandered by money? Is squandering something that can be done to freeloaders? Can it be done to money?* The fact that the latter questions have answers and that the former have none is proof that normal sentences have properties that are not present in the bones of those same sentences stripped of meaning. In fact, they have syntactic properties that are not present if the lexical items are not there to enrich the syntactic organization of the sentences.

The syntax of utterances seems to be just as intricately involved in the expression of meaning as the lexicon is, and to propose testing syntactic and lexical knowledge separately is like proposing to test the speed of an automobile with the wheels first and the engine later.

It makes little difference to the difficulties that discrete point testing creates if we change the focal point of the argument from the sentence level to the syllable level or to the level of full-fledged discourse.

Syllables have properties in discourse that they do not have in isolation and sentences have properties in discourse that they do not have in isolation and discourse has properties in relation to everyday experience that it does not have when it is isolated from such experience. In fact, discourse cannot really be considered discourse at all if it is not systematically related to experience in ways that can be inferred by speakers of the language. With respect to syllables, consider the stress and length of a given syllable such as /rɛd/ as in *He* read *the entire essay in one sitting* and in the sentence *He* read *it is what he did with it*, (as in response to *What on earth did you say he did with it?*).

Can a learner be said to know a syllable on the basis of a discrete test item that requires him to distinguish it from other similar syllables? If the learner knew all the syllables of the language in that sense would this be the same as knowing the language?

For the word *syllable* in the preceding questions, substitute the words *sound, word, syntactic pattern,* but one must not substitute the words *phrase, sentence,* or *conversation,* because they certainly cannot be adequately tested by discrete item tests. In fact it is extremely doubtful that anything much above the level of the distinctive sounds (or phonemes) of a language can be tested one at a time as discrete point theorizing requires. Furthermore, it is entirely unclear what should be considered an adequate discrete point test of knowledge of the sounds or sound system of a language. Should it include all possible pairs of sounds with similar distributions? Just such a pairing would create a very long test if it only required discrimination decisions about whether a heard pair of sounds was the same or different. Suppose a person could handle all of the items on the test. In what sense could it be said that he therefore knows the sound system of the tested language?

The fact is that the sounds of a language are structured into sequences that make up syllables which are structured in complex ways into words and phrases which are themselves structured into sentences and paragraphs or higher level units of discourse, and the highest level of organization is rather obviously involved in the lowest level of linguistic unit production and interpretation. The very same sequence of sounds in one context will be taken for one syllable and in another context will be taken for another. The very same sound in one context may be interpreted as one word and in another as a completely different word (e.g., 'n, as in *He's 'n ape,* and in *This 'n that 'n the other*). A given sequence of words in one context may be taken to mean exactly the opposite of what they mean in another context, (e.g., *Sure you will*, meaning either *No, you won't* or *Yes, you will*.)

All of the foregoing facts and many others that are not mentioned here make the problems of the discrete item writer not just difficult but insurmountable in principle. There is no way that the normal facts of language can adequately be taught or tested by using test items or teaching materials that start out by destroying the very properties of language that most need to be grasped by learners.

How can a person learn to map utterances pragmatically onto extralinguistic contexts in a language that he does not yet know (that is, to express and interpret information in words about experience) if he is forced to deal with words and utterances that are never related to extralinguistic experience in the required ways? The answer is that no one can learn a language on the basis of the principles advocated by discrete point theorists. This is not because it is very difficult to learn a language by experiencing bits and pieces of it in isolation from pragmatic contexts, it is because it is impossible to learn a language by experiencing bits and pieces of it in that way.

For the same reason, discrete test items that aim to test the knowledge of language independent of the use of that knowledge in normal contexts of communication must also fail. No one has ever proposed that instead of running races at the Olympics contestants should be subjected to a battery of tests including the analysis of individual muscle potentials, general quickness, speed of bending the leg at the knee joint, and the like – rather the speed of runners is tested by having them run. Why should the case be so different for language testing? Instead of asking, how well can a particular language learner handle the bits and pieces of presumed analytical components of grammar, why not ask how well the learner can use all of the components (whatever they are) in dealing with discourse?

In addition to strong logic, there is much empirical evidence to show that discrete point methods of teaching fail and that discrete point methods of testing are inefficient. On the other hand, there are methods of teaching (and learning languages) that work – for instance, methods of teaching where the pragmatic mapping of utterances onto extralinguistic contexts is made obvious to the learner. Similarly, methods of testing that require the examinee to perform such mapping of sequences of elements in the target language are quite efficient.

C. Examples of discrete point items

The purpose of this section is to examine some examples of discrete
point items and to consider the degree to which they produce the
kinds of information they are supposed to produce – namely,
diagnostic information concerning the mastery of specific points of
linguistic structure in a particular target language (and for some
testers, learners from a particular background language). In spite of
the fact that vast numbers of discrete point test categories are possible
in theory, they always get pared down to manageable proportions
even by the theorists who advocated the more proliferate test designs
in the first place.

For example, under the general heading of tests of phonology a
goodly number of subheadings have been proposed including:
subtests of phonemic contrasts, stress and intonation, subclassed still
further into subsubtests of recognition and production not to
mention the distinctions between word stress versus sentence stress
and so on. In actuality, no one has ever devised a test that makes use
of all of the possible distinctions, nor is it likely that anyone ever will
since the possible distinctions can be multiplied *ad infinitum* by
the same methods that produced the commonly employed distinctions. This last fact, however, has empirical consequences in the
demonstrable fact that no two discrete point testers (unless they have
imitated each other) are apt to come up with tests that represent
precisely the same categories (i.e., subtests, subsubtests, and the like).
Therefore, the items used as examples here cannot represent all of the
types of items that have been proposed. They do, however, represent
commonly used types.

First, we will consider tests of phonological skills, then vocabulary,
then grammar (usually limited to a narrow definition of syntax – that
is, having to do with sequential relations between words or phrases,
or clauses).

1. *Phonological items.* Perhaps the most often recommended and
widest used technique for assessing 'recognition' or 'auditory
discrimination' is the minimal pair technique or some variation of it.
Lado (1961), Harris (1969), Clark (1972), Heaton (1975), Allen and
Davies (1977), and Valette (1977) all recommend some variant of the
technique. For instance, Lado suggests reading pairs of words with
minimal sound contrasts while the students write down 'same' or
'different' (abbreviated to 'S' or 'D') for each numbered pair. To test
'speakers of Spanish, Portuguese, Japanese, Finnish' and other

language backgrounds who are learning English as a foreign or second language, Lado proposes items like the following:

1. sleep; slip
2. fist; fist
3. ship; sheep
4. heat; heat
5. jeep; gyp
6. leap; leap
7. rid; read
8. mill; mill
9. neat; knit
10. beat; bit (Lado, 1961, p. 53).

Another item type which is quite similar is offered by both Lado and Harris. The specific examples here are from Lado. The teacher (or examiner) reads the words (with identical stress and intonation) and asks the learner (or examinee) to indicate which words are the same. If all are the same, the examinee is to check A, B, and C, on the answer sheet. If none is the same he is to check O.

1. cat; cat; cot
2. run; sun; run
3. last; last; last
4. beast; best; best
5. pair; fair; chair (Lado, 1961, p. 74).

Now, let us consider briefly the question of what diagnostic information such test items provide. Suppose a certain examinee misses item 2 in the second set of items given above. What can we deduce from this fact? Is it safe to say that he doesn't know /s/ or is it /r/? Or could it be he had a lapse of attention? Could he have misunderstood the item instructions or marked the wrong spot on the answer sheet? What teaching strategies could be recommended to remedy the problem? What does missing item 2 mean with respect to overall comprehension?

Or suppose the learner misses item 4 in the second set given above. Ask the same questions. What about item 5 where three initial consonants are contrasted? The implication of the theory that highly focussed discrete point items are diagnostic by virtue of their being aimed at specific contrasts is not entirely transparent.

What about the adequacy of coverage of possible contrasts? Since it can be shown that the phonetic form of a particular phoneme is quite different when the phoneme occurs initially (after a pause or silence) rather than medially (between other sounds) or finally (before a pause or silence), an adequate recognition test for the sounds of

English should presumably assess contrasts in all three positions. If the test were to assess only minimal contrasts, it should presumably test separately each vowel contrast and each consonantal contrast (ignoring the chameleonic phonemes such as /r/ and /l/ which have properties of vowels and consonants simultaneously, not to mention /w/ and /y/ which do not perfectly fit either category). It would have to be a very long test indeed. If there were only eleven vowels in English, the matrix of possible contrasts would be eleven times eleven, or 121, minus eleven (the diagonal pairs of the matrix which involve contrasts between each element and itself, or the null contrasts), or 110, divided by two (to compensate for the fact that the top half of the matrix is identical to the bottom half). Hence, the number of non-redundant pairs of vowels to be contrasted would be at least 55. If we add in the number of consonants that can occur in initial, medial, and final position, say, about twenty (to be on the conservative side) we must add another 190 items times the three positions, or 1,470, plus 55 equals 1,525 items. Furthermore, this estimate is still low because it does not account for consonant clusters, diphthongs, nor for vocalic elements that can occur in initial or final positions.

Suppose the teacher decides to test only a sampling of the possible contrasts and develops a 100 item test. How will the data be used? Suppose there are twenty students in the class where the test is to be used. There would be 2,000 separate pieces of data to be used by the teacher. Suppose that each student missed a slightly different set of items on the test. How would this diagnostic information be used to develop different teaching strategies for each separate learner? Suppose that the teacher actually had the time and energy to sit down and go through the tests one at a time looking at each separate item for each separate learner. How would the item score for each separate learner be translated into an appropriate teaching strategy in each case? The problem we come back to is how to interpret a particular performance on a particular item on a highly focussed discrete point test. It is something like the problem of trying to determine the composition of sand in a particular sand box in relation to a certain beach by comparing the grains of sand in the box with the grains of sand on the beach – one at a time. Even if one were to set out to improve the degree of correspondence how would one go about it, and what criterion of success could be conceived?

Other types of items proposed to test phonological discrimination are minimal sentence pairs such as:

1. Will he sleep? Will he slip?
2. They beat him. They bit him.
3. Let me see the sheep. Let me see the sheep. (Lado, 1961, p. 53).

Lado suggests that these items are more valid than words in isolation because they are more difficult: 'The student does not know where the difference will occur if it does occur' (p. 53). He argues that such a focussed sort of test item is to be preferred over more fully contextualized discourse samples because the former insures that the student has actually perceived the sound contrast rather than merely guessing the meaning or understanding the context instead of perceiving the 'words containing the difficult sounds' (p. 54). Lado refers to such guessing factors and context clues as 'non-language factors'.

But let's consider the matter a bit further. In what possible context would comprehension of a sentence like, *Will he sleep?* depend on someone's knowledge of the difference between *sleep* and *slip*? Is the knowledge associated with the meaning of the word *sleep* and the sort of states and the extralinguistic situations that the word is likely to be associated with less a matter of language proficiency than knowledge of the contrast between /iy/ and /ɪ/? Is it possible to conceive of a context in which the sentence, *Will he sleep?* would be likely to be taken for the sentence, *Will he slip?* How often do you suppose slipping and sleeping would be expected to occur in the same contexts? Ask the same questions for each of the other example sentences.

Further, consider the difficulty of sentences such as the ones used in 2, where the first sentence sets up a frame that will not fit the second. If the learner assumes that the *they* in *They beat him* has the same referential meaning as the subsequent *they* in *They bit him* the verb *bit* is unlikely. People may beat things or people or animals, but *him* seems likely to refer to a person or an animal. Take either option. Then when you hear, *They bit him* close on the heels of *They beat him*, what will you do with it? Does *they* refer to the same people and does *him* refer to the same person or animal? If so, how odd. People might beat a man or a dog, but would they then be likely to bite him? As a result of the usual expectancies that normal language users will generate in perceiving meaningful sequences of elements in their language, the second sentence is more difficult with the first as its antecedent. Hence, the kind of contextualization proposed by Lado to increase item validity may well decrease item validity. The function of the sort of context that is suggested for discrete point items of phonological contrasts is to mislead the better language learners into false expectancies instead of helping them (on the basis of normally correct expectancies set up by discourse constraints) to make subtle sound distinctions.

The items pictured in Figures 9–13, represent a different sort of attempt to contextualize discrete point contrasts in a listening mode. In Figure 9, for instance, both Lado (1961) and Harris (1969) have in mind testing the contrast between the words *ship* and *sheep*. Figure 10, from Lado (1961), is proposed as a basis for testing the distinction between *watching* and *washing*. Figure 11, also from Lado, is proposed as a basis for testing the contrasts between *pin*, *pen*, and *pan* – of course, we should note that the distinction between the first two (*pin* and *pen*) no longer exists in the widest used varieties of American English. Figure 12 aims to test the initial consonant distinctions between *sheep* and *jeep* and the vowel contrast between *sheep* and *ship*. Figure 13 offers the possibility of testing several contrasts by asking the examinee to point to the *pen*, *pin*, *pan*, *picture*, *pitcher*, *the person who is watching the dishes* (according to Lado, 1961, p. 59) and *the person who is washing the dishes*.

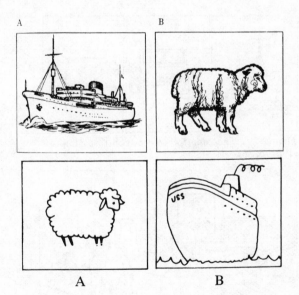

Figure 9. The *ship/sheep* contrast, Lado (1961, p. 57) and Harris (1969, p. 34).

Figure 10. The *watching/washing* contrast, Lado (1961, p. 57).

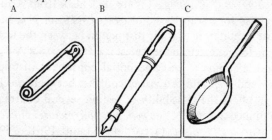

Figure 11. The *pin/pen/pan* contrast, Lado (1961, p. 58).

Figure 12. The *ship/jeep/sheep* contrast, Lado (1961, p. 58).

Figure 13. 'Who is *watching* the dishes?' (Lado, 1961, p. 59).

Pertinent questions for the interpretation of errors on items of the type related to the pictures in Figures 9–11 are similar to the questions posed above in relation to similar items without pictures. If it were difficult to prepare an adequate test to cover the phonemic contrasts of English without pictures it would surely be more difficult to try to do it with pictures. Presumably the motivation for using pictures is to increase the meaningfulness of the test items – to contextualize them, just as in the case of the sentence frames discussed two paragraphs earlier. We saw that the sentence contexts actually are apt to create false expectancies which would distract from the purpose of the items. What about the pictures?

Is it natural to say that the man in Figure 13 is watching the dishes? It would seem more likely that he might watch the woman who is washing the dishes. Or consider the man watching the window in Figure 10. Why is he doing that? Does he expect it to escape? To leave? To hatch? To move? To serve as an exit for a criminal who is about to try to get away from the law? If not for some such reason, it would seem more reasonable to say that the man in the one picture is *staring at a window* and the one in the other picture is *washing a different window*. If the man were watching the same window, how is it that he cannot see the man who is washing it? The context, which is proposed by Lado to make the contrasts meaningful, not only fails to represent normal uses of language accurately, but also fails to help the learner to make the distinctions in question. If the learner does not already know the difference between watching and washing, and if he was not confused before experiencing the test item he may well be afterward. If the learner does not already know the meaning of the words *ship*, *sheep*, *pin*, *pan*, and *pen*, and if the sound contrasts are difficult for the learner to perceive, the pictures in conjunction with meaningless similar sounding forms merely serve as a slightly richer basis for confusion. Why should the learner who is already having difficulty with the distinction say between *pin* and *pen* have any less difficulty after being exposed to the pictures associated with words which he cannot distinguish? If he should become able to perceive the distinction on the basis of some teaching exercise related to the test item types, on what possible basis is it reasonable to expect the learner to associate correctly the (previously unfamiliar) word *sheep*, for instance, with the picture of the sheep and the word *ship* with the picture of the ship?

The very form of the exercise (or test item) has placed the contrasting words in a context where all of the normal bases for the distinction in meaning have been deliberately obliterated. The learner is very much in the position of the child learning to spell to whom it is pointed out that the pairs of spellings *their* and *there*, *pare* and *pair*, *son* and *sun* represent different meanings and not to get confused about which is which. Such a method of presentation is almost certain to confuse the learner concerning which meaning goes with which spelling.

2. *Vocabulary items*. It is usually suggested that knowledge of words should be referenced against the modality of processing – that is, the vocabulary one can comprehend when reading. Hence, it is often claimed that there must be separate vocabulary tests for each of the traditionally recognized four skills, at least for receptive and productive repertoires. Above, especially in Chapter 3, we considered an alternative explanation for the relative availability of words in listening, speaking, reading, and writing. It was in fact suggested that it is probably the difficulty of the task and the load it places on memory and attention that creates the apparent differences in vocabulary across different processing tasks. Ask yourself the question whether you know or do not know a word you may have difficulty in thinking of at a particular juncture. Would you know it better if it were written? Less well if you heard it spoken? If you could understand its use by someone else how does this relate to your ability or inability to use the same word appropriately? It would certainly appear that there is room for the view that a single lexicon may account for word knowledge (whatever it may be) across all four skills. It may be merely the accessibility of words that changes with the nature of the processing task rather than the words actually in the lexicon.

In any event, discrete point theory requires tests of vocabulary and often insists that there must be separate tests for what are presumed to be different skill areas. A frequently-used type of vocabulary test is one aimed specifically at the so-called reading skill. For instance, Davies (1977) suggests the following vocabulary item:

> Our *tom* cat has been missing ever since that day I upset his milk.
>
> A. wild   C. name
> B. drum   D. male

One might want to ask how useful the word *tom* in the sense given is for the students in the test population. Further, is it not possible that a wild tom cat became the pet in question and was then frightened off by the incident? What diagnostic information can one infer (since this is supposed to be a diagnostic type of item) from the fact that a particular student misses the item selecting, say, choice C, *name*? Does it mean that he does not know the meaning of *tom* in the sense given? That he doesn't know the meaning of *name*? That he doesn't know any of the words used? That he doesn't understand the sentence? Or are not all of these possibilities viable as well as many other combinations of them? What is specific about the diagnostic information supposedly provided by such an item?

Another item suggested by Davies (1977) is of a slightly different type:

> *Cherry*: Red Fruit Vegetable Blue Cabbage
> Sweet Stalk Tree Garden

The task of the examinee is to order the words offered in relation to their closeness in meaning to the given word *cherry*. Davies avows, 'it may be argued that these tests are testing intelligence, particularly example 2 [of the two examples given immediately above] which demands a very high degree of literacy, so high that it may be entirely intelligence that is being tested here' (p. 81). There are several untested presuppositions in Davies' remark. One of them is that we know better what we are talking about when we speak of 'intelligence' than when we speak of language skill. (On this topic see the Appendix, especially part D.) Another is that the words in the proffered set of terms printed next to the word *cherry* have some intrinsic order in relation to cherries.

The difficulty with this item, as with all of the items of its type is that the relationship between cherries and cabbage, or gardens, etc., has a great deal more to do with where one finds the cherries at the moment than with something intrinsic to the nature of the word *cherry*. At one moment the fact that a cherry is apt to be found on a cherry tree may be the most important defining property. In a different context the fact that some of the cherries are red and therefore edible may carry more pragmatic cash value than the fact that it is a fruit. In yet another context sweetness may be the property of greatest interest. It is an open empirical question whether items of the sort in question can be scored in a sensible way and whether or not they will produce a high correlation with tests of reading ability.

Lado (1961) was among the first language testers to suggest vocabulary items like the first of Davies' examples given above. For instance, Lado suggested items in the following form:

Integrity
    A. intelligence   C. intrigue
    B. uprightness   D. weakness

Another alternative suggested by Lado (1961, p. 189) was:

The opposite of *strong* is
    A. short   C. weak
    B. poor   D. good

Similar items in fact can be found in books on language testing by Harris (1969), Clark (1972), Valette (1967, 1977), Heaton (1975) and in many other sources. In fact, they date back to the earliest forms of so-called 'intelligence' and also 'reading' tests (see Gunnarsson, 1978, and his references).

Two nagging questions continue to plague the user of discrete point vocabulary tests. The first is whether such tests really measure (reliably and validly) something other than what is measured by tests that go by different names (e.g., grammar, or pronunciation, not to mention reading comprehension or IQ). The second is whether the kind of knowledge displayed in such tests could not better be demonstrated in tasks that more closely resemble normal uses of language.

3. *Grammar items*. Again, there is the problem of deciding what modality is the appropriate one, or how many different modalities must be used in order to test adequately grammatical knowledge (whatever the latter may be construed to be). Sample items follow with sources indicated (all of them were apparently intended for a written mode of presentation):

    i. 'Does John speak French?'
       'I don't know what ...'
       A. does
       B. speaks
       C. he   (Lado, 1961, p. 180).
    ii. When _____?
       A. plan   C. to go
       B. do   D. you   (Harris, 1969, p. 28).
   iii. I want to _____ home now.
       A. gone   C. go
       B. went   D. going   (Davies, 1977, p. 77).

Similar items can be found in Clark (1972), Heaton (1975), and

Valette (1977). Essentially they concentrate on the ordering of words or phrases in a minimal context, or they require selection of the appropriate continuation at some point in the sentence. Usually no larger context is implied or otherwise indicated.

In the Appendix we examine the correlation between a set of tests focussing on the formation of appropriate continuations in a given text, another set requiring the ordering of words, phrases, or clauses in similar texts, and a large battery of other tests. The results suggest that there is no reasonable basis for claiming that the so-called vocabulary (synonym matching) type of test items are measuring anything other than what the so-called grammar items (selecting the appropriate continuation, and ordering elements appropriately) are measuring. Further, these tests do not seem to be doing anything different from what standard dictation and cloze procedure can accomplish. Unless counter evidence can be produced to support the super-structure of discrete point test theory, it would appear to be in grave empirical difficulty.

D. A proposed reconciliation with pragmatic testing theory

From the arguments presented in this chapter and throughout this entire book – especially all of Part Two – one might be inclined to think that the 'elements' of language, whatever they may be, should never be considered at all. Or at least, one might be encouraged to read this recommendation between the lines. However, this would be a mistake. What, after all, does a pragmatic test measure? Does it not in fact measure the examinee's ability to make use of the sounds, syllables, words, phrases, intonations, clauses, etc. in the contexts of normal communication? Or at least in contexts that faithfully mirror normal uses of language? If the latter is so, then pragmatic tests are in fact doing what discrete point testers wanted done all along. Indeed, pragmatic tests are the only reasonable approach to testing language skills if we want to know how well the examinee can use the elements of the language in real-life communication contexts.

What pragmatic language tests accomplish is precisely what discrete point testers were hoping to do. The advantage that pragmatic tests offer to the classroom teacher and to the educator in general is that they are far easier to prepare than are tests of the discrete point type, and they are nearly certain to produce more meaningful and more readily interpretable results. We will see in Chapter 9 that the preparation and production of multiple choice tests is no simple task. We have already seen that the determination of how many items of certain types to include in discrete point tests poses intrinsically insoluble and pointless theoretical and practical mind-bogglers. For instance, how many vocabulary items should be included? Is *tom* as in *tom cat* worth including? What is the relative importance of vowel contrasts as compared against morphological contrasts (e.g., plural, possessive, tense marking, and the like)? Which grammatical points found in linguistic analyses should be found in language tests focussed on 'grammar'? What relative weights should be assigned to the various categories so determined? How much is enough to represent adequately the importance of determiners? Subject raising? Relativization? The list goes on and on and is most certainly not even close to being complete in the best analyses currently available.

The great virtue, the important insight of linguistic analysis, is in demonstrating that language consists of complicated sequences of elements, subsequences of sequences, and so forth. Further, linguistic research has helped us to see that the elements of language are to a degree analyzable. Discrete point theory tried to capitalize on this insight and pushed it to the proverbial wall. It is time now to re-evaluate the results of the application. Recent research with pragmatic language tests suggests that the essential insights of discrete point theories can be more adequately expressed in pragmatic tests than in overly simplistic discrete point approaches which obliterate crucial properties of language in the process of taking it to pieces. The pieces should be observed, studied, taught, and tested (it would seem) in the natural habitat of discourse rather than in isolated sentences pulled out of the clear blue sky.

In Part Three we will consider ways in which the diagnostic information sought by discrete point theory in isolated items aimed at particular rules, words, sound contrasts and the like can much more sensibly be found in learner protocols related to the performance of pragmatic discourse processing tasks – where the focus is on communicating something to somebody rather than merely filling in some blank in some senseless (or nearly senseless) discrete item pulled from some strained test writer's brain. The reconciliation of discrete point theory with pragmatic testing is accomplished quite simply. All we have to do is acknowledge the fact that the elements of language are normally used in discourse for the purposes of communication – by the latter term we include all of the abstract, expressive, and poetic uses of language as well as the wonderful mundane uses so familiar to all normal human beings.

KEY POINTS

1. Discrete point approaches to testing derive from discrete point approaches to teaching. They are mutually supportive.
2. Discrete point tests are supposed to provide diagnostic input to specific teaching remedies for specific weaknesses.
3. Both approaches stand or fall together. If discrete point tests cannot be shown to have substantial validity, discrete point teaching will be necessarily drawn into question.
4. Similarly, the validity of discrete point testing and all of its instructional applications would be drawn into question if it were shown that discrete point teaching does not work.
5. Discrete point teaching is a notorious failure. There is an almost complete scarcity of persons who have actually learned a foreign language on the basis of discrete point methods of teaching.
6. The premise of discrete point theories, that language can be taken to pieces and put back together in the curriculum, is apparently false.
7. Any discourse in any natural language is more than the mere sum of its analyzable parts. Crucial properties of language are lost when it is broken down into discrete phonemic contrasts, words, structures and the like.
8. Nonsense, of the sort recommended by some experts as a basis for discrete point test items, does not exhibit many of the pragmatic properties of normal sensible utterances in discourse contexts.
9. The trouble is that the lowest level units of discourse are involved in the production and interpretation of the highest level units. They cannot, therefore, be separated without obliterating the characteristic relationships between them.
10. No one can learn a language (or teach one) on the basis of the principles advocated by discrete point theorists.
11. Discrete point tests of posited components are often separated into the categories of phonological, lexical, and syntactic tests.
12. It can easily be shown that such tests, even though they are advocated as diagnostic tests, do not provide very specific diagnostic information at all.
13. Typically, discrete items in multiple choice format require highly artificial and unnatural distinctions among linguistic forms.
14. Further, when an attempt to contextualize the items is made, it usually falls flat because the contrast itself is an unlikely one in normal discourse (e.g., *watching the baby* versus *washing the baby*).
15. Discrete items offer a rich basis for confusion to any student who may already be having trouble with whatever distinction is required.
16. Pragmatic tests can be shown to do a better job of what discrete point testers were interested in accomplishing all along.
17. Pragmatic tests assess the learner's ability to use the 'elements' of language (whatever they may be) in the normal contexts of human discourse.
18. Moreover, pragmatic tests are superior diagnostic devices.

DISCUSSION QUESTIONS

1. Obtain a protocol (answer sheet and test booklet) from a discrete point test (sound contrasts, vocabulary, or structure). Analyze each item, trying to determine exactly what it is that the student does not know on each item answered incorrectly.

2. Repeat the procedure suggested in question 1, this time with any protocol from a pragmatic task for the same student. Which procedure yields more finely grained and more informative data concerning what the learner does and does not know? (For recommendations on particular pragmatic tests, see Part Three.)

3. Interpret the errors found in questions 1 and 2 with respect to specific teaching remedies. Which of the two procedures (or possibly, the several techniques) yields the most obvious or most useful extensions to therapeutic interventions? In other words, which test is most easily interpreted with respect to instructional procedures?

4. Is there any information yielded by discrete point testing procedures that is not also available in pragmatic testing procedures? Conversely, is there anything in the pragmatic procedures that is not available in the discrete point approaches? Consider the question of sound contrasts, word usages, structural manipulations, and communicative activities.

5. What is the necessary relationship between being able to make a particular sound contrast in a discrete item test and being able to make use of it in communication? How could we determine if a learner were not making use of a particular sound contrast in conversation? Would the discrete point item help us to make this determination? How? What about word usage? Structural manipulation? Rhythm? Intonation?

6. Take any discrete point test and analyze it for content coverage. How many of the possible sound contrasts does it test? Words? Structural manipulations? Repeat the procedure for a pragmatic task. Which procedure is more comprehensive? Which is apt to be more representative? Reliable? Valid? (See the Appendix on the latter two issues, also Chapter 3 above.)

7. Analyze the two tests from the point of view of naturalness of what they require the learner to do with the language. Consider the implications, presuppositions, entailments, antecedents, and consequences of the statements or utterances used in the pragmatic context. For instance, ask what is implied by a certain form used and what it suggests which may not be stated overtly in the text. Do the same for the discrete point items.

8. Can the content of a pragmatic test be summarized? Developed? Expanded? Interpolated? Extrapolated? What about the content of items in a discrete point test? Which test has the richer forms, meaning wise? Which forms are more explicit in meaning, more determinate? Which are more complex?

SUGGESTED READINGS

1. John L. D. Clark, *Foreign Language Testing: Theory and Practice*. Philadelphia: Center for Curriculum Development, 1972.

2. Robert Lado, *Language Testing*. London: Longman, 1961.

3. Rebecca Valette, *Modern Language Testing*. New York: Harcourt, 1977.

9

Multiple Choice Tests

The main purpose of this chapter is to clarify the nature of multiple choice tests – how they are constructed, the subjective decisions that go into their preparation, the minimal number of steps necessary before they can be reasonably used in classroom contexts, the incredible range and variety of tasks that they may embody, and finally, their general impracticality for day to day classroom application. It will be shown that multiple choice tests can be of the discrete point or integrative type or anywhere on the continuum in between the two extremes. Some of them may further meet the naturalness requirements for pragmatic language tests. Thus, this chapter provides a natural bridge between Part Two (*contra* discrete point testing) and Part Three (an exposition of pragmatic testing techniques).

A. Is there any other way to ask a question?

At a testing conference some years ago, it was reported that the following exchange took place between two of the participants. The speaker (probably John Upshur) was asked by a would-be discussant if multiple choice tests were really all that necessary. To which

Upshur (according to Eugene Brière) quipped, 'Is there any other way to ask a question?' End of discussion. The would-be contender withdrew to the comfort and anonymity of his former sitting position.

When you think about it, conversations are laced with decision points where implicit choices are being constantly made. Questions imply a range of alternatives. Do you want to go get something to eat? Yes or no. How about a hamburger place, or would you rather have something a little more elegant? Which place did you have in mind? Are you speaking to me (or to someone else)? Questions just naturally seem to imply alternatives. Perhaps the alternatives are not usually so well defined as they are in multiple choice tests, and perhaps the implicit alternatives are not usually offered to confuse or trap the person in normal communication though they are explicitly intended for that purpose in multiple choice tests, but in both cases there is the fundamental similarity that alternatives (explicit or implicit) are offered. Pilot asked Jesus, 'What is truth?' Perhaps he meant, 'There is no answer to this question,' but at the same time he appeared to be interested in the possibility of a different view. Even abstract rhetorical questions may implicitly afford alternatives.

It would seem that multiple choice tests have a certain naturalness, albeit a strained one. They do in fact require people to make decisions that are at least similar in the sense defined above to decisions that people are often required to make in normal communication. But this, of course, is not the main argument in favor of their use. Indeed, the strain that multiple choice tests put on the flow of normal communicative interactions is often used as an argument against them.

The favor that multiple choice tests enjoy among professional testers is due to their presumed 'objectivity', and concomitant reliability of scoring. Further, when large numbers of people are to be tested in short periods of time with few proctors and scorers, multiple choice tests are very economical in terms of the effort and expense they require. The questions of validity posed in relation to language tests (or other types of tests) in general are still the same questions, and the validity requirements to be imposed on such tests should be no less stringent for multiple choice versions than for other test formats. It is an empirical question whether in fact multiple choice tests afford *any advantage whatsoever* over other types of tests. It is not the sort of question that can be decided by a vote of the American (or any other) Psychometric Association. It can only be decided by appropriate research (see the Appendix, also see Oller and Perkins, 1978).

The preparation and evaluation of specific multiple choice tests hinges on two things: the nature of the decision required by test items, and the nature of the alternatives offered to the examinee on each item. It is a certainty that no multiple choice test can be any better than the items that constitute it, nor can it be any more valid than the choices it offers examinees at requisite decision points. From this it follows that the multiple choice format can only be advantageous in terms of scoring and administrative convenience if we have a good multiple choice test in the first place.

It will be demonstrated here that the preparation of sound multiple choice tests is sufficiently challenging and technically difficult to make them impracticable for most classroom needs. This will be accomplished by showing some of the pitfalls that commonly trap even the experts. The formidable technical problem of item analysis done by hand will be shown to all but completely eliminate multiple choice formats from consideration. Further, it will be argued that the multiple choice format is intrinsically inimical to the interests of instruction. What multiple choice formats gain in reliability and ease of administration, in other words, is more than used up in detrimental instructional effects and difficulty of preparation.

B. Discrete point and integrative multiple choice tests

In Chapter 8 above, we already examined a number of multiple choice items of a discrete point type. There were items aimed at phonological contrasts, vocabulary, and 'grammar' (in the rather narrow sense of surface morphology and syntax). There are, however, many item types that can easily be put into a multiple choice format, or which are usually found in such a format but which are not discrete point items. For instance, what discrete elements of language are tested in a paraphrase recognition task such as the following?

> Match the given sentence with the alternative that most nearly says the same thing:
>> Before the turn of the century, the tallest buildings were rarely more than three storeys above ground (adapted from Heaton, 1975, p. 186).
>>> A. After the turn of the century, buildings had more storeys above ground.

B. Buildings rarely had as many as four storeys above ground up until the turn of the century.

C. At about the turn of the century, buildings became more numerous and considerably taller than ever before.

D. Buildings used to have more storeys above ground than they did at about the turn of the century.

It would be hard to say precisely what point of grammar, vocabulary, etc. is being tested in the item just exemplified. Could a test composed of items of this type be called a test of reading comprehension? How about paraphrase recognition? Language proficiency in general? What if it were presented in a spoken format?

As we have noted before, the problem of what to say a test is a test of is principally an issue of test validity. It is an empirical question. What we can safely say on the basis of the item format alone is what the test requires the learner to do – or at least what it appears to require. Perhaps, therefore, it is best to call the item type a 'sentence paraphrase recognition' task. Thus, by naming the task rather than positing some abstract construct we avoid *a priori* validity commitments – that is, we suspend judgement on the validity questions pending empirical investigation. Nevertheless, whatever we choose to call the specific item type, it is clearly more at the integrative side of the continuum than at the discrete point end.

There are many other types of multiple choice items that are integrative in nature. Consider the problem of selecting answers to questions based on a text. Such questions may focus on some detail of information given in the text, the general topic of the text, something implied by the text but not stated, the meaning of a particular word, phrase, or clause in the text, and so forth. For example, read the following text and then select the best answers to the questions that follow:

Black Students in Urban Canada is an attempt to provide information to urban Canadians who engage in educational transactions with members of this ethnicity. Although the OISE conference did not attract educators from either west of Manitoba or from Newfoundland, it is felt that there is an adequate minimum of relevance such that concerned urban teachers from all parts of this nation may uncover something of profit (D'Oyley and Silverman, 1976, p. vi).

(1) This paragraph is probably
    A. an introduction to a Canadian novel.
    B. a recipe for transactional analysis.

      C. a preface to a conference report.

      D. an epilog to ethnic studies.

(2) The word *ethnicity* as used in the paragraph has to do with

      A. sex.

      B. skin color.

      C. birthplace.

      D. all of the above.

(3) The message of the paragraph is addressed to

      A. all educators.

      B. urban educators.

      C. urban Canadians involved in education.

      D. members of the ethnic group referred to.

(4) The abbreviation OISE probably refers to the

      A. city in question.

      B. relevant province or state.

      C. journal that was published.

      D. sponsoring organization.

(5) It is implied that the ethnic group in question lives in predominantly

      A. rural settings.

      B. suburban areas.

      C. urban settings.

      D. ghetto slums.

(6) Persons attending the meetings referred to were apparently

      A. law enforcement officers.

      B. black students.

      C. educators.

      D. all of the above.

The preceding item type is usually found in what is called a 'reading comprehension' test. Another way of referring to it is to say that it is a task that requires reading and answering questions – leaving open the question of what the test is a test of. It may, for instance, be a fairly good test of overall language proficiency. Or, it may be about as good a test of listening comprehension as of reading comprehension. These possibilities cannot be ruled out in advance on the basis of the superficial appearance of the test. Furthermore, it is certainly possible to change the nature of the task and make it into a listening and question answering problem. In fact, the only logical limits on the types of tests that might be constructed in similar formats are whatever limitations exist on the creative imaginations of the test writer. They could be converted, for instance, to an open-ended

format requiring spoken responses to spoken questions over a heard
text.

Not only is it possible to find many alternate varieties of multiple
choice tests that are clearly integrative in nature, but it is quite
possible to take just about any pragmatic testing technique and
convert it to some kind of multiple choice format more or less
resembling the original pragmatic technique. For example, consider a
cloze test over the preceding text – or, say, the continuation of it. We
might delete every fifth word and replace it with a field of alternatives
as follows:

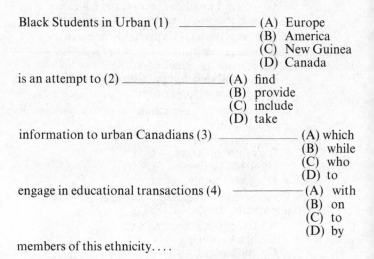

Black Students in Urban (1) _____ (A) Europe
(B) America
(C) New Guinea
(D) Canada

is an attempt to (2) _____ (A) find
(B) provide
(C) include
(D) take

information to urban Canadians (3) _____ (A) which
(B) while
(C) who
(D) to

engage in educational transactions (4) _____(A) with
(B) on
(C) to
(D) by

members of this ethnicity. . . .

Bear in mind the fact that either a printed format (see Jonz, 1974,
Porter, 1976, Hinofotis and Snow, 1977) or a spoken format would be
possible (Scholz, Hendricks, Spurling, Johnson, and Vandenburg, in
press). For instance, in a spoken format the text might be recorded as
'Black students in Urban blank one is an attempt to blank two
information to urban Canadians blank three engage in education
transactions blank four members of this ethnicity. . . .' The examinee
might see only the alternatives for filling in the numbered blanks, e.g.,

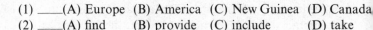

(1) ____(A) Europe (B) America (C) New Guinea (D) Canada
(2) ____(A) find   (B) provide   (C) include   (D) take

etcetera. To make the task a bit easier in the auditory mode, the
recorded text might be repeated one or more times. For some

exploratory work with such a procedure in an auditory mode see the Appendix, also see Scholz, *et al* (in press). For other suggestions for making the task simpler, see Chapters 10, 11, and 12 on factors that affect the difficulty of discourse processing tasks.

Once we have broached the possibility of using discourse as a basis for constructing multiple choice tasks, many variations on test item types can easily be conceived. For instance, instead of asking the examinee to select the appropriate continuation at a particular point in a text, he may be asked to select the best synonym or paraphrase for an indicated portion of text from a field of alternatives. Instead of focussing exclusively on words, it would be possible to use phrases or clauses or larger units of discourse as the basis for items. Instead of a synonym matching or paraphrase matching task, the examinee might be required to put words, phrases, or clauses in an appropriate order within a given context of discourse. Results from tasks of all these types are discussed in greater detail in the Appendix (also see the references given there). The important point is that any such tests are merely illustrative of a bare smattering of the possible types.

The question concerning which of the possible procedures are best is a matter for empirical consideration. Present findings seem to indicate that the most promising multiple choice tasks are those that require the processing of fairly extended segments of discourse – say, 150 words of text or more. However, a note of caution should be sounded. The construction of multiple choice tests is generally a considerably more complicated matter than the mere selection of an appropriate segment of discourse. Although pragmatic tasks can with some premeditation and creativity be converted into a variety of multiple choice tests, the latter are scarcely as easy to use as the original pragmatic tasks themselves (see Part Three). In the next section we will consider some of the technical problems in writing items (especially alternatives).

C. About writing items

There are only a handful of principles that need to be grasped in writing good items, but there are a great many ways to violate any or all of them. The first problem in writing items is to decide what sort of items to write. The second problem is to write the items with suitable distractors in each set of alternatives. In both steps there are many pitfalls. Professionally prepared tests are usually based on explicit instructions concerning the format for items in each section of the test. Not only will the superficial lay-out of the items be described and exemplified, but usually the kinds of fair content for questions will also be more or less circumscribed, and the intended test population will be described so as to inform item writers concerning the appropriate range of difficulty of items to be included in each part of the test.[1]

Unfortunately, the questions of test validity are generally consigned to the statistician's department. They are rarely raised at the point of item writing. However, as a rule of thumb, all of the normal criteria for evaluating the validity of test content should be applied from the earliest stages of test construction. The first principle, therefore, would be to ask if the material to be included in items in the test is somehow related to the skill, construct, or curriculum that the test is supposed to assess or measure. Sad to say many of the items actually included in locally prepared, teacher-made or multiple choice standardized tests are not always subjected to this primary evaluation. If a test fails this first evaluation, no matter how elegantly its items are constructed, it cannot be any better than any other ill-conceived test of whatever it is supposed to measure.

Assuming that the primary validity question has been properly considered, the next problem is to write the best possible items of the defined type(s). In some cases, it will not be necessary to write items from scratch, but rather to select appropriate materials and merely edit them or record them in some appropriate fashion. Let us assume that all test items are to be based on samples of realistic discourse. Arguments for this choice are given throughout the various chapters of this book. Other choices could be made – for instance, sentences in isolation could be used – but this would not change the principles directly related to the construction of items. It would merely change their fleshed-out realization in particular instances.

During the writing stage, each item must be evaluated for appropriateness of content. Does it ask for information that people would normally be expected to pay attention to in the discourse

---

[1] John Bormuth (1970) has developed an extensive argument for deriving multiple-choice items from curricula via explicit and rigorous linguistic transformations. The items in his methodology are directly tied to sentences uttered or written in the curriculum. The argument is provocative, However, it presupposes that the surface forms of the sentences in the curriculum are all that could be tested. Normal discourse processing, on the other hand, goes *far beyond* what is stated overtly in surface forms (see Frederiksen's recent articles and his references). Therefore, Bormuth's interesting proposal will not be considered further here. I am indebted to Ron Mackay (of Concordia University in Montreal) for calling Bormuth's argument to my attention.

context in question? Is the decision that is required one that really seems to exercise the skill that the test as a whole is aimed at measuring? Is the correct choice really the best choice for someone who is good at the skill being measured (in this case, a good language user)? Are the distractors actually attractive traps for someone who is not so good at the skill in question? Are they well balanced in the sense of going together as a set? Do they avoid the inclusion of blatant (but extraneous) clues to the correct choice? In sum, is the item a well-conceived basis for a choice between clear alternatives?

In addition to insisting that the items of interest be anchored to realistic discourse contexts, on the basis of research findings presented elsewhere in this text (especially the Appendix), we will disregard many of the discrete point arguments of purity in item types. In other words, we will abandon the notion that vocabulary knowledge must be assessed as if it were independent of grammatical skill, or that reading items should not include a writing aspect, etc. All of the available empirical research seems to indicate that such distinctions are analytical niceties that have no fundamental factual counterparts in the variance actually produced by tests that are constructed on the basis of such distinctions. Therefore, the distinctions that we will make are principally in the types of tasks required of the learner – not in the hypothetical skills or constructs to be tested. For all of these reasons, we should also be clear about the fact that the construction of a multiple choice test is not apt to produce a test that is more valid than a test of a similar sort in some other format. The point in building a multiple choice test is to attain greater economy of administration and scoring. It is purely a question of practicality and has little or nothing to do with reliability and validity in the broader sense of these terms.

Most any discourse context can be dealt with in just about any processing mode. For instance, consider a breakfast conversation. Suppose that it involves what the various members of a family are going to do that day, in addition to the normal 'pass the salt and pepper' kind of conversation at breakfast. Nine-year-old Sarah spills the orange juice while Mr Kowolsky is scalding his mouth on boiling coffee and remonstrating that Mrs Kowolsky can't seem to cook a thing without getting it too hot to eat. Thirteen-year-old Samuel wants to know if he can have a dollar (make that five dollars) so he can see that latest James Bond movie, and his mother insists that he not forget the piano lesson at four, and to feed the cat ... It is possible to talk about such a context; to listen to talk about it; to read about it; to write about it. The same is true for almost any context conceivable where normal people interact through the medium of language.

It might be reasonable, of course, to start with a written text. Stories, narratives, expository samples of writing, in fact, just about any text may provide a suitable basis for language text material. It is possible to talk about a story, listen to a story, answer questions about a story, read a story, retell a story, write a story, and so forth.

What kinds of limits should be set on the selection of materials? Obviously, one would *not* want to select test material that would distract the test taker from the main job of selecting the appropriate choices of the multiple choice items presented. Therefore, supercharged topics about such things as rape, suicide, murder, and heinous crimes should probably be avoided along with esoteric topics of limited interest such as highly technical crafts, hobbies, games, and the like (except, of course, in the very special case where the esoteric or super-charged topic is somehow central to the instructional goals to be assessed). Materials that state or imply moral, cultural, or racial judgements likely to offend test takers should also probably be avoided unless there is some specific reason for including them.

Let us suppose that the task decided on is a reading and question answering type. Further, for whatever reasons, let us suppose that the following text is selected:

> Oliver Twist was born in a workhouse, and for a long time after his birth there was considerable doubt whether the child would live. He lay breathless for some time, rather unequally balanced between this world and the next. After a few struggles, however, he breathed, sneezed and uttered a loud cry.
>
> The pale face of a young woman lying on the bed was raised weakly from the pillow and in a faint voice she said, 'Let me see the child and die.'
>
> 'Oh, you must not talk about dying yet,' said the doctor, as he rose from where he was sitting near the fire and advanced towards the bed.
>
> 'God bless her, no!' added the poor old pauper who was acting as nurse.
>
> The doctor placed the child in its mother's arms; she pressed her cold white lips on its forehead; passed her hands over her face; gazed wildly around, fell back – and died.
>
> 'It's all over,' said the doctor at last.
>
> 'Ah, poor dear, so it is!' said the old nurse.
>
> 'She was a good-looking girl, too,' added the doctor: 'where did she come from?'

'She was brought here last night,' replied the old woman. 'She was found lying in the street. She had walked some distance, for her shoes were worn to pieces; but nobody knows where she came from, or where she was going, nobody knows.'

'The old story,' said the doctor, shaking his head, as he leaned over the body, and raised the left hand; 'no wedding-ring, I see. Ah! Good night!' (Dickens, 1962, p. 1)

In framing questions concerning such a text (or any other) the first thing to be considered is what the text says. What is it about? If it is a story, like this one, who is referred to in it? What are the important events? What is the connection between them? What is the relationship between the people, events, and states of affairs referred to? In other words, how do the surface forms in the text pragmatically map onto states of affairs (or facts, imaginings, etc.) which the text is about? The author of the text had to consider these questions (at least implicitly) the same as the reader, or anyone who would retell the story or discuss it. Linguistically speaking, this is the problem of pragmatic mapping.

Thus, a possible place to begin in constructing test items would be with the topic. What is the text about? There are many ways of posing the question clearly, but putting it into a multiple choice format is a bit more complicated than merely asking the question. Here we are concerned with better and worse ways of forming such multiple choice questions. How should the question be put, and what alternatives should be offered as possible answers?

Consider some of the ways that the question can be badly put:

(1) The passage is about _____.

    A. a doctor

    B. a nurse

    C. an unmarried woman

    D. a child

The trouble here is that the passage is in fact about all of the foregoing, but is centered on none of them. If any were to be selected it would probably have to be the child, because we understand from the first paragraph of the text that Oliver Twist is the child who is being born. Further, the attention of every person in the story is primarily directed to the birth of this child. Even the mother is concerned merely to look at him before she dies.

(2) A good title for this passage might be _____.

    A. 'Too young to die.'

    B. 'A cross too heavy.'

    C. 'A child is born.'

    D. 'God bless her, no!'

Perhaps the author has C in mind, but the basis for that choice is a bit obscure. After all, it isn't just any child, and neither is it some child of great enough moment to justify the generic sense of 'a child'.

    Now, consider a question that gets to the point:

(3) The central fact talked about in the story is _____.

    A. the birth of Oliver Twist

    B. the death of an unwed mother

    C. an experience of an old doctor

    D. an old and common story

Hence, *the best choice must fit the facts well.* It is essential that the correct answer be correct, and further that it be better than the other alternatives offered.

    Another common problem in writing items arises when the writer selects facts that are in doubt on the basis of the given information and forces a choice between two or more possible alternatives.

(4) When the author says that 'for a long time after his birth there was considerable doubt whether the child would live' he probably means that _____.

    A. the child was sickly for months or possibly years

    B. Oliver Twist did not immediately start breathing at birth

    C. the infant was born with a respiratory disease

    D. the child lay still without breathing for minutes after birth

The trouble here is that the text does not give a sufficient basis for selecting between the alternatives. While it is possible that only B is correct, it is not impossible (on the basis of given information) that one of the other three choices is also correct. Therefore, the choice that is intended by the author to be the correct one (say, B) is not a very reasonable alternative. In fact, none of the alternatives is really a good choice in view of the indeterminacy of the facts. Hence, the facts *ought to be clear on the basis of the text, or they should not be used as content for test items.*

    Finally, once the factual content of the item is clear and after the correct alternative has been decided on, there is the matter of constructing suitable distractors, or incorrect alternatives. The distractors should not give away the correct choice or call undue attention to it. They should be similar in form and content to the correct choice and they should have a certain attractiveness about them.

For instance, consider the following rewrite of the alternatives offered for (3):

A. the birth of Oliver Twist
B. the death of the young unwed mother of Oliver Twist
C. the experience of the old doctor who delivered Oliver Twist
D. a common story about birth and death among unwed mothers

There are several problems here. First, Oliver Twist is mentioned in all but one of the alternatives thus drawing attention to him and giving a clue as to the correct choice. Second, the birth of Twist is mentioned or implied in all four alternatives giving a second unmistakable clue as to the correct choice. Third, the choices are not well balanced – they become increasingly specific (pragmatically) in choices B, and C, and then jump to a vague generality in choice D. Fourth, the correct choice, A, is the most plausible of the four even if one has not read the text.

There are several common ways item writers often draw attention to the correct choice in a field of alternatives without, of course, intending to. For one, as we have already seen, the item writer may be tempted to include the same information in several forms among the various alternatives. This highlights that information. Another way of highlighting is to include the opposite of the correct response. For instance, as alternatives to the question about a possible title for the text, consider the following:

A. 'The death of Oliver Twist.'
B. 'The birth of Oliver Twist.'
C. 'The same old story.'
D. 'God bless her, no!'

The inclusion of choice A calls attention to choice B and tends to eliminate the other alternatives immediately.

The tendency to include the opposite of the correct alternative is very common, especially when the focus is on a word or phrase meaning:

(5) In the opening paragraph, the phrase 'unequally balanced between this world and the next' refers to the fact that Oliver appears to be _____ .

A. more alive than dead
B. more dead than alive
C. about to lose his balance
D. in an unpleasant mental state

To the test-wise examinee (or any moderately clever person), A and B are apt to seem more attractive than C or D even if the examinee has not read the original text about Twist.

Yet another way of cluing the test taker as to the appropriate choice is to make it the longest and most complexly worded alternative, or the shortest and most succinct. We saw an example of the latter above with reference to item (3) where the correct choice was obviously the shortest and the clearest one of the bunch. Here is another case. The only difference is that now the longest alternative is the correct choice:

(6) The doctor probably tells the young mother not to talk about dying because _____.

    A. he doesn't think she will die

    B. she is not at all ill

    C. he wants to encourage her and hopes that she will not die

    D. she is delirious

The tendency is to include more information in the correct alternative in order to make absolutely certain that it is in fact the best choice. Another motive is to make the distractors short to save time in writing the items.

Another common problem in writing distractors is to include alternatives that are ridiculous and often (perhaps only to the test writer) hilarious. After writing forty or fifty alternatives there is a certain tendency for the test writer to become a little giddy. It is difficult to think of distractors without occasionally coming up with a real humdinger. After one or two, the stage is set for a hilarious test, but hilarity is not the point of the testing and it may be deleterious to the validity of the test *qua* test. For instance, consider the following item where the task is to select the best paraphrase for the given sentence:

(7) The pale face of a young woman lying on the bed was raised weakly from the pillow and she spoke in a faint voice.

    A. A fainting face on a pillow rose up from the bed and spoke softly to the young woman.

    B. The pale face and the woman were lying faintly on the bed when she spoke.

    C. Weakly from the pillow the pale face rose up and faintly spoke to the woman.

    D. The woman who was very pale and weak lifted herself from the pillow and spoke.

Alternative B is distracting in more ways than one. Choice C continues the metaphor created, and neither is apt to be a very good distractor except in a hilarious diversionary sense. Without reading the given sentence or the story, choice D is the only sane alternative.

In sum, the common foul-ups in multiple choice item writing include the following:

(1) Selecting inappropriate content for the item.

(2) Failure to include the correct answer in the field of alternatives.

(3) Including two or more plausible choices among the alternatives.

(4) Asking the test taker to guess facts that are not stated or implied.

(5) Leaving unintentional clues about the correct choice by making it either the longest or shortest, or by including its opposite, or by repeatedly referring to the information in the correct choice in other choices, or by including ridiculous alternatives.

(6) Writing distractors that don't fit together with the correct choice – i.e., that are too general or too specific, too abstract or too concrete, too simple or too complex.

These are only a few of the more common problems. Without doubt there are many other pitfalls to be avoided.

D. Item analysis and its interpretation

Sensible item analysis involves the careful subjective interpretation of some objective facts about the way examinees perform on multiple choice items. Insofar as all tests involve determinate and quantifiable choices (i.e., correct and incorrect responses, or subjectively determined better and worse responses), item analysis at base is a very general procedure. However, we will consider it here specifically with reference to multiple choice items and the very conveniently quantifiable data that they yield. In particular, we will discuss the statistics that usually go by the names of *item facility* and *item discrimination*. Finally, we will discuss the interpretation of *response frequency distributions*.

We will be concerned with the meaning of the statistics, the assumptions on which they depend in order to be useful, and their computation. It will be shown that item analysis is generally so tedious to perform by hand as to render it largely impracticable for classroom use. Nevertheless, it will be argued that item analysis is an important and necessary step in the preparation of good multiple choice tests. Because of this latter fact, it is suggested that every classroom teacher and educator who uses multiple choice test data should know something of item analysis – how it is done, and what it means.

(i) *Item facility*. One of the basic item statistics is *item facility* (IF). It has to do with how easy (or difficult) an item is from the viewpoint of the group of students or examinees taking the test of which that item is a part. The reason for concern with IF is very simple – a test item that is too easy (say, an item that every student answers correctly) or a test item that is too difficult (one, say, that every student answers incorrectly) can tell us nothing about the differences in ability within the test population. There may be occasions when a teacher in a classroom situation wants all of the students to answer an item (or all the items on a test) perfectly. Indeed, such a goal seems tantamount to the very idea of what teaching is about. Nevertheless, in school-wide exams, or in tests that are intended to reveal differences among the students who are better and worse performers on whatever is being tested, there is nothing gained by including test items that every student answers correctly or that every student answers incorrectly.

The computation of IF is like the computation of a mean score for a test only the test in this case is a single item. Thus, an IF value can be computed for each item on any test. It is in each case like a miniature test score. The only difference between an IF value and a part score or total score on a test is that the IF value is based on exactly one item. It is the mean score of all the examinees tested on that particular item. Usually it is expressed as a percentage or as a decimal indicating the number of students who answered the item correctly:

IF = the number of students who answered the item correctly divided by the total number of students

This formula will produce a decimal value for IF. To convert it to a percentage, we multiply the result by 100. Thus, IF is the proportion of students who answer the item in question correctly.

Some authors use the term 'item difficulty', but this is not what the proportion of students answering correctly really expresses. The IF increases as the item gets easier and decreases as it gets more difficult. Hence, it really is an index of *facility*. To convert it to a *difficulty* measure we would have to subtract the IF from the maximum possible score on the item – i.e., 1.00 if we are thinking in terms of decimal values, and 100 % if we are thinking in terms of percentage values. The proportion answering incorrectly should be referred to as the *item difficulty*. We will not use the latter notion, however, because it is completely redundant once we have the IF value.

By pure logic (or mathematics, if you prefer), we can see that the IF of any item has to fall between zero and one or between 0% and 100%. It is not possible for more than 100% of the examinees to answer an item correctly, nor for less than 0% to fail to answer the item correctly. The worst any group can do on an item is for all of them to answer it incorrectly (IF = .00 = 0%). The best they can do is for all of them to answer it correctly (IF = 1.00 = 100%). Thus, IF necessarily falls somewhere between 0 and 1. We may say that IF ranges from 0 to 1.

For reasons given above, however, an item that everyone answers correctly or incorrectly tells us nothing about the variance among examinees on whatever the test measures. Therefore, items falling somewhere between about .15 and .85 are usually preferred. There is nothing absolute about these values, but professional testers always set some such limits and throw away or rewrite items that are judged to be too easy or too difficult. The point of the test items is almost always to yield as much variance among examinees as possible. Items that are too easy or too difficult yield very little variance – in fact, the amount of meaningful variance must decrease as the item approaches an IF of 100% or 0%. The most desirable IF values, therefore, are those falling toward the middle of the range of possible values. IF values falling in the middle of the range guarantee some variance in scores among the examinees.

However, merely obtaining variance is not enough. Meaningful variance is required. That is, the variance must be reliable and it must be valid. It must faithfully reflect variability among tested subjects on the skill or knowledge that the test purportedly measures. This is where another statistic is required for item evaluation.

(ii) *Item discrimination.* The fundamental issue in all testing and measurement is to *discriminate* between larger and smaller quantities of something, better and worse performances, success and failure, more or less of whatever one wants to test or measure. Even when the objective is to demonstrate mastery, as in a classroom setting where it may be expected that everyone will succeed, the test cannot be a measure of mastery at all unless it provides at least an opportunity for failure or for the demonstration of something less than mastery. Or to take another illustration, consider the case of engineers who 'test' the strength of a railroad trestle by running a loaded freight train over it. They don't expect the bridge to collapse. Nonetheless, the test discriminates between the criterion of success (the bridge holding up) and failure (the bridge collapsing). Thus, any valid test must discriminate between degrees of whatever it is supposed to measure. Even if only two degrees are distinguished – as in the case of mastery versus something less (Valette, 1977) – discrimination between those two degrees is still the principal issue.

In school testing where multiple choice tests are employed, it is necessary to raise the question whether the variance produced by a test item actually differentiates the better and worse performers, or the more proficient examinees as against the less proficient ones. What is required is an index of the validity of each item in relation to some measure of whatever the item is supposed to be a measure. Clearly if different test items are of the same type and are supposed to measure the same thing, they should produce similar variances (see Chapter 3 above for the definition of variance, and correlation). This is the same as saying that the items should be correlated. That is, the people who tend to answer one of the items correctly should also tend to answer the other correctly and the people who tend to answer the one item incorrectly should also tend to answer the other incorrectly. If this were so for all of the items of a given type we would take the degree of their correlation as an index of their *reliability* – or in some terminologies their *internal consistency*. But what if the items could be shown to correlate with some other criterion? What if it could be shown that a particular item, for instance, or a batch of items were correlated with some other measure of whatever the items purport to measure? In the latter case, the correlation would have to be taken as an index of *validity* – not mere internal consistency of the items.

What criterion is always available? Suppose we think of a test aimed at assessing reading comprehension. Let's say the test consists of 100 items. What criterion could be used as an index of reading comprehension against which the validity of each individual item could be assessed? In effect, for each subject who takes the test there will be a score on the entire test and a score on each item of the test. Presumably, if the subject does not answer certain items they will be scored as incorrect. Now, which would be expected to be a better measure of the subject's true reading comprehension ability, the total score or a particular item score? Obviously, since the total score is a composite of 100 items, it should be assumed to be a better (more reliable and more valid) index of reading comprehension than any single item on the test. Hence, since the total score is easily obtainable and always available on any multiple choice test, it is the usual criterion for assessing individual item reliabilities. Other criteria could be used, however. For instance, the items on one test could easily be assessed against the scores on some different test or tests purporting to measure the same thing. In the latter instance, the other test or tests would be used as bases for evaluating the validity of the items on the first test.

In brief, the question of whether an individual test item discriminates between examinees on some dimension of interest is a matter of both reliability and validity. We cannot read an index of item discrimination as anything more than an index of reliability, however, unless the criterion against which the item is correlated has some independent claims to validity. In the latter case, the index of item discrimination becomes an index of validity over and above the mere question of reliability.

The usual criterion selected for determining item discrimination is the total test score. It is simply assumed that the entire test is apt to be a better measure of whatever the test purports to measure than any single test item by itself. This assumption is only as good as the validity of the total test score. If the test as a whole does not measure what it purports to measure, then high item discrimination values merely indicate that the test is reliably measuring something – who knows what. If the test on the whole is a valid measure of reading comprehension on the other hand, the strength of each item discrimination value may be taken as a measure of the validity of that item. Or, to put the matter more precisely, the *degree* of validity of the test as a whole establishes the limitations on the interpretation of item discrimination values. As far as human beings are concerned, a test is never perfectly valid, only more or less valid within limits that can be determined only by inferential methods.

To return to the example of the 100 item reading comprehension test, let us consider how an item discrimination index could be computed. The usual method is to select the total test score as the criterion against which individual items on the test will be assessed. The problem then is to compute or estimate the strength of the correlation between each individual item on the test and the test as a whole. More specifically, we want to know the strength of the correlation between the scores on each item in relation to the scores on all the items.

Since 100 correlations would be a bit tedious to compute, especially when each one would require the manipulation of at least twice as many scores as there are examinees (that is, all the total scores plus all the scores on the item in question), a simpler method would be desirable if we were to do the job by hand. With the present availability of computers, no one would be apt to do the procedure by hand any more, but just for the sake of clarity the Flanagan (1939) technique of estimating the correlation between the scores on each item and the score on the total test will be presented in a step by step fashion.

Prior to computing anything, the test of course has to be administered to a group of examinees. In order to do a good job of estimating the discrimination values for each test item the selected test population (the group tested) should be representative of the people for whom the test is eventually intended. Further, it should involve a large enough number of subjects to ensure a good sampling of the true variability in the population as a whole. It would not make much sense to go to all the trouble of computing item discrimination indices on a 100 item test with a sample of subjects of less than say 25. Probably a sample of 50 to 100 subjects, however, would provide meaningful (reliable and valid) data on the basis of which to assess the validities of individual test items in relation to total test scores.

Once the test is administered and all the data are in hand, the first step is to score the tests and place them in order from the highest score to the lowest. If 100 subjects were tested, we would have 100 test booklets ranking from the highest score to the lowest. If scores are tied, it does not matter what order we place the booklets in for those particular cases. However, all of the 98s must rank ahead of all of the 97s and so forth.

The next step (still following Flanagan's method) is to count off from the top down to the score that falls at the $82\frac{1}{2}$ percentile. In the case of our data sample, this means that we count down to the student that falls at the 28th position down from the top of the stack of papers. We then designate that stack of papers that we have just counted off as the High Scorers. This group will contain approximately $27\frac{1}{2}\%$ of all the students who took the test. In fact it contains the $27\frac{1}{2}\%$ of the students who obtained the highest scores on the test.

Then, in similar fashion we count up from the bottom of the booklets remaining in the original stack to position number 28 to obtain the corresponding group that will be designated Low Scorers. The Low Scorers will contain as near as we can get to exactly $27\frac{1}{2}\%$ of the people who achieved scores ranking at the bottom of the stack.

We now have distinguished between the $27\frac{1}{2}\%$ (rounded off in this case to 28 %) of the students who got the highest scores and the $27\frac{1}{2}\%$ who got the lowest scores on the test. From what we already know of correlation, if scores on an individual item are correlated with the total score it follows that for any item, more of the High Scorers should get it right than of the Low Scorers. That is, the students who are good readers should tend to get an item right more often than the students who are not so good at reading. We would be disturbed if we found an item that good readers (High Scorers) tended to miss more frequently than weak readers (Low Scorers). Thus, for each item we count the number of persons in the High Scorers group who answered it correctly and compare this with the number of persons in the Low Scorers group who answered it correctly. What we want is an index of the degree to which each item tends to differentiate High and Low Scorers the same as the total score does – i.e., an estimate of the correlation between the item scores and the total score.

For each item, the following formula will yield such an index:

ID = the number of High Scorers who answered the item correctly minus the number of Low Scorers who answered the item correctly, divided by $27\frac{1}{2}\%$ of the total number of students tested

Flanagan showed that this method provides an optimum estimate of the correlation between the item in question and the total test. Thus, as in the case of product-moment correlation (see Chapter 3 above), ID can vary from $+1$ to -1. Further, it can be interpreted as an estimate of the computable correlation between the item and the total score. Flanagan has demonstrated, in fact, that the method of comparing the top $27\frac{1}{2}\%$ against the bottom $27\frac{1}{2}\%$ produces the best estimate of the correlation that can be obtained by such a method (better for example than comparing the top 50% against the bottom 50%, or the top third against the bottom third, and so on).

A specific example of some dummy data (i.e., made up data) for one of the above test items will show better how ID is computed in actual practice. Suppose we assume that item (3) above, based on the text about Oliver Twist, is the item of interest. Further, that it is one of 100 items constituting the reading comprehension test posited earlier. Suppose we have already administered the test to 100 examinees and we have scored and ranked them.

After determining the High Scorers and the Low Scorers by the method described above, we must then determine how many in each group answered the item correctly. We begin by examining the answers to the item given by students in the High Scorers group. We look at each test booklet to find out whether the student in question got the item right or wrong. If he got it right we add one to the number of students in the High Scorers group answering the item correctly. If he got it wrong, we disregard his score. Suppose that we find 28 out of 28 students in the High Scorers group answered the item correctly. Then, we repeat the counting procedure for the Low Scorers. Suppose that 0 out of 28 students in the Low Scorers group answered the item correctly. The ID for item (3) is equal to 28 minus 0, divided by 28, or +1. That is, in this hypothetical case, the item discriminated perfectly between the better and not-so-good readers. We would be inclined to conclude that the item is a good one.

Take another example. Consider the following dummy data on item (5) above (also about the Oliver Twist text). Suppose that 14 of the people in the High Scorers group and 14 of the people in the Low Scorers group answered the item correctly (as keyed, that is, assuming the 'correct' answer really is correct). The ID would be 14 minus 14, divided by 28, or 0/28 = 0. From this we would conclude that the item is not producing any meaningful variance at all in relation to the performance on the entire test.

Take one further example. Consider item (4) above on the Twist text. Let us suppose that all of the better readers selected the wrong answer – choice A. Further, that all of the poorer readers selected the answer keyed by the examiner as the correct choice – say, choice D. We would have an ID equal to 0 minus 28, divided by 28, or −1. From this we would be inclined to conclude that the item is no good. Indeed, it would be fair to say that the item is producing exactly the wrong kind of variance. It is tending to place the low scorers on the item into the High Scorers group for the total score, and the high scorers on the item are actually ending up in the Low Scorers group for the overall test.

From all of the foregoing discussion about ID, it should be obvious that high positive ID values are desirable, whereas low or negative values are undesirable. Clearly, the items on a test should be correlated with the test as a whole. The stronger the correlations, the more reliable the test, and to the extent that the test as a whole is valid, the stronger the correlations of items with total, the more valid the items must be. Usually, professional testers set a value of .25 or .35 as a lower limit on acceptable IDs. If an item falls below the arbitrary cut-off point set, it is either rewritten or culled from the total set of items on the test.

(iii) *Response frequency distributions.* In addition to finding out how hard or easy an item is, and besides knowing whether it is correlated with the composite of item scores in the entire test, the test author often needs to know how each and all of the distractors performed in a given test administration. A technique for determining whether a certain distractor is distracting any of the students or not is simply to go through all of the test booklets (or answer sheets) and see how many of the students selected the alternative in question. A more informative technique, however, is to see what the distribution of responses was for the High Scorers versus the Low Scorers as well as for the group falling in between, call them the Mid Scorers. In order to accomplish this, a response frequency distribution can be set up as shown in Table 3 immediately below:

TABLE 3
Response Frequency Distribution Example One.

Item (3)	A*	B	C	D	Omit
High Scorers (top $27\frac{1}{2}\%$)	28	0	0	0	0
Mid Scorers (mid 45%)	15	10	10	9	0
Low Scorers (low $27\frac{1}{2}\%$)	0	7	7	7	7

The table is based on hypothetical data for item (3) based on the Oliver Twist text above. It shows that 28 of the High Scorers marked the correct choice, namely A, and none of them marked B, C, or D, and none of them failed to mark the item. It shows further that the distribution of scores for the Mid group favored the correct choice A, with B, C, and D functioning about equally well as distractors. No one in the Mid group failed to mark the item. Finally, reading across the last row of data in the chart, we see that no one in the Low group marked the correct choice A, and equal numbers marked B, C, and D. Also, 7 people in the Low group failed to mark the item at all.

IF and ID are directly computable from such a response frequency distribution. We get IF by adding the figures in the column headed by the letter of the correct alternative, in this case A. Here, the IF is 28 plus 15 plus 0, or 42, divided by 100 (the total number of subjects who took the exam) which equals .42. The ID is 28 (the number of persons answering correctly in the High group) minus 0 (the number answering correctly in the Low group) which equals 28, divided by $27\frac{1}{2}\%$ of all the subjects tested, or 28 divided by 28, which equals 1. Thus, the IF is .42 and the ID is 1.

We would be inclined to consider this item a good one on the basis of such statistics. Further, we can see that all of the distractors in the item were working quite well. For instance, distractors B and C pulled exactly 17 responses, and D drew 16. Thus, there would appear to be no dead wood among the distractors.

To see better what the response frequency distribution can tell us about specific distractors, let's consider another hypothetical example. Consider the data presented on item (4) in Table 4.

TABLE 4
Response Frequency Distribution Example Two.

Item (4)	A	B	C	D*	Omit
High Scorers (top $27\frac{1}{2}\%$)	28	0	0	0	0
Mid Scorers (mid 45%)	15	15	0	14	0
Low Scorers (low $27\frac{1}{2}\%$)	0	0	0	28	0

Reading across row one, we see that all of the High group missed the item by selecting the same wrong choice, namely A. If we look back at the item we can find a likely explanation for this. The phrase 'for a long time after his birth' does seem to imply alternative A which suggests that the child was sickly for 'months or possibly years'. Therefore, distractor A should probably be rewritten. Similarly, distractor A drew off at least 15 of the Mid group as well. Choice C, on the other hand, was completely useless. It would probably have changed nothing if that choice has not been among the field of alternatives. Finally, since only the low scorers answered the item correctly it should undoubtedly be completely reworked or discarded.

E. Minimal recommended steps for multiple choice test preparation

By now the reader probably does not require much further convincing that multiple choice preparation is no simple matter. Thus, all we will do here is state in summarial form the steps considered necessary to the preparation of a good multiple choice test.

(1) Obtain a clear notion of what it is that needs to be tested.
(2) Select appropriate item content and devise an appropriate item format.
(3) Write the test items.
(4) Get some qualified person to read the test items for editorial difficulties of vagueness, ambiguity, and possible lack of clarity (this step can save much wasted energy on later steps).
(5) Rewrite any weak items or otherwise revise the test format to achieve maximum clarity concerning what is required of the examinee.
(6) Pretest the items on some suitable sample of subjects *other than the specifically targeted group.*
(7) Run an item analysis over the data from the pretesting.
(8) Discard or rewrite items that prove to be too easy or too difficult, or low in discriminatory power. Rewrite or discard non-functional alternatives based on response frequency distributions.
(9) Possibly recycle through steps (6) to (8) until a sufficient number of good items has been attained.
(10) Assess the validity of the finished product via some one or more of the techniques discussed in Chapter 3 above, and elsewhere in this book.
(11) Apply the finished test to the target population. Treat the data acquired on this step in the same way as the data acquired on step (6) by recycling through steps (7) to (10) until optimum levels of reliability and validity are consistently attained.

In view of the complexity of the tasks involved in the construction of multiple choice tests, it would seem inadvisable for teachers with normal instructional loads to be expected to construct and use such tests for normal classroom purposes. Furthermore, it is argued that such tests have certain instructional drawbacks.

F. On the instructional value of multiple choice tests

While multiple choice tests have rather obvious advantages in terms of administrative and scoring convenience, anyone who wants to make such tests part of the daily instructional routine must be willing to pay a high price in test preparation and possibly genuine instructional damage. It is the purpose of the multiple choices offered in any field of alternatives to trick the unwary, illinformed, or less skillful learner. Oddly, nowhere else in the curriculum is it common procedure for educators to recommend deliberate confusion of the learner – why should it be any different when it comes to testing?

It is paradoxical that all of the popular views of how learning can be maximized seem to go nose to nose with both fists flying against the very essence of multiple choice test theory. If the test succeeds in discriminating among the stronger and weaker students it does so by decoying the weaker learners into misconceptions, half-truths, and Janus-faced traps.

Dean H. Obrecht once told a little anecdote that very neatly illustrates the instructional dilemma posed by multiple choice test items. Obrecht was teaching acoustic phonetics at the University of Rochester when a certain student of Germanic extraction pointed out the illogicality of the term 'spectrogram' as distinct from 'spectro-graph'. The student observed that a spectrogram might be like a telegram, i.e., something produced by the corresponding -graph, to wit a telegraph or a spectrograph. On the other hand, the student noted, the 'spectrograph' might be like a photograph for which there is no corresponding photogram. 'Now which,' asked the bemused student, 'is the machine and which is the record that it produces?' Henceforth, Dr. Obrecht often complained that he could not be sure whether it was the machine that was the spectrograph, or the piece of paper.

What then is the proper use of multiple choice testing? Perhaps it should be thoroughly re-evaluated as a procedure for educational applications. Clearly, it has limited application in classroom testing. The tests are difficult to prepare. Their analysis is tedious, technically formidable, and fraught with pitfalls. Most importantly, the design of distractors to trick the learners into confusing dilemmas is counter productive. It runs contrary to the very idea of education. Is this necessary?

In the overall perspective multiple choice tests afford two principal advantages: ease of administration and scoring. They cost a great deal on the other hand in terms of preparation and counter productive instructional effects. Much research is needed to determine whether the possibly contrary effects on learning can be neutralized or even eliminated if the preparation of items is guided by certain statable principles – for instance, what if all of the alternatives were set up so that only factually incorrect distractors were used? It might be that some types of multiple choice items (perhaps the sort used in certain approaches to programmed instruction) are even instructionally beneficial. But at this point, the instructional use of multiple choice formats is not recommended.

KEY POINTS

1. There is a certain strained naturalness about multiple choice test formats inasmuch as there does not seem to be any other way to ask a question.
2. However, the main argument in favor of using multiple choice tests is their supposed 'objectivity' and their ease of administration and scoring.
3. In fact, multiple choice tests may not be any more reliable or valid than similar tests in different formats – indeed, in some cases, it is known that the open-ended formats tend to produce a greater amount of reliable and valid test variance, e.g., ordinary cloze procedure versus multiple choice variants (see Chapter 12, and the Appendix).
4. Multiple choice test may be discrete point, integrative, or pragmatic – there is nothing intrinsically discrete point about a multiple choice format.
5. Pragmatic tasks, with a little imagination and a lot of work, can be converted into multiple choice tests; however, the validity of the latter tests must be assessed in all of the usual ways.
6. If one is going to construct a multiple choice test for language assessment, it is recommended that the test author begin with a discourse context as the basis for test items.
7. Items must be evaluated for content, clarity, and balance among the alternatives they offer as choices.
8. Each set of alternatives should be evaluated for clarity, balance, extraneous clues, and determinacy of the correct choice.
9. Texts, i.e., any discourse based set of materials, that discuss highly technical, esoteric, super-charged, or otherwise distracting content should probably be avoided in most instances.
10. Among the common pitfalls in item writing are selecting inappropriate content; failure to include a thoroughly correct alternative; including more than one plausible alternative; asking test takers to guess facts not stated or implied; leaving unintentional clues as to the correct choice among the field of alternatives; making the correct choice the longest or shortest; including the opposite of the correct choice among the alternatives; repeatedly referring to information in the correct choice in other alternatives; and using ridiculous or hilarious alternatives.
11. Item analysis usually involves the examination of item facility indices,

item discrimination indices, and response frequency distributions.

12. Item facility is simply the proportion of students answering the item correctly (according to the way it was keyed by the test item writer).

13. Item discrimination by Flanagan's method is the number of students in the top $27\frac{1}{2}\%$ of the distribution (based on the total test scores) minus the students in the bottom $27\frac{1}{2}\%$ answering the item correctly, all divided by the number corresponding to $27\frac{1}{2}\%$ of the distribution.

14. Item discrimination is an estimate of the correlation between scores on a given item considered as a miniature test, and scores on the entire test. It can also be construed in a more general sense as the correlation between the item in question and any criterion measure considered to have independent claims to validity.

15. Thus, ID is always a measure of reliability and may also be taken as a measure of validity in the event that the total test score (or other criterion) has independent claims to validity.

16. Response frequency distributions display alternatives against groups of respondents (e.g., high, mid, and low). They are helpful in eliminating non-functional alternatives, or misleading alternatives that are trapping the better students.

17. Among the minimal steps for preparing multiple choice tests are the following: (1) clarify what is to be tested; (2) decide on type of test to be used; (3) write the items; (4) have another person read and critique the items for clarity; (5) rewrite weak items; (6) pretest the items; (7) item analyze the pretest results; (8) rewrite bad items; (9) recycle steps (6) through (8) as necessary; (10) assess validity of product; (11) use the test and continue recycling of steps (7) through (10) until sufficient reliability and validity is attained.

18. Due to complexity of the preparation of multiple choice tests, and to their lack of instructional value, they are not recommended for classroom applications.

19. Oddly, multiple choice tests are the only widely used educational devices deliberately conceived to confuse learners.

DISCUSSION QUESTIONS

1. Examine a multiple choice test that is widely used. Consider the alternatives offered to some of its items. In what ways are the distractors composed so as to be maximally attractive to the unwary test takers?

2. Have you ever used multiple choice tests in your classroom? Or, better still, have you ever taken a multiple choice test prepared by an amateur? Have you been subjected to final examinations in a multiple choice format? What were your reactions? What was the reaction of your students? Were there any students that did well on the test who did not know the subject matter supposedly being tested? How can this be accounted for? Were there any points about which you or your students seemed to be more confused after testing than before?

3. What uses of multiple choice tests can you conceive of that are not confusing to learners? What experiments would be necessary to test the validity and utility of multiple choice tests of the proposed type in

comparison with tests in other formats?

4. In what ways are multiple choice tests more practical than pragmatic tests? In what ways is the reverse true? What are the key factors to be considered?

5. Can you conceive of ways of short-cutting the recommended steps for multiple choice test preparation? For instance, consider the possibility of using more items in the pretest setting than are necessary for the final test format. What are the costs and benefits?

6. Find out how much money, how many man hours, and how much overall expense goes into the preparation of a single standardized test that is widely used in the schools where you work, or where your children attend, or in the area where you live. How does the expense compare with the time, money, materials, and equipment available to the average classroom teacher?

7. Have you ever done an item analysis of a multiple choice test by hand? Would you consider doing one once a week? Once a month? Twice a year? What kinds of changes in instructional load, equipment availability and the like would be necessary to make regular multiple choice testing in the classroom a reasonable teacher initiated and teacher executed chore? What other alternatives exist? District wide tests? Professionally prepared tests to go with particular curricula? How about teacher made tests of an entirely different sort?

SUGGESTED READINGS

1. John Bormuth, *On the Theory of Achievement Test Items.* Chicago: University of Chicago Press, 1970.

2. Alan Davies, 'The Construction of Language Tests,' in J. P. B. Allen and Alan Davies (eds.) *Testing and Experimental Methods. Volume 4 of the Edinburgh Course in Applied Linguistics.* London: Oxford University, 1977, pp. 38–104.

3. J. B. Heaton, *Writing English Language Tests.* London: Longman, 1975.

4. Rebecca Valette, *Modern Language Testing.* New York: Harcourt, 1977.

PART THREE
Practical Recommendations for Language Testing

10

Dictation and Closely Related Auditory Tasks

In Part Two, we considered some of the shortcomings of discrete point approaches to language testing. Now we come to the question that has no doubt been on the minds of many readers ever since the beginning of the discussion of pragmatic language testing in Chapter 1 of Part One. That question is how to do it reliably and validly.

This chapter focusses attention on a family of auditory testing procedures. The best researched of them is a variety of dictation which we will refer to as *standard dictation*. This variety and others related to it are described in some detail below, but it should be noted early that the few testing techniques which are discussed in this and in following chapters are scarcely indicative of the range of possible pragmatic testing procedures. More particularly, the few auditory tasks described in this chapter are far from a complete accounting of possible tests. In fact, no complete listing can ever be obtained because their number is unbounded in principle. The techniques discussed are intended merely to introduce some of the possibilities that are known to work well. It is not to set the limits of the range of pragmatic auditory tasks that are possible.

A. Which dictation and other auditory tasks are pragmatic?

Any proposed testing procedure which is to qualify as a pragmatic language processing task must meet the two naturalness criteria laid down in Chapter 3 above: (1) It must require the processing of temporal sequences of elements in the language constrained by the normal meaningful relationships of such elements in discourse, and (2) it must require the performer of the task to relate the sequences of elements to extralinguistic context via what we defined above as pragmatic mappings. More succinctly, pragmatic tasks require time constrained processing of the meanings coded in discourse.

In order for such a pragmatic task to be used as a testing procedure, it is necessary that it be quantifiable by some appropriate and feasible scoring technique. It is assumed that all pragmatic tasks insofar as they have external manifestations from which processing can be observed or inferred are more or less quantifiable. The adequacy of the quantification process is part of the assessment of the reliability and validity of any such procedure used as a testing technique. Of course, some techniques are more easily converted to scores than are others, so if we have our choice, we are better off with the ones that are most easily quantifiable.

It is not necessary, however, that pragmatic tasks single out any particular skills or hypothesized component of grammar. Neither is it necessary that the task require the processing of stimuli in only one sensory modality or in only one productive output mode. Various skills, more than one input/output channel, and all of the presumed components of language proficiency are apt to be involved in any pragmatic task.

Among the family of dictation procedures that have been used in a variety of ways as testing techniques are standard dictation, partial dictation, dictation with competing noise, dictation/composition, and elicited imitation. The first of these, and probably the best known, requires examinees to write verbal sequences of material as spoken by an examiner or played back from a recording. If the material is presented at a conversational rate and if it is given in sequences of sufficient length to challenge the examinee's short term memory, we can be assured that a deeper level of pragmatic processing must take place. If the material, on the other hand, is dictated very slowly and with very short sequences of words or one word at a time syllable-by-syllable, the task does not meet the naturalness criteria.

Partial dictation is similar to standard dictation except that the examinees are given a written version of the text (along with the spoken version) where the written passage has certain portions left out. The examinees must listen to the spoken material and fill in the blanks in the written version. In this case, the task resembles a cloze test except for the fact that all of the text is presented in the oral version (which may by some methods be presented more than once) and portions of it are also written down for the examinees in advance. Other factors being equal, partial dictation is an easier task from the examinee's point of view though it takes more effort to prepare from the vantage point of the examiner. It is easier to perform because more sensory information is given concerning the message – a partial written version and a complete spoken version.

Dictation may be made more difficult by reducing the signal-to-noise ratio. As Miller, Heise, and Lichten (1951) had thoroughly demonstrated many years ago, the speech signal is remarkably resistant to distortion. Normally we can understand spoken messages even under very noisy conditions (as when carrying on a conversation in an automobile speeding along a freeway). And, we can understand speech or writing when the signal itself is very weak (as in listening to a distant radio station with a lot of competition from static, or when reading the text of a badly faded duplicated copy). Spolsky, Sigurd, Sato, Walker, and Arterburn (1968) showed that dictation with added noise was a feasible language testing procedure. Pragmatic versions of the technique are possible so long as the naturalness criteria are met.

Another form of dictation is what has sometimes been called the dicto-comp, or dictation/composition. Examinees are instructed to listen to a text one or more times while it is presented either live or on tape at a conversational rate. Then they are asked to write from memory what they have heard. Verbatim scoring procedures are less applicable to this technique, and it presents many of the same scoring difficulties that we will encounter in reference to essays in general in Chapter 13. Scoring is more difficult than with standard dictation, but detailed procedures have been worked out with reference to specific texts (Frederiksen, 1975a, 1975b, and his references). Most applications of this procedure have been in studies of discourse processing in cognitive psychology, though the procedure (or at least a variant of it) has been used in Freshman English testing (Brodkey, 1972).

Elicited imitation is an auditory task that is similar to dictation in terms of the material presented to the examinee but dissimilar with respect to the response mode. In this case, the examinee hears the material, the same as in dictation (and with equal possibilities for variation), but instead of writing down the material the examinee is asked to repeat it or otherwise recount what was said. Both verbatim tasks and more loosely constrained retelling tasks have been used (Slobin and Welsh, 1967, pioneered the former technique in studies of child language which is the more scorable of the two approaches; see also Miller, 1973, for an excellent list of references on verbatim tasks). The more loosely constrained retelling tasks run into the formidable scoring problems of the dictation/composition technique and essay grading or rating of free speech. A significant difference, however, in favor of the elicited imitation and dictation techniques is that the examiner at least knows fairly well what the examinee should be trying to say or write. In the essay and free speech cases, the limits of possible messages are less well defined.

B. What makes dictation work?

As testing procedures, simple dictation and its derivatives may seem a little too simple. Some may object that it is possible to write down (or repeat) sequences of material in a language that one does not even understand. This is an important objection and it deserves to be dealt with early in this discussion. A potential examiner may argue, for example, that some learners can take dictation in a certain language almost flawlessly, but that they cannot understand that language under conversational conditions. This is an interesting way of stating the objection because in this form the objection gratuitously offers its own solution: describe the 'conversational conditions' that the learner finds difficult and translate them into an appropriate dictation procedure. It follows that such a dictation must by definition constitute a challenge to the limits of the learner's ability in the language and it remains only to quantify the technique (i.e., develop a scoring procedure).

The reason that dictation works well is that the whole family of auditory tasks that it comprises faithfully reflect crucial aspects of the very activities that one must normally perform in processing discourse auditorily. In fact, in the case of dictation in particular and pragmatic testing procedures in general, language tests are much more direct measures of the competence underlying such performances than is the case with almost any other kind of educational testing. Performing a dictation task is a lot closer to understanding spoken discourse than answering multiple choice questions on a so-called aptitude test is to displaying an aptitude for learning or for whatever the aptitude test purports to measure. Consider the case of displaying memory for certain pairings of English words with Turkish words in a subtest of the *Modern Language Aptitude Test*. Such an activity is considerably less similar to learning a foreign language than dictation is to processing discourse. This same argument can be extended to a comparison of any pragmatic test with any other sort of educational measure.

If pragmatic language tests require examinees to do the kinds of tasks that a pragmatic theory of language use and language learning defines as characteristic of human discourse, then the tests should be as good as the theory depending on how faithfully they mirror the performances that the theory tries to explain. The theory is vulnerable to other sorts of empirical tests but the information from studies of language tests *qua* tests is also *one* of the sources of data to test the theory. The reasoning may seem circular, but it is certainly not viciously so. The theory itself can be used as an argument for the validity of proposed testing procedures that accord well with it because the theory itself is anchored to empirical reality through validity checks other than language test data and research. This is the requirement of the theoretical basis advocated by Cronbach and Meehl (1955) in their classic article on construct validity.

A second validity criterion concerns the pattern of inter-relationship between tests that purport to measure the same construct. Cronbach and Meehl (1955) argued that if a variety of tests are believed (according to some theoretical reasoning) to assess the same construct (in our case the expectancy grammar of the language user), they should produce a corresponding pattern of intercor-relation. That is, they should intercorrelate strongly, demonstrating a high degree of variance overlap. This sort of validity evidence for dictation and closely related procedures was discussed in Chapter 3 above (also see the Appendix). In fact, the degree of correlation between dictation and other pragmatic testing procedures in many studies has approached the theoretical ideal given the estimated degree of reliability of the tests investigated (see especially Oller, 1972, Stubbs and Tucker, 1974, Irvine, Atai, and Oller, 1974, Hinofotis, 1976, Oller and Hinofotis, 1976, Bacheller, in press, LoCoco, in press, and Stump, 1978).

A third validity criterion suggested by Cronbach and Meehl (1955) pertains to the kinds of errors that examinees make in performing the tasks circumscribed by a procedure or set of testing procedures. Data from studies of learner errors (or better, learner protocols including all of the learner outputs) are supportive of the interpretation that pragmatic tasks of all sorts share a considerable amount of variability in terms of what they require learners to do. Comparisons of the types and quantities of errors reveal substantial similarities in performance across different pragmatic tasks (see the discussion of error analysis in Chapter 3 above).

In a nutshell, dictation and closely related procedures probably work well precisely because they are members of the class of language processing tasks that faithfully reflect what people do when they use language for communicative purposes in real life contexts. That class of tests is large, but it excludes many co-called 'language' tests that do not meet the pragmatic naturalness criteria.

C. How can dictation be done?

1. *Selecting the material and the procedure.* The first step is to determine the purpose for testing. What is to be done with the test data once gathered? Failure to deal adequately with this question results in the collection of far more data than can be analyzed in many cases, or else it leads to the collection of data that cannot be used to address the principal questions or needs. Once it has been determined what the test is for, the next step is to decide which of the many possible

procedures to use and how to calibrate the test appropriately to the purpose for testing and the subject population to be tested. Both of these decisions should be informed by the educator's (or other person's) knowledge of the subjects to be tested, how the testing is to be articulated within the total curricular setting, and the practicalities of how many people and what amount of time (and possibly money) is to be spent in collecting, analyzing and interpreting the test data.

In relation to the foregoing decisions, some of the questions that should probably be considered are: How many times will the testing be done? If it is part of an instructional program, how can the test data be used to improve the efficiency of that program? Is the test data to be used for placement purposes? As a basis for diagnosing levels of overall proficiency and prescribing instruction accordingly? Is it to be used to assess specific instructional goals? There are many other questions, but perhaps these provide some clues as to how to attack the decision-making problem. Some examples of specific testing problems may also help.

Suppose the purpose of testing is to assess the ability of children to understand the language of the classroom, and possibly to assess the degree of bilinguality of children with more than one language. We might want to know, for instance, whether it makes sense to deliver instruction in English to children whose home language is, say, Spanish. The test should be defined in terms of the kinds of discourse tasks the children will be expected to perform in classroom contexts. If an estimate of dominance is desired it will be necessary to devise similar tasks of roughly equivalent difficulty in both languages and to obtain a proficiency estimate in each language along the lines suggested in Chapter 4 above. If the children are preliterate, or if they are still involved in the difficult process of acquiring literacy, an elicited imitation task might be selected. Other forms of dictation would be ruled out. Below, we consider in more detail one of the ways of doing elicited imitation.

Another possible purpose for institution-wide testing is the case of testing foreign students in a college or university admissions and placement procedure. The principal question might be whether the incoming students can understand the sorts of speech events they will be required to deal with in the course of their study in a certain degree program. If it is determined that college lecture material is the sort of discourse that should be used as a basis for test material, then it may make sense to use one or more texts drawn from typical lecture material as a basis for testing.

In many school contexts, and for many purposes, it would make a lot of sense to try to find out more about the ability of learners to process discourse of varying degrees of difficulty and concerning different subject matter domains. Dictation at an appropriate rate, of the kinds of material that learners are expected to cope with, is a promising way of investigating how well learners can handle a variety of school-related discourse processing tasks. Many educators may be surprised if not dismayed at the level of comprehension exhibited by students.

In some cases learners may be able to handle substantially richer verbal material than they are being exposed to. In an important study (discussed in greater detail in Chapter 14) Hart, Walker, and Gray (1977b) have shown that preliterate children are capable of dealing with texts of substantially greater pragmatic complexity than the ones with which they are presented in most reading programs. Their research shows that children who are exposed to richer and more complex materials, that are better articulated in relation to the kinds of discourse children are able to handle, learn to read and write much more readily (Hart, 1976). In other cases it may be that the language of the curriculum is too complex and needs to be simplified. If this were the case, however, it would probably be true only in a limited sense – e.g., perhaps certain concepts should be taught rather than taken for granted. In most instances, though, learners are probably capable of handling a great deal more information and of considerably greater complexity than any particular curriculum has found ways of expressing.

Or, consider the problem of testing foreign students at the college level. Probably the standard dictation procedure is about as appropriate as any testing technique to determine the relative abilities of foreign students to follow spoken English in whatever contexts are defined. Scores can be made more meaningful in relation to the general problem of admission by finding out how well the broad spectrum of entering students who are native speakers of English perform on the same task. There is evidence that there may be considerably more variability in the performance of native speakers on pragmatic processing tasks than could ever have been discovered with discrete point test procedures. Whereas it was reasonable to insist that the average native speaker should be able to answer all or nearly all of the items on a discrete point grammar test correctly, or on a phonological discrimination task, there is considerable room for variability in discourse processing skills that involve the higher integration of knowledge and verbally coded information. Recent evidence suggests that native speakers may tend to make the same kinds of errors in dictation that non-natives make (Fishman, in press), though the natives do make fewer errors.

Another possible purpose for wanting to test with some variety of dictation is to evaluate the acquisition of information of some more specific sort. For instance, a foreign language teacher, or an English teacher (or a math or statistics teacher) may want to know how well the students in a particular class are able to follow the discussion of a particular topic or segment of course material. A standard dictation of material (with fairly long bursts of sequences at a conversational rate) or perhaps better, a dictation/composition may be informative both to the teacher and to the students. If the sequences of verbal material are presented at a normal conversational speed and in fairly long bursts, it will be exceedingly difficult for learners to write down what they do not understand, or to recall and rephrase material that they cannot process at a fairly deep level of comprehension.

The research of Frederiksen (1975a, 1975b, and see his references) and that of Gentner (1976, also see his references) suggests strongly that the process of understanding discourse is considerably more constructive than sentence interpretation models of speech understanding would have led us to believe. Furthermore, learner performances probably vary much more and due to many more factors than the speech processing models of the 1960s would have led us to believe. Learning in any academic setting may be far more a matter of language comprehension in a fairly literal sense than traditional models might have led us to suppose (for some pioneering work on this topic, see Freedle and Carroll, 1972).

(i) *Standard dictation.* For the purpose of illustrating the most widely used dictation procedure, the following texts taken from dictation materials used in the testing of foreign students at UCLA in the spring of 1971 are selected:

(a) SAMPLE MATERIALS
Will Rogers (Text 1)

Will Rogers grew up in the western part of the United States. He was a real cowboy, riding horses around his father's ranch all day. When he was very young, his parents worried about him because he was always doing something wrong.

No one could control him. His father finally sent him to a military school in the South. When the director of the school noticed Will's cowboy rope lying on top of his suitcase, he expected trouble with this new boy, and he was right.

A Taste for Music (Text 2)

A taste for music, a taste for anything, is an ability to consume it with pleasure. Taste in music is preferential consumption; a greater liking for certain kinds of it than for others. A broad taste in music involves the ability to consume with pleasure many kinds of it. Vast numbers of persons, many of them highly intelligent, derive no pleasure at all from organized sound. An even larger number can take it or leave it. They find it agreeable for the most part, stimulating to the sentiments, and occasionally interesting to the mind.

It can be said that neither of these texts is very characteristic of college level reading material and they may even be less representative of college classroom discourse. Nonetheless, both worked very well in discriminating English abilities of foreign students entering UCLA, which was their original purpose as dictation materials, and which is further testimony to the robustness of dictation as a testing technique.

(b) ADMINISTRATION PROCEDURES

However the decision concerning the selection of materials is reached, the next step is to decide how to set up the dictation task. There are many ways to influence the difficulty level of the task even after the difficulty level of the materials has been set by the selection process. Factors influencing the task difficulty are: (1) the conceptual difficulty of the word sequences themselves (other factors being held constant); (2) the overall speed of presentation; (3) the length of sequences of material that are presented between pauses; (4) the signal-to-noise ratio; (5) the number of times the text is presented; (6) the dialect and enunciation of the speaker and the dialect the hearer is most familiar with; and (7) a miscellany of other factors.

The determination of difficulty level is scarcely algorithmic. Rigorous criteria do not exist and quite possibly cannot ever be established. This is partly due to the tremendous variability of the experience of populations of subjects for which one might like to set such criteria. However, the fact that rigorous decision-making criteria do not exist does not prevent testers from reaching practical decisions concerning relevant factors. The main reason for mentioning such factors is to provide the reader with some notion concerning the remarkable spread of difficulty levels that may be obtained with a single text. Within certain ill-defined limits, the difficulty level of any text is more or less continuously variable.

Concerning the first factor mentioned in the preceding paragraph, we can easily see that Text 1 above (the one about Will Rogers) is easier than Text 2 (about music appreciation). The vocabulary in Text 1 is simpler and the ideas expressed are less abstract. However, by varying the overall speed of presentation, the length of sequences between pauses, and/or the signal-to-noise ratio, Text 1 could be made into a dictation task that would be more difficult than a different dictation task over Text 2.

Fortunately, the difficulty level of any given task is not the principal thing. If a group of examinees is observed to display a certain rank order of proficiency levels on, say, a particular chunk of Mark Twain's prose from a certain novel, chances are extremely good that they will display a similar rank order of levels on almost any other portion of text from the same novel, or another novel, or in fact any similar text or any other passage of discourse. (This is assuming that in each case the text in question is about equally familiar or unfamiliar to all of the tested subjects.)

It is not the difficulty level of the passage for a group of subjects or for any particular examinee that matters most, rather it is the tendency for examinees to perform proportionately well or poorly in relation to each other. This tendency for examinees to differ in performance, somewhat independently of the difficulty of any particular task, is what accounts for the robustness of the dictation procedure. In a word, it is the *variance* in test scores, not the mean of a certain group or the score of a particular subject on a particular task that is the main issue. Therefore, the purpose of the examiner is not to find a text or define a task that will produce a certain mean score (i.e., a certain difficulty level), rather, it is to find a text and define a task over it that will generate a desirable amount of variance between subjects in the performance of that task.

If the examiner is looking for an indication of degree of overall proficiency, the object may be to set a task that is not too difficult for the examinees who are lowest in proficiency nor too easy for the examinees who are highest in proficiency. Fortunately again, the dictation procedure is sufficiently robust normally to satisfy this need regardless which point in a range of difficulty levels is struck upon in the materials selection process. We return to this topic below in the discussion of the interpretation of scores on dictation tasks. If, on the other hand, the purpose of the test is to measure ability to comprehend a particular text that may have been assigned for study, a task over that same text would seem to be called for.

In the standard dictation procedure, the task set the examinees is to write down sequences of heard material. Usually, the text to be written is read once at a conversational rate while the examinees just listen. The second time it is read with pauses at pre-established break points, and sometimes with marks of punctuation given by the examiner. The third time it is read either with or without pauses (and/or punctuation) while the examinees check what they have written. An important step in setting up the procedure is deciding on break points in the text or texts to be dictated.

There are no absolute criteria for deciding where to place the pauses, but some general principles can be suggested as heuristic guidelines. Breaks should be spaced far enough apart to challenge the limits of the short term memory of the learners and to force a deeper level of processing than mere phonetic echoing. The amount of material that can easily be held in short term memory without really understanding its meaning will vary from learner to learner somewhat according to the proficiency level of the learners. More proficient examinees will be able to handle longer sequences with the same ease that less proficient examinees handle shorter ones. Probably sequences much less than seven words in length should be avoided. In some cases sequences in excess of twenty words in length may be desirable.

Pauses should *always* be inserted at natural break points. They should not be inserted in the middle of a phrase, e.g., '... grew up in the / Western part of the United States. . . .' (where the inserted slash mark represents a pause, or break point in the presentation of the dictation). Pauses should be inserted at natural points where pauses might normally occur in a discourse, e.g. at the period after the phrase 'the United States'. Sometimes it may be necessary to break in the middle of a clause, or even in the middle of a series of phrases within a clause, e.g., a break might be set between 'grew up' and 'in the western part of the United States''. In all cases, the most natural break points are to be preferred.

In Text 1, the following break points were selected (as indicated by slash marks):

Will Rogers (Text 1)

Will Rogers grew up in the western part of the United States./ He was a real cowboy, riding horses around his father's ranch all day./ When he was very young, his parents worried about him/ because he was always doing something wrong./ No one could control him./ His father finally sent him to a military school in the South./ When the director of the school noticed Will's cowboy rope/ lying on top of his suitcase,/ he expected trouble with this new boy, and he was right./

Since the purpose of the test is decidedly not to assess the speed with which examinees can write, the pauses must be long enough not to turn the task into a speed writing contest. A rule of thumb that seems to work fairly well is for the examiner to subvocalize the spelling of each sequence of verbal material twice during the pause while the examinees are writing it. If the material is to be tape-recorded this process will generally provide ample time. For instance, the examiner would read aloud (either live in front of the examinees or onto a tape recording) the first designated sequence of words of the preceding text: 'Will Rogers grew up in the western part of the United States.' Then he would silently rehearse the spelling of the sequence: 'W-I-L-L-R-O-G-E-R-S-G-R- . . .' and so on twice through. Then he would proceed to the next sequence beginning 'He was a real cowboy, . . .' and so on throughout the passage.

In some dictation tasks, the punctuation marks are given as part of the reading of the dictation. If this is done, and it usually is done in standard dictation, the examinees should be appropriately instructed to expect marks of punctuation to be given. For instance, the following instructions might be given either orally or in written form:

This is a test of your ability to comprehend and write down orally presented material. It is a dictation task. You will hear a paragraph read aloud three times. The first time it will be read at a conversational speed. Just listen and try to understand as much as you can. The second time the passage will be read with pauses for you to write down what you hear. Marks of punctuation will be given wherever they occur. When you hear the word 'period' at the end of a sentence, put a period (.) at that point in the paragraph. Do not write out the word P-E-R-I-O-D. Other marks of punctuation that will be given are 'comma' (,) and 'semicolon' (;). (The instructor should make sure the examinees are forewarned about all of the marks of punctuation that actually appear in a given passage, at least until they are familiar with the procedure to be followed.) The third time you will hear the same paragraph without pauses while you check what you have written down. You should write exactly what you hear.

Alternative forms of the dictation procedure would be to read the passage twice, or only once. Another possibility would be to require the examinee to write the passage with no marks of punctuation indicated. If this latter option were followed, it would probably be best to disregard punctuation altogether in the scoring or to allow as many forms of punctuation as possible for the given text. Including the marks of punctuation as part of the dictation procedure is one way around the difficulty of scoring punctuation (if at all). If the marks are indicated clearly in the oral procedure, putting them in becomes a part of the overall listening comprehension task.

If the object of the test is to measure overall ability to deal with auditorily presented material that is new or relatively unfamiliar, probably the methods of reading the material once, twice, or three times will produce roughly equivalent results though it is expected that a second or third reading will make the task progressively easier. Research needs to be done on this question, but we might expect an increase in mean score on the same passage if it is read a second time, and possibly another increase if it is read a third time, but the variance in scores should be largely overlapping (highly correlated) in all three cases. That is, the tendency of scores to differ from their respective means on each of the three tasks should be roughly similar. The choice of how many presentations of the material to use may make little difference in some cases, but in others there may be good reasons for preferring to read the material only once – for instance, when trying to simulate closely an actual listening task.

(c) SCORING PROCEDURES

If the examiner chooses to make a live presentation of the dictation material, he should make every effort to avoid slips of the tongue, unnecessary disfluencies, and the like, and should be prepared to compensate for his own errors in whatever scoring system is devised. It is possible for the examiner to say something different than what is actually in the written passage. Usually when this happens, the examiner is unaware of it until it is time to score the tests. The problem may then become obvious when the examiner discovers that all of the students tried in fact to write what he said and not what the passage actually contained. In such cases, it is appropriate to score the test for what was said rather than what appeared in the script.

Standard dictation is usually scored by allowing one point for every word in the text. It can be done in either of two roughly equivalent ways. If there are few correct sequences in the examinees' protocols, it is probably best (easiest and most reliable) to count only the correct words that appear in the appropriate sequence. If there are few errors on the other hand and many correct words in sequence, it is probably best to count errors and subtract their number from the total number of points. Because of the possibility of inserting words not in the text, it is possible by the error counting method to derive scores less than zero. Therefore, the error-counting method and the correct words-in-sequence method are not perfectly equivalent if intrusions are counted as errors. For reasons to be discussed below, it is best not to count spelling errors unless they seem to indicate a problem in the perception of distinctive sounds or knowledge of different word meanings.

Word-for-word scoring goes somewhat slowly for the first several papers (or protocols), but as the scorer becomes more familiar with the text, it goes considerably faster. Errors include deletions, distortions of form or sequence, and intrusions. Spelling errors can be distinguished as a special category as will be illustrated.

Examples of deletions in protocols generated by dictating the Will Rogers text (see above) to foreign students being admitted at UCLA in the spring of 1971 include the following:

1. 'In the western, He was a real cowboy, all day. . . .' in place of, 'Will Rogers grew up in the western part of the United States. He was a real cowboy, riding horses around his father's ranch all day. . . .' for a total of 15 deletion errors, or

10 correct words in sequence from a possible 25 (freehand circles above the line indicate deletions);

2. 'in western part of United States. ...' instead of 'in the western part of the United States' scored as 2 deletion errors or alternatively as 6 correct words in sequence out of a possible 8;

3. 'He was real cowboy, ...' for 'He was a real cowboy' with 1 deletion error or 4 out of 5 points.

Some examples of distortions of form and their scoring are:

4. 'Will Rogers grow up in the western part of the United States. He was a real cowboy, reading horses in his father ranch all day. ...' In this protocol there are distortion errors in the words 'grew', 'riding', 'in', and 'father's' for a total of 4 errors or 21 of 25 possible points;

5. 'When the director of the school saw this real cowboy lying on top of his suitcase, ...' instead of 'when the director of the school noticed Will's cowboy rope lying on top of his suitcase ...' where the word 'noticed' has been transformed into 'saw this' (1 error), and 'Will's cowboy rope' has been rendered as 'real cowboy' (2 errors);

6. 'rinding horseback in his fathers range all day' for 'riding horses around his father's ranch all day' (3 errors, 'rinding' for 'riding', 'in' for 'around', and 'range' for 'ranch');

7. 'Wilcablerook' for 'Will's cowboy rope' (3 errors).

Distortions of sequence are less common, but they do occur (frequently they are interlaced with a variety of other errors):

8. 'He was a real cowboy, reading horses around all day in his fathers ranch' instead of 'He was a real cowboy riding horses around his father's ranch all day' (the adverbial 'all day' is transposed to an earlier position; 'reading' is substituted for 'riding'; and 'in' is inserted where it did not appear at all – total score is 10 out of a possible 13 or a total of 3 errors);

9. 'he always was doing' for 'he was always doing' (1 error);
10. 'writing horses his around father's ranch all day' instead of 'riding horses around his father's ranch all day' ('his' out of order for 1 error and 'writing' for 'riding' for a second error);
11. 'new trouble with this poor boy' instead of 'trouble with this new boy' (2 errors: 1 order, 1 intrusion or distortion);
12. 'to send him military school' for 'sent him to a military school' (3 errors; 1 order, 1 distortion of form, 1 deletion).

Intrusions of words that did not appear in the text also occur occasionally:

13. 'expected the trouble with this new boy' for 'expected trouble with this new boy' (1 error, intrusion of 'the');
14. 'noticed Wills cowboy's rope' for 'noticed Will's cowboy rope' (1 error for the intrusion of the possessive morpheme apparently copied from 'Will's' to 'cowboy');
15. 'all day long instead of 'all day' (1 error);
16. 'he will cowboy rope lying on the top' for 'Will's cowboy rope lying on top' (2 intrusion errors, 1 distortion).

The foregoing merely illustrate some of the common types of errors that occur in non-native attempts at writing dictation of the standard variety. There is one further type of error that we should consider before we proceed to look at several actual examinee protocols. It is possible to distinguish (generally) spelling errors from other types of errors.

(d) WHY SPELLING ERRORS ARE NOT COUNTED

A general rule of thumb is to ask of any potential spelling error whether it could be made by someone who really knows the language well and is capable of making all the appropriate sound distinctions, e.g., the distinction between /l/ and /r/ or between /w/ and /v/ and /b/, or say between the vowel sound of 'beat' versus the vowel of 'bit' and so forth. English is not an easy language to spell, and it is not the purpose of dictation (normally) to be a test of knowledge of English spelling. Below, examples of spelling errors appear in the left hand column; the correct spelling appears in the center column; and examples of lexical or phonological errors that are not classifiable as spelling errors are given in the third column. Practically all the examples are genuine errors from examinee protocols. Contrived examples are asterisked.

SPELLING ERRORS	CORRECT SPELLING	PHONOLOGICAL ERRORS
Will Rodgers	1. Will Rogers	Bill Roger(s)
Wil Radgers		Will Radios
Wil Rogers		Will Lagerse
		William Roger
		We ride
		Willi Rogers
fathers	2. father's	farmer's
		father
		farther's
al day	3. all day	hole day
		whole day
notest	4. noticed	notice
noteced		*know this
roap	5. rope	robe
*expekted	6. expected	excepted
		espected
yung	7. young	*lung
directer	8. director	*dractor
rannch	9. ranch	ransh
		range
suitecase	10. suitcase	*suitscase
somthing	11. something	somsing
		*some think
rong	12. wrong	*long
wright	13. right	write
abillity	14. ability	a meladic
abilitie		
abilaty		
militery	15. military	emelitery
millitary		omilitary

Of course, there are cases where it is difficult to decide whether an error is really a spelling problem or is indicative of some other difficulty besides mere spelling. In such cases, for instance, 'pleshure' for 'pleasure', 'teast' for 'taste', 'ridding' for 'riding', 'fainaly' for 'finally', 'moust' for 'must', 'whit' for 'with' and similar instances, perhaps it is best to be consistently lenient or consistently stringent in scoring. In either case it is a matter of judgement for the scorer. Fortunately, such doubtful cases account for only a small portion of the total variance in dictation scores. For 145 foreign students tested at UCLA in 1971 on the texts illustrated above, the average number of spelling errors was 1.30 on the first passage (Will Rogers) and 1.61 on the second (A Taste for Music). Compare these figures against the average number of all other errors on the two passages which was in excess of 50 on each passage. Furthermore, the number of errors classed as spelling errors concerning which there is doubt is only a small fraction of the total number of spelling errors.

Why not include spelling errors as part of the total score? That is, why not subtract them from the total score the same as any other type of errors? Table 5 shows that spelling errors are uncorrelated with the other types of errors that learners make in taking dictation, and they are also unrelated to performance on a variety of other tasks included in the UCLA *English as a Second Language Placement Examination (Form 2D)*. The test consisted of four multiple choice sections in addition to the two dictations. It was administered to 145 subjects in the spring of 1971. The table reports the intercorrelations between the two dictations (Dictation 1, Dictation 2), a multiple choice synonym matching task (Vocabulary), a multiple choice reading comprehension task (Reading), a multiple choice grammar test requiring subjects to select the one appropriate word, phrase, or clause to fill a blank in a larger verbal context (Grammar Select), and a multiple choice task requiring subjects to put words, phrases, or clauses in an appropriate order (Grammar Order). Also included in the table are two spelling scores, one for each of the respective dictations. Since the spelling scores (Spelling 1, Spelling 2) are negative, that is, the worse the subject did the higher the score, and since all of the other test scores are expressed as the number of correct answers on the respective portion of the test, correlations between the spelling scores and the other test scores should be negative.

The table reveals, however, that in fact the spelling scores are slightly positively correlated with the other test scores represented in the correlation matrix. The spelling scores on the two dictations are substantially correlated with each other, but are scarcely correlated at all with any other test in the table. This would suggest that spelling errors on the two dictations used are not related to overall proficiency in English as measured by the dictations and the other parts of the UCLA *ESLPE 2D*. For this reason, it is recommended that spelling errors not be included as part of the total score computation for dictation tests. Whitaker (1976) and Johansson (1973) make similar recommendations.

TABLE 5

Intercorrelations between Two Dictations, Spelling Scores on the Same Dictations, and Four Other Parts of the UCLA *English as a Second Language Placement Examination Form 2D* Administered to 145 Foreign Students in the Spring of 1971.

UCLA ESLPE 2D Subparts	UCLA ESLPE 2D Abbreviated Subparts	V	GS	GO	R	D1	D2	S2	S1
Vocabulary		1.00	.71	.64	.85	.47	.71	−.03	.04
Grammar Selection			1.00	.79	.75	.69	.64	.04	.08
Grammar Order				1.00	.73	.61	.61	.06	.07
Reading					1.00	.47	.68	.06	.11
Dictation 1						1.00	.68	.06	.03
Dictation 2							1.00	.06	.03
Spelling 1								1.00	.55
Spelling 2									1.00

From Table 5 we can see that the tendency to make spelling errors in the two dictations is substantially correlated. That is, the correlation between Spelling 1 and Spelling 2, see row 7 and column 8 of the correlation matrix, is .55. Thus, about .30 of the variance in spelling errors on Dictation 1 is also present in the variance in spelling errors on Dictation 2. A relationship of this strength would not be expected to occur by chance as often as one time in one thousand tries. That is, if we repeated the testing procedure with a thousand different groups of subjects of about 150 in number, we would not expect a correlation of .55 to occur by chance even one time. Hence, the correlation must be produced by some empirically reliable factor – say, ability to spell English words.

However, none of the correlations between the spelling scores and the other subtests reaches significance. Correlations of the observed magnitudes (ranging from −.03 to .11) would be expected to occur by chance more than ten times in 100 tries. Besides, if the correlations were produced by some real relation between the cognitive ability underlying English language proficiency and ability to spell English words, the correlations ought to be stronger (i.e., of greater magnitude) and they ought to be consistently negative. If ability to spell English words is related to overall proficiency as assessed by the *ESLPE 2D*, then the greater the number of spelling errors in a dictation, the lower should be the proficiency of the examinee who made the errors. In fact, the slight positive correlations suggest that the greater the number of errors the higher the overall proficiency score.

Although spelling errors are uncorrelated with scores on any of the language proficiency subtests, the latter are all quite strongly correlated with each other. That is, a higher score on one part of the test will tend to correspond to a higher score on every other part of the test, while a lower score will tend to correspond to a lower score on all subtests. Along the lines of the argument presented in Chapter 3 of Part One, the correlations observed in Table 5 should strengthen our confidence in the various testing procedures represented there. The strongest relationship exists between the Reading subtest and the Vocabulary subtest. All of the tests, however, appear to have substantial reliability and validity.

(e)   SAMPLE SCORED PROTOCOLS

To give a clearer notion of how the scoring of a standard dictation task might be done, three protocols for each of the sample texts from section 1 above are given in their entirety below. All are actual renditions by foreign students at the university level. The native language of the learner who wrote the protocol is given at the top left in parentheses. Cross-outs are the learner's own in each case. In some cases, error types are indicated in cursive script above the line as *deletions, distortions, intrusions, spelling errors,* and so on. Punctuation and capitalization have been corrected or ignored. In no case do they contribute to the total score. The marking method used is to encircle errors and place circles above the line where words are deleted. Intrusions above the number of errors in any given line of text are not counted toward the total score. The total score is then the number possible minus the number of errors. (Depending on how intrusions are treated, this method may result in a slightly different score than merely counting the total number of correct words in correct sequence.) It is not possible to get a score lower than zero so long as intrusions in excess of the number of errors in a given line of text do not count.

Protocol 1

(Japanese)   SCORE: _80/87_

Will Rogers grew up in the Western part of the United States. He was a real cowboy, riding horses ~~on~~ *around* his *(farther's)* [distortion] *(ranches)* [distortion] all day. When he was very young, his parents worried about him because he was always doing something [distortion] wrong. No one could control him. His *(farther)* [distortion] finally sent him to a military school in the South. When the director of the school noticed *(will)* [distortion] cowboy ~~wrote~~ [distortion] lying on the top of his suitcase, he expected *(to)* [intrusion] *(travel)* [distortion] trouble with this new boy and he was ~~wright~~.

Protocol 2

(Chinese) *phonological distortion*   SCORE: _68/87_

Will *(Lagerse)* grewup in the western part *(s)* of the United *spelling (no points off)* States. He was a *reall* cowboy, riding horses around *(in)(the)* ranch *(ows)* [intrusion] all day. When he was *(a)-* [intrusion] very young, his parents worried about him, because he was alway *(s)* [intrusion] *doing* something wrong. No one could contro *(led)* [intrusion] him. His father finally sen ~~t~~ *(d)* him to *(O)* military school *(OO)* south. When the director of the school noticed a cowboy *(group)(line)(of)* top of *(the)* suitcase, he expected *(to)* trouble with new boy, and he was right.

Protocol 3

(Armenian)   SCORE: _66/87_

Will Roger *(s)* *(grow)* *phonological* in Western part of United States. He was a real cowboy, riding horses around *(O)* father's *(house)* all day. When he was ~~we~~ very young, his parents *(vorried)* about him *phonological (not spelling)* because he always doing *somthing* wrong. No ~~a~~ one could *spelling (no points off)*.

control him. His father finally send him to melitery school
in the Shout. When the director of school known the cowboy
rod line the suitcase, he expected trouble with this new boy,
and he would wrig write. — *lexical (not spelling)*

To check the assigned scores, the reader may want to look back at the
exact text given above on p. 274. Three examples from the second text
follow:

Protocol 4

(Japanese – same subject as in Protocol 1) SCORE: 84/94
A taste of music, a taste for anything, is an ability to
consume with the pleasure. Tasted in music is proporential
consamption, a greater liking on certain kinds of it than for
others. A broad taste of in music involves the ability to
consume with the pleasure many kinds of it. Vast numbers of
persons, many of the highly intelligent, derive no pleasure at
all from organized sound. An even larger number can take at
leave it. They find it agreeable for the most part, stimulating
for the synemoms, and occasionally interested in mind.

Protocol 5

(Chinese – same as Protocol 2)   SCORE: 38/94
A taste of music, a taste anything is ability A taste music
consumptions great of lighten than others. A brought tast
music in ability consupmtion pleasure many kinds of it. Base
number's persons, many of highly intelegence, divised all
parts from organized sound. Even large number can take a
live They finded great for most part. Stimulating setlements,
and occasional of mine

Protocol 6

(Armenian – see Protocol 3)   SCORE: 60/94
A taste for music, a tate for anything, is ability to consure for
pleasure. Taste for music consumtion, a greater line circle

than for other. A brought taste of music in volver in ability to consure for pleasure many kinds of it. Last number of persons, many of them high inteligent devide no pleasure of for organize sound. An even larger number can take it or leav it. They find it a new robol for most part, stemlery to OO, and occasionaly for a mind.

2. (ii) *Partial dictation.* This technique is actually a combination of dictation and the cloze procedure (see Chapter 12 for a more detailed discussion of the latter). In partial dictation, actually *all* of the material is presented in an auditory version, and *part* of it is also presented in a printed form. The portions of text that are missing in the printed version are the criterion parts where the examinee must write what is heard – hence, though all of the material is presented in an auditory form, only part of it is really dictated for the learner to write down. The technique has a great deal of flexibility and may be done in such a way as to break up the text somewhat less than the standard form of dictation.

Johansson (1973) suggests two methods for selecting materials. One way is to tape a portion of natural discourse – a lecture, a radio program, a conversation, or some other verbal exchange. Another is to concoct a text or script to be tape recorded as if it were one of the foregoing, or merely to tape record a script, say, a paragraph of prose. In the first case it is necessary to transform the auditory version into a written form, that is, write the script. In the second, one starts with the script and then makes a recording of it. Another step in either case is to decide what portions of the script to leave blank. Once those decisions are reached, pauses of sufficient length must be inserted in the taped version. Probably the same rule of thumb recommended for standard dictation pauses can also be applied for partial dictation – namely, spell out the deleted portion twice in creating each respective pause. This method creates a pause length that is consistently related to the length of the deleted material (as consistent at least as the speller's timing in subvocally uttering the sequence of letters twice through).

In the samples that follow, the material which would be heard but which would not actually appear on the script placed in the hands of the examinees is in italics and enclosed in parentheses. The slash mark at the end of each italicized portion of the text indicates the location of a pause on the tape. Both samples were used by Johansson (1973) in his research with Swedish learners of English as a foreign language (at the college level). The first sample was created from a text by making a recording of it. The second sample originated as a radio program that was recorded and then subsequently transcribed for the purpose of the test.[1]

(a) SAMPLE MATERIALS
Partial Dictation Sample 1
(Book Review: 'The Fetterman Massacre' by Dee Brown.)

The Fetterman Massacre is the story of Red Cloud's completely victorious ambush of 80 soldiers of the United States army in December 1866. Red Cloud, commanding armies of Sioux and Cheyenne, decoyed a troop of 80 men from Fort Phil Kearny on the Montana road. No one returned alive. The man who took the news of the massacre to the head of the telegraph near Fort Laramie was Portugee Phillips who, (*at below-zero temperatures and through continuous blizzards*)/, rode 236 miles in four days. Portugee Phillips survived. The horse died. Captain Brown and Colonel Fetterman, obviously by agreement, (*shot each other to avoid capture*)/. The Indians (*had very few rifles*)/, the United States soldiers (*were reasonably well armed*)/. They did not (*run out of ammunition*)/. Red Cloud's (*victory was complete*)/. It was, of course, (*only temporary*)/. The Montana road was opened again within ten years. (*Westward pressure was inexorable*)/. Dee Brown, as in Bury My Heart at Wounded Knee, (*conveys the vast genocidal tragedy of the period*)/. He is not (*sentimental or sensational*)/. He draws together (*the pertinent facts with skill and clarity*)/. In a sense he lets the facts tell the story, but to say this is (*doing him less than justice*)/. It is (*his arrangement and presentation of the facts*)/ that gives both books (*their excitement and distinction*)/. It is possible that some readers may think that Dee Brown (*lacks the sweep and the eloquence*)/ of the great American historian Francis Parkman but he has an eloquence of his own (*rather more closely related to the literary taste of 1972*)/, and I suspect that in the future it will be with writers like Parkman that Dee Brown (*will be compared*)/.

Partial Dictation Sample 2
(Book Review: 'The Scandaroon' by Henry Williamson.)

[1] Johansson credits Stig Olsson, Lund University, with the selection of the materials and the creation of the text of the second sample.

This book is about some very unusual relationships, not between men and women nor even between men and men, but between men and birds. The workpeople in the small town of Thirby in North Devon keep racing pigeons. That sport has made them deadly enemies of the peregrine falcons, which have lived and hunted along that stretch of the Devon coast for a thousand summers. The falcons swoop on the pigeons as they return home but Sam Baggott, keeper of the Black Horse Inn and a dedicated pigeon racer, has his own deterrent against 'they bloody hawks'. He (*sends up decoy birds impregnated with strychnine*)/, and dances for joy when the falcons tumble out of the sky, (*having succumbed to his poisoned bait*)/. The Scandaroon itself is a (*rather unusual migrant from distant shores*)/, something of a (*brightly plumed cross between a pigeon and a crow*)/. Its arrival in Thirby is greeted with considerable interest. Sam Baggott (*lusts after it as a potential bait for the falcons*)/. The local doctor regards it with great interest (*as a natural history specimen*)/. But the Scandaroon eventually becomes the property of (*an elderly admiral's young son*)/. That of course, is only the beginning of the story, and since it is rather a good one (*I don't propose to repeat all of it here*)/. In this short novel, set just after the First World War, Henry Williamson presents us with several contrasting views of the English countryside – that of (*the dedicated naturalist*)/, that of (*the equally dedicated sportsman*)/, and that of (*the less passionately involved observer*)/. Henry Williamson is not a sentimental nature writer. He knows the countryside and its people too well to lapse into the (*casual urban dream of some rural Arcadia*)/. He recognizes that (*cruelty and beauty fuse together*)/ when a peregrine falcon (*swoops on a straggling pigeon*)/. In his novels (*he exhibits a telescopic eye for detail*)/, and one feels that he cares more too. Our concern for the environment is essentially a social concern. It derives from the social problem (*of providing ledger-space for the urban millions*)/.

Before going on to discuss some of the details of the administration and scoring of partial dictations, a few words need to be said about the placement of blanks. Johansson (1973) says on the basis of his research with the procedure that it is important that blanks not be left in the middle of a sentence several words before the pause is inserted. For instance, items like the following should (according to Johansson) be avoided:

(1) Britain has the (*fastest rising cost of living*) of any country in the world./

He urges that if omission of material is to be made in the middle of a sentence, it should be preceded by a pause – otherwise, such items (where 'item' refers to each deleted portion in a text) prove to be excessively difficult. Perhaps, the same hip-pocket principle used in the placement of breaks in standard dictation should also be followed in determining what to delete and what to leave in with partial dictation. However, it may be worth noting that by following Johansson's recommendation, the unacceptable item given above could theoretically be converted to an acceptable (but somewhat more difficult item) as follows:

(2) Britain has the (*fastest rising cost of living of any country in the world*)./

In general, therefore, it would seem that items for partial dictation can be made as difficult or easy (within certain illdefined limits) as the examiner would like them to be. The most striking difference between either of the foregoing items and the following (3) is the length of the sequence between the beginning of the deletion and the pause:

(3) Britain has the fastest rising cost of living of (*any country in the world*)./

In (1) and (2) the number of words between the beginning of the deleted portion and the pause is 11 words in each case, whereas it is only 5 in (3). Hence, (1) and (2) ought to be somewhat more difficult than (3).

(b) ADMINISTRATION PROCEDURES

In the research by Johansson, the recorded material was played only once. Subjects were instructed to listen to the tape and fill in the blanks in the text. They were told that a pause would occur at each slash mark (/). Examinees were also given 'a few minutes for final revision' (1973, p. 52) after the tape finished playing. Johansson used a language laboratory with separate headsets for each examinee, but a single tape playback should work equally well so long as the room accoustics are good. Live presentation is also possible with partial dictation and may be preferred by classroom teachers (as it usually is with standard versions of dictation).

The scoring methods employed with partial dictation are quite similar to those used with standard dictation. Johansson allowed one point for each correct word in the correct sequence. He did not subtract any points for words that were misspelled but clearly recognizable as the correct form. His 'guiding principle' was to 'disregard errors which would not affect pronunciation, provided that the word is clearly recognizable and distinct from other words with a similar spelling' (1973, p. 15). Examples of incorrect spellings for which no points were subtracted included: *strycnine* (strychnine), *poisened* (poisoned), *repeate* (repeat), *rifels* (rifles), *elequence* (eloquence), *sentimentel* (sentimental) and *frosen* (frozen). Examples that illustrate genuine non-spelling errors include: *strickney* (strychnine), *speciment* (specimen), *repit* (repeat), *exapit* (exhibit), and *causal* (casual).

2. (iii) *Elicited imitation.* Perhaps the most widely used research technique with preliterate or barely literate children is elicited imitation. It has not always been a favored technique for language proficiency testing, however. Like dictation, it has seemed too simple to some of the experts. Some argued that it was not anything more than a test of very superficial levels of processing. The research with the technique, however, simply does not support this narrow interpretation. It certainly can be done in such a way as to challenge the short term memory of the examinees and to require a deeper level of processing.

The technique is called 'imitation' because it requires the examinees to repeat or 'imitate' utterances that are presented to them (usually the scoring system requires a verbatim repetition). Sometimes children or others imitate utterances spontaneously, but in the test situation the imitation is asked for by the adult or instructor who is giving the test – therefore, it is *'elicited* imitation'. One of the most interesting applications of elicited imitation is in the determination of language variety dominance in children whose language varieties include forms other than the typical middle class standard varieties of English.

The two samples of discourse which have been used as elicited imitation tasks to distinguish levels of language variety proficiency (or dialect dominance) in children are from Politzer, Hoover, and Brown (1974). The first passage is the text of a story in a widely spoken variety of American English. It is about a man who was a slave and a great folk hero. The second sample of discourse is a more widely known story of another black hero whose exploits and courage are also told in a well-known ballad. The stories are probably about equally appropriate to the preliterate kindergarten and early primary grade children for whom they were intended.

(a) SAMPLE MATERIALS
High John the Conqueror
(from Politzer, Hoover, and Brown, 1974)

This here be a story. This story 'bout High John the Conqueror. High John might could be call a hero. High John he could go to all the farms. He could go where the black people was. This was because he was a preacher and a doctor. Couldn't none of the other black folk do that. High John was really smart. High John master wanted him to fight a black man. High John didn't really want to be fighting another slave like hisself. So High John he say to hisself: 'Master crazy. Why he want me to do that? I bet he be hoping we kill each other.' So High John he use his head to get out of fighting. He wait till the day of the fight. Peoples was coming from miles around. Black folk and white folk was there. Everybody get seated in they place. High John he walkeded [wɔktəd] up to the master daughter. Then he slap her. This take so much nerve that the other slave run away and refuse to fight. He refuse to fight anybody bad and nervy as High John.

John Henry
(from Politzer, Hoover, and Brown, 1974)

This is a story about John Henry. You have probably heard this story in school. John Henry could be called a hero. He was a worker on the railroad. John Henry was a leader. So he was always where the other workers were. None of the other workers knew as many people. John Henry's boss wanted John Henry to race a machine. At first John Henry didn't want to do it himself. John Henry says to himself: 'The boss is crazy. Why does he want me to do this? I'll bet he hopes I kill myself.' But he used his hammer anyway. He practiced till the day of the race. People were coming from miles around. Working folks and other folks were there. Everybody gets settled in his seat. John Henry picks up his hammer. Then he walks up to his boss and tells him he's ready to start. John Henry has so much strength that he hammers long hours till he beats the machine. He dies at the end, though.

It is probably apparent to the reader that the two passages are rather deliberately similar. In fact, the parallelism is obviously contrived. John Henry muses to himself concerning his boss much the way High John does concerning the master. The intent of these two passages was to test certain contrasts between the surface forms of the language variety used in the first text against the corresponding forms used in the second text. In this sense, the two texts were contrived to test *discrete points of surface grammar*. For all of the reasons already given in previous chapters, this use is not recommended. Furthermore, if the two passages are to be used to assess the dominance of a group of children in one language variety or the other, they should be carefully counterbalanced for an order effect. If all children were tested on one of the passages before the other, it is likely that performance on the second passage would be affected by previous experience with the first. Another possible problem for the intended application of the two sets of materials (that is, the application recommended by Politzer, *et al*) is that the John Henry story in all probability is more familiar to start with. It would not be improbable that the familiar story might in fact cause confusion in the minds of the children. It is a well known fact that similar stories such as the ones exemplified would be more apt to interfere with each other (become confused in the retelling for instance) than would dissimilar ones.

Why then use these texts as samples? The answer is simple. If the materials are used as tests of the ability to comprehend auditorily presented material (in either language variety) and if the imitation task is scored for comprehension, either set of materials will probably work rather well. However, attention to certain surface forms of grammar (e.g., whether the child says 'himself' or 'hisself' or whether he says 'might could' or simply 'could') should not be the point of a comprehension task. If the question is what forms does the child prefer to use (that is, if the legitimate focus of the test is on surface grammar) then perhaps attention to such matters could be justified. In either case, the issues come to loggerheads in the scoring procedure. We will return to them there.

(b) ADMINISTRATION PROCEDURES

Politzer, Hoover, and Brown (1974) first recorded the texts. Then, the tape was played to one child at a time and the recording was stopped at each point where a criterion sentence was to be repeated. Not all of the sentences contained surface forms of interest. Since Politzer *et al* were interested only in whether the children could repeat the criterion surface forms, only the attempts at repeating those forms were transcribed by the examiner. If the form was correct, that is, if it corresponded perfectly with the form given on the tape, this was merely noted on the answer sheet. If not, the incorrect form was transcribed.

Another approach would be to use two tape recorders, one to play the tape and the other to record the child's responses. This approach was used in a study by Teitelbaum (1976) in an evaluation of a bilingual program in Albuquerque, New Mexico. If this is done the scoring of the child's responses should probably be done immediately after each session in order that the child's attempt be still fresh in the memory of the examiner when it comes time to score it. Furthermore, instead of scoring the attempts merely for some of the words, it could be scored for all of the attempted material. Alternative methods of scoring are taken up below.

In order to try to insure that the first performance did not interfere with the second, Politzer *et al* allowed a week to elapse between testings. However, all children were tested first on one test and then on the other (apparently, as the authors are not perfectly clear on this point). If there were an order effect, that is, if children automatically do better on the second passage because of having practiced the technique, it would tend to inflate scores on the second passage unrealistically. Therefore, in dominance testing it is recommended that half the children be tested first on one passage and half on the other or that there be a warm up testing that does not count. If the first option is chosen this will tend to spread the practice effect evenly over both tests. If the second option is selected it will tend to eliminate the practice effect by making the children equally familiar with the testing technique before either of the actual tests occurs. The first option would be appropriate if one is merely interested in the dominance characteristics of a group of children while the latter would be more appropriate if one is interested in making individual decisions relative to the language-variety dominance of individual children.

The notion of allowing a time lapse between testings makes some sense, but there is no guarantee that the children will forget the first story during the time lapse. If in fact the first story is still fresh in their minds when the second one is encountered, they may very well experience some problems of comprehension. They may, for instance, expect the events of the story the second time around to correspond to the events on the first test. The best way to eliminate the problem thoroughly is to select materials that are less similar than the examples given above but which are known to be comparable in difficulty level according to other criteria – e.g., sentence complexity, vocabulary difficulty, and content.

This can be achieved in the following way. (1) Find two texts of roughly equivalent difficulty and appropriateness for the test population. (2) Create versions of the texts in both languages (or language varieties) of the population to be tested (e.g., in English and in Spanish, or in the majority variety of English and in some non-majority variety of English). (3) Test each examinee on one of the texts in one language (or language variety) and on the other text in the other language (or language variety). (4) Test approximately equal numbers of students on each possible combination of text with language (or language variety). That is, suppose that L1 = language or language variety number one, and L2 = language or language variety number two. Further that TA = the first text and TB = the second text. No examinee would take the same text twice. By requirement (3) they would take L1TA and L2TB, or L2TA and L1TB. By requirement (4) about half would take the first combination of tests and one half would take the second combination. The language (or language variety) dominance of the population can then be estimated by comparing the mean scores of all subjects on L1 (over both texts) with the mean scores on L2 (again over both texts). If the texts are of equivalent difficulty (and this can be determined by comparing the mean of all scores on TA (over both languages) with the mean on TB (over both languages), then the dominance score for each individual subject can be estimated.

In situations where multilingualism and language dominance estimates are not the main point of the testing, the problem is much simpler. The question is more apt to be, how well can these children understand this story and similar ones? Or, how well does a certain child perform in relation to his own previous performances or in relation to other children who use the same language? In such cases decisions concerning how to set up and administer the elicited imitation task probably allow as much flexibility as standard or partial dictation which we have already discussed above. Among the pertinent decisions are where to place the pauses and how long a burst of speech to expect the child to be able to repeat and how accurately.

(c) SCORING PROCEDURES

If the object of the testing is to assess the child's ability to comprehend and restate the meaning of each sentence in, for instance, one of the discourse chunks given above as samples, a score based on content rather than verbatim repetition would seem to make more sense. In all probability, scores based on content and scores based on verbatim repetition will be highly correlated in any case.

In the task as devised by Politzer *et al* (1974) only certain sentences were supposed to be repeated, and only certain words in those sentences were scored. For instance, in the text about High John the Conqueror, the first sentence, '*This here be* a story,' was to be repeated and the italicized words were scored. If the subject got all three words in exactly the form they were presented originally, the 'item' was scored correct. The same procedure was followed for all items (15 in all, many of them single words). Thus, scores might range from 0 to 15. Clearly, this method is based on discrete point test philosophy. It is appropriate only to find out whether the children in question normally use the surface forms tested or (perhaps more accurately) whether or not they can repeat them accurately when they encounter them in sentences as part of a story. Note that this may have little or nothing to do with their actual comprehension of the story in question. In fact, the child might comprehend all of the story and get none of the criterion forms 'correct' because he may transform them all to the surface forms characteristic of his own language variety. Alternatively, the child might get a reasonably high score on the criterion forms and not understand the material very well. This is because Politzer *et al* did not pay any attention in the scoring to the rest of the sentence. It could be missing or distorted – e.g., a form like 'This here be,' would get a score of 1 while a form·like 'This is a story,' would get a score of 0.

If comprehension is the key thing, another scoring procedure seems to be called for. It is possible to use a verbatim scoring method that requires an exact repetition of the forms used in each sentence. This scoring would correspond roughly to the technique illustrated above with respect to standard dictation. By such a method, there would be as many points possible as there are words in the text to be repeated. For High John the Conqueror there would be 186 points possible. Such a scoring would give a much wider range of variability and a much better indication of the degree of overall comprehension of the passage than the discrete point scoring with a maximum of only 15 points possible relating to only a small number of words in the passage. It would also be possible to ask the children to repeat only certain sentences in the text. In this case, the technique might be set up like a partial dictation. In such a case, the verbatim scoring would be applied just as it is in partial dictation.

Another scoring technique and one that would seem to make even more sense in relation to the assessment of comprehension would be to allow full credit for full restatements of the content of sentences even if the form of the restatement is changed. For example, if the child hears, 'This here be a story,' and he repeats, 'This is a story,' he could be allowed full credit – say 1 point for each word in the presented material which would be a score of 5. The next sentence is 'This story 'bout High John the Conqueror.' If he repeats, 'This story is about High John the Conqueror,' or 'This here story be about High John the Conqueror,' in either case he would get full credit of 7 points. In fact, if the child said, 'It is about High John the Conqueror,' he should also receive full credit. But suppose he said, 'This story 'bout somebody name John,' or 'This story is about someone named John,' in either case the child should receive less than full credit. A practical system might be to count off one point for each of the additional words necessary to specify more fully the original meaning – e.g., *High* John *the Conqueror*, where the italicized portions are in a sense deleted from the child's response. Hence, the score would be 7 minus 3 or 4 for either rendition. By this scoring system, the child might be bidialectal in terms of auditory comprehension and might prefer to speak only one of the two dialects or language varieties represented. This scoring technique would give a measure of the child's level of comprehension of the story rather than his preference for one dialect or the other.

It would of course be possible to obtain both a language preference score and a language comprehension score by scoring the same subject protocols by the content method just illustrated, and by the verbatim method illustrated above. The scores would probably be highly correlated for a group of children, but there would probably be some exceptional cases of children who differ markedly in their scores by the two methods. For instance, some children may be truly bidialectal both in comprehension and in production of the surface forms of both dialects. Others may be equally good at comprehending both dialects (or both languages in the case of say Spanish and English) but they may prefer to produce forms only in one variety (or only in one language).

3. *Interpreting scores and protocols.* We come now to the most important, and probably the most neglected aspect of the testing procedures discussed in this chapter. What does a score mean for a given subject? What does an average score mean for a given group of subjects? What can or should be done differently in an educational program, or in a classroom that is suggested by the outcomes of the

testing? What can be learned from a study of individual learner protocols, or groups of them?

Answers to the foregoing questions will vary significantly from population to population and depending on the purpose of the testing. This does not mean that meaningful generalizations are impossible, however. The principle purpose in any of the hypothesized testing situations referred to in this chapter is to find out how well a learner or group of learners can comprehend auditorily presented materials. In fact, it is to find out how completely they can process one or another form of discourse. Therefore, the interpretation of scores should relate to that basic underlying purpose.

In relation to the main question just defined, it is possible to look at the performance of a given learner (or group) from several possible angles, among them are: (1) How does the learner do at time one in relation to time two, three, etc.? More succinctly in relation to a classroom situation, does the learner show any real improvement across time? This question can be phrased with reference to language learning in the foreign language classroom, the ability to follow narrative prose about historical events in a history class, the capacity to comprehend complex mathematical formulas talked about in a statistics class, or whatever other educational task that can be translated into a discourse processing task. Hence, the focus may be on improvement in language skill *per se*, or it may be on improvement in the ability to handle some subject matter that can be expressed in a linguistic form. (2) How does learner skill in the discourse processing task defined by the test tend to vary across learners? That is, how does learner A compare with learner B, C, D, and so on. Where does learner A fit on a developmental scale of language development (or any other sort of learning that is closely related to the ability to use language), and more specifically, where does learner A rank on the scale defined by test scores relative to other learners who were also tested. (3) What skills or kinds of knowledge does the learner exhibit or fail to exhibit in the protocols relative to a given discourse processing task? For instance, is a general problem of language proficiency indicated? E.g., the learner does not understand language x or variety x. Is a deficit of specific content indicated? E.g., the learner does not understand some concept or has not had some relevant prerequisite experience?

With respect to question (1) raised in the preceding paragraph, a few comments are necessary on the possibility of improving on dictation (or one of the other tasks derived from it) without a corresponding improvement in language skill or in the knowledge base that language skill provides access to. Valette (1973) states that the repeated use of dictation (and presumably any closely related assessment technique) should not be recommended. She apparently believed, at that time, learners who are exposed to repeated testing by dictation may improve only in their ability to take dictation and not in their knowledge of the language or anything else. However, Kirn (1972) reported that the repeated use of dictation did not result in spurious gains. Kirn tested students in ESL classes at UCLA repeatedly during the course of a ten week quarter with dictation and was somewhat disappointed that there was no apparent gain from the beginning of the quarter to the end. This would tend to suggest the happy result that dictation is relatively insensitive to a practice effect, and the sad result that all of the practice in English that ESL students were getting in the UCLA ESL classes used in the study was not helping them much if at all. Valette (1973) apparently based her contrary conclusion on a study with French as a foreign language in (1964). The question deserves more investigation, but it would seem on the strength of Kirn's more extensive study and the larger population of subjects used in her work that dictation scores are not likely to improve without a concomitant improvement in language proficiency.

It is possible to learn a great deal from a systematic study of the protocols of a group of learners on a dictation task. The maximum learning comes only at considerable costs in time and effort, however. There is no easy way to do a thorough analysis of the errors in a dictation without spending hours closely examining learner protocols. Learners themselves, however, may benefit greatly from doing some of the work in studying their own errors. A classroom teacher too, can readily form some general impressions about learner comprehension and rates of progress by occasionally scoring dictation tasks himself.

To illustrate the point briefly, consider what can be learned from only two samples of data – in particular, consider protocols 2 and 5 above on p. 283f. Both are protocols from the Chinese subject. We can see immediately from a thoughtful look at the learner's output that he is having a good deal of trouble with a number of phonological, and structural elements of English. For instance, he hears *Rogers* as *Lagerse* probably [lajɽs].[2] Two problems are

---

[2] See William A. Smalley, *Manual of Articulatory Phonetics*, 1961.

apparent here. First the /l/ /r/ distinction is not clear to him. This is borne out later in the text on music where he writes *setlements* for *sentiments*. Apparently the flap pronunciation of the *nt* in [sɛ̃ñəmənts] is close enough to an *lt* combination to cause difficulty in an unfamiliar phonological setting – namely, in the lexical item *sentiments* which he either does not know at all or does not know well. He also deletes the final /r/ on *larger* in the same text, and distorts *derive* to get *devised*. A second problem is the final voiced sibilant /z/ on *Rogers*. He is usually unsure of consonant clusters at the ends of words – witness *parts* for *part*, *alway* for *always*, *controled* for *control*, *send* for *sent*, *consumptions* for *consumption*, *base* for *vast*, *intelligence* for *intelligent*, *finded* for *find it*, *mine* for *mind*. He often devoices final voiced consonants as in *brought* for *broad*. He reveals a general failure to comprehend the sense of tense markers such as the *-ed* in relation to modals like *could* as in *could controled* instead of *could control*, also *send* for *sent*, and *devised* for *derive*. He is unsure of the meaning and use of determiners of all sorts – *a very young* instead of *very young*, *omilitary school south* for *a military school in the South*, *with new boy* for *with this new boy*, *is ability* for *is an ability*. The use and form of prepositional phrases and intersentential relations of all sorts can also be shown to be weak in his developing grammatical system.

In addition, many other highly specific diagnoses are possible. Each can be checked and corroborated or revised on the basis of other texts and other discourse processing tasks. Nevertheless, it should be obvious here and throughout the subsequent chapters in Part Three that pragmatic tests are vastly richer sources of diagnostic data than their discrete point rivals. Further, as we will see especially in Chapter 13, specific workable remedies can be devised more readily in relation to texts than in relation to isolated bits and pieces of language.

KEY POINTS

1. Dictation and other pragmatic tasks are unbounded in number.
2. Examples given in this chapter merely illustrate a few of the procedures that have been used and which are known to work rather well.
3. Pragmatic tests require time constrained processing of meanings coded in discourse.
4. They don't need to single out a posited component of a skill or even one of the traditionally recognized skills.
5. Standard dictation, partial dictation, dictation with noise, dictation/composition, and elicited imitation are closely related techniques.
6. Dictation and the other procedures described are more similar to the

performances they purport to assess than are most educational tests.

7. Language tests like dictation meet three stringent construct validity criteria: (a) They satisfy the requirements of a theory; (b) they typically show strong positive correlations with tasks that meet the same theoretical requirements; (c) the errors that are generated by dictation procedures correspond closely to the kinds of errors learners make in real life language uses.

8. The choice of method and material in dictation testing depends primarily on the purpose to which the test is to be put.

9. Possible purposes for the auditory testing techniques discussed include determining the ability of children in a school to understand the language of instruction, placing foreign students in an appropriate course of study at the college level, and measuring levels of comprehension for discourse concerning specific subject matter.

10. Processing of discourse is a constructive and creative task which goes beyond the surface forms that are given.

11. Connected chunks of discourse are recommended for testing purposes because they display certain crucial properties of normal constraints on language use that cannot be expressed in disconnected sentences.

12. Factors known to affect the difficulty of a dictation task are: (a) the difficulty of the text itself; (b) speed of presentation; (c) length of bursts between pauses; (d) signal-to-noise ratio; (e) number of presentations; (f) dialect of speaker and of listener; and (g) others.

13. Setting a difficulty level for a task for a particular group of learners is a matter of subjective judgement – rigorous criteria for such a decision cannot be set (at least not at the present state of our knowledge).

14. It is the variance in test scores, however, rather than the difficulty of a particular task that is the principal thing.

15. In giving standard dictation, word sequences between pauses should probably be seven words of length or more, and the pauses should be inserted at natural break points.

16. One technique for setting the length of pauses is to spell, letter-by-letter each word sequence sub-vocally twice before proceeding to the next word sequence in the text.

17. By some methods the material is read three times and the marks of punctuation are given during the second and possibly also the third reading. Neither of these points, however, is essential.

18. Standard dictation may be scored allowing one point for each correct word that appears in the correct sequence.

19. Errors include distortions of various sorts, intrusions of extraneous words into the text, and deletions. Usually, no more errors are counted for any given sequence of words than the number of words it contains. This prevents scores lower than zero.

20. Spelling errors which do not indicate difficulties in perception of distinct sounds of the language or which do not affect the lexical identity of a word should not be counted.

21. Spelling errors are probably not at all correlated with other types of errors in dictations or with language proficiency.

22. An example of a spelling error is *sumpthing* for *something*. An example of

an error that affects word meaning is *write* for *right*. An example of an error that indicates a sound perception problem is *somsing* for *something*.

23. Partial dictation, a technique developed by Johansson in Sweden, combines dictation with cloze procedure.

24. The text of a passage is provided with some portions deleted. A complete auditory version is presented and the examinee must fill in the missing portions of the written version of the text.

25. Elicited imitation is similar to dictation and partial dictation except that the response is oral instead of written. Therefore, it can be conveniently used with preliterate children or non-literate adults.

26. Discrete point scoring procedures are not recommended, however, as they do not necessarily reflect comprehension of the text.

27. Testing bilingual (or bidialectal) populations presents some special problems. See Chapter 4 Part One. Special steps must be taken in order to insure test equivalence across languages. (See discussion question 10 below.)

28. Two scoring procedures are suggested for elicited imitation: a word-by-word (verbatim) scoring is suggested to determine which language or language variety a child (or group) prefers to speak (and simultaneously how well they can produce it); and a more lenient content scoring is recommended to determine how well a child (or group) comprehends a text in a given language (or language variety).

29. The meanings of scores and the interpretation of specific learner protocols are points that require much individual attention depending on the special circumstances of a given test situation and test population.

30. Questions related to rate of progress, degree of comprehension of specific subject matter, and ability to process discourse in a particular language or language variety can all be addressed by appropriate study of scores and learner protocols on the types of tests discussed in this chapter.

DISCUSSION QUESTIONS

1. Consider the stream of speech. Take any utterance of any sequence of words and ask where the word boundaries are represented in the speech signal. How does the listener know where one word ends and another begins?

2. Try recording an utterance on an electronic recording device while there is a great deal of noise in the background. Listen to the tape. Can you recognize the utterance? Listen to it repeatedly. What happens to the sound of the speech signal? Does it remain constant? Play the tape for some of your students, classmates, or friends and ask them to tell you (or better, write down) what they hear on the tape. Read and study the protocols. Ask in what sense the words in a dictation are given.

3. Why is time such an essential feature of a dictation, partial dictation, elicited imitation, or other auditory discourse processing task? What are the crucial facts about the way attention and memory work that make time such an important factor?

4. Try listening to a fairly long burst of speech and repeating it. Can you do

it without comprehending what is said? Try the same task with a shorter burst of speech. Up to about how many words can you repeat without understanding? Can you do better if you do not have to give a word for word (verbatim) repetition? Why or why not?

5. Discuss spelling. To what extent does it seem to your mind to be a language based task? How is spelling a word like (or unlike) knowing how to use it or understand it in a speech context? Ask the same question for punctuation. Do you know anyone who is highly fluent in a language but who cannot spell? Do you know anyone who is a reasonably good speller but who does not seem to be very highly verbal?

6. What are some of the factors that must be taken into consideration in translating a text (or a chunk of discourse) from one language into another? What are some of the factors that make such translation difficult? Are some texts therefore more easily translated than others? Is highly accurate translation usually possible or is it the exception? Consider translating something like the life story of Alex Haley into a language other than English. What kinds of things would translate easily and what kinds would not? Or take a simpler problem: consider translating from English to Spanish, the directions for getting from the gymnasium to the cafeteria on a certain college campus that you know well. What is the difference between the two translation problems? Can you relate them to the distinctions introduced in Part One above?

7. Use one of the testing procedures discussed in this chapter and analyze the protocols of the learners. Try the task yourself and reflect on the internal processes you are executing in order to perform the task. Try to develop a model of how the task must be done – that is, the minimal steps to be executed.

8. In relation to question 7, pick some other educational testing procedure and do the same for it. Then compare the discourse processing task with the other procedure. How are they similar and how are they different?

9. Analyze a dictation protocol of some learner studying a foreign language. Compare your analysis with the results of a discrete point test.

10. Perform a language dominance study along the following lines: Select two texts (TA and TB) say TA is in language (or language variety) one (L1) and TB is in L2. Two more texts are created by carefully translating TA into L2 and TB into L1. The four texts are then used as the basis for four tests. Each learner is tested on two of the four, either TA in L1 and TB in L2, or TB in L1 and TA in L2. Approximately equal numbers of subjects are tested on the two pairs of tests. The success of the equating procedure for the two texts can be roughly determined by averaging all scores on TA regardless of the language of the test, and all scores on TB also disregarding the language of the test. The relative proficiency of the group in L1 as compared against L2 can be determined roughly by similar averages over both tests in L1 and both tests in L2. (That is, disregarding the language of the text.) The relative proficiency of a given subject in L1 and L2 may be estimated by examining his score on the two texts and taking into account the relative difficulty of the texts. Relate the difference scores in L1 and L2 to the dominance scale suggested above in Chapter 4.

SUGGESTED READINGS

1. H. Gradman and B. Spolsky, 'Reduced Redundancy Testing: A Progress Report.' In R. Jones and B. Spolsky (eds.) *Testing Language Proficiency*, Arlington, Va.: Center for Applied Linguistics, 1975, 59–70.

2. Stig Johansson, 'An Evaluation of the Noise Test: A Method for Testing Overall Second Language Proficiency by Perception under Masking Noise,' *International Review of Applied Linguistics* 11, 1973, 109–133.

3. Stig Johansson, *Partial Dictation as a Test of Foreign Language Proficiency*. Lund, Sweden: Department of English. *Contrastive Studies Report No. 3*, 1973.

4. Diana S. Natalicio and Frederick Williams. *Repetition as an Oral Language Assessment Technique*. Austin, Texas: Center for Communication Research, University of Texas, 1971.

5. B. Spolsky, Bengt Sigurd, H. Sato, E. Walker, and C. Arterburn, 'Preliminary Studies in the Development of Techniques for Testing Overall Second Language Proficiency.' In J. A. Upshur and J. Fata (eds.) *Problems in Foreign Language Testing. Language Learning, Special Issue No. 3*, 1968, 79–101.

6. Thomas A. Stump, 'Cloze and Dictation as Predictors of Intelligence and Achievement Scores.' in J. W. Oller, Jr. and Kyle Perkins (eds.) *Language in Education: Testing the Tests*. Rowley, Mass.: Newbury House, 1978.

7. R. M. Valette, 'Use of Dictée in the French Language Classroom,' *Modern Language Journal* 49, 1964–431–434.

8. S. F. Whitaker, 'What is the Status of Dictation?' *Audio Visual Journal* 14, 1976, 87–93.

11

Tests of Productive
Oral Communication

A. Prerequisites for pragmatic
   speaking tests
   1. Examples of pragmatic
      speaking tasks
   2. The special need for oral
      language tests
B. *The Bilingual Syntax Measure*
C. *The Ilyin Oral Interview* and the
   Upshur *Oral Communication Test*
D. The *Foreign Service Institute Oral
   Interview*
E. Other pragmatic speaking tasks
   1. Reading aloud
   2. Oral cloze procedure
   3. Narrative tasks

While it is not claimed anywhere in this book that speaking and listening tasks are based on independent skills (nor that reading and writing tasks are), in this chapter we focus attention on tasks that require the production of utterances in overt response to discourse contexts. The issue, however, is the outward manifestation of discourse processing in the form of speech. We avoid hypothesizing the existence of a special 'speaking' skill as distinct from language ability in general. In the preceding chapter the focus was on listening tasks, but the principal examples involved reading and writing as well as listening and speaking. In later chapters we will focus attention on reading (see Chapter 12) and writing (see Chapter 13) as distinct forms of discourse processing. However, we continue to work from the premise that all of the traditionally recognized language skills are based on the same fundamental sort of language competence or expectancy grammar.

303

A. Prerequisites for pragmatic speaking tests

People usually talk both because they have something to say and because they want to be heard. Sometimes, however, they talk just because they want someone to listen. The child who talks his way through a stone stacking and dirt piling project may prefer no one to be listening. An adult doing the same sort of thing is said to be thinking out loud. There is a tale about a certain famed linguist who once became so engrossed in a syntactic problem at a Linguistic Society meeting that he forgot he had an audience. He had turned to the blackboard and had begun to mutter incoherently until the noise of the would-be audience rose to a level that disturbed his concentration. These are examples of talk that arises from having something to say but without much concern for any audience besides one's self.

It is also possible to have nothing much to say and nevertheless to want someone to listen, or to feel compelled to speak just because someone appears to be listening. Lovers tell each other that they are in love. The words do not carry much new cognitive information, but who is to say that they do not convey meaning? The lecturer who is accused of saying nothing in many different ways is apparently filling some ill-defined need. Perhaps he is escaping the uneasy feeling that comes when the air waves are still and all those students are sitting there expectantly as if something should be said. The audience's presence goads the speaker to talk even if he has nothing to say.

But these are unusual cases. In the normal situation, speech is motivated by someone's having something to say to someone else. Even the muttering and incoherent linguist had something to say, and he had an audience at all times consisting of at least himself. Lovers certainly feel that they are saying something when they tell each other well known truths and trivia called 'sweet nothings', and the uneasy lecturer who blithers on saying nothing in many ways also feels that he is saying something even though his audience may not know or care what it might be. Hence, even in these special cases of phatic communion or verbalization of thoughts, there is something to say and someone to say it to.

What is to be said and the person to whom it is said are among the principal things in communicative acts. Words and sequences of them find their reason for being (regardless whether they are eloquent or drab) in contexts where people express meanings to one another. Song and poetry may be special cases, but they are not excluded.

For all of these reasons, in testing the ability of a person to speak a language, it is essential that the test involve something to say and someone to say it to. It is possible to imagine what one would say if one wanted to convey a certain meaning, but it is easier to find the right words when they are called for in the stream of experience. 'Take care of the sense,' the Duchess said, 'and the sounds will take care of themselves' (quoth Miller and Johnson-Laird, 1976, p. v). And, she may well have added, 'Forget the sense or ignore the context and the sounds will scarcely come out at all.' If this were not so, anyone could perform any part in any play and without having to memorize any lines.

Therefore, the more contrived the task and the more it taxes the imagination and conjuring powers of the examinees, the less it is apt to be an effective test of their ability to perform in appropriate speech acts. For these pragmatic reasons, we seek testing procedures that provide the crucial props of something to say and someone to say it to, or at least that faithfully reflect situations in which such factors are present. Put somewhat more narrowly, we require testing techniques that will afford opportunities for examinees to display their ability to string sequences of elements in a stream of speech in appropriate correspondence with extralinguistic context. In short, we need tests that meet the pragmatic naturalness criteria.

1. *Examples of pragmatic speaking tasks.* Along with a modified scoring of the *Bilingual Syntax Measure* we consider the *Ilyin Oral Interview* and the Upshur *Oral Communication Test*. It is argued that the scoring technique for such tests should relate to the totality of the discourse level meanings and not exclusively to discrete points of morphology or syntax. Interview procedures, it is suggested, constitute special cases of conversations that are examiner directed.

Attention is often focussed on picture-based contexts interpreted jointly by the examiner and the examinee. By their very nature, such conversational episodes usually involve listening comprehension (the converse is not necessarily true, however). In effect, the examiner confronts the examinee with verbal problem-solving tasks that require the pragmatic mapping of utterances to context and the reverse. As we will see below, the scoring of interviews is usually analogous to scoring elicited imitation tasks for content rather than surface form.

Less structured speaking tests can be conducted along the lines of the *Foreign Service Institute Oral Interview*. The *FSI* approach is discussed in some detail because it is probably the best known and most widely researched technique for testing oral language skills of adult second language learners. Though the extension of such oral language tests to native speakers has not been discussed widely, it already exists in certain individual measures of 'IQ' such as the Wechsler Intelligence Scale for Children. In any case, classroom teachers and other educators can learn much about assessing day-to-day conversational exchanges and educational tasks from a careful consideration of interview procedures such as the *FSI* technique. (See also the Appendix for a consideration of how the *FSI Oral Interview* relates to other testing techniques.)

It is fairly obvious why conversational techniques such as structured and unstructured oral interviews constitute pragmatic speaking tasks (for the examiner at least if not always for the examinee), but it is less obvious how certain other pragmatic tasks can qualify. For instance, can reading aloud be construed as a pragmatic language task? What about an oral fill-in-the-blank test (i.e., an oral cloze test)? What about a narrative repetition or retelling task (e.g., the spoken analogue of dictation/composition)? Or how about a creative construction task such as inventing a story on the spot? All of these have been tried though not all seem equally promising for reasons that relate more or less directly to the pragmatic naturalness criteria, and to technical difficulties of quantification or scoring.

2. *The special need for oral language tests.* Interestingly, speech is the most manifest of language abilities. If a person cannot write we do not consider him as not having language, but speaking ability is more fundamental. We are apt to say that a person who cannot fluently produce a language does not know or has not fully learned the language. One who has thoroughly mastered the spoken form of a language on the other hand is said to know it in some fundamental sense independent of whether or not he can read or write it. Indeed, in many cases many thousands of speakers of at least many hundreds of languages can neither read nor write them because the languages in question have never been transcribed and systematized orthographically. They are languages nonetheless.

Furthermore, speech is important in another sense. A person may indicate comprehension and involvement in human discourse by merely appearing bright-eyed and interested, but these evidences of comprehension are generally quite subordinate to speech acts where the same person puts into words the evidence of comprehension and participation. In fact, comprehension is not merely understanding someone else's words, it is profoundly more. It is carrying thoughts to a deeper level and expressing meanings that were not stated. It involves reaching beyond the given in the personalization of meanings. As John Dewey (1929) pointed out, even deductive reasoning typically involves discovery in the sense of going beyond what is known. Speech is the principal device for displaying human knowledge through discourse in the present tense and it is simultaneously a mutually engaging method of intelligent discovery of that knowledge.

This is not to say that other forms of human discourse are not important and effective methods for displaying and participating in intelligent activity, but it is to say that in an important sense, speech is the method par excellence of having on-going intelligent interaction with other human beings. Further, speech is the common denominator that makes written and other symbolic systems intelligible to normal human beings. Signing systems of the deaf are special cases, but they do not disprove the role of speech in normals, they merely demonstrate the severity of the lack in persons who are deprived of the blessings of speech that hearing persons are able to enjoy.

The special importance of speech is manifested in the increasing concern among educators and legislators for the language development of children in the schools. Cazden, Bond, Epstein, Matz, and Savignon (1976) report that any California school receiving state money for Early Childhood Education must 'not only include an oral language component but also evaluate it' (p. 1). The same authors view with some trepidation the fact that 'evaluation instruments become an implicit in-service curriculum for teachers, an internalized framework that influences the mini-tests that teachers continuously construct in the classroom as they take children's words as indicators of what they have learned' (p. 1). It is therefore imperative that the testing techniques used in the schools be as effective and humane as can be devised.

A recent monograph published by the Northwest Regional Educational Laboratory evaluates 24 different tests that purport to assess oral language skills (Silverman, Noa, Russell, and Molina, 1976). It is disappointing to note that none of the fourteen measures evaluated among those listed as commercially available was rated above 'fair' (on a three point scale ranging from 'poor' to 'good') in terms of either 'validity' or 'technical excellence'.

It seems clear that there is a serious need for better oral tests. It is the intent of this chapter to offer some techniques that can be adapted to specific classroom or other educational needs to help fill the gap. Here, more than elsewhere in the book, we are forced into largely unresearched territory. For ways of checking the adequacy of techniques that may be adapted from suggestions given here, see the Discussion Questions at the end of this chapter. (Also see references to recent research in the Appendix.)

In addition to the growing need for effective oral language assessment in relation to early childhood education and especially multilingual education, there is the constant need for assessment of oral language skills in foreign language classrooms and across the whole spectrum of educational endeavors. The oral skills of teachers are probably no less important than those of the children, not to mention those of the parents, administrators, and others in the larger school comunity.

B. The *Bilingual Syntax Measure*

Among bilingual measures, the colorful cartoon-styled booklet bearing the label, the *Bilingual Syntax Measure*, has already become a pace setter. It has several appealing qualities. Its cartoon drawings were probably inspired by the Sesame Street type of educational innovation and they are naturally motivating to preschoolers and children in the early grades. Compare for instance the picture shown as Figure 1 in Chapter 3, p. 48 with its drab counterpart from the *James Language Dominance Test* shown as Figure 14 or the equally unmotivating pictures from the *New York City Language Assessment Battery, Listening and Speaking Subtest* shown as Figure 15. It is not just the color that differentiates the test illustrations as bases for eliciting speech. In both the James and the New York City test, the intent of the pictures displayed is to elicit one-word names of objects. There is something unnatural about telling an experimenter or examiner the name of an object when it is obvious to the child that the examiner already knows the correct answer. By contrast the question 'How come he's so skinny?' (while the examiner is pointing to the skinny man in Figure 1, p. 48 above) requires an inference that a child is usually elated to be able to make. The question has pragmatic point. It makes sense in relation to a context of experience that the child can relate to, whereas questions like, 'What's this a picture of?' or 'Point to the television,' have considerably less pragmatic appeal. They do not elicit speech in relation to any meaningful context of discourse

Figure 14.   Pictures from the *James Language Dominance Test.*

Figure 15.   Pictures from the *New York City Language Assessment Battery, Listening and Speaking Subtest.*

where facts are known to have antecedents and consequences. Both types of questions require relating words to objects or object situations, but only the sort of question asked in the BSM requires the pragmatic mapping of utterance onto an implied context of discourse. Further, it requires the stringing together of sequences and subsequences of meaningful elements in the tested language.

The questions asked in relation to the series of pictures that comes at the end of the BSM suggest possibilities for elicitation of meaningful speech in a connected context of discourse where a chronological and cause-effect type of relationship is obtained between a series of events. In Figure 16, where all three of the pertinent pictures are displayed, in the first picture the King is about to take a bite out of a drumstick. In the same picture the little dog to his left is eyeing the fowl hungrily. In the next picture, while the King turns to take some fruit off a platter the dog makes off with the bird. In picture three the King drops the fruit and with eyes wide is agape over the missing meat. Sly Mr Dog with winking eye is licking ye olde chops. The story has point. It is rich in linguistic potential for eliciting speech from children. It has a starting point and a picture punch line. If the child is willing to play the examiner's game, the pictured events provide an interesting context for discourse.

The relative complexity of pragmatic mappings of utterances onto context that can be achieved is suggested by paraphrases of the questions asked in the BSM. In order to protect the security of the test, only questions 5, 6, and 7 below are given in the exact form in which they appear in the BSM.

(1) The examiner points to the first picture in the sequence (picture 5) and asks the child to point out the King.
(2) Then the child is asked to point to the dog in the second picture (picture 6).
(3) Next, the last picture (picture 7) is indicated and again the child is asked to point out the King.
(4) The first scored question in relation to these pictures asks why the dog is looking at the King (picture 5).
(5) 'What happened to the King's food?' (Picture 3.)
(6) 'What would have happened if the dog hadn't eaten the food?' (No particular picture indicated.)
(7) 'What happened to that apple?' Examiner points to the third picture.
(8) Finally, the child is asked why the apple fell.

Because of the discrete-point theory that Burt, Dulay, and Hernandez (1975, 1976) were working from, they recommend scoring only questions 5, 6, and 7. Further, they are actually concerned with the past irregular forms ('ate' in question 5, 'fell' in question 7) and the perfect conditional ('would have' in question 6, see Burt *et al* 1976, p. 27, Table 9). By their scoring method, if the child uses those

Figure 16.
Pictures 5, 6, and 7 reproduced from the *Bilingual Syntax Measure* by permission, copyright © 1975 by Harcourt, Brace, Jovanovich, Inc. All rights reserved.

forms correctly he has performed perfectly on the three test items in question. In effect, their intent in including questions 5, 6, and 7 on their test was to elicit *obligatory* uses of the grammatical forms indicated above. If the child is to answer the questions correctly he is likely to use the verb forms sought. There are other possibilities, however.

For instance, in response to question 5 the child *might* say something like, 'The King ate it all up,' which is by their scoring syntactically correct but is pragmatically inaccurate. Or he might say, 'The dog eated it,' where the syntactic form is not quite right but the pragmatic sense is impeccable. In response to question 7 the child might say, 'It dropped from the plate,' or 'The King dropped it,' where the child does not use the desired irregular verb form 'fell'. From reading the Technical Handbook and the other published materials, it is not completely clear how such cases are to be handled. With the syntactic scoring where any 'grammatically correct' form is counted correct 'even though the child's response seems strange or contrary to fact,' (Burt *et al*, 1975, p. 9 of the Manual, English Edition) the emphasis is quite different than it might be if the test were scored for meaning. For instance, it would be possible to score every criterion question for whether or not the response makes sense and tells everything necessary to answer the question adequately. Better still, it would be possible to ask questions that are designed to elicit more complex pragmatic mappings to exhaust completely the potential meanings in the context.

For example, the first three questions might be kept as warm-ups and followed by,

(A) What is the King getting ready to do? (E is pointing to picture one.)

(B) What is the dog doing? (E points to one.)

(C) What is the dog gonna do? (E points to two.)

(D) Why didn't the dog just take the food in this picture? (E points back to one.)

(E) What's the King doing in this picture? (E points to two.)

(F) What is the King so surprised about in this picture? (Picture three.)

(G) Why do you think the dog is winking his eye in this picture? (Picture three.)

(H) What do you think would have happened if the King had kept his eye on his food in this picture? (Picture two.)

Questions (A) and (B) can be answered in one word each. The child may say, 'Eat,' or 'Eat his dinner,' or 'Eat some turkey,' etc. in response to A and 'Watching,' or 'Watching the King eat,' or 'Looking at the King,' or 'Wishin' he was eatin' the turkey instead of the King,' and so on. Pragmatic scoring of subject's responses could be done in a variety of ways. Probably (though the research has not been done to back up this guess) a considerable variety of scoring techniques would produce similar variances (i.e., strongly correlated scores).

A practical solution might be to allow one point for each phrasal unit required to respond adequately to the question. Questions A and B would count for one point each. Question C requires at least two phrasal units ('Steal the chicken,' 'Take the meat,' 'Swipe the food,' or the like) so it might be awarded two points. D is worth a minimum of three points ('Because the King was watching' or 'He didn't want to get caught,' etc.). E is worth two points ('Getting an apple,' or 'He's not lookin',' etc.) by the same system, and F would probably count for at least three ('Because his food is gone'). G is worth three ('He ate the turkey') and H is worth four ('The dog wouldn't have stolen it').

Partial credit for partially correct responses might be considered though it would make the scoring of protocols more complicated. It would be possible by this method to compute separate scores for grammatical accuracy (in the syntactic sense of grammar) and contextual appropriateness, but the latter should have priority. The sense of what the child says should be the main thing – not its form. No credit should be given for correct forms that do not fit the sense of the context and the question.

It is a safe bet that a pragmatic scoring of the BSM or any test that is conducive to discourse chunks constrained by event chronology, cause-effect relations, and the like, will be superior in reliability and validity to syntactic scorings that rely on a few points of morphology and syntax. Consider the fact that the syntactic scoring of the BSM questions 5, 6, and 7 above allows for only three possible points of variability in the data while the pragmatic scoring of questions A to H allows 19 points. Because of the greater possibility for variance and the kind of variance likely to emerge from a pragmatic scoring, reliability and validity indices would probably increase. Partial credit for partially correct answers would allow for even more meaningful variability in the data provided the scoring were done reliably.

Perhaps what is most important from all of the foregoing remarks about the BSM is that similar picture tasks that depict events with meaningful sequence constraints could easily be adapted to similar testing techniques by a creative teacher. Many tasks could be devised. The example selected for discussion here is therefore offered only as an illustration of how one might begin.

C. The *Ilyin Oral Interview* and the Upshur *Oral Communication Test*

Research with techniques like the BSM for assessing the relative ability of children in two or more languages has probably been less extensive than work with techniques for second language oral assessment, but the latter are also relatively unresearched in comparison to techniques that rely mainly on response modes other than speaking. Among the recently developed structured interview techniques are the *Ilyin Oral Interview* (1976) developed by Donna Ilyin in San Francisco and the *Oral Communication Test* developed at the English Language Institute of the University of Michigan chiefly under the direction of John A. Upshur. The Ilyin interview is the more typical and the more pragmatically oriented of the two so we will consider it first.

A page from the student's test booklet used during the interview is displayed as Figure 17. The pictures attempt to summarize several days' activities in terms of major sequences of events on those days. For instance, the first sequence of events pictured across the top of the page was supposed to have occurred 'Last Sunday' as indicated at the left. The first pictured event was supposed to have taken place at 9:55 in the morning as indicated by the clock under the picture (The man getting out of bed); the second at 10:25 (the man eating breakfast); and the third between 11:00 am and 5:00 pm (off to the beach with a female friend). Ilyin explains in the Manual (1976) that the examinee is to relate to the pictures in terms of whatever day the test is actually administered on. Therefore, she has constructed a form to be administered on any weekday except Friday and another to be given on any weekday except Monday (this is so the referents of 'Yesterday' and 'Tomorrow' will fall on weekdays or weekends as desired). The two forms may be used separately in test-retest studies or together to obtain higher reliability. Each consists of a 50 item version recommended for lower level students and a 30 item version which may be used at intermediate and advanced levels.

The set of pictures given in Figure 17 are actually used in orienting the examinee to the overall procedure. They will serve the purpose

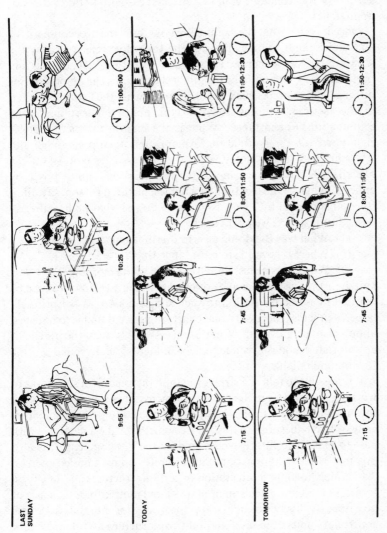

Figure 17. Sample pictures for the *Orientation* Section of the *Ilyin Oral Interview.* (1976)

here, however, of illustrating the testing technique. The point is not to recommend the particular procedures of Ilyin's test, but rather to show how the technique could be adapted easily to a wide variety of approaches.

Once it is clear that the examinee knows how the procedure works and understands the meanings of the time slots referred to by the separate picture sequences as well as the picture sequence on any particular day, a number of meaningful questions can be posed. For instance, the examinee may be asked to tell what the fictitious person in the pictures is doing today at the approximate time of the examination. For instance, 'What is the man in the picture doing right now? It's about 10:00 am.' An appropriate response might be: 'He's in class taking notes while the professor is writing on the blackboard.' From there, more complex questions can be posed by either looking forward in time to what the pictured person, say, 'Bill' (the name offered by Ilyin), is going to do, or what he has already done. For instance, we might ask:

(1) What was Bill doing at 7:15 this morning?
(2) Where is he going to be at lunch time?
(3) Where was he last Sunday at 7:45 in the morning?

and so forth. The number and complexity of the questions that can be reasonably posed in relation to such simple contexts is surprisingly large. Neither is it necessary that every single event that is to be asked about also be pictured. What is necessary is that the range of appropriate responses is adequately limited so as to make scoring feasible and reliable.

It is possible to follow a strategy in the construction of such tasks of working outward from the present moment either toward the past or toward the future. Or one might follow the strategy of chronologically ordered questions that generate something like a narrative with past to present to future events guiding the development. It is also possible and tempting for the discrete point minded person deliberately to plan the elicitation of certain structures and linguistic forms, but to opt for such an organizational motive for a sequence of questions is likely to obliterate the sense of normal discourse constraints unless the discrete points of structure are planned very cleverly into the sequence.

If, on the other hand, one opts for one of the more pragmatic strategies, say of merely following the chronology of events in the series, asking simpler questions at the beginning and more complex ones later in the series, it is likely that the discrete points of syntax one might have tried to elicit more deliberately will naturally fall out in the pragmatically motivated sequence. An example of a relatively simple question would be: 'Where is Bill now? It's 10:00.' A more complex question would be: 'What was Bill doing yesterday at 10:25?' A still more complex question would be: 'What would Bill be doing today, right now, if it were Sunday?' Or even more complex: 'What would Bill have been doing Sunday at 7:45 if he had thought it was a regular week-day?'

Oral tests built around actual or contrived contexts of discourse afford essentially unlimited possibilities. The examples given above in relation to the *Ilyin Oral Interview* merely display some of the options. Clearly the technique could be modified in any number of ways to create more difficult or less difficult tasks. For instance, the procedure could easily be converted into a story retelling task if E were to tell the examinee just what is happening in each pictured event (say, starting from past and working up to future events). Then the examinee might be asked to retell the story, preferably not to the same E, but to someone else. To make the task simpler, the second person might prompt the examinee concerning the pictures by asking appropriate leading questions. Or, to make the task simpler still, it could easily be converted to an elicited imitation task.

Another testing technique that has been used with non-native speakers of English is the *Oral Communication Test* developed by John A. Upshur at the University of Michigan. It is a highly structured oral interview task where the examinee is tested on his ability to convey certain kinds of information to the examiner. In the development of the test, Upshur (1969a) defined 'productive communication' as a process whereby 'as a result of some action by a speaker (or writer) his audience creates a *new* concept' (p. 179). The criterion of successful communication was that there must be 'a correspondence between the intentions of a speaker and the concept created by his audience' (p. 179).

Upshur and his collaborators set up a test to assess productive communication ability as follows: (1) examinee and examiner are presented with four pictures which differ in certain crucial respects on one or more 'conceptual dimensions'. (Figure 18 displays three sets of four pictures each.) (2) The examinee is told which of the four he is to describe to the examiner. They are separated from each other so that the examiner cannot see which of the four pictures has been designated as the criterion for the examinee. Further, the pictures are in different orders in the examiner's set otherwise the examinee could

Figure 18.   Items from the Upshur *Oral Communication Test.*

merely say, 'The one to the far left,' or 'The second one from the left,'
and so forth. (3) The examinee tells the examiner which picture to
mark and the examiner makes a guess. (4) The number of hits, that is,
correct guesses by the examiner is the score of the examinee.
Interestingly, Upshur found in experimental uses of this testing
technique that time was a crucial factor. If examinees were given
unlimited amounts of time there was little difference in performance
between speakers who were more proficient and speakers who were
less proficient as judged by other assessment techniques. However, if

time constraints were imposed (i.e., if subjects were given only a certain number of seconds for each task, say a few seconds more than native speakers require to perform the same task) there was good discrimination between more and less proficient examinees.

Apparently, the normal time constraints associated with oral communication are not otherwise intrinsically involved in the performance of the *Oral Communication Test*. It seems likely that this is so because the *Oral Communication Test* violates the pragmatic naturalness constraint of meaningful sequence. That is, there is no temporal connection of the sort characteristic of normal discourse between consecutive items on the test. The question that arises is whether the task could be modified in such a way that meaningful connection between consecutive items on the task could be obtained. Artificial imposition of time limits on items is one way of dealing with the problem, but some of the artificiality can be done away with if there are more natural reasons for progressing from one item to the next at a normal conversational rate. Further, as will be explained below, discourse constraints ranging across several events or utterances in a text (where 'text' is taken to refer to chunks of discourse in general) constitute intrinsic temporal constraints.

Pragmatically more viable forms of the *Oral Communication Test* could be constructed by setting up a sequential connection between the items of the test. Instead of going from a set of four pictures where someone is pictured in various postures relative to an observer, to a set of pictures where the observer is looking at different hair styles, the sequence of criterion items might tell a story. For instance, in the first set of pictures a man might be displayed in various relations to a doorway (as in the first set of pictures in Figure 18). Say the criterion item is the one where the man is entering a corridor. The next items might depict the man (a) coming out of the other end of the same corridor, (b) walking down the corridor, (c) stopping to talk with some other man, (d) turning aside at a doorway leading to an adjoining room. Any these latter possibilities are logically possible sequiturs for the antecedent event of entering the corridor. The next set of pictures might include any events that could logically follow from the event that is designated as the criterion from the set described in (a) – (d), and so forth throughout the test.

With such a modification, it would probably still be necessary to impose time constraints on each set of pictures, and perhaps the examiner would have to exercise more judgemental discretion concerning what constitutes an acceptable description of the criterion. The technique would, however, afford more realistic testing of the kinds of discourse constraints that emerge in normal conversation. Further, it would be possible to consider additional scoring techniques that discriminate responses of the examinee in greater detail.

D. The *Foreign Service Institute Oral Interview*

Perhaps the most widely used oral testing procedure is one developed by the Foreign Service Institute. It involves, usually, two interviewers and a candidate in a room set aside for the purpose of the interview. Sessions are tape recorded for future reference and to establish a permanent record for possible validity studies and other purposes. The main objective of the oral interview is to determine the level of 'speaking' proficiency of candidates on a five point scale defined roughly as follows:

(1) *Able to satisfy routine travel needs and minimum courtesy requirements.* Can ask and answer questions on topics very familiar to him; within the scope of his very limited language experience can understand simple questions and statements, ...

(2) *Able to satisfy routine social demands and limited work requirements.* Can handle with confidence but not with facility most social situations including introductions and casual conversations about current events, as well as work, family, and autobiographical information ...

(3) *Able to speak the language with sufficient structural accuracy and vocabulary to participate effectively in most formal and informal conversations on practical, social, and professional topics.* Can discuss particular interests and special fields of competence with reasonable ease; comprehension is quite complete for a normal rate of speech; vocabulary is broad enough that he rarely has to grope for a word; accent may be obviously foreign; control of grammar good; errors never interfere with understanding and rarely disturb the native speaker.

(4) *Able to use the language fluently and accurately on all levels normally pertinent to professional needs.* Can understand and participate in any conversation within his range of experience with a high degree of fluency and precision of vocabulary; would rarely be taken for a native speaker, but can respond appropriately even in unfamiliar situations; errors of pronunciation and grammar quite rare; can handle informal interpreting from and into the language.

(5) *Speaking proficiency equivalent to that of an educated native*

speaker. Has complete fluency in the language such that his speech on all levels is fully accepted by educated native speakers in all of its features, including breadth of vocabulary and idiom, colloquialisms, and pertinent cultural references (ETS, 1970, pp. 10–11).[1]

The interview normally does not take more than about thirty minutes and except in cases where subjects simply are not able to carry on a conversation in the language it usually takes at least fifteen minutes. While the *Manual for Peace Corps Language Testers* prepared by ETS in 1970 stresses that the conversation should be natural, it also emphasizes the point that 'it is *not* simply a friendly conversation on whatever topics come to mind ... It is rather, a specialized procedure which efficiently uses the relatively brief testing period to explore many different aspects of the student's language competence in order to place him into one of the categories described' (ETS, 1970, p. 11).

The influence of discrete point theory is not lacking in the FSI procedure. Candidates are rated separately on scales that pertain to accent, grammar, vocabulary, fluency, and comprehension. In the Appendix we will show that these separate ratings apparently do not contribute different types of variance and that in fact they appear to add little to what could be obtained by simply assigning an overall rating of oral language proficiency (also see Callaway, in press, and Mullen, in press b). Nevertheless, in order to provide a fairly comprehensive description of the FSI procedure, we will look at the five separate scales that FSI uses 'to supplement the overall rating'. (As we will see below, the ratings on these scales are weighted differentially. We will see that the grammar scale receives the heaviest weighting, followed by vocabulary, then comprehension, then fluency, then accent which receives the lowest weighting.)

Accent

1. Pronunciation frequently unintelligible.
2. Frequent gross errors and a very heavy accent make understanding difficult, require frequent repetition.
3. 'Foreign accent' requires concentrated listening and mispronunciations lead to occasional misunderstanding and apparent errors in grammar or vocabulary.

---

[1] This quote and subsequent materials from the same publication (*Manual for Peace Corps Language Testers*, 1970) is reprinted by permission of Educational Testing Service.

4. Marked 'foreign accent' and occasional mispronunciations which do not interfere with understanding.
5. No conspicuous mispronunciations, but would not be taken for a native speaker.
6. Native pronunciation, with no trace of 'foreign accent'.

Grammar
1. Grammar almost entirely inaccurate except in stock phrases.
2. Constant errors showing control of very few major patterns and frequently preventing communication.
3. Frequent errors showing some major patterns uncontrolled and causing occasional irritation and misunderstanding.
4. Occasional errors showing imperfect control of some patterns but no weakness that causes misunderstanding.
5. Few errors, with no patterns of failure.
6. No more than two errors during the interview.

Vocabulary
1. Vocabulary inadequate for even the simplest conversation.
2. Vocabulary limited to basic personal and survival areas (time, food, transportation, family, etc.).
3. Choice of words sometimes inaccurate, limitations of vocabulary prevent discussion of some common professional and social topics.
4. Professional vocabulary adequate to discuss special interests; general vocabulary permits discussion of any nontechnical subject with some circumlocutions.
5. Professional vocabulary broad and precise; general vocabulary adequate to cope with complex practical problems and varied social situations.
6. Vocabulary apparently as accurate and extensive as that of an educated native speaker.

Fluency
1. Speech is so halting and fragmentary that conversation is virtually impossible.
2. Speech is very slow and uneven except for short or routine sentences.
3. Speech is frequently hesitant and jerky; sentences may be left uncompleted.
4. Speech is occasionally hesitant, with some unevenness caused by rephrasing and groping for words.
5. Speech is effortless and smooth, but perceptibly non-native in speed and evenness.
6. Speech on all professional and general topics as effortless and smooth as a native speaker's.

Comprehension
1. Understands too little for the simplest type of conversation.
2. Understands only slow, very simple speech on common social and touristic topics; requires constant repetition and rephrasing.
3. Understands careful, somewhat simplified speech directed to him, with considerable repetition and rephrasing.
4. Understands quite well normal educated speech directed to him, but requires occasional repetition and rephrasing.
5. Understands everything in normal educated conversation except for very colloquial or low-frequency items, or exceptionally rapid or slurred speech.
6. Understands everything in both formal and colloquial speech to be expected of an educated native speaker (ETS, 1970, pp. 20–22).

Although the *Manual* seems to insist that the above verbal descriptions of points on the various scales are merely 'supplementary' in nature, there is a table for converting scores on the various scales to a composite total score which can then be converted to a rating on the overall five levels given above. The conversion table is given below:

WEIGHTING TABLE

Proficiency Description	1	2	3	4	5	6	
Accent	0	1	2	2	3	4	_____
Grammar	6	12	18	24	30	36	_____
Vocabulary	4	8	12	16	20	24	_____
Fluency	2	4	6	8	10	12	_____
Comprehension	4	8	12	15	19	23	_____
						Total:	_____

CONVERSION TABLE

Total Score (from Weighting Table)	FSI Level
16–25	0+
26–32	1
33–42	1+
43–52	2
53–62	2+
63–72	3
73–82	3+
83–92	4
93–99	4+

For example, suppose a given candidate is interviewed and it is decided that he rates a 2 on the scale for Accent. According to the verbal description this means that the candidate makes 'frequent gross errors' has 'a very heavy accent' and requires 'frequent repetition'. From the Weighting Table the tester will determine that a rating of 2 on the Accent scale is worth 1 point toward the total overall rating and the eventual determination of the overall level on the FSI rating system. Suppose further that the examinee is rated 3 on the Grammar scale ('Frequent errors showing some major patterns uncontrolled and causing occasional irritation and misunderstanding'). By the Weighting Table this score is worth 18 points toward the total. Say then that the same examinee is rated 3 on Vocabulary for an additional 12 points; 3 on Fluency for 6 points; and 3 on Comprehension for 12 points. The examinee's total score would thus be $1 + 18 + 12 + 6 + 12 = 49$. This score according to the Conversion Table would rank the candidate at level 2. That is, the candidate would be judged to be '*Able to satisfy routine social demands and limited work requirements.*'

Is it fair to say that the technique is already formidable? There are many problems in the interpretation of the verbal descriptions of the various scales, and there are many more in the interpretation of the meaning of the overall ratings once they are arrived at. Nonetheless, the procedure seems to work fairly well. The examiners of course are required to complete a fairly rigorous training program, and there are a number of procedural niceties that we have omitted discussing. The interested reader should obtain further information from the ETS *Manual for Peace Corps Language Testers* (1970) and other ETS and FSI publications. The point in discussing the procedure here has not been to recommend it in particular, but rather to suggest some ways that similar testing techniques that would be more feasible for a broader spectrum of educational assessment problems might be constructed.

Surely if raters can be trained to agree substantially on what qualifies as 'the simplest type of comprehension', 'very simple speech', 'somewhat simplified speech', 'everything in normal educated conversation except for very colloquial or low-frequency items', 'everything in both formal and colloquial speech' (see the verbal descriptions of the six point Comprehension scale given above), they can do the simpler task of rating subjects on a five or six point scale where the points are defined in terms of assigning the lowest ratings to the worst performers and the highest to the highest.

If interview performance is also compared against performance on a more structured oral test, the meanings of points on the interview scale can be referenced against scores on the other task and vice versa.

Obviously, the FSI Oral Interview was conceived with adults in mind. Further, it was aimed toward adults who were expected to fill governmental posts at home or abroad. However vague the verbal descriptions of performances may be in relation to the target population and the requisite skills, they nonetheless work rather well. There is every reason to believe that similar techniques referenced against different target populations and different performances might work equally well.

The essential features of the Oral Interview procedure used by FSI are perhaps difficult to identify. However, if we desire to extend what has been learned from that technique of evaluation to other similar techniques, we must decide what the parameters of the similarity are to be. What techniques in other words can we expect to produce results similar to those achieved with the FSI Oral Interview? Obviously, not all of the results are desirable. The ones that would be useful in a wide range of oral testing settings are the attainment of highly reliable ratings of speech samples in ways that are at least related to the performance of specific educational tasks. In this sense, the generalizability of the procedure to the rating of speech samples in a wide range of contexts seems possible.

As we show in the Appendix, the FSI Oral Interview is not dependent for its reliability on the componential breakdown of skills. In fact, it is apparently dependent on the ability of intelligent speakers of a language (namely, the raters) to assign scores to performances that are not defined in any adequate descriptive terminology. It is apparently the case that the utility of the FSI procedure is dependent primarily on the ability of raters to differentiate performances on one basic dimension – the pragmatic effectiveness of speech acts.

One hesitates to propose any particular example of an extension of the FSI rating procedure to other speech acts because the range of possibilities defies the imagination. It is probably the case that suitable rating scales can be created for almost any spontaneous speech act that tends to recur under specifiable circumstances. For instance, repetitive interactions in the classroom between children and teachers, or between children and other children, or outside the classroom between children and others. Formal interview situations of a wide variety could be judged for pragmatic complexity, affective arrousal (say, enthusiasm and effectiveness in creating the same feelings in the interlocutor) and confidence. Or perhaps they should be judged only in terms of pragmatic complexity of utterances and át the same time the effectiveness of those same utterances.

People are constantly engaged in evaluating the speech of other people. It is not so strange an occurrence that it is exclusively the domain of language testing *per se*. Viewers of television and movies judge the performances of actors to be more or less effective. Readers implicitly or often explicitly judge the effectiveness of a narrator in telling a story, or of an expositor in explaining something clearly. Some speakers are said to be articulate and others less so. Some performances of speech acts are judged to be particularly adept, others inept. All of these judgements presumably have to do with the appropriateness of usages of words in contexts of speech. Hence, the FSI type of rating scales would appear to be generalizable to speech acts of many different sorts.

Requisite decisions include how the speech acts are to be elicited; what the rating scale(s) will be referenced against; and who is a qualified rater. Speech acts may be contrived in interview settings (as they are in the case of the FSI Oral Interview), or they may be taped or simply observed interactions between the examinee and some other or others. The rating scale may refer to the surface form of the utterances used by the examinee – i.e., focussing on questions of well-formedness (by someone's definition), or it may refer to questions of pragmatic effectiveness – i.e., how well does the examinee communicate meanings in the setting of the speech act.

Persons who are asked to rate performances of examinees should be speakers of the language in question and should be able to demonstrate their ability to differentiate poor performances from good ones in agreement with other competent judges. The latter requirement can be met by taking samples of better and worse performances and asking judges (or potential judges) to rate them. If judges consistently agree on what constitutes a better performance or more succinctly on how to rank order a series of clearly differentiated performances ranging from weak to strong, the necessary rudiments of reliability and validity are probably implicit in such judgements.

E. Other pragmatic speaking tasks

Clearly, the specific tasks discussed to this point were all designed with special purposes in mind. There are other testing procedures that can be applied to a wider variety of testing purposes and which were not designed with any special population or testing objective in mind. For instance, a generally applicable oral language task is reading aloud. Another is oral cloze procedure. Still another is narrative repetition, the oral analogue of what was discussed in Chapter 10 above under the term dictation/composition. In this section, we turn our attention to these techniques in particular as tasks for eliciting speech. Reading aloud and oral cloze have the distinct advantage of being somewhat more easily quantifiable than some of the more open-ended procedures discussed above. Elicited imitation which was discussed in Chapter 10 can also be used as a speaking task, and it too, like oral cloze testing, is relatively easy to score.

1. *Reading aloud.* It will be objected early that reading and speaking are dissimilar tasks. This is largely true if one reads silently, and even if one reads aloud, there are differences between reading aloud and speaking. Therefore, reading aloud can only be used for persons who are known to be good readers in at least one language besides the one they are to be tested in, and in situations where the learners have had ample opportunity to become literate in the language in which they are to be tested.

Paul A. Kolers (1968) reported results with a reading aloud task which he used in a study of the nature of bilingualism. He asked subjects to read a paragraph in English and also its translation in French. His purpose was to discover whether there was a significant difference in the amount of time required to read the text in English or in French and the time required to read the same material mixed together in both French and English. The latter detail is of interest to this discussion only insofar as Kolers' study showed that the efficiency of processing is related to the amount of time it takes to convert the printed form to a spoken stream of speech. The English passage and its French translation are given below:

> His horse, followed by two hounds, made the earth resound under its even tread. Drops of ice stuck to his cloak. A strong wind was blowing. One side of the horizon lighted up, and in the whiteness of the early morning light, he saw rabbits hopping at the edge of their burrows.
>
> Son cheval, suivi de deux bassets, en marchant d'un pas égal faisait résonner la terre. Des gouttes de verglas se collaient à son manteau. Une brise violente soufflait. Un côté de l'horizon s'éclaircit; et, dans la blancheur du crépuscule, il aperçut des lapins sautillant au bord de leur terriers.

How could reading aloud be used as a measure of speaking ability or at least of fluency in reading aloud? There are a variety of conceivable scoring procedures. One easy way to score such a task would be to record the reading protocols on tape and then measure the amount of time from the onset of the first word to the termination of the last word in the spoken protocol. This can be done with a stop watch or with the timing mechanism on the tape recorder provided the latter is accurate enough. There must also be some method for taking into account the accuracy of the rendition. A word by word scoring for recognizability (and/or accuracy of pronunciation) could be recorded along with the amount of time required for the reading. The average time required by a sample of fluent native speakers would provide a kind of ceiling (as opposed to a baseline) performance against which to compare the performance of non-natives on the same task.

Another possible scoring technique would be to rate the reading aloud protocols the way one would rate speech protocols in an interview setting – subjectively according to loosely stated criteria. For instance, the reading could be rated for accuracy and this rating could be reported along with the amount of time required to complete the task.

Reading aloud is probably easier than speaking. That is, a person should be expected to be able to read fluently things that he could not say fluently without the aid of a written text. However, it is unlikely that a person who cannot speak fluently in any context without a script will be able to do so with a script. A foreign language learner, for example, who cannot carry on a simple conversation fluently will probably not be able to read a somewhat more complex text with fluency either. Hence, the technique deserves investigation as a pragmatic speaking task.

It may be true that a fluent native speaker can read aloud while thinking about something else and that in this special case the task violates the pragmatic naturalness criterion of meaningfulness. However, the important question for the possible use we are discussing is whether the non-native speaker who does not know the language well can read a passage of text fluently without understanding it in the sense of mapping the sequences of words onto appropriate extralinguistic context. If the non-native must comprehend what he is reading in order to do so fluently, then reading aloud to that extent qualifies as a pragmatic testing procedure. (For some preliminary data on reading aloud as a language proficiency measure, see the Appendix, especially section D.)

2. *Oral cloze procedure.* One of the most versatile and least used

oral testing procedures is the oral cloze test (Taylor, 1956). It can be constructed in a multitude of forms. Oral cloze procedures have been applied in a variety of ways to special research interests, but only recently to problems of language proficiency assessment. For instance, Miller and Selfridge (1950) used a variety of oral cloze technique to construct texts of differing degrees of approximation to normal English. Aborn, Rubenstein, and Sterling (1959) used an oral cloze approach in a study of constraints on words in sentences. Craker (1971) used an oral cloze test to study the relationship between language proficiency and scores on educational tests for children in Albuquerque, New Mexico. A pioneering study by Stevenson (1974) used an oral cloze test as a measure of the English proficiency of foreign students at Indiana University. Scholz, *et al* (in press) used oral cloze tests for a similar purpose at Southern Illinois University (again see the Appendix, section D).

Although no thoroughgoing study of the properties of oral cloze tests has been done, on the strength of the extensive work with written cloze tasks and the few successful applications of oral cloze tests, the technique can be recommended with some confidence. To be sure, there are important differences in the oral applications of the technique and the more familiar reading and writing procedures (see Chapter 12), but there are also some substantial similarities. Whereas in the written task examinees can utilize context on both sides of a blank (or decision point), in an oral cloze test usually only the preceding context is available to help the examinee infer the appropriate next word at any decision point. This difference can be minimized by allowing the test subjects to hear the passage once or twice without any deletions before they actually attempt to fill in blanks in the text. Someone might object that this modification of oral cloze procedure would make it more of a test of listening comprehension, but for reasons given in Part One above, this is not a very significant objection. Normal speaking always involves an element of listening comprehension. However, even if the decisions in an oral cloze test must be made only on the basis of preceding context and without reference to the material to follow, there are still fundamental similarities between written and oral cloze tests. Probably the most important is that in both tasks it is necessary to generate expectancies concerning what is likely to come next at a given point. This requires knowledge of discourse constraints concerning the limits of sequiturs.

There are many ways of doing oral cloze tests. We will begin by considering a variant that derives in fairly straightforward fashion from the well-known written cloze test procedures. As in the case of dictation, a first step is to select an appropriate text. The considerations that were discussed in Chapter 10 would also generally apply to the selection of material for an oral cloze task. Because speaking tasks place a heavier burden on short term memory and on the attention of the speaker, however, the text for an oral cloze test should probably be pitched at a somewhat lower level other things being equal. The text may be a tape-recording of a radio or television broadcast, a segment of a drama, or a portion of some written text converted to an oral form.

An example of a fairly difficult text for an oral cloze test follows. Slash marks indicate pause points. Deletions are italicized.

> Each year since the 1960s hospitals in the United States have had to accommodate about one million additional/ (*patients*). As a result, hospitals across the/ (*country*) have searched for new ways to/ (*be*) more efficient in order to provide/ (*the*) best possible patient care.
> Harris Hospital, a 628-bed institution/ (*in*) Fort Worth, Texas, has successfully/ (*met*) this need using a computer-based system. Key to the/ (*system*) is an IBM computer and more/ (*than*) 100 terminals located at the admitting/ (*desk*), all nursing stations and in key/ (*departments*) throughout the hospital.
> Staff members can now/ (*enter*) or retrieve all pertinent medical information/ (*on*) every patient from any authorized location in the hospital (from the text of an IBM advertisement, *Reader's Digest*, February, 1977, p. 216).

A text like this one can be administered in a variety of ways. Probably most of the variations in the way the task is done would tend to affect its overall difficulty level more than anything else. For instance, the text may be presented in its entirety (without any deletions) one or more times before it is presented with pauses for the examinee(s) to fill in the missing portions. After each decision point, where the examinee is given a certain amount of time to guess the next word in the sequence, the correct form may or may not be given before progressing to the next decision point.

It is also possible to test examinees over every word in the text by systematically shifting the deletion points and by making a new pass through the material for each new set of deletion points. For instance, if every fifth word is deleted on the first pass, it is only necessary to shift all blanks one word to the left, make another pass, and repeat this procedure four times (that is, for a total of five passes) in order to test examinees over every word in the text.

Another technique which can be used to test subjects over every word in a given text is what may be called a forward build-up. The examinee is given a certain amount of lead-in material, say, the first ten words of text, and then is required to guess each successive word of the text. After each guess he is given the material up to and including the word just attempted. Obviously, there are many possible variations on this theme as well. It could be done sentence by sentence throughout a text, or it could be used over the entire text. It has the drawback of seeming tedious because of the number of times that the lead-in material preceding each guess has to be repeated. The word just preceding the word to be attempted at any decision point may have been heard only once (twice if the examinee guessed correctly on the preceding attempt), but the word before that has been heard at least twice, the word before that three times, and so on, such that the word n words before a given decision point will have been heard n times when that decision point is reached in the text.

Yet another possibility is for the examinee to guess not the next word, but the next sensible phrase or unit of meaning. This type of oral cloze test seems to be closer to the sort of hypothesizing that normal language users are always doing when listening to speech with full comprehension.

If every word in a text is to be tested, which necessitates one of the iterative procedures with multiple passes through the same material, a passage of no more than 100 words will probably provide substantial reliability as a testing device. The reliability attained, of course, will vary according to the degree of appropriateness of the difficulty level of the text, and a number of related parameters that affect difficulty (see Chapter 10 on the discussion of selecting a dictation text). If an every nth word deletion procedure is to be used without iterative passes through the text, a passage of n times fifty will probably provide adequate reliability for most any purpose. For classroom tests with more specific aims – e.g., assessing comprehension of a particular instruction, a given lesson, a portion of a text, or the like – it is quite possible that much shorter tasks would have sufficient reliability and validity to be used effectively.

Oral cloze tasks could conceivably be done live, but for many reasons this is not generally recommended. Tape-recorded texts offer ample time for editing on the part of the examiner which is simply not available in face-to-face live testing. If examinees can be tested in a language laboratory where individual responses are recorded, this too is an advantage generally. Testing can be done one-on-one, but for many obvious reasons this is less economical in most educational settings.

It is also possible to have examinees write responses to oral cloze items. This possibility requires investigation, however, before it can be seriously recommended as an alternative to elicited speech. Further, if the responses are to be written, many of the techniques that are applicable in the case of spoken responses cannot be used for testing. For instance, if the examinee is asked to write responses, no feedback can be given concerning the correct form before proceeding to the next decision point – that would be giving away the answers. In the oral situation by contrast, if the examinee is required to speak his answer into a microphone in so many seconds, subsequent feedback concerning the appropriate word will not impinge on the word or words spoken onto the tape some seconds before by the examinee. Iterative techniques are generally less applicable also if responses are written. We should note, however, that the written response possibility has much appeal because it would allow the testing of many subjects simultaneously without the need for more than one tape recorder.

Oral cloze test protocols may be scored in several ways of which we will only briefly consider two. Responses may be scored for the exact word to appear at a particular point in a text, or they may be scored for their appropriateness to the preceding (and/or total) context. Both of these options are discussed in considerably greater detail along with several other options in Chapter 12 on written cloze tasks. Therefore, only two recommendations will be made here, and the reader is encouraged to consider the discussion in Chapter 12 on the same topic. It is believed to be generally relevant to the scoring problem regardless of the testing mode. However, for oral cloze tests, it is suggested that (1) contextually appropriate responses should be scored as correct unless there is some compelling reason to use the exact word scoring technique; and (2) in determining what constitutes an appropriate response, *all of the context* to which the learner has been exposed at a given point in the text should be taken into account (this is assuming that the text is meaningfully sequenced to start with – that it does not consist of disjointed and unrelated sentences). If the learner has been exposed to the entire text on one or more readings, then the entire text is the context to be taken into account in judging the appropriateness of responses.

3. *Narrative tasks*. Normally, describing a picture is not a narrative task. It only becomes one if the picture fits into a stream of experience where certain events lead to other events. Where causes have effects, and effects have causes – where there is a meaningful and non-random sequential development of one thing leading to another. It is not necessary that the progression be a strictly logical one – experience is not strictly logical – but it is necessary that there be some sort of discoverable connection between events in a sequence in order for the sequence to serve as an appropriate basis for narrative.

As we noted in Chapter 10, story retelling tasks are merely a special kind of elicited imitation task. There are many other sorts of narrative tasks however. A very interesting example is offered by Cazden, *et al* (1976). A child is given a set of materials and is instructed to build or make whatever he wants to with them. The materials in experimental trials included some 'plastic foam, fasteners, paper, pipe cleaners, tape, etc.' and some 'tools' including 'magic markers and scissors'. The children were given about 30 minutes for the construction project, then they were asked to write about '"how" they made whatever they made' (p. 7f). The writing task was allotted 35 minutes.

An oral form of this testing procedure could be conducted by asking children to tell how they made what they made to a non-threatening interlocutor. If desired, the protocols could be tape-recorded for later analysis and scoring. One possible simplification of the scoring of such protocols would be to use a rating procedure comparable to the kinds of scales invented by the FSI (see above) for the oral assessment of adult protocols. Scales for creativity, communicative effectiveness, and whatever else the teacher might subjectively want to evaluate could be constructed. These should be carefully researched, however, to assess their validity. Perhaps a single overall scale would make the most sense. See Callaway (in press) and Mullen (in press b).

Another type of narrative task consists of retelling a story. This technique is probably most applicable for children, but appropriate versions can also be constructed for adults (e.g., telling someone how to follow a set of complicated instructions that have just been presented by a third party). The Gallup-McKinley School District in New Mexico has recently collaborated with the Lau Center in Albuquerque in developing a pilot test that includes a story retelling task. Children are interviewed one at a time by two adults.

First the child is asked non-threatening questions about himself and things that he likes. Then the examiner tells the child a story preceded by the instruction that the child is to listen carefully so that he can retell the story to another person who has ostensibly not heard the story before. As much as possible, the story relates to things that represent familiar objects in the reservation environment of Gallup, New Mexico. The things used include a toy pick-up (of which one child avowed 'Every kid should have one o' them'), a string doubling for a rope, a horse made of plastic, a toy dog, and some other objects. The story involves going on a trip to a place designated by the child as a place that he or she would like to visit more than any other place in the world. The pick-up gets stuck. The horse is unloaded and hitched to the bumper to pull it out. Meanwhile the dog gets lost chasing rabbits. After a search he is located on a desert road where he is being chased by a giant jackrabbit.

The first adult who told the story then leaves the room and the second adult who has not heard the story enters and the child (usually with considerable alacrity) tells the second person the story. It is important that the second adult be someone who (from the child's point of view) has not heard the story. It seems odd even to a child to turn around and retell a story to someone who just made it up, but it is not unnatural at all to tell a story just heard to a party that has not heard it before.

The scoring of protocols (which are usually recorded on tape) is only slightly less difficult than it is in the case of narrative tasks where the content is less well defined. At least in the case of story retelling, the content that the child is supposed to express is fairly well defined. It must be decided whether to subtract points for insertion of extraneous material or in fact to reward it as a case of verbal creativity. It must be determined how to weight (if at all) different portions of the content. Some events may be more salient than others – e.g., the jackrabbit chasing the dog is a chuckler for any reservation child. One possible solution is to assign overall subjective ratings to the child based on predetermined scales – e.g., overall communicative effectiveness may be rated on a scale of one to five where the points on the scale are defined in terms of nothing more specific than better and worse performances of different children attempting the task. Another possibility is to score protocols for major details of the story and the comprehensibility of the rendition of those details by the child. A perfect rendition would receive full credit for all major facts. A rendition that omits a major fact of the story would have a certain number of points subtracted depending on the subjectively determined weighting of that fact in the story. A rendition of a particular fact that is distorted or only partly comprehensible would receive partial credit, and so forth.

Versions of narrative tasks for adults or for more advanced learners can easily be conceived. Interpretive tasks are actually not so uncommon as the opponents of translation as a testing device have sometimes argued. A text may be presented in either the target language (that is, the target of the testing procedure) or in some other language known to the examinee(s). The task then is telling someone else what the text contained – that is reiterating it to some third party. In this light, translation of a substantial text (say, fifty words or more) is merely a special kind of retelling or paraphrasing task. The reader is left to explore the many other possibilities that can be developed along these lines. It is suggested that the scoring considerations discussed in Chapter 13 with reference to essay tasks be taken as a foundation for investigating alternative scoring methods for other productive tasks such as narrative reporting, etc. Also, see Chapter 14 for sample speech protocols from the Mount Gravatt Australian research project and for suggestions concerning the relationship of speech to literacy and school tasks in general.

KEY POINTS
1. Pragmatic speaking tasks should generally involve something to say and someone to say it to.
2. Examples of pragmatic speaking tasks include structured and unstructured interviews, and a wide range of text processing and construction tasks including oral cloze procedures, narrative based tasks, and for some purposes perhaps, reading aloud.
3. Speaking tests are important because of the special importance associated with speech in all aspects of human intercourse.
4. There is a serious need for better oral language tests.
5. *The Bilingual Syntax Measure* is an example of one published test that affords the possibility of meaningful sequence across test items.
6. Its colorful illustrations and surprise value make it a naturally suitable basis for eliciting discourse type protocols from children.
7. Alternative question formats and non-discrete point scoring procedures, however, are recommended.
8. *The Ilyin Oral Interview* is used as an example of how pictured sequences of events can be used to elicit discourse in a somewhat more complex form than the *Bilingual Syntax Measure*.
9. A possible modification of the *Oral Communication Test* is discussed.
10. The FSI Oral Interview technique is suggested as a procedure with many possible applications.

11. Its focus on discrete point categories of traditional testing (e.g., distinct rating scales for 'Accent', 'Vocabulary', 'Grammar', and so on) is generally rejected as an unnecessary complication.

12. However, the rating scale technique of the FSI Oral Interview is viewed as being easily adaptable to the evaluation of almost any spoken protocol – e.g., classroom or playground interactions between children and others, or story retelling protocols.

13. Other pragmatic speaking tasks that are discussed include various devices for eliciting speech from examinees.

14. Reading aloud is considered to have applicability with literate language users.

15. A variety of oral cloze tasks based mostly on extensions of well-studied written tasks are considered.

16. Among them are iterative and non-iterative procedures.

17. Two narrative tasks are discussed in some detail and a number of others are implied: for instance, the child may determine what is to be said, or the examiner may tell a story and ask the child to repeat it. Similar procedures can easily be extended to adults.

18. Many other pragmatic tasks can be inferred from the examples that are discussed – among them are various translation and paraphrasing tasks that are similar to the other narrative tasks offered.

DISCUSSION QUESTIONS

1. In what ways is talk a means for discovering thoughts? Without speech or its surrogate, writing, how could thoughts be made public? Consider the possibility of thought without words. Introspect on the question. About how much of your thinking is of the non-verbal sort? Can you conceptualize or imagine the meaning of the phrase *10,000,000 people* without words? Try the Pythagorean theorem. Or consider the interconvertibility of matter and energy.

2. Consider a picture. Say everything that naturally comes to mind about it. Would you say that talking about a picture is a very natural sort of thing to do? What elements of normal discourse are missing? How can they be supplied? Consider the difference between talking about a movie you've seen recently and talking about a painting or a photograph. Why does the movie offer more interesting talking material? But suppose you are the painter of the painting or the photographer who took the photograph. You might have somewhat more to say about it. Are the factors that make the movie a conducive topic of conversation similar to the ones that might make a photograph an interesting topic under special circumstances?

3. Consider the pragmatic difficulty of judging the effectiveness of someone's speaking ability if he is not motivated to talk, or if he is only mildly motivated to do so.

4. It has sometimes been argued that an oral interview is not a natural conversational situation but is rather a contrived one. Consider the pros and cons of the issue. What similar situations arise in real life settings?

What kinds of motives and pressures are present in casual conversations as compared against test interviews? Job interviews? Oral examinations in school?

5. Consider the various forms and uses of language. Which form do you consider to be primary (speech, writing, sign language, secret languages of various sorts, codes that relate to written or spoken language, etc.)? What do you suppose are the reasons for preferring one form over another and thinking of it as the principal form of language? Consider some arguments both for writing and for speech.

6. Why is it more natural for a child to tell an examiner what objects are in a sack that the examiner cannot see into than it is for the child to name objects that the examiner can plainly see? How about telling a story to someone you know has heard it before as opposed to telling it to someone who has not heard it? What is the principle involved? Is it similar in the two cases? Are there special pragmatic occasions where naming objects that are plainly visible is not unnatural, or where telling the same story over and over is not unnatural?

7. Why is a counterfactual conditional (e.g., 'If such and such had not happened, then thus and so would have happened') pragmatically more complex than a simple declarative statement (e.g., 'Such and such happened and thus and so did not')? Or consider the contrast between the statements, 'The dog bit the man,' versus 'James said that the dog bit the man,' versus 'I thought that James said that the dog bit the man,' versus 'Sarah said that she thought that I said that I thought that James said that the man bit the dog.' Can you suggest a weighting system for scoring such statements in a speaking test protocol? Could the implicit criteria for the scoring of such a set of sentences be used for scoring speech protocols in general?

8. What differences exist between a discrete point scoring of the questions on the *Bilingual Syntax Measure* and a pragmatic scoring of the same task? Is one necessarily apt to be more reliable than the other? Consider the number of test items (or opportunities to get or to lose points) by the different scoring methods. If there are fewer points to be gained or lost, what is the generally predictable effect on test reliability?

9. What are the advantages and disadvantages of counting grammatically correct responses even when they do not express meanings that fit the context of the question in relation to the discourse implied in the test situation?

10. In relation to the *Ilyin Oral Interview* and the *Oral Communication Test*, why are sequentially related events superior to unrelated pictures of unrelated events as test materials? As an exercise, take a picture out of its context in the Ilyin oral test and try to conceive of all the meaningful and reasonable questions that an examiner might pose concerning it. Then put the same picture back in its context and consider the range of possibilities for test questions.

11. Why is it natural or unnatural to impose time constraints on a test of speaking ability? Consider the Upshur oral test.

12. Take any two points defined verbally on the FSI sub-scales, e.g., points 5 and 6 on the Fluency scale (see p. 322 above). How confident would you

feel in differentiating those two points with reference to the speech of non-native speakers you have observed? Or try constructing scales for the speech of another reference population. Ask the same question concerning the scales you come up with.

13. It is known that experienced raters make quite reliable overall judgements concerning the speech of non-native speakers in an oral interview of the FSI type. To what do you attribute the reliability of such judgements?

14. Why should reading aloud be an easier task than speaking? Following a similar line of reasoning, and assuming that other factors were held constant, how would you expect elicited imitation, story retelling, and creative construction to rank as speech tasks?

15. Do an oral cloze test along with one or more other measures of oral proficiency. Compute scores in all tasks by several methods and examine the correlations between scoring methods on the same task and between scores across tasks. With the help of a person trained in statistical techniques, try to determine which of the scoring methods is providing the greatest amount of the desired sort of information, and which of the two or more techniques is providing the most reliable sort of information. Among the techniques that might be studied are cloze, elicited imitation, reading aloud, narrative, and so on. Another method of checking the usability of the various techniques is by examining learner protocols elicited by the different testing methods. One might ask which of the various techniques seems to be most characteristic of what is known and expected of different examinees tested.

SUGGESTED READINGS

1. Courtney B. Cazden, J. T. Bond, A. S. Epstein, R. T. Matz, and Sandra J. Savignon. 'Language Assessment: Where, What, and How.' Paper presented at the workshop for explaining next steps in qualitative and quantitative research methodologies in education. Monterey, California. July 21–23, 1976. In *Anthropology and Education Quarterly* 8, 1977, 83–91.

2. Donna Ilyin, 'Structure Placement Tests for Adults in English Second Language Programs in California,' *TESOL Quarterly* 4, 1970, 323–330. Reprinted in Leslie Palmer and Bernard Spolsky (Eds.) *Papers in Language Testing 1967–1974*. Washington, D.C.: TESOL, 1975, 128–136.

3. Veronica Gonzales-Mena LoCoco, 'A Comparison of Three Methods for the Collection of L2 Data: Free Composition, Translations, and Picture Description,' *Workingpapers in Bilingualism* 8, 1976, 59–86.

4. Diana S. Natalicio and Frederick Williams. *Repetition as an Oral Language Assessment Technique*. Austin, Texas: Center for Communication Research, 1971.

5. Sandra Savignon, *Communicative Competence*. Montreal: Marcel Didier, 1972.

6.   John A. Upshur, 'Objective Evaluation of Oral Proficiency in the ESOL
      Classroom,' *TESOL Quarterly* 5, 1971. Reprinted in Palmer and Spolsky
      (1975), 53–65. See reference 2 above.
7.   John A. Upshur, 'Productive Communication Testing: A Progress
      Report,' in G. E. Perren and J. L. M. Trim (Eds.) *Selected Papers of the
      Second International Congress of Applied Linguistics*. Cambridge,
      England: Cambridge University Press, 1971, 435–441. Reprinted in J.
      W. Oller and J. C. Richards (Eds.) *Focus on the Learner: Pragmatic
      Perspectives for the Language Teacher*. Rowley, Mass.: Newbury House,
      1973, 177–183.

12

Varieties of Cloze Procedure

In this chapter we continue to apply the pragmatic principles discussed in earlier chapters, but we focus our attention on a written testing technique known as cloze procedure. Though many of the findings of studies with written cloze tests are undoubtedly generalizable to other types of tests and to other modalities of language processing, the written cloze procedure is largely a reading and writing task. Among the questions addressed are: (1) What is the cloze procedure and why is it considered a pragmatic task? (2) What are some of the applications of the cloze procedure? (3) What scoring procedures are best? (4) How can scores on cloze tasks be interpreted?

A. What is the cloze procedure?

W. L. Taylor is credited with being the inventor of the cloze technique. He is also responsible for coining the word 'cloze' which is rather obviously a spelling corruption of the word 'close' as in 'close the door'. It has been a stumbling stone to many a typesetter and has often been misspelled by an overzealous and unknowing editor who found it difficult to believe that anyone would really intend to spell a word C–L–O–Z–E. The term is a mnemonic or perhaps a humorless pun intended to call to mind the process of closure celebrated by Gestalt psychologists. In the cloze technique blanks are placed in prose where words in the text have been deleted. Filling the blanks by guessing the missing words is, according to Taylor's notion, a special kind of closure – hence the term *cloze*. The reader's guessing of missing words is a kind of gap filling task that is not terribly unlike the perceiver's completion of imperfect visual patterns (for instance, the square, the letter A, and the smiling face of Figure 19).

Compare the ability of a perceiver to complete the patterns in Figure 19 with the ability of a reader to complete the following mutilated portions of text:

   (1) one, t__, t____, f____, __ive, __x, ____n, . . .

   (2) Four _____ and seven _____ ago _____ _____ . . .

   (3) After the mad dog had bitten several people he was finally
       sxghtxd nxxr thx xdgx xf txwn xnd shxt bx a local farmer.

   (4) It is true that persons _____ view the treatment of
       mental _____ from a clinical perspective tend _____
       explain socioeconomic and ethnic differences _____
       biological terms.

In example (1) the reader has no difficulty in supplying the missing letters of the words 'two', 'three' and so on. The series is highly redundant, which is similar to saying that the reader's expectancy grammar anticipates the series on the basis of very little textual information. Example (2) is also highly redundant if one happens to know the first line of Lincoln's Gettysburg address. If the text is unfamiliar to the reader, (2) is considerably more difficult to fill in

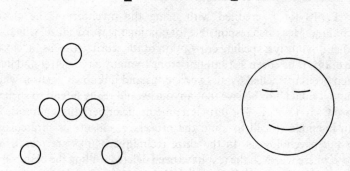

Figure 19. Some examples of visual closure – seeing the overall pattern or Gestalt.

than (3) or (4), otherwise it is probably somewhat easier. In any case, even when the original text is not stored in its entirety or at least in some recoverable form in memory, missing or mutilated portions may nonetheless be recoverable by a creative process of construction as is illustrated by examples (3) and (4). The mutilated words in (3) are 'sighted near the edge of town and shot by' and in (4) the missing words are 'who', 'retardation', 'to', and 'in'.

The above examples do not even begin to exemplify the range of possible distortions that readers can cope with in the processing of print, but perhaps they provide a basis for the comparison of the notion of pattern completion in Gestalt psychology and the concept of closure in relation to the processing of text. It would seem that the perceiver's ability to fill in gaps in imperfect patterns such as the ones examplified in Figure 19 (or in more complicated visual examples) may be related to the ability to construct the same patterns. In any event, it would seem that the ability to fill in gaps in prose is characterizable in that way. The reader can supply the missing portions by a constructive process similar to the way the writer put the text together in the first place. When the material is almost completely redundant, e.g., filling in the missing letters in the series of words in example (1), or filling in the missing words in a text that has been committed to memory, the task would seem to be somewhat like the process of filling in the gaps in imperfect visual patterns. However, when the material is not so familiar and is therefore less redundant, the power of the generative mechanisms necessary to fill in the gaps or to restore distorted portions of text would seem to be more complex by orders of magnitude than the simple visual cases.

Consider the kinds of information that have to be utilized in order to fill the blanks in example (4) above, or to restore the mutilated portion of example (3). In the processing of (3), the first mutilated word could probably be guessed by spelling clues alone. However, there is much more information available to the reader who knows the language of the text. He can infer that a mad dog who has bitten several people is a menace to be disposed of. Further, if he knows anything of mad dogs he is apt to infer correctly that once the hydrophobia expresses itself in the slobbering symptoms of vicious madness, the dog certainly cannot be saved. Therefore, an intelligent community of human beings interested in protecting their own persons and the well-being of pets and livestock would in all probability actively hunt the diseased animal and dispose of the threat. The range of possible meanings at any point in the text is expected to conform to these pragmatic considerations. Semantic and syntactic constraints further limit the range of possible continuations at any particular point in the text. Hence, when the reader gets to the word 'sxghtxd' he is actively expecting a past participle of a verb to complete the verb phrase 'was finally _____'. Subsequent possibilities are similarly limited by the expectancy grammar of the learner and by the textual clues of word spaces and unmutilated letters.

In example (4), the restoration of missing words is dependent on a host of complex and interrelated systems of grammatical knowledge. The reader may easily infer that the appropriate pragmatic mapping of the sentence relates to the clinical treatment of some mental disorder. Further, that it relates to the characterization of a way of dealing with such disorders by persons taking the clinical perspective as the point of departure for explaining socioeconomic and ethnic differences. On the basis of semantic and syntactic constraints the reader can determine (if not consciously, at least intuitively and subconsciously) that a relative pronoun is required for the first blank to subordinate the following clause to the preceding and also to serve as the surface of the verb 'view'. On the basis of semantic and syntactic clues, the reader knows that the second blank in the text of example (4) requires a noun to serve as the head of the noun phrase that starts with the adjective 'mental'. Moreover, the reader knows that the noun phrase 'mental _____' is part of a prepositional phrase 'of mental _____' which serves as a modifier of the preceding noun 'treatment' telling in fact what the treatment in question is a treatment of. On the basis of such information, the reader may be inclined to fill in the blank with words such as 'disorders', 'retardates', or possibly with the correct word 're-tardation'. If 'treatment' is read in the sense of 'consideration' 'health' is a possibility.

From all of the foregoing, we may deduce that the cloze procedure – that is, the family of techniques for systematically distorting portions of text – is a method for testing the learner's internalized system of grammatical knowledge. In fact the cloze technique elicits information concerning the efficiency of the little understood grammatical processes that the learner performs when restoring missing or mutilated portions of text. Wilson Taylor viewed the cloze procedure in this way from its inception. His notion of 'grammatical expectation' was necessarily less refined than it has come to be in the last twenty years, but he very clearly had the same idea in mind when he cited the following argument which he attributed to Charles E. Osgood:

> Some words are more likely than others to appear in certain patterns or sequences. 'Merry Christmas' is a more probable combination than 'Merry birthday'. 'Please pass the _____' is more often completed by 'salt' than by 'sodium chloride' or 'blowtorch'. Some transitions from one word to the next are, therefore, more probable than others (Taylor, 1953, p. 419).

According to Taylor, Osgood argued that the foregoing was a product of the redundancy of natural language:

> 'Man coming' means the same as 'A man is coming this way now'. The latter, which is more like ordinary English, is redundant; it indicates the singular number of the subject three times (by 'a', 'man', 'is'), the present tense twice ('is coming' and 'now'), and the direction of action twice ('coming' and 'this way'). Such repetitions of meaning, such internal ties between words, make it possible to replace 'is', 'this', 'way', or 'now', should any one of them be missed (p. 418).

B. Cloze tests as pragmatic tasks

Not all fill-in-blank tests are pragmatic. It is possible to set up fill-in-blank items over sentences that are as disjointed as a poorly planned pattern drill. Cloze items may also be arranged to focus on certain discrete points of structure or morphology. Davies (1975), for instance, reports results with a variety of cloze procedure that deletes only certain grammatical categories of words. He also clued the examinee by leaving in the first letter of the deleted word – e.g., 'T_____ i_____ a test o_____ reading comprehension' (p. 122). Frequently, blanks were placed contiguously in spite of the fact that research has shown that a deletion ratio of greater than one word in five creates many items that even native speakers of English cannot complete and Davies was working with non-natives. Consider the first sentence of one of his tests: 'B_____ changes i_____ t_____ home are less revolutionary, a_____ easier t_____ assimilate, t_____ changes i_____ industry. ....' These items may work fairly well, but they cannot be taken as indicative of the sort of items that appear in more standard cloze items. Since Davies' items are placed only on function words, they cannot be expected to produce as much reliable variance as items placed, say, every fifth word over an entire text.

What sorts of cloze tests do qualify as pragmatic? There are many types. The most commonly used, and therefore, the best researched type, is the cloze test constructed by deleting every nth word of a passage. This procedure has been called the *fixed-ratio method* because it deletes $1/n$th of the words in the passage. For instance, an every 5th word deletion ratio would result in 1/5th of the words being blanked out of the text. By this technique, the number of words correctly replaced (by the exact-word scoring procedure) or the number of contextually appropriate words supplied (by the contextually appropriate scoring method) is a kind of overall index of the subject's ability to process the prose in the text. Or alternatively the average score of a group of examinees on several passages may be taken as an indication of the comprehensibility of each text to the group of subjects in question. Or from yet another angle, constraints within any text may be studied by comparing scores on individual items.

Another type of cloze procedure (or family of them) is what has been called the *variable-ratio method*. Instead of deleting words according to a counting procedure, words may be selected on some other basis. For instance, it is possible to delete only words that are richly laden with meaning, typically these would include the nouns, verbs, adjectives, adverbs, or some combination of them in the text in question. Another version leaves out only the so-called function words, e.g., the prepositions, conjunctions, articles and the like.

It is also possible to use an every *n*th word procedure with some discretionary judgement. This is probably the most commonly used method for classroom testing. Instead of only deleting words on a counting basis, the counting technique may be used only as a general guide. Thus, it is common practice to skip over items such as proper nouns, dates, and other words that would be excessively difficult to replace. When the test constructor begins to edit many items in a text, however, he should be aware of the fact that the cloze test thus derived is not necessarily apt to generate the usual reliability and validity. Neither are all of the previous generalizations about other properties of cloze tests apt to be true in such a case.

Because of the fact that cloze items are usually scattered over an entire text on some fixed or variable ratio method, cloze tests are generally tests of discourse level processing. Further, it has been shown that performance on cloze items is affected by the amount of text on either side of a blank up to at least fifty words plus (Oller, 1975). Apparently cloze items reflect overall comprehension of a text. Not every item is sensitive to long-range constraints (Chavez, Oller, Chihara, and Weaver, 1977), but enough items apparently are sensitive to such constraints to affect overall performance.

It is difficult to imagine anyone filling in the blanks on a cloze test correctly without understanding the meaning of the text in the sense of mapping it onto extralinguistic context – hence, cloze tests seem to meet the second of the two pragmatic naturalness constraints. But what about the temporal sequence of cloze items and cloze test material? Are there time constraints that challenge short term memory? In response to this second question, consider the following brief text:

> (5) 'The general content and overall plan of the previous edition have proved so well adapted to the needs of its users that an attempt to change its essential character and form _____ inadvisable' (from the Preface to *Webster's Seventh New Collegiate Dictionary*, 1969, p. 4a).

The word deleted from the blank is 'seems'. In order to answer the item correctly, the reader has to process the preceding verb 'have proved' twenty words earlier. Further, he presumably has to hold in attention the subject noun phrase 'an attempt' which appears seven words back. The example illustrates the considerable length of segments that must be taken into account in order to fill in some of the blanks in a passage of text. Unless the short term memory is aided by a fairly efficient grammatical system that processes segments fairly quickly leaving the short term memory free to handle new incoming segments, errors will occur. At least some of those errors will be the result of a breakdown in the processing of long range temporal constraints.

Thus, it can be reasoned that there are time constraints on cloze items. Therefore, cloze tests generally satisfy the first pragmatic naturalness requirement: they require the learner to process temporal sequences of elements in the language that conform to normal contextual constraints. Although it has sometimes been argued that cloze items are only sensitive to contexts of about five to ten words on either side of a blank (Aborn, Rubenstein, and Sterling, 1959, Schlesinger, 1968, Carroll, 1972, and Davies, 1975), these claims have been shown to be generally incorrect (Oller, 1975, Chihara, *et al*, 1977, Chavez, *et al*, 1977).

It is interesting to note that Wilson Taylor was intuitively aware of the fundamental difference between fill-in-blank tests over single sentences and cloze tests ranging over substantial portions of connected discourse. In his first paper on the topic of cloze procedure, he included a subsection entitled, '*Not a Sentence-Completion Test*' (1953, p. 417). After noting the superficial similarities between these two types of tests, Taylor points out the basic differences: first, 'cloze procedure deals with contextually interrelated series of blanks, not isolated ones'; and second, 'the cloze procedure does not deal directly with specific meaning. Instead it repeatedly samples the likeness between the language patterns used by the writer to express what he meant and those possibly different patterns which represent readers' guesses at what they *think* he meant' (p. 417).

Perhaps the distinguishing quality of cloze tests can be stated somewhat more succinctly: they require the utilization of discourse level constraints as well as structural constraints within sentences. Probably, it is this distinguishing characteristic which makes cloze tests so robust and which generates their surprisingly strong validity coefficients in relation to other pragmatic testing procedures (see Chapter 3 above and the Appendix below).

C. Applications of cloze procedure

Among the applications of the cloze procedure which we will consider
briefly are the following: judging readability of textual materials,
estimating reading comprehension, studying the nature of contextual
constraints, estimating overall language proficiency (especially in
bilinguals and second language learners), and evaluating teaching
effectiveness.

   1. *Judging the difficulty of texts.* According to Klare (1976), the
interest in judging the readability of texts has been around for a long
long time 'Lorge (1944), for example, reports attempts by the
Talmudists in 900 AD to use word and idea counts to aid them in this
task' (p. 55). Apparently, the motive for this interest has always been
to make written materials more effective for communicative
purposes. In the service of this objective, many readability formulas
have been developed – most of them in this century. Klare (1974–5)
reports that before 1960 there were already at least 30 formulas of
various sorts in the extant literature. Since 1960, many other formulas
have been developed. All of them tend to rely on one or more of the
following criteria: sentence length, vocabulary difficulty, references
to persons, and possibly indices of syntactic and morphological
complexity. A recently developed formula by Botel and Granowski
(1972) requires the rating of syntactic units on a scale of zero to three.
The most widely used formulas, however, the Dale-Chall (Dale and
Chall, 1948a, 1948b) and the Flesch (1948) rely on the average
sentence length in words plus one or two other criteria. For the Dale-
Chall formula only one additional index is required – the number of
unfamiliar words. The Flesch formula requires two additional pieces
of information – the number of affixes and the number of references
to people. Detailed instructions for both formulas are given in the
original sources.

   On the whole, the readability formulas have not been as successful
as it was originally hoped they might be. Glazer (1974) contends that
the formulas are inaccurate because of the fact that 'all language
elements can, in some way, be involved in the reading comprehension
process' (p. 405), but only a few of the elements can easily be
incorporated in the indices of the formulas. She goes on to say,
'attempts to develop formulas to include these [additional] variables
has resulted in the development of complex instruments too
cumbersome for practical use' (p. 405). One of the shortcomings of

practically all of the formulas is that a pivotal element is sentence length, yet it has been shown that sentence length *per se* does not necessarily make content less recoverable. In fact, increasing the length of sentences may improve readability in many cases as has been shown experimentally by Pearson (1974). For example, two sentences like, 'The chain broke. The machine stopped,' are not necessarily easier to comprehend than a single sentence such as, 'Because the chain broke, the machine stopped.' Pearson concludes that 'readability studies must begin with the question: what is the best way to communicate a given idea?' (p. 191).

Other solutions, frequently discussed in the literature, include appeal to subjective judgements and attempts to measure the comprehensibility of different texts via a variety of testing techniques. There is some evidence that subjective judgements of sentence complexities, word frequencies, and overall passage difficulties may have some validity. However, in order to attain necessary levels of reliability, many judges are required, and even then, the judgements are not very precise.

Klare (1976) showed that the overall ranking of five passages from the McCall-Crabbs *Standard Test Lessons in Reading* (1925) by fifty-six professional writers were identical to the ranking based on multiple choice questions over the passages and another ranking based on the Flesch Reading Ease formula (Flesch, 1948). Richards (1970b) similarly demonstrated that judgements of familiarity of words were fairly reliable (.775 for the last list of 26 words presented in different dummy lists on two different occasions two weeks apart for forty judges). Glazer (1974) argues that similar judgements can reliably be made for sentence difficulties.

However, comprehension questions and judgements of difficulty are apparently too imprecise for some purposes. Though both seem to offer higher validities than the formulas, neither is a very consistent measuring technique. Klare (1976) for instance notes wide discrepancies in the judgements of difficulty levels offered by the fifty-six professional writers who participated in his study. Only one of the five passages was not ranked in all possible positions by at least some of the judges. That was the most difficult passage. No one rated it the easiest. But, every possible rank was assigned to each of the four remaining passages.

Multiple choice questions are similarly fraught with problems. Who is to say that questions written for different passages are themselves of equivalent difficulty? That is, suppose a set of multiple choice questions is constructed for the first passage in Klare's study, another set for the second, and so forth for all five passges of text, as in fact was done in order to create the McCall-Crabbs widely used *Standard Test Lessons in Reading*. How can we be certain that the questions asked in relation to passage one are of the same difficulty as those asked in relation to passage two? Three? Four? And so forth. In judging the various sets of multiple choice questions for difficulty, we are in precisely the same boat as in judging the passages. Is there no escape from this circle?

It was these kinds of considerations that led Wilson Taylor (1953) to propose the cloze procedure as a basis for measuring the readability of prose. Klare, Sinaiko, and Stolurow (1972) point out that the average score of a group of subjects on a cloze test is an *actual measure* of readability whereas the formulas, and even the multiple choice question techniques, are probably best regarded only as methods for *estimating* difficulty levels. Indeed, the cloze procedure is a suitable device for validating (that is, testing the validity of) the other techniques. In anticipation of the well aimed criticism of the formulas by Glazer (1974), twenty-one years ago, Taylor pointed out that 'a cloze score appears to be a measure of the aggregate of influences of *all factors* [his italics] which interact to affect the degree of correspondence between the language patterns of transmitter and receiver' (1953, p. 432). The formulas, on the other hand (as Glazer, 1974 noted) take into account only some of the superficial aspects of the text.

Taylor (1953) and Klare (1974–5) recommend that the best estimates of readability may be obtained by 'clozing' every word in sample texts. To keep our reasoning simple, suppose that someone wants to measure the readability of three stories for fourth grade children in a certain school. If there are 75 fourth graders in the school in three separate classrooms with 25 in each, the tests might be set up as follows: first construct five test forms over each text. Assuming that each text is at least 250 words long, with an every fifth word deletion procedure, it is possible to construct five forms over each text by deleting the fifth, tenth, fifteenth, ... and so forth on the first pass; the fourth, ninth, fourteenth, ... on the second; the third, eighth, ... on the third; the second, seventh, ... on the fourth; and the first, sixth, ... on the fifth pass. Suppose then that the test forms are stacked and distributed as follows:

Form	Text	Student	Class
1	1	1	1
1	2	2	1
1	3	3	1
2	1	4	1
.	.	.	.
.	.	.	.
.	.	.	.
5	3	15	1
1	1	16	1
.	.	.	.
.	.	.	.
.	.	.	.
3	3	25	1
4	1	26	2
.	.	.	.
.	.	.	.
.	.	.	.
5	3	75	3

The first student receives form 1 of text 1. The second student gets form 1 of text 2. The third student receives form 1 of 3. The fourth student then gets form 2 of text 1 and the procedure continues recycling until all twenty-five children in class 1 have received tests. The procedure is then continued for student number 26 through 50 (i.e., all of those in class 2), and for 51 through 75. Each child then takes one form of the five possible forms over one of the three texts. The selection of subjects who take the test over text 1 as opposed to text 2 or text 3 is quite random. It is exceedingly unlikely that all of the better readers happen to be seated in every third seat – or that all of the not-so-good readers are seated in a similar arrangement.

Thus, after testing, the average score of the 25 children who attempted text 1 can be compared against the average of the 25 who did one of the tests over text 2 and the 25 who did one of the tests over text 3. In short, the difficulties of the three texts can thus be directly compared.

If it is desired to obtain a finer degree of accuracy, the measures can be repeated by administering a new set of tests stacked as follows on two additional occasions:

	Form	Text	Student	Class
	1	2	1	1
	1	3	2	1
on the	1	1	3	1
second test day	2	2	4	1
	.	.	.	.
	.	.	.	.
	.	.	.	.

	Form	Text	Student	Class
	1	3	1	1
	1	1	2	1
on the	1	2	3	1
third test day	2	3	4	1
	.	.	.	.
	.	.	.	.
	.	.	.	.

Hence, on occasion one, the first, fourth, seventh, ... through the seventy-third students take one of the five forms over text 1; the second, fifth, eighth, ... and seventy-fourth students take one of the five forms over text 2; the third, sixth, ninth, ... and seventy-fifth students take one of the forms over text 3. On the second occasion, the situation is adjusted so that the first, fourth, ... through seventy-third students take one of the five tests over text 2 and the remaining two groups take tests over text 3 and text 1 in that order. On the third occasion of testing, the situation is once more adjusted so that the first, fourth, ... through seventy-third students take one of the five forms over text 3 and the remaining two groups take one of the tests over texts 1 and 2 respectively.

By this latter method, the learning effect of taking one of the tests on day one, and another on day two and yet another on day three is spread equally over all three texts. In fact, the experimenter would have 75 points of reference over which to average in order to compare the readability of the three passages. Further, if there were any reason to do so, the experimenter could compare performance over the fifteen separate tests – that is, the five forms over text 1, the five over 2, and the five over 3. For each of those comparisons, there would be ($75 \times 3 = 225$ divided by $5 = 45$) exactly 45 different scores.

Ultimately the teacher or educator doing the testing will have to make intelligent decisions about what procedure will be best suited to measuring readability levels in a given educational setting. However, some general guidelines can be offered based on the extensive research literature using the cloze procedure as a measure of readability. A minimum of 50 blanks in a given cloze test, and at least 25 points of reference (that is, individual subject scores) for every desired comparison, will generally assure sufficient reliability. By now the research has made it abundantly clear (see Potter, 1968, Klare, Sinaiko, and Stolurow, 1972, Klare 1974–5) that the cloze procedure affords substantially more trustworthy information about the difficulty levels of samples of text than any other method yet devised. Other pragmatic text processing tasks may work equally well, but this has not been demonstrated. What has been shown convincingly is that the cloze technique works much better than the readability formulas.

Anderson (1971b) offers the following suggestions for determining what a given cloze score means with respect to a non-native student's understanding of a particular passage. A cloze score of .53 or above (by the exact word method, see below) corresponds to what has traditionally been called the 'independent level of reading'. A score between .44 and .53, he suggests, is in the appropriate range for instructional materials, the so-called 'instructional level'. However, a score less than .44 falls into the 'frustrational level' and would not, according to Anderson, be appropriate for instructional use.

Presumably, the percentages of correct items required for similar judgements concerning native speakers should be adjusted downward somewhat. No comparison between natives and non-natives is given in the Anderson (1971b) paper, but Potter (1968) may offer a clue. He suggests that a widely accepted rule of thumb concerning multiple choice comprehension questions is to judge reading materials suitable 'for a pupil's instructional use if he responds correctly to 75 percent or more of the items' (p. 7). In a study of native speakers, Bormuth (1967) found that 'cloze scores between 40 and 45 percent have been found comparable to the 75 percent criterion' (Potter 1968, p. 7).

Thus, it would appear that the lower bound on materials in the instructional range for native speakers (.40 to .45) is about the same as for non-natives (.44). This is contrary to the expectation that it might be lower for natives. Of course, it is important to realize that guidelines of this type can never be made any more accurate than the meanings of the terms 'independent', 'instructional', and 'frust-rational'. Nevertheless, insofar as such terms have determinate meanings, they may help in interpreting either the cloze score of an individual or the average score of a group over a given text or perhaps a range of texts.

2. *Rating bilinguals.* Although the first applications of cloze procedure were to the measurement of readability levels of texts, it became apparent almost immediately that the technique would find many other uses. Osgood and Sebeok (1965) suggested that it might be used for assessing the relative proficiency of a bilingual person in his two languages. Taylor had hinted at this possibility even earlier in an article reviewing research results in 1956. He had suggested that 'it also seems possible to use the cloze method ... for testing the progress of students learning a foreign language' (p. 99).

A not very encouraging conclusion along the line of testing foreign language proficiency was reached by Carroll, Carton, and Wilds (1959). Cloze tests were developed in English, French, and German. The authors claimed that the cloze technique measures language skill quite indirectly and that there may be a specific skill involved in taking cloze tests that is not strongly correlated with language proficiency. There were several problems which may have led them to this conclusion, however. First, the criterion measure (against which the cloze tests were correlated) was not another language test, but was in fact the *Modern Language Aptitude Test* – which itself has surprisingly weak validity (Carroll, 1967). A second difficulty was that the tests developed were not of the standard every nth deletion ratio. (We discuss below the fact that other procedures seem to work less well on the whole.) A third problem was that the generalizations were based on quite small sample sizes with subjects who may have been atypical in the first place. (See the discussion in Chapter 7 above concerning the problems of referencing tests against the performance of non-natives who have had only a classroom exposure to the language.) In any event, in spite of these facts, the conclusions of Carroll, *et al* probably were the main factor in discouraging much further research with cloze as a measure of language proficiency *per se* until the late 1960s and early 1970s. Since then, the cloze technique has proved to be a very useful measure of language proficiency.

Holtzman and Hopf presented a paper to the Speech Association of America in December 1965 on cloze procedure as a test of English language proficiency, but it was not until 1968 that Darnell published his study revealing some of the potential merits of cloze as a measure of proficiency in English as a second language. After 1968, many researchers began to take interest. Spolsky (1969b) almost immediately summarized the results of Darnell's 1968 study in the *TESOL Quarterly*.

For 48 non-native speakers of English, Darnell found a reliability of .86 for a cloze test (scored by a somewhat complex scoring procedure which we will return to below in section D.4.iii) and a correlation of .83 with the Test of English as a Foreign Language. In view of the estimated reliability of the *TOEFL* and of the cloze test Darnell used, the correlation of .83 between the two tests approximates the maximum correlation that could be found even if the two tests were perfectly correlated – i.e., if the *TOEFL* did not produce any variance not also generated by the cloze test.[1]

Shortly after Darnell's study was completed, several reports pointing to similar conclusions began to appear. An Australian doctoral dissertation by Jonathon Anderson was completed in 1969 showing remarkably high reliability and validity coefficients for cloze tests of 50 items or more used with non-native speakers of English. A Master's thesis at UCLA by Christine Conrad yielded similar results in 1970.

Subsequent research by Oller, Bowen, Dien, and Mason (1972) extended the technique to tests across languages and provided evidence that the method could be used to develop roughly equivalent tests in different languages. Their study investigated tests in English, Thai, and Vietnamese. The fact that the extension was made to such unrelated and vastly different language systems provided empirical support for the hope that parallel tests could be developed by a simple translation procedure.[2] Encouraging results have also been reported by McLeod (1975). He produced tests in Czech, English, French, German, and Polish. The translation method of deriving equivalent tests has been further researched by Johansson (in press) who used cloze tests in English and Swedish as a basis for what he called a 'bilingual reading comprehension index'.

---

[1] Any readers who may have skipped over the statistical portion of Chapter 3, section E. 1 may want to return to it before pressing on.

[2] Osgood and Sebeok (1965) had suggested just such a procedure 7 years before the first data became available. Interestingly, Osgood is credited by Taylor (1963) as having inspired the development of the cloze procedure in the first place. Johansson (in press), cites Osgood and Sebeok with reference to the translation, but Oller *et al* (1972), McLeod (1975), and Klare (1974–5, esp. p. 95f) were all apparently unaware of the suggestion by Osgood and Sebeok.

Johansson (in press), however, voiced an old skepticism concerning the standard every nth word deletion procedure for the assessment of reading comprehension. Therefore, he created tests by deleting only content words (i.e., nouns, verbs, adjectives, adverbs, and generally words that appeared to be heavily laden with meaning). He reasoned that deletion of function words (e.g., prepositions, conjunctions, particles, and the like) would create difficulties that would not reflect the true comprehensibility of a text to a non-native speaker of the language in question. This would lead to incorrect assessment of relative rates of reading comprehension across languages. Perhaps Johansson's argument has merit if applied exclusively to some notion of 'reading comprehension' across languages. However, if we are interested in global language proficiency, the very reasons offered against the standard every nth deletion procedure would vie in favor of it.

Interestingly, the inventor of the cloze technique was also the first to investigate the important questions concerning optimum deletion procedures. Taylor (1957) addressed the following question raised by 'certain skeptics': 'Wouldn't sampling points created by deleting only "important" words such as nouns or verbs yield more discriminating results than the practice of counting out words without regard for their differing functions?' (Taylor, 1957, p. 21). To answer the question, Taylor constructed three cloze tests of 80 items each over the same text. The first test consisted of items derived by the standard cloze procedure. The second was based on content deletions only (adverbs, verbs, and nouns) over words that had proved in previous cloze tests over the same text to be difficult to replace – i.e., they generated a greater number of incorrect responses. The third test was based on function word deletions (verb auxiliaries, conjunctions, pronouns, and articles) over items that had proved relatively easy to replace – i.e., they generated fewer incorrect responses than content words.

Taylor administered the three tests to randomly selected subgroups of a sample of 152 Air Force trainees. Criteria against which the cloze scores were correlated included pre and post comprehension questions of the multiple choice variety over the same article that the cloze tests were based on, and the Armed Forces Qualification Test (purportedly a measure of IQ). On the whole, the cloze test constructed by the standard method yielded higher reliability and validity coefficients. Each test was administered twice – once before the article was studied, and again after study and after about a week had elapsed. The pre and post correlations for the cloze tests were .88 (standard version), .80 (function word version), and .84 (content version). The pre and post correlations for the comprehension questions (also administered once before the article was studied and a week later after study) were .83, .74, and .74 for the respective groups of subjects. Overall, the validity coefficients were highest for the standard procedure. Similar results have been attained with non-native speakers of English (compare correlation coefficients reported by Oller and Inal, 1971 with a test of prepositions and verb particles with corresponding coefficients for standard cloze tests reported by Oller, 1972, Stubbs and Tucker, 1974, LoCoco, in press, Hinofotis and Snow, in press).

3. *Estimating reading comprehension.* Ever since Taylor's first studies in 1953, it has been known that cloze scores were good indices of reading comprehension. Taylor's original argument was to show that the differences between subjects tended to remain constant across different texts. This is the same as saying that the cloze scores of the same subjects on different texts were correlated. Since then, it has been demonstrated many times over that cloze scores are extremely sensitive measures of reading ability. Correlations between cloze scores and multiple choice reading comprehension tests are consistently strong – usually between .6 and .7 and sometimes higher (Ruddell, 1965, Potter, 1968, Anderson, 1971a). This is consistently true for both native and non-native subjects, though poorer results are sometimes reported when the method of test construction is radically altered (Davies, 1975, Weaver and Kingston, 1963).

Cloze scores have also been used in attempts to assess the amount of information gained through study of a given text. The question asked is, how much do scores improve if subjects are allowed to study the unmutilated text before taking a cloze test over it. Taylor (1956, 1957) reported significant gains in cloze scores as a result of students having the opportunity to study the text between test occasions. In addition to the two administrations of the cloze tests, a multiple choice test on the same article was also administered before study and after study.

The cloze test seemed to be more sensitive to gains due to study than was the multiple choice test. The average gain on the cloze test was 8.46 points while on the multiple choice test the gain was 4.79 points. Though Taylor does not mention the number of points allowed on the multiple choice comprehension test, it is possible to infer that the cloze scores were in fact more sensitive to the study effect from the statistics that are given relative to the respective variances of the gain scores (for the statistically minded readers, these were the t-ratios of 9.55 for the cloze test gains and 6.43 for the multiple choice test gains). Further, the reliability of the cloze test was higher judging from the test and re-test correlation of .88, compared against .83 for the multiple choice test.

Also, though both tests were substantially correlated with each other in the before-study condition (.70), they were even more strongly correlated in the after-study condition (.80). This would seem to indicate that whatever both tests were measuring in the after condition, they measured more of it after subjects studied the article than before they studied it. Perhaps this is because multiple choice comprehension questions can sometimes be answered correctly without reading the article at all (Carroll, 1972), but this is hardly possible in the case of cloze scores since the cloze test *is* the article.

The fact that the correlation between the cloze test and the multiple choice test is higher in the after-study condition than it is in the before-study condition may suggest that the multiple choice test becomes a more valid test after the material has been studied. In other words, that the multiple choice test may become more sensitive to the meaningful variance between subjects after they have studied the article. Of course, it is not the test itself that has changed, rather the way it impresses the minds of the subjects who are responding to it. Along this same line, the multiple choice comprehension test and the Armed Forces Qualification Test (an IQ test modeled after the Stanford-Binet) correlated at .65 before study but at .70 after study. The cloze scores, incidentally, were somewhat more strongly correlated with the AFQT in both conditions (.73 and .74, for the before and after conditions respectively).

4. *Studying textual constraints.* Aborn, Rubenstein, and Sterling (1959) investigated constraints within sentences. They concluded that the predictability of a word in a given context was generally inversely proportional to the size of the grammatical class. That is, the larger the number of words in a given grammatical class, the harder it is to predict a particular member of that class in a sentence context. Prepositions, for instance, are generally easier to predict than adjectives. They also demonstrated that a blank with context on both sides of it was easier to fill in than one with context only preceding or only following. Their study, however, had one major limitation: they

were examining sentences in isolation from any larger context of discourse.

MacGinitie (1961) criticized the study by Aborn *et al* for their failure to examine contexts longer than single disconnected sentences. It is interesting that Aborn *et al* had also criticized some of the work prior to their own because it had failed to look beyond contexts longer than 32 consecutive letters of text. MacGinitie took a step further and suggested looking at contexts of prose materials up to 144 words in length. He concluded, among other things, that 'context beyond five words did not help in the restoration of ... missing words' (p. 127). However, he noted that 'this does not mean that constraints never operate over distances of more than four or five words' (p. 128). For instance, 'knowing the topic may have a ... generalized influence that does not decline with decreasing length of context in an easily specifiable way' (p. 128).

Among the important questions raised by the studies just cited are: first, what sorts of contraints are cloze items sensitive to? And, second, what sorts of constraints exist? These questions are intertwined, but perhaps their intermingling is not hopelessly confounded. We may be sure, at least, that if the cloze procedure is sensitive to some sort of contextual constraint or other that the constraint exists. Thus, the cloze procedure can be used both to assess the existence of certain sorts of constraints (namely the ones that it is sensitive to) and it may be used along with other techniques to measure the strength of the effect of those contextual constraints.

MacGinitie (1961) cites M. R. Trabue as saying that 'the difficulty of a test sentence is influenced rather markedly by the number and character of sentences near it' (p. 128), but the evidence that this is so is not very convincing in the MacGinitie study. Coleman and Miller (1967) reached a conclusion very similar to the one MacGinitie came to. On the basis of three different deletion procedures, they concluded that guesses are 'constrained very slightly, if at all, by words' across sentence boundaries. In fact, they argued that contexts beyond five words did not affect cloze scores very much and that contexts beyond twenty words from a given cloze item (in texts of 150 words in length) did not significantly affect item scores at all.

There are some interesting contrary results, however. For example, Darnell (1963) found that if the fifteen sentences of a certain passage of prose that consisted primarily of what he called 'because' relations were presented in orders other than the original so-called 'because' order, cloze scores were adversely affected. That is, if the order of the sentences was logically consistent with a deductive form of argument, it was easier to fill in cloze blanks over the text than if the sentences were presented in any one of six other orders investigated. Similarly, Carroll, Carton, and Wilds (1959) showed that if a text were divided into ten word segments with one cloze item inserted in each segment, the items were much easier to fill in if the segments were presented in the original order of the text than if they were presented in a scrambled order. However, as MacGinitie (1961) noted, 'scrambling the order of the segments probably not only obscures the paragraph topic, ... but also reduces restoration scores through misdirection and confusion' (p. 128).

Oller (1975) set out to show that cloze items are indeed sensitive to constraints across contexts that exceed the five to ten word limit suggested by previous research. The technique used was also a cut and scramble procedure similar to that of Carroll *et al* (1959), except that five separate lengths of context were investigated. Five prose passages each of 100 words plus were successively cut into five, ten, twenty-five, and fifty word segments. It was demonstrated that items inserted in the five word segments were significantly more difficult than the very same items in the ten word segments, and so on. In fact, the difference between items in the full texts and items in scrambled presentations of the fifty word segments was greater than the corresponding difference between items in the twenty-five word segments and in the fifty word segments, and so on.

While it is true that a cut and scramble procedure may create false leads which will make the restoration of missing words more difficult than it would be if there were no misleading contexts, is this not part of the question – that is, whether or not cloze items are sensitive to contexts beyond a certain number of words? Indeed it would seem that cloze items *are* sensitive to constraints that range beyond the previously estimated limits of five to ten words on either side of a blank. If this is so, the procedure can be used to study the effects of discourse constraints ranging across single sentence boundaries. Incidentally, this result was also hinted at in the study by Miller and Coleman (1967). They found that on the average, words were 9.2 percent easier to guess when none of their surrounding context (up to a total of 149 words before and after) was mutilated than when an every fifth word deletion technique was used. Furthermore, when only preceding context was given, the average loss in predictability was 30 percent.

One of the difficulties with the cut and scramble techniques used by

Carroll, Carton, and Wilds (1959) and by Oller (1975) could be overcome if whole sentences were used as the criterial segments. If cloze items are not sensitive to constraints ranging beyond the boundaries of a single sentence, items inserted in a prose text should be equally difficult regardless of the order of sentences in the text. Chihara, Oller, Weaver, and Chavez (1977), however, have shown that this is not true. Cloze items were inserted in texts on an every nth word deletion basis. For text A every sixth word was deleted, and for text B every seventh word was deleted. Then, the sentences of both texts were systematically reordered. Forty-two native speakers of English and 201 Japanese studying English as a foreign language completed one of the texts in the sequential condition and the other in the scrambled condition. In spite of the fact that the sentence boundaries were left intact in both presentations, the scrambled sentence versions were considerably more difficult.

Since unlike the Darnell (1963) study there was no attempt to select passages that would maximize the effect of sentence order, perhaps it is safe to infer that cloze items are in fact generally sensitive to constraints across sentence boundaries in prose. Consider the following example items from one of the texts used in the Chihara *et al* study:

> Joe is a freshman and he (1) IS having all of the problems that most (2) FRESHMEN have. As a matter of fact, his (3) PROBLEMS started before he even left home. (4) HE had to do a lot of (5) THINGS that he didn't like to do (6) JUST because he was going to go (7) AWAY to college ...

Not all of the foregoing items proved to be easier in the normal text condition than in the scrambled sentence condition, but items 3 and 4 were considerably easier in the full text condition. It is not too difficult to see why this is so. Since the fact that Joe was having problems is mentioned in the first sentence, it constrains the possible responses to item 3. Similarly, the fact that Joe is the person being talked about in sentences one and two constrains the possible responses to item 4. By contrast, items 1, 2, 5, and 6 proved to be about equally difficult in the normal textual condition and in the scrambled sentences version.

On the whole, items that proved to be maximally sensitive to discourse constraints were simply those that involved meanings that were expressed over larger segments of discourse. Interestingly, they were not limited to contentives (e.g., nouns, verbs, and the like). For instance, the word 'the' was sensitive to long-range constraints in a context where it implied reference to a pair of slacks that had been mentioned previously. The words 'still' and 'so' in the phrases '*still* growing' and '*so* fast' also proved to be sensitive to discourse constraints (i.e., constraints beyond sentence boundaries) in a context where Joe's father was talking about whether or not Joe should buy a certain pair of slacks.

Many questions remain unanswered. Perhaps the rapidly growing interest in textual constraints and their effects on memory (see Tulving, 1972) and the corresponding research on discourse grammars (Frederiksen, 1975a, 1975b, Schank, 1972, and Rummelhart, 1975) will help to shed some light on the questions that can now be formulated more clearly than before. There is every reason to believe that the cloze procedure will continue to make an important contribution to our meager but growing knowledge of the effects of contextual constraints. What appears to be needed are clearer notions of just what sorts of conceptual dependencies exist within discourse.

5. *Evaluating teaching effectiveness.* If cloze scores are sensitive to some of the sorts of variables discussed under earlier applications, they must also be sensitive to many of the things that teachers are trying to accomplish in the way of instructional objectives. For instance, if cloze scores can be used to judge the readability of texts, they can probably be used to evaluate the appropriateness of certain curricular decisions concerning materials selected for instructional use. If cloze scores are sensitive indices of language proficiency, they can be used to measure attainment in foreign language classes, or in bilingual educational settings.

Although much of what has been said in earlier portions of this book questions the usefulness of discrete point objectives in the teaching of grammar (in the narrow sense of phonology, morphology and syntax), cloze tests are more useful than competing discrete point alternatives for the evaluation of the effectiveness of an instructional program in achieving such specific objectives. Furthermore, cloze tests have the virtue (if applied to normal texts rather than isolated sentences or highly artificial, contrived tests) of assessing points of grammatical knowledge in normal contexts of usage. (See Chapter 8 section D above.)

A more appropriate application of the cloze technique in the evaluation of instruction, however, would seem to be in relation to particular contexts of discourse rather than points of grammar in the abstract (not in real discourse contexts). For instance, if a language learner has been taught to perform certain speech acts (e.g., ordering a meal at a restaurant, buying a ticket at the airport, taking a telephone message, and the like), cloze tests over samples of discourse exemplifying such acts might be appropriate indicators of the effectiveness of instruction. Or if a student has been asked to study a certain text or article, a cloze test over portions of the text might be an appropriate index of the effectiveness of study. If specific points of grammar have been emphasized in the instruction, these could be tested specifically with reference to actual usages in real contexts.

Oller and Nagato (1974) used a cloze test to determine the effect of English as a foreign language in the elementary schools in a certain prefecture in Japan. It was demonstrated that by the time children who had been exposed to EFL in the elementary grades reached the eleventh grade in high school, any advantage gained by having studied EFL in the elementary grades had been overcome by students who had not had EFL exposure prior to the secondary level. Although the children who had received EFL instruction in the elementary grades showed an initial advantage over children who had not been exposed to such instruction, their advantage seemed to be lost by the eleventh grade. The loss of advantage was attributed to the fact that the children who got EFL in elementary grades were placed together with children who had not had EFL and were in fact forced to repeat materials they had already studied in earlier grades.

To date, the applications of cloze procedure to individual classroom studies, though they may have been fairly widespread in the last few years, have not been widely published. Nevertheless, Kirn's research at UCLA (1972) suggests that cloze tests are not generally sensitive to any practice effect, and, therefore, they should be quite applicable to routine classroom studies with repeated testing.

D. How to make and use cloze tests

We have already discussed several varieties of cloze testing procedures in earlier parts of this chapter. Further, we have discussed some of the advantages of what might be called the 'standard' procedure. Here we outline some specific suggestions that may be used as general guidelines in constructing cloze tests for a variety of purposes.

1. *Selecting material for the task*. In spite of the natural feeling that just any old text will not do, or that a suitable text must be a carefully chosen and possibly edited text, research has shown that the cloze procedure is probably appropriate to just about any text. True, some may be more difficult than others, but it has been demonstrated that for some purposes (e.g., testing ESL proficiency of university level foreign students) the level of difficulty of the task does not greatly affect the spread of scores that will be produced. This does not mean that a teacher or other educator would ever want to use a cloze task without some sense of the level of skill of the students for whom the test was intended, but it does mean that a fairly wide latitude can be tolerated by the technique.

If the purpose is to assess the readability of a certain book for children at a certain grade level, then the sampling technique that would be most appropriate would be one that selected portions of the text most representative of the entire book. According to Klare, Sinaiko, and Stolurow (1972), the technique that best assures representativeness is a random one. For instance, if the text is long, say more than a few thousand words, samples may be taken at intervals by some arithmetic procedure. If a book is divided into chapters, it might make sense to take at least one sample from each chapter, or one from each of ten equal portions of textual material (i.e., divide the number of pages by ten and take a sample of material from each of the ten sections). Following the general guidelines suggested earlier, portions of running text long enough to produce tests of at least fifty blanks each should be constructed over each sample, and at least twenty-five subjects should be tested on each cloze passage.

If the purpose is to assess overall language proficiency of students in a foreign language classroom, the most appropriately gauged material would depend on the level of the students in the class. However, unless the material used in the teaching of the language is quite idiomatic and natural, it would probably be best to select a passage from a book intended for a comparable level of native speakers of the language in question. For example, if the students are studying English as a foreign language, it may well be that reading material intended for fifth grade geography students would be usable for cloze material.

Some of the things to be avoided are texts that involve topics that are intrinsically disturbing or so emotionally charged that they would distract the attention of the students from the main problem set by the test – filling in the blanks. Passages that require esoteric or technical knowledge not generally available or which is available only to some of the students should also be avoided. Texts that contain arguments or statements that some of the students may strongly disagree with (e.g., texts that state strong pro or con views on controversial issues such as capital punishment, abortion, religion, politics, and the like) should also probably be avoided. Passages that do not contain enough words of running text to provide a sufficient number of blanks (about 50) should probably be set aside in favor of longer texts. Of course, there may be special circumstances where any or all of the foregoing suggestions should be disregarded. For instance, it would make no sense to avoid using a short text when it is that same short text that has been studied. It would not make sense to avoid a religious topic when the class is a course on religion, and so forth.

2. *Deciding on the deletion procedure.* Unless the purpose of the testing involves a need to assess student performance on some particular grammatical form, type of content or the like, an every nth deletion procedure will probably work best. The length of the selected text is also a factor to be taken into account when deciding on a deletion procedure. If the text is 250 words or thereabouts, five 50 item cloze tests are possible with an every fifth word deletion technique.

Simply begin counting from a word near the beginning of the text and delete every fifth word thereafter until 50 blanks are obtained. It matters little where the counting begins. Though some researchers have left the first sentence intact and have begun their deletions on the second sentence of a text, Klare, Sinaiko, and Stolurow (1972) contend that this is not necessary – though there is no harm in it either. For similar reasons, some have also left a certain amount of unmutilated lead out at the end of the text – i.e., one or more unmutilated sentences at the end of the test. This too is unnecessary, though again, there is no harm in it.

If an every nth deletion ratio is desired, and if it is desired to leave blanks in the entire text at roughly equal intervals, the test preparer may simply count the number of words in the text and divide by fifty to arrive at a suitable deletion ratio. For approximately 350 words of text an every seventh word deletion ratio will produce 50 blanks (i.e., 350 divided by 50 equals 7). For 400 words of text an every eighth word deletion ratio will yield 50 blanks, and so on.

If the purpose is proficiency testing, there is probably nothing to be gained by preparing multiple forms over a given cloze passage. Such forms might have some instructional value, but Jongsma's 1971 review of cloze tests as instructional procedures *per se* expresses skepticism. However, if multiple forms are desired, they can easily be prepared, by an every *n*th word deletion procedure as described above in section C. 1.

3. *Administering the test*. The following instructions to test takers are appropriate to cloze tests constructed over normal sequential passages of text. (Cloze items over isolated sentences, of course, do not qualify as pragmatic tests at all and are not recommended.)

> In the following passage, some of the words have been left out. First, read over the entire passage and try to understand what it is about. Then, try to fill in the blanks. It takes exactly one word to fill in each blank. Contractions like *can't*, or words written with a hyphen like *well-being* count as single words. If you are not sure of the word that has been left out, guess. Consider the following example:
> The _____ barked furiously, and the _____ ran up the tree.
> The words that correctly fill in the blanks are *dog* and *cat*.

These directions, of course, would have to be simplified for children in the early grades, and probably they should be given orally and with an example at the blackboard. However, they are quite adaptable to almost any cloze test procedure for most any purpose. For instance, if the subjects to be tested are non-native speakers of the language of the test, and if they all happen to speak a common language as in a foreign language classroom situation, the test instructions can be presented in their native language.

If the test is gauged appropriately in difficulty, it is usually possible for even the slowest students to have ample time to attempt every item of a 50 item cloze test within a 50 minute class period. If the text is easier, much less time may be required – as little as ten minutes per 50 item test for the fastest students. Non-native speakers, of course, take longer than fluent natives, but unless the test is inappropriately calibrated for the group, a 50 minute class period is usually long enough for every student in a class to attempt every item on a 50 item test. If the test is much too difficult on the other hand, there is little point in extending the amount of time allowed to complete the test.

Fortunately, cloze tests are extremely robust measures, and even if a test is on the whole more difficult than would normally be appropriate, or if it is too easy for a given group of students, it will still provide some meaningful discrimination. Regardless of the difficulty level of the test, the weakest students usually make some points, and the strongest rarely make perfect scores. Thus, the test will usually provide some meaningful discrimination even if it is poorly judged in difficulty level. The scoring technique, of course, may greatly affect the difficulty level of the test. A test that is too difficult by the exact word technique may not be too difficult at all if a more lenient scoring technique is used.

4. *Scoring procedures*. It should be noted at the outset that all of the scoring methods that have ever been investigated produce highly correlated measures. The bulk of the change in scores that results from a more lenient scoring procedure is simply a change in the mean score. Usually, there is little change in the relative rank order of scores – that is, high scorers will remain high scorers and low scorers will remain low relative to all of the subjects taking the test. If a more lenient scoring technique is used, all of the examinees may tend to improve by about 15 points, say, but if they all improve equally, it follows that the high scorers will still be at the high end of the rank and the low scorers will still be at the low end.

Correlations as high as .99 have been observed between exact word scores and scores that allowed synonyms for the exact words as correct answers (Miller and Coleman, 1967). Usually the correlations are in the .9 and up range (Klare, Sinaiko, and Stolurow, 1972) and this also holds for non-native speakers of the language in question (Stubbs and Tucker, 1974, Irvine, Atai, and Oller, 1974, Oller, Baca, and Vigil, 1977, and their references). Thus, the exact word technique, which is generally the easiest to apply, is usually (but not always) to be preferred.

(i) *The exact word method*. The rationale behind the exact word scoring method goes back to Taylor (1953). He reasoned that the ability of a reader to fill in the very word used by a writer would be a suitable index of the degree of correspondence between the language system employed by the writer and that employed by the reader. However, it can be argued that requiring the reader to replace the very word used by the writer is too stringent a requirement. It certainly places a severe limit on the range of possible responses. In fact, it would keep the creative reader from supplying an even better word in some cases.

For instance, consider item (3) exemplified above in the text about Joe and his problems. The line reads, 'As a matter of fact, his _____ started before he even left home.' The correct word by the exact word criterion is 'problems'. Other alternatives which seem equally good, or possibly better by some standards, such as 'difficulties', 'troubles', 'trials', 'tribulations', or 'worries', would have to be marked wrong – just as wrong, in fact, as such clearly off the wall fill-ins as 'methods', 'learning', or worse yet 'of', 'be', or 'before'. Many writers would have preferred to use some word other than 'problems' to avoid repeating that word in two consecutive sentences.

Nonetheless, in spite of the fact that it does seem counter-intuitive to give more credit for the very word the author used at a particular point in a text than for some other equally or possibly even more appropriate word, this whole line of argument is easily countered by the fact that the exact word method of scoring cloze tests correlates so strongly with all of the other proposed methods. As Swain, Lapkin, and Barik (1976) note, however, when very fine discrimination is desired, or for instructional purposes, it may make more sense to use a scoring method that is more lenient.

If the total score on a composite of 50 items or more is the main object of interest (e.g., in judging the difficulty of reading materials, or possibly in rating the proficiency of non-native speakers of a language, or in evaluating the relative proficiency of bilinguals in their two languages), the exact word method probably loses very little of the available information. However, if one is interested in specific performances of examinees on particular items, much information may be lost by the exact word technique. It would seem that some of the other methods have some instructional advantages and there is evidence to show that they are somewhat more strongly correlated with other proficiency criteria than the exact word method is.

(ii) *Scoring for contextual appropriateness*. The exact word scoring method is simple enough, but how do you score for something as vague as 'contextual appropriateness'? The general guideline that is usually stated is to count any word that fully fits the total surrounding context as correct. There is no escaping the fact that such a suggestion invokes the subjective judgement of some interpreter – namely, the person or persons must do the scoring.

It is not enough simply to say, count the exact word or any synonym for it as correct. The notion of synonymy makes sense in relation to some nouns, verbs, adjectives, and adverbs, but what is a synonym for the word 'even' as in, 'He couldn't *even* arrive on time'? There are other words that could replace it, such as 'just', 'barely', 'quite', and so on, but they are not synonyms of 'even'. Some of the possible alternatives would be ruled out by other facts mentioned or implied in the context. Usually the kinds of constraints that a native speaker of a language is intuitively aware of cannot be easily made explicit – but this does not mean that they are not real nor does it mean that they cannot be used to good effect in scoring cloze tests.

Some general guidelines can be stated: first, see if the word in a given blank is the exact word, if so, score it as correct; second, if it is not the exact word, check to see if it fits the immediately surrounding context, that is, whether or not it violates any local constraints in the same sentence or surrounding phrases; third, ask if it is consistent with all of the preceding and subsequent text (this includes previous and subsequent responses in other blanks as filled in by the examinee). If the response passes all of these checks, score it as correct. Otherwise score it as incorrect. For example, consider the following item:

> He couldn't _____ arrive on time. He was always late to everything she ever planned for him. It made little difference that he was the Governor – he could have shown some consideration for his wife.

A response like 'have' is clearly incorrect. It violates what we have called 'local constraints'. It would require a past tense marker on the verb 'arrive' but none is there, so 'have' would be an incorrect response.

What about the word 'still' inserted in the same blank? It doesn't violate any local constraints, but it does seem inconsistent with the meanings that are stated and implied in the subsequent lines of the text. There is nothing to indicate that the man referred to ever arrived on time, and there is plenty to indicate that in fact he never did. Thus, 'still' is an inappropriate response.

On the other hand, 'ever' would be appropriate to all of the stated and implied meanings. The word 'barely' would seem to fit the local constraints, but not the long range ones. 'Just' seems inappropriate to the total context, but it might be difficult to say exactly how it is inappropriate.

Because of the subjectivity of such a method, some might fear that it would prove unreliable. If it were very unreliable, however, the high correlations that are observed between scores generated on this basis and scores based on the exact word technique could not arise. Furthermore, careful research has shown that the technique is sufficiently reliable that even test scores generated by different raters may be regarded as equivalent for all practical purposes (see Hanzeli, 1976, and Naccarato and Gilmore, 1976). In addition, it has been shown that fewer items fail to discriminate between degrees of proficiency with the appropriate word scoring technique than with the exact word technique (Oller, 1972).

Nacarrato and Gilmore (1976) showed by a very stringent statistical technique that one rater working alone could achieve substantial reliability and that the scores generated by two raters working separately were about equally reliable. In fact, if a different native speaker scored each test in a batch of tests, the scores would closely approximate the set of scores over all the tests that would be obtained if any one of the raters scored all of the tests.

This result is important because it makes it possible for large populations of subjects to be tested by the cloze technique and still use the contextually appropriate scoring method. For instance, if 1,000 subjects were tested in a given educational setting, the problem of scoring all the tests by the contextually appropriate method would be nearly insurmountable if all of it had to be done by one person, but if 100 scorers could be used, each one would only have to score 10 tests. This can easily be done in less than an hour.

Research has also shown that the contextually appropriate scoring method does generate some meaningful variance that is lost if an exact-word scoring technique is used. In spite of the very high degree of variance overlap between the exact-word and the contextually-appropriate scoring method (sometimes referred to as the 'acceptable-word method'), the latter often produces slightly higher correlations with external criteria of validation – i.e., with other tests that purport to measure similar abilities (Oller, 1972, Stubbs and Tucker, 1974, Swain, Lapkin, and Barik, 1976, and LoCoco, in press).

(iii) *Weighting degrees of appropriateness*. Some responses seem to be more appropriate than others. In general, it seems that responses which violate local constraints are more serious errors than responses that violate longer range constraints. In fact, several schemas for weighting responses for their degree of conformity to contextual constraints have been suggested and in fact used. In this section, we will consider two kinds of weighting systems. The first is based on distinctions between types of errors in relation to some linguistic analysis of the text, and the second is based on the performance of a group of native speakers on the same items. In the latter case, the frequency of occurrence of a given word in response to a given cloze item by a specified reference group (e.g., native speakers) is used as a basis for assigning a weighted score to responses to each item made by a test group (e.g., non-natives).

The first method of weighting scores is based on an analysis (whether implicit or explicit) of the text. Categories of errors are distinguished along the following lines. The most serious is the sort that violates the strongest and most obvious contextual constraints. The least serious is the sort that violates the weakest and least obvious contextual constraints. If a response violates constraints in its immediately surrounding context, it will usually violate longer range constraints as well, but this is not always the case. It is possible, for instance, for a response to fit the sense of the text but to violate some local constraint – e.g., the use of a plural form where a mass noun has been deleted, as in 'the *peoples* of the world' instead of the '*people*'. If groups of people were the intended signification, the first form would be correct, but if all the people of the world in the collective sense were intended, the second form would be more correct. In either case, the sense of the text is partly preserved even if the wrong morphological form is selected.

A scale of degrees of appropriateness can be exemplified best with reference to a particular cloze item in a particular context. Suppose we consider item (3) from the text about Joe and his problems: 'His _____ started before he even left home.'

a. The best response (perhaps) is the very word used by the author of the text – namely, 'problems'.

b. The second best (or perhaps, an equally good) response is a close synonym for the deleted word – say, the word 'difficulties'.

c. Perhaps the next best response would be one that preserves the overall intent of the text, but does so with an incorrect form of the lexical item used – e.g., 'bewildering', instead of, for instance, 'bewilderment'.

d. A response that is appropriate to the local constraints of the item but which is not appropriate to the meaning of the text as a whole would probably be judged more severely (certainly it would be more incorrect than type b or c) – e.g., 'methods'.

e. An even more severe error would be one that failed to fit either the local or the long range constraints – e.g., 'before'.

On the basis of some such scale, points could be awarded differentially. For example, a score of 4 could be awarded for the exact word (category a), 3 for a perfectly acceptable substitute, 2 for category c, 1 for d, and 0 for e. Or, categories a and b could be equally weighted – say, 3 for a or b, 2 for c, 1 for d, 0 for e. Or, categories c and d could be equally weighted – say, 2 for a or b, 1 for c or d, and 0 for e.

All of the foregoing systems of scoring tests for adult foreign students studying English as a second language were investigated by Oller (1972). The results showed all of the methods to be either equivalent or slightly inferior to a method that counted categories a and b worth 1 point and all the rest worth nothing – i.e., for scoring purposes, differentially weighting degrees of appropriateness had no significant effect on the overall variance produced. Not only were all of the methods investigated highly correlated with each other, but all were about equally correlated with scores produced by other language tests. The contextually appropriate method yielded slightly better results than the exact word method, however. Thus it is probably safe to conclude that complex weighting systems do not afford much if any improvement over the simpler methods of scoring.

One other system of weighting responses deserves discussion. It is the technique referred to as 'clozentropy' by D. K. Darnell. No doubt Darnell's system is the most complex one yet proposed as a basis for scoring cloze tests, but it has a great deal of intuitive appeal. Moreover, if computer time and programming expertise are available, the technique is feasible – at least for research purposes. The reason for discussing it here is not to recommend it as a classroom procedure, but rather to show that it is roughly equivalent to simpler methods that are more appropriate for classroom use.

Darnell was interested in testing the English skill of non-native speakers – in particular, foreign students at the University of Colorado at Boulder. Because of the negative results reported by Carroll, Carton, and Wilds (1959, see the discussion in section C. 2 above), Darnell shied away from the exact word scoring method, and opted to develop a whole new system based on the responses of native speakers. He administered a cloze test to native speakers (200 of them) on the assumption that the responses given by such a group would be a reasonable criterion against which to judge the adequacy of responses given by non-native foreign students to the same test items. He reasoned that the responses given more frequently by native speakers should be assigned a heavier weighting than less frequent responses.

Without going into any detail, Darnell showed that his method of scoring by the clozentropy technique generated surprisingly high correlations with the *Test of English as a Foreign Language* (Educational Testing Service and the College Entrance Examination Board) – to be exact, .83 for a group of 48 foreign students. The only difficulty was that Darnell's method required about as much work as the preparation of an objectively scorable test of some other type (that is, other than a cloze test). In short, the virtue of the ease of preparing a cloze test was swallowed up in the difficulty of scoring it.

Fortunately, Pike (1973) showed that there was a very high correlation between Darnell's scoring technique and an exact word scoring technique. Both scoring methods produced strong correlations with the *TOEFL*. This latter result has been further substantiated by Irvine et al (1974). It follows that if both exact and contextually appropriate methods are substantially correlated with each other (at .9 or better), and if exact and contextually appropriate scores as well as exact and clozentropy scores are strongly correlated with *TOEFL* (at .6 to .8 or better), it follows that exact, contextually appropriate, and clozentropy scores are all strongly correlated with each other.

From all of the foregoing, we may conclude that except for special research purposes there is probably little to be gained by using a complex weighting scale for degrees of appropriateness in scoring cloze tests. Either an exact word or contextually appropriate method should be used. The choice between them should be governed by the purpose to which the scores are to be put. If the intent is to use only the overall score, probably the exact word method is best. If the intent is to look at specific performances on particular test items or in particular student protocols, probably the contextually appropriate scoring should be used.

(iv) *Interpreting the scores and protocols.* Robert Ebel (1972) has argued that test validity in the traditional sense of the term may not be as important as test interpretability. An important question that is too often overlooked is what the test scores mean. In this chapter we have examined what cloze scores mean with reference to a wide variety of other tests that involve the use of written forms of language. We have seen, for instance, that it is possible to form a rough idea about the readability of a text on the basis of a particular group's performance on cloze items formed over the text. We have also seen that it is possible to form a notion of a given learner's ability to comprehend textual material of a defined level of difficulty. Further, we have seen that specific hypotheses about contextual constraints can be tested via performance on cloze tests. Finally, group scores can be used to assess the effectiveness of instructional methods.

There are yet other diagnostic uses of cloze tests. For instance, it is possible to form specific hypotheses about individual learner competencies. It is sometimes even possible to see precisely where a given student went awry and with study it is sometimes possible to form a good guess as to what led to the error – e.g., inappropriate instructional procedures, or incomplete learning of constraints on certain linguistic forms. As an example, consider the following items from a cloze test protocol (the answers were given by a Japanese adult studying English as a second language):

> ... A responsible society wants (30) _punishment_, not revenge. It does (31) _neither_ need to get revenge (32) _____ itself, nor should it (33) _____ to do so ...

The learner has seemingly been led to believe that the 'neither/nor' construction is appropriate for such contexts. This could be the fault of inappropriate pattern practice (i.e., incomplete exemplification of usages of such a construction). It would certainly appear that the learner is clued to place 'neither' in the blank for item 31 because of the 'nor' that follows seven words later. The word 'punishment' in item 30 reveals a partial understanding of the text, but an incomplete understanding of the meaning of the word. Although 'punishment' may not be synonymous with 'revenge', still it involves an element of vengeance or retribution. The word that was actually deleted from blank 30 was 'justice'.

In another test item, from another cloze test, the same student reveals another interesting effect of instruction:

> ... 'I think Daddy (43) _should_ do the dishes tonight.' 'Your father (44) _are_ worked hard all day.' 'But so have (45) _you_, Mother. You've worked hard all day too, (46) _haven't_ that so?' asked the oldest. ...

Item 46 is the one of greatest interest (though there is an error in item 44 as well). The learner, apparently having been trained by pattern drilling of the sort exemplified in Chapter 6, notices the auxiliary 'have' in 'You've worked ...' and inappropriately forms the tag question 'haven't that so?' Item 44 is also revealing inasmuch as it shows an inadequate comprehension of the meaning of the present perfect. No obvious explanation suggests itself for the learner's failure to notice that the subject is singular. However, a study of other protocols by this same learner shows that he often has difficulty with the complex verb forms involving auxiliaries and modals, e.g.,

> ... marijuana has (3) ___been___ effects on people ....
> .... simple punishment is one of the most often (28) ___use___ arguments for the death penalty[3] .....
> .... Abortion (66) ___is___
> freed women from unwanted (67) ___baby___. ...

Note in the last example that the problem of the plural/singular distinction arises again in item 67.

The foregoing examples do not begin to exhaust the richness of even the sample protocols referred to for the single subject selected. Perhaps they will serve, however, to illustrate some of the kinds of information that can be inferred from learner protocols on cloze tests.

KEY POINTS

1. The cloze technique was invented by Wilson Taylor who likened it to the kind of closure characteristic of visual perception of incomplete patterns.
2. A cloze test is constructed by deleting words from a text or segment of discourse.
3. It is not a mere sentence completion task, however, because cloze items are not independent and range across the sequentially related sentences of a discourse.
4. Closure of blanks left in text is possible because of the redundancy of discourse and the internalized expectancy system that speakers of a language possess.
5. The standard test construction technique, known as the *fixed ratio method*, involves deleting every *n*th word (where *n* usually varies from 5 to 10) and replacing each one with a standardized blank (usually about 15 typed spaces).
6. The standard length of the cloze test is 50 items – thus the passage length must be approximately 50 times *n*.
7. Another procedure, the properties of which are less determinate, is to delete words on some *variable ratio* usually decided by a rational selection procedure – e.g., delete only content words.

---

[3] As we noted above, topics such as the decriminalization of marijuana, capital punishment, and abortion are not universally recommendable. They may be distracting because of their controversial nature. They were used in several tests exemplified here, however, to test the effects of attitude variables in cloze tests over precisely such topics (see Doerr, in press).

8. Cloze tests can be shown to require both temporally constrained sequential processing and pragmatic mapping of linguistic elements onto extralinguistic contexts; therefore, they are pragmatic tests.

9. It is possible to construct fill-in-blank tests that do not meet one or both of the pragmatic naturalness criteria.

10. Cloze procedure has been shown to be a highly reliable method of distinguishing the readability of texts; in fact, the technique appears to be a good measure of the redundancy of discourse to particular audiences.

11. The cloze method as a measure of readability is superior in validity to any of the other techniques that have been proposed and studied carefully: the readability formulas are less accurate.

12. As a rough guideline it is suggested that at least 25 scores on tests of at least 50 items be used for comparative purposes – e.g., for comparing the readability of texts, the language proficiency of groups and the like.

13. Anderson (1971b) suggests that cloze scores at .53 or above (by the exact-word scoring) can be equated with an 'independent' level of reading for the material tested; a score between .44 and .53 falls within the 'instructional' range; and below .44 in the 'frustrational' range.

14. Research by Bormuth (1967) indicates that scores in the .4 to .45 range and up are suitable for instruction with native speakers insofar as they are roughly equivalent to scores of .75 on the traditional multiple choice tests of reading comprehension.

15. Osgood and Sebeok (1965) suggested using the cloze method for assessing the relative proficiency of bilinguals in each of their languages.

16. Only recently has it been demonstrated that a simple translation procedure may yield roughly comparable tests in two or more languages. (However, see the equating procedure recommended in Chapter 10 p. 292f.)

17. Taylor (1957) demonstrated that the every nth word deletion technique yielded cloze items of somewhat greater reliability and validity than deliberate selection of words to be deleted – e.g., deleting only content or only function words.

18. Subsequent research with non-native speakers suggests that cloze tests based on an every nth word procedure are also superior for bilingual testing.

19. Cloze scores are known to be good indicators of whatever is measured by standardized reading comprehension tests, and appear to be somewhat more sensitive to gains attributable to study than are standard multiple choice items.

20. Deletion techniques that operate over every word in a text seem especially well-suited to the study of contextual constraints.

21. Although there is some controversy in the literature, it seems empirically established that cloze tests are sensitive to constraints that range across sentences – though some items are more sensitive than others.

22. Cloze scores can also be used to evaluate the effectiveness of an instructional procedure.

23. For most purposes, the standard method of deleting every nth word of a text is best.

24. For an every 5th word deletion ratio, 250 words of text will yield 50 items; in general, the length of text needed can be roughly determined by multiplying the number of desired blanks by the number of words between deletions.
25. Instructions should encourage examinees to read the entire text before attempting to fill in blanks and should inform them that there is no penalty for guessing.
26. Most adult students (native or non-native) can fill in, or at least attempt, 50 items in a 50 minute period – perhaps a general guideline of one minute per item could be followed for shorter tests, though for longer tests such a rule of thumb would probably be overgenerous. For younger subjects, on the other hand, it might be on the stingy side.
27. Correlations between exact-word scores and contextually appropriate scores are sufficiently strong to recommend the exact-word scoring for most purposes – however, research has shown that slightly finer discrimination can be achieved by the contextually appropriate method.
28. Techniques that weight responses for degrees of appropriateness or for degrees of conformity to native speaker performance do not seem to yield finer degrees of discrimination for practical purposes.
29. It has been shown that contextually appropriate scoring can be done either by a single rater working alone or by several raters, with equivalent results (Naccarato and Gilmore, 1976).
30. In addition to the more common uses, cloze scores can also be interpreted for diagnostic information concerning individual learner performances.

DISCUSSION QUESTIONS

1. Discuss the factors that contribute to the difficulty (or the ease) of filling in the blanks on a cloze test. Compare these with the factors discussed in Chapters 10 and 11. To what extent can such factors be generalized to all discourse processing tasks? What are the factors that contribute to the differences across such tasks – e.g., what factors might make an oral cloze task more difficult than a dictation over the same text?
2. Taylor (1953, 1956, 1957) believed that the cloze testing concept could be extended to visual processing. Consider the possibility of a text accompanied by audio-visual aids used as a basis for a cloze procedure that might leave out whole phrases, clauses, or even exchanges between persons, i.e., if the picture were left intact but the sound were intermittently interrupted.
3. What does a person have to know in order to fill in the missing portions of the items in Figure 19? How does that knowledge resemble (or fail to resemble) the knowledge necessary to fill in the blanks in a cloze test over the numbers 'one, two, ...' or the Gettysburg address, or some less familiar text?
4. Construct and administer a cloze test to a group of students. Analyze the students' responses with a view to determining the strategies they employed in filling in the items. Compare the responses of different

students. Compare the difficulty of different items and the constraints operating on each. Which items do you think are sensitive to constraints across sentences?

5. Construct multiple forms of cloze tests over a single text using an every fifth word deletion procedure. Administer the tests in such a way that the practice effect is distributed roughly equally over all parts of the text. This can be done by handing out the five forms of the test so that the first student gets form one, the second gets two, the third three, the fourth four, the fifth five, the sixth one, and so on. On the second test day, hand out the tests so that student one gets form two, the second gets form three, the third gets form four, the fourth five, the fifth one, and so on. This procedure is repeated three more times. At the end of the five test sessions, each student will have completed all five forms of the cloze passage. However, student one will have completed them in the order one, two, ... five; the second will have completed them in the order two, three, four, five, one; the third in the order three, four, five, two, one; and so on. Thus, the practice of having taken one of the forms on day one and a different one on occasion two is nearly equally spread over all five forms of the cloze passage. Score all of the tests and count the percentage of right answers (say, by the exact-word scoring to make it simpler) to each item in each form. Write the percentage of correct answers above each word in a full copy of the text. Which words were easiest and why? Which were the hardest? What sorts of constraints seem to be operating within phrases, across phrases, within clauses, across clauses, and so on?

6. If you are a foreign language teacher, you might want to try the following: select a passage you think your students can handle in the target language (i.e., in the foreign language in this case); translate it into English; construct cloze tests over each text; use the same deletion procedure (e.g., every fifth word, say); give both tests to your students (target language passage first, then the passage in English). The scores your students make in English should be roughly comparable to the scores native speakers of the target language would have made on the test in the target language. How do your students compare to native speaker performance on the task? In other words, the difference between their scores in English and their scores in the target language is roughly equivalent to the difference between their scores in the target language and scores that would have been achieved by a socioeconomically and educationally comparable group of native speakers of the target language.

7. What effect would you predict if the distance between blanks on a cloze text were increased? Would it make the task easier or harder? Why?

8. Try cutting a text into five word segments and inserting a cloze item in the middle of each segment. Type each segment on a separate card and shuffle the cards – or use some other scrambling procedure. Then try running the items together to form a text. What sorts of false leads are set up by such a contrived cloze passage? How does such a text differ from normal prose? Repeat the procedure with different lengths of segments. Is the effect any different? When does the effect cease to be significant to the reader? Consider shuffling the chapters of a book into a new order.

That is, consider the effects that would be produced. It isn't a very practical experiment to suggest.

9. No one, to the knowledge of this writer, has ever investigated the effects of different instructions on scores on cloze tests. What if learners were not instructed to read over the entire text before attempting items? What effect would you expect? What if they were told not to guess – that there would be a penalty for guessing incorrectly? How would such changes in instructions be likely to affect scores?

10. Try to conceptualize a scoring schema that assigns points for different degrees of correctness. What advantages would your system have for diagnostic purposes? Could such a schema be based on the errors that learners are actually observed to make? Could the method you propose be taught to someone else? Try it out with another scorer over a batch of cloze tests. See how much the two of you agree or disagree in assigning particular responses to the weighted categories you have set up.

11. Analyze the responses of a single student on various pragmatic tasks including cloze tests completed by that student. Try to devise special drills or exercises (based on discourse processing tasks) that will help this student overcome certain determined deficiencies. For instance, if the learner makes errors in the use of articles across all of the tasks, try to determine with respect to particular texts what information exactly the student is not attending to that the native speaker would have noticed – e.g., the fact that a particular pair of slacks had been mentioned prior to a certain item requiring 'the' in reference to that same pair of slacks (see the text about Joe's problems and the discussion above on pp. 361–362).

SUGGESTED READINGS

1. Jonathon Anderson, 'Selecting a Suitable "Reader": Procedures for Teachers to Assess Language Difficulty,' *Regional English Language Center Journal* 2, 1971, 35–42.

2. John E. Hofman, *Assessment of English Proficiency in the African Primary School.* Series in Education, University of Rhodesia, Occasional Paper Number 3, 1974.

3. Stig Johansson, *Partial Dictation as a Test of Foreign Language Proficiency.* Swedish–English Contrastive Studies, Report Number 3, 1973.

4. George R. Klare, 'Assessing Readability,' *Reading Research Quarterly* 10, 1974–1975, 62–102.

5. Bernard Spolsky, 'Reduced Redundancy as a Language Testing Tool,' paper presented at the 2nd International Congress of Applied Linguistics, Cambridge, England, September, 1969. ERIC ED 031–702.

6. Joseph Bartow Stubbs and G. Richard Tucker, 'The Cloze Test as a Measure of English Proficiency,' *Modern Language Journal* 58, 1974, 239–241.

7. Merrill Swain, Sharon Lapkin, and Henri C. Barik, 'The Cloze Test as a Measure of Second Language Proficiency,' *Working Papers on Bilingualism* 11, 1976, 32–43.

8. Wilson L. Taylor, '"Cloze Procedure": A New Tool for Measuring Readability,' *Journalism Quarterly* 30, 1953, 415–433.
9. Wilson L. Taylor, 'Recent Developments in the Use of "Cloze Procedure",' *Journalism Quarterly* 33, 1956, 33, 42–48, 99.

13

Essays and Related Writing Tasks

A. Why essays?
B. Examples of pragmatic writing tasks
C. Scoring for conformity to correct prose
D. Rating content and organization
E. Interpreting protocols

For many reasons writing is one of the foundational skills of educated persons. Tests of writing skills are therefore needed. This chapter explores traditional essay techniques and suggests both objective and subjective scoring methods. It is recognized that the problem of quantifying essay tasks is a crucial difficulty in school applications. A method of interpreting learner protocols with a view toward helping learners to overcome language difficulties is discussed. Though essay testing may require more work of the teacher and of the students than many other testing procedures, it is considered to be a profitable assessment technique. Certainly it affords a rich yield of diagnostic information concerning the learner's developing expectancy grammar.

A. Why essays?

One of the most often used and perhaps least understood methods of testing language skills is the traditional essay or composition. Usually a topic or selection of topics is assigned and students are asked to write an essay of approximately so many words, or possibly to write an essay within a certain time limit. Sometimes, in the interest of controlling the nature of the task, students may be asked to retell a narrative or to expand on or summarize an exposition. For example, the student might be asked to discuss the plot of a novel or short

382 LANGUAGE TESTS AT SCHOOL

story, or to report on the major themes of a non-fictional book or passage of prose.

Essays are probably used so frequently because of the value placed on the ability to organize and express our ideas in written form. This ability is counted among the most important skills imparted by any educational system. Witness the three R's. It is not known to what extent the acquisition of writing skill carries over into other aspects of language use – e.g., being an articulate speaker, a good listener, or an insightful reader – but there is evidence that all of these skills are substantially interrelated. Moreover, there is much evidence to suggest that practice and improvement in one skill area may rather automatically result in a corresponding gain in another skill area. There is even some suggestion in the data from second language learning that practice in speaking and listening (in real life communication) may have as much of an effect on reading and writing as it does on speaking and listening and conversely, pragmatic practice in reading and writing (where communication is the goal) may affect performance in speaking and listening at least as much as reading and writing (see Murakami, in press).

However, in spite of their popularity, there is a major problem with free composition tasks as tests. It is difficult to quantify the results – i.e., to score the protocols produced by examinees. We will see below that reliable methods of scoring can be devised, and that they are only slightly more complex conceptually than the methods suggested in Chapter 10 for the scoring of dictation protocols. Perhaps we should not stress the difficulty of obtaining reliable scores, but rather the ease and likelihood of obtaining unreliable (and therefore invalid) scores on essay tasks.

As we noted earlier, in Chapters 10 and 11, tasks that require the production of sequences of linguistic material that are not highly constrained all present similar scoring problems. For instance, a dictation/composition task, or a hear and retell task, or a creative story telling task, and all similar production tasks whether written or oral entail stubborn scoring problems. The oral tasks require an extra step that is not present in the scoring of written protocols – namely transcribing the protocols from tape or scoring them live (an even more difficult undertaking in most cases). Further, the scorer must in many cases try to infer what the examinee intended to say or write instead of merely going by what appears in the protocol. If the examinee intends to say 'he did it by a hammer', then there is no error – i.e., if the person referred to performed the act near a hammer rather than 'with' a hammer. On the other hand, if the examinee intended to encode the instrumental meaning (i.e., the hammer was the instrument used in the action performed) there is at least one error.

In this chapter we are concerned with defining methods of scoring essay tasks in particular, and productive language tasks in general. It is assumed that essay tasks are fundamentally similar to speaking tasks in certain respects – namely in that both types of discourse processing usually presuppose someone's saying (or writing) something for the benefit of someone else. If the writer has nothing to say he is in very much the same boat as the speaker holding forth on no particular topic. If the writer has something to say and no prospective audience, he may be in the position of the child describing its own performances with no audience in mind, or the adult who is said to be thinking out loud.

Of course, these parallels can be drawn too closely. There are important differences between acts of speaking and acts of writing as any literate person knows all too well. The old saw that a person should write as he would speak, or the popular wisdom that unclear writing is the result of unclear thinking, like all forms of proverbial wisdom require intelligent interpretation. Nonetheless, it is taken for granted here that much of what was said in Chapter 11 concerning productive oral testing is applicable to writing tasks and need not be repeated here, and conversely that much of what is suggested here concerning the scoring of written protocols (especially essays) can be applied to transcriptions of oral protocols or to tape recorded oral performances.

B. Examples of pragmatic writing tasks

Just as it is possible to conceive of non-pragmatic tests of other sorts, it is also possible to invent testing procedures that may require writing, but which are not in any realistic sense pragmatic. Sentence completion tasks, for instance, do not necessarily involve pragmatic mapping onto extra-linguistic context, and they do not generally involve higher order discourse constraints ranging beyond the boundary of a single sentence. A typical school task that requires the utilization of words in sentences (e.g., as a part of a spelling exercise) would not qualify as a pragmatic task. Neither would a written transformation task that requires changing declarative sentences into questions, passives into actives, present tense statements into past tense statements, etc. In general, any manipulative exercise that uses isolated sentences unrelated to a particular pragmatic context of discourse does not constitute a pragmatic writing task.

The key elements that must be present in order for a writing task to qualify are similar to those for speaking tasks. The writer must have something to say; there must be someone to say it to (either explicitly or implicitly); and the task must require the sequential production of elements in the language that are temporally constrained and related via pragmatic mapping to the context of discourse defined by (or for) the writer. Probably such tasks will be maximally successful when the writer is motivated to write about something that has personal value to himself and that he would want to communicate to someone else (preferably the intended readership). Contrived topics and possibly imagined audiences can be expected to be successful only to the extent that they motivate the writer to get personally (albeit vicariously) involved in the production of the text. An unmotivated communicator is a notoriously poor source of information. To the degree that a task fails or succeeds in eliciting a highly motivated performance, it will probably fail or succeed in eliciting valid information about the writing ability of the examinee.

In this chapter we will consider writing tasks to be pragmatic if they relate to fullfledged contexts of discourse that are known to the writer and that the writer is attempting to make known to the reader. Protocols that meet these requirements have two important properties that disjointed sentence tasks do not have. First, as Rummelhart (1975) points out, 'Connected discourse differs from an unrelated string of sentences ... in that it is possible to pick out what is important in connected discourse and summarize it without seriously altering the meaning of the discourse' (p. 226). Second, and for the same reasons, it is possible to expand on a discourse text and to interpolate facts and information that are not overtly stated. Neither of these things is possible with disjointed strings of sentences.

Writing about a poignant experience, a narrow escape, recollections of childhood, and the like all constitute bases for pragmatic essay tasks. Of course, topics need not focus on the past, nor even on what is likely. They may be entirely fictional predicated on nothing but the writer's creative imagination. Or, the writing may be analytical or expository. The task may be to summarize an argument; retell a narrative; recall an accident; explain a lecture; expand on a summary; fill in the details in an incomplete story; and so on.

There really is no limit to the kinds of writing tasks that are potentially usable as language tests. There is a problem, however, with using such tasks as tests and it has to do with scoring. How can essays or other writing tasks be converted to numbers that will yield meaningful variance between learners? Below we consider two methods of converting essay protocols and the like to numerical values. The first method involves counting errors and determining the ratio of the number of errors to the number of opportunities for errors, and the second technique depends on a more subjective rating system roughly calibrated in the way the FSI rating scales for interview protocols are calibrated.

C. Scoring for conformity to correct prose

It is possible in scoring essays to look only at certain so-called grammatical 'functors'. Such a scoring method would be similar to the one used in scoring the *Bilingual Syntax Measure* (discussed in Chapter 11, above). It would, however, be a discrete point scoring method. For instance, the rater might check certain morphemes such as plurals, tense indicators, and the like on 'obligatory occasions'. The subject's score would be the ratio of correct usages to the number of obligatory occasions for the use of such functors. This method, however, does not necessarily have any direct relationship to how effectively the student expresses intended meanings. Therefore, it is considered incomplete and is rejected in favor of a method that focusses on meaning (see Evola, Mamer, and Lentz, in press).

To score an essay for its conformity to correct prose, it is first necessary to determine what the essay writer was trying to say. In making such a determination, there is no way to avoid the inferential judgement of someone who knows the language of the essay. Further, it helps a great deal if the reader studies what is said in its full context. Knowledge of the topic, the outline of the material, or any other clues to intended meanings may also be helpful. To illustrate the importance of context to the reader's task of discovering (or rather inferring) the writer's intended meanings, consider the following excerpts of unclear prose:

> (1) I woke up when I was in the hospital with broken legs because I had a flat tire.
> (2) Adaptation is the way how to grow the plant or the animals in their environments.

In the first case the task was to 'write about an accident you have witnessed'. In studying the protocol, from the text surrounding the sentence given as example (1) it is clear that the author was driving carelessly when he had an accident. He blew a tire going seventy miles per hour on an expressway. The next thing he knew he was in a hospital with two broken legs. In the second case, the task was to study a text and then write it from recall. The sentence given as example (2) above was apparently an attempt to reproduce from memory the sentence: 'An adaptation is a body structure that makes an animal or plant more likely to survive in its environment.'

Once the reader has developed a notion of what the writer had in mind (or what the writer should have had in mind, as in the case of example 2 where the task is to recall a given text), it is possible to assess the degree of conformity of what the author said to what a more skilled writer might have said (or to what the text actually said when the task is recall).

A simple method that can be used with essay scoring is to restate any portion of the protocol that does not conform to idiomatic usage or which is clearly in error. The error may be in saying something that does not express the intended meaning – for instance, the author of example (1) above did not wake up because he had a flat tire – or the error may be in simply saying something quite incorrectly – for instance, adaptation is not 'the way how to grow the plant or the animals' as stated in example (2) above, rather it is a change that makes plants or animals better suited to their environments.

Rewriting the protocol to make it conform to standard usage and also to express the intended meaning of the author may be difficult, but it is not impossible, and it does provide a systematic basis for evaluating the quality of a text. Furthermore, rewriting an essay to express the intended meanings (insofar as they can be determined by the scorer) requires evaluation not just in terms of how well the text conforms to discrete points of morphology and syntax, but how well it expresses the author's intended meanings. There is guesswork and inference in any such rewriting process, but this reflects a normal aspect of the interpretation of language in use whether it is spoken or written. Indeed, the difficulties associated with making the right guesses about intended meanings should reflect the degree of conformity of the essay to normal clear prose. Hence, the guessing involved is not a mere artefact of the task but reflects faithfully the normal use of language in communication.

In a classroom situation, there are many reasons why the rewriting of each learner's protocol should be done in consultation with the writer of the essay. However, due to practical considerations, this is not always possible. Nonetheless, whether the procedure can be done consultatively or not, rewriting the text to make it express the scorer's best guess as to the intended meaning and to make it do so in idiomatic form is apt to be a much more useful procedure pedagogically than merely marking the errors on the student's paper and handing the paper back. In the latter case, the attention is focussed on the surface form of the language used in the essay, in the former, the attention is focussed on the intended meaning and the surface form is kept in proper perspective – as a servant to the meaning.

Once the rewriting has been carefully completed – deleting superfluous or extraneous material, including obligatory information that may not have been included in the protocol, changing distorted forms or misused items, and so forth – a score may be computed as follows: first, count the number of error-free words in the examinee's protocol; second, subtract from the number of error-free words, the number of errors (allowing a maximum of one error per word of text); third, divide the result of step two by the number of words in the rewritten text. These steps can be expressed simply as shown in the following formula:

ESSAY SCORE = [(the number of error-free words in the student's protocol) minus (the number of errors in the student's protocol)] divided by (the number of words in the rewritten text)

In general there are three types of errors. There are words that must be deleted from the student's protocol; there are words that must be added; and there are words that must be changed.

Below, the suggested scoring method is applied to three protocols of essays written by college level students at Southern Illinois University in the Center for English as a Second Language. The protocols are genuine and have not been changed except to transform them from their original cursive script to print. The cursive notes above the line are my suggested rewrites. Other scorers might have made some different suggestions for changes. Or, they might have been more or less lenient. The point of the method, however, is not to attempt to provide a scoring system that will be equivalent across all possible scorers. This would not even be a reasonable objective. Differences across readers cannot be dissolved nor would an attempt to eradicate such differences reflect the normal use of language in written form or any other form. The point of the scoring method is to provide a technique of converting essay protocols to a quantity that reflects (in the view of at least one proficient reader) the degree of conformity of those protocols to effective idiomatic prose.

More research is needed to test the reliability and validity of the recommended scoring method, but it has been shown to be substantially reliable and valid in recent work at Southern Illinois University (see Scholz, Hendricks, Spurling, Johnson, and Vandenburg, in press, and Kaczmarek, in press). In brief, the method probably works as well as it does because it very clearly assesses the overall conformity of the student's writing to idiomatic prose.

Protocol 1

Score: (124–24)/142 = .70

(An advanced ESL student at Southern Illinois University)

I was going to my home from the school. When I was standing before a red light at the corner, a yellow car passed the red light and hit a blue car passing the corner going through the intersection. Obviously the driver of yellow car was at fault. It was about noon and there was heavy traffic. The blue car was almost damaged destroyed. The driver of yellow car was calm. He came to the other driver and begged his pardon. But the driver of blue car was nervous. Someone called the police. After five minutes a police car came and towed the two cars away The guilty driver was taken a given a fifty dollar ticket. The blue car had many a lot of damages that estimated at about five hundred dollars. Though I was late to my getting home that day, but I had an interesting story to tell my parents.

Rewrite of 1

I was going home from school. When I was standing at a red light at the corner, a yellow car ran the light and hit a blue car going through the intersection. Obviously, the driver of the yellow car was at fault. It was about noon and there was heavy traffic. The blue car was almost destroyed. The driver of the yellow car was calm. He came over to the other driver and begged his pardon. But the driver of the blue car was nervous. Someone called the police. After five minutes a police car came and towed the two cars away. The guilty driver was given a fifty dollar ticket. The blue car had a lot of damage estimated at about five hundred dollars. Though I was late getting home that day, I had an interesting story to tell my parents.

Protocol 2

Score: $(127–70)/188 = .30$

(An intermediate ESL student at Southern Illinois University)

Four years ago befor I got my diploma I had very bad accident that I am going to deseribe. In that time my father had two cars and it was at 8 p.m. that my father and my mother went out to visit some our relative. I said to my young brother open the dore of garage and lets drive for a little whail and I hadn't driving licence I was driving in high way and in this time I dicid to came back to home I turn the car back very fast and I couldn't controled and one car was parked there and I both to that car very hard, becaus I hadn't a driver's license I tought its better to go and I went very fast to my home when my father came and He asked me what happend to the car I told him I had accident with wall and he blive me but the day after that the police got my father when He was driving by that car and He paid a lot of mony to the police and the man that I had accident with his car.

Rewrite of 2

Four years ago, before I got my diploma, I had a very bad accident that I am going to tell about. At that time my father had two cars. One evening, about 8 p.m. my father and my mother went out to visit some of our relatives. I told my younger brother to open the door of the garage and we would drive for a little while. I didn't have a driver's license. We drove off on a highway, but finally decided to go home. I turned the car around very fast and I couldn't control it. Another car was parked there and I ran into it very hard. Because I didn't have a driver's license, I thought I'd better go. I went home very fast. When my father came home, he asked me what happened to the car. I told him I had run into a wall and he believed me. But the day after that the police stopped my father when he was driving in that car. He paid a lot of money to the police and to the man whose car I had run into.

Protocol 3

Score: $(12–21)/33 = -.27$

(A beginning student of ESL at Southern Illinois University)

I have a car. I go to stret and another car he's titesh me. I call to the Police man he's cam in. He's gav to the another ticet becuas he's titesh me.

Rewrite of 3

I have a car. I was backing into the street and another car hit me. I called the police. They came. They gave a ticket to the other man because he hit me.

Just as in the case of dictations (and cloze tasks) spelling errors are counted only when they distort a word's morphology or pronunciation (e.g., the word 'happened' spelled 'happend' is not scored as an error, whereas the word 'believed' spelled 'blive' is scored as an error). In the above protocols, punctuation errors are corrected, but do not contribute to the total score of the examinee. This is not to suggest that punctuation and spelling are not important aspects of writing skill, but for the same reasons that spelling is not scored in dictation these mechanical features are not counted in the essay score either. Because of the results with non-native speakers of English, it is assumed that learning to spell English words and learning to put in appropriate punctuation marks in writing are relatively independent of the more fundamental problem of learning the language. Research is needed to see if this is not also true for native speakers of English.

It can readily be seen from the three sample protocols that the scores reflect the presumed range of abilities of the examinees. The most advanced student got the highest score (.70), the beginner got the lowest score ($-.27$); and the intermediate student got a score in the middle (.30). The beginner's negative score reflects the fact that the free writing task (students were asked to write about an accident for fifteen minutes) was so difficult that his errors outnumbered the correct sequences he was able to generate. It is probably true that the task was too difficult and therefore was frustrating and to that extent pedagogically inappropriate for this student and for others like him, but it does not follow from this that the test was invalid for this student. Quite the contrary, the test was valid inasmuch as it revealed the difference between the ability of the beginner, the intermediate, and the advanced student to perform the essay writing task – namely, to describe an accident within a fifteen minute time limit.

Many scoring methods besides the one exemplified could be used. For instance, if for whatever reason the examiner wanted to place a premium on quantity of output, the examinee might be awarded points for errorless words of text. The score might be the number of errorless words of text written in a certain time period. Brière (1966) even argued that the mere quantity of output regardless of errors should be considered. In an experimental study he claimed to have shown that learners who were encouraged to write as much as they could as fast as they could within a time limit learned as much as students who received corrective feedback (i.e., whose papers were marked for errors). However, from a testing point of view, it would have to be shown that a mere word count would correlate with other presumed valid measures of writing skill. In the three examples given above, the best essay is not the longest.

On the whole it would seem best to use a scoring method that awards positive points for error-free words and subtracts points for errors. To keep the focus of the examinee and the scorer on the intended meanings and the clear expression of them, some attention should be paid to the amount of deviation from clear prose in any given attempt at written expression. The scoring method proposed above reflects all of these considerations.

D. Rating content and organization

It has long been supposed that subjective ratings were less accurate than more objective scoring methods. However, as we have seen repeatedly, subjective judgements are indispensable in decisions concerning whether a writer has expressed well his intended meaning and, of course, in determining what that intended meaning is. There is no escape from subjective judgement in the interpretation of normal expression in a natural language. In fact, there are many reasons to suppose that a trained judge may be the most reliable source of information about how well something is said or written. The crucial question in any appeal to such judgements is whether or not they are reliable – that is, do different judges render similar decisions concerning the same samples of writing, and do the same judges render similar decisions concerning the same samples of writing on different occasions. The question of the reliability of ratings is the same whether we are thinking of written or spoken (possibly recorded) samples of language.

Research with the FSI oral testing procedure discussed in Chapter 11 above has indicated that trained judges can render highly reliable evaluations of samples of speech acquired in oral interview settings. More recent work with oral ratings and with the evaluation of written protocols has indicated that even untrained raters tend to render fairly reliable judgements though trained raters do still better. Although Mullen found substantial variability across judges in the calibration of their evaluations, reliability across judges (that is, the correlation of the ratings of the same subjects by different judges) was consistently high. For both written and oral protocols, the correlation across pairs of judges working independently was consistently above .5 and for most pairs was above .8 (Mullen, in press a, and Mullen, in press b). Callaway (in press) similarly showed that the correlation across judges in the evalutation of spoken protocols was consistently above .7 for more than half of the raters in a sample of 70.

The work of both Callaway and Mullen indicates further that judges always seem to be evaluating communicative effectiveness, regardless whether they are trying to gauge 'fluency', 'accentedness', 'nativeness', 'grammar', 'vocabulary', 'content', 'comprehension', or whatever. Moreover, this is apparently true both for naive (untrained) raters *and* for ESL teachers (trained raters, in Callaway's study). The variance overlap across scales aimed at, say, 'accentedness' versus 'vocabulary' was nearly perfect within the estimated limits of the reliability of the separate scales. This suggests that whatever it is that judges are assessing when they evaluate the 'accentedness' of a speech sample, it is the same thing that they are considering when they attempt to evaluate the 'vocabulary' used in it. Similarly for written protocols, whatever it is that judges are evaluating when they assess the 'content' is nearly perfectly correlated (within the estimated error of measurement) with whatever they are assessing when they judge the 'organization' or the 'grammar' and so on. Both of the studies by Mullen, and the Callaway research as well as recent work by Oller and Hinofotis (1976) and by Scholz *et al* (in press) point to the conclusion that trained and untrained judges alike listen for the communicative effect of speech and they read for the communicative effect of writing. Put very simply, the judges all seem to agree that what is most important in the evaluation of the use of language is how well a person says what he means. They may not agree on this consciously or overtly, but their behaviour in evaluating protocols of speech and writing supports the conclusion that they agree on this implicitly at the very least.

But isn't it true that judges may differ widely in their ratings of the same subjects on the same rating scale? The answer, of course, is that they do sometimes differ widely. Well, doesn't this prove that their judgements are therefore unreliable? No, it doesn't prove that at all. Consider a scale that asks judges to rate the three sample protocols given earlier in this chapter on degree of communicative effectiveness. Suppose that the scale allows for points to be assigned between zero and ten. Suppose further that two different judges are asked to assign scores on the same ten point scale to each of the three protocols. Let's say that judge A is somewhat more severe than judge B. The two judges assign scores as follows:

	Judge A	Judge B
Protocol 1 (advanced)	3	10
Protocol 2 (intermediate)	2	9
Protocol 3 (beginning)	1	8

Judge A consistently assigned lower scores than B, yet the two judges ranked the students in exactly the same order. In both cases the advanced student was ranked ahead of the intermediate student who was ranked ahead of the beginning student. The judges may have disagreed about how to calibrate the scale, but nonetheless, their evaluations are perfectly correlated.

The correlation is perfect because the relative distance of any given score in the set from the mean score for that set is exactly the same across the two sets of scores. That is, the advanced student is rated one point above the mean by both of the judges and the beginner is rated one point below the mean. In both cases, the intermediate student is rated at the mean. Hence, there is perfect agreement (in this hypothetical example) about the relative proficiencies of the three subjects tested even though the scores assigned are quite different when compared directly. The same remarks would hold true if a third judge, C, were added who rated the protocols 10, 5, and 0 on the same scale. The reader can check the correlations between judges by computing the correlations between judge A and B, A and C, and B and C (see Chapter 3, section E. 1 above for an explanation of the computational procedure).

If the scores are expressed in terms of units of deviation from the mean score for each set of scores, it can be seen that the judges are in fact in perfect agreement about how the subjects' performances should be ranked relative to each other. In all three cases, the advanced student is rated as one standard deviation above the mean; the intermediate student is rated at the mean; and the beginner is rated at one standard deviation below the mean. Thus, it is possible for judges to agree substantially on ratings of speech or writing even if they disagree substantially on the particular score that should be assigned to a given subject.

The available research indicates that subjective ratings that evaluate the overall communicative effect of a piece of writing (or speech) are about as informative as objective scores in terms of differentiating between better and worse performances of the individuals in a group of students. However, subjective ratings are summative in nature and do not provide the diagnostic detail that is possible with the more objective type of scoring outlined earlier in this chapter. Another factor to be considered is that the more objective type of scoring is probably less sensitive to individual differences of calibration.

E. Interpreting protocols

Essay tasks have often been favored as classroom testing techniques. Educators sometimes appeal to them as a kind of ultimate criterion against which other tests must be judged. However, the greatest virtue of essay tasks may also be their greatest liability. While it is true that such tasks confer the freedom and responsibility of choice on the examinee, they also require thoughtful evaluation on the part of the examiner. The writer may elect to express very simple ideas only in words that he is sure of, or he may venture into more complex or profound meanings that stretch his capacity to put things into words. Whether the writer has charted a conservative or a daring course is left to the judgement of the examiner. For this reason, equal scores may not represent equivalent performances, and unequal scores do not necessarily imply that the higher score represents the better performance.

The main question in interpreting an essay protocol is, 'What was the writer trying to say, and how well did he say it?' There may seem to be two questions here, but for good reasons readers tend to treat them as one. If a writer does not express things fairly well, it will be hard to tell what he is trying to say; similarly, if a writer has little or nothing to say, how can he say it well? It does not take a sage to see the wisdom of saying nothing unless there is something to say. In fact, a person has to go to school for a very long time to become able to write on topics which do not naturally elicit a desire to communicate (though this is not because people lack things to talk and write about).

Once the evaluator is fairly confident that he knows what the writer was trying to express, it is possible to evaluate how well the job was done. Obviously, the evaluator cannot be much better at evaluating than he himself is at writing and this is where the teeth of subjectivity bite hard. The examiner must place himself in the shoes of the writer and try to figure out precisely what the writer meant and whether he said it well, or how he could have said it better. Thus, the largest part of evaluating essays or other written protocols is inferential, just as the interpretation of speech and writing in other contexts is inferential.

In spite of the criticism that essay tasks allow the writer the freedom to avoid 'difficult structures', such tasks are nonetheless usually quite revealing. A number of problems can be diagnosed by studying a protocol such as number 1 above. Among the glaring errors is the failure to use the definite article where it is required in such expressions as 'The driver of yellow car'. The surface aspect of this error lies in the fact that any noun phrase with a countable head noun (such as 'car' or 'yellow car') requires an article. The deeper aspect of this same error is that without the article, in fact without a definite article, the writer fails to call attention to the fact that the reader knows which yellow car the writer is referring to – namely, the one that ran the red light. If the writer can be made to see this, he can learn to use the article correctly in such cases.

Another noun phrase problem occurs in the phrase 'many damages'. Here, the trouble is that we normally think of damage as a kind of amorphous something which is uncountable. The word 'damage' does not usually appear in the plural form because the referent is not discrete and countable. There can be a little damage or a lot of damage, but not few or many damages. The reader should note that this has no more to do with the syntax of countable and uncountable nouns than it has to do with the concept of what damage is. If we were to conceptualize damage differently, there is nothing in the grammar of the English language that would keep us from counting it or saying 'many damages'. The problem involves meaning and goes far beyond 'pure syntax' even if there were such a thing. If the writer can see the sense or meaning the way the native speaker does, this kind of error can be overcome.

The writer confuses 'give' and 'take'. This distinction has puzzled if not bewildered many a grammarian, yet native speakers have little or no difficulty in using the terms distinctly and appropriately. In this context, 'give' is required because the police were there at the scene. There was no need to take the ticket anywhere. The policeman just handed it to the driver who was presumed to be at fault. Had the driver who was to receive the ticket left the scene of the accident and, say, gone home to Chicago (from Carbondale), it is possible that someone might have *taken* him the ticket. It would appear that the cop *gave* the ticket to the man, and the man to whom he *gave* it *took* it home to Chicago or wherever he was going.

Two other errors involved clause connectors of sorts. The writer says, 'The blue car had a lot of damage that estimated about five hundred dollars'. The problem the writer needs to be made to see is that the way he has it written, the damage is doing the estimating. Another difficulty in joining clauses together appropriately, occurs in the last sentence of the protocol where the learner avows, 'Though I was late getting home that day, but I had an interesting story to tell my parents'. Perhaps the learner does not realize that 'though' and 'but' in this sentence both set up the condition for another statement offering contrary information. In the case of 'but' the contrast has a kind of backward look whereas with 'though' an anticipatory set is cued for information yet to come.

How can the diagnostic information noted above be applied? Surely it is not enough to offer grammatical explanations to the learner. In fact, such explanations may not even be helpful. What can be done? For one thing, factual pattern drills may be used. For instance, using only the facts in the story as told by the writer (and well known to the writer) it is possible to set up the following pattern drill with 'the' following a preposition and elsewhere.

1. I was waiting at a light. The color of *the* light was red.
2. A car ran the light. The color of *the* car was yellow.
3. It hit another car. The color of *the* car that it hit was blue.
4. The color of *the* car that hit the blue one was yellow.
5. The driver of *the* blue car was nervous.
6. He came over to the driver of *the* yellow car and apologized.
7. The police gave the driver of *the* blue car a ticket. The amount of *the* fine was fifty dollars.

In addition to the above sentences it is possible to set up meaningful question and answer drills. For example,

1a. Where were you waiting?
   At a light.
1b. What color was the light?
   It was red.
1c. What was red?
   The light was red.
2a. What happened next?
   A car ran the light.
2b. What color was the car?
   It was yellow.
2c. What was yellow?
   The car was.
3a. Which car ran the light?
   The yellow car did.

and so forth.

The key advantage to the above type of pattern drill is the meaning. The writer knows what the facts are. The deep structure, or the sense, is known. It is how to express the sense in terms of surface structure that the writer needs to discover. The drills should be designed to help the learner see how to express meanings by using certain surface forms. The main difference between the type of drill illustrated above (and the number and variety of such drills is unlimited) and the type so often found in ESL or foreign language curricula is where the learner's attention is focussed. In the drills recommended here, the focus is on the meaning. In the disconnected and relatively meaningless sentences of typical pattern drills, on the other hand, the focus is on the surface form – with scarcely a thought for the meaning.

(See Chapter 6, section C above.) Here the learner knows what the meaning is and can discover what the surface form should be. With meaningless sentences, by contrast, the meaning is not known to the learner and cannot be discovered (unless he already knows the language).

Much remains to be discovered concerning the nature of writing and the discourse processing skills that underlie it. However, there is little reason to doubt the utility of essay writing as a reasonable testing procedure to find out how well learners can manipulate the written forms of a language. In fact, there are many more arguments in favor of essay writing as a testing technique than there are against it. Its usefulness as a diagnostic tool for informing the organizers of a curriculum cannot be overlooked. Further, such tests can easily (though not effortlessly) be integrated into a sensible curriculum.

KEY POINTS

1. The freedom allowed by essay tasks may be both their greatest strength and weakness – a strength because they require a lot of the examinee, and a weakness because of the judgement required of the examiner.
2. Except for the greater accessibility of the written protocols of learners, the evaluation of writing performances is similar to the evaluation of spoken protocols.
3. The fundamental problem in using essay tasks as tests is the difficulty of quantification – converting performances to scores.
4. A technique for evaluating the conformity of a text to normal written discourse is for a skilled writer (presumably the language teacher) to read the text and restate any portions of it that do not seem to express the author's intended meaning, or which do not conform to idiomatic usage.
5. For instructional value and also to insure the most accurate possible inferences concerning intended meanings, such inferences are best made in consultation with the author of the text in question.
6. Something to say and the motivation to say it are crucial ingredients to pragmatic writing tasks.
7. A recommended scoring procedure is to count the number of error-free words in the text; subtract the number of errors; and divide the result by the number of words in the error-free version of the text.
8. Research has shown that subjective ratings of written protocols are about as reliable as objective scoring techniques and that the subjective methods generate about as much valid test variance as the objective techniques do.
9. Research has also shown that attempts to direct attention toward presumed components or aspects of writing ability (e.g., vocabulary, grammar, organization, content, and the like) have generally failed.
10. Apparently, whatever is involved in the skill of writing is a relatively unitary factor that does not lend itself easily to componential analysis.

11. It must be noted that the reliability of ratings of essays by different judges is only marginally related to the calibration of the ratings – it is principally a matter of whether different judges rank subjects similarly. Judges that differ widely in the specific ratings they assign to a set of protocols may agree almost entirely in what they rank as high and what they rank as low in the set.

12. A given learner's protocol may serve as a basis for an in depth analysis of that learner's developing grammatical system. Further, it may provide the basis for factual pattern drills designed to help the learner acquire difficult structures and usages.

13. Indeed, factual pattern drills, derived directly from the facts in the contexts can serve as a basis for preparing materials for an entire class or a whole curriculum to be used in many classes.

14. Essays are reasonable testing devices that have the advantage of being easily incorporated into a language curriculum.

DISCUSSION QUESTIONS

1. How did you learn to write essays in your native language? What experiences in and out of school helped you to acquire skill as a writer? What was the relationship of the experiences you had as a talker to your becoming a writer?

2. To what extent do you agree or disagree with the suggestion that people would do well to write the way they talk?

3. Consider a task where you read a book and summarize in written form what you have read. How would the written form compare with a summary you might give to someone who wanted to know what the book was about? Or, consider seeing a movie and writing a narrative of what happened in it. What is the relation between writing and experience? Introspect on the task of writing a brief autobiography.

4. Assign an essay task to a group of students and analyze the protocols. Try to find group tendencies that would justify drills (factual pattern practices) which would benefit the maximum number of students.

5. Compare the protocols of learners on the essay task with protocols from dictation, cloze procedure, oral interview and the like.

6. What would you predict concerning a comparison of a discrete point method for scoring essay protocols and a more comprehensive scoring method focussed on meaning? What sort of experiment would be necessary to test the validity of the two methods? How could correlation be used to assess which of the two methods was producing the greater quantity of reliable and valid variance? How could it be determined that the variance produced was in fact attributable to the learner's communicative effectiveness in performing the essay task?

7. Discuss your own experiences as a teacher of writing skills or the notions that you would try to employ if you were such a teacher. What methods of instruction have been (or would be, in your view) most effective? What evidence can you offer? Is it your opinion that writing classes *per se* usually teach people to be good writers? If not, what is lacking? How can

people learn to express their ideas in writing, and how can they be instructed so that they will improve?

8. Discuss the differences and similarities between a recall task, such as the one briefly described in Chapter 13, and an essay task where a topic and major points to be covered are suggested by the examiner or instructor. Consider also the case where no topic is offered.

9. Construct scales for evaluating essays that try to sort out all of the things that you think contribute to good or effective writing. For instance, you might have a scale that assesses content and organization; another for vocabulary; another for syntactic and morphological correctness, etc. Apply the scales as diligently as you can to the essays written by a group of students (natives, non-natives, pre-secondary, secondary, or post-secondary, no matter). Compute correlations between the scales. Examine the correlations and the individual protocols to evaluate the success with which you have partitioned the writing skill into components, aspects, or elements.

SUGGESTED READINGS

1. William E. Coffman, 'The Validity of Essay Tests,' in Glenn H. Bracht, Kenneth D. Hopkins, and Julian C. Stanley (eds.), *Perspectives in Educational and Psychological Measurement*. Englewood Cliffs, New Jersey: Prentice-Hall, 1972, 157–63.

2. Celeste M. Kaczmarek, 'Scoring and Rating Essay Tasks,' in J. W. Oller and Kyle Perkins (eds.), *Research in Language Testing*. Rowley, Mass.: Newbury House, in press.

3. Nancy Martin, Pat D'Arcy, Bryan Newton, and Robert Parker, *Writing and Learning across the Curriculum* 11–16. Leicester, England: Woolaston Parker, 1976.

4. Karen A. Mullen, 'Evaluating Writing Proficiency in ESL,' in Oller and Perkins (op cit).

14

Inventing New Tests in Relation to a Coherent Curriculum

    A. Why language skills in a school curriculum?
    B. The ultimate problem of test validity
    C. A model: the Mount Gravatt reading program
    D. Guidelines and checks for new testing procedures

Tests in education should be purposefully related to what the schools are trying to accomplish. For this to be so, it is necessary to carry the validation of testing techniques beyond the desk, chalkboard, and classroom to the broader world of experience. The tests and the curriculum which they are part of are both designed to serve the interests of students and of the larger community beyond the school grounds. They constitute the planned part of the educational effort to instill values, and to impart skills and knowledge to the populace at large. Education in this sense is not an accident and there is no excuse for its effects to remain as poorly understood as they are at the present time. In this chapter we will see that the curriculum is subject to validation by research just as the tests are. Whereas the purpose of the tests is to measure variance in performances of various sorts, it is the purpose of the curriculum to produce such variances over the course of time, or possibly to eliminate them. In all of this, language plays a crucial pivotal role – the curriculum and the tests are largely dependent upon language. In this chapter, we will consider some of the factors necessary to valid language curricula and tests.

A. Why language skills in a school curriculum?

Doesn't the question seem rhetorical? Isn't it obvious why language skills are crucial to the whole business of education? Perhaps it is obvious *that* language skills are important to what happens in the schools, but it may not be obvious just *how* important they are. Stump (1978) observes that language is central to at least two of the three R's, and we may add that it may be of nearly equal importance in the early stages of all three. Reading requires knowledge of language in a fundamental and obvious way. Writing similarly requires language. Furthermore, it isn't enough merely to be able to recognize and form the shapes of letters. Consider the difficulty of writing something coherent about something of which you know absolutely nothing, or alternatively, consider the difficulty of writing something intelligible in a language that you do not know (albeit on a topic of which you may have vast knowledge).

It has often been observed by math teachers that a big part of the problem is simply learning how to read, interpret, and refer to the symbology. As a statistics instructor put it recently, 'Once you have learned the language of multiple regression, you will have the course in your pocket.' Before that? That is, until the language is comprehensible, presumably you will not have understood the content of the course. Thus, it isn't just 'Readin' 'n Writin'' that require language skills. 'Rithmetic' requires language skills too.

Stump's milestone study of fourth and seventh grade children in the Saint Louis schools demonstrates that *all* of the major standardized tests used in that school district (including the Lorge-Thorndike IQ Test, Verbal and Non-Verbal; and the Iowa Tests of Basic Skills, with subtests aimed at language, arithmetic, and reading) are principally measures of the same language factor that is common to cloze tests and dictations – the same sort used with non-native speakers in many of the studies referred to in earlier chapters of this book. Further, Stump's study shows that the distinction between verbal and non-verbal IQ (as expressed in the items of the Lorge-Thorndike) is quite suspect. At the seventh grade level, non-verbal IQ was as strongly correlated with the cloze and dictation scores as was verbal IQ.

Could it be that Stump's results are spurious? Is it possible that the particular tests investigated are not characteristic of similar educational tests in general? The content and the history of the development of the tests make any such explanation unlikely. As Robertson (1972) has shown, nearly every widely used IQ test in existence was modeled after the same pattern – namely the original Binet, later modified to become the Stanford-Binet. The Lorge-

Thorndike test is no exception, rather, it is typical of group administered IQ tests. The same argument can be offered for the Iowa Tests of Basic Skills. It is very similar to many other batteries of achievement tests. Furthermore, as Gunnarsson (1978) has demonstrated, it can be concluded directly from the items on standardized tests that purport to measure 'intelligence', 'achievement', and 'personality' that they are scarcely distinguishable from tests that purport to measure various aspects of 'language ability'.

Unfortunately, the similarities between educational tests generally and tests that are known to measure language proficiency reliably and validly are not usually taken into account in the interpretation and application of the tests in placement, counseling and guidance, remedial teaching, and the curriculum in general. IQ tests may be used to label a child as 'mentally deficient' rather than as not knowing a certain language. Personality tests may be used to identify children who 'have problems of adapting' rather than children who for whatever reason have not learned a certain language or perhaps who have not become very proficient in that language. Achievement tests are usually interpreted in relation to how much of the *curriculum* has been learned or not learned rather than in relation to how much of the *language of the curriculum* the child understands.

Language pervades education. This is no doubt a fact that motivated a book of papers on the topic of *Language Comprehension and the Acquisition of Knowledge* edited by Roy O. Freedle and John B. Carroll (1972). Being able to use a language or even a particular variety of a language seems to be a prerequisite for anything that education attempts to accomplish; or viewed from a slightly different angle, we might say that the ability to use language in a variety of ways is the principal thing that education tries to instill. It is never true to say that language is a mere adjunct of the curriculum, for without language, there could be no curriculum at all. The three R's and all the benefits to which they provide access are founded in language ability.

B. The ultimate problem of test validity

It is said in a widely used book on foreign language testing that the final criterion of test validity in foreign language teaching is whether or not the test assesses what is taught in the foreign language classroom. There is a problem with this criterion of validity, however. It relates to the fact that most of what is taught in foreign language

404   LANGUAGE TESTS AT SCHOOL

classrooms is apparently not language. At least it is not language as it is known outside foreign language classrooms. Few, if any, of the many thousands of students who study foreign languages in classroom settings are able to pass as native speakers of those languages even though they may have been among the best students in their classes. The ones who do acquire the foreign language fluently usually have had to supplement their classroom experience by many hours of experience outside the classroom on their own time and creating their own curriculum. Many will report that they learned next to nothing in the classroom context and that they only acquired the language after travelling to the country where it was spoken.

Merely requiring language tests (or other educational tests) to measure what the curriculum teaches may not be enough. It will be enough only if the curriculum teaches what it is supposed to teach. Most foreign language curricula do not. They do not produce people who can understand and use the foreign languages they try to teach. Hence, there must be a deeper validity requirement. It must be more abstract, more profound, more fundamental than any particular curriculum. The ultimate validity criterion is not a mere requirement for tests alone, but it must be a requirement for the curriculum itself.

If the purpose of a curriculum is to teach children to read in a certain variety of English, the ultimate criterion of success (and the very definition of valid tests for assessing success) is whether or not children who have had the program can read in that variety of English. If the purpose of the curriculum is to teach people to communicate in a foreign language, the criterion of success is how well they can communicate in the language after they have had the course. Thus, the validity of tests in education must be referenced against the skill, performance, ability, or whatever the educational program purports to instill. Anything less will not do. The curriculum itself is subject to validation just as the tests are.

What is the ultimate criterion of validity for language tests? To many it will seem presumptuous even to pose such a question, but putting the question clearly should not be more objectionable than merely offering a glib answer to a vaguer form of the question in an implicit unstated form as is usually done in the testing literature. Certainly the ultimate criterion of validity in language testing cannot be the curriculum because the language teacher's curriculum is also subject to validation. The ultimate criterion must be what people do when they use language for the purpose of communication in all of its ramifications – from poetry and song to ordinary conversation.

But how can the facts of language usage be clarified so that they can serve as the basis for validating curricula and tests? Part of the difficulty is that the 'facts of language usage' are so pervasive and so thoroughly a part of everyday experience that even the most essential research may seem trivial to the casual observer. Why bother to find out how people learn and use language? Everyone who is not an imbecile already knows how people learn and use language. There is a danger that to the casual observer the most fundamental aspects of language will not seem worth the investigative effort, yet there is no rational activity of man that is more profound and abstract than the use and learning of language. The latter generalization follows as a logical entailment of the fact that any cognitive activity can be talked about. Whether it be the conception of theory of relativity or figuring out why the key won't turn in the lock, from the least abstract cognitions to the most profound thoughts, language remains at least one level above, because we can always talk about whatever the activity may be and however abstract it may be. We can turn language inward on itself and talk about talking about talking to any degree of abstraction our minds can handle.

Carl Frederiksen (1977a) urges research into the nature of discourse processing. He suggests that

> the ability to produce and comprehend discourse is among the most important areas of cognitive development. ... Discourse is the natural unit of language, whether a discourse is produced by a single speaker, as in stories or school texts, or by more than one speaker as in conversations. Consequently, the development of communicative competency intimately involves processes which operate across sentences, conversational turns, and larger stretches of language. ... Discourse processing skill is ... central to children's learning and cognitive development (p. 1).

If discourse is the natural unit of language use, and if discourse processing skill is the principal objective of child language learning, it would make sense to propose discourse processing as the prime object of study for the validation of language based curricula. Teaching a child to read in his native language can be viewed as a problem of teaching him to process discourse in an unfamiliar mode. Teaching a person (whether a child or an adult) another language can be viewed as a problem of teaching him to process discourse in that other language. Superficially the tasks appear to be radically different, but they may not be nearly as different as they appear on the surface. Reading curricula, foreign language curricula, and many other language based educational programs are fundamentally similar in their aim to instill discourse processing skill. Therefore, at a deep level, the ultimate validity criterion for evaluating such programs is how well they succeed in enabling students to process discourse in different modes or different languages, and possibly on certain topics or concerning certain subjects. By the same token, the ultimate criterion for the validity of language tests is the extent to which they reliably assess the ability of examinees to process discourse.

Tests that purport to be measures of language ability that do not assess discourse processing skill can hardly be called 'language tests' at all. Neither can curricula that purport to teach language or language skills (e.g., reading) be called 'language curricula' unless they really do teach people to use language in the normal ways that language is used. It would seem to be axiomatic that instructional or testing procedures that do not relate to discourse processing skill in demonstrable ways can scarcely be called 'language teaching' or 'language testing'. Further, instructional and evaluational procedures that are principally oriented toward discourse processing tasks can scarcely be called anything else. So-called 'intelligence', 'achievement', 'aptitude', and 'personality' tests that require complex discourse processing skills should be considered language tests until it is clearly demonstrated by empirical research that they are actually measures of something else. This is imperative because we have a much better chance as educators of bringing about therapeutic changes in language proficiency than we have of changing 'innate intelligence' or 'aptitude' or perhaps even 'personality'. The stakes are too high to base decisions on untested theoretical opinions. Moreover, there are a number of promising methods of empirically determining just what the nature of discourse processing actually is. Why should we rely on opinions when empirical answers are accessible?

Two kinds of investigation are currently yielding informative results. The first type of study involves the analysis of discourse with a view to determining precisely what sorts of processes would be necessary to produce or comprehend it, and the second method of investigation involves detailed examination of the inputs to and outputs from human beings involved in the activity of discourse processing. Examples of the first type of study include the investigation of the constraints underlying stories, narratives, and other forms of discourse currently being done by psychologists and others who are attempting to simulate human discourse processing with computational procedures. Rummelhart's attempt to characterize the grammatical systems underlying stories (1972) offers many insights into the nature of discourse processing and how it is distinct from mere knowledge of words or sentence patterns. Schank and Colby (1973) and Grimes (1975) demonstrate the crucial role of knowledge of the world and the relationships that hold between things, people, events, states-of-affairs, and so on, to the notion of coherence in discourse. Frederiksen (1977a) has demonstrated convincingly that inference plays an important role in both the production and comprehension of some of the simplest aspects of utterances and surface forms of discourse – such as pronoun reference to take a simple case in point.

Frederiksen argues, partly on the basis of requisite assumptions for computer simulation, that normal discourse processing is usually guided by inferential assumptions about intentions, meanings, topics, and the like. Such assumptions or hypotheses about meaning must often be inferred at an abstract level utilizing information that is not given anywhere in the text. Thus, he reasons that overemphasis of surface correspondence of sound and symbol, or visual pattern and word, in the early stages of reading curricula may quite logically produce non-readers – children who have many of the superficial skills that may be necessary to the process, but who cannot comprehend text because they get bogged down in trying to decode forms at the surface while the sense of the discourse eludes them.

The argument can easily be extended to language curricula in general. If the teaching methods focus on relations between surface forms without making it possible for the learner to discover the relationship between discourse and the contexts of discourse, they are bound to fail. Further, we may relate Frederiksen's point to language testing procedures. If a proposed task does not require processing that involves relating discourse to contexts of experience outside the linguistic forms *per se*, then the task cannot legitimately be called a language test in the normal sense of the word 'language'.

A second type of empirical study that is relevant to the questions associated with human discourse processing involves an examination of the human activity itself. Goodman's work with reading miscues (1965, 1968, 1970) is a good example of a technique for discovering something of the way that human beings actually process discourse. There are, of course, many other angles of approach. Frederiksen (1976a, 1976b, 1977a, 1977b) has coupled his work in computer modeling with investigations of actual protocols of children reporting discourse. He used a story retelling technique to elicit samples of data. Other techniques that have been used widely, though they have certainly not yet been wrung dry, include samples of writing, conversation, etc. Indeed, any pragmatic language test offers a suitable basis for eliciting data for the investigation of discourse processing. Conversely, any discourse processing study *is* in a fundamental sense an investigation of both the nature and the validity of pragmatic language testing.

C. A model: the Mount Gravatt reading program

By the arguments already presented in this chapter we are led to conclude that teaching and testing are merely aspects of the same basic problem. With respect to language curricula the crucial problem for teaching is to instill discourse processing skill. The central problem for testing is to assess the extent of such skill. If the objective of the curriculum is to teach children to read in their native language, the objective of the tests must be to assess their ability to do so. At the surface, teaching and testing may look like quite different activities, but down underneath the apparent differences there is an important sameness – indeed an identity of purpose. If that sameness is not obtained for whatever reason, there must be a validity problem either in the teaching or in the testing.

Just as the fundamental sameness of teaching and testing activities in schools may escape notice, the relationship between educational tasks and normal experience outside the classroom may similarly be neglected. If learning to read is a problem of learning to process discourse in a different mode, then it would make sense to capitalize on the discourse processing skill that the learner already has. Yet most curricula do not fully capitalize on the natural relationship between what Hart, Walker, and Gray (1977) have termed 'oracy and literacy'. That is to say, reading curricula should take advantage of what the child already knows about the processing of discourse in an oral mode. They should maximize his chances of success in learning to read by building on what he already knows.

Of course, it would be important to have an understanding of the mechanics of the reading process itself, but this understanding would necessarily remain subordinate to the main goal of teaching children to comprehend and produce written discourse. The mechanics of surface processing compared with the deeper processing of meaning pale to a much lesser significance. The central question becomes how to capitalize on what the child already knows of oral language in teaching him to read. Traditional answers have been based on guesses. Vast experience of educators with failures in initial reading programs indicates that the guesses have not always been very helpful. Another alternative would be to examine empirically the language of children prior to an attempt to set up a reading curriculum.

The intent of a research program might well be to discover the kinds of things children can say and understand in normal contexts of oral discourse prior to the presentation of written forms. Hart, Walker, and Gray (1977) report on a ten year study of child language that has offered many insights for reading curricula. They examined sizable samples of data from $2\frac{1}{2}$, $3\frac{1}{2}$, $4\frac{1}{2}$, $5\frac{1}{2}$, and $6\frac{1}{2}$ year old children. For each child included in the study, data consisted of every utterance spoken to or by the child from the time he got up in the morning until he went to bed that night. In addition to the tape recording of all utterances, a running commentary was kept on the contexts in which the utterances occurred. Thus it was possible to link utterances with contexts taking into account the normal antecedent constraints of previous contexts, their consequences, and so forth.

The recorded protocols of children's discourse provide a basis for testing many specific hypotheses and for answering many questions about the nature of child language acquisition. Further, on the basis of such data it is possible to test existing curricula for their degree of similarity to the kinds of uses normal children put language to – at, say, age $5\frac{1}{2}$. For instance, are the utterances and contexts of child language experience similar to those found in widely used reading programs? Hart et al have found that in fact child language in some important respects bears a closer resemblance to newspaper copy, or to the text of an article likely to be found in a popular magazine than to the language of widely used reading curricula.

Fortunately, the Australian project provides an alternative curriculum for the teaching of reading and suggests an approach to the validation of curricula of many sorts. Indeed, it affords a model, or at least one possible way, of relating the curricula employed in school to the experience of children outside the school. As they point out in *Child Language: A Key to Literacy*, it is a widely accepted notion that teaching should begin with what is known and build upon it. It certainly should not begin by tearing down or throwing away what is known.

Well, where should the reading curriculum begin? There have been many answers. For instance, the so-called 'phonics method' insists that it is sounding out the words that the child must learn to do. The 'phonetic' system on the other hand asserts that it is the relationship between sound and symbol itself that the curriculum must simplify by making sure that each phoneme of the language in question has only one spelling instead of many as in traditional orthographic systems (especially English where the spellings of words are notorious for their diversity of pronunciation, and similarly, the pronunciations are notorious for the diversity of representations). Another method emphasizes the recognition of 'whole words'. Yet another stresses the 'experience of the child' outside of school. Another author may suggest the pot-pourri approach or the eclectic method, taking a little from here and a little from there according to personal preference.

The Australian research program at Mount Gravatt is refreshingly empirical. It is predicated on the belief of Norman Hart and other members of the team that the best foundation for teaching children to read is what they already know about talking and understanding talk. This idea is not new, but their use of it is new. They reasoned that if the language used in beginning readers were pragmatically mapped onto experiences, facts, events, and states of affairs of known or discoverable sorts (from the child's vantage point), and if the utterances that appeared in written form in the texts also conformed to the kinds of utterances (that is pragmatic shapes) already known to the children, they would have an easier time of learning to recognize and manipulate the printed forms of those utterances.

The task Hart *et al* set themselves was, therefore, two-fold: first, to determine the nature of children's utterances in contexts of normal communication; second, to develop a reading curriculum that would utilize such utterance forms. Probably the most striking difference between the utterances of children and the reading curricula to which they are usually exposed (subjected?) has to do with the deep structure of children's discourse – that is, the meanings they are capable of understanding and expressing. In particular, it is obvious in comparing samples of actual child speech with samples of school book material that the children's language is far richer, more interesting and more complex than the language of the books. Children are capable of understanding, and producing more abstract, more complex, and more intriguing plots, situations, relationships, and states of affairs than they are usually presented with in school texts. A second contrast has to do with the forms of utterances. The

actual protocols of child language reveal a very different surface form
than the typical early reading lessons in most school books.

To illustrate the aforementioned contrasts, it may be useful to
compare actual transcripts of child language discourse with samples
of text taken from reading curricula for the early grades. The child
language samples are from the Mount Gravatt Language Research
Program. They are excerpted from the transcripts associated with $5\frac{1}{2}$
year old children from the Brisbane area. In the first example of child
discourse, Jason is at school doing a kind of show-and-tell about a
trip to a Japanese restaurant, The Little Tokyo. Jason begins with
what is apparently a practiced introduction for such occasions:

> 'Mrs Simmons, Boys and Girls, we went to the restaurant
> and got chopsticks. Ah ...' The teacher interrupts, 'They're at
> school here somewhere, aren't they?' Jason answers, 'In my
> port.' He is referring to a lunch-box type of affair that the
> Australian children carry their school things in back and forth
> between home and school. The teacher suggests, 'Go and find
> them so you can show them to us.' While Jason is getting the
> chopsticks Mrs Simmons says, 'We're just waiting for Jason.'
> He returns holding up the chopsticks and announces, 'These're
> chopsticks.' The teacher interprets, 'You like those. They're
> chopsticks. Chinese people eat with them.' The teacher aide
> interjects, 'Jason will show you how he eats with them.'
> Another child puts in, 'We got some.' Mrs Simmons responds,
> 'You've got some at home too?' Then, turning to Jason, she
> urges, 'Show them how you use them, Jason. That's right.' The
> aide puts in, 'Did you like the Chinese food you had?' Jason
> answers, 'Aw, aw, some chicken.' Mrs Simmons answers, 'Oh,
> that was nice,' and the aide asks, 'What did Mummy have?'
> 'Ah, rice,' Jason replies. 'She had rice,' Mrs Simmons answers:
> 'Right. Thanks, Jason.'

Throughout the school day, Jason makes repeated references to the
experience at the restaurant. For instance, later, during free time, he
says,

> 'I'm doing a restaurant first. I'm gonna do the sukiaki. The
> Little Tokyo. Mrs Simmons!' She answers, 'Yes.' 'Um, the
> restaurant's called The Little Tokyo ...'

Compare the discourse in which Jason participates with the following
material from McCracken and Walcutt (1969), *Lippincott's Basic
Reading*:

> Ann ran. A man ran. A ram ran (p. 9).
> Run, rat, run, run, run, run. Run to a red sun. Run to a red
> sun. Run, run, run (p. 17).

412   LANGUAGE TESTS AT SCHOOL

Interestingly, on the following pages the text seems to ramble from one context to another with no thought for meaning or context. At least there is no apparent attempt to maintain an experientially sensible flow. For instance, the authors jauntily jump from dropping eggs and spinning tops to a ram running at two boys whose names begin with *T* and who happen to be resting in a tent. In the end a dog named Rags chases Red, the squirrel, up a tree.

The next sample of actual child discourse comes from a different $5\frac{1}{2}$ year old child. He's having breakfast with Mom and the experimenters who are collecting the data sample:

Mom says, 'That's a good boy. Don't pull the cloth. You've got it all crooked.' The child responds, 'Mr. Fraser's bigger 'n you. Oh, who pulling the table?' Mother replies, 'You are!' He answers, 'I'm not.' She says, 'Sit up and be quiet.' He repeats, 'I'm not. Something under the table what's pulling.' Mother answers, 'All right, fine.' One of the experimenters approaches. 'Can I sit anywhere?' Mother says, 'Just anywhere. Anywhere, yes. You've got a spoon, right?' The experimenter (apparently Mr. Fraser) answers, 'Yes.' The child interjects, 'I'm beat you.' Mr. Fraser responds, 'You beat me, did you?' 'Yeah,' the child answers. 'You've got your other course yet, so you might be beaten yet,' the experimenter challenges. 'I only want one thing and then nothing,' the child responds indicating that he is almost through. Now, Mother addresses the other experimenter, 'Did your father find his way all right, Donelle?' 'Yes,' Donelle replies. 'Oh, beaut,' says the child's mother in typical Australian slang. Donelle continues, 'We missed the street first, but, ah, when we were going past, and I said, "That's it." He said, "No it isn't." We looked past. Yes, that was it.' The other experimenter puts in, 'You were right, oh?' The child adds, 'You still remember where my house is, cause I told you, but you didn't know, did you, a while ago?' Donelle says, 'No.' The child continues, 'You thought you didn't, they did.' Donelle says, 'Mmmm.' 'But, but I told you. Then you know,' the child continues and then adds as an afterthought, 'You didn't drive here.' Donelle asks, 'Hmmm?' 'You didn't drive here, cause you haven't got any license.' 'Mmm. That's right,' Donelle answers. 'If you drive . . .' the child begins but is interrupted by his mother. 'Do you have a license, Donelle?' she asks. 'No,' says Donelle. 'You haven't,' Mother says rhetorically. 'I wish I had now,' Donelle laments. 'Cause too bad!' the child interjects, 'I would put a match in the car.' Donelle says, 'Oh!' and he continues, 'and put in three bags of dynamite.' 'Don't be rude, Brenton,' his mother remonstrates, but he continues undaunted. 'And push the gear lever up, and I will blow up.' 'Mmmm,' says Donelle. Now Brenton warms to the con-

versation, 'That will be the last of the powerline. It will blow up.
. . . Even pour some pepper in your nose, and you will go achoo
and I will . . .' Mother interrupts, 'I think you're being a rude
little boy.' He goes on, 'and I will put some salt down in your
nose. And I will put some wire and some matches. I will light the
match, put it in, and you will blow up to pieces.' 'Then I
wouldn't be able to come and visit you,' Donelle suggests. But
Brenton has a solution, 'Cause I think you could, cause I'd
make you back into the same pieces and put black hair on you.'
'Oh,' she says. 'I started to find, cause I started to find some
black chalk under the house . . .' he continues.

Now, compare the foregoing discourse with a sample of text from
Rasmussen and Goldberg (1970), *A Pig Can Jig*, published by Science
Research Associates (a subsidiary of IBM) designed for use in reading
curricula in the early grades:

man Dan ran fan can I the (p. 1).
I ran. Dan ran. The man ran (p. 2).
I can fan. Dan can fan. The man can fan (p. 3).

4. The text continues with declarative sentences with several possible
permutations of Dan and the man being fanned. Later, near the end
of the book a character named 'Jim' has a remarkable conversation
with 'Dad' about fitting a big rag in a bag. Dad asks if it can fit. Jim
says it can if he rips the bag – so 'rip! rip! rip! zip! zip! zip!' And with
rags in his lap Jim finally gets the big one in the bag (see p. 83). Strange
discourse, isn't it? Hardly like what children really say.

A final example of child discourse comes from a little girl in the
same unpublished Mount Gravatt data sample. She too is $5\frac{1}{2}$. At
school on the playground she begins to talk with one of the
experimenters who is helping to record the speech sample:

'That's what Mark taught me,' she says, 'karate chops.' 'Oh,
did he,' says the adult. 'He used, he used to have his arm in
plaster. He got ran over by a car. He got knocked over by a car.
And guess what he was doin'. Ridin' a motor bike with one
hand.' 'Yeh,' says the adult. 'He's clever,' continues the little
girl. 'He's clever, is he?' says the adult. 'He changed hands and
he fell off. He nearly broke the other arm. He fell in the water
and wet all the plaster.'

Compare this data protocol with the following excerpt of text from
Early, Cooper, Santeusanio, and Adell (1974), *Sun Up Reading Skills
1*, which is part of the Bookmark Reading Program published by
Harcourt, Brace, Jovanovich:

The sun was up (p. 5). Sandy [the dog] was up (p. 6). Bing [the
cat] was up (p. 7).

This unusual beginning is followed by all possible combinations of the greeting 'Good Morning' with the sun, Sandy, Bing, Bing and Sandy, and Sandy and Bing. Then on page 41 there is a sequence where Bing, the dog, and a certain grasshopper, each in their turn go 'hop, hop, hop'. Later, near the end of the book, a turtle, a duck, a rabbit, and a character known as 'Little Pig' all fall down the hill, 'down, down, down' (p. 72).

There are some remarkable differences between the sorts of things children say, the kinds of conversations they engage in, and the texts they are expected to learn to read from. In the children's speech samples, there is a rich system of organization whereby utterances are tied to meanings – present events, previous events, persons, objects, causes and effects. In the reading texts there is a near total disregard for such organization. The point of such texts, apparently, is to present forms of language that use a small inventory of elements (letters and sequences of them as surrogates for sounds and syllables). The object is certainly not to say anything a child would be likely to think of saying. The materials exemplified from widely used readers, rather, display a near complete disregard for intelligent communication. They lack any sense of flow or coherence which is so characteristic of actual language use. They say the most unusual things for the sake of being able to use certain syllables, consonants, or vowels with practically no attention whatsoever to the highly developed expectancies of children concerning the likely relationships between utterances and meanings.

The reading materials developed by Hart, Walker, Gray and the other members of the Mount Gravatt research team on the other hand are predicated on the assumption that the texts should contain utterance forms and meanings that are systematically related to the sorts of meanings that children commonly communicate spontaneously, and in the normal school contexts of their everyday experience. They contend that in order to make the reading materials meaningful to the child, 'he has to be placed in a practical situation which clearly demonstrates contextual meaning' (Hart and Gray, 1977, p. 2). The approach which they have developed on the basis of 'Pragmatic Language Lessons' is systematically rooted in key concepts of the total curriculum as well as the linguistic experience of the child. It has profited much from the failures of other reading programs that lacked the pragmatic emphasis, and it stands on the shoulders of those programs that have emphasized the language experience of children.

Although it is impossible to do justice to the full scope of even a single lesson in the Mount Gravatt program in the short space that is available here, it may be instructive to note the contrast between the first lesson in their program and the examples cited earlier. With suitable illustrations displaying the pragmatic sense of the language forms used, in the first lesson, the children read:

> I'm five. I'm walking to school. That's my teacher. I've got friends (see Hart and Gray, 1977, p. 24 of the Teacher's Manual).

Preliminary results reveal that children are not only learning to read in very short order, but they are spontaneously writing as well.

But what has all of this to do with language testing? Everything. If we are interested in valid tests of how people actually use language, the ultimate validity criterion is *how they actually use language*. The question of how to develop new testing procedures (or how to test existing ones) is intimately related to what we want the tests to be tests of. The latter question, at least in education, is related to the equally important question concerning what the curriculum is supposed to be accomplishing. The problems of teaching and testing are as closely linked in a coherent philosophy of education as are time and space in modern physics.

The above samples of children's discourse illustrate a remarkable complexity and abstractness as well as coherence and sense. The speech of children is not empty as the old time Dick and Jane readers might have led us to suppose. Neither is it dull and insipid as many of the modern approaches imply. It does not repeat endlessly ideas that have already been made clear or which can be easily inferred by ordinary people from the context. It does not jump aimlessly about from topic to topic like a pattern drill. Child discourse arises within meaningful contexts that spark interest and set the genius of language off and running. It has coherence in the sense of meaningful sequence where events, things, people, relationships, and states of affairs are connected by causal and other relations. It has sense because the utterances of children are related to present and implied contexts in sensible non-random ways.

D. Guidelines and checks for new testing procedures

In the preceding chapters we have discussed quite a number of tests that have been shown to meet the two naturalness criteria for pragmatic language tests. Further, we have noted in the case of each type of testing procedure discussed that it is really a family of testing procedures rather than a single test. For instance, dictation can be done in a vast variety of ways, as can cloze testing, oral interview, and essay writing. There are potentially many other procedures that will work as well or possibly even better than the ones considered in this book. It seems likely that the specific procedures recommended here will be improved on as more research is done in the coming years. It is, therefore, probably safe to say that the best pragmatic testing procedures have yet to be invented. It is the purpose of this final section to suggest some heuristic guidelines on the basis of which new procedures might be developed. Of course, any technique that is proposed will have to be tested the same as the existing procedures have been and are being tested. When dealing with such empirically vulnerable quantities as test scores, it is never safe merely to assume that a test is a good test of whatever it purports to be a test of. Tests must be tested.

By now it may be obvious to the reader that the first guideline to be recommended must be to select a discourse processing task that faithfully mirrors things that people normally do when using language in natural contexts. Deviation from normal uses of language requires justification in every case – whereas adherence to normal uses of language is an initial basis for asserting test validity. Scoring conversational exchanges for communicative effectiveness on a subjective basis requires less justification than scoring conversational exchanges on the basis of certain discrete points of surface form singled out by a linguistic analysis. The question of whether a person can or cannot make himself understood is a common sense question that relates easily to normal uses of language. However, the question of whether or not a person knows and uses certain functors (e.g., the plural morpheme, articles, the possessive morphemes, pronominal forms, prepositions, tense markers and the like) is less obviously and less directly related to how well he can speak or use a language. The latter type of question thus requires more justification as a basis for testing than does the former.

Discourse processing tasks of all sorts are logical choices for tasks that may reasonably be converted into procedures that might justifiably be called language tests. It is necessary that such tasks be quantifiable in some way in order for them to be used for measurement and evaluation in the usual ways – for instance, to assess the student's ability; to evaluate the effectiveness of the teacher; and to judge the instructional validity of the curriculum. Quantification may be accomplished by virtue of a scoring procedure that counts certain units in the surface form of the discourse such as the counting procedures that are used with dictation and cloze testing, or it may be achieved on a more subjective basis in relation to a judgement of communicative effectiveness as in the evaluation of oral interview protocols.

The two principal properties of discourse that language tests must reflect are related to the naturalness criteria iterated and reiterated in relation to each of the testing procedures discussed in preceding chapters. First, the task must require the processing of sequences of language elements in temporal relationships, and second, they must require the mapping of those sequences of elements onto extra-linguistic contexts (and vice versa). This is tantamount to saying as Frederiksen (1977a) does that a major property of discourse is its 'coherence'. There is a meaningful sequence of words, phrases, and so on that corresponds to ordered relationships between states of affairs, events, objects, persons, etc. in the world of experience which is distinct from the linguistic forms *per se*. Further, the connections that exist between linguistic forms of discourse and extra-linguistic context, that is the pragmatic mapping relationships, are distinguished by the fact (as Frederiksen also points out) that they are discoverable only by 'inference'.

What sources of data can be investigated as bases for proposing new pragmatic language testing procedures? The Mount Gravatt research program is suggestive. If we want to know how people use language in school, it would make sense to investigate the uses of language in school settings. Similarly, if we want a test of a particular type of discourse processing – e.g., the ability to understand the language of the courts in the U.S., sometimes called 'legalese' – it would make sense to go to the contexts in which discourse of the type in question arises naturally. Examine it. Analyze it. Synthesize it. Develop some likely procedures and try them. Evaluate, revise, retest and refine them.

But how can we test the tests? We have already suggested several heuristics. Among them are the requirements of natural discourse processing tasks, but we must go further before we claim validity for any proposed language test. It needs to be demonstrated that the test produces the kind of test variance that it claims to produce. It must be shown that the test is reliable in the sense defined above in Chapter 3, and it must be shown that the test is valid in the sense of correlating with other tests that are known to produce reliable and valid measures of the same skill or of a skill that is known to be strongly correlated with the skill tested.

In the end we have to make practical choices. We run the risk of a certain amount of inescapable error. We cannot, however, afford to avoid the risk. Decisions are required. The schools are now in session and the decisions are presently demanded. They cannot be neglected. Not deciding on testing procedures is merely a form of a decision that itself is fraught with the potential for irreparable harm to school goers. The decisions cannot be avoided. The best course, it would seem, is to make the best choices available and to keep on making them better.

KEY POINTS

1. Language processing skills are essential in obvious ways to reading and writing, and they are also important in less obvious but easily demonstrable ways to arithmetic – hence to all of the three R's.

2. Stump's research shows that traditional educational measures (in particular the ones used in the Saint Louis schools) are principally measures of language skill.

3. Gunnarsson has demonstrated that tests of many different types including so-called measures of 'intelligence', 'achievement', and 'personality' include item types that are often indistinguishable from each other, though they appear in tests with different labels, and which are also indistinguishable from items that appear on standardized tests aimed at measuring language proficiency.

4. The ultimate problem of test validity is a matter of what the curriculum tries to teach – not the curriculum itself.

5. The validity criterion for language tests can be shown to be identical to the validity criterion for language teaching curricula.

6. Discourse processing skill is central to all sorts of learning and to human cognition in general.

7. Investigations of human discourse processing skills are presently proceeding on two related fronts: first, there are simulation studies where the objective is to get a machine or an appropriately programmed device to produce and/or interpret discourse; second, there are investigative studies that actually collect data on inputs to and outputs from human beings during their production and comprehension of discourse.

8. Research into the nature of discourse processing suggests that it is guided by attention to hypotheses about meaning or plans for communicating meanings – not a very surprising fact in itself.

9. But, if the foregoing fact is not realized by curriculum designers, it is possible that they will neglect the meanings and requisite inferential processes associated with their encoding and decoding and will plan curricula that focus too narrowly on surface forms of language.

10. Reading curricula that train children to concentrate on decoding symbols into sounds, or words into sequences of sounds, and the like may result in children who can laboriously read sounds and words without understanding what the text they are reading is about.

11. Language teaching curricula that focus on the surface forms of language and neglect the pragmatic mapping of those surface forms onto extra-linguistic contexts and the inferential processes that the normal pragmatic mappings require must necessarily fall short of their primary goal – namely, enabling learners to understand, produce, read, and write sensible discourse in the language.

12. The Mount Gravatt reading program was developed out of research into the discourse of children. Among other things, the research demonstrated that the children were typically able to handle considerably more complex ideas than they are usually exposed to in books designed to teach them how to read. Further, the surface forms used in the books are scarcely similar to those actually used by children in normal discourse.

13. It can be effectively argued that the accurate characterization of real discourse processing has everything to do with the development not only of curricula for instilling discourse processing skill, but also for tests that purport to assess such skill.

14. Conformity to normal discourse processing is a natural criterion to require of language tests – related to it are the criteria of coherence and inference, meaningful sequence and pragmatic mapping.

15. In the final analysis tests must be tested in empirical contexts to determine whether they measure what they are supposed to measure.

DISCUSSION QUESTIONS

1. Consider ways in which language skills are crucial to the development of knowledge within a particular area of the curriculum at your school. Analyze the written materials presented to students, collected from them, spoken explanations and lectures presented to them, and responses orally elicited from them. Where do the students get practice in developing the language skills necessary to hear about, talk about, read about and write about mathematics? Geography? Chemistry? Social studies? Literature?

2. Consider a difficult learning task that was set for you in school. How did you conquer it, or why did it conquer you? Did language figure in the problem? Was it written? Spoken? Heard? Read?

3. If IQ tests are principally measures of language proficiency, how can their present uses be modified to make them more meaningful and more valid educational tools?

4. If achievement tests are as much a measure of language proficiency as of unique subject matter areas, what does this imply for the interpretation and use of achievement batteries? What remedies would you recommend, for instance, if a child got a low score in a certain subject matter, or in all of them (which is usually the case for low scorers)?

5. Do you believe that IQ can be modified? Do you think that language

proficiency can be modified? Do you think that what IQ tests measure can be modified? How could you test your opinions?

6. If there can be shown to be no test variance produced by so-called measures of IQ that is not also produced by so-called measures of language proficiency, what can be deduced about both types of test? Now, consider inserting other labels in relation to the same empirical result. For instance, consider personality tests in relation to language tests? Achievement tests in relation to language tests?

7. Which sort of construct, as an abstract object of psychometric theory, is more difficult to define – language proficiency or intelligence? Personality or language proficiency? Defend your answers with empirical data. What will you take as evidence for intelligence, language, or personality? Which sort of evidence is most readily accessible to the senses? Which is most accessible to test? To experimentation? To change? To therapeutic intervention?

8. Invent a testing technique for use in your classroom to assess student knowledge, your success as a teacher, the effectiveness of the curriculum you are using (or that your school is using), or pick one of the many evaluation procedures that you have already used. Evaluate the procedure. Does it conform to the normal requirements on pragmatic tests? Does it require normal language use? Does it relate the curriculum to normal contexts of discourse that the learner can relate to as a human being (with intelligence)? Does it require the manipulation of meanings and forms under normal temporal constraints? Could another task that meets these requirements be constructed to do what you want done?

9. Analyze samples of test data – learner outputs in response to tests used in your school. Do the learner protocols reflect normal communicative processes? Is the learner trying to say something, or write something meaningful for the benefit of someone? Or is the task devoid of the essential communication properties of normal language use? Are the tests of a discrete point, analytical, take-things-apart type? Or do they require the use of information in relation to normal contexts of human experience?

10. Write a letter to your school principal, head administrator, or the school board asking them to explain the purpose behind the standardized or other testing procedures used in your school or school district. Ask for the rationale behind the use of IQ measures, personality inventories, aptitude batteries, and any other tests that may be used for prognostic purposes. Ask him, or them, to explain how the achievement batteries that may be used reflect what the school is or should be teaching in the curriculum. If you are dissatisfied with the response, as you are likely to be, then why not get involved in trying to change the tests and the curriculum in your own classroom, school, district, state, or nation to make them more responsive to the main objective of education – namely, enabling people to enjoy fully the benefits of the negotiation of human discourse.

SUGGESTED READINGS

1. J. Britton, *Language and Learning*. New York: Penguin, 1973.
2. Bjarni Gunnarsson, 'A Look at the Content Similarities Between Intelligence, Achievement, Personality, and Language Tests,' in J. W. Oller, Jr. and Kyle Perkins (eds.) *Language in Education: Testing the Tests*. Rowley, Mass.: Newbury House, 1978.
3. Norman W. M. Hart, R. F. Walker, and B. Gray, *The Language of Children: A Key to Literacy*. Reading, Mass.: Addison-Wesley, 1977.

Appendix

The Factorial Structure
of Language Proficiency:
Divisible or Not?

This Appendix is included for several reasons. It discusses the recent findings of several research studies that support some of the implications and suggestions offered in the earlier chapters of the book, and it clarifies some of the avenues of empirical investigation that have only just begun to be explored. It is included as an appendix rather than as a part of the body of the text because of the statistical technicality of the arguments and data presented. There are many related questions that could be discussed, but the main focus of attention here will be whether or not language ability can be divided up into separately testable components.

Among the closely related issues that are considered peripheral to the main question is whether or not first language learning and second language learning are essentially similar or fundamentally different processes. The evidence that can be amassed from the data discussed here would seem to suggest that the similarities across the two learning tasks outweigh the differences – that inferences concerning second language acquisition (the attainment of second language proficiency) are usually also applicable to first language acquisition (attainment of first language proficiency), and vice versa. Further, the data do not seem to support the view that what has sometimes been called 'acquisition' (language learning in the natural contexts of communication) is distinct from 'learning' (language learning in formal classroom contexts, insofar as the latter can ever be said actually to take place). About the only distinction that seems supported by the data is that learning in the classroom is *usually* far less efficient than learning in more natural communication contexts.

A. Three empirically testable alternatives

Is language proficiency, however it may be attained, divisible into components that may be assessed separately, for instance, by different testing procedures? Another way of putting the question is to ask whether language processing tasks of diverse sorts tend to produce overlapping variances or whether they tend to produce unique variances (in the algebraic sense of 'variance', as defined in Chapter 3, above). Or putting it in yet another way, we might ask, what is the extent of correlation between a variety of language processing tasks, or tests that purport to measure different aspects of language proficiency? The usual assumption is that tests which have the same name, or which purport to measure the same thing, should be highly correlated, whereas tests that purport to measure different things need not be highly correlated, and in some cases should not be.

With respect to language proficiency, three possibilities can be suggested. It has been suggested that language skill might be divided up into components much the way discrete point testers have suggested. We will refer to this possibility as the *divisibility hypothesis*. For instance, it might be possible to differentiate knowledge of vocabulary, grammar, and phonology. Further, it might be possible to distinguish test variances associated with the traditionally recognized skills of listening, speaking, reading, and writing, or aspects of these skills such as productive versus receptive competencies *vis-à-vis* the hypothesized components (e.g., productive phonology in an oral mode, or receptive vocabulary in a written mode). But this is only the first of three possibilities.

A second alternative is that the construct of language proficiency may be more like a viscous substance than like a machine that can readily be broken down into component parts. We will refer to this second possibility as the *indivisibility*, or *unitary competence hypothesis*. It may be that language proficiency is relatively more unitary than the discrete point testers have contended. Perhaps what has been called 'vocabulary' knowledge (as measured by tests that have been called 'vocabulary' tests) cannot in fact be distinguished from 'grammar' knowledge (as measured by 'grammar' tests). This alternative is not apt to be found as appealing as the first mentioned one, but it cannot be excluded by pure logic.

A third possibility is to take a kind of middle ground. Actually, there are many points between any two well-defined positions, so logically, this third alternative could express itself at any point between the two extreme possibilities already defined. It will be called the *partial divisibility hypothesis*. It could be argued that in addition to a general component common to all of the variances of all language tests (at least those with some claim to validity), there ought to be portions of variance reliably (consistently) associated with tests in a listening mode that would not also be associated with tests in, say, a reading mode. That is, the 'reading' tests ought to share some variance among them that would not be common to 'listening' tests; 'vocabulary' tests should share some variance not common to 'grammar' tests; and so on for all of the contrasts between all of the posited components assumed to exist over and above the general component presumed to be common to all of the language tests.

Whether we take the first alternative or the third, we must find testing procedures that will generate variances that are unique to tests that are supposed to measure different things. Either the indivisibility hypothesis or the partial divisibility hypothesis allows for a large general factor (or component of variance) common to all language tests. The difference between these alternatives is that the indivisibility hypothesis allows *only* for a general component of test variance. Once such a component is accounted for, the indivisibility hypothesis predicts that no additional reliable variance will remain to be accounted for.

Hence, the three alternatives allow for three kinds of variance – error variance (random variance), reliable variance common to all of the tests, and reliable variance common only to some of the tests. They can be summarized as follows:

> The Divisibility Hypothesis (H_1): there will be reliable variance shared by tests that assess the same component, skill, aspect, or element of language proficiency, but essentially no common variance across tests of different components, skills, aspects, or elements;
> The Indivisibility Hypothesis (H_2): there will be reliable variance shared by all of the tests and essentially no unique variance shared by tests that purport to measure a particular skill, component, or aspect of language proficiency;
> The Partial Divisibility Hypothesis (H_3): there will be a large chunk of reliable variance shared by all of the tests, plus small amounts of reliable variance shared by only some of the tests.

In all three cases, some non-reliable variance must be allowed for. Thus, it is important to the question of test validity to determine whether the error variance is large or small in relation to the reliable variance attributable to a particular construct or skill. If, for instance, the reliable variance attributable to a general factor were as large as the estimated reliable variance of any single test in, say, a large battery of diverse tests, it would seem reasonable to assume that the only variance left over after the general factor was accounted for would have to be error variance, or unreliable variance.

B. The empirical method

Thus, we can see that the question posed at the outset – namely, whether or not language proficiency is divisible into components – can be construed as an empirical issue with at least three alternative outcomes. The crucial experimental method from the point of view of language proficiency measurement is to examine the correlations among a battery of tests administered to a large enough sample of language learners to provide the necessary statistical reliability. Actually, such an empirical study can be viewed as a method of evaluating the theoretical hypotheses and at the same time assessing the construct validity of the various tests that might be included in such a study. If the tests employed were not demonstrably reliable in their own right, and if they had no independent claims to validity, a failure to clarify the choice between the theoretical positions would hardly be conclusive. On the other hand, if the tests employed in the research can be shown on independent grounds to be valid measures of language ability, the results may indeed discriminate convincingly between the several theoretical positions, and at the same time, further substantiate the claims to validity of some or all of the tests employed. Similarly, if tests that purport to measure different things can be shown to measure essentially the same thing, the construct validity of those tests must be re-evaluated.

Some of the evidence concerning the above hypotheses was discussed briefly in Chapter 3 of this volume. However, the technicality of the procedures used in some of the data analyses requires that they be discussed in somewhat more detail than seemed appropriate in the main body of the text. Most of the studies that are pertinent to the central question rely on the statistical technique of factor analysis – or in fact on the family of techniques that go by that name. In particular, the most appropriate method for testing for a general factor is the one originally developed by Charles Spearman at about the turn of the century. It is the method often referred to as 'principal components analysis'.

Factor analysis is a family of statistical procedures that examine many correlations simultaneously to sort out patterns of relationships. All factoring methods are concerned with variances in the statistical and algebraic sense of the term. Especially, they are concerned with determining what patterns of common and unique variances exist for a given set of measures. The principal components method was originally conceptualized by Spearman in an attempt to determine whether or not there existed a general factor of what he called 'intelligence'. This factor was often spoken of in the literature and at professional meetings, and came to be referred to as 'g'. The empirical evidence for 'g' consisted in factoring a battery of tests to a principal components solution. When this was done repeatedly, it was determined that a general factor existed which 'explained' or 'accounted for' a substantial portion of the variance in just about any complex problem solving test. Whether it was a matter of finding a route through a maze or discussing a verbal analogy or matching abstract visual patterns, 'g' always seemed to emerge as the first and largest principal component of just about any such test. Thus, it came to be believed that there was indeed a general factor of intelligence, call it 'g'.

As Nunnally (1967) points out, the notion of a general factor of intelligence though popular for a season lost its luster after a few years and in the 1960s and early 1970s was rarely referred to in the literature. Jensen (1969) mentioned it simply to note that it remains 'like a Rock of Gibraltar', undaunted by the several theoretical attacks launched against it. Nunnally, however, points out a method of extending and simplifying the technique of principal components analysis to test for a single general factor. He shows that if there were only one factor, it is a mathematical necessity that the correlation between any two tests in the set used in the definition of the general factor must equal the product of the separate correlations of each of the tests with the general factor. It sounds complex, but at base it is quite simple.

The first principal component extracted in the factor analysis is actually a linear combination of the variables (or tests) entered into the computations in the first place. The correlation of each contributing variable with that factor is an index of the contribution which that variable makes to the definition of the factor. The same correlation can also be used as an estimate of the validity of the contributing variable as a measure of the posited factor supposed to underlie that principal component. Suppose we call that factor an expectancy grammar (or any other name that signifies the internalized knowledge of language). To the extent that the posited factor actually exists, the 'loadings' (another name for the correlations of the individual contributors with that factor) of the respective variables input to the analysis can be read directly as validity coefficients. Further, if we assume that the general factor, that is the expectancy grammar, exhausts the available meaningful variance, it follows as a mathematical necessity that the product of the loadings of any pair of variables on that factor must equal the correlation between them. Without going into any of the details, this is similar to saying that the general factor (if it exists, and if the indivisibility hypothesis stated above is correct) is either the only factor that exists, or it is the only one that the tests are capable of measuring.

Fortunately, even if the indivisibility hypothesis should turn out to be incorrect, the factoring methods applicable subsequent to a principal components analysis can conveniently be used to test hypothesis three. As we will see shortly, there is no hope whatsoever for the first hypothesis (the divisibility hypothesis). Other statistical techniques can also be used, but the most obvious approach is the one used here. Multiple regression techniques that treat individual language tests as repeated measures of the posited general component of expectancy grammar can be used to sharpen up the picture (for this approach see Kerlinger and Pedhazur, 1973), but the conceptualization of the problem with regression techniques is considerably more complex and is not as easily accessible in computer programs. Of course, without computing facilities neither approach would be very feasible. Both techniques are computationally so complex that they could scarcely be done at all by hand.

C. Data from second language studies

The first application of Nunnally's proposed modification of Spearman's test for a general factor was to several versions of the UCLA *English as a Second Language Placement Examination*. That test consisted of at least five subtests in each of its administrations. The data were collected between 1969 and 1972, and were analyzed in 1974 with the Nunnally method. The results were reported in a

European psycholinguistics journal, *Die Neuren Sprachen*, and were also presented at a meeting of the Pacific Northwest Conference on the Teaching of Foreign Languages sponsored by the American Council of Teachers of Foreign Languages in April of 1976. (See Oller, 1976a.)

In brief, the findings showed that once the general factor predicted by the indivisibility (or unitary competence) hypothesis was extracted, essentially no meaningful variance was left in any of the tests on the several batteries of UCLA *ESLPE*'s examined. The first principal component extracted accounted for about .70 of the total variance produced by all of the tests (in each of five separate batteries of tests), and whatever variance remained could not be attributed to anything other than error of measurement. In other words, both the divisibility and partial divisibility hypotheses (H_1 and H_3, above) were clearly ruled out. Since all five of the test batteries investigated were administered to rather sizable samples of incoming foreign students the results were judged to be fairly conclusive. Whatever the separate grammar, reading, phonology, composition, dictation, and cloze tests were measuring, they were apparently all measuring it. Some of them appeared to be better measures of the global language proficiency factor, but all appeared to be measures of that factor and not much else.

The second application of the Nunnally technique to second language data came in 1976. Data from the Test of English as a Foreign Language were available from a study reported by Irvine, Atai, and Oller (1974). The battery of tests investigated included the five subtests of the *TOEFL* – Listening Comprehension, English Structure, Vocabulary, Reading Comprehension, and Writing Ability – along with a cloze test and a dictation. The subject sample consisted of 159 Iranian adults in Tehran. Again the results supported H_2, the indivisibility hypothesis. A single global factor emerged and practically no variance whatsoever remained to be accounted for once that factor was extracted.

A third application of Nunnally's suggested technique was to data collected as part of a doctoral dissertation study by Frances Hinofotis at the Center for English as a Second Language at Carbondale, Illinois in 1975–6. Hinofotis (1976) investigated the pattern of relationships among the various parts of the placement test used at CESL (SIU in Carbondale), the *TOEFL*, the five subscales on the Foreign Service Institute Oral Interview, plus a cloze test (in a standard written format). Her study, together with the Irvine, *et al* data, provided the basis for a report presented at the Linguistic Society winter meeting in Philadelphia (Oller and Hinofotis, 1976). The results with the CESL data were somewhat less clearcut than with the Iranian subjects. A major difference in the test batteries examined was that the Hinofotis data included the measures from the FSI Oral Interview procedure.

While a general factor emerged from the Hinofotis data, it was not possible to rule out the alternative that a separate factor, possibly associated with speaking skill, also existed. The data were examined from several different angles, and in each case, the general factor accounted for no less than .65 of the total available variance.[1] However, a rotated varimax solution seemed to justify the suggestion that the five subscales of the FSI Oral Interview were measuring something other than what was measured by the nine other tests studied. The question that arose at this point was whether the apparently separate oral factor could reliably be associated with a 'speaking skill' rather than the mere subjective judgement of the interviewers who provided the five ratings on each subject. Clearly, if a speaking skill factor could be isolated or at least partially separated from the general factor, this result would force a rejection of the strong version of the indivisibility hypothesis in favor of the partial divisibility option. There was also some hint in the Hinofotis data that perhaps a 'graphic skills' factor could be distinguished from the general factor.

Although the Hinofotis data raised the possibility of separate skills (e.g., listening, speaking, reading, and writing, or possibly oral skills as distinct from graphic skills) it seemed to rule out conclusively the possibility of separable components (e.g., phonology versus

---

[1] We should take note of the fact that the data reported by Oller (1976a) and by Oller and Hinofotis (1976) used slightly different statistical procedures. Whereas the first study used a non-iterative procedure with communality estimates of unity in the diagonals for the principal components solution, the latter studies reported by Oller and Hinofotis, used an iterative procedure which successively refined the communality estimates through a procedure of repeated calculations. As a result, all of the available variance in the correlation matrix for the *TOEFL*, cloze and dictation from the Iranian subjects was explained by a single general factor. This seemingly anomalous finding is due to the iterative procedure and to the fact that once the error variance was discarded, nothing remained that was not attributable to the general factor. Whereas this procedure (factoring with iterations) is a common one, Nunnally argues that the method of using unities in the diagonal is mathematically preferable. For this reason, and because of the desire to avoid the seeming anomaly of a single factor explaining all of the variance in a battery of tests (which disturbed at least one psychometrist consulted) subsequent analyses reported here revert to the non-iterative method of placing unities in the diagonal of the initial correlation matrix.

vocabulary versus grammar and the like). There was no evidence whatsoever to support the claim that the so-called 'vocabulary' measures were producing any reliable variance that was not also attributable to the so-called 'grammar' or 'structure' tests.

In fact, there was no basis for claiming that the five separate scales of the FSI Oral Interview were measures of different things at all. Since the Hinofotis study, this latter result has been confirmed independently by Mullen (in press a, in press b) and Callaway (in press). When people try to judge speech for vocabulary, or for grammar, or for fluency, or even for accent, they apparently are so influenced by the overall communicative effect that all of the judgements turn out to be quite indistinguishable. This is a serious validity problem for the FSI Oral Interview – it could be resolved by condensing all of the scales to one single scale. It is important to realize that the failure of the FSI technique to distinguish components of oral skill is doubly significant because at least one of the contributing judges must be a trained linguist. If trained linguists cannot make such distinctions, who can?

D. The Carbondale Project, 1976–7

It remained to determine whether the variance produced by the oral interview procedure used in the Hinofotis study was merely a subjective consistency possibly unrelated to speaking skill, or whether it was a genuine source of variance in a separable component of language skill that could be called 'speaking ability'. A suitable empirical approach would be to devise a battery of speaking tests – or at least tasks that require speaking – along with a battery of tests aimed at the other traditionally recognized skills of listening, reading, and writing. At the same time, it would be desirable to include only tasks known to produce reliable variance and which had independent claims to validity as language tests.

The opportunity for the latter sort of study came in 1976–7 during the author's visiting appointment in the Department of Linguistics at Southern Illinois University on a grant from the Center for English as a Second Language. Several other reports discussing aspects of the research undertaken are to be published in two separate volumes, *Language in Education: Testing the Tests* and *Research in Language Testing* (Oller and Perkins, 1978, and in press). Therefore, only the relevant non-redundant data will be discussed here.

The project began by assembling a team of researchers, mostly volunteers, with the able help of Richard Daesch, Administrative Director CESL at SIU, and Charles Parish, Academic Director of CESL. Other major contributors included Professor Kyle Perkins, who was a driving force behind the attitudinal research incorporated, and George Scholz, who headed a group of instructors and staff responsible for much of the oral testing that was done. Reports by many other contributors to the work are included in the volumes mentioned above. The second task was to assemble a battery of tests aimed at four skills and, at Charles Parish's urging, important points of grammatical knowledge.

Early on there was considerable discussion about whether or not the test should be aimed at discrete points of structure exclusively or whether they should have a broader focus. In the end, the desirability of including discourse processing tasks was agreed to by all, and the desire to assess specific points of grammatical knowledge was bent to the mold of a modified cloze testing procedure with selected points of deletion. Professor Parish prepared the latter test.

The enormity of the task of preparing tests of listening, speaking, reading, and writing (not to mention the grammar test battery) was enough to discourage many potential participants and some of them fell by the wayside. However, the objective of producing a battery of tests that would answer certain crucial questions about the factorial structure of language proficiency and which would also eventuate in the possibility of constructing a better placement instrument for the CESL program provided sufficient incentive to keep a surprisingly large number of teaching assistants, research assistants, and faculty doggedly plodding on.

In all, 182 students were tested. A total of 60 separate discourse processing tasks were used. Not every student was tested on all 60 tests. This turned out to be impossible due to the fact that all of the tests had to be administered to small groups meeting in separate classes. Because of absences, occasional equipment failures, inevitable scheduling difficulties, etc., it was not possible to get test data on every subject for every task. However, the smallest group of subjects that completed any sub-battery of tests (i.e., the sub-batteries aimed at listening, at speaking, and so forth), was never less than 36 and in some cases was as high as 137. Students tested were only those enrolled in CESL classes – they ranged in placement from the lowest level (1) to the highest level (5). There was a considerable tendency for the drop-outs to be students who were at the lower end of the distribution of scores. Hence, the students who completed most or all of the tests tended to be at the high end of the distribution. According to Rand (1976) this should bias things against the indivisibility hypothesis by reducing the total spread of scores.

Since the tests (or samples of them) are reproduced in *Research in Language Testing*, only brief descriptions will be given here. Further, only the factor analyses using list-wise deletion of missing cases will be reported. Although separate computations based on the pair-wise option were also done corresponding to each of the analyses reported, the patterning of the data was nearly identical in every case for the principal component (or 'g' factor) solution. Moreover, the list-wise deletion of missing cases has the advantage of selecting cases for analysis which are quite comparable across all of the tests included in that particular analysis. The pair-wise deletion of missing data on the other hand produces correlations across pairs of tests that may be based on quite different sub-groups drawn from the total population (Nie, Hull, Jenkins, Steinbrenner and Bent, 1975). Hence, the list-wise procedure affords a more straightforward interpretation of the factorial composition of the variance produced by the several tests – it is less apt to be confounded by differences that might pertain merely to contrasts across sub-groups accidentally selected by the sampling technique.

First we will look at the factorial structure of the various sub-batteries taken as a whole – the entire battery of tests – then we will examine the subscores pertaining to the separate tests within each sub-battery. It should be kept in mind that the tests discussed in this first analysis in many cases are composite scores derived from several separate sub-tests.

i. Overall pattern.

Five types of tests can be distinguished. First, there were five sets of tests aimed at listening tasks. They included the subtest called Listening Comprehension on the Comprehensive English Language Test (henceforth referred to as CELT-LC); an open-ended cloze test in a listening format (Listening Cloze); a multiple choice cloze test in a listening format (Listening MC Cloze); a multiple choice listening comprehension test based on questions over three different texts that the examinees heard (MC Listening Comprehension); and three dictations (Dictation).

Second, there were four speaking tasks. The first was an oral interview which resulted in at least five relatively independent scores for accent (OI Accent), grammar (OI Grammar), vocabulary (OI

Vocabulary), fluency (OI Fluency), and comprehension (OI Comprehension), respectively. The other three consisted of first a composite repetition score over three separate texts (Repetition); three fill-in-the-blank oral cloze tests (where the responses were spoken into a microphone, Oral Cloze); and a reading aloud task over three separate texts (Reading Aloud).

Third, there were three types of reading tasks. The first was the Reading subtest from CELT (CELT-R). The second type of reading task involved identifying a synonym or paraphrase for a word, phrase, or clause in a text (actually there were three tests of this type, each over a different text (MC Reading Match). The third reading task was actually a composite of eight open-ended cloze tests in a written format (Standard Cloze).

Fourth, three writing test scores were included. The first type of writing task was actually an essay scored in two ways – first by a subjective rating on a five point scale (Essay Rating), and second by an objective scoring technique (number of error-free words minus number of errors, all divided by the number of words required for a fully intelligible rewrite by a native speaker, Essay Score). The second type of so-called 'writing' test was actually the result of an attempt to analyze writing tasks into three subtasks – namely, selecting the appropriate word, phrase, or clause to continue a test at any given point; editing texts for errors in choice of words, phrases, or clauses; and ordering words, phrases, and clauses appropriately at certain decision points in given texts (MC Writing). The third type consisted of a teacher's rating on a five point scale of the accuracy and completeness of written recalls of three separate texts that were displayed in a printed format for exactly one minute each (Recall Rating).

The fifth, and last type of test included in the overall analysis, included two tasks aimed at grammatical knowledge. The first of these was the Structure subtest on the CELT (CELT-S), and the second was a modified cloze test (126 items) aimed at specific points of grammatical usage (Parish's Grammar test, referred to above).

Following the program of test analysis discussed above, two factor solutions are presented – the result of a principal components analysis is given in Table 1, and of a varimax rotation method in Table 2. In the first column of Table 1, the loadings of each test on the hypothesized 'g' factor are given. In column two, the squares of those loadings can be read to determine the amount of variance shared by the 'g' factor and the test in question. The sum of the squared loadings or Eigen value is given at the bottom of column two, and can be divided by the total number of tests in the analysis to get the total amount of explained variance equal to .52.

TABLE 1
Principal Components Analysis over Twenty-two
Scores on Language Processing Tasks Requiring
Listening, Speaking, Reading, and Writing as well
as Specific Grammatical Decisions (N = 27).

SCORES	LOADINGS ON g	SQUARED LOADINGS
Listening		
CELT-LC	.64	.41
Listening Cloze	.78	.61
Listening MC Cloze	.40	.16
MC Listening Comprehension	.62	.38
Dictation	.83	.69
Speaking		
OI Accent	.42	.18
OI Grammar	.88	.77
OI Vocabulary	.80	.64
OI Fluency	.62	.38
OI Comprehension	.88	.77
Repetition	.59	.35
Oral Cloze	.76	.56
Reading Aloud	.56	.31
Reading		
CELT-R	.64	.41
MC Reading Match	.83	.69
Standard Cloze	.83	.69
Writing		
Essay Rating	.71	.50
Essay Score	.77	.59
MC Writing	.85	.72
Recall Rating	.77	.59
Grammar		
CELT-S	.55	.30
Grammar (Parish test)	.88	.77
	Eigen value = 11.49	

The loadings on g given in Table 1 reveal that there are good tests of g in each of the batteries of tests or scores. For instance, both the Listening Cloze and the Dictation tasks produce substantial loadings on g. Similarly, the OI Grammar, OI Vocabulary, OI Comprehension, and Oral Cloze scores produce substantial loadings on the same factor. Two of the reading tasks load heavily on the g factor – both the MC Reading Match task, and the Standard Cloze. Among the writing tasks, the best measure of g appears to be the MC Writing test, but all four tasks produce substantial loadings – noteworthy among them are the two subjective scores based on Essay Rating and Recall Rating. Finally, the Parish Grammar test loads heavily on g.

It is worth noting that the 27 subjects included in the analysis reported in Table 1 are a relatively small sub-sample of the total number of subjects tested. In particular, this sub-sample is relatively higher in the distribution than would be likely to be chosen on a random basis – hence, the variability in the sample should be depressed somewhat, and the g factor should be minimized by such a selection. This kind of selection, according to some writers (especially Rand, 1976), should reduce the importance of g, yet it does not. Furthermore, as we noted above, the results of a pair-wise deletion of missing cases (thus basing computations of requisite correlations on different and considerably larger sub-samples subjects) was essentially similar. Hence, the pattern observed in Table 1 appears to be quite characteristic of the population as a whole. Nonetheless, for the sake of completeness a varimax solution over the same twenty-two tests is presented in Table 2.

The patterning of correlations (factor loadings, in this case) in Table 2 is somewhat different than in Table 1. However, the total amount of explained variance is not a great deal higher (at least not for the interpreted loadings). Further, the patterning of loadings is not particularly easy to explain on the basis of any existing theory of discrete point notions about different components or skills. For instance, although both Reading Aloud and OI Fluency are supposed to involve an element of speed, it does not emerge as a separate factor – that is, the two types of scores load on different factors, namely, 1 and 3. Similarly, the OI Comprehension scale does not tend to load on the same factor(s) as the various Listening tests (especially factor 3), rather it tends to load on factor 1 with a considerable variety of other tasks.

One might try to make a case for interpreting factors 4 and 5 as

TABLE 2
Varimax Rotated Solution for Twenty-two Language Scores (derived from the principal components solution partially displayed in Table 1, only loadings above .47 are interpreted).

SCORES \ FACTORS	1	2	3	4	5	h^2
Listening						
CELT-LC	.49				.48	.47
Listening Cloze				.57		.32
Listening MC Cloze				.88		.77
MC Listening Comp				.80		.64
Dictation	.55					.30
Speaking						
OI Accent				.88		.77
OI Grammar	.69					.48
OI Vocabulary	.78					.61
OI Fluency	.77					.59
OI Comprehension	.80					.64
Repetition				.68		.46
Oral Cloze				.47		.22
Reading Aloud			.85			.72
Reading						
CELT-R		.57	.48			.55
MC Reading Match	.71	.52				.77
Standard Cloze		.67				.45
Writing						
Essay Rating			.56			.31
Essay Score	.56			.49		.55
MC Writing	.51	.61				.76
Recall Rating			.74			.55
Grammar						
CELT-S		.87				.76
Grammar (Parish Test)	.55	.64				.89
				Eigen value	= 13.22	

being primarily associated with speaking and listening whereas 2 and 3 seem to be predominantly reading and writing factors – however, there are exceptions. Why for example does the essay score load with the speaking and listening tests on factor 4? Why does the Reading Aloud test load so heavily on factor 3 and not at all on 1, 2, 4, or 5?

One possible explanation for the patterning observed in Table 2 is that it may be largely due to random variances attributable to error in the measurement technique. Interestingly, the varimax solution presented here is not strikingly similar to the one that emerged in the Hinofotis study (see Oller and Hinofotis, 1976). If the patterning is not due to random variation, it should tend to reappear in repeated studies. However, for the varimax rotation (though not for the principal components solution) the pair-wise deletion procedure tended to produce a somewhat different pattern of factors than the list-wise procedure. This too lends support to the possibility that the varimax patterning may be a result of unreliable variance rather than valid differences across tasks.

A final bit of evidence favoring the unitary competence hypothesis is the fact that the loadings on g (see Table 1) are higher than the loadings on any other factor (see Table 2) for 15 of the 22 scores input to the original analysis. Thus, it would appear that g is the better theoretical explanation of the available non-random variance for well over half of the tasks or scales studied. It is also a surprisingly good basis for explaining substantial amounts of variance in all of the scores except possibly the Listening MC Cloze which only loaded at .40, and the OI Accent scale which loaded at .42 on the g factor.

ii. Listening.

Among the listening tasks investigated were the CELT-LC; three open-ended cloze tests in a listening format (Listening Cloze A, Listening Cloze B, and Listening Cloze C); three multiple choice cloze tests in a listening format (Listening MC Cloze A, Listening MC Cloze B, Listening MC Cloze C); three listening comprehension passages with multiple choice questions following each (MC Listening Comprehension A, B, and C); and three dictations (Dictation A, B, and C). There were several ulterior motives that guided the selection of precisely these tasks. For one, it was assumed that listening tasks that required the use of full-fledged discourse were preferable to tasks requiring the processing of isolated sentences and the like (see the argument in Part Two of the text above in the main body of the book). A second guiding principle was the need to develop tests that could be scored easily with large numbers of subjects. Yet another motivation, and the one that is of prime importance to this Appendix, was to include tasks that were known to have some reliability and validity along with the more experimental tests (the latter being the cloze tests in listening format).

The results of a principal components solution extracting the first principal factor are given in Table 3. The problem here, as before, is to select the solution that best explains the patterning of the data – i.e., that maximizes the explained variance in the tests investigated. It is not sufficient merely to find factors. One must also account for them on the basis of some reasonable explanation. An alternative factor solution is given in Table 4. There, four factors are extracted, but no particularly satisfying pattern emerges. Why, for instance,

TABLE 3
Principal Components Analysis over Sixteen
Listening Scores (N = 36).

SCORES	LOADINGS ON g	SQUARED LOADINGS
CELT-LC	.50	.25
List Cloze A (Exact)*	.70	.49
List Cloze B (Exact)	.80	.64
List Cloze C (Exact)	.66	.44
List MC Cloze A	.76	.58
List MC Cloze B	.52	.27
List MC Cloze C	.71	.50
List Comprehension A	.63	.40
List Comprehension B	.59	.35
List Comprehension C	.68	.46
Dictation A	.69	.47
Dictation B	.73	.53
Dictation C	.71	.50
List Cloze A (Appropriate)**	.44	.19
List Cloze B (Appropriate)	.58	.34
List Cloze C (Appropriate)	.19	.04
		Eigen value = 6.47

* The exact word scoring method was used to obtain the values for each protocol (12 items in each subsection).
** The so-called 'appropriate' scores used here were actually obtained by counting *only* the words that had not already been included in the exact score. This, of course, is not the usual method, but was easier to apply in this case due to the computer program used at the SIU Testing Center where the data was initially processed. The exact word method and the more usual appropriate word method are explained in greater detail in Chapter 12 above.

should the CELT-LC load on factor 2 while the multiple choice Listening Comprehension tests A, B, and C all load on factor 1? Why is it that Listening Cloze A scatters over three factors (2, 3, and 4) while the other two load consistently on factor 2? It would appear that the patterning in Table 3 is due to reliable variance attributable to the g factor while the patterning in Table 4 results from the partitioning of unreliable variances. Interestingly, the multiple choice tests all tend to load on factor 1 in Table 4, except for the CELT-LC. The Dictations load primarily on factor 2 in Table 4, but hardly as strongly as the composite Dictation score loaded on g in Table 1 above.[2]

TABLE 4
Varimax Rotated Solution for Sixteen Listening
Scores (N = 36).

SCORES / FACTORS	1	2	3	4	h^2
CELT-LC		.67			.45
List Cloze A (Exact)		.53	.49	.46	.73
List Cloze B (Exact)			.78		.61
List Cloze C (Exact)			.84		.71
List MC Cloze A	.80				.64
List MC Cloze B	.84				.71
List MC Cloze C	.76				.58
List Comprehension A	.69				.48
List Comprehension B	.71				.50
List Comprehension C	.72				.52
Dictation A		.67			.45
Dictation B		.84			.71
Dictation C		.79			.62
List Cloze A (Appropriate)				.78	.61
List Cloze B (Appropriate)			.80		.64
List Cloze C (Appropriate)				−.69	.48
				Eigen value = 9.44	

[2] It may be worth noting here that the listening tasks were the very last tasks to be administered in the series. Because of the extensive testing done during the project, the order may be significant due to a fatigue factor. The latter tests in the series seemed to be somewhat less reliable on the whole and also produced the weakest correlations. The order for the remaining test types reported below was Writing, Grammar, Reading, with the Speaking tests interspersed among all the rest.

iii. Speaking.

The speaking tasks were the result of the collaboration of a group of graduate students and staff at CESL under the capable leadership of George Scholz. Lela Vandenburg was also very much involved in the initial stages of the data collection and her responsibilities were later largely taken over by Deborah Hendricks. Together, they and two other students have compiled two extensive reports related to the tests aimed at speaking skills (see Scholz, Hendricks, *et al*, in press, and Hendricks, et al, in press). The summary offered here incorporates their major findings and relates them to aspects of the total project outside of the purview of their reports.

The speaking tasks used by Scholz *et al* included an interview procedure modeled after the FSI technique. Five rating scales were used (OI Accent, OI Grammar, OI Vocabulary, OI Fluency, and OI Comprehension – see Chapter 11 above for elaboration on each of these). Over and above the scales an FSI Oral Proficiency Level was assessed for each interview. In addition to the oral interview procedure, three other types of task were used – repetition, oral cloze, and reading aloud. It was reasoned that since all three of the latter tasks involved speaking in the target language they would be suitable procedures against which to compare the scores on the oral interview scales. Each of the latter tasks employed three texts – one judged to be easy in relation to the supposed level of skill of CESL students, another judged to be moderately difficult, and finally, one of considerable difficulty. In all, then, nine texts were required – three for the repetition tasks (Repetition A, B, and C); three for oral cloze tasks (Oral Cloze A, B, and C); and three for the reading aloud texts. The latter three were used to generate three scores each – the amount of time (in seconds) required to read the text (Reading Time A, B, and C); the number of fully recognizable words (Reading Accuracy Exact A, B, C); and the number of additional words that were appropriate to the sense of the text though they did not actually appear in it (Reading Accuracy Appropriate A, B, C).

Repetition tasks were scored in two ways. The first set of scores were based on the number of words reproduced in recognizable form that actually appeared in the original text (Repetition Exact A, B, C). The second set of scores consisted of the number of additional words produced that were actually appropriate to the sense of the original text though they did not appear in it (Repetition Appropriate A, B, C). Similarly, the oral cloze tasks were scored both for exact word responses (Oral Cloze Exact A, B, C), and for words other than the exact word that fit the context (Oral Cloze Appropriate A, B, C).[3]

In all there were twenty-seven scores computed over the speaking tasks. A principal components analysis over those scores is given in Table 5 followed by a varimax rotation to an orthogonal solution revealing seven factors with an Eigen value greater than one in Table 6.

There are several facts that should be considered in interpreting the factor analyses in Tables 5 and 6. Foremost among them are the methods used for obtaining the various scores.

Consider Table 5 first. Repetition exact scores over texts A and B load substantially on the g factor – however, the 'appropriate' scores are scarcely correlated with that factor at all. This is because of the nature of the task. The more an examinee tended to answer with an exact word repetition of the original, the less he was apt to come up with some other appropriate rendition – hence, the low correlation between appropriate scores for the repetition tasks, and also for the reading aloud tasks over all three texts. In fact, in the case of the appropriate scores for the reading aloud texts, the correlation with g tended to be negative. This is not surprising if the method of obtaining those scores is kept in mind. Similarly, the correlations (loadings) of the time scores for reading aloud tasks tended to be substantial and negative for all three of the texts in question. This is not surprising since we should expect lower proficiencies to result in longer reading rates. The appropriate scores over oral cloze tests, however, were on the whole slightly better measures of g than the exact scores. This is also a function of the way the appropriate scores were computed in this case (see footnote 3 below) by adding the exact word score and any additional acceptable words to obtain the appropriate score.

Thus, the best measures of g appear to be ratings based on the oral interview procedure, exact scores of the A and B repetition texts, appropriate cloze scores, especially A and C, reading aloud times, and for some reason the accuracy score (exact) on texts B and C. Due partly to the unreliability of some of the measures, and no doubt also to the fact that some of the scores computed are not actually measures of g at all, the total amount of explained variance in all of the scores is

---

[3] Here, the appropriate score is the sum of exact plus additional appropriate words. In fact, this 'appropriate' scoring method is the only one that includes the exact word score. In subsequent tests (see Tables 7–12 below), cloze scores that are called 'appropriate' word scores are actually a count of the words over and above (not including) the exact words restored in the text in question.

TABLE 5
Principal Components Analysis over Twenty-seven
Speaking Scores (N = 64).

SCORES	LOADINGS ON g	SQUARED LOADINGS
OI Accent	.59	.35
OI Grammar	.83	.69
OI Vocabulary	.79	.63
OI Fluency	.80	.64
OI Comprehension	.87	.76
FSI Oral Proficiency Level	.87	.76
Repetition Exact A	.71	.50
Repetition Appropriate A	.07	.00
Repetition Exact B	.87	.76
Repetition Appropriate B	.29	.08
Repetition Exact C	.39	.15
Repetition Appropriate C	−.06	.00
Oral Cloze Exact A	.54	.29
Oral Cloze Appropriate A	.66	.44
Oral Cloze Exact B	.59	.35
Oral Cloze Appropriate B	.43	.18
Oral Cloze Exact C	.38	.14
Oral Cloze Appropriate C	.67	.45
Reading Aloud Time A	−.65	.42
Reading Aloud Exact A	.39	.15
Reading Aloud Appropriate A	−.10	.01
Reading Aloud Time B	−.65	.42
Reading Aloud Exact B	.70	.49
Reading Aloud Appropriate B	−.36	.13
Reading Aloud Time C	−.54	.29
Reading Aloud Exact C	.52	.27
Reading Aloud Appropriate C	−.17	.03

Eigen value = 9.39

relatively small (.34). However, if we eliminate the scores that are not expected to correlate with g (in particular, the appropriate word scores for the repetition and reading aloud tasks), the total amount of variance explained by the g factor jumps to .44. All four types of tasks appear to be measuring g within the limits of reliability of the various scores derived from them.

TABLE 6
Varimax Rotated Solution over Twenty-seven
Speaking Scores (N = 64).

SCORES \ FACTORS	1	2	3	4	5	6	7	h²
OI Accent	.48							.23
OI Grammar	.89							.79
OI Vocabulary	.90							.81
OI Fluency	.83							.69
OI Comp	.87							.76
FSI Oral Level	.92							.85
Rep Exact A		.45			.46			.41
Rep Approp A						.73		.53
Rep Exact B	.48	.50						.48
Rep Approp B		.49				.46		.45
Rep Exact C							.69	.48
Rep Approp C						.58		.34
OC Exact A					.49			.24
OC Approp A		.75						.56
OC Exact B		.52			.45			.47
OC Approp B		.86						.74
OC Exact C					.72			.52
OC Approp C		.56						.33
RA Time A			−.82					.67
RA Exact A				.61	.44	.45		.77
RA Approp A				.87				.76
RA Time B			−.84					.71
RA Exact B					.63			.40
RA Approp B				.72				.52
RA Time C			−.82					.67
RA Exact C			.45		.56			.51
RA Approp C				.73				.53
							Eigen value = 15.22	

In Table 6, the varimax rotated factors reveal a possible fluency factor (see factor 3) associated strongly with all three of the reading aloud time scores, but oddly, not associated with the fluency scale on the oral interview. The exact scores for oral cloze, reading aloud, and one of the repetition tasks all load on factor 5. Factor 7 appears to be a throw out created by some sort of unreliable variance in the exact score over repetition text C. Perhaps this is due to the fact that the task turned out to be too difficult for most of the examinees. Similar unreliabilities emerge with reference to several of the subscores.

Considering the fact that the g factor displayed in Table 5 accounts for substantial variance in all of the sub-tasks investigated, and taking into account that the more reliable tests seem to load very substantially on that factor, the results of the speaking subtests on the whole seem to support the indivisible competence hypothesis rather than the partial divisibility hypothesis.

iv. Reading.

The first reading score was the Reading subtest on the CELT (CELT-R). The second type of reading test was a matching task in a multiple choice format. It involved selecting the nearest match in meaning for an underlined word, phrase, or clause from a field of alternatives at various decision points in a text. There were three texts (MC Reading Match A, B, C). Finally, there were eight cloze tests in an every fifth word format scored by the exact and appropriate word methods. The appropriate word score here, however (see footnote 3 above), did not include the exact word score as a subpart – rather it was simply the count of appropriate responses over and above the exact word responses.

There was an ulterior motive for including so many different cloze tests. We wanted to find out if agreeing or disagreeing with controversial subject matter would affect performance. Therefore, pro and con texts on the legalization of marijuana (Marijuana Pro, Marijuana Con), the abolition of capital punishment (Cap Pun Pro, Con), and the morality of abortion (Abortion Pro, Con) were included along with two neutral texts on non-controversial subjects (Cloze A and B). Results on the agreement versus disagreement question are reported by Doerr (in press). In a nutshell, it was determined that the effect of one's own belief though possibly significant is apparently not very strong. In fact, it would appear from the data to be quite negligible. Furthermore, the correlation between scores over texts with which subjects agreed and with which they disagreed was very strong, .91, and there was no significant contrast in scores. Similarly, the correlation across pro and con texts (independent of the subjects' agreement or disagreement) was .90. The pro texts were significantly easier, however. These results at least mollify if they do not in fact controvert the findings of Manis and Dawes (1961) concerning the sensitivity of cloze scores to differences in beliefs. Further research is needed with a more sensitive experimental design, and with more proficient examinees.

As before, the data were factor analyzed to a principal components solution and then rotated to a varimax solution. Results of these procedures are given in Tables 7 and 8. Whereas the loadings on g account for 47% of the total available variance, the interpreted loadings on the four factor rotated solution only account for an additional 6% (for a total of 53%). Again, the pattern of loadings in the rotated solution seems to indicate a considerable amount of unreliable variability in the data. As noted above, this is partly attributable to the data collection procedures, and partly to the shortness of some of the subtests for which scores are reported. In the cloze scores reported here (Table 7, especially) and above in Table 5,

TABLE 7
Principal Components Solution over Twenty Reading Scores (N = 51).

SCORES	LOADINGS ON g	SQUARED LOADINGS
CELT-Reading Subtest	.57	.32
MC Reading Match A	.74	.55
MC Reading Match B	.75	.56
MC Reading Match C	.77	.59
Cloze Exact A	.66	.44
Cloze Exact B	.69	.48
Marijuana Pro Exact	.68	.46
Marijuana Con Exact	.79	.62
Cap Pun Pro Exact	.77	.59
Cap Pun Con Exact	.77	.59
Abortion Pro Exact	.85	.72
Abortion Con Exact	.74	.55
Cloze A (Approp)	.54	.29
Cloze B (Approp)	.63	.40
Marijuana Pro (Approp)	.71	.50
Marijuana Con (Approp)	.55	.30
Cap Pun Pro (Approp)	.74	.55
Cap Pun Con (Approp)	.62	.38
Abortion Pro (Approp)	.63	.40
Abortion Con (Approp)	.64	.41
		Eigen value = 9.40

TABLE 8
Varimax Rotated Solution over Twenty Reading
Scores (N = 61).

SCORES \ FACTORS	1	2	3	4	h^2
CELT-R	.65				.42
MC RM A	.79				.62
MC RM B	.65				.42
MC RM C	.55				.30
Cloze Exact A	.77				.59
Cloze Exact B	.68				.46
MP Exact			.81		.66
MC Exact	.49	.41	.50		.66
CP Exact	.63		.47		.62
CC Exact		.54			.29
AP Exact	.52	.67			.72
AC Exact	.47		.57		.55
Cloze A (Approp)			.48	.58	.57
Cloze B (Approp)		.70			.49
MP (Approp)		.49	.49		.48
MC (Approp)			.72		.52
CP (Approp)		.81			.66
CC (Approp)	.43				.18
AP (Approp)		.73			.53
AC (Approp)				.85	.72
				Eigen value = 10.46	

the appropriate scores appear to be contributing about as strongly to g as the exact scores. Further, in neither of the rotated solutions (see Tables 6 and 8) do the appropriate and exact scores over the cloze texts clearly differentiate themselves – that is, they do not load exclusively on separate orthogonal factors.

Therefore, in view of all of the foregoing, it seems reasonable to conclude that the indivisibility hypothesis is again to be preferred. In other words, little or no explanatory power is gained by the rotated solution over the single factor principal component solution. These results also accord well with the findings of Anderson (1976). He found that a single factor accounted for 65 % of the variance in ten different measures of what were presumed to be eight different aspects of reading ability. His subjects were 150 children spread evenly over three grade levels in elementary schools in Papua New Guinea. For many of them, English was a second language.

v. Writing.

Eighteen writing scores were generated. In this analysis three separate scores were obtained over the essay task referred to above in Tables 1 and 2. First, the results were rated on a five point scale by the instructors in the classes in which the subjects originally wrote the essays (see Kaczmarek, in press, for a more complete description of the procedure). Second, the same essays were judged for content and organization on a different five point scale by a different rater. Third, the person assigning the latter subjective rating also computed an objective score by counting the number of error-free words in the subject's protocol, subtracting the number of errors, and dividing the result by the total number of words in an errorless rewrite of the text. These scores are referred to below as Instructor's Essay Rating, Content and Organization Rating, and Essay Score.

Next, a battery of multiple choice tests aimed at components of writing skill were included. Each task was based on decisions related to text. The first task was to select the appropriate word, phrase, or clause to fill in a blank in a text. It was, thus, a kind of multiple choice cloze test. This task was repeated over three texts – one supposed to be easy for the subjects tested (Select A), a second supposed to be moderately difficult (Select B), and a third expected to be difficult (Select C).

The second type of test included in the multiple choice battery required editorial decisions concerning errors systematically implanted in texts. The errors were of the type frequently made by native and non-native writers. The format was similar except that the criterial word, phrase, or clause was underlined in each case and followed by several alternatives. The first alternative in every case was to leave the underlined portion alone – i.e., no change. In addition, four other options were provided as possible replacements for the underlined portion. Again, easy, moderate, and difficult texts were used (Edit A, B, and C).

The third type of test included in the multiple choice battery required subjects to place words, phrases, or clauses in an appropriate order within a given text. In each case four words, phrases, or clauses (or some combination) were provided and the subject had to associate the correct unit with the appropriate blank in a series of four blanks. As before, three texts were used (Order A, B, and C).

A final type of writing task used was a read and recall procedure. Again, three texts were used. Each one was displayed via an overhead projector for one minute. Then subjects (having been instructed beforehand) wrote all that they could recall from the text. The resulting protocols were scored in two ways. First, they were rated on a simple five point scale (see Kaczmarek, in press, for elaboration); second, they were scored by allowing one point per word of text that conformed to something stated or implied by the original text. The rating was done by the instructors who also rated the essay task and is thus referred to as Instructor's Rating of Recall A, B, and C. The scoring, on the other hand, was done by the same team of graders who scored the essay task (Recall Score A, B, and C).

The principal components solution is presented in Table 9 and the rotated solution in Table 10. Whereas 49% of the total available variance is explained by g, only 4 additional percentage points are explained by the rotated solution which accounts for a total of 53%. Furthermore, the patterning displayed in Table 10 certainly appears to be due largely to chance. There is no clear tendency for the same

TABLE 9
Principal Components Analysis over Eighteen Writing Scores (N = 137).

SCORES	LOADINGS ON g	SQUARED LOADINGS
Instructors' Essay Rating	.80	.64
Content and Organization Rating	.80	.64
Essay Score	.77	.59
Select A	.63	.40
Select B	.74	.55
Select C	.71	.50
Edit A	.67	.45
Edit B	.62	.38
Edit C	.45	.20
Order A	.75	.56
Order B	.69	.48
Order C	.62	.38
Recall Rating A	.78	.61
Recall Rating B	.69	.48
Recall Rating C	.78	.61
Recall Score A	.74	.55
Recall Score B	.66	.44
Recall Score C	.62	.38
	Eigen value = 8.84	

TABLE 10
Varimax Rotated Solution over Eighteen Writing
Scores (N = 137).

SCORES \ FACTORS	1	2	3	h^2
Instructors' Essay Rating	.45	.57		.60
Content and Organization Rating		.70		.49
Essay Score		.77		.59
Select A	.49			.24
Select B		.70		.49
Select C			.65	.42
Edit A	.45	.52		.52
Edit B	.49	.53		.59
Edit C			.71	.50
Order A		.69		.48
Order B			.55	.30
Order C		.46	.60	.66
Recall Rating A	.57	.65		.75
Recall Rating B	.75			.56
Recall Rating C	.81			.66
Recall Score A		.70		.49
Recall Score B	.64			.41
Recall Score C	.71			.50
			Eigen value = 9.25	

types of scores to load on the same factors. For instance, the Select
scores scatter over three uncorrelated factors. Thus, again the
indivisibility hypothesis seems to be the better explanation of the
data.

vi. Grammar.

Two kinds of grammar scores were used. First, the subtest on the
CELT labeled Structure was included, and second, there were several
subscores computed over Parish's Grammar test. Except for the fact
that it was possible to compute subscores over the latter test, there
would have been no need for this section. However, it serves a very
useful purpose in providing a straightforward test of the view that
discrete points of grammar can be usefully distinguished whether for
teaching or for testing purposes. Further, it is worth noting that the
author of the grammar items began with (and perhaps still maintains)

a sympathetic view toward the discrete point analysis of grammatical 'knowledge' (whatever the latter turns out to be).

Among the subscores on the Parish Grammar test were sums of scores over selected items representing particular grammatical categories believed to be functionally similar by the test author. For instance, noun modifiers such as adjectives and determiners were extracted by a computer scoring technique to obtain a subscore called Adj Det. It is important to note that the items did not include any heavily laden content adjectives but rather were limited to highly redundant demonstratives and the like. The entire text of the test with items used in computing subscores are given in the Appendix to *Research in Language Testing*. The other subscores are named in Tables 11 and 12 which report the requisite factor analyses. It is apparent from an examination of both tables that there is no basis whatever for claiming that separately testable grammatical categories exist. In the principal components solution and in the varimax rotation, all of the exact scores over all of the various categories load on the same factor. Again, the additional factors that are required for the rotated solution add little new information to what is already contained in g. Further, it is *only* the appropriate scores which tend to sort out randomly onto different factors. This is undoubtedly due to the fact that there was little reliable variance in those scores. There could not be, because the exact word scores exhausted nearly all of the variability in the performance of different examinees. If they didn't know the correct answer (in fact, the exact word deleted), chances were good that they could not get the item correct even if they were allowed to put in some other response. Hence, the appropriate scores here as in the cases of the repetition tasks and the reading aloud tasks added little new information.

E. Data from first language studies

The relationship between measures of language ability and IQ has often been examined in empirical studies of children and adults who are native speakers of English (and no doubt other languages). However, for some reason, high correlations between IQ tests and other tests – e.g., vocabulary tests, listening comprehension tests, reading tests, achievement batteries, personality indices, cloze procedure, etc. – have usually been interpreted to mean that the other tests were also incidentally testing IQ. This interpretation is unassailable from the point of view of pure statistics, but it leaves

TABLE 11
Principal Components Analysis over Twenty-three
Grammar Scores (N = 63).

SCORES	LOADINGS ON g	SQUARED LOADINGS
CELT-Structure	.70	.49
Adjectives & Determiners Exact	.78	.61
Adverbs & Particles Exact	.83	.69
Copula Forms ('Be') Exact	.77	.59
'Do' Forms Exact	.78	.61
Inevitable Nouns (as in idioms) Exact	.67	.45
Interrogatives Exact	.83	.69
Modals Exact	.80	.64
Prepositions Exact	.86	.74
Pronouns Exact	.91	.83
Subordinating Conjunctions Exact	.74	.55
Verbals Exact	.89	.79
Adjectives & Determiners Approp	.15	.02
Adverbs & Particles Approp	.23	.05
Copula ('Be') Approp	.08	.01
'Do' Forms Approp	.08	.01
Inevitable Nouns Approp	.24	.06
Interrogatives Approp	.08	.01
Modals Approp	.28	.08
Preposition Approp	.06	.00
Pronouns Approp	.00	.00
Subordinating Conjunction Approp	.19	.04
Verbals Approp	−.08	.01
		Eigen value = 7.97

open another alternative which is equally acceptable and worthy of consideration.

That other possibility is that the so-called 'IQ' tests are very likely measures of something other than innate intelligence. Although no-one would be apt to deny that in fact 'IQ' tests measure language proficiency to a great extent, the tests are rarely applied and interpreted as if they were measures of language proficiency – an attained skill as opposed to an innate, immutable, genetically

TABLE 12
Varimax Rotated Solution over Twenty-three
Grammar Scores (N = 63).

SCORES \ FACTORS	1	2	3	4	5	h²
CELT-Structure	.70					.49
Adj Det Exact	.77					.59
Adv Part Exact	.85					.72
Copula (be) Exact	.81					.66
Do Exact	.77					.59
Inevitable N Exact	.70					.49
Interrog Exact	.81					.66
Modals Exact	.79					.62
Prep Exact	.88					.77
Pronouns Exact	.90					.81
Subord Conj Exact	.72					.52
Verbals Exact	.87					.76
Adj Det Approp		.68				.46
Adv Part Approp				.59		.35
Copula Approp		.64				.41
Do Approp		.68				.46
Inevitable N Approp		.64				.41
Interrog Approp		.55				.30
Modals Approp		.63				.40
Prep Approp		.60				.36
Pronouns Approp				.70		.49
Subord Conj Approp			.63			.40
Verbals Approp			.69			.48
				Eigen value = 12.20		

determinable quantity. For instance, the San Diego twins (CBS News, August 1977) whose language system was incomprehensible to anyone but themselves were wrongly diagnosed as mentally retarded on the strength of so-called 'IQ' tests. Indeed, for thousands of children, the meaning of variance in IQ scores (not to mention other educational tests which are equally suspect) is crucial to the kind of educational experience which they are apt to receive.

Put simply, the question is whether or not intelligence in the abstract can or cannot be identified with what IQ tests measure. Related to this first question is the important matter as to whether or not what IQ tests measure can be modified by experience. If it can be shown that what IQ tests measure is principally language proficiency and nothing else, it will be excessively difficult for Jensen and others to keep maintaining that 'IQ' (that is, whatever is measured by IQ tests so-called) is genetically determined (or even largely so). This would make about as much sense as claiming that the fact that an Englishman speaks English and not Chinese or something else is genetically determined, and has nothing to do with the fact that he grew up in England and just happened to learn English. It would be tantamount to the claim that attained language proficiency is not attained. In the case of second language learners, this latter claim is patently false – even in the case of first language learners it is likely to be false also for all practical purposes.

With respect to first language acquisition it might be reasonable to ask whether language skill can be componentialized just as we have done in relation to second language learning. For instance, is there a component of vocabulary knowledge that is demonstrably distinct from syntactic knowledge? Can a component of intelligence be distinguished from a component of reading ability? Can either of these be distinguished from specific kinds of knowledge typically displayed through the use of language – e.g., social studies, history, biology, etc.? One might suppose these questions to be a bit ridiculous since they seem to challenge the very core of accepted educational dogma, but that in itself only increases the shock value of posing the questions in the first place. It certainly does not decrease their importance to educators. Indeed, if anything, it makes it all the more imperative that the widely accepted dogmas be empirically supported. If no empirical support can be offered (save that 'this is the way we've been doing it for two hundred years or more'), the dogmas should perhaps be replaced by more defensible notions. In any event, the strength of the distinctions common to educational practices should be founded on something other than precedent and opinion.

Is there any reason to suppose that the g factor of intelligence so widely recognized by educational psychologists and psychometrists might actually be something other than global language proficiency? There are a great many relevant studies. So many that we cannot do more than mention a smattering of them. For instance, Kelly (1965) found that a certain form of the Brown-Carlsen Listening Comprehension Test correlated more strongly with the Otis Test of Mental Abilities than it did with another form of the Brown-Carlsen. This raised the serious question whether the Brown-Carlsen test was measuring anything different from what the Otis test was measuring. However, since the Otis test was supposed to be a measure of IQ the author questioned the Brown-Carlsen's validity rather than that of the Otis test. Presumably this course of action was due to the mystique associated with the concept of intelligence – a mystique that listening tests apparently lack.

Concannon (1975) compared results on the Stanford-Binet and the Peabody Picture Vocabulary Test with 94 preschoolers. Correlations at grades 3, 4, and 5 were .65, .55, and .61. These figures roughly approximate the maximum possible correlations that could be achieved if the tests were measuring the very same thing given the limitations on the reliability of both tests. In other words, it is doubtful that correlations of significantly greater magnitude would be obtained if the tests were merely administered twice and the corresponding sets of scores on the same tests were correlated.

Hunt, Lunneberg, and Lewis (1975) investigated various aspects of what they considered verbal intelligence. In particular they were interested in whether or not a verbal IQ test could be taken as a measure of IQ independent of acquired knowledge. They

> conclude that although a verbal intelligence test is directly a measure of what people know, it is indirectly a way of identifying people who can code and manipulate verbal stimuli rapidly in situations in which knowledge *per se* is not a major factor (p. 233).

Does this not sound reminiscent of one of the naturalness constraints on pragmatic language tests? But, what about the other side of the same coin? Don't the so-called IQ tests also require pragmatic mapping of utterances onto contexts? Gunnarsson (1978) at least has demonstrated for many so-called verbal *and* non-verbal IQ tests that pragmatic mapping is involved.

Ultimately, it is a matter of investigating the nature of test variances and their patterns of intercorrelation with other tests. In a study of high school seniors, Stinson and Morrison (1959) found a correlation of .85 between a reading test and the Wechsler Intelligence Scale for Adults. Does this mean that the reading test is actually an IQ test, or that the IQ test is a reading test? Or could it be that both are measuring the same global factor of language proficiency? In another study, Wakefield, Veselka, and Miller (1974–5) found that a single canonical variate accounted for 75% of the variance in the several subtests on the Iowa Tests of Basic Skills and the Prescriptive Reading Inventory. One of the test batteries is supposedly aimed at achievement. Nevertheless, it would appear that both are doing pretty much the same thing.

In another study focussed on quite different questions, Chansky (1964) found a range of correlations between .58 and .68 between presumed tests of personality and so-called reading tests. Is it possible that as much as 45 % of the variance in so-called personality tests is attributable to reading ability? To global language proficiency? It is noteworthy that the amount of variance thus attributable to a language factor approximates the estimated total available non-random variance (i.e., the square of the estimated reliability) of the personality measures (see Chapter 5, above).

Until recently all that was lacking in terms of empirical data needed to link IQ and language proficiency tests of the sort discussed in Part Three of this book was an empirical study of native speakers employing pragmatic language tests in combination with a battery of IQ and achievement tests. The results of such a study are now available in the master's thesis of Tom Stump. He showed that a single factor of language proficiency accounted for about equal amounts of variance in the dictations and cloze tests included, as well as in the IQ scores (both verbal and non-verbal) and the various achievement scores. The test batteries used were the Lorge-Thorndike Intelligence Test, and the Iowa Tests of Basic Skills. A few scores were also available on the Stanford-Binet IQ Test, but only enough to indicate the possibility that the language tests were apparently better measures of whatever the IQ tests were measures of, than were the IQ tests. Interestingly, for the 109 seventh graders tested, the non-verbal portion of the Lorge-Thorndike correlated more strongly with the language scores (cloze and dictation) than did the verbal portion of the same test. Further, for the two samples of data (109 fourth graders and the nearly equal number of seventh graders – native speakers of English enrolled in middle class Saint Louis Schools) a single principal component accounted for .54 of the total variance in all of the tests in the one case, and .67 in the other.

In sum it would seem that the data from first language studies do not support either a componentialization of language skills nor do they support a differentiation of IQ and language tests. Apparently, the g factor of intelligence is indistinguishable from global language proficiency. Moreover, the relative indivisibility of the g factor seems to hold either for first or second language proficiency.

F. Directions for further empirical research

Implications of the foregoing findings for education are sweeping.

They suggest a possible need for reform that would challenge some of the most deeply seated notions of what school is about – how schools fail and how they succeed. The potential reforms that might be required if these findings can be substantiated are difficult to predict. Clearly they point us in the direction of curricula in which the focus is on the skills required to negotiate symbols rather than on the 'subject matter' in the traditional senses of the term. They point away from the medieval notion that psychology, grammar, philosophy, English, history, and biology are intrinsically different subject matters. Physics and mathematics may not be as reasonably distinct from English literature and sociology as the structure of universities implies.

Because of the potency of the implications of language testing research for the whole spectrum of educational endeavor it is of paramount importance that the findings on which decisions are based be the most carefully sought out and tested results that can be obtained. If it is not reasonable to make the traditional distinction between language and IQ, then the distinction should be done away with or replaced by an updated version consistent with available empirical findings. If vocabulary is not really distinct in a useful sense from syntax then the texts and the tests should abandon that distinction or replace it with one that can be empirically defended. Certainly, when we are dealing in an area of education where empirical answers are readily accessible, there is no defence for untested opinions. There is no room for appeal to authority concerning what a test is a test of. It doesn't matter a great deal what someone (anyone) thinks a test is measuring – what does matter is how people perform on the test and how their performance on that test compares with their performance on other similar and dissimilar tasks.

The research discussed here only begins to scratch the surface. Many unanswered questions remain, and many of the answers proposed here will no doubt need to be refined if not in fact discarded. The Stump project needs to be replicated in a large range of contexts. The study in Carbondale with second language learners needs to be refined and repeated in a context where more stringent controls can be imposed on the administration of the tasks employed. Other tasks need to be thoroughly studied. Especially, the nature of variability in the proficiency of native speakers in a greater variety of languages and dialects needs to be studied.

In spite of all the remaining uncertainties, it seems safe to suggest that the current practice of many ESL programs, textbooks, and curricula of separating listening, speaking, and reading and writing activities is probably not just pointless but in fact detrimental. A similar conclusion can be suggested with respect to curricula in the native language. It would appear that every teacher in every area of the curriculum should be teaching all of the traditionally recognized language skills.

References

Aborn, M., H. Rubenstein, and T. D. Sterling. 1959. 'Sources of contextual constraint upon words in sentences.' *Journal of Experimental Psychology* **57,** 171–180.

Adorno, T. W., Else Frenkel-Brunswick, D. J. Levinson, and R. N. Sanford. 1950. *The authoritarian personality.* New York: Harper.

Ahman, J. Stanley, and Marvin D. Glock. 1975. *Measuring and evaluating educational achievement.* Boston: Allyn and Bacon, 2nd ed.

Allen, Harold B., and R. N. Campbell (eds.). 1972. *Teaching English as a second language: a book of readings* . New York: McGraw Hill.

Allen, J. P. B., and Alan Davies. 1977. *Testing and experimental methods.* London: Oxford University Press.

Anastasi, Anne. 1976. *Psychological testing.* New York: Macmillan.

Anderson, D. F. 1953. 'Tests of achievement in the English language'. *English Language Teaching* **7,** 37–69.

Anderson, Jonathon. 1969. *Application of cloze procedure to English learned as a foreign language.* Unpublished doctoral dissertation, University of New England, Australia.

Anderson, Jonathon, 1971a 'Research on comprehension in reading'. In Bracken and Malmquist (eds.) *Improving reading ability around the world.* Newark, Delaware: International Reading Association.

Anderson, Jonathon. 1971b 'Selecting a suitable "reader": procedures for teachers to assess language difficulty'. *Regional English Language Center Journal* **2,** 35–42.

Anderson, Jonathon. 1976. *Psycholinguistic experiments in foreign language testing.* Santa Lucia, Queensland, Australia: University of Queensland Press.

Angoff, William H., and Auriel T. Sharon. 1971. 'Comparison of scores earned by native American college students and foreign applicants to U.S. colleges'. *TESOL Quarterly* **5,** 129–136. Also in Palmer and Spolsky (1975), 154–162.

Anisfeld, M., and W. E. Lambert. 1961. 'Social and psychological variables in learning Hebrew'. *Journal of Abnormal and Social Psychology* **63,** 524–529. Also in Gardner and Lambert (1972), 217–227.

Asakawa, Yoshio, and John W. Oller, Jr. 1977. 'Attitudes and attained proficiency in EFL: a sociolinguistic study of Japanese learners at the secondary level'. *SPEAQ Journal* 1. 71–80.

Asher, J. J. 1969. 'The total physical response approach to second language learning'. *Modern Language Journal* **59**, 3–17.

Asher, J. J. 1974. 'Learning a second language through commands: the second field test'. *Modern Language Journal* **58**, 24–32.

Bacheller, Frank. In press. 'Communicative effectiveness as predicted by judgements of the severity of learner errors in dictations'. In Oller and Perkins.

Backman, Nancy. 1976. 'Two measures of affective factors as they relate to progress in adult second language learning'. *Working papers. On Bilingualism* **10**, 100–122.

Bally, Charles, Albert Sechehaye, and Albert Riedlinger (eds.) 1959. *Course in general linguistics: Ferdinand de Saussuré.* Translated by Wade Baskin. New York: McGraw Hill.

Banks, James A. 1972. 'Imperatives in ethnic minority education'. *Phi Delta Kappan* **53**, 266–269.

Baratz, Joan. 1969. 'A bidialectal task for determining language proficiency in economically disadvantaged Negro children'. *Child Development* **40**, 889–901.

Barik, Henri C. and Merrill Swain. 1975. 'Three-year evaluation of a large scale early grade French immersion program: the Ottawa study'. *Language Learning* **25**, 1–30.

Barrutia, Richard. 1969. *Linguistic theory of language learning as related to machine teaching.* Heidelberg: Julius Groos Verlag.

Bass, B. M. 1955. 'Authoritarianism or acquiescence?' *Journal of Abnormal Social Psychology* **51**, 616–623.

Bereiter, C. and S. Engelmann. 1967. *Teaching disadvantaged children in the preschool.* Engelwood Cliffs, N.J.: Prentice-Hall.

Bernstein, Basil. 1960. 'Language and social class'. *British Journal of Sociology* **11**, 271–276.

Bezanson, Keith A. and Nicolas Hawkes. 1976. 'Bilingual reading skills of primary school children in Ghana'. *Workingpapers in Bilingualism* **11**, 44–73.

Bird, Charles S. and W. L. Woolf. 1968. *English in Mali.* Edited by James E. Redden. Carbondale, Illinois: Southern Illinois University Press.

Bloom, Benjamin S. 1976. 'Human characteristics and school learning'. New York: McGraw Hill.

Bloomfield, Leonard. 1933. *Language.* New York: Holt, Rinehart, and Winston.

Bogardus, E. S. 1925. 'Measuring social distance'. *Journal ·of Applied Sociology* **9**, 299–308.

Bogardus, E. S. 1933. 'Social distance scale'. *Sociology and Social Research* **17**, 265–271.

Bolinger, Dwight L. 1975. *Aspects of language.* Second edition. New York: Harcourt, Brace, and Jovanovich.

Bormuth, John. 1967. 'Comparable cloze and multiple choice comprehension test scores'. *Journal of Reading* **10**, 291–299.

Bormuth, John. 1970. *On the theory of achievement test items.* Chicago: University of Chicago Press.

Botel, M. and Alvin Granowsky. 1972. 'A formula for measuring syntactic complexity: a directional effort'. *Elementary English* **49**, 513–516.

Bower, T. G. R. 1971. 'The object in the world of the infant'. *Scientific American* **225,** 30–38.

Bower, T. G. R. 1974. *Development in infancy.* San Francisco: Freeman.

Bracht, Glenn H., Kenneth D. Hopkins, and Julian C. Stanley (eds.) 1972. *Perspectives in educational and psychological measurement.* Engelwood Cliffs, N.J.: Prentice-Hall.

Brière, Eugene. 1966. 'Quantity before quality in second language composition'. *Language Learning* **16,** 141–151.

Brière, Eugene. 1972. 'Cross cultural biases in language testing'. Paper presented at the Third International Congress of Applied Linguistics in Copenhagen, Denmark. Reprinted in Oller and Richards (1973), 214–227.

Britton, J. 1973. *Language and learning.* New York: Penguin.

Brodkey, Dean. 1972. 'Dictation as a measure of mutual intelligibility: a pilot study'. *Language Learning* **22,** 203–220.

Brodkey, Dean and Howard Shore. 1976. 'Student personality and success in an English language program'. *Language Learning* **26,** 153–162.

Brooks, Nelson. 1964. *Language and language learning.* New York: Harcourt, Brace, and World.

Brown, H. Douglas. 1973. 'Affective variables in second language acquisition'. *Language Learning* **23,** 231–244.

Bung, Klaus. 1973. *Towards a theory of programmed language instruction.* The Hague: Mouton.

Buros, Oscar K. (ed.) 1970. *Personality: tests and reviews.* Highland Park, N.J.: Gryphon Press.

Buros, Oscar K. (ed.) 1974. *Personality tests and reviews II: a monograph consisting of the personality sections of the seventh mental measurements yearbook 1972 and tests in print 1974.* Highland Park, N.J.: Gryphon Press.

Burt, Marina K., Heidi C. Dulay, and Eduardo Hernandez-Chavez. 1973. *The bilingual syntax measure. With illustrations by Gary Klaver.* New York: Harcourt, Brace, and Jovanovich.

Burt, Marina K., Heidi C. Dulay, and Eduardo Hernandez-Chavez. 1975. *Bilingual syntax measure: Manual.* New York: Harcourt, Brace, and Jovanovich.

Burt, Marina K., Heidi C. Dulay, and Eduardo Hernandez-Chavez. 1976. *Bilingual syntax measure: technical handbook.* New York: Harcourt, Brace, and Jovanovich.

Callaway, Donn. In press. 'Accent and the evaluation of ESL oral proficiency'. In Oller and Perkins.

Carroll, John B. 1961. 'Fundamental considerations in testing for English proficiency of foreign students'. *Testing the English proficiency of foreign students.* Washington, D.C.: Center for Applied Linguistics, 31–40. Reprinted in Allen and Campbell (1972), 313–320.

Carroll, John B. 1967. 'Foreign language proficiency levels attained by language majors near graduation from college'. *Foreign Language Annals* **1,** 131–151.

Carroll, John B. 1972. 'Defining language comprehension: some speculations'. In Freedle and Carroll (1972), 1–29.

Carroll, John B., Aaron S. Carton, and Claudia P. Wilds. 1959. 'An investigation of cloze items in the measurement of achievement in foreign languages'. *College Entrance Examination Board Research and Development Report*. Laboratory for Research in Instruction, Harvard University.

Carroll, Lewis. 1957. *Alice in wonderland and through the looking glass*. New York: Grosset and Dunlap.

Cazden, Courtney B., James T. Bond, Ann S. Epstein, Robert D. Matz, and Sandra J. Savignon. 1976. 'Language assessment: where, what, and how'. Paper presented at the Workshop for Exploring Next Steps in Qualitative and Quantitative Research Methodologies in Education, Monterey, California. Also in *Anthropology and Education Quarterly* **8**, 1977, 83–91.

Chansky, Norman. 1964. 'A note on the validity of reading test scores'. *Journal of Educational Research* **58**, 90.

Chapman, L. J. and D. T. Campbell. 1957. 'Response set in F scale'. *Journal of Abnormal and Social Psychology* **54**, 129–132.

Chase, Richard A., S. Sutton, and Daphne First. 1959. 'Bibliography: delayed auditory feedback'. *Journal of Speech and Hearing Disorders* **2**, 193–200.

Chastain, Kenneth. 1975. 'Affective and ability factors in second language acquisition'. *Language Learning* **25**, 153–161.

Chavez, M. A., Tetsuro Chihara, John W. Oller, Jr., and Kelley Weaver. 1977. 'Are cloze items sensitive to constraints across sentences?' II Paper read at the Eleventh Annual TESOL Convention Miami, Florida.

Cherry, Colin. 1957. *On human communication: a review, a survey, and a criticism*. Second edition, 1966. Cambridge, Mass.: MIT Press.

Chihara, Tetsuro and John W. Oller, Jr. 1978. 'Attitudes and attained proficiency in EFL: a sociolinguistic study of adult Japanese learners'. *Language Learning* **28**, 55–68.

Chihara, Tetsuro, John W. Oller, Jr., Kelley Weaver, and Mary Anne Chavez. 1977. 'Are cloze items sensitive to constraints across sentences?' I *Language Learning* **27**, 63–73.

Chomsky, Noam A. 1957. *Syntactic structures*. The Hague: Mouton.

Chomsky, Noam A. 1964. 'Current issues in linguistic theory'. In Fodor and Katz (1964), 50–118.

Chomsky, Noam A. 1965. *Aspects of the theory of syntax*. Cambridge, Mass.: MIT Press.

Chomsky, Noam A. 1966a. *Topics in the theory of syntax*. The Hague: Mouton.

Chomsky, Noam A. 1966b. 'Linguistic theory'. In R. G. Mead (ed.) *Northeast conference on the teaching of foreign languages*. Menasha, Wisconsin: George Banta. Reprinted in Oller and Richards (1973), 29–35.

Chomsky, Noam A. 1972. *Language and mind*. New York: Harcourt, Brace, and Jovanovich.

Christie, R. and Florence Geis. 1970. *Studies in machiavellianism*. New York: Academic Press.

Chun, Ki Taek, Sidney Cobb, and J. R. P. French Jr. 1975. *Measures for psychological assessment: a guide to 3,000 original sources and their applications*. Ann Arbor, Michigan: Survey Research Center of the Institute for Social Research. (Foreword by E. Lowell Kelly.)

Clark, John L. D. 1972. *Foreign language testing: theory and practice.* Philadelphia: Center for Curriculum Development.

Coffman, William E. 1966. 'The validity of essay tests'. *Journal of Educational Measurement* **3**, 151–156. Reprinted in Bracht, Hopkins and Stanley (1972), 157–163.

Cohen, Andrew. 1973. 'The sociolinguistic assessment of speaking skills in a bilingual education program'. Paper read at the International Seminar on Language Testing sponsored jointly by the AILA Commission on Tests and the TESOL organization, San Juan, Puerto Rico. In Palmer and Spolsky (1975), 173–186.

Coleman E. B. and G. R. Miller. 1967. 'The measurement of information gained during prose learning'. *Reading Research Quarterly* **3**, 369–386.

College Entrance Examination Board and Educational Testing Service. 1968. *Test of English as a foreign language: interpretive information.* Princeton, N.J.: Educational Testing Service.

College Entrance Examination Board and Educational Testing Service. 1969. *Manual for studies in support of score interpretation.* Princeton, N.J.: Educational Testing Service.

College Entrance Examination Board and Educational Testing Service. 1973. *Manual for TOEFL score recipients.* Princeton, N.J.: Educational Testing Service.

Concannon, S. J. 1975. 'Comparison of the Stanford-Binet scale with the Peabody Picture Vocabulary Test'. *Journal of Educational Research* **69**, 104–105.

Condon, Elaine C. 1973. 'The cultural context of language testing'. Paper read at the International Seminar on Language Testing sponsored jointly by the AILA Commission on Tests and the TESOL organization, in San Juan, Puerto Rico. In Palmer and Spolsky (1975), 204–217.

Condon, W. S. and W. D. Ogston. 1971. 'Speech and body motion synchrony of the speaker-hearer'. In David L. Horton and James J. Jenkins (eds.) *The perception of language.* Columbus, Ohio: Merrill, 150–173.

Conrad, Christine. 1970. *The cloze procedure as a measure of English proficiency.* Unpublished master's thesis, University of California, Los Angeles. Abstracted in *Workpapers in TESL: UCLA* **5**, 1971, 159.

Cooke, W. (ed.) 1902. *The table talk and bon-mots of Samuel Foote.* London: Myers and Rogers.

Cooper, Robert L. 1968. 'An elaborated language testing model'. In John A. Upshur and Julia Fata (eds.) *Problems in foreign language testing. Language Learning, Special Issue Number* **3**, 15–72. Reprinted in Allen and Campbell (1972), 330–346.

Cooper, Robert L. 1969. 'Two contextualized measures of degree of bilingualism'. *Modern Language Journal* **53**, 172–178.

Cooper, Robert L. and Joshua A. Fishman. 1973. 'Some issues in the theory and measurement of language attitude'. Paper read at the International Seminar on Language Testing sponsored jointly by the AILA Commission on Tests and the TESOL organization, San Juan, Puerto Rico. In Palmer and Spolsky (1975), 187–197.

Copi, Irving. 1972. *An introduction to logic.* Fourth edition. New York: Macmillan.

Cowan, J. Ronayne and Zahreh Zarmed. 1976. 'Reading performance of bilingual children according to type of school and home language'. *Working papers on Bilingualism* **11,** 74–114.

Craker, Viola. 1971. *Clozentropy procedure as an instrument for measuring oral English competencies of first grade children.* Unpublished doctoral dissertation, University of New Mexico.

Cronbach, Lee J. 1970. *Essentials of psychological testing.* New York: Harper and Row.

Cronbach, Lee J. and P. E. Meehl. 1955. 'Construct validity in psychological tests'. *Psychological Bulletin* **52,** 281–302.

Crowne, D. P. and D. Marlowe. 1964. *The approval motive.* New York: Wiley.

Dale, E. and J. S. Chall. 1948a 'A formula for predicting readability'. *Educational Research Bulletin* **27,** 11–20, 28.

Dale, E. and J. S. Chall. 1948b. 'A formula for predicting readability: instructions'. *Educational Research Bulletin* **27,** 37–54.

Darnell, Donald K. 1963. 'The relation between sentence order and comprehension'. *Speech Monographs* **30,** 97–100.

Darnell, Donald K. 1968. *The development of an English language proficiency test of foreign students using a cloze-entropy procedure.* ERIC ED 024039.

Davies, Alan. 1975. 'Two tests of speeded reading'. In Jones and Spolsky, 119–130.

Davies, Allen. 1977. 'The construction of language tests'. In Allen and Davies, 38–104.

Dewey, John. 1910. *How we think.* Boston: D. C. Heath.

Dewey, John. 1916. *Essays in experimental logic.* New York: Dover.

Dewey, John. 1929. 'Nature, communication, and meaning'. Chapter 5 in *Experience and nature.* Chicago: Open Court. Reprinted in Hayden and Alworth (1965), 265–296.

Diana vs. California State Education Department. 1970. CA No. C-7037 RFD (n.d. Cal., February 3).

Dickens, C. 1962. *Oliver Twist.* Edited and abridged by Latif Doss. Hong Kong: The Bridge Series, Longman.

Doerr, Naomi. In press. 'The effects of agreement/disagreement on cloze scores'. In Oller and Perkins.

D'Oyley, Vincent and H. Silverman (eds.) 1976. Preface to Black Students in urban Canada. TESL Talk 7, January.

Dumas, Guy and Merrill Swain. 1973. 'L'apprentisage du francais langue seconde en class d'immersion dans un milieu torontois'. Paper read at the Conference on Bilingualism and Its Implications in the West, University of Alberta.

Early, Margaret, Elizabeth K. Cooper, Nancy Santeusanio, and Marian Young Adell. 1974. *Teacher's edition for sun-up and reading skills 1.* New York: Harcourt, Brace, and Jovanovich.

Ebel, Robert L. 1970. 'Some limitations on criterion referenced measurement'. Paper read at a meeting of the American Educational Research Association. In G. H. Bracht, Kenneth D. Hopkins, and Julian C. Stanley (eds.) *Perspectives in Educational and Psychological Measurement.*

Engelwood Ciffs. New Jersey: Prentice-Hall, 1972, 74–87.

Educational Testing Service. 1970. *Manual for peace corps language testers.* Princeton, N.J.: ETS.

Ervin-Tripp, Susan M. 1970. 'Structure and process in language acquisition'. In James F. Alatis (ed.) *Report of the twenty-first annual round table meeting on linguistics and language studies.* Washington, D.C.: Georgetown University Press, 312–344.

Evola, J., E. Mamer, and R. Lentz. In press. 'Discrete point versus global scoring for cohesive devices.' In Oller and Perkins.

Ferguson, Charles A. 1972. 'Soundings: some topics in the study of language attitudes in multilingual areas'. Paper read at the Tri-university Meeting on Language Attitudes, Yeshiva University.

Ferguson, Charles A. and John Gumperz. 1971. 'Linguistic diversity in South Asia'. In Anwar S. Dil (ed.) *Language structure and language use: essays by Charles A. Ferguson.* Palo Alto, California: Stanford University Press.

Fishman, Joshua A. 1976. *A series of lectures on bilingualism and bilingual education.* University of New Mexico.

Fishman, M. In press. 'We all make the same mistakes: a comparative study of native and non-native errors'. In Oller and Perkins.

Flanagan, J. C. 1939. 'General considerations in the selection of test items and a short method of estimating the product-moment coefficient of correlation from data at the tails of the distribution'. *Journal of Educational Psychology* **30,** 674–680.

Flesch, Rudolf. 1948. 'A formula for predicting readability: instructions'. *Journal of Applied Psychology* **32,** 221–233.

Fodor, J. A. and J. J. Katz (eds.) 1964. *The structure of language: readings in the philosophy of language.* Englewood Cliffs, N.J.: Prentice-Hall.

Fraser, Colin, Ursula Bellugi, and Roger Brown. 1963. 'Control of grammar in imitation, comprehension, and production'. *Journal of Verbal Learning and Verbal Behavior* **2,** 121–135.

Frederiksen, Carl H. 1975a. 'Effects of context induced processing operations on semantic information acquired from discourse'. *Cognitive Psychology* **7,** 139–166.

Frederiksen, Carl H. 1975b. 'Representing logical and semantic structure of knowledge acquired from discourse'. *Cognitive Psychology* **7,** 371–459.

Frederiksen, Carl H. 1977a. 'Inference and the structure of children's discourse'. Paper read at the Symposium on the Development of Discourse Processing Skills, at a meeting of the Society for Research in Child Development in New Orleans.

Frederiksen, Carl H. 1977b. 'Discourse comprehension and early reading'. Unpublished paper available from the National Institute of Education, Washington D.C.

Freedle, Roy O. and John B. Carroll (eds.) 1972. *Language comprehension and the acquisition of knowledge.* Washington, D.C.: V. H. Winston, and New York: Wiley.

Gardner, Robert C. 1975. 'Social factors in second language acquisition and bilinguality'. Paper read at the invitation of the Canada Council's Consultative Committee on the Individual, Language, and Society at a conference in Kingston, Ontario.

Gardner, Robert C. and Wallace E. Lambert. 1959. 'Motivational variables in second language acquisition'. *Canadian Journal of Psychology* **13**, 266–272. Reprinted in Gardner and Lambert (1972), 191–197.

Gardner, Robert C. and Wallace E. Lambert. 1972. *Attitudes and motivation in second language learning*. Rowley, Mass.: Newbury House.

Gardner, Robert C., R. Smythe, R. Clement, and L. Gliksman. 1976. 'Second language learning: a social psychological perspective'. *Canadian Modern Language Review* **32**, 198–213.

Gattegno, Caleb. 1963. *Teaching foreign languages in schools: the silent way*. New York: Educational Solutions.

Gentner, Donald R. 1976. 'The structure and recall of narrative prose'. *Journal of Verbal Learning and Verbal Behavior* **15**, 411–418.

Glazer, Susan Mandel. 1974. 'Is sentence length a valid measure of difficulty in readability formulas?' *The Reading Teacher* **27**, 464–468.

Goodman, Kenneth S. 1965. 'Dialect barriers to reading comprehension'. *Elementary English* **42**, 8.

Goodman, Kenneth S. 1968. 'The psycholinguistic nature of the reading process'. In K. S. Goodman (ed.) *The psycholinguistic nature of the reading process*. Detroit, Michigan: Wayne State University Press, 13–26.

Goodman, Kenneth S. 1970. 'Reading: a psycholinguistic guessing game'. In Harry Singer and Robert Ruddell (eds.) *Theoretical models and processing in reading*. Newark, Delaware: International Reading Association, 259–272.

Goodman, Kenneth S. and Catherine Buck. 1973. 'Dialect barriers to reading comprehension revisited'. *The Reading Teacher* **27**, 6–12.

Gradman, Harry L. and Bernard Spolsky. 1975. 'Reduced redundancy testing: a progress report'. In Jones and Spolsky (1975), 59–70.

Grimes, Joseph Evans. 1975. *The thread of discourse*. The Hague: Mouton.

Guiora, A. Z., Maria Paluszny, Benjamin Beit-Hallahmi, J. C. Catford, Ralph E. Cooley, and Cecelia Yoder Dull. 1975. 'Language and person studies in language behavior'. *Language Learning* **25**, 43–62.

Gunnarsson, Bjarni. 1978. 'A look at the content similarities between intelligence, achievement, personality, and language tests'. In Oller and Perkins, 17–35.

Haggard, L. A. and R. S. Isaacs. 1966. 'Micro-momentary facial expressions as indicators of ego-mechanisms in psychotherapy'. In L. A. Gottschalk and A. H. Auerbach (eds.) *Methods of research in psychotherapy*. New York: Appleton, Century and Crofts, 154–165.

Hanzeli, Victor E. 1976. 'The effectiveness of cloze tests in measuring the competence of students of French in an academic setting'. Paper read at the University of Kentucky Foreign Language Conference. Also in the *French Review*, **50**, 1977, 865–74.

Harris, David P. 1969. *Testing English as a second language*. New York: McGraw Hill.

Harris, Zellig. 1951. *Structural linguistics*. Chicago: University of Chicago Press.

Hart, Norman W. M. 1974. 'Language of young children'. *Education News* December. 29–31.

Hart, Norman W. M. 1976. 'Reading as languaging in print'. Paper read at the Sixth World Congress on Reading sponsored by the International Reading Association in Singapore.

Hart, Norman W. M. and B. N. Gray. 1977a. *The Mount Gravatt developmental language reading program: teacher's manual.* Reading, Mass.: Addison-Wesley.

Hart, Norman W. M., Richard F. Walker, and B. N. Gray. 1977b. *The language of children: a key to literacy.* Reading, Mass.: Addison-Wesley.

Heaton, J. B. 1975. *Writing English language tests.* London: Longman.

Herrnstein, R. 1971. IQ. *Atlantic Monthly,* September. 43–64.

Hinofotis, Francis Ann Butler. 1976. *An investigation of the concurrent validity of cloze testing as a measure of overall proficiency in English as a second language.* Unpublished doctoral dissertation, South Illinois University.

Hinofotis, Francis Ann Butler and Becky Gerlach Snow. 1977. 'An alternative cloze testing procedure: multiple choice format'. Paper read at the Eleventh Annual Meeting of TESOL, Miami, Florida. In Oller and Perkins (in press).

Hofman, John E. 1974. *Assessment of English proficiency in the African primary school. Series in Education, University of Rhodesia, Occasional Paper Number 3.*

Huff, D. 1954. *How to lie with statistics,* New York: Norton.

Hunt, Earl, Clifford Lunneberg, and Joe Lewis. 1975. 'What does it mean to be high verbal?' *Cognitive Psychology* 7, 194–227.

Illyin, Donna. 1976. *Ilyin oral interview.* Rowley, Mass.: Newbury House.

Ilyin, Donna. 1970. 'Structure placement tests for adults in English second language programs in California'. *TESOL Quarterly* 4, 323–330. Reprinted in Palmer and Spolsky (1975), 128–136.

Ingram, Elisabeth. 1977. 'Basic concepts in testing'. In Allen and Davies, 11–37.

Irvine, P., Parvin Atai, and John W. Oller, Jr. 1974. 'Cloze, dictation, and the Test of English as a Foreign Language'. *Language Learning* 24, 245–252.

Jackson, D. N. and S. J. Messick. 1958. 'Content and style in personality assessment'. *Psychological Bulletin* 55, 243–252.

Jackson, D. N., S. J. Messick, and C. M. Solley. 1957. 'How "rigid" is the "authoritarian"?' *Journal of Abnormal and Social Psychology* 54, 137–140.

James, William. 1890. *Principles of psychology, I and II.* New York: Henry Holt.

Jensen, Arthur R. 1965. 'Review of the Rorshach'. In Buros (1970), 1306–1314. Reprinted in Bracht, Hopkins and Stanley (1972), 292–308.

Jensen, Arthur R. 1969. 'The nature of intelligence'. *Harvard Educational Review* 39, 5–28. Reprinted in Bracht, Hopkins, and Stanley (1972), 191–213.

Johansson, Stig. 1972. 'An evaluation of the noise test: a method for testing overall second language proficiency by perception under masking noise'. Paper read at the Third International Congress of Applied Linguistics, Copenhagen, Denmark. In *IRAL* 11, 1973, 109–133.

Johansson, Stig. 1973. 'Partial dictation as a test of foreign language proficiency'. Department of English, Lund University, *Swedish-English Contrastive Studies Report Number 3.*

Johansson, Stig. In press. 'Reading comprehension in the native language and the foreign language: on an English-Swedish reading comprehension index'. In Arne Zettersten (ed.) *Language testing*. Copenhagen, Denmark: Department of English, University of Copenhagen.

John, Vera and Vivian J. Horner. 1971. *Early childhood bilingual education*. New York: Modern Language Association.

Johnson, Thomas Ray and Kathy Krug. In press. 'Integrative and instrumental motivations: in search of a measure'. In Oller and Perkins.

Jones, R. L. and Bernard Spolsky (eds.) 1975. *Testing language proficiency*. Arlington, Virginia: Center for Applied Linguistics.

Jongsma, Eugene R. 1971. 'The cloze procedure: a survey of the research'. *Occasional Papers in Reading*, Bloomington, Indiana: Indiana University School of Education. ERIC ED 050893.

Jonz, Jon. 1974. 'Improving on the basic egg: the multiple choice cloze test'. Paper read at the Eighth Annual Meeting of TESOL, Denver, Colorado. Also in *Language Learning* **26**, 1976, 255–65.

Kaczmarck, Celeste. In press. 'Rating and scoring essays'. In Oller and Perkins.

Katz, J.J. and J.A. Fodor. 1963. 'The structure of a semantic theory'. *Language* **39**, 170–210. Reprinted in Fodor and Katz (1964), 479–518.

Katz, J.J. and P.M. Postal. 1964. *An integrated theory of linguistic descriptions*. Cambridge, Mass.: MIT Press.

Kelly, C.M. 1965. 'An investigation of the construct validity of two commercially published tests'. *Speech Monographs* **32**, 139–143.

Kerlinger, Fred N. and Elazar J. Pedhazur. 1973. *Multiple regression in behavioral research*. New York: Holt, Rinehart, and Winston.

Kinzel, Paul. 1964. *Lexical and grammatical interference in the speech of a bilingual child*. Seattle: University of Washington Press.

Kirn, Harriet. 1972. *The effect of practice on performance on dictations and cloze tests*. Unpublished master's thesis, University of California, Los Angeles. Abstracted in Workpapers in TESL: UCLA **6**, 102.

Klare, George R. 1974–5. 'Assessing readability'. *Reading Research Quarterly* **10**, 62–102.

Klare, George R. 1976. 'Judging readability'. *Instructional Science* **5**, 55–61.

Klare, George R., H.W. Sinaiko, and L. M' Stolurow. 1972. 'The cloze procedure: a convenient readability test for training materials and translations'. *International Review of Applied Psychology* **21**, 77–106.

Kolers, Paul A. 1968. 'Bilingualism and information processing'. *Scientific American* **218**, 78–84.

Labov, William. 1972. *Language in the inner city: studies in the black English vernacular*. Philadelphia: University of Pennsylvania Press.

Labov, William and P. Cohen. 1967. 'Systematic relating of standard and non-standard rules in the grammar of negro speakers'. *Project Literacy 7* (as cited by Politzer, Hoover, and Brown, 1974).

Lado, Robert. 1957. *Linguistics across cultures*. Ann Arbor, Michigan: University of Michigan.

Lado, Robert. 1961. *Language testing*. New York: McGraw Hill.

Lado, Robert. 1964. *Language teaching: a scientific approach*. New York: McGraw Hill.

Lado, Robert and Charles C. Fries. 1954. *English pronunciation*. Ann Arbor: University of Michigan.

Lado, Robert and Charles C. Fries. 1957. *English sentence patterns*. Ann Arbor: University of Michigan Press.

Lado, Robert and Charles C. Fries. 1958. *English pattern practices*. Ann Arbor: University of Michigan Press.

Lambert, Wallace E. 1955. 'The measurement of linguistic dominance of bilinguals'. *Journal of Abnormal and Social Psychology* **50**, 197–200.

Lambert, Wallace E., R. C. Gardner, H. C. Barik, and K. Tunstall. 1962. 'Attitudinal and cognitive aspects of intensive study of a second language'. *Journal of Abnormal and Social Psychology* **66**, 358–368. Reprinted in Gardner and Lambert (1972), 228–245.

Lambert, Wallace E., R. C. Hodgson, R. C. Gardner, and S. Fillenbaum. 1960. 'Evaluational reactions to spoken language'. Journal of Abnormal and Social Psychology **55**, 44–51.

Lambert, Wallace E. and G. Richard Tucker. 1972. *Bilingual education of children: the St. Lambert experiment*. Rowley, Mass.: Newbury House.

Lapkin, Sharon and Merrill Swain 1977. 'The use of English and French cloze tests in a bilingual education program evaluation: validity and error analysis'. *Language Learning* **27**, 279–314.

Lashley, Karl S. 1951. 'The problem of serial order in behavior'. In L. A. Jeffress (ed.) *Cerebral mechanisms in behavior*. New York: Wiley, 112–136. Also in Sol Saporta and Jarvis R. Bastian (eds.) *Psycholinguistics: a book of readings*. New York: Holt, Rinehart, and Winston, 1961, 180–197.

Lau vs. Nichols. 1974. 414 U. S. 563, 94 S. Ct. 786, 38 L. Ed. Zd 1.

Lett, John. 1977. 'Assessing attitudinal outcomes'. In June K. Phillips (ed.) *The language connection: from the classroom to the world*. ACTFL Foreign Language Education Series. National Textbook.

Liebert, R. M. and Michael D. Spiegler. 1974. *Personality: strategies for the study of man*. Revised edition. Homewood, Illinois: Dorsey Press.

Likert, R. 1932. 'A technique for the measurement of attitudes'. *Archives of Psychology*, Number **40**.

LoCoco, Veronica Gonzalez-Mena. 1976. 'A comparison of three methods for the collection of L2 data: free composition, translation, and picture description'. *Working papers on Bilingualism* **8**, 59–86.

LoCoco, Veronica Gonzalez-Mena. 1977. 'A comparison of cloze tests as measures of overall language proficiency'. *Modern Language Journal*, in press.

Lofgren, Horst. 1972. 'The measurement of language proficiency'. *Studia psychologica et pedagogica, Series altera* **57**. Lund, Sweden: CWK Gleerup Berlingska Boktryckerict.

Lorge, Irving. 1944. 'Word lists as background for communication'. *Teachers College Record* **45**, 543–552.

Lukmani, Yasmeen. 1972. 'Motivation to learn and language proficiency'. *Language Learning* **22**, 261–274.

Luria, A. R. 1959. 'The directive function of speech, in development and dissolution.' *Word* **15**, 341–52.

MacGinitie, W. H. 1961. 'Contextual constraint in English prose paragraphs'. *Journal of Psychology* **51,** 121–130.

MacKay, D. M. 1951. 'Mindlike behavior in artefacts'. *British Journal of the Philosophy of Science* **2,** 105–121.

McCall, W. A. and L. M. Crabbs. 1925. *Standard test lessons in reading: teacher's manual for all books.* New York: Bureau of Publications, Teacher's College, Columbia University.

McCracken, Glenn and Charles C. Walcutt. 1969. *Teacher's edition: Lippincott's basic reading.* Philadelphia: J. B. Lippincott.

McLeod, John. 1975. 'Uncertainty reduction in different languages through reading comprehension'. *Journal of Psycholinguistic Research* **4,** 343–355.

Manis, M. and Dawes, R. 1961. 'Cloze score as a function of attitude'. *Psychological Reports* **9,** 79–84.

Martin, Nancy, Pat D'Arcy, Bryan Newton, and Robert Parker. 1976. *Writing and learning: across the curriculum 11–16.* Foreword by James Britton. Leicester: Woolaston Parker.

Menyuk, Paula. 1969. *Sentences children use.* Cambridge, Mass.: MIT Press.

Miller, G. A. 1956. 'The magical number seven plus or minus one or two'. *Psychological Review* **63,** 81–97.

Miller, G. A. 1964. 'The psycholinguists: on the new scientists of language'. *Encounter* **23,** 29–37. Reprinted in Osgood and Sebeok (1965), as an appendix.

Miller, G. A., G. A. Heise, and W. Lichten. 1951. 'The intelligibility of speech as a function of the context of the test materials'. *Journal of Experimental Psychology* **41,** 81–97.

Miller, G. A. and Phillip N. Johnson-Laird. 1976. *Language and perception.* Cambridge, Mass.: Harvard University Press.

Miller, G. A. and Jennifer Selfridge. 1950. 'Verbal context and the recall of meaningful material'. *American Journal of Psychology* **63,** 176–185.

Miller, G. R. and E. B. Coleman. 1967. 'A set of thirty-six prose passages calibrated for complexity'. *Journal of Verbal Learning and Verbal Behavior* **6,** 851–854.

Miller, Jon F. 1973. 'Sentence imitation in pre-school children'. *Language and Speech* **16,** 1–14.

Morton, Rand. 1960. *The language lab as a teaching machine: notes on the mechanization of language learning.* Ann Arbor: University of Michigan.

Morton, Rand. 1966. 'The behavioral analysis of Spanish syntax: toward an acoustic grammar'. *IRAL* **4,** 170–177.

Mullen, Karen. In press a. 'Evaluating writing proficiency in ESL'. In Oller and Perkins.

Mullen, Karen. In press b. 'Rater reliability and oral proficiency evaluations'. Paper read at the First International Conference on Frontiers in Language Proficiency and Dominance Testing April, 1977. In Oller and Perkins.

Murakami, Mitsuhisa. In press. 'Behavioral and attitudinal correlates of progress in ESL'. In Oller and Perkins (b).

Naccarato, R. W. and G. M. Gillmore. 1976. 'The application of generalizability theory to a college level French placement test'. Paper read at the Fourth Annual Pacific Northwest Educational Research and Evaluation Conference, Seattle, Washington.

Nadler, Harvey, Leonard R. Marelli, and Charles S. Haynes. 1971. *American English: grammatical structure book I*. Paris: Didier.

Naiman, N. 1974. 'The use of elicited imitation in second language acquisition research'. *Working papers on Bilingualism* **2**, 1–37.

Nakano, Patricia J. 1977. 'Educational implications of the Lau vs. Nichols decision'. In Marina K. Burt, Heidi C. Dulay, and Mary Finocchiaro (eds.) *Viewpoints on English as a second language*. New York: Regents, 219–234.

Natalicio, Diana S. and F. Williams. 1971. *Repetition as an oral language assessment technique*. Austin, Texas: Center for Communication Research.

National Council of Teachers of English. 1973. *English for today*. Second edition, W. R. Slager, Lois McIntosh, Harold B. Allen, and Bernice E. Leary. New York: McGraw Hill.

Newcomb, T. M. 1950. *Social psychology*. New York: Holt, Rinehart, and Winston.

Nie, Norman H., C. Hadlai Hull, Jean G. Jenkins, Karen Steinbrenner, and Dale H. Brent. 1975. *Statistical package for the social sciences*. Second edition. New York: McGraw Hill.

Norton, Darryl E. and William R. Hodgson. 1973. 'Intelligibility of black and white speakers for black and white listeners'. *Language and Speech* **16**, 207–210.

Nunnally, J. C. 1967. *Psychometric theory*. New York: McGraw Hill.

'OCR sets guidelines for fulfilling Lau decision'. 1975. *The Linguistic Reporter* **18**, 1, 5–7.

Oller, John W. Sr. 1963. *El español por el mundo; primer nivel: la familia Fernández*. Chicago: Encyclopedia Britannica Films.

Oller, John W. Sr., and Angel González. 1965. *El espanol por el mundo; segundo nivel: Emilio en España*. Chicago: Encyclopedia Britannica Films.

Oller, John W. Jr. 1970. 'Dictation as a device for testing foreign language proficiency'. *Workpapers in TESL: UCLA* **4**, 37–42. Also in *English Language Teaching* **25**, 1971, 254–259.

Oller, John W. Jr. 1972. 'Scoring methods and difficulty levels for cloze tests of proficiency in ESL'. *Modern Language Journal* **56**, 151–158.

Oller, John W. Jr. 1975. 'Cloze, discourse, and approximations to English'. In Marina K. Burt and Heidi C. Dulay (eds.) *New directions in second language teaching and bilingual education: on TESOL '75*. Washington, D.C.: TESOL, 345–355.

Oller, John W. Jr. 1976a. 'Evidence for a general language proficiency factor: an expectancy grammar'. *Die Neuren Sprachen* **2**, 165–174.

Oller, John W. Jr. 1976b. 'Language testing'. In Ronald Wardhaugh and H. Douglas Brown (eds.) *Survey of applied linguistics*. Ann Arbor: University of Michigan Press, 275–300.

Oller, John W. Jr. 1976c. 'A program for language testing research'. In H. Douglas Brown (ed.) Papers in second language acquisition: proceedings of the sixth annual conference on applied linguistics at the University of Michigan. *Language Learning, Special Issue Number* **4**, 141–165.

Oller, John W. Jr. 1977. 'The psychology of language and contrastive linguistics: the research and the debate'. *Foreign Language Annals*, in press.

Oller, John W. Jr., Lori Baca, and Fred Vigil. 1977. 'Attitudes and attained proficiency in ESL: a sociolinguistic study of Mexican-Americans in the Southwest'. *TESOL Quarterly* **11**, 173–183.

Oller, John W. Jr., J. Donald Bowen, Ton That Dien, and Victor Mason. 1972. 'Cloze tests in English, Thai, and Vietnamese: native and non-native performance'. *Language Learning* **22**, 1–15.

Oller, John W. Jr. and Christine Conrad. 1971. 'The cloze procedure and ESL proficiency'. *Language Learning* **21**, 183–196.

Oller, John W. Jr. and Francis Ann Butler Hinofotis. 1976. 'Two mutually exclusive hypotheses about second language proficiency: factor analytic studies of a variety of language tests'. Paper read at the Winter Meeting of the Linguistic Society of America, Philadelphia. Also in Oller and Perkins (in press).

Oller, John W. Jr., Alan J. Hudson, and Phyllis Fei Liu. 1977. 'Attitudes and attained proficiency in ESL: a sociolinguistic study of native speakers of Chinese in the United States'. *Language Learning* **27**, 1–27.

Oller, John. W. Jr. and Nevin Inal. 1971. 'A cloze test of English prepositions'. *TESOL Quarterly* **5**, 315–326. Reprinted in Palmer and Spolsky (1975), 37–49.

Oller, John W. Jr. and Naoko Nagato. 1974. 'The long-term effect of FLES: an experiment'. *Modern Language Journal* **58**, 15–19.

Oller, John W. Jr. and Kyle Perkins (eds.) 1978. *Language in education: testing the tests.* Rowley, Mass.: Newbury House.

Oller, John W. Jr. and Kyle Perkins (eds.) in press. *Research in language testing.* Rowley, Mass.: Newbury House.

Oller, John W. Jr. and Jack C. Richards (eds.) 1973. *Focus on the learner: pragmatic perspectives for the language teacher.* Rowley, Mass.: Newbury House.

Oller, John W. Jr., Bruce Dennis Sales, and Ronald V. Harrington. 1969. 'A basic circularity in traditional and current linguistic theory'. *Lingua* **22**, 317–328.

Oller, John W. Jr. and Virginia Streiff. 1975. 'Dictation: a test of grammar based expectancies'. *English Language Teaching* **30**, 25–36. Also in Jones and Spolsky (1975), 71–88.

Osgood, Charles E. 1955. 'A behavioristic analysis of perception and language as cognitive phenomena'. In Ithiel de Sola Pool (ed.) *Contemporary approaches to cognition: a report of a symposium at the University of Colorado 1955.* Cambridge, Mass.: MIT Press, 1957, 75–118.

Osgood, Charles E. and Thomas A. Sebeok. 1965. *Psycholinguistics: a survey of theory and research problems.* Bloomington, Indiana: Indiana University Press.

Osgood, Charles E., G. T. Suci, and P. H. Tannenbaum. 1957. *The measurement of meaning.* Urbana: University of Illinois Press.

Palmer, Leslie and Bernard Spolsky (eds.) 1975. *Papers on language testing: 1967–1974.* Washington, D.C.: TESOL.

Paulston, Christina B. and Mary Newton Bruder. 1975. *From substitution to substance: a handbook of structural pattern drills.* Rowley, Mass.: Newbury House.

Pearson, David P. 1974. 'The effects of grammatical complexity on children's comprehension, recall, and conception of certain semantic relations'. *Reading Research Quarterly* **10**, 155–192.

Petersen, Calvin R. and Francis A. Cartier. 1975. 'Some theoretical problems and practical solutions in proficiency test validity'. In Jones and Spolsky (1975), 105–118.

Pike, Lewis. 1973. *An evaluation of present and alternative item formats for use in the TOEFL*. Princeton, N.J.: Educational Testing Service (mimeo).

Pimsleur, Paul. 1962. 'Student factors in Foreign Language Learning: A Review of the Literature'. *Modern Language Journal* **46**, 160–9.

Platt, John R. 1964. 'Strong inference'. *Science* **146**, 347–353.

Politzer, Robert L., M. R. Hoover, and D. Brown. 1974. 'A test of proficiency in black standard and non-standard speech'. *TESOL Quarterly* **8**, 27–35.

Politzer, Robert L. and Charles Staubach. 1961. *Teaching Spanish: a linguistic orientation*. Boston: Ginn.

Porter, D. 1976. 'Modified cloze procedure: a more valid reading comprehension test'. *English Language Teaching* **30**, 151–155.

Potter, Thomas C. 1968. *A taxonomy of cloze research, Part I: readability and reading comprehension*. Inglewood, California: Southwestern Regional Laboratory for Educational Research and Development.

Rand, Earl. 1969a. *Constructing dialogs*. New York: Holt, Rinehart, and Winston.

Rand, Earl. 1969b. *Constructing sentences*. New York: Holt, Rinehart, and Winston.

Rand, Earl. 1972. 'Integrative and discrete point tests at UCLA'. *Workpapers in TESL: UCLA* **6**, 67–78.

Rand, Earl. 1976. 'A factored homogeneous items approach to the UCLA ESL Placement Examination'. Paper read at the Tenth Annual Meeting of TESOL, New York City.

Rasmussen, Donald and Lynn Goldberg. 1970. *A pig can jig*. Chicago: Science Research Associates.

Reed, Carole. 1973. 'Adapting TESL approaches to the teaching of written standard English as a second dialect to speakers of American black English vernacular'. *TESOL Quarterly* **7**, 289–308.

Richards, Jack C. 1970a. 'A non-contrastive approach to error analysis'. Paper read at the Fourth Annual Meeting of TESOL, San Francisco. Also in *English Language Teaching* **25**, 204–219. Reprinted in Oller and Richards (1973), 96–113.

Richards, Jack C. 1970b. 'A psycholinguistic measure of vocabulary selection'. *IRAL* **8**, 87–102.

Richards, Jack C. 1971. 'Error analsis and second language strategies'. *Language Sciences* **17**, 12–22. Reprinted in Oller and Richards (1973), 114–135.

Richards, Jack C. 1972. 'Some social aspects of language learning'. *TESOL Quarterly* **6**, 243–254.

Rivers, Wilga. 1964. *The psychologist and the foreign language teacher*. Chicago: University of Chicago Press.

Rivers, Wilga. 1967. 'Listening comprehension'. In Mildred R. Donaghue (ed.) *Foreign languages and the schools: a book of readings*. Dubuque,

Iowa: William C. Brown, 189–200.

Rivers, Wilga. 1968. *Teaching foreign language skills*. Chicago: University of Chicago Press.

Robertson, Gary J. 1972. 'Development of the first group mental ability test'. In Bracht, Hopkins, and Stanley (1972), 183–190.

Ruddell, Robert B. 1965. 'Reading comprehension and structural redundancy in written material'. *Proceedings of the International Reading Association* **10,** 308–311.

Rummelhart, D. E. 1975. 'Notes on a schema for stories'. In D. G. Bobrow and A. M. Collins (eds.) *Representation and understanding: studies in cognitive science*. New York: Academic Press, 211–236.

Rutherford, William E. 1968. *Modern English: a textbook for foreign students*. New York: Harcourt, Brace, and Jovanovich.

Sapir, Edward. 1921. *Language: an introduction to the study of speech*. New York: Harcourt, Brace, and World.

Sarason, I. G. 1958. 'Interrelationships among individual difference variables, behavior in psychotherapy, and verbal conditioning'. *Journal of Abnormal and Social Psychology* **56,** 339–344.

Sarason, I. G. 1961. 'Test anxiety and intellectual performance of college students'. *Journal of Educational Psychology* **52,** 201–206.

Savignon, Sandra J. 1972. *Communicative competence: an experiment in foreign language teaching*. Montreal: Marcel Didier.

Schank, Roger. 1972. 'Conceptual dependency: a theory of natural language understanding'. *Cognitive Psychology* **3,** 552–631.

Schank, Roger and K. Colby (eds.) 1973. *Computer models of thought and language*. San Francisco: W. H. Freeman.

Schlesinger, I. M. 1968. *Sentence structure and the reading process*. The Hague: Mouton.

Scholz, George, D. Hendricks, R. Spurling, M. Johnson, and L. Vandenburg. In press. 'Is language ability divisible or unitary? A factor analysis of twenty-two language proficiency tests'. In Oller and Perkins.

Schumann, John H. 1975. 'Affective factors and the problem of age in second language acquisition'. *Language Learning* **25,** 209–235.

Schumann, John H. 1976. 'Social distance as a factor in second language acquisition'. *Language Learning* **26,** 135–143.

Scoon, Annabelle. 1974. *The feasibility of test translation – English to Navajo*. Unpublished doctoral dissertation, University of New Mexico, Albuquerque.

Selinker, Larry. 1972. 'Interlanguage'. *IRAL* **10,** 209–231.

Shaw, Marvin E. and Jack M. Wright. 1967. *Scales for the measurement of attitudes*. New York: McGraw Hill.

Shore, M. 1974. *Final report of project BEST: the content analysis of 125 Title VII bilingual programs funded in 1969 and 1970*. New York: Bilingual Education Application Research Unit, Hunter College (mimeo, as cited by Zirkel, 1976, 328).

Silverman, Robert J., Joslyn K. Noa, Randall H. Russell, and John Molina. 1976. *Oral language tests for bilingual students: an evaluation of language dominance and proficiency instruments*. Washington, D.C.: United States Office of Education.

Skinner, B. F. 1953. *Science and human behavior*. New York: Macmillan.

Skinner, B. F. 1957. *Verbal behavior*. New York: Appleton, Century, Crofts.

Skinner, B. F. 1971. *Beyond freedom and dignity*. New York: Alfred K. Knopf.

Slobin, D. I. 1973.'Introduction to chapter on studies of imitation and comprehension'. In C. A. Ferguson and D. I. Slobin (eds.) *Studies of child language and development*. New York: Holt, Rinehart, and Winston, 462–465.

Slobin, D. I. and C. A. Welsh. 1967. 'Elicited imitation as a research tool in developmental psycholinguistics'. Paper presented at the Center for Research on Language and Language Behavior, University of Michigan, March, 1967. In C. A. Ferguson and D. I. Slobin (eds.) *Studies of child language and development*. New York: Holt, Rinehart, and Winston, 1973, 485–497.

Smalley, William A. 1961. *Manual of articulatory phonetics*. Ann Arbor, Michigan: Cushing-Malloy.

Somaratne, W. 1957. *Aids and tests in the teaching of English*. London: Oxford University Press.

Spearman, Charles E. 1904. '"General intelligence" objectively determined and measured'. *American Journal of Psychology* 15, 201–293.

Spolsky, Bernard. 1968. 'What does it mean to know a language? Or how do you get someone to perform his competence?' Paper read at the Second Conference on Problems in Foreign Language Testing, University of Southern California. Reprinted in Oller and Richards (1973), 164–176.

Spolsky, Bernard. 1969a. 'Attitudinal aspects of second language learning'. *Language Learning* 19, 271–283. Reprinted in Allen and Campbell (1972), 403–414.

Spolsky, Bernard. 1969b. 'Recent research in TESOL'. *TESOL Quarterly* 3, 355.

Spolsky, Bernard. 1969c. 'Reduced redundancy as a language testing tool'. Paper read at the Second International Congress of Applied Linguistics, Cambridge, England. ERIC ED 031702.

Spolsky, Bernard. 1974. 'Speech communities and schools'. *TESOL Quarterly* 8, 17–26.

Spolsky, Bernard. 1976. 'Language testing: art or science'. Paper read at the Fourth International Congress of Applied Linguistics. In *Proceedings of the fourth international congress of applied linguistics*. Stuttgart, Germany: Sonderdruck, 9–28. Also appears as 'Introduction: Linguists and language testers,' in *Advances in language testing: Series 2, Approaches to language testing*. Arlington, Virginia: Center for Applied Linguistics, 1978, v-x.

Spolsky, Bernard, Bengt Sigurd, M. Sato, E. Walker, and C. Arterburn. 1968. 'Preliminary studies in the development of techniques for testing overall second language proficiency'. In Upshur and Fata. 79–101.

Spolsky, Bernard, Penny Murphy, Wayne Holm, and Allen Ferrel. 1972. 'Three functional tests of oral proficiency'. *TESOL Quarterly* 6, 221–235. Reprinted in Palmer and Spolsky (1975), 75–90.

Srole, Leo. 1951. 'Social dysfunction, personality, and social distance attitudes'. Paper read at a meeting of the American Sociological Society,

Chicago (as cited by Gardner and Lambert, 1972).

Srole, Leo. 1956. 'Social integration and certain corollaries: an exploratory study'. *American Sociological Review* 21, 709–716.

Stevens, J. H., K. F. Ruder, and Roy Jew. 1973. 'Speech discrimination in black and white children'. *Language and Speech* 16, 123–129.

Stevenson, Douglas. 1974. *A preliminary investigation of construct validity and the Test of English as a Foreign Language.* Unpublished doctoral dissertation, University of New Mexico, Albuquerque.

Stinson, P. and M. Morrison. 1959. 'Sex differences among high school seniors'. *Journal of Educational Research* 53, 103–108.

Streiff, Virginia. 1977. *Reading comprehension and language proficiency among Eskimo children: psychological, linguistic, and educational considerations.* Doctoral dissertation, Ohio University. To appear in New York: Arno Press.

Strevens, Peter. 1965. *Papers in language and language teaching.* London: Oxford University Press.

Strickland, G. 1970. *Attitude to school questionnaire.* Los Angeles: Cooperative Research Project at UCLA. ERIC ED 051260.

Stubbs, Joseph Bartow and G. Richard Tucker. 1974. 'The cloze test as a measure of English proficiency'. *Modern Language Journal* 58, 239–241.

Stump, Thomas. 1977. 'Cloze and dictation tasks as predictors of intelligence and achievement scores'. Paper read at the First International Conference on Frontiers in Language Proficiency and Dominance Testing, Southern Illinois University. Also read at the Eleventh Annual Meeting of TESOL, Miami, Florida. In Oller and Perkins (1978), 36–63.

Swain, Merrill. 1976a. 'Bibliography: research on immersion education for the majority child'. *The Canadian Modern Language Review* 32, 592–596.

Swain, Merrill. 1976b. *Lecture on the bilingual experiments in Canada.* University of New Mexico, Albuquerque.

Swain, Merrill, Guy Dumas, and N. Naiman. 1974. 'Alternatives to spontaneous speech: elicited translation and imitation as indictors of second language competence'. *Working papers on Bilingualism: Special Issue on Language Acquisition Studies* 3, 68–79.

Swain, Merrill, Sharon Lapkin, and Henri C. Barik. 1976. 'The cloze test as a measure of second language proficiency for young children'. *Workingpapers in Bilingualism* 11, 32–44.

Tate, Merle. 1965. *Statistics in education and psychology: a first course.* New York: Macmillan.

Taylor, Wilson L. 1953. '"Cloze procedure": a new tool for measuring readability'. *Journalism Quarterly* 30, 415–433.

Taylor, Wilson L. 1956. 'Recent developments in the use of "cloze procedure"'. *Journalism Quarterly* 33, 42–48, 99.

Taylor, Wilson L. 1957. '"Cloze" readability scores as indices of individual differences in comprehension and aptitude'. *Journal of Applied Psychology* 41, 19–26.

Teitelbaum, Herta. 1976. *Testing bilinguality in elementary school children.* Unpublished doctoral dissertation, University of New Mexico, Albuquerque.

Thorndike, Robert L. 1972. 'Reliability'. In Bracht, Hopkins, and Stanley,

66–73.

Tucker, G. Richard and Wallace E. Lambert. 1973. 'Sociocultural aspects of language study'. In Oller and Richards, 246–250.

Tulving, E. 1972. 'Episodic and semantic memory'. In E. Tulving and W. Donaldson (eds.) *Organization and memory*. New York: Academic Press.

Upshur, John A. n. d. *Oral communication test*. Ann Arbor: University of Michigan (mimeo).

Upshur, John A. 1962. 'Language proficiency testing and the contrastive analysis dilemma'. *Language Learning* **12,** 123–127.

Upshur, John A. 1969a. 'Productive communication testing: a progress report'. Paper read at the Second International Congress of Applied Linguistics, Cambridge, England. In G. E. Perren and J. L. M. Trim (eds.) *Selected papers of the second international congress of applied linguistics*. Cambridge University Press, 1971, 435–441. Reprinted in Oller and Richards (1973), 177–183.

Upshur, John A. 1969b. 'TEST is a four letter word'. Paper read at the EPDA Institute, University of Illinois.

Upshur, John A. 1971. 'Objective evaluation of oral proficiency in the ESOL classroom'. *TESOL Quarterly* **5,** 47–60. Also in Palmer and Spolsky (1975), 53–65.

Upshur, John A. 1973. 'Context for language testing'. In Oller and Richards (1973), 200–213.

Upshur, John A. 1976. 'Discussion of "A program for language testing research"'. In H. Douglas Brown (ed.) *Papers in second language learning: proceedings of the sixth annual conference on applied linguistics at the University of Michigan. Language Learning, Special Issue Number* **4,** 167–174.

Upshur, John A. and Julia Fata (eds.) 1968. *Problems in foreign language testing. Language Learning, Special Issue Number* **3**.

Vachek, J. 1966. *The linguistic school of Prague*. Bloomington, Indiana: Indiana University Press.

Valette, Rebecca M. 1964. 'The use of dictée in the French language classroom'. *Modern Language Journal* **39,** 431–434.

Valette, Rebecca M. 1973. 'Developing and evaluating communication skills in the classroom'. *TESOL Quarterly* **7,** 407–424.

Valette, Rebecca M. 1977. *Modern language testing*. Second edition. New York: Harcourt, Brace, and Jovanovich.

Wakefield, J. A., Ronald E. Veselka, and Leslie Miller. 1974–5. 'A comparison of the Iowa Tests of Basic Skills and the Prescriptive Reading Inventory'. *Journal of Educational Research* **68,** 347–349.

Watzlawick, Paul, Janet Beavin, and Kenneth Jackson. 1967. *Pragmatics of human communication: a study of interactional patterns, pathologies, and paradoxes*. New York: Norton.

Weaver, W. W. and A. J. Kingston. 1963. 'A factor analysis of the cloze procedure and other measures of reading and language ability'. *Journal of Communication* **13,** 252–261.

Whitaker, S. F. 1976. 'What is the status of dictation?' *Audio Visual Journal* **14,** 87–93.

Wilson, Craig. 1977. 'Can ESL cloze tests be contrastively biased:

Vietnamese as a test case'. Paper read at the First International Conference on Frontiers in Language Proficiency and Dominance Testing, Southern Illinois University. In Oller and Perkins (in press).

Woods, William A. 1970. 'Transition network grammars for natural language analysis'. *Communications of the Association for Computing Machinery* **13**, 591–606.

Wright, Audrey L. and James H. McGillivray. 1971. *Let's learn English*. Fourth edition. New York: American Book.

Zirkel, Perry A. 1973. *Black American cultural attitude scale*. Austin, Texas: Learning Concepts.

Zirkel, Perry A. 1974. 'A method for determining and depicting language dominance'. *TESOL Quarterly* **8**, 7–16.

Zirkel, Perry A. 1976. 'The why's and ways of testing bilinguality before teaching bilingually'. *The Elementary School Journal*, March, 323–330.

Zirkel, Perry A. and S. L. Jackson. 1974. *Cultural attitude scales: test manual*. Austin, Texas: Learning Concepts.

Index

479

narrative repetition (see also elicited imitation), 326, 336
narration (see also story telling), 332–335
Natalicio, Diana, 65, 302, 338, 470
National Council of Teachers of English, 161, 470
native language, 2, 12
native speaker, 2, 62
criterion for test performance, 6, 8, 199–208
nativeness, rating scale, 392
naturalness criteria, 6, 28, 33, 34, 36, 38, 42, 44, 46, 70, 72, 180, 221, 263–265, 267, 305, 306, 319, 346, 376, 415, 417
Navajo, tests in, 88ff, 93
negatives, 44
Newcomb, J. M., 137, 471
Newton, B., 400, 470
New York City Language Assessment Battery, 308–309
Nie, N. H., 433, 471
Noa, Joslyn K., 172, 180, 307, 474
noise procedure, 45, 70, 72, 264, 298
nominal validity, 109–110, 128, 176
non-native performance as a criterion for tests, 199–208
nonsense, 214, 229
normal distribution, 54
Norman, Donald, 35
Northwest Regional Educational Laboratory, 307
Norton, Darry, 86, 471
noun, 44
phrases, 395, 396
Nunnally, J. C., 53, 427–429, 431, 471

objectivity, 232, 257
obligatory occasions, 385
Obrecht, H., 256
oracy, 408
oral cloze, (see cloze)
Oral Communication Test, 9, 49, 305, 314, 317–320, 335, 337
oral interview, 9, 47–49, 60, 70, 176, 301–338, 416, 433ff
oral modality, 9, 37, 47, 68, 70, 301–338
need for oral language tests, 306–308
Ogston, W. D., 28, 463

Oller, D. K., 22
Oller, J. W., 2, 13, 35, 50, 58, 59, 61–62, 73, 87, 92, 95, 134–136, 140–141, 155, 172, 175, 195, 233, 267, 302, 339, 346–347, 355, 357, 360–361, 363, 370, 372, 393, 421, 429–431, 438, 459–462, 464–465, 467–468, 470–473, 475–477
Oller, J. W. Sr., 23, 32, 177, 400, 471
Olsson, Stig., 286
Osgood, Charles E., 13, 22, 25, 134, 344, 354–355, 376, 472
other concept (see interpersonal relationships)
Otis Test of Mental Abilities, 454f

Palmer, Leslie, 104, 148, 338, 459, 463, 467, 472, 475, 476
Paluszny, Maria, 113, 133, 466
paralinguistics, 18
paraphrasing, 336
paraphrase recognition, 46, 50, 70
sentence, 234
Parish, C., 432, 434, 451
Parker, R., 400, 470
partial dictation, 264, 285–289, 298, 300
administration, 288–289
spelling errors, 289
partial divisibility hypotheses, 425–458
pattern drills, 32, 157–165, 179, 204, 415
factual, 397, 399
Paulston, C. B., 160, 163, 472
Peabody Picture Vocabulary Test, 455
Pearson, D., 349, 472
Pedhazur, Elazar J., 53, 428
percept, 31
perceptual-motor skills, 65
Perkins, Kyle, 2, 50, 62, 79, 195, 233, 302, 400, 421, 431–432, 460–461, 464, 465, 468, 470, 472, 476, 477
Perren, G. E., 339, 476
personality, 3, 5, 12, 105, 109, 403, 406, 418, 420
(see also attitudes)
Peterson, Calvin R., 182, 184–185, 208, 472
Pharis, Keith, 79